Praise for *Where Dragons Dance*

Kory Varlen's exciting research into the effects of the 47 Lunar Saros Series has brought an entirely new dimension to my understanding of my life's purpose. Her original research and sophistication as a writer have made me fall in love with astrology.

–Paulette Tomasson, RN RCC MA
author of *Sensuous and Sultry: Sex is for the Courageous*

I have so many people to be grateful to but there is one special person that has helped me to discover hidden assets within me that I didn't even know existed. She is a constant source of inspiration and energy to me, and perhaps more importantly, my guide to see things more clearly, read signs, and utilize what is already there. Actually, in a way you could say that she has helped me to change my future to what I believe was actually meant to happen in the first place. Her name is Kory Varlen.

–Erik Olsson, CEO, Redtienda Corporation, Sweden

I met Kory Varlen in Quito, Ecuador, while on assignment for National Geographic *Adventure* magazine. My photographer partner and I met her outside of the South American Adventure's Club and I was instantly drawn in by her smile, open eyes, and her insights as an ex-pat living in a country she called "the face of God." She did my astrological chart and shocked me with a series of startling insights. Given that my astrology expertise runs to three line epithets I read in the local newspaper, I was amazed by the hard science aspect of this cultivated art. And more impressed by her ability to interpret the information she read from my chart. Kory's insights ran deep. I highly encourage anyone eager to learn more about astrology to consult with this wise and loving woman.

–Joe Glickman, freelance journalist Brooklyn, NY

I have known Kory since 1983 and I can say with confidence that she is "simply the best." She has consistently been invaluable in both my personal and business life. Regrettably, there were times when I didn't listen to her and paid handsomely for my obstinance.

–Lance Shaler, President Sci-Com Data Services Ltd. Canada

Where Dragons Dance

Lunar Eclipse Pathways to Personality & Prediction

KORY VARLEN

Foreword by David Cochrane

Published in 2023 by Ibis Press, an imprint of Nicolas Hays, Inc.
P. O. Box 540206
Lake Worth, FL 33454-0206
www.nicolashays.com

Distributed to the trade by
Red Wheel/Weiser, LLC
65 Parker St. • Ste. 7
Newburyport, MA 01950
www.redwheelweiser.com

ISBN: 978-089254-231-4
Ebook ISBN: 978-0-89254-298-5

Library of Congress Cataloging-in-Publication Data
available upon request

Book design and production by
Sky Peck Design
Edited by Scott Silverman

Printed in the U.S.A.

MP

"It does not do to leave a
live dragon out of your calculations,
if you live near him."

-J. R. R. TOLKIEN

Contents

Part Three—Dancing with Air

Part Four – Dancing with Water

Foreword

BY DAVID COCHRANE

If you are lucky, at least a few times during your lifetime you will see the Sun on a cloudless day suddenly start to become obscured and then become increasingly covered and then reappear a few hours later. Similarly, you are lucky if you are able to watch the Full Moon on a very clear night gradually become obscured for a period of time. These dramatic events, of course, are the solar eclipse and lunar eclipse.

Solar eclipses tend to get more attention than lunar eclipses. From the point of view of astrology, this is unfortunate! The brilliant, extensive research conducted by Kory Varlen shows us that lunar eclipses are not second-class citizens that stand in the shadow (pardon the pun) of solar eclipses. The power of lunar eclipses has been overlooked for millennia and this groundbreaking book reveals spectacular new insights into how lunar eclipses are relevant to our lives.

One reason why lunar eclipses have been overshadowed by solar eclipses is that the Sun disappearing during the day is visually more conspicuous than a disappearing Full Moon. You do not need to be looking up at the sky to notice that the day has suddenly become dark. You look up and see something extraordinary: the Sun is becoming hidden by something. That "something" is the Moon, but that is not obvious if you are just looking up at the sky without having tracked the movement of the Sun and Moon. A second reason why solar eclipses get more attention is because a solar eclipse is visible only on a particular path across the Earth. The opportunity to see a solar eclipse comes on very rarely, and eclipse aficionados will travel great distances to get the best view of one. If it is cloudy, then the trip is disappointing, but worth the risk.

However, how visually stunning something is may not be necessarily a measure of how important it is astrologically. Many things that are given great importance astrologically are visually unimpressive or even insignificant. The Ascendant is an abstract point in space. The tropical zero degree Aries point from which the zodiac is created is also an abstract point. Planets do not lose most of their power after they set and we do not see them. The vast majority of modern astrologers find that Uranus and Neptune and even Pluto have a very dramatic effect, and Uranus is only faintly visible under nearly perfect conditions for a person with excellent eyesight. Neptune and Pluto are not visible.

An example of how solar eclipses have gotten most of the attention is how we think of the Saros Cycle. The Saros Cycle is a kind of celestial heartbeat where eclipses occur with great regularity. I will not discuss the details of this here because it is explained very beautifully in this book. My point here is that we often think of the Saros Cycle as a feature of solar eclipses. However, lunar eclipses also occur in a Saros Cycle! The Lunar Saros Cycle has largely been overlooked. This book shakes up our assumptions and shows how the Lunar Saros Cycle plays an important part in our lives.

Good investigations in astrology start with good observations. Kory has utilized the full power of modern astronomy and computer software to track these celestial cycles. She uses a database of people to identify the Saros Cycle that a person is connected to, and she provides clear and simple rules for identifying what cosmic cycle an individual is connected to. We then proceed to see if the information is useful in specific cases. As I looked at my own Lunar Saros Cycle, I felt as if I was traversing a kind of DNA structure that reaches back into some kind of ancestral past upon which my life is built. Being of a very scientific temperament, this experience inspires me to seek more information.

I can count on my fingers of one hand the number of astrologers I am aware of who have dived deep into the study of eclipses. Frankly, most astrological ideas we encounter are simply ideas that a person learns from other astrologers, finds that they make sense in their lives, and then they trust that they work. This faith in a tradition of ideas based only on a tradition and limited personal experience is not adequate. One must persevere for years in some specialized area of astrology and must question, doubt, analyze, and reanalyze repeatedly before Mother Nature gives up her secrets. Kory Varlen is one of the very few investigators with the education, dedication, perseverance, and will power to open a door to new insights in astrology. This book is a gem, and it will be of interest to people far into the future because of the great time, care, and attention given to it.

Welcome to the future of astrology. The future of astrology lies in advanced analysis using all of the tools available to us in the 21st century. We open doors to a new world of understanding with creative thinking, decades of dedication, and the humility to obtain help from wherever we can. Currently there are relatively few on the path to this new world of astrology, but the numbers of people seeking an understanding of what astrology is and how it works using the highest levels of academic rigor and creative thinking are growing. This is a book, then, for that expanding and exciting movement whose goal is to actualize advances in astrology. *Where Dragons Dance* paves the way forward as it hacks a path through the overgrowth of untended astrological ideas and beliefs. This book shines a light into the mystery of astrology and helps untangle the complex web of celestial threads. Enjoy the journey that it takes you on as Kory shows us how the cosmic heartbeat of the Lunar Saros Cycle establishes a vital rhythm for all our lives.

Introduction

Lunar eclipses wield a power that make solar eclipses stand back in awe. A solar eclipse is localized to just one area upon the Earth whereas a lunar eclipse occurs when the Moon moves into Earth's shadow. Anyone on Earth facing the Moon can see a lunar eclipse, giving this type of celestial event a huge potential audience of observers. Our solar star, meanwhile, can only yearn for such magnified participation numbers. In addition, the Moon in eclipse mode is just a lot friendlier and magical to look at in comparison to the terrifying solar flare ejections shooting out in all directions from the eclipse Sun's corona, which, from all historical accounts, scared the living hell out of anyone bold enough to look up.

Throughout many cultures it is the lunar eclipse, rather than the dreaded and often feared solar eclipse, that marks a time of rejuvenation. Our ancestors have watched the Moon's monthly phases and have literally merged our daily rhythms to be in simpatico with her ever-changing orb. In the process, either by osmosis or via a celestial syncopation not yet fully understood, we have internalized her ever morphing essence and incorporated it into our atomic structure. We are one with the cosmos; living in the realms of both the sacred and mundane, our lives personify the ancient dictum, "As above, so below." We are star stuff in flux, outrageously entangled in a process of continual cosmic intercourse that unites our innate well-being to that of our expanding universe.

Twenty-first-century scholarship is now opening the door to an exciting world that connects all of us to a greater web of life that is our cosmic heritage. In his book, *Living with The Stars: How the Human Body is Connected to the Life*

Cycles of the Earth, the Planets and the Stars, astrophysicist Karel Schrijver states how many of our atoms ". . . started out on the Moon, on Mars, in asteroids and comets or elsewhere in the solar system, and fell to the Earth sometime between the birth of the planet and days ago."[1] Every atom in our bodies can be traced back to stars and their cataclysmic supernovae explosions billions of years ago. Our universal DNA is undeniable. The pounding of our hearts and the rise and fall of our breath are fellow travelers with the cosmic waves that continuously reshape our earthly shores. We are intimately linked to the rhythms and magnetic energy fields not only of our planet but to the nuclear furnace that is our Sun and its family of planets, moons, asteroids, and comets.

Karel Schrijver's co-author, Stanford University professor Iris Schrijver, concludes that "Everything we are and everything in the universe and on Earth originated from stardust, and it continually floats through us even today. It directly connects us to the universe, rebuilding our bodies over and again over our lifetimes."[2] We all participate in this dance of undivided wholeness as our life essence, however defined, is anchored in the reality of indivisible unity. Our body has always known this great truth; the lunar rhythms have always linked us to the great mother mysteries. Our human body is inescapably intertwined with the cycles of Nature and so too do our dreams and aspirations find a home within the lunar orbs' heavenly firmament.

Many astrologers use lunar eclipses to time key transitional time periods for themselves and their clients. I have for years noted their placements and their effectiveness and never thought much more about them. They worked. That was enough for me considering all the other predictive tools and theories I was mastering. But then, as the old saying goes, the light went on and I had my Oprah *Ahah!* moment. It was May of 2013 and several world events (most notably among them NSA whistleblower Edward Snowden) arrived on the scene along with the newest member of the lunar eclipse family: LS150. Lunar Saros 150 would rock my world and bring me to a totally new way of understanding not only how lunar eclipses work but *why* they work. This book is the result of that moment.

You might be assuming you know how lunar eclipses work. But you'd be wrong. Even after watching them for years in the charts of clients, their presence and potency eluded my quest for understanding. However, everything changed when I realized that the lunar eclipses were functioning as distinct families in their own right, with their own special qualities, needs, characteristics, concerns, challenges, and gifts. I saw the immediate value of what their range of expression could add to an individual's life story, whether from the dynamic dimensions of a natal birth chart perspective or from a transiting contact. I began to write this book because *I* needed it. And if I needed it, I was sure that I could help all astrologers to understand better what I wanted them to understand well. To that end, may the stories and compelling characteristics of these 47 Lunar Saros Series eclipses become a welcome addition to your cosmic toolkit.

No one, not even Harry Potter, is an orphan. We all have our earthly parents, but now we also belong to a heavenly family—a family of dragons, or galvanizing lunar eclipse patterns, many of which are ancient and have been returning for centuries to check up on us, their earthly kin. Get ready to meet your dragon family and maybe for the first time you'll discover life patterns that have been dancing you through such elaborate cosmic steps heretofore unknowable by any conventional means of astrological analysis.

Patterns—that is what a horoscope highlights and that is especially what a lunar eclipse field is all about and what I am so excited to share with you, dear reader, because what is this world made up of but patterns? Multiple patterns layered one on top of one another in a harmonious manner and in a manner that indicates that there is communication going on between all the patterned layers because they *have to* work together. And when you stand back and really see how these patterned layers are functioning, well, a new level of meaning emerges. It's much like music and music is an analog of the structure of existence itself. When you move your body to a piece of music, you're moving in sync, you're moving in tune to the rhythm of that pattern.

And that is exactly how lunar eclipse fields work. Their unique patterns are musical in nature and coax even the most reluctant wallflower to take part in their dance. Through the talisman of your chart, when your energy field and its complexity of patterns connects into theirs, a multi-layered harmony is created that indicates that you can play. While it is all quite unpredictable what might happen, the thing I can tell you for sure is that when your chart connects into the energy field of a lunar eclipse—either by birthright or rite of passage (they return every eighteen years)—you will be dancing on the edge of creation. Every lunar eclipse brings its own sphere of consciousness along to the party (as full of life as we are, yet seemingly spontaneous and unstructured). We are their freestyle dance partners and through the act of bringing ourselves into harmony with their field's highest potentiality, our own sphere of consciousness expands. A six-month fling on the dance floor is the perfect time period—not too short or too long, just enough time to learn some new steps and feel the rhythm of a new beat.

If you're looking for a precision instrument that is useful, reliable, and will function 100 percent of the time, the forty-seven families of lunar eclipses outlined in this book have quite the stories to tell. Some are ancient, some are new, and some are yet to be born. But they each have the power to illuminate your sphere of influence. We all want to fulfill the highest, truest expression of ourselves as human beings and a knowledge of how these Lunar Saros Series eclipses work shines a special quality of light upon our personality and our pathway through the world.

Each eclipse presents the astrological criteria for determining not only how and when a particular Lunar Saros eclipse will impact your life but what possibilities arrive with its activation. And since each Lunar Saros eclipse belongs, like all of us, to a distinct family, you'll be surprised and impressed by its unique contribution to your basic character.

In preparation for your journey through the fascinating energy fields of these forty-seven awe-inspiring and unique lunar eclipses, here are some ground rules for how special events and new ideas get seeded into our psyche. For any shift in our collective or personal consciousness to occur, one of two things (and sometimes both) has to happen. A lunar eclipse field has to activate a significant planet, angle, asteroid, or midpoint, either in a personal chart or in the birth chart of a nation. Since the analysis of the forty-seven Lunar Saros Series eclipses presented here, to my knowledge, has never been approached from a family dynamic perspective, I leave my findings and hypothesis for future generations to validate, improve upon, or reject.

To conduct research on Lunar Saros Series eclipses I would encourage anyone to begin with their personal journals as they reveal our deepest hopes, wishes, dreams, and inspirations, along with our darkest hours of inner turmoil. The best sources are always diary entries, journals, letters, and anything that speaks to the inner life as that is when the value of lunar eclipses rises to the surface.

As we will see in the lives of so many of the people in these case studies, our charts, vis à vis their unique spheres of appearance, hold a consciousness as viable as our own. In fact, due to their extended lifespan (of up to almost fifteen hundred years in some cases), Lunar Saros Series charts may have an even better claim on consciousness than we mortals feel entitled to hold. Our corporeal forms vanish within a century, but these magnificent lunar eclipse spheres continue well past the millennium marker.

In the meantime, these lunar dragons continue on their global expeditions, appearing anywhere from two to four times per year. With every eighteen-year return to the spotlight of our night skies and our terrestrial endeavors, they offer all of us an exciting if not liberating opportunity to experience and try on new thoughts, feelings, sensations, sights, sounds, and styles of behavior. How exciting that we get to be a part and play a part in the updating of not only our own but the global zeitgeist. I've come to regard each and every one of them as a muse helping me to add new pages and adventures to my life's story.

All of these lunar eclipses are time travelers, offering a diversity of experience along their continuum. At every stage of their journey, be it the beginning, middle or end, their unique essence is part of the grand galactic highway upon which we all travel. As such, their character and temperament are valuable assets helping us all to better navigate the expressways of our life. In the pages that follow, you'll meet people who launched, struggled, celebrated, reassessed, and ended relationships and careers in the company and trajectory of one of them. None of these lunar eclipses are overtly good or bad but, like us, they do seem to have their individual personalities and preferences, which I hope you'll find insightful.

All data used to construct the foundational charts for all forty-seven Lunar Saros Series eclipses has been sourced from NASA's official eclipse website *eclipse.gsfc.nasa.gov*. There you will find a five millennium catalog of lunar eclipses that range from 2000 BCE to 3000 CE. All charts and reference data are in the New Style (Gregorian) calendar.

---

1. Karel Schrijver and Iris Schrijver, *Living with the Stars: How the Human Body is Connected to the Life Cycles of the Earth, the Planets and the Stars* (Oxford, UK: Oxford University Press, 2015), p. 192.
2. Ibid.

How to Use This Book

Top 10 Steps for How to Live with Dragons

1. Find your Dragon Family in the chart of 200 Years of Lunar Saros Dragon Degrees that follow—some of us have two!
2. Find the eclipse that occurred BEFORE your birth. This is your pre-birth lunar eclipse (PREBLE). If your birth occurred within three weeks either side of an eclipse you get two PREBLEs.
3. Read the entire analysis, examples, summary, and list of luminaries to get a feel for your Dragon family DNA.
4. Create a Bi-Wheel of you and your Dragon family chart.
5. Note all 1st and 2nd Harmonics (aka Cosmic Bridges):
   6 degree orb for Sun/Moon/Nodes to planets, nodes, and angles
   5 degree orb for same planet to planet contacts
   4 degree orb for planets to planets and midpoints
   3 degree orb for planets to asteroids
6. Pay attention to any patterns in your Dragon family's chart: Kite, T-Square, Grand Trine/Cross, Boomerang, or Anchor. Look at how these connect into your own chart, as you will be able to sync to that entire pattern.
7. Find your Space Lanes (described on page 13). These connectors are the strongest and come through the eclipse nodes and eclipse axis on any of the four angles of your chart.
8. Rank your Cosmic Bridges (described on page 15). The strongest connectors are from the eclipse nodes and the eclipse axis to your Moon, Sun, planets, midpoints, and asteroids.
9. Find your Global Gateways (described on page 17). Go to the Reference Section at the back of the book and note all the Dragon Families who share your nodal axis.

   Mark in RED the ones whose SNode activates your SNode and NNode to NNode. (These are difficult and constrained). Mark in GREEN all Dragon Families whose SNode activates your NNode and NNode to SNode.(These are wonderful and unconstrained)
10. Go to the Reference Section at the back of the book. Note all the lunar eclipses whose eclipse axis (Moon and Sun) connect to your Moon or Sun by 1st or 2nd Harmonics. 6 degree orb.

200 Years of Lunar Saros Dragon Degrees

1899	17 Dec	133S	24♊									
1900	13 Jun	138N	21♐	6 Dec	143S	13♊						
1901	3 May	110N	12♏	27 Oct	115S	3♉						
1902	22 Apr	120N	1♏	17 Oct	125S	22♈						
1903	12 Apr	130N	20♎	6 Oct	135S	12♈						
1904	2 Mar	102N	11♍	31 Mar	140N	10♎	24 Sep	145S	1♈			
1905	19 Feb	112N	0♍	15 Aug	117S	22♒						
1906	9 Feb	122N	20♌	4 Aug	127S	11♒						
1907	29 Jan	132N	9♌	25 Jul	137S	1♒						
1908	18 Jan	142N	27♋	14 Jun	109S	23♐	13 Jul	147S	21♑	7 Dec	114N	15♊
1909	4 Jun	119S	13♐	27 Nov	124N	4♊						
1910	24 May	129S	2♐	17 Nov	134N	24♉						
1911	13 May	139S	21♏	6 Nov	144N	13♉						
1912	1 Apr	111S	12♎	26 Sep	116N	3♈						
1913	22 Mar	121S	1♎	15 Sep	126N	22♓						
1914	12 Mar	131S	21♍	4 Sep	136N	11♓						
1915	31 Jan	103S	10♌	1 Mar	141S	10♍	26 Jul	108N	2♒	24 Aug	146N	1♓
1916	20 Jan	113S	29♋	15 Jul	118N	22♑						
1917	8 Jan	123S	17♋	4 Jul	128N	12♑	28 Dec	133S	6♋			
1918	24 Jun	138N	2♑	17 Dec	143S	25♊						
1919	15 May	110N	23♏	7 Nov	115S	15♉						
1920	3 May	120N	12♏	27 Oct	125S	4♉						
1921	22 Apr	130N	2♏	16 Oct	135S	22♈						
1922	13 Mar	102N	22♍	11 Apr	140N	21♎	6 Oct	145S	12♈			
1923	3 Mar	112N	12♍	26 Aug	117S	3♓						

1924	20 Feb	122N	1♍	14 Aug	127S	22♒						
1925	8 Feb	132N	20♌	4 Aug	137S	12♒						
1926	28 Jan	142N	8♌	25 Jun	109S	4♑	25 Jul	147S	2♒	19 Dec	114N	27♊
1927	15 Jun	119S	23♐	8 Dec	124N	16♊						
1928	3 Jun	129S	13♐	27 Nov	134N	5♊						
1929	23 May	139S	2♐	17 Nov	144N	24♉						
1930	13 Apr	111S	23♎	7 Oct	116N	14♈						
1931	2 Apr	121S	12♎	26 Sep	126N	3♈						
1932	22 Mar	131S	2♎	14 Sep	136N	22♓						
1933	10 Feb	103S	21♌	12 Mar	141S	21♍	5 Aug	108N	13♒	4 Sep	146N	11♓
1934	30 Jan	113S	10♌	26 Jul	118N	3♒						
1935	19 Jan	123S	29♋	16 Jul	128N	23♑						
1936	8 Jan	133S	17♋	4 Jul	138N	13♑	28 Dec	143S	6♋			
1937	25 May	110N	4♐	18 Nov	115S	26♉						
1938	14 May	120N	23♏	7 Nov	125S	15♉						
1939	3 May	130N	12♏	28 Oct	135S	4♉						
1940	23 Mar	102N	3♎	22 Apr	140N	2♏	16 Oct	145S	23♈			
1941	13 Mar	112N	23♍	5 Sep	117S	15♓						
1942	3 Mar	122N	12♍	26 Aug	127S	2♓						
1943	20 Feb	132N	1♍	15 Aug	137S	22♒						
1944	9 Feb	142N	19♌	6 Jul	109S	14♑	4 Aug	147S	12♒	29 Dec	114N	8♋
1945	25 Jun	119S	4♑	19 Dec	124N	27♊						
1946	14 Jun	129S	23♐	8 Dec	134N	16♊						
1947	3 Jun	139S	12♐	28 Nov	144N	5♊						
1948	23 Apr	111S	3♏	18 Oct	116N	25♈						
1949	13 Apr	121S	23♎	7 Oct	126N	13♈						

1950	2 Apr	131S	12♎	26 Sep	136N	3♈						
1951	23 Mar	141S	2♎	17 Aug	108N	23♒	15 Sep	146N	22♓			
1952	11 Feb	113S	21♌	5 Aug	118N	13♒						
1953	29 Jan	123S	10♌	26 Jul	128N	3♒						
1954	19 Jan	133S	28♋	16 Jul	138N	23♑						
1955	8 Jan	143S	17♋	5 Jun	110N	14♐	29 Nov	115S	7♊			
1956	24 May	120N	3♐	18 Nov	125S	26♉						
1957	13 May	130N	23♏	7 Nov	135S	15♉						
1958	4 Apr	102N	14♎	3 May	140N	13♏	27 Oct	145S	4♉			
1959	24 Mar	112N	3♎	17 Sep	117S	23♓						
1960	13 Mar	122N	23♍	5 Sep	127S	13♓						
1961	2 Mar	132N	12♍	26 Aug	137S	3♓						
1962	19 Feb	142N	0♍	17 Jul	109S	24♑	15 Aug	147S	22♒			
1963	9 Jan	114N	19♋	6 Jul	119S	14♑	30 Dec	124N	8♋			
1964	25 Jun	129S	3♑	19 Dec	134N	27♊						
1965	14 Jun	139S	23♐	8 Dec	144N	16♊						
1966	4 May	111S	14♏	29 Oct	116N	6♉						
1967	24 Apr	121S	4♏	18 Oct	126N	24♈						
1968	13 Apr	131S	23♎	6 Oct	136N	13♈						
1969	2 Apr	141S	13♎	27 Aug	108N	4♓	25 Sep	146N	3♈			
1970	21 Feb	113S	2♍	17 Aug	118N	24♒						
1971	10 Feb	123S	21♌	6 Aug	128N	14♒						
1972	30 Jan	133S	10♌	26 Jul	138N	3♒						
1973	18 Jan	143S	29♋	15 Jun	110N	25♐	15 Jul	148N	22♑	10 Dec	115S	18♊
1974	4 Jun	120N	14♐	29 Nov	125S	7♊						
1975	25 May	130N	3♐	18 Nov	135S	26♉						

1976	13 May	140N	23♏	6 Nov	145S	15♉						
1977	4 Apr	112N	14♎	27 Sep	117S	4♈						
1978	24 Mar	122N	4♎	16 Sep	127S	24♓						
1979	13 Mar	132N	23♍	6 Sep	137S	13♓						
1980	1 Mar	142N	11♍	27 Jul	109S	5♒	26 Aug	147S	3♓			
1981	20 Jan	114N	0♌	17 Jul	119S	25♑						
1982	9 Jan	124N	19♋	6 Jul	129S	14♑	30 Dec	134N	8♋			
1983	25 Jun	139S	3♑	20 Dec	144N	28♊						
1984	15 May	111S	24♏	13 Jun	149S	22♐	8 Nov	116N	16♉			
1985	4 May	121S	14♏	28 Oct	126N	5♉						
1986	24 Apr	131S	4♏	17 Oct	136N	24♈						
1987	14 Apr	141S	24♎	7 Oct	146N	13♈						
1988	3 Mar	113S	13♍	27 Aug	118N	4♓						
1989	20 Feb	123S	2♍	17 Aug	128N	24♒						
1990	9 Feb	133S	21♌	6 Aug	138N	14♒						
1991	30 Jan	143S	10♌	27 Jun	110N	5♑	26 Jul	148N	3♒	21 Dec	115S	29♊
1992	15 Jun	120N	24♐	9 Dec	125S	18♊						
1993	4 Jun	130N	14♐	29 Nov	135S	7♊						
1994	25 May	140N	4♐	18 Nov	145S	26♉						
1995	15 Apr	112N	25♎	8 Oct	117S	15♈						
1996	4 Apr	122N	15♎	27 Sep	127S	4♈						
1997	24 Mar	132N	4♎	16 Sep	137S	24♓						
1998	13 Mar	142N	22♍	8 Aug	109S	15♒	6 Sep	147S	14♓			
1999	31 Jan	114N	11♌	28 Jul	119S	5♒						
2000	21 Jan	124N	0♌	16 Jul	129S	24♑						
2001	9 Jan	134N	19♋	5 Jul	139S	13♑	30 Dec	144N	8♋			

2002	26 May	111S	5♐	24 Jun	149S	3♑	20 Nov	116N	27♉			
2003	16 May	121S	24♏	9 Nov	126N	16♉						
2004	4 May	131S	14♏	28 Oct	136N	5♉						
2005	24 Apr	141S	4♏	17 Oct	146N	24♈						
2006	14 Mar	113S	24♍	7 Sep	118N	15♓						
2007	3 Mar	123S	13♍	28 Aug	128N	4♓						
2008	21 Feb	133S	1♍	16 Aug	138N	24♒						
2009	9 Feb	143S	21♌	7 Jul	110N	15♑	6 Aug	148N	13♒	31 Dec	115S	10♋
2010	26 Jun	120N	4♑	21 Dec	125S	29♊						
2011	15 Jun	130N	24♐	10 Dec	135S	18♊						
2012	4 Jun	140N	14♐	28 Nov	145S	6♊						
2013	25 Apr	112N	5♏	25 May	150N	4♐	18 Oct	117S	25♈			
2014	15 Apr	122N	25♎	8 Oct	127S	15♈						
2015	4 Apr	132N	14♎	28 Sep	137S	4♈						
2016	23 Mar	142N	3♎	16 Sep	147S	24♓						
2017	11 Feb	114N	22♌	7 Aug	119S	15♒						
2018	31 Jan	124N	11♌	27 Jul	129S	4♒						
2019	21 Jan	134N	0♌	16 Jul	139S	24♑						
2020	10 Jan	144N	20♋	5 Jun	111S	15♐	5 Jul	149S	13♑	30 Nov	116N	8♊
2021	26 May	121S	5♐	19 Nov	126N	27♉						
2022	16 May	131S	25♏	8 Nov	136N	16♉						
2023	5 May	141S	14♏	28 Oct	146N	5♉						
2024	25 Mar	113S	5♎	18 Sep	118N	25♓						
2025	14 Mar	123S	23♍	7 Sep	128N	15♓						
2026	3 Mar	133S	12♍	28 Aug	138N	4♓						
2027	20 Feb	143S	2♍	18 Jul	110N	25♑	17 Aug	148N	24♒			

2028	12 Jan	115S	21♋	6 Jul	120N	15♑	31 Dec	125S	10♋			
2029	26 Jun	130N	4♑	20 Dec	135S	29♊						
2030	15 Jun	140N	24♐	9 Dec	145S	17♊						
2031	7 May	112N	16♏	5 Jun	150N	14♐	30 Oct	117S	6♉			
2032	25 Apr	122N	5♏	18 Oct	127S	25♈						
2033	14 Apr	132N	25♎	8 Oct	137S	15♈						
2034	3 Apr	142N	14♎	28 Sep	147S	5♈						
2035	22 Feb	114N	3♍	19 Aug	119S	25♒						
2036	11 Feb	124N	22♌	7 Aug	129S	15♒						
2037	31 Jan	134N	12♌	27 Jul	139S	4♒						
2038	21 Jan	144N	1♌	17 Jun	111S	26♐	16 Jul	149S	24♑	11 Dec	116N	19♊
2039	6 Jun	121S	15♐	30 Nov	126N	8♊						
2040	26 May	131S	5♐	18 Nov	136N	27♉						
2041	16 May	141S	25♏	8 Nov	146N	16♉						
2042	5 Apr	113S	15♎	29 Sep	118N	6♈						
2043	25 Mar	123S	4♎	19 Sep	128N	26♓						
2044	13 Mar	133S	23♍	7 Sep	138N	15♓						
2045	3 Mar	143S	13♍	27 Aug	148N	4♓						
2046	22 Jan	115S	2♌	18 Jul	120N	25♑						
2047	12 Jan	125S	21♋	7 Jul	130N	15♑						
2048	1 Jan	135S	10♋	26 Jun	140N	5♑	20 Dec	145S	29♊			
2049	17 May	112N	27♏	15 Jun	150N	25♐	9 Nov	117S	17♉			
2050	6 May	122N	16♏	30 Oct	127S	6♉						
2051	25 Apr	132N	5♏	19 Oct	137S	26♈						
2052	13 Apr	142N	24♎	8 Oct	147S	15♈						
2053	4 Mar	114N	14♍	28 Aug	119S	6♓						

2054	21 Feb	124N	3♍	18 Aug	129S	25♒						
2055	11 Feb	134N	23♌	7 Aug	139S	14♒						
2056	1 Feb	144N	12♌	27 Jun	111S	6♑	26 Jul	149S	4♒	22 Dec	116N	1♋
2057	17 Jun	121S	26♐	11 Dec	126N	19♊						
2058	6 Jun	131S	16♐	30 Nov	136N	8♊						
2059	26 May	141S	6♐	19 Nov	146N	27♉						
2060	15 Apr	113S	26♎	9 Oct	118N	17♈	8 Nov	156N	16♉			
2061	4 Apr	123S	15♎	29 Sep	128N	6♈						
2062	25 Mar	133S	4♎	18 Sep	138N	26♓						
2063	14 Mar	143S	24♍	7 Sep	148N	15♓						
2064	2 Feb	115S	13♌	28 Jul	120N	6♒						
2065	22 Jan	125S	2♌	17 Jul	130N	25♑						
2066	11 Jan	135S	21♋	7 Jul	140N	15♑	31 Dec	145S	10♋			
2067	28 May	112N	7♐	27 Jun	150N	5♑	21 Nov	117S	28♉			
2068	17 May	122N	27♏	9 Nov	127S	17♉						
2069	6 May	132N	16♏	30 Oct	137S	7♉						
2070	25 Apr	142N	5♏	19 Oct	147S	26♈						
2071	16 Mar	114N	25♍	9 Sep	119S	17♓						
2072	4 Mar	124N	14♍	28 Aug	129S	6♓						
2073	22 Feb	134N	4♍	17 Aug	139S	25♒						
2074	11 Feb	144N	23♌	8 Jul	111S	17♑	7 Aug	149S	14♒			
2075	2 Jan	116N	12♋	28 Jun	121S	6♑	22 Dec	126N	0♋			
2076	17 Jun	131S	26♐	10 Dec	136N	19♊						
2077	6 Jun	141S	16♐	29 Nov	146N	8♊						
2078	27 Apr	113S	7♏	21 Oct	118N	28♈	19 Nov	156N	27♉			
2079	16 Apr	123S	26♎	10 Oct	128N	17♈						

2080	4 Apr	133S	15♎	29 Sep	138N	6♈						
2081	25 Mar	143S	4♎	18 Sep	148N	25♓						
2082	13 Feb	115S	25♌	8 Aug	120N	16♒						
2083	2 Feb	125S	14♌	29 Jul	130N	6♒						
2084	22 Jan	135S	2♌	17 Jul	140N	26♑						
2085	10 Jan	145S	21♋	8 Jun	112N	18♐	7 Jul	150N	15♑	1 Dec	117S	9♊
2086	28 May	122N	7♐	20 Nov	127S	29♉						
2087	17 May	132N	27♏	10 Nov	137S	18♉						
2088	5 May	142N	16♏	30 Oct	147S	7♉						
2089	26 Mar	114N	6♎	19 Sep	119S	27♓						
2090	15 Mar	124N	25♍	8 Sep	129S	16♓						
2091	5 Mar	134N	15♍	29 Aug	139S	5♓						
2092	23 Feb	144N	4♍	19 Jul	111S	27♑	17 Aug	149S	25♒			
2093	12 Jan	116N	23♋	8 Jul	121S	17♑						
2094	1 Jan	126N	11♋	28 Jun	131S	7♑	21 Dec	136N	0♋			
2095	17 Jun	141S	26♐	11 Dec	146N	19♊						
2096	7 May	113S	18♏	6 Jun	151S	16♐	31 Oct	118N	9♉	29 Nov	156N	8♊
2097	26 Apr	123S	7♏	21 Oct	128N	28♈						
2098	15 Apr	133S	26♎	10 Oct	138N	17♈						
2099	5 Apr	143S	15♎	29 Sep	148N	6♈						
2100	24 Feb	115S	6♍	19 Aug	120N	27♒						

Space Lanes (SLs)

Larry King hit the celestial jackpot on the day he was born: his PREBLE-LS146 lit up his ASC/DSC axis. This alignment offers an individual a celestial speedway that sets before them a unique path or portal into the entire field of the eclipse, allowing for made-to-order downloads that can set life into motion. These celestial pathways are "Space Lanes," an original concept that I have discovered to be stunningly effective. There are two styles of Space Lanes (SLs): the first is created when the lunar eclipse axis connects into the angles of the chart—i.e., through contact with the ASC/DSC/MC/IC. The second SL is created when the nodal axis of the lunar eclipse connects into the angles of the chart. When they occur through a transiting eclipse activation, SLs provide an acceleration of energy that is hard to resist.

Eclipse Axis to ASC/DSC/MC/IC

Aretha Franklin has Space Lanes that run right through her Fourth House IC foundation to the roof of her world Tenth House MC giving her, from birth, a road to stardom. Similar but different is the case of Roman Polanski who also has SLs through his IC to MC, but the impact his Dragon Family LS108 DNA wielded gave his life a completely different path. There are so many more but let's give a shout out to Tony Robbins who was born, like Larry King, with SLs across his ASC/DSC and, thanks to the sphere of consciousness running through his mighty LS117 Air Dragons, we are all the better for Tony's liberation.

Bill Clinton would experience a different style of liberation as SLs arrived on August 8, 1998, via the Air Dragons of LS109; they rose up through his Fourth House IC and literally took him out of the game of politics. And then there's Winston Churchill who got back into power thanks to the illustrious SLs of LS140 arriving on April 22, 1940, to light up his DSC/ASC axis and make him once again a beloved public figure. Finally, there is the ignoble case of Prince Andrew who, in the spring of 2022 would be taken out of the game by the aptly named Air Dragons of LS126—Game Changers—as their eclipse axis lit up both "Randy Andy" and Virginia Giuffre's identical 11 degree Leo ASC/DSC axis.

Eclipse Nodes to ASC/DSC/MC/IC

Susan Boyle is a wonderful example of SLs created by the eclipse nodal axis running through her birth chart via the Fourth/Tenth axis thanks to her Air Dragon LS143 family's nodal axis laying down a path for her to follow "when she was good and ready." There is often a delay with the nodal axis falling on the angles of a birth chart. It is understandably an energy that seems to collect its strength and direction given enough time and life experience. This is especially the case when the North Node attaches to the IC making it a struggle but an even sweeter victory when its soulful song emerges and never truer than in the life of Susan Boyle.

We have one of the greatest comedians of all time—Lenny Bruce born with SLs running right across his ASC/DSC axis from the Water Dragons of LS137 whose tidal flows and flux were the story of his turbulent career. And if you're going to court or waging a public feeding frenzy like Johnny Depp did in the spring of 2022 against his ex Amber Heard, it helps to have the reigning dragons in charge—LS131 and their "Pursuit of Truth" nodal punch running SLs of support through his Tenth MC to his Fourth IC axis. SLs are particularly effective when they activate the ASC/DSC axis by a returning transit as you'll read about in the case of Clint Eastwood and his extraordinary encounter in the spring of 2013 with the arrival of the Fire Dragons of LS150 in Part One.

Three Styles of Cosmic Bridges (CBs)

Eclipse Axis to Nodes, Planets, Midpoints, and Asteroids

When it comes to natural born talent it's hard to beat a Cosmic Bridge created from the eclipse Moon in a 1st or 2nd Harmonic to the nodal axis, Moon, or any one of the planets. Think of this bridge style as the San Francisco Golden Gate Bridge of CBs, a classic in every sense of the word. A CB from the eclipse Moon to the nodal axis or to the Moon is a destiny marker with enough power to either set the course of your life or change it simply by experiencing one of its returns. Here are some examples of the people you'll meet who have an eclipse Moon contact to their nodal axis: Larry Page, Sergey Brin, and Oskar Schindler LS109; Alexandra Elbakyan LS118; Nikola Tesla LS121; Margaret Atwood LS135; Kathryn Bigelow LS141; and Dr. Robert Gallo LS149. Examples of the eclipse Moon to a natal Moon are extremely potent and are found in the charts of such public figures as Tony Robbins LS117, Donald Trump LS129, and Oprah Winfrey LS133. A transiting lunar eclipse activation can change your life as it did with Fidel Castro LS102, Nikola Tesla LS121, Adele LS130, and Queen of Camelot's Jackie Kennedy Onassis and Queen of France's Marie Antoinette both of LS136.

The eclipse axis Moon making contact to the Sun seems to create an international field of experience for all event charts as well as for those receiving contact by birthright or rite of passage. This eclipse contact can take hold on the psyche and individuals touched by its essence can reach across the globe to fascinate and frustrate all those held captive by their presence. Here are a few examples: Roman Polanski LS108, William Shatner (aka Captain Kirk) from LS116, Volodymyr Zelenskyy LS126, J. P. Getty LS129, Steven Spielberg LS130, Brexit LS144, Tim Berners-Lee and Richard Nixon LS148, and Taylor Swift from LS149.

The eclipse axis Sun making contact to the Sun in a chart is a sign that you are ahead of the social curve and have to wait for the zeitgeist to catch up with your brilliance. Here are a few examples: Bob Fosse and Alan Turing from LS128, Steven Spielberg from LS130, and Mahatma Gandhi from LS139. All other eclipse axis Sun contacts are a sure sign of success with dozens of examples in this book. Here is a taste of what's to follow.

Adele	LS130's Sun	1st H to her Moon
J. P. Getty	LS129's Sun	2nd H to his Sun
Leonardo DiCaprio	LS120's Sun	2nd H to his Mercury
Audrey Hepburn	LS134's Sun	1st H to her Venus
Chien Shiung Wu	LS125's Sun	1st H to her Mars
J. R. R. Tolkien	LS124's Sun	2nd H to his Ceres
Martin Luther King	LS119's Sun	2nd H to his Jupiter
Edith Piaf	LS149's Sun	1st H to her Saturn
Edward Snowden	LS150's Sun	1st H to his Chiron
Jack Dorsey	LS113's Sun	2nd H to his Uranus
Orson Welles	LS125's Sun	1st H to his Neptune
Bonnie Parker	LS129's Sun	1st H to her Pluto

Cosmic Bridges

Eclipse Nodes to Planets, Midpoints and Asteroids

As impressive as the CBs are from the eclipse axis, you don't want to miss out on what the eclipse nodal axis has to offer. Think of these CBs like New York's illustrious Brooklyn Bridge that gives access and mobility to the millions that cross that span every day. These CBs are just as critical since they can literally launch or reboot a career or relationship with one mighty link. There are dozens of examples in the book that highlight how one transiting lunar eclipse node connection has provided a key link to a better place and even space if you're an astronaut like LS141's Sally Ride. To have the nodal axis of your PREBLE resonating to the energies within your chart can give you a path to follow for life. These are rocket boosters capable of blasting off or finishing off whatever needs doing and most of the time there doesn't seem to be much choice in the matter. It is as if a higher power knows best and is on the job. If you need a change of direction, look forward to the next lunar eclipse whose nodal axis links to your chart. And again, here is a taste of what awaits in the land of Lunar Nodes.

Harry Houdini	147	NN	Moon	Jack Dorsey	113	SN	Moon
V. Zelenskyy	126	NN	Mercury	Jim Henson	138	SN	Mercury
Oskar Schindler	109	NN	Venus	Jean-Paul Sartre	112	SN	Venus
Larry King	146	NN	Mars	Ricky Gervais	132	SN	Mars
Billy Crystal	144	NN	Ceres	Einstein	112	SN	Ceres
J. K. Rowling	147	NN	Jupiter	Bear Stearns	133	SN	Jupiter
Akiane Kramarik	140	NN	Saturn	Neil Peart	120	SN	Saturn
The Red Baron	123	NN	Chiron	Aretha Franklin	122	SN	Chiron
Elon Musk	121	NN	Uranus	Putin	126	SN	Uranus
William Shatner	116	NN	Neptune	Johnny Depp	131	SN	Neptune
Brexit	144	NN	Pluto	Tiger Woods	127	SN	Pluto

Cosmic Bridges

Planets and PREBLES

The Dragon Bridge of Da Nang, Vietnam, is the perfect metaphor to represent the nobility, power, and prosperity that has always been associated with dragons. This style of CB is in fact the most abundant and there are over 142 celestial combinations that provide fascinating examples of how planets from the lunar eclipse field can interact and breathe life into your unique sphere of awareness. These are the "meat and potatoes" backbone of interaction that provides the structure and stability for what is possible when a Lunar Saros Series comes calling. And when you do connect with one, either by way of its eighteen year return or through a get together with your PREBLE, remember to take into account the widely and wildly different fates available to any two energetic systems coming together: it's Einstein's Quantum Entanglement at its best. And don't think for a minute that those 2nd Harmonic connections are playing hard to get. When working with lunar eclipses you'll find them to be masters of manifestation, eager to bring a taste of their world to your doorstep. Here are some examples:

H. G. Wells	125	Uranus-Moon	Roddenberry	130	Uranus-Moon
David Letterman	142	Mercury-Mercury	Louis Theroux	113	Mercury-Mercury
Audrey Hepburn	134	Moon-Venus	Angelina Jolie	134	Moon-Jupiter
Robert Downey	123	Venus-Mars	Jackie "O"	136	Venus-Mars
Aretha Franklin	122	Uranus-Mars	Salvador Dalí	144	Mars-Uranus
Nelson Mandela	133	Ceres-Jupiter	MrBeast	142	Jupiter-Ceres
Princess Diana	117	Saturn-Jupiter	Matt Damon	118	Jupiter-Saturn
Alice A. Bailey	115	NNode-Jupiter	Johnny Depp	131	Jupiter-SNode
V. Zelenskyy	126	Saturn-Saturn	Eve Ensler	135	Saturn-Saturn
J. F. K.	132	Uranus-Saturn	The Red Baron	123	Uranus-Saturn
Pablo Picasso	128	Neptune-Sun	Steve Jobs	143	Neptune-Saturn
Paul Newman	134	Pluto-Moon	Jordan Peterson	142	SNode-Pluto

Global Gateways

The Problematical GGs

There are four possible GGs created from contact to a nodal axis and two of them are kind of a drag. The problematical ones are created when an eclipse NNode or SNode makes contact with another NNode or SNode in the same polarity. It all looks friendly but they're a portal to frustration. There's hardly any charge and this type of contact has fewer options to speak of and is often frustrating and anxiety producing. I discovered this well into my research as I began noticing the powerful effect that an opposite nodal polarity had on one's level of effectiveness and fulfillment. It seemed counter-intuitive since I had always worked from the premise that a similar nodal axis was a connection of agreement and harmony. But the research proved that this is not in fact true—in fact the opposite is true, at least for lunar eclipses.

Let's use Pablo Picasso as an example; his nodal axis is South Node Gemini, North Node Sagittarius, the same nodal polarity found in his Earth Dragon LS128—Coming Into Existence family. Now Picasso was the most iconic artist of the 20th century, so this doesn't seem to affect your status in the outer world. In fact, Donald Trump shares the same fate, as does J. K. Rowling, Richard

Nixon, Wayne Gretzky, H. P. Lovecraft, Shailene Woodley, Anne Frank and Amber Heard. It may offer the Midas touch or celebrity status, but it doesn't seem to bring a lot of happiness in one's emotional world, at least not until one overcomes some major career setbacks and emotional hurdles. If this is part of your dragon DNA, you have to embrace either the struggle that invariably comes with your professional path or the frustration that surrounds your personal and intimate relationships.

You might want to start by finding all the Dragon families who share your nodal axis so you can circle in RED all the families whose South Node activates your South Node and North Node to North Node as these are just plain difficult families for you. I never thought of this until now but I'm thinking this could be worth looking into for compatibility profiles. You know, certain years, certain dragon families that have the same polarity to yours (to avoid) and those that have the opposite polarity (to attract) might be worth looking into.

Global Gateways

The Fun and Fabulous GGs

Now that you've met the first two GGs you know that juice flows from an eclipse node in contact with another node but in the opposite polarity. There are many luminaries in the book who have benefited from a highly charged opposite polarity GG including Matt Damon, Steven Spielberg, Alexandra Elbakyan, Bob Fosse, Brad Pitt, Thomas Merton, and the fabulously outrageous MrBeast. I'm sure you'll want to eagerly find and circle in GREEN all the Dragon families who have the reverse polarity of your nodal axis, where their South Node activates and "charges up" your North Node and vice-versa. There's solid science behind this as it works on the same principle as a battery where the current in the circuit flows from the positive to the negative electrode. Ohm's law states that current flows from a positive to negative electric potential; this is like the flow of electrons in a battery, where one side of the battery is pushing and the other side is pulling electrons, creating an electric charge.

Midpoints

The joy of writing a book comes from all the discoveries made along the way. I started using midpoints in my lunar eclipse research when there were no obvious direct hits to planets or angles from the eclipse activation degree. I knew something had to be going on but what was it? As providence or dumb luck would have it, midpoint activations would play a major role in hundreds of case studies undertaken for this book. You'll be amazed at how potent and precise they are once they are activated. Never fail to include them. Each introduction to a Lunar Saros Series includes the top two midpoint structures along with the two tightest isotrap patterns. I have noticed that with every return of a lunar eclipse, its midpoint structures seem to act with a greater degree of finesse and control; it is as if the consciousness of the entire sphere is evolving. All of which contributes to my hypothesis that these are families with distinct personalities and in their lifetimes, like us, are moving through states of awareness in terms of sensitivity, sophistication, and effectiveness.

Isosceles Trapezoid Diagonals aka Isotraps

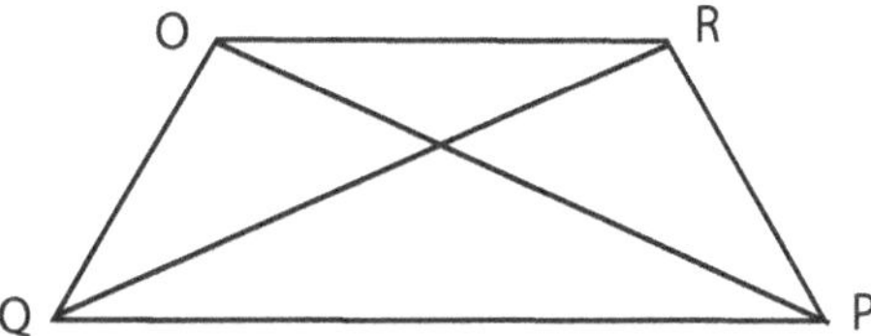

Here's the math stuff first: The bases (top and bottom) of an isosceles trapezoid are parallel. The opposite sides of an isosceles trapezoid are the same length and are thus congruent, which makes the diagonals also congruent. If lines were drawn between each of the opposite corners, this would create isosceles trapezoid diagonals. If planets were placed at the O and P diagonal they would hold the same relationship to planets at the Q and R diagonal, making the planets at the O and R as well as the Q and P placements in resonance, greatly enhancing the entire pattern. Astrologers call such a pattern an isotrap. Many have noticed that there is something almost magical going on with the diagonals and planets at those energetic placements, creating a resonance much like a tuning fork. David Cochrane calls it an anti-entropy function as it creates complexity and gives a huge resonance through the entire pattern as well as setting a basic foundational tone. The Sun/Mars conjunct Saturn/Neptune isotrap of 2023's LS141 holds the potential to empower individualistic achievement based on service and inspiration.

Critical Degree Theory (CDT)

I've tried almost every technique in astrology that comes across my laptop and have to say the surprise of 2021 was to discover the work of Serbian astrologer Nikola Stojanovic and his Critical Degree Theory. Sadly, Nikola died of COVID-19 on April 5, 2021, just as I was making plans to go to Europe to study with him. But even from the basic knowledge that he so generously shared with the world, truly amazing and highly accurate statements and predictions can be made from using his CDT. In essence, the first degree is an Aries influence, the second carries a Taurean vibe and around the wheel we go. Every degree past twelve restarts the Zodiac sequence where thirteen as well as twenty-five hook and hold the Aries template beginning anew the celestial dance. Zero is an intriguing degree: it represents the basic characteristics as well as the full potential inherent in the archetypal structure of the sign in which it is placed. All 0° placements are a ticket to adventure and function within an enormous range of expression. There are multiple references throughout this book that demonstrate the effectiveness and revelatory nature of Stojanovic's Critical Degree Theory.

PREBLE Protocol

When evaluating the strength of a PREBLE here is a protocol that I find helpful and have used consistently throughout my research: Start with a basic understanding of the chart. Next, immerse yourself in the meaning of the PREBLE that is its Dragon DNA. This will help you to immediately start making sense of the connections that you'll find between their respective fields.

Start your list with the highest value connections: The Space Lanes, the Cosmic Bridges, and the high or low energy levels of the Global Gateways. The CBs created by the nodal axis and eclipse axis to your natal and progressed nodes and luminaries are the most dynamic. Finish by noting any phase angle similarities—these are subtle yet significant. If you were born within three weeks of an eclipse you will have two PREBLES—twice the work but twice the fun.

To recap: Start by finding your Dragon Family. You just might have two. To be born within days or even hours of a lunar eclipse doesn't always leave the deepest impressions as you'll see with Donald Trump's analysis. Whatever element your dragon family hails from, read the Introduction to that section first and then your dragon family Lunar Saros Series. For example, I was born on May 6, 1953, which means that my birth occurred between the lunar eclipse of January

29, 1953, and the next lunar eclipse of July 26, 1953. My birth makes me part of the Air Dragon clan of LS123—so that is my PREBLE. I would then go to Part Three—Dancing with Air—and read the Introduction to find out what these Air Dragons are all about. Then it's on to your PREBLE to learn more.

When you're ready, create a Bi-Wheel of you and your Dragon family. After admiring the two of you, get down to the nitty-gritty of what makes you and your family tick. Start your list of connections and remember to always put the eclipse energy first as you'll see in all the examples in the book. Remember the orbs:

6 degree orb for Sun/Moon/Nodes to planets, nodes, and angles
5 degree orb for the same planet to planet contacts
4 degree orb for planets to planets and midpoints
3 degree orb for planets to asteroids

Pay attention to any patterns in your Dragon family's chart: T-Squares, Kites, Grand Trines, Crosses, Fans, Yods, Boomerangs (aka Anchors) that connect into your chart. You will be able to sync to that pattern if you have resonance with it. A lot of connectors/tie-ins doesn't necessarily make for a strong resonance. What makes the resonance strong are the SLs, CBs, and GGs.

Traveling Back in Time

Now it's time to travel back in time. To do that you simply refer to the 200 Years of Lunar Saros Dragon Degrees (see page 7): all the activation degrees are listed. Find the degrees that sync with your chart. Note all the activation degrees that either conjunct or oppose any of your planets, angles, midpoints, and asteroids; those will be outstanding three to six month periods of high activity or of intense inner focus. Another suggestion is to go through the entire set of forty-seven lunar eclipses and find the eclipses that have your Moon sign as this basic resonance instantly opens the door to their domain, and of course the tighter the contact the stronger the resonance.

Traveling Forward in Time

And when the time is right and you have a few hours or days to spare, check out the lunar eclipses that are on the horizon and especially those that have strong resonance to your chart. If you've noticed that a certain Lunar Saros Series or maybe a few of them have consistently produced events or experiences that have made an impact on your life, chances are good that they will bring forth similar results in their next return. There are so many ways to dance with these eclipses and I feel like I am just getting started on figuring them out. Meanwhile, there are plenty of lunar eclipses to keep us engaged and dancing through time.

Keeping Track of the Tribe

At the end of each Part Introduction, you'll find a listing of all the eclipses in that element by Zodiac sign for a quick and easy reference. For example, Part One holds the largest cache of eclipses—fifteen—and out of those fifteen, ten are fueled by the expansive and optimistic tenor of Sagittarius. Now, if you have a Moon in Sagittarius, you'll want to know where to find the rest of your clan. If you have an Aries Moon, same deal, you'll want to know where to find the Lunar Saros Series that are powered up by the fire Moons of Aries. Sad to say there are currently no active Lunar Saros Series that feature Moon in Leo designation. And there is nothing on the horizon until at least the 31st century.

Lunar Eclipse Phases

The forty-seven Lunar Saros Series eclipses you are about to meet have a lifespan of anywhere from 1,260 to 1,496 years. LS126, LS147, and LS148 have only seventy returns; only one eclipse, LS102 holds the distinction of being the longest lived with eighty-four returns. But no matter how long lived they may be, they all fall into phases that are marked by the lunar cycle itself, namely its New Moon, Crescent, First Quarter, Gibbous, Full Moon, Disseminating, Last Quarter to its closing Balsamic Dark of the Moon phase. As Michael Erlewine has stated, all cycles can be broken down into phases and because astrology is all about the study of cycles, it is worth our time to study them.[1]

To appreciate the impact your lunar eclipse family has, it is helpful to know what particular phase of evolution your dragon family is at, especially since the phases shift every seventy-two to ninety years and bring with those changes an updated agenda and style of behavior. And in case you are wondering where we start the clock, as Dane Rudhyar has said, you can pick any point in the phases of a cycle because there isn't just one way to do this.[2] Because all the Lunar Saros Series eclipses begin at the moment of Full Moon, the clock starts at this moment and proceeds to unfold from there. It is fascinating to live through a dragon phase shift; as their priorities change, so too will yours

As an example, here are the dates for Lunar Saros 122 as it unfolds through an ancient, eight-fold rhythm. During their lifespan of 1,316 years, we get to experience their take on the world as they share their sphere and hold us dear on the terrestrial dance floor that marks out each and every one of their seventy-four returns. With every return we get better and better at learning to move in sync with their cosmic rhythms. LS122 entered a Disseminating Phase on April 4, 1996. This fifty-fifth visit opened at 15 Libra with every return that follows advancing through the Zodiac by ten to twelve degrees. You can refer back to the 200 Year Lunar Saros Dragon Degrees on page 12 to watch their trek across the Zodiac until the year 2100.

Lunar Saros 122

54th visit	March 24, 1978	03 ♎
55th visit	April 4, 1996	15 ♎
56th visit	April 15, 2014	25 ♎
57th visit	April 25, 2032	05 ♏
58th visit	May 6, 2050	16 ♏

Here is an 8-Phase unfoldment of Lunar Saros 122's lifespan of 1,316 years in 74 returns:

New Moon Phase

Return	Date	Degree
1st	August 14, 1022	26 ♒
34th	August 16, 1617	23 ♒
67th	August 13, 2212	20 ♒

Crescent Phase

Return	Date	Degree
5th	October 2, 1094	09 ♈
38th	September 29, 1689	06 ♈
71st	September 25, 2284	03 ♈

First Quarter Phase

Return	Date	Degree
9th	November 16, 1166	23 ♉
42nd	November 12, 1761	20 ♉

Gibbous Phase

Return	Date	Degree
13th	December 29, 1238	08 ♋
46th	December 26, 1833	04 ♋

Full Moon Phase

Return	Date	Degree
17th	February 12, 1311	23 ♌
51st	February 20, 1924	01 ♍

Disseminating Phase

Return	Date	Degree
21st	March 27, 1383	06 ♎
55th	April 04, 1996	15 ♎

Last Quarter Phase

Return	Date	Degree
26th	May 21, 1473	00 ♐
59th	May 16, 2068	27 ♏

Balsamic Phase

Return	Date	Degree
30th	July 4, 1545	11 ♑
63rd	June 30, 2140	09 ♑

1. Michael Erlewine, *Astrology's Mirror Full-Phase Aspects* (Big Rapids, MI: e-book Startypes.com) 1998, p. 45.
2. Ibid.

PART ONE

DANCING WITH FIRE

The Fire Eclipses

"Set your life on fire. Seek those who fan your flame."

-Mevlana Rumi

Discover your potential. Turn on the air conditioning because these Dragons bring the heat. And they don't understand the word moderation. Their presence is a reminder that life must be larger than life, and that there is always a new beginning happening somewhere. The patterns and fields of energy produced by these fearless fire eclipses bring out our heroic self and magically, the world of myth becomes a part of our daily life. We awaken with renewed vigor, purpose, and connection to something deeper, higher, and greater than ordinary reality. These lunar eclipse families and their foundation birth charts all carry a magnificent entanglement of possibility, as befits their capacity to generate will, ambition, power, and excitement.

All the lunar eclipses in Part One dance around the central flame of purpose and the importance of being alive. You'll feel potent and more confident about being able to make things happen when you notice a lunar fire eclipse on the horizon. And for those fire eclipses that may seem to have passed you by, perhaps you'll be able to draw forth a better understanding of the meaning of that time period as you look back with appreciation for the mythic dimension of life that you were experiencing. Many of the fire eclipses are challenging as they relentlessly accept nothing less than the highest and best within us. If you've been drifting in and out of focus, a lunar fire eclipse may just be the cosmic tonic to get you up, out, and back in the game.

If you still seem to be on the sidelines after an encounter with a fire eclipse, it's nothing to worry about. Trust me, you're processing all the million and one sparks of inspiration, ideas, feelings, intuition, and gut reactions that these fire babies bring to the table of life. Because of the nature of fire and its connection with the ecstatic but often private mythic imagery of our inner world, it can seem as though nothing of any great consequence is going on in the outer world. However, internally, nothing could be further from the truth: life is gathering momentum, speeding up by the inevitable friction produced by the contrast of what is versus what could be. Encounters with a lunar fire eclipse are made even more poignant by perceived gaps or deficiencies in our state of affairs. Our sense of reality or entitlement can now be challenged and channeled as internal pressure seeks to find pathways that can express the emerging creative life force associated with shifts in awareness.

Part One holds the largest cache of lunar eclipses—fifteen fire dazzlers that inspire and roar with invigorating self-confidence. Each lunar eclipse presented here draws from a mixed profile of celebrities who either belong to that eclipse family or who were affected by one of its returns. In addition, there are historical moments that define the meaning of boldness of vision, while attempting to push the boundaries of acceptable gain and loss. Included as well in the profile is the occasional News Flash; these will show that our dragon families are in sync with the times.

The following example charts reflect only the smallest glimpse of possibility or outcome potentials and are given in the spirit of exploring key elements of the personality and purpose of each lunar eclipse family. To that end, Part One is replete with tales of inspiring people and their memorable life-turning moments. From revolutionary figures such as Fidel Castro and thousands of fed-up commoners who participated in England's Peasants' Revolt of 1384 to visionaries like Albert Einstein and Carl Jung, these eclipses changed the way we think about ourselves, our nations, and our place in the world.

Lunar Saros 129—Fame and Fortune—with its Moon at 26 degrees Sagittarius seemed more than predisposed to help out a family member, especially one born on the exact day of its return on June 14, 1946. Donald Trump was born into this most fortunate of lunar eclipse families as his natal chart reflects a deep resonance to this dragon family, which arrived on June 10, 1351. But Trump carries a double allegiance as do all who are born within a two to three week eclipse window where the incoming lunar eclipse saturates the pre-birth inner landscape. In Trump's case, this is PREBLE LS124—Imagine—a Water Dragon family you'll meet in Part Four.

A lunar eclipse not only affects your personality but also specific areas of interest and activities that you'll be drawn toward. To be born within hours or days of a lunar eclipse seems to mark and magnify its unique character into the energy stream of the emerging Being, regardless of time spent immersed in the previous lunar eclipse field. There is no pressure to choose as both are important; however, one dragon family's character traits do seem to dominate. A framework is given below to help determine which lunar family will take precedence.

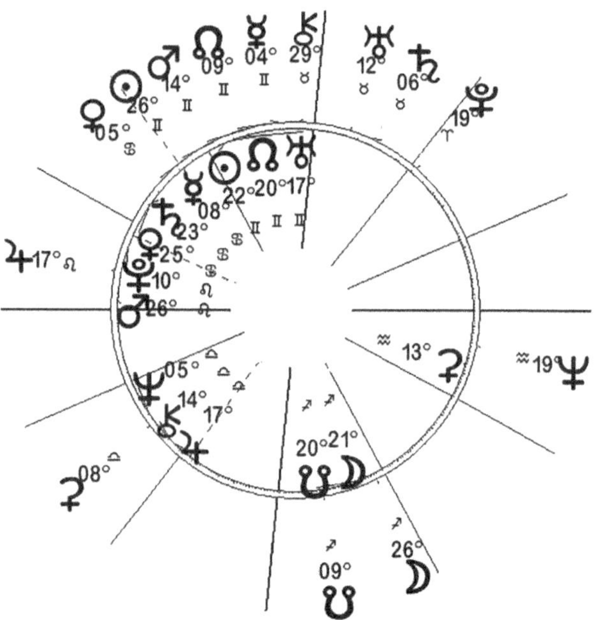

Donald Trump's Connections to the Dragons of LS129
↓SNode with SNode↓

1st Harmonics: Moon/Sun – Moon/Sun, Venus – Mercury, Ceres – Neptune, Mars – Uranus
2nd Harmonic: Pluto – Jupiter

People born within hours of a lunar eclipse, such as Trump, have the ability to experience the full range of personality and persuasion that belongs to a particular lunar eclipse. They are in essence fully paid up, cosmic card-carrying members who delight in flaunting the best and worst qualities of their cosmic relations. Lunar Saros 129 has an OOB Moon and Venus, imparting an "outlier-over-the-top" quality to Trump's core essence and an eagerness to assimilate experience.

The eclipse Pluto and its double-dipped Leo trine to Jupiter in 2nd Harmonic to Trump's Jupiter offers a collective power of worldly proportion that seeks drama and fosters great expectations. The only difficulty with LS129 is that the charts carry the same nodal polarity, which is not the best as it brings agitation and discord into the life.

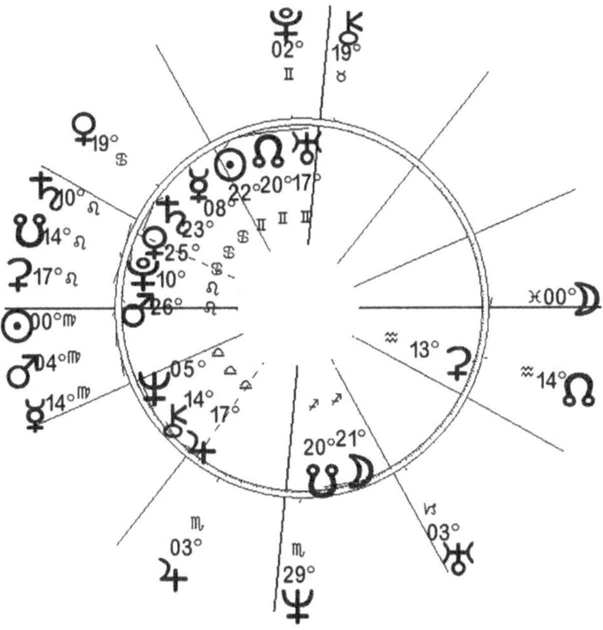

Donald Trump's Connections to the Dragons of LS124
Space Lanes via DSC/ASC
Venus with Venus
Ceres to Ceres

1st Harmonics: NNode – Ceres, SNode – Pluto, Moon – DSC, Saturn – Pluto, Chiron – MC
2nd Harmonics: Moon – Mars, Saturn – Ceres

If I had to make a case for which lunar eclipse was stronger in the life of Donald Trump, it would be his PREBLE LS124. Both charts carry Venus and Ceres ties to each other; this reinforces similar styles of value, especially as the eclipse NNode is practically sitting on his Ceres. I cannot stress enough the importance of giving Ceres her due as she is the de facto progenitor of what makes you happy! LS124's formidable Saturn-SNode to Trump's Pluto provides a talent bank of ambition and the need for public attention. But the standout connector of all connectors are the Space Lanes created by the eclipse axis falling on his DSC/ASC axis, which set his life on a unique and clearly directed path toward advancing his own agenda. Take a moment to look at the 2nd Harmonic infinity degree of his dragon family's Piscean Moon to his flamboyant and celebrity-driven Mars in Leo at the twenty-sixth degree with its Taurean overtones, and you'll see his lust for glitz and glamor really starts to make sense. You'll learn more about LS124 and its powerful scene stealer Royal Fixed Star that lights the way for opportunity to find you in the Water Dragons of Part Four.

Within each one of these fifteen lunar eclipses, you'll find brave souls shining their radiant self out into the world. Their actions are a beacon of hope, sparking life-enhancing moments for others buoyed by the confidence of their courage. Decisions made in the umbra of a fire eclipse have changed the entire trajectory of individual and national destinies. Weaving throughout these pages you'll meet a few of my clients, who wanted to contribute a personal story to share in the wonder of how lunar eclipses opened doors to new dimensions of possibility never before imagined.

If you are fortunate enough to have a feisty fire moon in your natal chart, pay attention to the lunar fire eclipses scheduled to activate your chart as they will most certainly push your panic buttons—causing all manner of conflict and arguments with others. They are not above making alliances for the sake of self-promotion as they can be a vain and proud lot. In the world of lunar eclipses, alarms and emergencies provide the necessary complications and turmoil that forge the will and help the soul to gain greater independence, insight, and higher values. Their style and manner are anything but meek, and the commotion they cause is simply exhilarating.

The Lunar Saros Series featuring a Moon in Aries will be of special interest to anyone with their natal Moon in Aries.

Lunar Saros 102
Lunar Saros 119
Lunar Saros 120
Lunar Saros 121
Lunar Saros 140

The Lunar Saros Series featuring a Moon in Sagittarius will be of special interest to anyone with their natal Moon in Sagittarius.

Lunar Saros 110
Lunar Saros 111
Lunar Saros 112
Lunar Saros 129
Lunar Saros 130
Lunar Saros 132
Lunar Saros 133

Lunar Saros 149
Lunar Saros 150
Lunar Saros 151

There are currently no active Lunar Saros Series from the 20th and 21st centuries that feature a Moon in Leo and nothing on the horizon until at least the 31st century according to NASA's official eclipse website that provides a five-millennium catalog of lunar eclipses that range from 2000 BCE to 3000 CE.

Fire Dragon Allegiance

Lunar Saros 102
Fidel Castro, The Peasant's Revolt of 1381, Robin—The Boy Wonder

Lunar Saros 110
Tina Turner, Sir Isaac Newton, Client's Story—Alannis

Lunar Saros 111
Arthur Miller, Carl Jung, *News Flash!* George Floyd

Lunar Saros 112
Albert Einstein, J. P. Sartre, Jason Collins

Lunar Saros 119
Martin Luther King, Atomic Bomb Drop,
Oumuamua—An Interstellar Visitor

Lunar Saros 120
Leonardo DiCaprio, Neil Peart, Richard Nixon

Lunar Saros 121
Nikola Tesla, Elon Musk, *News Flash!* Pulitzer Prize to Darnella Frazier

Lunar Saros 129
Donald Trump, J P Getty, Bonnie Parker

Lunar Saros 130
Gene Roddenberry, Adele, Steven Spielberg

Lunar Saros 132
Ricky Gervais, Caitlyn Jenner, John F. Kennedy

LUNAR SAROS 102

"All the heavens, all the hells are within you."

-JOSEPH CAMPBELL

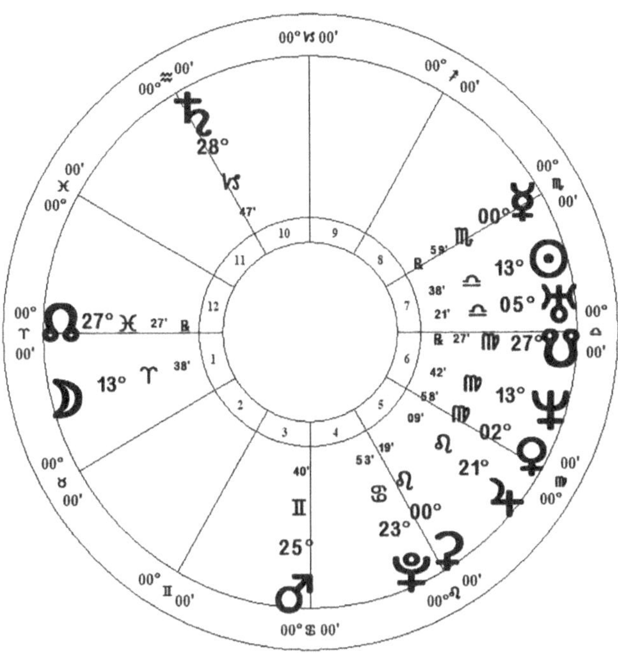

Lunar Saros 102

October 6, 461 • 1:34:43 PM • North Pole

Fires of Freedom

Lunar Saros 102 was a call to adventure for both individuals and societies unwilling to accept authoritarian rulers and archaic restrictions. Driving this NNode Aries eclipse was its Out-of-Bounds (OOB) Mars in Gemini in mutual reception (MR) with Mercury in Scorpio. Together, both planets danced in and out of military campaigns, waves of insurgencies, armed rebellions, and a plethora of hostilities too numerous to name. Confident and decidedly righteous, an atmosphere of brotherhood heightened ideological agendas and stirred the passion, pride, and pragmatism of people willing and ready to fight.

The stage was set for a noble cause to emerge as Mars tangoed with a sensitive and service-oriented Virgo/Pisces nodal axis highly attuned to the suffering of others. Mars in square to the nodes would have to face many logistical problems and fluctuating levels of resolve from communities, special interest groups and organizations. However, thanks to the hail-Mary MR effect where contingency plans reside, obstacles and delays were often miraculously sorted by unseen hands.

LS102 carried a See-Saw pattern, one of seven chart types devised by the well-known American astrologer Marc Edmund Jones in his book *The Guide to Horoscope Interpretation.*[1] Jones postulated that there were at least seven distinct personality patterns that could be gleaned just from evaluating the type of pattern formed by the planets in a chart. LS102's eclipse field had the capacity to generate tremendous internal conflict along with the ability to manipulate situations to avoid having to compromise. Self-destructive behavior was often the result thanks to the Moon at the critical, double-dipped thirteenth degree of Aries.

Critical degrees have shown their worth time and time again and in conjunction with Nikola Stojanovic's Critical Degree Theory, a world of accurate predictive patterns and places quickly emerges. The Moon's ego-centric thirteenth degree makes an almost perfect quincunx to the eclipse Neptune in Virgo, always a sign of serious dissatisfaction with the status quo along with enough irritation to do something about it. People born within the firing range of this eclipse would find their sympathies easily aroused and eager to provide service at the first threat of danger. Active in any personal, social, or environmental concerns, they exhibited a deep social and spiritual response to the challenges of their time believing that their sacrifices would not be in vain. Famous people born with the Moon in Aries include Dante, Friedrich Nietzsche, and Jacqueline Kennedy Onassis who you'll find in the Air Dragons of LS136—Risk and Reward in Part Three.

LS102 had centuries to refine its field of privilege with Saturn's power plays of tyranny and toughness. Pluto's extreme OOB (28N12) holding steady at the 23rd degree of Cancer would push Saturn's patriotic 28th degree to the outer limits of fanaticism and intolerance. Even Saturn's square to an alpha zero degree Mercury with its MR to Mars would finally have to yield the field to the vitality and leadership of a more youthful and mobile power base positioned within the sphere's Mars and its sextile to Jupiter. Decisions were made that impelled individuals to prioritize and vigorously promote either their own self-interests or social causes. The family's midpoints danced to deeply ingrained religious, spiritual, and philosophical traditions that carried a patina of righteousness that only shone brighter with every advancing return. Notice how both isotraps feature the OOB Pluto: its potential for superhuman power and exceptional ability is held within its Moon/Uranus conjunct Mars/Pluto matrix. 18th-century writer Charles-Guillaume Étienne, born under this lunar eclipse, famously remarked, "n'est jamais servi si bien que par soi-même." It has been widely translated as "If you want something done right, do it yourself."

Closest Midpoints: Jupiter/Saturn-Neptune, Eclipse/Mercury-Node
Isotraps: Moon/Uranus conjunct Mars/Pluto
Mercury/Pluto conjunct Jupiter/Uranus

1900—2100 Eclipses: Lunar Saros—102

1904, 1922, 1940, 1958
Length of cycle —1,496 years
Series ended—April 4, 1958

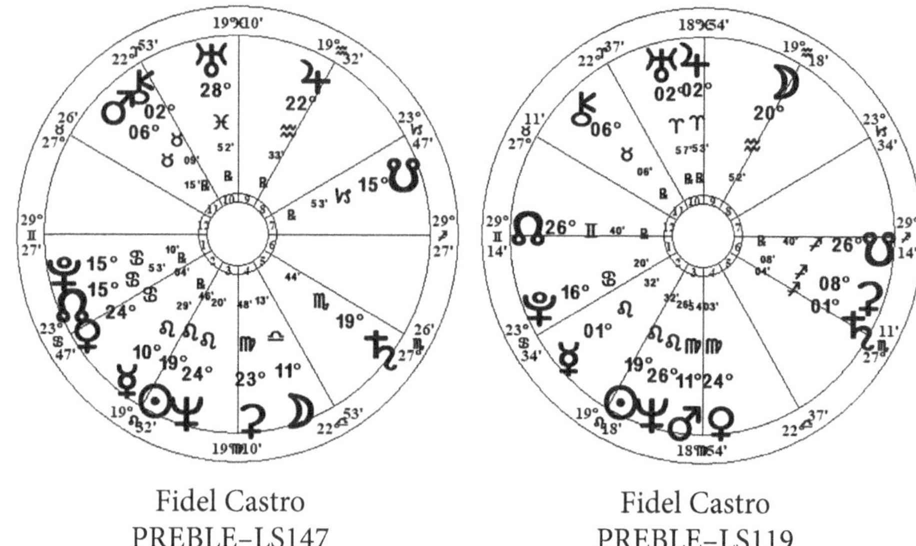

Fidel Castro
PREBLE–LS147

August 13, 1926 • 2:00 AM • Biran, Cuba

Fidel Castro
PREBLE–LS119

August 13, 1927 • 2:00 AM • Biran, Cuba

Cuban Communist Revolutionary

"Men do not shape destiny. Destiny produces the man for the hour."

–Fidel Castro

1926 is the official year of Castro's birth, however 1927 has also been put forward and that chart is included here–(see the Notes section on page 584 for more information and analysis). After a bungled attack on a military garrison in 1953, Fidel Castro was tried, convicted and sentenced to serve fifteen years in prison. He was released in 1955 on an amnesty deal with the Batista government and left for Mexico, where he would meet Che Guevara.[2] Together, they returned to Cuba in December 1956, and reignited their revolution.[3] The lunar eclipse of April 4, 1958, at 14 Libra on his Moon would mark a critical tipping point; within days, Castro would unite his forces in a compelling act of patriotic revolution.

What appeared to be a failure at creating an island-wide strike after the eclipse in April was the catalyst for the strategic turnarounds in July and August for the Rebel Army.[4] By the end of 1958, Batista's forces were on the run; in January 1959, Batista fled the country and Castro assumed command of the military.[5] Fidel's years of active commitment to social reforms had finally found success; he would be Prime Minister from 1959 to 1976 and President from 1976 to 2008.

Fidel Castro's 1926 Connections to the Lunar Dragons of LS102
Pluto with Pluto

1st Harmonics: NNode – Uranus, SNode – Ceres, Sun – Moon, Jupiter – Sun/Neptune, Uranus – Moon, Pluto – Venus, Mars – ASC, Neptune – IC
2nd Harmonics: Mercury – Chiron, Jupiter – Jupiter, Saturn – Venus

By empowering his Moon, the 1958 lunar eclipse affirmed Castro as a man of the people, especially with his Venus/Moon and Uranus/Jupiter MR, the latter of which was triggered by LS102's Jupiter activating Neptune at the fulcrum of his "Anchor." What's an Anchor you ask? It's an updated Boomerang with very tight orbs that functions in the here and now. Look for three planets that may include a node or asteroid in three consecutive signs all within a two degree orb. The fulcrum will be making an opposition to a planet, node, or asteroid at the apex of the pattern, giving it the distinctive look of an anchor. A persuasive Cosmic Bridge CB from the eclipse NNode to his Uranus and LS102's Pluto to his Venus flung open the gates for revolution.

Castro has three more CBs: the eclipse SNode to his Ceres which must have been the source of both deep pain and deep joy as Ceres in Virgo wants nothing more than to nourish loved ones, especially because, at its core, Virgo is drawn to the finest of details and often gets caught up in the minutiae of life. A SNode-Ceres combo is akin to having an on-off switch that can quickly turn darkness into light. As destiny would show, his CB eclipse Sun's 1st Harmonic to his Moon would ennoble his cause and bring his political platform, along with his magnetism and flair, to a country ready to appreciate his point of view.

The 2nd Harmonic connections are the true gift givers that emerge from our dragon families. In Castro's case, he received a 2nd Harmonic from the eclipse Moon to his natal Moon which is a 100 percent guarantee that your life is about to change and change fast. I have never seen this fail. A 2nd Harmonic Moon to a natal or progressed Moon is worth its weight in gold; it's a cosmic green light that reignites your soul, refreshes your spirit and recharges your body.

Born from the womb of an evolutionary Pluto/NNode in Cancer, and a powerful Sun-Saturn-Jupiter Fixed T-Square, he was destined to turn stressors into strength. LS102's deeply resourced Mercury in opposition to Castro's Chiron would play a critical role in outmaneuvering his political opponents in that fateful year of revolution. In its final appearance and moving into a Full Moon Harvest phase, LS102's flames of freedom would find Fidel Castro reaping the rewards and ready to enjoy the rest of the ride as he became the undisputed revolutionary leader of the first communist state in the Western Hemisphere.

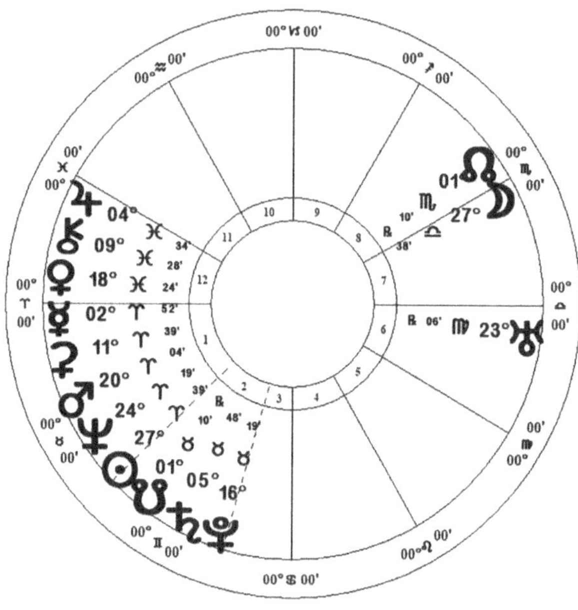

Lunar Saros 102
52nd Return

April 17, 1381 • 12:27:38 PM • London, UK

The Peasants Revolt

"One of the most portentous events in the whole of our history."

–William Stubbs, Medievalist

After decades of misery, the 14th century had become a wasteland decimated by the Black Death of 1348 when more than half of England and Europe's population perished. This period was further aggravated by wide-spread famine, foul weather, and the on-going 100 Years War between England and France.[6] By the spring of 1381, a hated Poll Tax enforced by heavy-handed tax commissioners set off the rebellion, igniting fires of freedom that would eventually lead to the end of serfdom and Medieval society in England and across Europe.[7] The historical chronicles state that riots quickly spread across the counties of Kent, Norfolk, Essex, and beyond starting on May 30, 1381; by the first week of June, a mob not just of peasants but prosperous "rural entrepreneurs—reeves, millers, smiths, bakers, brewers, independent agricultural contractors, small landholders, and more" were on the march to London, daring to challenge the injustice of the Poll Tax.[8] By June 14, an army of rebels, in an act never before seen or duplicated since, captured the Tower of London and, in armed rebellion, brought the government of London to its knees.[9]

The Peasants' Revolt did not end well: gains were summarily won and lost, and thousands of individuals were systematically hunted down in a campaign of terror. Nevertheless, it contributed to the pattern for later revolts that would ultimately dismantle serfdom and empower ordinary people in bringing down institutionalized tyranny.

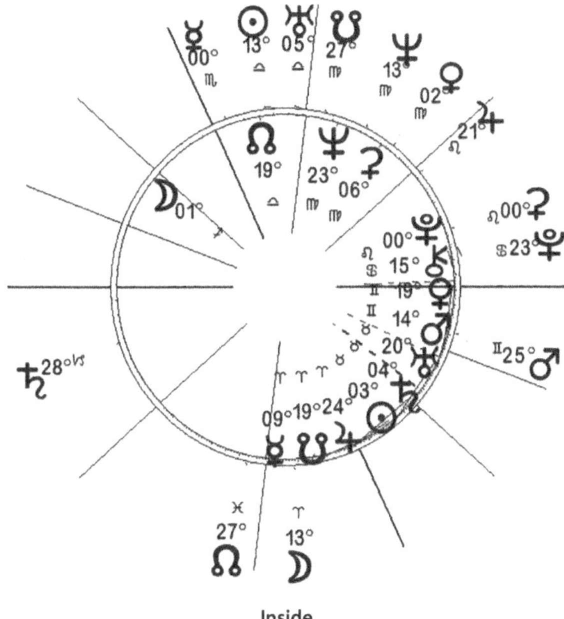

Inside

Robin—The Boy Wonder

April 24, 1940 • 12:01 AM • Manhattan, NY, USA

Outside

LS102

October 6, 461 • 1:34:43 PM • North Pole

Detective Comics (DC) Edition No. 38, launched in April 1940 introduced the world to *The Sensational Character Find of 1940 . . . Robin-The Boy Wonder,* partner in crime-fighting and Batman's famous superhero sidekick.[10] The emergence of Robin the crime-fighter is an example of how a comic book craze became part of the cosmic cult zeitgeist of its time. He is a fictional character perfectly aligned to the spirit of LS102's NNode Aries eclipse and its Mars in Gemini. His debut in DC's Edition No. 38, published for spring 1940 was made available on newsstands on April 24, 1940, one month to the day of LS103's penultimate return on March 23 at 3 Libra.

Here are some ground rules for how special events like this and new ideas get seeded into our psyche. For any shift in our collective or personal consciousness to occur, one of two things (and sometimes both) have to happen. A lunar eclipse field has to activate a significant planet or angle either in a personal chart or in the birth chart of a nation. Since, to my knowledge, the analysis of the forty-seven Lunar Saros Series eclipses presented in this book have never been approached from a family dynamic perspective, I leave my findings and hypothesis for future generations to validate, improve upon or reject. In the meantime, the lunar eclipses continue on their global traversing appearing anywhere from two to four times per year. They offer all of us an exciting if not liberating opportunity to experience and try on new styles of behavior while simultaneously updating the global zeitgeist.

Then, there are many occasions when an event simply happens, and its emergence seems to be synchronized to the most recent lunar eclipse energy field holding court either through its activation degree and/or its resonance to the foundational energy patterns of the current dragon family. The arrival of Robin on the fictional world stage satisfies both requirements, so let's take a look at the above chart and see what a story it tells.

First, we create a Bi-Wheel using the chart of the event in tandem with the mother chart or dragon family chart—here we're using LS102's foundation chart. The next step is to list all the 1st and 2nd Harmonics between the fields, placing the nodal connectors (if any) at the top of the list followed by Sun/Moon connectors. When designing your list put the eclipse planet first followed by its target planet, angle, asteroid or midpoint. Here's our list of Harmonics for Robin and LS102:

Robin's Connections to the Lunar Dragons of LS102
Mars with Mars
Neptune with Neptune

1st Harmonics: SNode – Neptune, Moon – SNode, Ceres – Pluto
2nd Harmonics: Mercury – Sun, Saturn – Pluto

Always start with the activation degree of the lunar eclipse that preceded the event. In our case that degree was 3 Libra in the sign of partnerships. How lucky for Batman. Looking at the event chart for Robin's first appearance on the world stage we find it resonated by an opposition (2nd Harmonic) to Mercury at 9 Aries, a strong position for Mercury because Aries loves to throw itself into the brink, often appearing brilliant in the process. It holds a novile (40 degree) aspect to Uranus in Taurus adding charisma and a sense of its evolutionary part in the development of the DC franchise. Since the event chart is cast for one minute past midnight, the actual placement of the Moon in Sagittarius would have moved along during the day to reach a respectable and life-affirming trine to Mercury. The planet that gets "zapped" by the activation degree of the lunar eclipse must always be interpreted within the context of the entire energy field of either the event or the individual.

The real fun begins as you examine all the vectors across the two fields, noting if there is a planet or planets getting more than their fair share of attention. You need to pay attention as that energy functions much like a coach, helping you to victory. In our example, the nodal axis from both charts is taking the lead with strong resonance coming from the solar side of both eclipse fields adding to the solar hero motif. The SNode connector to Neptune in Robin's chart is a sweet salute to the characters that fill the pages of the comic book genre. Again, to get an accurate reading, the planets in play from both fields must be evaluated through their own matrix of interlocking relationships.

To end this brief introduction, take a quick look at LS102's Mercury at the infinity zero degree alpha 00 Scorpio position. It brings a fresh perspective to any of its pursuits while fighting for a cause, often to the death. Its square to Saturn in rulership entangles it with all the troubles and trials of the day but gives it both the political and moral clout to get the job done while working through the established social conventions of its time.

At the time of LS102's eighty-third return, it was moving through its final leg of its last journey through the Gibbous phase. This is a time when the lights really come on and we get to experience a good working relationship with our base of knowledge and skill set. It is a time to pull it all together; it encourages faith, stability, and confidence even in the face of adversity. It is a time to "punch up."

How appropriate then to have Batman's famous superhero sidekick Robin, The Boy Wonder, become his partner and zap the comic book zeitgeist with his tales and talent for crime-fighting. He was a fictional character completely in sync with the times, especially considering the dark clouds of war that were moving across the globe.

LS102 Summary

The Fire Dragons of LS102 brought fresh infusions of ambition, controversy, and radical leadership with every return. Their energy fields resonated with fiery inspiration and the courage of vivacious conviction. Acts of conquest were won and lost on the strength of one's ideals and ability to express moral outrage and garner immediate support that inspired acts of bravery. Their way in the world was always through endeavors that required boldness; to be born into this fiery clan was a guarantee that your character would be defined by willfulness, self-interest and having an opinion on pretty much everything.

This eclipse field nurtured the spirit of individuality and often required bouts of seclusion if not self-indulgent solitude. Forged in the fires of truth and integrity, LS102 guarantees a life of uncompromised individualism but always with the caveat that one needs to be aware that a sense of entitlement is never far afield. Regardless of social, sexual, economic, or political leanings, any area of interest could/can prosper if one was/is inventive enough, persistent enough or creative enough to put one's ideas forward. This last characteristic is crucial because the energy field of this lunar eclipse has a remarkable ability to manifest its ideas and manifest them rather quickly due to its total integration into the mainstream mode of any era, time period or culture. If you are a member of the LS102 Fire Dragon family or have an attraction to a historical figure or time period linked to their returns, know this: Matters of fate, destiny, and individual effort are fuel for the fires that continue to blaze through every time period, person, and personality blessed by their vigor and ability to take action in service of any personal, social, or environmental concerns. The record is replete with both historical and contemporary people who exhibited a deep social and spiritual response to the challenges of their time believing that their efforts and sacrifices would not be in vain.

Phase	Return	Year
Crescent	72nd	1741
First Quarter	76th	1814
Gibbous	80th	1886
Full Moon	84th	1958

LS102 Luminaries

Édouard Manet	January 23, 1832
Evangeline Adams	February 8, 1868
Dr. Seuss[E1]	March 2, 1904
B F Skinner	March 20, 1904
Forrest Mars Sr.	March 21, 1904
Joseph Campbell	March 26, 1904
Jack Kerouac[E1]	March 12, 1922
Carl Reiner	March 20, 1922
Doris Day	April 3, 1922
"Mongo" Santamaría	April 7, 1922
James Caan	March 26, 1940
Herbie Hancock	April 12, 1940
Claire Bretécher	April 17, 1940
Pilar Miró	April 20, 1940
Christa Johnson	April 25, 1958
Marc Randolph	April 29, 1958
Doreen Virtue	April 29, 1958

PREBLE—LS135
Evangeline Adams
Dr. Seuss
Jack Kerouac
Carl Reiner
James Caan

1. Marc Edmond Jones, *The Guide to Horoscope Interpretation* (Philadelphia: David McKay, 1941), p. 8.
2. https://www.biography.com/dictator/fidel-castro. Retrieved Jan. 11, 2022.
3. Ibid.
4. Fidel Castro, *My Life* (London: Penguin Books, 2007), p. 636.
5. Ibid.
6. Paul Strohm, A "Peasants' Revolt"? in *Misconceptions About the Middle Ages*, Stephen J. Harris and Bryon L. Grigsby, eds. (New York: Routledge, 2008), p. 197.
7. Ibid.
8. Tony Robinson, *The Peasants' Revolt.* Documentary. https://www.youtube.com/watch?v=4kq9sbt-FCR8. Retrieved Jan. 11, 2022.
9. Ibid.
10. https://dc.fandom.com/wiki/Batman_Vol_1_1. Retrieved Jan. 11, 2022.

LUNAR SAROS 110

"Any human anywhere will blossom in a hundred unexpected talents and capacities simply by being given the opportunity to do so."

–Doris Lessing

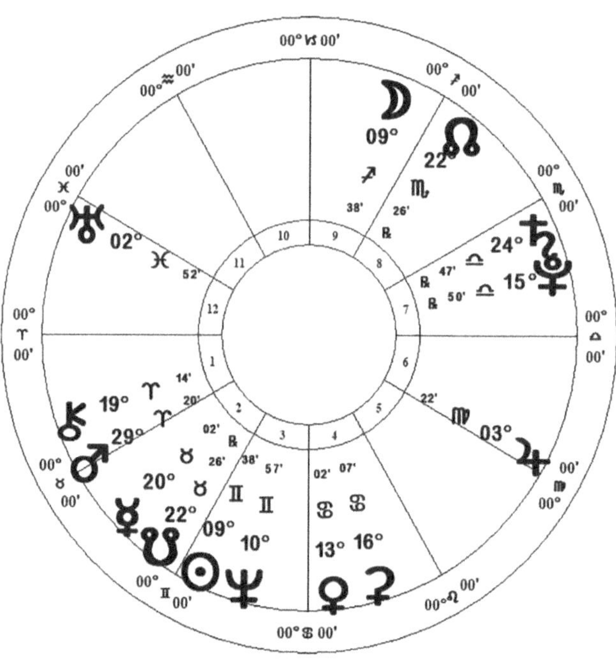

Lunar Saros 110

June 1, 747 • 9:09:21 PM • North Pole

Twisty Tales

This Sagittarian eclipse is incredibly special because out of all the 45 Lunar Saros Series currently active, this is the only one that features a lunar conjunction to the Galactic Center of our Milky Way Galaxy. Astronomers speculate that a super massive black hole resides in this area also known as Sagittarius A. To have either the Sun or Moon located here is a celestial event not to be missed as it can determine the entire course of an individual's life.

The eclipse field's Jupiter is part of a dynamic Mutable Cross with Uranus and Neptune, giving dreams a greater role to play in our daily lives. All levels and types of intelligence now come into play as psychology, law, education, travel, sales, religion, and philosophy all benefit from the enormous talent bank of these Sagittarian dragons.

Mercury's conjunction to the SNode in Taurus offers a bedrock of real world experience, especially since the nodal axis sits at the 21-22 Fixed Critical Degree zone. Planets, asteroids, nodes, and midpoints struggle or shine under these degrees. Lucky for Mercury it can draw down strength and devotion from its midpoint with Mars and Neptune. In point of fact, Mars is especially potent here as it not only holds a wealth of experience—being at the intuitive twenty-ninth degree of Aries and in rulership—but it also is in a one degree parallel declination to Jupiter, magnifying its search engine capacity for challenges

The Venus/Ceres conjunction in Cancer is a perfect foil for the adventurous spirit that dominates the landscape, especially since Venus is an OOB (24N49) Evening Star holding court at thirteen Cancer, a Cardinal Critical Degree and in that very Arian "take no prisoners" thirteenth degree zone that requires personal attention. This conjunction is perfectly poised to kick down any domestic door if its square to retrograde Pluto demands redress or better still—satisfaction. The eclipse field's Grand Mutable Cross and its energized Jupiter in Virgo are ready to get the job done especially with its Venus/Saturn midpoint that is "all in" and in no mood for slouchers. Now is the time to meet all adversity with courage, knowing your particular skill set and creativity are your greatest assets as seen through the foundational Mars/Pluto and Jupiter/Neptune isotrap.

Born into this lunar eclipse, Whoopi Goldberg has the right idea when she stated: "I used my imagination to make the grass whatever color I wanted it to be." Momentary setbacks are everywhere, and challenges are to be welcomed with a Sun/Uranus opposition Moon/Jupiter isotrap seeking expression within the sphere. What's important here is that the synchronistic seeds of success sown in this high-flying "747" year of its birth, have been providing a reliable harvest of creative self-expression (Sun conjunct Neptune) for centuries.

Do not be hindered by a lack of appreciation from those who have previously benefited from your talent and tenacity. Under no circumstances allow your sense of self-worth to be demoralized by the opinions of others. There is a life-affirming quality to this family of eclipses that is hinted at by its *Splash* chart pattern, a planetary classification system made famous by Marc Edmond Jones in *The Guide to Horoscope Interpretation.* His work established a new baseline from which temperament could be judged by examining the overall picture or pattern of a chart. LS110's Splash pattern is associated with a temperament that requires a wide variety of interests in life. A general sense of optimism, wellbeing, and ability to find a path through difficulty, along with talent in any number of areas is typical of this pattern.

Closest Midpoints: Mercury/Mars-Neptune, Jupiter/Venus-Saturn
Isotraps: Mars/Pluto conjunct Jupiter/Neptune
Sun/Uranus opposition Moon/Jupiter

1900—2100 Eclipses: Lunar Saros—110

1901, 1919, 1937, 1955, 1973, 1991, 2009, 2027
Length of cycle —1,280 years
Series ends—July 18, 2027

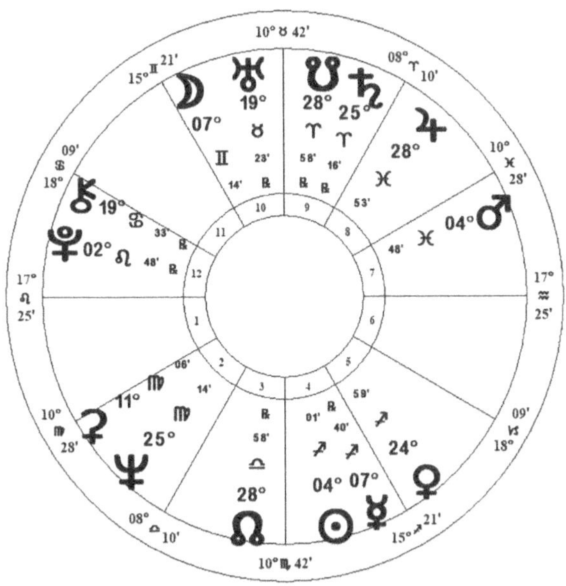

Tina Turner
PREBLE—LS135

November 26, 1939 • 10:10 P.M. • Nutbush, TN, USA

The Queen of Rock n' Roll

"This is what I want in heaven... words to become notes and conversations to be symphonies."

-Tina Turner

Tina Turner's life began to rapidly change gears thanks to the arrival of LS110 on June 15, 1973, at 25 Sagittarius. The lunar eclipse's OOB Venus (24N49) conjunct Ceres threw a spotlight on her own OOB Venus (24S19) bringing a new friendship into her life that would nourish and revive her embattled self-worth. LS110 marked *the* critical turning point in her life from which she would begin to restore and strengthen her wounded spirit. Tina's PREBLE is one of the more difficult lunar eclipses to be born under as it carries an energy punch packed with setbacks, pitfalls and endings. It brings a fair share of dissension and disorder but also a compensating silver lining within the turmoil.

Tina would dance her way through life by the sheer gutsiness of her personal values and choices as all fellow Air Dragon clan members of PREBLE-LS135 can attest to.

June of 1973 marked the release of "Nutbush City Limits," a song written by the former Anna Mae Bullock, from Nutbush, Tennessee.[1] It would be the last hit that Ike and Tina Turner had together. According to Tina's autobiography, *I, Tina,* the marriage was sliding downhill fast, steadied solely by her own search for spiritual meaning and the comfort and insights that she received from readers of cards, palms, and the stars. Tina says of this time:

> And I prayed every night, you can believe that. But now I was really seeking a change, and I knew that it had to come from the inside out—that I had to understand myself, and accept myself, before anything else could be accomplished. The readers—the good ones—helped me do that. I'm not talking about fortune-telling or witchcraft. I was looking for the truth of a future that I could feel inside of me.[2]

By the fall of 1973, Tina was introduced to Valerie Bishop and Nichiren Buddhism and would later credit her new-found faith and chanting *Nam Myoho Renge Kyo,* to awakening the power within her that would eventually set her free.[3] The fact that Tina's center-stage Full Moon across the Gemini/Sagittarius axis is mirrored by LS110's Sagittarius/Gemini eclipse axis would have been enough to make this eclipse a dazzler. But Tina's ties to this magnificent lunar eclipse family are through her double-dipped Saturn at 25 Aries to LS110's Saturn at 25 Libra, confirming undeniable patriarchal strength. Add in Tina's Uranus conjunct the family eclipse Mercury and there are no shortages of hereditary codes to testify that Tina is one of their own.

The dying of light for Tina could only be temporary. On May 24, 2023, the Queen of Rock n' Roll slipped "the surly bonds of Earth" into what I can only imagine would be her next glorious gig. If there's a heaven, Tina is without a doubt commanding center stage, enjoying ovations of love as the celestial crowd chants: Tina—you're simply the best! . . . with words as musical as notes and conversations as [star-studded as] symphonies.

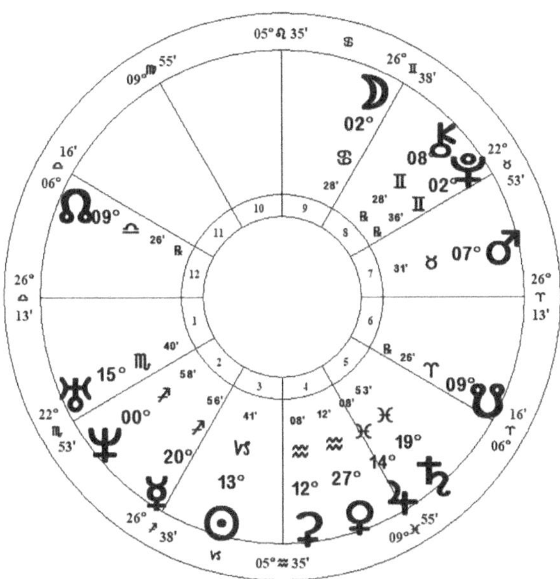

Sir Isaac Newton
PREBLE—LS121

January 4, 1643 • 1:38 AM • Woolsthorpe, UK

Mathematical Magician/Genius

"If I have seen further it is by standing on the shoulders of Giants."

- Sir Isaac Newton

Within two weeks of Isaac Newton's 41st birthday, LS110 arrived on December 21, 1684 at 1 Cancer, scoring a direct hit to his natal Moon at 2 Cancer. A friendship was fast forming between Edmond Halley PREBLE LS114—Carried by the Tide (of comet Halley fame) and Newton over discussions of an astronomical nature that would result in Halley becoming "one of Newton's "staunchest supporters."[4] This critical activation would set off an eighteen month period of intense discovery, resulting in Newton's masterpiece theory: (*The Mathematical Principles of Natural Philosophy*) or *Principia.*[5] Finished in July 1686, it would be published in 1687 establishing his reputation as one of the greatest mathematicians of his time.[6] Newton's legacy is often that of father to modern science and in that respect he "essentially invented many elements of the modern scientific method."[7] Newton's PREBLE is LS121—Sparks of Inspiration, a family of technological wizards.

LS110's 2nd Harmonic Venus/Ceres activates his Sun at 13 Capricorn while its Sun/Neptune sparks his Chiron at 8 Gemini. The potent eclipse Saturn opposition Mars with its parallel declination to Jupiter falls across his ASC/DSC bringing down to earth the bounty of universal wisdom.

Client Spotlight

Alannis is a global open educationalist born February 16, 1972. Her PREBLE, LS133, isn't the easiest one to be born under. Like Tina, both PREBLE 135 and PREBLE 133 carry the soul energy of a first decan/face Sagittarian Moon. (All references to the decans or decanates are based on the concepts of modern Western Astrology.) Its highly focused centaur aim can take an individual far away from their starting place on a journey that has deep repercussions not only for themselves but for the collective. When LS110 arrived in July 2009, her Sun/Neptune and Mercury/ Neptune midpoints were activated at 15 Capricorn. A month earlier she had just been awarded a prestigious doctoral research grant that led to a very high profile but boring "dull as dishwater" job at a university in England. Sadly, her intent to make a meaningful contribution to education never materialized. But all that was to change with the arrival of these twist turning, non-linear dragons.

In July she was having serious misgivings about not only the job but the usefulness of traditional education when, just before leaving, her boss funded her attendance at a conference in Cambridge where she immediately connected into an international community with an open education movement where education is viewed as a human right. July was the pivotal month; since then, Alannis has been working on open education projects around the world, and living her dream where innovation is being guided by the need to share the world's abundant resources to educate, nourish, and develop ourselves.

LS110 Summary

A philosophical nature and a love of knowledge are the twin characteristics of these vibrant and venerable Fire Dragons. They have seen enough of life to know that all great journeys are completed by placing one foot in front of the other while taking care of basic self-maintenance. New emotional experiences and a flux in domestic partners and patterns all work to stimulate the flow of information, self-knowledge, and a desire for personal autonomy. Lucky breaks and a greater capacity for tolerance are features of this lunar family as is a buoyant and progressive spirit able to enjoy whatever life brings to your doorstep.

When these Fire Dragons light up your life by birthright or rite of passage, their knock on your door is an invitation to get yourself in shape, mentally, physically, financially, and soul-wise, spiritually. For sure you're about to encounter a lot of twists and turns but be grateful for they are the drivers of your evolutionary process. Their contribution to your character will always be seen through an increase in emotional intelligence and a willingness to explore some of life's most compelling and perplexing mysteries.

Phase	Return	Year
Last Quarter	59th	1793
Balsamic	63rd	1865
New Moon	67th	1937
Crescent	72nd	2027

LS110 Luminaries

Johann Sebastian Bach	March 31, 1685
Harriet Beecher Stowe	June 14, 1811
William Butler Yeats	June 13, 1865
Willie Sutton	June 30, 1901
Louis Armstrong	August 4, 1901
Salvatore Quasimodo	August 20, 1901
Enrico Fermi	September 29, 1901
Sir Edmund Hillary	July 20, 1919

Malcolm Forbes	August 19, 1919
Pierre Elliott Trudeau	October 18, 1919
Doris Lessing	October 22, 1919
Morgan Freeman	June 1, 1937
Richard Petty	July 2, 1937
Charles Schwab	July 29, 1937
Dustin Hoffman	August 8, 1937
Willem Dafoe	July 22, 1955
Allan Border	July 27, 1955
Bill Gates	October 28, 1955
Whoopi Goldberg	November 13, 1955
Neil Patrick Harris[E]	June 15, 1973
Juliette Lewis	June 21, 1973
Michal Sýkora	July 5, 1973
Madylin Sweeten[E]	June 27, 1991
Anastasia Pavlyuchenkova	July 03, 1991
Devon Conway	July 08, 1991

PREBLE—LS143
Morgan Freeman
Juliette Lewis

1. Tina Turner with Kurt Loder, *I, Tina.* (New York: William Morrow and Company, 1986), p. 154.
2. Ibid.
3. Ibid, p.155.
4. https://www.biography.com/scientist/isaac-newton. Retrieved Jan. 11, 2022.
5. Ibid.
6. Peter Tyson, *Newton's Legacy.* https://www.pbs.org/wgbh/nova/article/newton-legacy. Retrieved Jan. 11, 2022
7. Ibid.

LUNAR SAROS 111

"Any fool can make something complicated. It takes a genius to make it simple."

-WOODY GUTHRIE

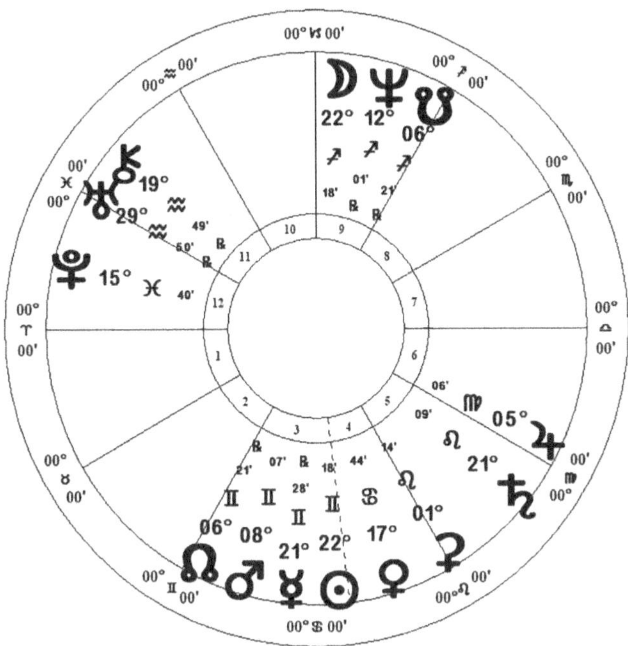

Lunar Saros 111

June 14, 830 • 6:04:23 AM • South Pole

Summon Your Muse

Renew your passport: these Sagittarian dragons love to shake their tails. This SNode fire eclipse reinvigorates positivity. It holds a Splay pattern, one of seven chart types devised by the well-known American astrologer Marc Edmund Jones in his book *The Guide to Horoscope Interpretation*. Jones postulated that there were at least seven distinct personality types that could be gleaned just from evaluating the kind of pattern formed by the planets in a chart. LS111's Splay pattern inculcates unusual tastes and interests along with an ability to generate fresh perspectives, all of which are heightened by Jupiter's nodal axis squares and in particular its waning square to Mars.

The Sun/Saturn conjunct Mars/Jupiter isotrap sets a pattern of discipline that can tame the fearless courage resonating within the sphere's restless spirit. Mercury in rulership and retrograde is a heterodox marker; in waning sextile to Saturn at critical degree 21 Leo encourages concentration and practical platforms so that others may reap the benefits of its vast accumulation of knowledge. Mars in opposition to Neptune opens the floodgates to imagination and even martyrdom if the need arises. Following a dream isn't always a stairway to heaven or a descent into hell. Take comfort from the wise words of Honoré de Balzac when he said, "Our worst misfortunes never happen, and most miseries lie in anticipation." Solid advice for an eclipse field whose mutable mode is more in tune with jazz than a stately waltz.

The eclipse Moon in Sagittarius is OOB (24S49) giving its breadth of vision an eagle-eye perspective that borders on CRISPR technology tinkering. It's sparkling lucidity and capacity for extraordinary insights has been up-regulated not only by its OOB status but also by its dynamic opposition to the Mercury/Sun conjunction in Gemini. Together, these patterns supply a rush of energy and enthusiasm that can literally take you into space, as travel, whether foreign, domestic, or inter-galactic is well within their celestial mandate. LS111's Saturn holds a tender trine to this third decan goal-seeking Moon reinforcing its capacity to reach for the stars regardless of any opposition. Saturn's reputation for putting the brakes on projects and dampening enthusiasm does not apply here as its fear of the unknown has been completely nullified by the vitality and adaptability of the Sagittarius/Gemini eclipse axis that is pretty much up for anything. All told, these are kind, open-hearted, no-strings-attached folk who need to enjoy life. They are one of the finest and friendliest of all the dragon families.

Make it a priority to summon your muse because nobody is "doing" it alone. Set a time and place every day when you will show up. Chances are, so will your muse with its cadre of invisible helping hands. And if by chance your muse is on vacation, take heart as you can always count on your earthly friends. This is a friendly family, famous for its random acts of kindness—its Venus/Uranus square Node is a perfume of pleasure that lingers in the air; its willingness to share is bolstered by Pluto's waxing trine to an OOB (24N00) Venus, one of the best indicators for success as people just love having you around. The thrill of discovery and the call to adventure are what gets you out of bed and your dragon family traversing the Earth on their 1,262 lifespan. When a grand vision strikes, be ready.

Closest Midpoints: Pluto/Eclipse-Mars, Venus/Uranus-Node
Isotraps: Sun/Saturn conjunct Mars/Jupiter
Sun/Jupiter opposition Neptune/Pluto

1900—2100 Eclipses: Lunar Saros—111

1912, 1930, 1948, 1966, 1984, 2002, 2020, 2038, 2056, 2074, 2092
Length of cycle —1,262 years
Series ends—July 19, 2092

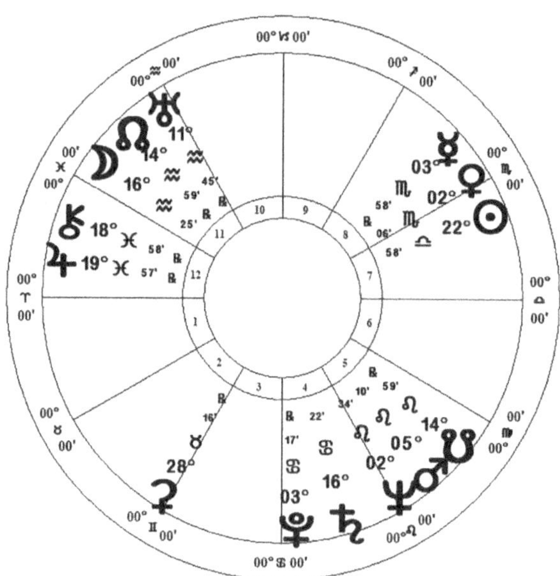

Arthur Miller
PREBLE—LS146

October 17, 1915 • 5:12 AM • New York, NY, USA

American Playwright

"Everybody likes a kidder, but nobody lends him money."

-Arthur Miller

In his autobiography, *Timebends: A Life*, Arthur Miller recounts how a chance meeting with an uncle in the winter of 1948 rekindled an idea he had for a story. When LS111 arrived in April at 3 Scorpio, it scored a direct hit to his Venus and his Mercury at 3 Scorpio. Miller wrote: "By April of 1948 I felt I could find such a form, but it would have to be done, I thought, in a single sitting, in a night or a day, I did not know why."[1] Miller may not have known the "why" of it, but an astrologer with knowledge of how lunar eclipse activations work would certainly know why. When your chart connects into a lunar eclipse field so precisely, you can bet stuff happens and stuff happens fast. Miller's play unfolded at hurricane velocity fueled by the drive not only of his dramatic Tenth House

Mars/Neptune conjunction in Leo square his "born to be a writer" Venus/Mercury conjunction in Scorpio but the man has an exact trine from Pluto to that artistic, articulate Venus/Mercury energy.

His inspiration rode on the essence of Dragon Tail eclipses which favor activities that move toward completion. By returning to his idea to write a play about a salesman, he was completing a project that had lain dormant for over a decade, thus drawing favor from a SNode eclipse. *Death of a Salesman* opened on Broadway on February 10, 1949. By the time it closed after 742 performances, the play had won Miller a Pulitzer Prize for Drama.[2] Miller would go on to write many more successful plays, but it was LS111 and *Death of a Salesman* that launched his career and established his reputation as an American playwright.

Arthur Miller's Connections to the Lunar Dragons of LS111

1st Harmonics: Chiron – NNode/Moon, Venus – MC/Saturn, Ceres – Neptune/Mars, Pluto – Chiron/Jupiter
2nd Harmonic: Saturn – Moon

Patterns of energy that are found in both charts increase the potential for the lunar eclipse field to activate. The tighter the link, the stronger is its capacity to manifest. In Miller's chart, the creative potential of his Mars-Neptune conjunction comes alive in the fires of LS111's Mars-Neptune opposition. As well, both fields enjoy the creative confidence of a waxing Pluto trine Venus.

The cosmic codes shared by Miller and the Dragons of LS111 reveal three Cosmic Bridges (CBs) that include the eclipse Chiron to Miller's NNode as well as to his Moon that initiate a new adventure filled with the twists and turns of emotional turbulence. The latter is reinforced by the eclipse Venus at 17 Cancer on Miller's MC and Saturn at 16 Cancer. This is an outstanding link that would promote a work of deep sentimentality, especially since the sixteenth degree carries Cancerian overtones that provide a basis for the dramatic seventeenth degree overtones of the eclipse Venus. The third CB comes from the eclipse Saturn's complex relationships with Chiron, the Moon and Mercury that together help to create a practical platform where critical thinking and concentration can be given free rein to explore and redefine lines of inquiry.

How fitting that on the sixty-third return of the Fire Dragons of LS111, they would find themselves entering, for the last time, a closing Balsamic Phase famous for encouraging the mind-body-spirit trinity to let go and let the universe lead. It is a time to go inward, to rest, to surrender, and to dream.

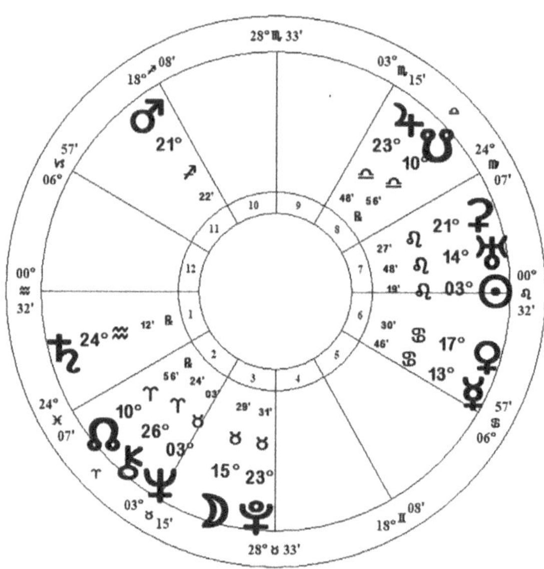

Carl Gustav Jung
PREBLE—LS139

July 26, 1875 • 7:29 PM • Kesswil, Switzerland

Founder of Analytical Psychology

"In knowing ourselves to be unique, we possess the capacity for becoming conscious of the infinite. But only then!"

-Carl Jung

Lunar Saros 111's impact on the life of Carl Jung is remarkable. After thirty-six years and two eclipse cycles, LS111 returned on April 24, 1948, at 3 Scorpio, directly opposing his mystical Neptune and squaring his Leo Sun. This is Jung's signature aspect, defining his solar hero quest for wholeness. However, Jung's first encounter with this series began on April 1, 1912, as it perfectly synced to his 10 Libra SNode allowing its accumulation of energy and information to cross the Cosmic Bridge that was created by LS111's activation degree on his SNode. In that year, Jung's successful American lectures on the theory of psychoanalysis would be published as *The Psychology of the Unconscious* and translated into English in 1916.[3]

In Ronald Hayman's biography, *A Life of Jung*, he writes that on April 24, 1948, Jung addressed his first class of thirteen students at the newly opened Bollingen Institute in Switzerland and named 1912 "as the year he discovered the collective unconscious."[4] The concept of archetypes and the use of synchronicity in psychotherapy were among Jung's many contributions to psychology.[5] What is key to the discovery process of how lunar eclipse activations work is the fact that the newly opened classes at Bollingen occurred within hours of LS111's arrival on April 23, 1948. A synchronicity like this calls for a closer look.

Carl Jung's Connections to the Lunar Dragons of LS111

1st Harmonics: Moon – Mars, Venus – Venus/Mercury, Ceres – Sun, Saturn – Ceres
2nd Harmonics: Mercury – Mars, Chiron – Ceres, Saturn – Saturn

The impact field of the eclipse had more than just its activation degree at 3 Scorpio opposing Jung's Neptune to grant significance. What is frankly startling, apart from the 1st Harmonic Moon to his Mars, are all the Ceres contacts, the first from the eclipse to his Sun, the second from the eclipse Saturn to his Ceres and the third and most fascinating is the 2nd Harmonic eclipse Chiron to his Ceres.

The Venus to Venus tie is extremely significant as its near perfect alignment boosts the amplitude of the signal as its trine to Pluto seeks an experience of transformation. But the tie that tells the tale can always be found in the 2nd Harmonics. The lunar eclipse Chiron adds more fuel to the fire of Jung's solar hero quest by activating his Ceres/Mars/Chiron Grand Fire Trine that was set ablaze by LS111's Moon to his double-dipped twenty-first degree Sagittarian Mars. And like Arthur Miller, Carl Jung benefited from the eclipse moving into the wondrous dreamtime and incubation leg on its Balsamic Phase journey.

News Flash!

Police Brutality Shocks the World
George Floyd—October 14, 1973 to May 25, 2020

George Floyd, born into the Fire Dragons of LS148—Webs of Wonder—died on May 25, 2020 in Minneapolis, Minnesota after police officer Derek Chauvin pinned him to the ground and knelt on his neck for almost nine minutes.[6] A groundswell of national outrage and civil protest erupted across the United States along with a crackdown against protesters reminiscent of the 1960s. By June 2, international communities around the world were protesting in support of Floyd.

LS111 arrived on June 5, 2020 blazing away at 15 Sagittarius ready to light up the world with their commitment to doing good for one another. Within a month, fellow Fire Dragons from LS149—Breakthroughs and Comebacks—would arrive to turn up the heat, setting the world aflame with indignation. Chauvin was convicted of murder in April 2021 and sentenced to 22 and a half years in prison.[7]

LS111 Summary

Gifts that lead to originality of expression are the rewards bestowed from this brilliant family of Fire Dragons. Their well-defined sense of self-worth is contagious as is their love of pleasure. They're known for jump-starting ideas that have fallen by the wayside or giving one a totally new track to run on. Whether born under their fiery gaze or enjoying one of their eighteen year visits, you need to think on a grand scale—spread your wings and the dreamer within will lift you skyward. Stay open and cultivate a sense of possibility. Fan the flames of inquiry. Effort will be rewarded, especially if backed up with some basic preparation and planning. Many touched by this lunar eclipse find that their status has suddenly and often dramatically changed and changed for the better, increasing their connectivity to and often representing a wider group of people.

Life pulses to a hotter, cosmological beat either by your birthright or by rite of passage. Serendipity and synchronicity seem to follow your every footstep and a six month visit from these lucid and expressive lunar dragons could change your life forever. There is a noted up-tick in energy levels and optimism that can be dramatic, giving your life a sense of renewal and invigoration. Don't be surprised if you suddenly discover you have a talent for acting or a desire to be in the public eye as all that is a manifestation of the field's desire to explore and discover.

Phase	Return	Year
Disseminating	55th	1804
Last Quarter	59th	1876
Balsamic	63rd	1948
New Moon	68th	2038

LS111 Luminaries

George Washington	February 22, 1732
George Sand	July 1, 1804
Max Planck	April 23, 1858
Alfred Kinsey	June 23, 1894
Wu Chien-Shiung	May 31, 1912
Alan Turing	June 23, 1912
Woody Guthrie	July 14, 1912
Julia Child	August 15, 1912
Gene Kelly	August 23, 1912
Harvey Milk	May 22, 1930
Clint Eastwood	May 31, 1930
Yuan Longping	September 7, 1930
Ray Charles	September 23, 1930
Brian Eno	May 15, 1948
Stevie Nicks	May 26, 1948
Kathy Bates	June 28, 1948
Avery Brooks	October 2, 1948
Gretchen Carlson	June 21, 1966
Moises Alou	July 3, 1966
Jimmy Wales	August 7, 1966
Adam Sandler	September 9, 1966
Mark Zuckerberg[E1]	May 14, 1984
Mickie Knuckles[E1]	May 16, 1984
Laverne Cox	May 29, 1984

PREBLE—LS144
Mark Zuckerberg
Mickie Knuckles

---

1. Arthur Miller, *Timebends, A Life* (New York: Grove Press, 1987), p.182.
2. https://www.ibdb.com/broadway-production/death-of-a-salesman-2111. Retrieved Jan. 9, 2022.
3. https://openlibrary.org/books/OL7147819M/Psychology_of_the_unconscious. Retrieved Jan. 9, 2022.
4. Ronald Hayman, *A Life of Jung* (London: W.W. Norton & Company, 2002), p. 396.
5. Ibid., p. 503.
6. https://www.theguardian.com/us-news/2020/jun/02/abuse-of-power-global-outrage-grows-after-death-of-george-floyd. Retrieved Jan. 2, 2022.
7. https://www.nytimes.com/article/george-floyd.html. Retrieved Jan 2, 2022.

LUNAR SAROS 112

"I invented 'it's a good thing' before you were ever born."

-Martha Stewart

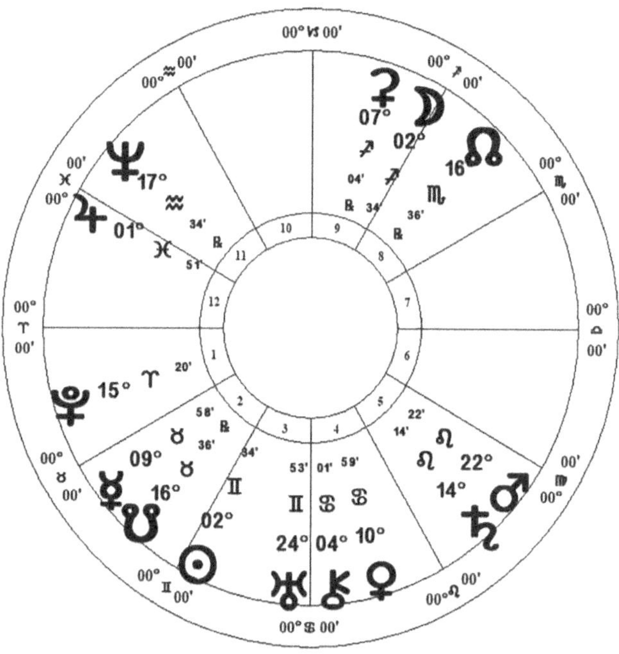

Lunar Saros 112

May 24, 859 • 1:12:31 PM • North Pole

Follow Your Bliss

Expanding the realm of possibility is what you were made for as this is a North Node Jupiter-ruled eclipse that has its own search engine of discovery. As ruler and at the leg of the Mutable T-Square to the eclipse axis, Jupiter needs to be moving humanity forward in whatever way possible. Seeking wisdom and high ideals is second nature to members of this tribe and Jupiter in this position is a magnet for popularity and success. The demands of this configuration are constant and thus it creates many opportunities to develop great strengths and conviction.

Powering up LS112's search engine are two very special sextiles: The first is Mercury to an OOB Venus (25N15) and the second is Mars to an OOB Uranus (23N43). These two OOB planets are only found here and nowhere else in the entire Lunar Saros series giving this eclipse an outlier feel thanks to Venus and Uranus playing by their own rules. Because the T-Square is mutable there is little down time as one is fully engaged if not overwhelmed by the minutiae of life. Thank goodness for Mercury's working sextile to an OOB Venus as it brings a comforting form of organic truth, pared down and singularly sensational. The Mars sextile to OOB Uranus has its own style of delivering last-minute resources that manage to save the day and will, time and time again, be a pillar of strength.

Standing in the light of self-acceptance is made a little easier by LS112's Bucket pattern with the eclipse Moon as singleton at the handle. In almost all Bucket pattern temperaments, life generally swings around the nature of the planet at the handle, giving a single-minded drive and leg up toward achieving a goal. Lighting the way along that path is the lunar eclipse Moon and its conjunction to Ceres in Sagittarius. Together this duo will stoke the creative fires to touch the deep body of fertility within. In their book *Asteroid Goddesses*, Demetra George and Douglas Bloch write: "Astrologically Ceres describes the ways in which we face the issues of self-worth and self-esteem, relationship to our parents and children, attachment, dependency, loss, separation, rejection, grief, sharing, work and productivity."[1] All are legitimate paths to nurturing self-discovery and in the process may transform the world.

LS112's Saturn/Neptune opposition to the nodal axis can literally make our dreams come true if we are *not* defeated by the multiplicity of false starts they inevitably attract. Such trials, tribulations and failure need to be viewed as fuel for the fires of inspiration. An antidote to the frustration that this pattern seeds into the eclipse field is to simply take on more responsibility and shoulder, what bestselling author Jordan B. Peterson says is "a noble burden." Peterson has a lot to say about the role of responsibility and our failure to appreciate its significance. He elaborates: ". . . the meaning that sustains life in all its tragedy and disappointment is to be found in shouldering a noble burden."[2] This is not what most people want to hear. Peterson is featured in the Water Dragons of Part Four.

LS112, after all, holds a Mars/Saturn conjunction in Leo in trine to Pluto which practically guarantees success if you can accept your responsibilities and their wider implications for social change. You are by birthright or soon to be by their return, more than capable of expressing your self-assured style of leadership to the spirit of the times. Think of their qualities as guides and gurus that have your back. And please, please, oh pretty please—pick up your noble burden.

Closest Midpoints: Node/Saturn-Neptune, Eclipse/Mercury-Uranus
Isotraps: Mars/Neptune opposition Uranus/Pluto
Mercury/Pluto conjunct Jupiter/Uranus

1900—2100 Eclipses: Lunar Saros—112

1905, 1923, 1941, 1959, 1977, 1995, 2013, 2031, 2049, 2067, 2085, 2103
Length of cycle —1,280 years
Series ends—July 12, 2139

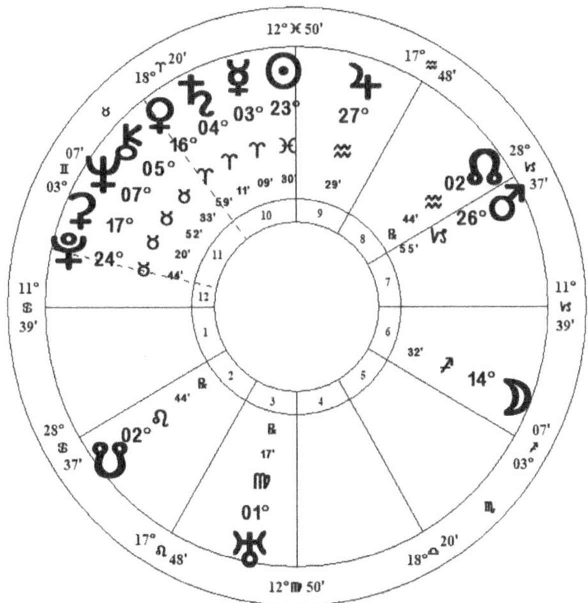

Albert Einstein
PREBLE—LS141

March 14, 1879 • 11:30 AM • Ulm, Germany

Nobel Laureate/Scientist/Genius

"The only thing that interferes with my learning is my education."

-Albert Einstein

1905 is often called Einstein's Miracle Year.[3] While working full time at the Swiss patent office he produced "his first theory of relativity, and $E=mc^2$, as well as his work that helped lay the path for lasers, computer chips, key aspects of the modern pharmaceutical and bio-engineering industry, and all Internet switching devices."[4]

The Miracle Year was launched by a lunar eclipse on February 19, 1905 at 1 degree Virgo that completely electrified his Third House Uranus as the handle on his Bucket. By its activation, his Saturn/Uranus/Neptune midpoint came online with its stability, innovation and imagination to challenge the accepted notions of the day that supported a Newtonian worldview of reality. As a brief aside, Stephen King, with his unparalleled chops as a storyteller, has the same midpoint structure that allows him to write unique and often bizarre tales of fantasy. For Einstein, this midpoint structure gave unflappable staying power amidst the surge of insignificance that marked his early career. He retained a notable childlike wonder and belief in his own significance, sustained by his Jupiter/Sun-Node and Mercury/Jupiter-Neptune midpoints working optimistically toward the day when his theories would be fully realized.

Einstein's Connections to the Lunar Dragons of LS112
Moon with Moon

1st Harmonics: SNode – Ceres, Venus – ASC, Mercury – Chiron/Neptune, Jupiter – Jupiter
2nd Harmonic: Jupiter – Uranus

1905 was an extraordinary year for Einstein. It was made even more amazing by the fact that his Uranus received a catalytic bolt of lightning that energized a link to the foundational field of LS112 and in particular its Arian infused Jupiter at the first degree of Pisces through its activation hit at Virgo's refreshing "Be all you can be" first degree. Considering his Sagittarian OOB Moon (26S22) resonated to LS112's Sagittarian Moon, along with six other sets of connectors, Einstein was perfectly positioned to revel in the light of cosmic expansion. His Theory of Special Relativity (encapsulated in $E=mc^2$) would soon be surpassed by his stellar 1907 General Theory of Relativity, which would end up making Einstein the most famous scientist in the world.[5]

The eclipse 2nd Harmonic Jupiter in Pisces to his Uranus encapsulates all the dignity of its rulership along with all the demands of its position at the leg of the Mutable T-Square that requires constant devotion to an area of specialization. Joanna Martine Woolfolk's *The Only Astrology Book You'll Ever Need* has this to say about Jupiter in Pisces:

> Jupiter also accentuates imagination, wisdom, and high ideals. In general, you do your best work in fields in which you help humanity. Jupiter-Pisceans are singled out for success in social or religious work, politics, and philanthropic organizations.[6]

Einstein's Uranus/Jupiter opposition along with his Jupiter/Sun-Node midpoint couldn't have been happier to have experienced this activation that would lead to public recognition and success. All of this excitement occurred while LS112 had just entered its fifty-ninth return and its second and final Last Quarter Phase, with its emphasis on high productivity and public responsibility. More than anything else, it marks a turning point in the life. It has always been associated with the one key idea that sums up this entire phase the best—Reorientation.

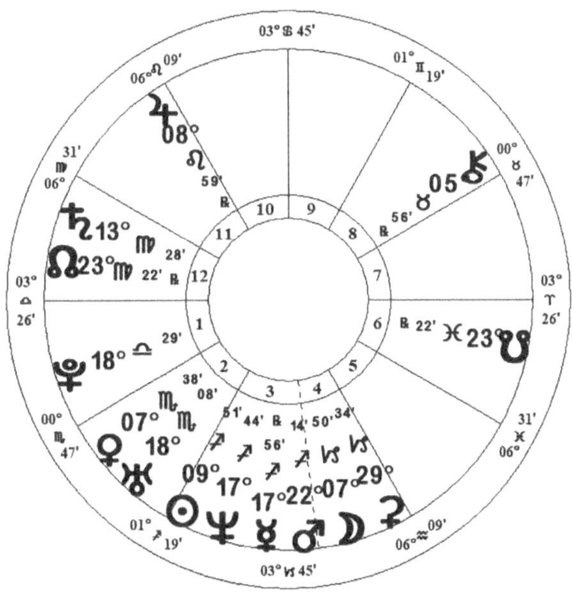

Jason Collins
PREBLE—LS127

December 2, 1978 • 1:27 AM • Northridge, CA, USA

NBA's First Openly Gay Player

"The most you can do is stand up for what you believe in.
I'm much happier since coming out to my friends and family.
Being genuine and honest makes me happy."

-JASON COLLINS

On April 29, 2013, Jason Collins, while still playing in the major leagues, came out as the first major North American professional gay athlete. His announcement came with LS112's opening shot at 6 Scorpio on April 25, 2013—a slam dunk to Collins' Venus at 7 Scorpio. The eclipse continued to rack up points on his Chiron at 6 Taurus. Saturn's transit through Scorpio in the fall of 2012 had witnessed the training and dedication that would set Collins firmly on a path of unwavering conviction. On the very day of his announcement, retrograding Saturn was within twenty-five minutes of exactitude to his natal Venus. Transiting Jupiter at 17 Gemini was part of the media blitz as it formed an exact opposition to Collins' retrograde Mercury/Neptune conjunction in Sagittarius. In an article with Franz Lidz for *Sports Illustrated* in May 2013, Jason Collins wrote:[7]

> It takes an enormous amount of energy to guard such a big secret. I've endured years of misery and gone to enormous lengths to live a lie. I was certain that my world would fall apart if anyone knew. And yet when I acknowledged my sexuality I felt whole for the first time.

Jason Collins is part of a cohort of PREBLE-LS127—Fired in the Kiln prodigies whose mastery comes from a deep well of discipline that attracts recognition and social success. Collins has found the faith and conviction to follow his bliss. He has a Bundle pattern, the rarest of all seven types which makes an individual a specialist—someone who can focus on a single area of interest and become expert at it.

Collin's ties to LS112 are extensive with six distinct vectors of resonance. His eclipse family's NNode Cosmic Bridge to his Uranus joyfully supports his life style choices and further, the eclipse Ceres is right there on his Sun, proudly nourishing his solar essence. What is most satisfying to find in all these patterns of resonance, however, is the eclipse outlier Venus in opposition to his Moon, which helps him establish a new personal hierarchy of needs that prioritize his concerns over the concerns of others.

LS112's appearance on April 25, 2013 coincided with its sixty-fifth return as it was moving deep into the darkness of its final Balsamic Phase, famous for its desire and ability to release from the life all that has heretofore been repressed and held back within the true spirit of an individual or nation. At this time, anyone moving in sync with the rhythms of this phase will want to strip down and get to the bare bones of who and what they are all about. It is a time to drop all the burdens of pretense and face oneself in the light of pure consciousness. The key concept given for this phase of the journey is often best summed up by one word—Release.

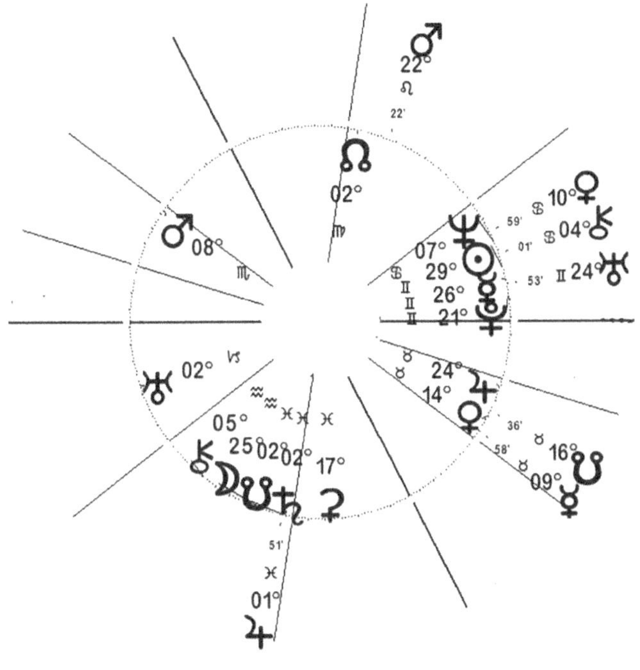

Jean-Paul Sartre
PREBLE—LS112

June 21, 1905 • 6:45 PM • Paris, France

The "Pope" of Existentialism

"Three o'clock is always too late or too early for anything you want to do."

-Jean-Paul Sartre

The term "existentialism," coined in the mid-1940s, is most often identified with Sartre. He was one of the most brilliant and beloved public intellectuals of the 20th century; a reported crowd of 50,000 lined the streets and followed the hearse to Montparnasse cemetery the day of his funeral.[8] On the topic of the meaning of life, Sartre said that "man first of all exists, encounters himself, surges up in the world—and defines himself afterwards." Emphasizing individualism, existentialism focuses on the self and one's ability to confront, engage, and direct the choice-maker within who holds the ultimate responsibility and power for decision-making.

Jean-Paul Sartre was born under LS112—these are his dragon people. His chart is presented to illustrate resonance across their respective fields. For the sake of simplicity, only the vectors from the lunar eclipse field that connected into his chart have been included for the diagnosis. Feel free to refer back to the Top 10 List of How to Live with Dragons.

First, start with a Bi-Wheel. Then make a list of all the 1st and 2nd Harmonics between the fields, placing the nodal connectors (if any) at the top of the list followed by Sun/Moon connectors. When designing your list put the eclipse planet first followed by its target planet, angle, midpoint or asteroid. Here's our list of Harmonics for Jean Paul Sartre and LS112:

Jean-Paul Sartre's Connections to the Dragons of LS112

1st Harmonics: SNode – Venus, Jupiter – SNode, Uranus – Sun, Venus – Neptune, Jupiter – Saturn, Uranus – Mercury, Uranus – Pluto
2nd Harmonics: Mars – Moon, Mercury – Mars, Chiron – Uranus

Now we're ready to note any patterns in the eclipse field that Sartre's activated planets hooked into. Start with the highest value connections—here it's the eclipse field's SNode conjunct Sartre's Venus and the eclipse Jupiter to his SNode/Saturn. First we position Sartre's Venus within the eclipse field and find it falls within LS112's Saturn/Neptune opposition to the nodal axis, a pattern that can literally make our dreams come true if we are not defeated by the multiplicity of false starts they inevitably attract. Sartre suffered from depression and was a heavy drug and alcohol user as well as a sexaholic for the majority of his adult life. Lucky for him his talent bank SNode/Saturn was powerfully attuned to the good will of Jupiter and its T-Square to the eclipse axis on its mission to discover the secrets of the universe. He was a magnet for success—his popularity only increased as he continually engaged in public discourse while immersing himself in the fields of literature, art, and politics.

Next we look for contacts to the Sun or Moon and here we have a 1st Harmonic between the eclipse Uranus to Sartre's Sun and a 2nd Harmonic from the eclipse Mars to his Moon. That, dear reader, is astounding when you find both lights in your chart activated because those energetic elements of the field can truly be said to be deeply embedded in your character and personality structure. LS112's Mars sextile to OOB Uranus can be relied upon to faithfully pull your chestnuts out of the fire as it refuses to be defeated. This was an on-going and highly noted characteristic of Sartre's life, especially considering that his natal Sun at the AP held an opposition to Uranus. The 2nd Harmonic Mars to his Moon had to have been a torrent of trouble in his domestic affairs. Sartre never married, never had children, and lived for over fifty years in a scandalous and well-publicized partnership with feminist and fellow existentialist Simone de Beauvoir, famous for her 1949 treatise *The Second Sex*.

Although the list is long, let's take one more example to showcase how these connectors and their resonance can be so valuable in analyzing and better still articulating their effects on personality and character development.

LS112's Venus is within a three degree 1st Harmonic to Sartre's Neptune. This contact is a key reveal of his character because Sartre's Neptune is involved in a Grand Water Trine which, knowing his infatuation with drugs, alcohol, and sex, was made even more intense and problematic by its activation from the eclipse OOB Venus. The heightened outlier effect of the eclipse Venus and its sextile to Mercury certainly contributed to a nervous system sensitized and predisposed to craving the effects of chemically induced states of ecstasy. Indeed, the man had a long history of drug abuse, especially amphetamines along with narcotics that he consumed on a daily basis. According to the diaries and books written by Simone de Beauvoir, he never slept for more than four hours in any twenty-four hour period.[9]

Jean Paul Sartre was born into a Last Quarter phase in the life of his Fire Dragon family's journey. Born in 859 CE, by 1905, the dragons of LS112 had already been making the rounds of the planet for over a thousand years; their appearance in 1905 would mark their fifty-ninth return. Refer back to the remarks given for Einstein as to what he experienced in that remarkable year of his life as he synced to the resonance of LS112's emerging Last Quarter Phase: this would constitute the essence of what Jean Paul Sartre experienced for his *entire life* being born into a Last Quarter Phase.

LS112 Summary

The conviction to follow your passion pretty much sums up the essence of these wise old Fire Dragons. If you are lucky enough to get a visit, feel fortunate: they nurture creativity, faith, knowledge, and the confidence to follow your truth. Be responsible, aim high, ignore all the critics and naysayers, and follow your bliss. Focus on your strengths and fan the flames of your passion. New enterprises undertaken are both soulful and innovative. A little effort goes a long way and success can now blossom in outlandish proportion to the endeavors undertaken. Friendships, gurus, and guides now appear to help you on your way and encourage soulful sustenance.

Whether by birth or by transit, this eclipse field draws one into the realms of exploration, be it through science, prophecy, spirituality, or culture: all paths take us on a journey to better ourselves and to work to improve conditions for others. A pioneering spirit is present throughout the lifespan of this lunar eclipse as it encourages a playful participation in the zeitgeist of our times. There is a distinct architectural quality to this field that encourages all of us to become builders of a future where we can all share in a life that values both individual freedoms and the collective rights of those members to live in peace. UN Secretary-General and Nobel Prize laureate Dag Hammarskjöld held a belief that might prove helpful in this regard. He is credited with saying, "I would rather live my life as though there is a God and die to find out that there isn't, than to live my life as though there is no God and die to find out there is."[10] Sounds like a conviction worth embracing.

Phase	Return	Year
Disseminating	55th	1833
Last Quarter	59th	1905
Balsamic	63rd	1977
New Moon	67th	2049

LS112 Luminaries

Gustav Ludwig Hertz	July 22, 1887
Viktor Frankl	March 26, 1905
Dag Hammarskjöld	July 29, 1905
Jean-Paul Sartre	June 1, 1905
Hjalmar Andersen	March 12, 1923
Estelle Getty	July 25, 1923
Richard Dawkins	March 26, 1941
Pete Rose	April 14, 1941
Nora Ephron	May 19, 1941
Emma Thompson	April 15, 1959

Wim Hof	April 20, 1959
Hugh Laurie	June 11, 1959
Magic Johnson	August 14, 1959
John Oliver	April 23, 1977
Kanye West	June 8, 1977
Liv Tyler	July 1, 1977
Tom Brady	August 3, 1977

PREBLE—LS145
Hjalmar Andersen

---

1. Demetra George and Douglas Bloch, *Asteroid Goddesses—The Mythology, Psychology and Astrology of the Re-emerging Feminine* (Lake Worth, FL: Ibis Press, 2003), p. 61.
2. Jordan B. Peterson, *Beyond Order 12 More Rules For Life* (Toronto: Random House Canada, 2021), p. 161.
3. David Bodanis, *E = mc2: A Biography of the World's Most Famous Equation* (New York: Anchor Canada, 2001) p. 85.
4. Ibid, p. 161.
5. Ibid, p. 204.
6. Joanna Martine Woolfolk, *The Only Astrology Book You'll Ever Need* (Lanham, MD: Scarborough House, 1990)p. 203.
7. Jason Collins with Franz Lidz, "I'm a 34-year old NBA center. I'm black. And I'm gay," *Sports Illustrated,* May 6, 2013, pp. 34-41.
8. Thomas Flynn, "Jean-Paul Sartre," *The Stanford Encyclopedia of Philosophy (Fall 2013 Edition)*, Edward N. Zalta (ed.), https://plato.stanford.edu/archives/fall2013/entries/sartre/ Retrieved March 16, 2022.
9. https://en.wikipedia.org/wiki/Simone_de_Beauvoir. Retrieved March 1, 2022.
10. https://westernmystics.files.wordpress.com/2015/04/dag-hammarskj.jpg. Retrieved Jan. 9, 2022.

LUNAR SAROS 119

"Madness need not be all break-down. It may also be break-through. It is potential liberation and renewal as well as enslavement and existential death."

-R. D. Laing

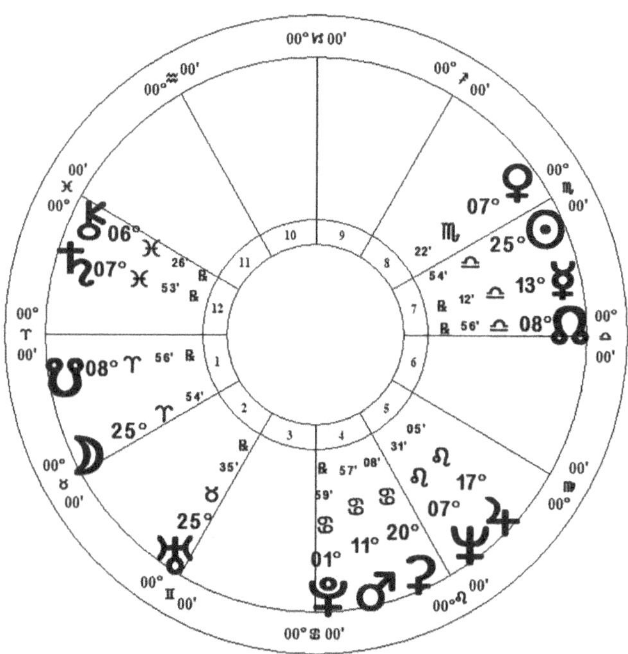

Lunar Saros 119

October 19, 935 • 7:08:02 PM • South Pole

Who's Your Daddy?

This is a SNode Aries eclipse featuring Ruler Mars in a fast flowing Grand Trine with Venus and a retrograde Saturn/Chiron in Pisces. An air of allegiance to king, country, God, or an inflated ego fires up the field. The Moon/Mars MR is highly disruptive as their reciprocity gives the upper hand to the combative nature of Mars. Its potency accelerated as its OOB (24N09) declination can't resist pushing past acceptable norms of behavior. The Moon always seeks safety; in her MR to Mars she'll take a back seat for the sake of security. When repositioned within the Grand Water Trine with Saturn and Chiron, the element of sacrifice can never be ignored, especially since this is a "releasing" eclipse.

LS119 holds a Locomotive pattern, one of seven chart types devised by the well-known American astrologer Marc Edmund Jones in his book *The Guide to Horoscope Interpretation*. Jones postulated that there were at least seven distinct personality patterns that could be gleaned from the type of pattern formed by the planets in a chart. LS119's Locomotive adds a power punch of energy driven by an almost mad scientist Saturn in Pisces engine whose midpoints with Pluto help to uncouple it from the constraints of reality.

There are a number of planets at Critical Degrees in the lunar eclipse field. Mercury retrograde at 13 Libra is the most obvious as it is part of the T-Square from the nodal axis to Mars. The Cardinal Critical Degree zone at 0, 13 and 26 degrees all seem to require help, healing, or hallelujah, often at the same time. The eclipse axis adds weight to the Critical Count giving restlessness, impatience, and the will to dominate front row seats. When you factor in the Moon's MR with Mars and Mercury's square to the nodal axis, constant change is the daily diet for this family and for you if this is your clan. A Moon in Aries feeds on the hustle of enterprise. Brando, Al Capone, and Salvador Dalí are stellar examples. Dalí is featured in LS144—Real Surreal, the most incredible of all the Air Dragons in Part Three.

Neptune's square to Venus in Scorpio adds charisma especially as both planets are located in the Fixed (8-9 and 21-22) Critical Degree zone. This waxing square carries the drive and courage that only fixed-fire Neptune in Leo, with its taste for glamor and leadership, is willing to chase to make a dream come true. In the 20th century, Neptune in Leo again occurred with LS119's return in 1927 with the birth of American Baseball Hall of Fame manager Tommy Lasorda, born on September 22, 1927. His character is deeply dipped in the vibrancy, loyalty, and loquaciousness of his dragon family's Neptune/Venus square. His personality exhibited the best and worst of their traits. He was beloved by his players, and he said that "he made it his business to know the names of all of his players' wives and children and to ask about them regularly."[1]

Because the LS119 family is still learning how to self-regulate, not yet having had the benefit of reaching middle age, they need to work on what psychologists loosely refer to as "state management." This is essential considering that Pluto's presence in the field's midpoints benefits from its returning cycles. Its part in the isotrap configurations draws it to dance with danger, or at the very least the shadow world within. Given enough time, their Libran NNode will master the high art of diplomacy. In the meantime, if this is your clan remember: No matter how big a star you are (and you are a shining star), the path forward is always through reciprocity, sharing, and learning to play nice with others.

Closest Midpoints: Saturn/Neptune-Node, Pluto/Eclipse-Saturn
Isotraps: Mars/Neptune conjunct Jupiter/Pluto
Moon/Mercury conjunct Neptune/Pluto

Lunar Eclipses 1900—2100

1909, 1927, 1945, 1963, 1981, 1999, 2017, 2035, 2053, 2071, 2089
Length of cycle —1,460 years Series ends—March 25, 2396

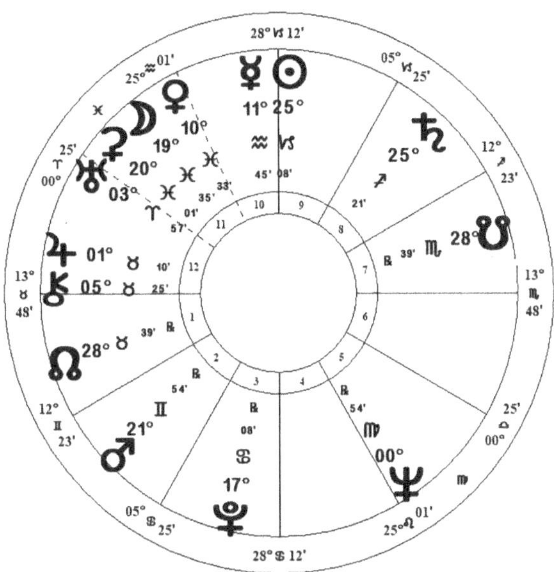

Martin Luther King
PREBLE—LS134

January 15, 1929 • 12:00 PM • Atlanta, GA, USA

Nobel Peace Laureate

"We may have all come on different ships, but we're all in the same boat now."

-Martin Luther King

On August 28, 1963, Martin Luther King Jr. delivered his famous *I Have a Dream* speech to over a quarter-million people at the national mall in Washington, DC. James Reston with the *New York Times* reported that "He was full of the symbolism of Lincoln and Gandhi, and the cadences of the Bible. He was both militant and sad, and he sent the crowd away feeling that the long journey had been worthwhile."[2] The following year, Dr. King's status as a leader of the civil rights movement earned him the Nobel Peace Prize.

On July 6, 1963, the impact of LS119's return at 14 Capricorn would light up Dr. King's visionary Neptune/NNode midpoint at 14 Cancer along with his natal Pluto at 17 Cancer. *The Sabian Symbols*, created by Marc Edmond Jones and Elsie Wheeler, give the following image for 17 Cancer: "A hen clucks among her chicks,"[3] a fitting refrain for a brooding Neptune/NNode/Pluto confluence of collective consciousness. As such, Dr. King's speech was a time bomb set to explode into the moral and social landscape of all those who were present that day.

Martin Luther King, Jr. represented a turbulent turning point in the space-time continuum that was the sixties, a time when people still believed in Lyndon Johnson's "just society" and were willing to stand up and challenge the power elites. King's PREBLE-LS134—The Attractor Factor—was a huge factor in both his desire and ability to serve the world because of its enormous capacity to connect and to care. This social conscience is a noted characteristic of fellow LS134 alumni Noam Chomsky, David Bowie, and Edward Snowden.

Martin Luther King's Connections to the Lunar Dragons of LS119

1st Harmonics: SNode – Uranus, Uranus – NNode,
Moon – Jupiter, Ceres – Pluto, Chiron/Saturn –Venus
2nd Harmonics: Ceres – Sun, Venus – Chiron, Neptune – Mercury

Four Cosmic Bridges establish irrefutable connections across their respective fields. Both charts are driven by Locomotive patterns that push and pull them forward, presenting a "smooth" feel regardless of what else is going on. Mutable Saturn at the leading edge of their Locomotives gives them a double tap of "saving the world" ambition.

Dr. King's hungry NNode is fed by LS119's Uranus, satisfying a need to explore life's greater potential and "is more a wild-eyed god whose intuitive power crackles with electrical vitality," as Bil Tierney writes in *Alive and Well with Uranus.*[4] In turn, the eclipse SNode on King's Uranus-Aries/Neptune-Virgo "anything goes" zero degrees quincunx feels deeply disturbing and deeply karmic. The eclipse 1st Harmonic Moon on Dr. King's Jupiter trine anything goes Neptune greatly expands the scope of disruption giving the eclipse Moon/Mars MR a greater range in which to operate. At the first degree of Taurus, and in the Twelfth House, Jupiter is more than willing to sacrifice.

Lunar Saros 119's return in the summer of 1963 and its impact on Dr. King's life can best be summed up by the eclipse Ceres 1st Harmonic to his Pluto and its 2nd Harmonic to the Sun. This is cosmic complexity of death-defying magnitude made even more defiant by Dr. King's 25 degree Capricorn Sun which, when factored into the eclipse field, creates a Grand Cardinal Cross that is capable of releasing upsetting amounts of intense energy. A person willing to use this formidable power must embrace German philosopher Friedrich

Nietzsche's adage that "what does not kill me makes me stronger." Martin Luther King Jr. would die within five years; he was assassinated on April 4, 1968.

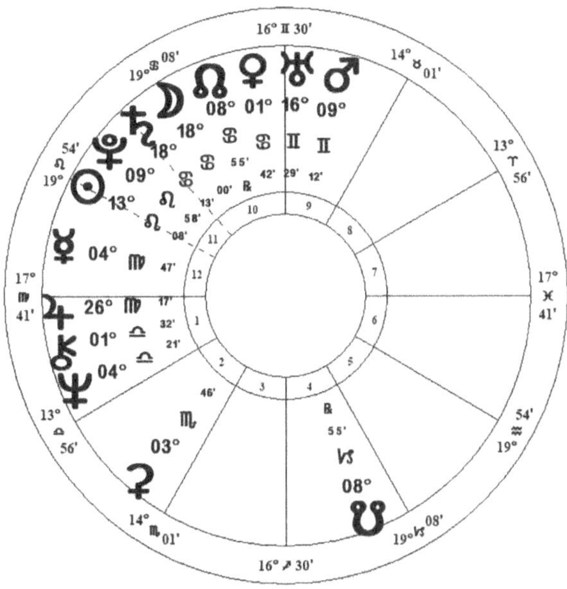

Atomic Bomb Drop

August 6, 1945 • 8:15 AM • Hiroshima, Japan

Dropping "Little Boy"

When LS119 arrived on June 26, 1945, for Hiroshima, Japan, the Moon had reached the zenith in full ambition-driven Capricorn. Its waxing square to Neptune would not offer much escape from the horror that was to come. On August 6, 1945, at 8:15 a.m., Uranus reached the zenith degree over Hiroshima at the exact moment the atomic bomb was dropped. Transiting Venus would conjunct LS119's Dragon DNA Pluto, opening the gates to Hell where destructive power reigns supreme.

In moments that hold stunning and startling revelations, Uranus can often be found holding a key position in the cosmos. Here, Uranus is channeling two behemoths of war—the great warrior stars Bellatrix and Rigel. Our English words "belligerent" and "bellicose" are derived from the Latin root *bellum*, "war," and impart a commanding and opportunistic presence. Similarly, Rigel is battle-scarred and has always had an association with foreign encounters on its journey to high adventure and knowledge. Rigel is the sixth brightest star in the sky and holds court in the constellation of Orion, the Hunter. The Arabic name for Rigel was Al Najid, "the Conqueror."

Another chaos contender is LS131—Pursuit of Truth—in Part Four of the Water Dragons. Here you'll find the chart for the Chernobyl disaster on April 26, 1986, with Uranus dead-steady and rising on the horizon at the exact moment of nuclear meltdown.

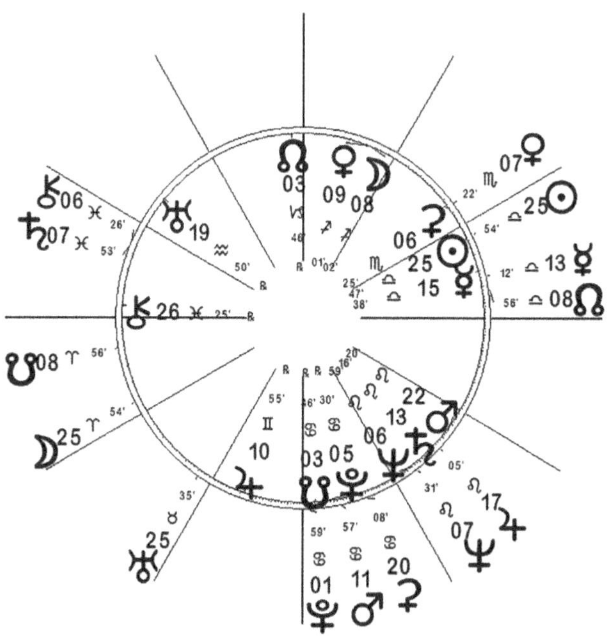

Inside

Oumuamua

October 19, 2017 • Discovery Time Unknown • Haleakala Observatory, Hawaii

Outside

LS119

October 14, 935 • 7:00:02 PM • South Pole

An Interstellar Visitor

Extraterrestrial: The First Sign of Intelligent Life Beyond Earth

-Avi Loeb

Oumuamua is the first interstellar object detected passing through our solar system. It was discovered by Robert Weryk at the Haleakala Observatory, Hawaii, on October 19, 2017. Astrophysicist Avi Loeb (longest-serving Chair of Harvard's Astronomy department) reacted to the discovery of Oumuamua by calling it an artifact, an extra-terrestrial bottle from interstellar space with a message that we are not alone. Loeb writes, "Oumuamua must have been designed, built, and launched by an extraterrestrial intelligence."[5]

LS119's arrival on August 7, 2017, at 15 Aquarius held and opened a space that would resonate to Oumuamua's discovery with Uranus at 19 Aquarius. But just look at all the links to the mother chart of LS119. It is truly one of the most astounding resonances presented in this entire book, and I leave it in your most capable hands to enjoy finding all the links.

LS119 Summary

Take off your blinders because power in all its fabulous and frightening forms seems to follow in the footsteps of these Fire Dragons. Acting against norms using bold, blatant, and often unparalleled procedure, ambitious, large scale projects can now be undertaken. Able to function under great strain and duress, these dragons often herald tumultuous times that bring together divergent people and ideas. Pivotal creative forces are generated within the matrix of this eclipse field that allows for ambitious and often large scale challenges to be undertaken. Management and leadership skills emerge that highlight originality and an appreciation for one's unique identity as viewed through the lens of social justice and civil society. Themes of aggression, audacity, loss, and suffering often emerge when these powerful dragons engage. Their arrival coincides with a cosmic appreciation for the greater forces that flow through the world and how little control most of us have regarding our ultimate fate. A word to the wise: Be on the lookout for abuses of authority and power. Don't be alarmed if bereavement, debt, divorce, injury, sacrifice, separation, and trouble seem to be circling the wagons. Relocations and cross-country moves are common.

The Aries impact of independence is so strong in this eclipse field that practically anyone who holds a Moon in Aries, an Aries ascendant, or at least two personal planets in this frequency will be able to pick up on LS119's dynamic, vibrant—and above all else—optimistic life force. The research indicates that you don't need an activation degree from the returning lunar eclipse field to experience a significant shift in levels of self-confidence. To that end, it won't require much effort to be in harmony with these fiery fellows; their force field is more than willing to sweep you up into its tidal flux of frenzy and fabulousness. You might want to fasten your seat belt.

Phase	Return	Year
Full Moon	50th	1819
Disseminating	55th	1909
Last Quarter	59th	1981
Balsamic	63rd	2053

LS119 Luminaries

Catherine the Great	May 2, 1729
Queen Victoria	May 24, 1819
Jessica Tandy	June 7, 1909
Homi J. Bhabha	October 30, 1909
Johnny Mercer	November 18, 1909
Peter Drucker	November 19, 1909
Neil Simon	July 4, 1927
Tommy Lasorda	September 22, 1927
R D Laing	October 7, 1927
George C Scott	October, 18, 1927
Carly Simon[E1]	June 25, 1945
Helen Mirren	July 26 1945
Steve Martin	August 14, 1945
Bette Midler	December 1, 1945
Whitney Houston	August 9, 1963
Alejandro Iñárritu	August 15, 1963
Brad Pitt	December 18, 1963
Meghan Markle	August 4, 1981

Roger Federer	August 8, 1981
Beyonce Knowles	September 4, 1981
Ivanka Trump	October 30, 1981
Britney Spears	December 2, 1981

PREBLE—LS114
Jessica Tandy
Carly Simon

---

1. https://en.wikipedia.org/wiki/Tommy_Lasorda. Retrieved March 21, 2022.

2. James Reston, "*I Have a Dream...*" *Peroration by Dr. King Sums Up a Day the Capital Will Remember* http://graphics8.nytimes.com/packages/pdf/topics/MLK/washdream.pdf. Retrieved Jan. 20, 2022.

3. Diana E. Roche, *The Origin and History of the Sabian Symbols.* https://sabian.org/sabian_symbols.php Retrieved Jan. 20, 2022.

4. Bil Tierney, *Alive and Well with Uranus, Transits of Self-Awakening* (St. Paul, MN: Llewellyn Publications, 1999), p. 101.

5. https://en.wikipedia.org/wiki/Extraterrestrial:_The_First_Sign_of_Intelligent_Life_Beyond_Earth.

LUNAR SAROS 120

"I don't try to describe the future. I try to prevent it."

-Ray Bradbury

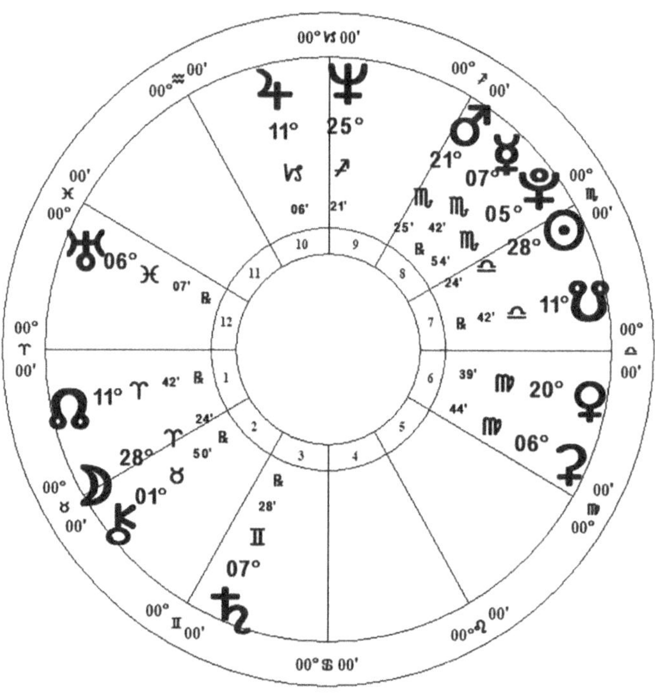

Lunar Saros 120

October 22, 1000 • 1:24:50 AM • North Pole

Burn Baby Burn

Intensity is what you get when Ruler Mars and Pluto, both in Scorpio, announce this North Node Aries lunar eclipse. Pluto's conjunction to retrograde Mercury in Scorpio greatly increases the chances that mythic tales of might and struggle, victory and defeat will fill and thrill while Mars in sextile to Venus makes sure that creative opportunities are realistic and grounded in the earthiness of efficiency. The Moon's trine and the Sun's sextile to Neptune give tremendous imaginative potential, a love of drama and the ability to "fine tune and fit in" with almost any situation. The Moon's conjunction with Chiron in Taurus is solid and secure, able to work toward any worthwhile goal.

This eclipse marks a time of returning to and often reworking old ideas. Sifting through the seeds of discontent is the job of the retrograde Saturn/Uranus/Ceres T-Square as it eliminates inefficiency in its efforts to build in greater understanding and capacity to work within a larger cultural context. Accordingly, be prepared for failure as many ideas fall by the wayside as one grows in self-discovery. Failure is a prerequisite for success, and no one understands that better than Soichiro Honda who, with his own Pluto/Mars-Saturn, built a global empire starting out from a wooden shack. Soichiro Honda is from LS127—Fired in the Kiln—and like LS120, used this challenging midpoint (which has one of the highest failure ratings of them all) to rise to the top. In Honda's case, on balance, he made the most out of his Venus/Mercury OOB conjunction in Sagittarius along with an OOB Uranus in Capricorn.

Many who are new to astrological analysis may not yet have discovered the literal fountain of creativity that lies within a tightly bound inconjunct/quincunx with its reputation for frustration and delays. Mercury's trine to Uranus and its inconjunct to Saturn in Gemini at the seventh degree—and all in retrograde—speak to the "reversals in thinking" theme already noted, with special emphasis on turnarounds/delays and the potential for overturning of legal decisions.

Making life even more interesting is an extremely rare OOB (23S35) Jupiter found only in this eclipse field and in LS121—Sparks of Inspiration. Here the OOB Jupiter is in a Cardinal T-Square to the nodal axis, unfolding a complex of ambition in an endless array of real time events and characters that both delight and exacerbate; such notable gangsters as Meyer Lansky born on July 4, 1902 as well as Carlo Gambino on August 24, 1902 belong to this family. 1902 appears to have been a very good year for gangsters. Action junkie Evel Knievel, born October 17, 1938, is a stellar example and member of the tribe.

In matters of personal relationships and social standing, this family offers a wide assortment of role reversals and changes of attitude. Many will benefit from the natural cycles of life experience that allow for the juvenile and vitriolic prejudices of youth to be replaced by a more rational and mature perspective. If that maturation is slow to come on line, pursuing satisfaction in any cultural sense may prove frustrating as seen through the Eclipse/Venus-Saturn midpoint. But take heart as the Sun/Moon opposition Venus/Saturn isotrap rewards all those who labor long and are in fact strengthened by the adversity that comes their way.

The struggles that emerge from Lunar Saros 120 all lead toward personal freedom. In spite of the many challenges that this eclipse represents, its Splash chart offers bold versatility and an aptitude for finding order in the field of chaos. Unappreciated during his lifetime, we can take comfort in the words of French Post-Impressionist artist Paul Gauguin who said: "I shut my eyes in order to see."

Closest Midpoints: Mercury/Venus-Neptune, Mars/Saturn-Pluto
Isotraps: Mars/Neptune conjunct Jupiter/Pluto
Sun/Moon opposition Venus/Saturn

1900—2100 Eclipses: Lunar Saros—120

1902, 1920, 1938, 1956, 1974, 1992, 2010, 2028, 2046, 2064, 2082, 2100
Length of cycle —1,478 years
Series ends—April 7, 2479

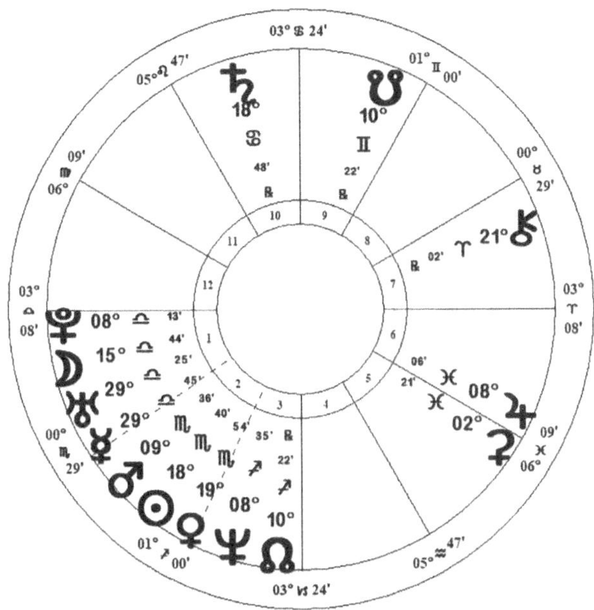

Leonardo DiCaprio
PREBLEs—LS120 & LS125

November 11, 1974 • 2:47 AM • Los Angeles, CA, USA

More Than Just a Pretty Face

"I don't think there's anybody better than Leonardo DiCaprio, and I've been saying that since before anyone knew who he was."

-Michael Keaton

Let's take a look at how the lunar dragons of LS120 have left their mark on, and contributed to, the legacy of this superstar's life.

Leonardo DiCaprio's Connections to the Lunar Dragons of LS120

1st Harmonics: SNode – Pluto, SNode – Moon, Saturn – SNode,
Sun – Mercury/Uranus, Mercury – Mars, Mars – Sun, Mars – Venus
2nd Harmonics: Moon – Mercury, Moon – Uranus,
Ceres – Jupiter, Chiron – Mercury, Chiron – Uranus, Saturn – Neptune

The SNode of the lunar eclipse links to his ruler Pluto, forming the all-important Cosmic Bridge that, in itself, is all you need. The eclipse Cardinal T-Square to the nodal axis and its complex of ambition finds a foothold in DiCaprio's beautiful and charming Libran First House where his creative endeavors get a super-charged boost of energy. The aesthetic perceptions of his Moon in Libra are greatly enhanced, bringing into his daily life a keen appreciation for beauty and art in a way that is unmatched by any other Moon position.

The eclipse field's Saturn and its Mars/Saturn-Pluto midpoint attaches to DiCaprio's SNode in an extremely positive manner. This gave him the ability, confidence, and support early on to continue to work at his craft regardless of setbacks. LS120's Sun/Neptune on his Mercury/Uranus inspired an unfailing love of drama and the ability, from a very young age, to become a chameleon to fit the needs of any role he played. Mercury/Uranus is always about following your intuition. Placed at the critical 29th degree, his keen sense of intuition would have been a guiding force in his rise to stardom.

DiCaprio's 1st and 2nd Harmonics from Mercury to his Mars and Chiron increase his romantic allure thanks to the eclipse Mercury/Venus-Neptune midpoint. Conversely, the eclipse Mars with its potent Mars/Neptune conjunct Jupiter/Pluto isotrap ties directly into his Sun/Venus conjunction, increasing his life force and vitality and at the same time intensifying a creative drive that demands that one live not simply for oneself but to be in service to others. Leonardo's compassion and generosity flow into his environmental and political activism and his philanthropy. These are exemplary examples of how this dynamic energy pattern from his lunar dragon family continues to shape his life choices.

Finally, the eclipse Moon with its conjunction to Chiron and its trine to Neptune points the way to redemption and healing through developing empathy and the capacity to identify with another person's feeling states. The mother chart of LS120 is a reminder, with its Moon/Neptune trine, that all members of this clan must be aware of their social obligations. DiCaprio has always stepped up to be a solar hero in this regard and gives his own mother all the credit; he is often quoted as saying, "My mother is a walking miracle."[1] These overlapping patterns dance through DiCaprio's futuristic Uranus/Mercury in Libra's sense of fair play, and through the 2nd Harmonic bring into his life partnerships that support his vision and humanitarian projects, making Leonardo much more than just a pretty face.

And one more thing. Leo was born just as his Fire Dragon family was entering, for the second time around, their final Disseminating Phase making them, by this stage of their evolution, masters at getting the word out. As you've read by now, the Disseminating Phase has a special skill set that involves being able to convey awareness— it has a natural attraction to education, both for oneself and the public writ large. These folks just love to impart their knowledge as they practice the high art of stewardship. And if publicity is involved, so much the better.

Neil Peart
PREBLE—LS118

September 12, 1952 • TOB Unknown • Hamilton, ON, Canada

Drummer Extraordinaire

"If the future's looking dark, we're the ones who have to shine."

-NEIL PEART

On July 29, 1974, Canadian drummer Neil Peart joined the group RUSH; two weeks later, on August 14, he was at the Civic Arena in Pittsburgh, Pennsylvania, as part of an opening act for Uriah Heep and Manfred Mann.[2] This was definitely providence in action since Neil had just returned to Canada after spending eighteen months in the UK, completely disenchanted and disillusioned about the music business.[3]

The lunar eclipse that would restore his passion and revitalize his career was LS120. The eclipse fired up on June 4, 1974, rebooting not only his drummer's technical expertise by activating his extraordinary Mars square Mercury with its exquisite body-centric timing, but more importantly it awakened his sleeping Ceres to begin again the process of nurturing his musical imagination and reviving his lyrical soul. By energizing 14 Sagittarius, the lunar eclipse made an exact opposition to Peart's Ceres at 14 Gemini, putting the spotlight on the role that communication played in his ability to nurture himself and others. Ceres holds three trines to Venus, Saturn, and Neptune in Libra and all in turn trine his brotherhood fan based NNode in Aquarius. His craftsmanship as a drummer can be seen in many ways: his dignified Venus/Saturn vortex reflects a master's touch of timing and harmony and in tandem to Jupiter in Taurus square a Pluto/SNode conjunction in Leo gives his musical talent a stage for dramatic, artistic expression. Not only did he get the gig and was able to work as a musician, but he also quickly found his gift for writing.

Neil Peart went on to become the dominating force behind the lyricism of RUSH thanks to his talent, confidence, and a helping hand from the driving urgency and rebirth that is LS120. Working away in the background is his PREBLE 118—The Marketplace—one of the hardest working and diligent lunar eclipses of the entire Saros Series, and a source of many self-made success stories.

Neil Peart's Connections to the Lunar Dragons of LS120

1st Harmonics: SNode – Venus,
SNode – Saturn, Venus – Sun, Ceres – Mercury
2nd Harmonics: Mars – Jupiter, Uranus – Mercury

Neil Peart's family ties could never be in doubt starting with double strands of sweetness; LS120's Venus to his Sun and his Venus to the nodes form a critical Cosmic Bridge. Here we find the timeless tenderness of the lunar eclipse SNode to his Venus, reinforcing bonds of affection and aesthetic expression. The SNode is also synchronized to Peart's Saturn in Libra, giving him access to a well-provisioned, past life store of self-control and talent. The lunar eclipse 2nd Harmonic Uranus opens its arms to his Mercury and its partile square to

Mars, a drummer's dream of dexterity that would only accelerate his already fast-paced and high-energy motor control. In 1974, the Fire Dragons of LS120 returned for their 55th appearance on the global stage, entering a Disseminating Phase that would continue to rock the world for the next seventy-two years. This phase, as we've already seen in DiCaprio's life, carries high levels of awareness and loves to impart knowledge; the majority of its energy is often associated with publicity, making it a perfect springboard that would launch Peart and RUSH to the top of the charts.

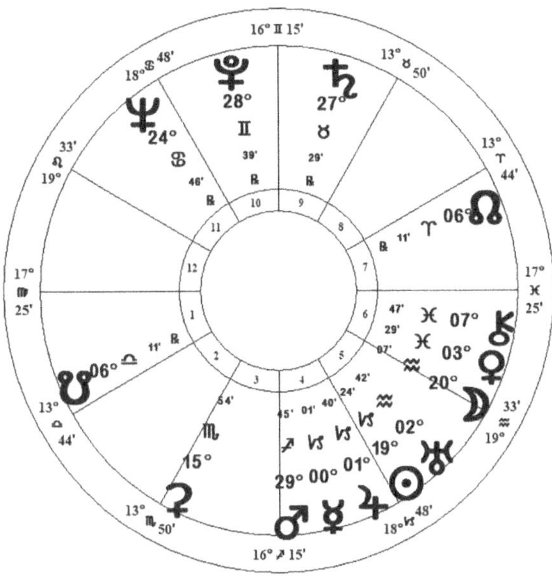

Richard Nixon
PREBLE—LS116

January 9, 1913 • 9:35 PM • Yorba Linda, CA, USA

"I can take it. The tougher it gets, the cooler I get."

-Richard Nixon

35th President of the United States

"Anyone can grow up to be president."

-American Adage

On August 9, 1974, under the looming threat of impeachment and halfway through his second term, Richard Nixon resigned, bringing his presidency to an abrupt end, following accusations of obstructing justice in the now infamous Watergate scandal.[4] After a year of intensive negotiation, legal haranguing, and court battles to get access to Nixon's tapes, on July 24, 1974, the Supreme Court ordered the President to release the tapes; this was followed on July 27 by charges of obstruction of justice and "the first of three articles of impeachment."[5]

Adding fuel to the fire that would burn his house to the ground, LS120 landed on June 4, 1974, at 14 Sagittarius, scoring a direct hit to Nixon's Fourth House IC cusp. The activation set off his unstable Midheaven MC/Ceres/Sun Finger of Fate Yod, a precarious if not dangerous situation for a world leader. In the land of Yod, one can find themselves in need of an immediate compromise, adjustment, trade-off, or in worst case scenarios, sacrifice. Ambition is an integral factor in the psychology of LS120's eclipse field with its OOB Jupiter in T-Square to the nodes. Nixon's Mercury/Jupiter at the AP along with his Pluto matched the eclipse field's ambitious profile. But Nixon's options were quickly running out, leaving his Yod to step up to make the required sacrifice. With impeachment proceedings underway and criminal prosecution waiting in the wings, Richard Nixon resigned in the wake of LS120's disruptive currents of setbacks and loss.

To appreciate the finer nuances of this critical period of Nixon's political career, a look through the lens of lunar eclipse analysis is insightful. As always, put the eclipse energies first and then its contact in Nixon's chart. Here's our list:

Richard Nixon's Connections to the Lunar Dragons of LS120
↓South Node with South Node↓

1st Harmonics: SNode – SNode, NNode – NNode,
Venus – ASC, Uranus – Venus, Uranus – Chiron
2nd Harmonic: Ceres – Venus

LS120's SNode to Nixon's SNode is a Global Gateway (GG) that opens to a field full of constraint. The GG activating through the same polarity is known to produce states of anxiety along with disruptive experiences; it holds the potential to either neutralize or temporarily impede an individual's sense of accomplishment.

However, the tie that truly bound Nixon's fate to LS120's celestial wheel is found through the eclipse Uranus at 6 Pisces to his Chiron. It is essential to keep in mind that Nixon's SNode is in exact quincunx to his Chiron in Pisces in the Sixth House where it lives in an environment of perpetual paranoia. Adding to this was his notoriously ill-fitted nature and reputation for inflexibility and deception. The eclipse Saturn square with retrograde Uranus definitely went to work to redefine and relocate Nixon within a larger cultural context. When one considers that his PREBLE is LS116—Persuasion—with its core issues and concerns about being liked and even loved, the stage was set for a political as well as psychological breakdown.

Nixon is a good example of LS120's relationship to role reversals and changes in attitude that so often accompany their returns and even more so considering the lunar eclipse had just entered its Disseminating Phase with its need for re-evaluation. This phase, while still being very public oriented, begins a time for internal and reflexive synthesis. Also, at this time we find Nixon's progressed Moon at the twelfth devotional and despondent degree of Taurus *exactly* on his progressed DSC axis.

LS120 Summary

These are intense times as an inner compulsion drives us forward to achieve our goals, aspirations, and even dreams. Delays, disappointments, and disillusionment are all in service to this ancient lunar family, providing essential experiences in the process of maturation. Frustration for these Fire Dragons is a valuable tool and wonderfully redemptive. It is a noted characteristic of this family and highly underrated, as it is a crucial component in their ability to activate and accelerate any new stage of growth. The necessity to fail is almost a requirement, if not a badge of honor, for these wise fire breathers. They have made it their mission to make it OK to fail. Their attitude toward failure is extremely positive and hopefully, after a cycle of return or two or indeed, a lifetime under their influence, failure will be perceived as an open door to surprising insights and the development of character.

To get the best from this lunar family whether by birthright or rite of passage requires one to dig deep and build a strong emotional foundation that can withstand the inevitable disruptions of life. To be in harmony with their dance moves, it is always best to throw yourself headfirst into the storm of your life. There will be no talk of stress here—only that of inspiration and amazement. Have faith and when the burdens get too heavy to carry, call home.

Phase	Return	Year
Full Moon	50th	1902
Disseminating	55th	1974
Last Quarter	59th	2046
Balsamic	63rd	2118

LS120 Luminaries

René Descartes	March 31, 1596
Paul Gauguin	June 7, 1848
David O Selznick	May 10, 1902
Paul Dirac	August 8, 1902
Carlos Gracie	September 14, 1902
Ray Kroc	October 5, 1902
David Brinkley	July 10, 1920
Maureen O'Hara	August 17, 1920
Ray Bradbury	August 22, 1920
Timothy Leary	October 22, 1920
Joyce Carol Oates	June 16, 1938
Natalie Wood	July 20, 1938
Alberto Fujimori	July 28, 1938
Evel Knievel	October 17, 1938
Björn Borg	June 6, 1956
Anthony Bourdain	June 25, 1956
David Copperfield	September 16, 1956
Martina Navratilova	October 18, 1956
Carrie Fisher	October 21, 1956
Alanis Morissette[E3]	June 1, 1974
Hilary Swank	July 30, 1974
Joaquin Phoenix	October 28, 1974
Leonardo DiCaprio	November 11, 1974
Selena Gomez	July 22, 1992
Miley Cyrus	November 23, 1992

PREBLE—LS115
Alanis Morissette

---

1. https://www.biography.com/actor/leonardo-dicaprio. Retrieved April 2, 2022.
2. http://www.drumlessons.com/drummers/neil-peart/ Retrieved Jan 26, 2022.
3. Ibid.
4. https://www.history.com/this-day-in-history/house-begins-impeachment-of-Nixon. Retrieved Jan. 26, 2022.
5. https://www.history.com/topics/1970s/Watergate. Retrieved Jan. 26, 2022.

LUNAR SAROS 121

"The only place success comes before work is in the dictionary."

-Vince Lombardi

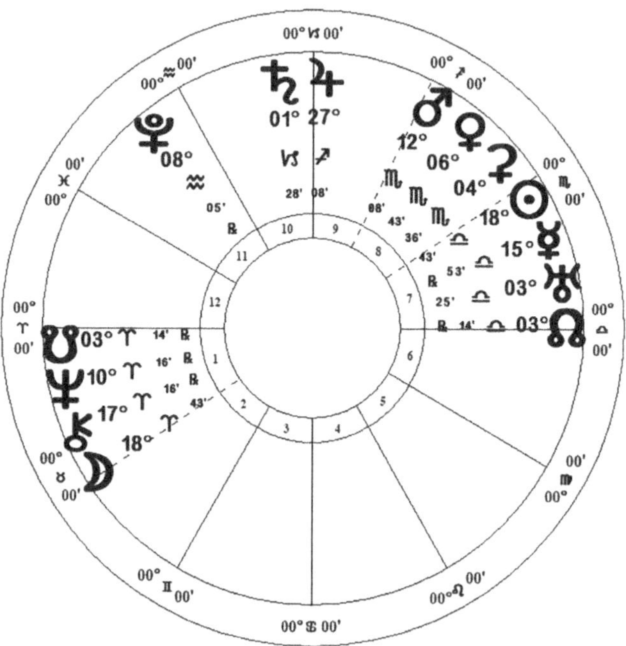

Lunar Saros 121

October 12, 1047 • 7:01:02 PM • South Pole

Sparks of Inspiration

Sparks fly to light up our space and our place within those worlds with the arrival of these exciting Aries SNode dragons. This series offers illumination with its Promethean Mercury rising ahead of the Sun. There is never a dull moment in this family because Saturn, Jupiter, and Mars are all in rulership and Jupiter conjuncts Saturn at the AP, an energetic signature unique to this lunar family. The NNode/Uranus conjunction is a tonic that continually refreshes the eclipse field, empowered by challenging life refits—courtesy of Saturn's "at the bends" square to the nodal axis. This trio is inspired by the perceptive Neptune/ Mercury-Uranus midpoint that continually grows in both intellectual and metaphysical curiosity as the eclipse unfolds through its 1,460 year lifespan. Highly focused and self-contained, individuals born within LS121's Bowl pattern, one of only three in the entire 47 lunar eclipse series, can always be counted on to go in search of work that is personally relevant.

Retrograde Mercury opposition Chiron and the Moon is constantly updating the field. A quick look at the isotraps promotes a paradoxical portrait of both gain and loss exemplified by Jupiter's closing conjunction to Saturn which, as Marc Robertson in *Cosmopsychology 1* writes: "You could be called crazy, but you could also originate the systems that the future demands when the past has failed."[1] Jupiter benefits enormously from the Saturn/ Node square since it is constantly at work building in resilience aided by an extremely rare OOB (23s41) Jupiter. The only other OOB Jupiter belongs to LS120—Burn Baby Burn. Jupiter's conjunction to Saturn and the nodal axis gives all clan members an optimistic sense of adventure. In the realm of high adventure, LS121's fifty-second return brought forth The Outer Space Treaty, signed into international law in 1967, declaring that nations cannot own celestial bodies and prohibiting any weapons of mass destruction to be placed in orbit, on the Moon, or on other bodies in space.

Making the ordinary extraordinary is LS121's OOB Pluto; at 27S23 it holds the most extreme Pluto declination of any Lunar Saros Series with only one other, Earth Eclipse LS128—Coming Into Existence—in Part Two. Extreme declinations for Pluto are rare and underscore the need for intensity. Membership requires depth of character and serious thought. Pluto's waning square with Venus in Scorpio is a celestial blueprint that requires one to forsake superficiality.

The essence of the Moon in Aries is to be a truth teller, no matter the price one must pay. Famous people born with the Moon is Aries include Charles de Gaulle, Robespierre, and the great Albert Schweitzer. One of the most famous astronauts in the world is Gordon Cooper who has a Moon/ Chiron conjunction at 29 Aries. In 1963 Cooper became the first American to spend an entire day in space. He would be the last American to experience a solo mission, a telling reveal to the nature of the 29th degree of Aries that represents his first and solo achievement as well as it being the critical last ever flight of its kind.

What matters most is the answer to the question: "What am I learning now from what is happening in my life?" Such existential considerations are part of the psychological makeup of LS121. Membership in this clan makes you a passionate soul, fully engrossed in your current obsession. Just be aware that others may be as fixated as you are and are allowed to have their own opinions.

Closest Midpoints: Eclipse/Venus-Node, Neptune/Mercury-Uranus
Isotraps: Venus/Saturn conjunct Mars/Jupiter
Moon/Mercury opposition Jupiter/Pluto

1900—2100 Eclipses: Lunar Saros—121

1913, 1931, 1949, 1967, 1985, 2003, 2021, 2039, 2057, 2075, 2093
Length of cycle —1,460 years
Series ends—March 18, 2508

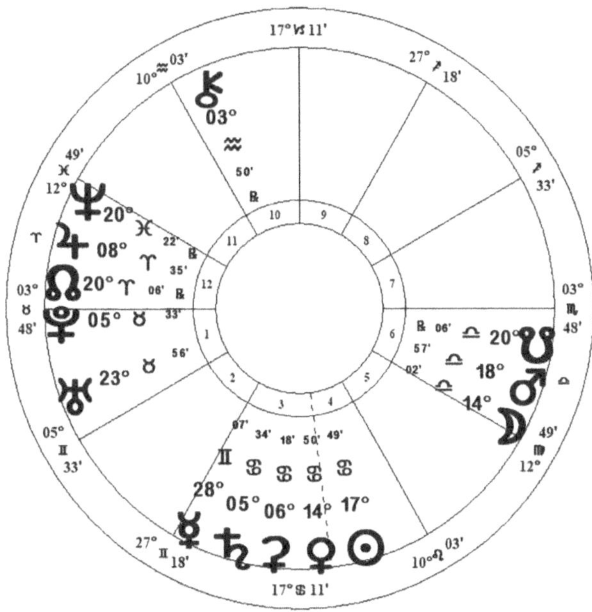

Nikola Tesla
PREBLE—LS129

July 10, 1856 • 12:01 AM • Smiljan, Croatia

Visionary Inventor/Genius

"Let the future tell the truth, and evaluate each one according to his work and accomplishments. The present is theirs; the future, for which I have really worked, is mine."

-NIKOLA TESLA

Nikola Tesla was reportedly born during a violent electrical storm, which is fascinating because energy became the story of his life. At the turn of the twentieth century, Tesla, the inventor of the AC motor and wireless power, was one of America's most dazzling and eccentric celebrity scientists. With his vision of free energy for the world along with a quirkiness for extraterrestrial communications, he was an acknowledged genius who seemed to be a man from the future. Of countless articles and biographies written about Tesla, most memorable is W.

Bernard Carlson's *Tesla: Inventor of the Electrical Age,* wherein the author remarks on Tesla's unusual and powerful visual imagination. Carlson sources original documents from Tesla's private and public life, wherein the inventor, at age nineteen stated that he, "observed to my delight that I could visualize with the greatest facility," and later claimed "I needed no models, drawings, or experiments. I could picture them all as real in my mind."[2] Tesla's Uranus/Mercury-Node midpoint certainly contributed to this unprecedented ability.

On March 11, 1895, LS121 arrived at 20 Virgo exactly opposing Tesla's Neptune in Pisces. Two days later, under mysterious conditions, Tesla's laboratory completely burned to the ground—his notes, data, tools, photographs, and hundreds of invention models valued between $80,000 to $100,000 were lost forever. Unfortunately, he had no fire insurance.[3] At the time, the press reported that Tesla, using one of his oscillating coils, gave himself regular shocks to keep "from sinking into a state of melancholia."[4]

Within a month of the fire, Tesla was fully recovered. On April 15, 1895, the first test of the largest AC generators ever installed at the Niagara Falls Power Plant successfully came online, an event which would make his name and over forty of his patents a legacy for the coming age of illumination.[5] On April 4, 1931, LS121 returned at 12 Libra, illuminating Tesla's Moon at 14 Libra. In recognition of his life-long achievements and to mark his 75th birthday, *Time Magazine* put his portrait on the cover in July. Tesla received "congratulatory letters from more than seventy pioneers in science and engineering including Albert Einstein."[6]

Nikola Tesla's Connections to the Lunar Dragons of LS121
↑NNode with SNode↓

1st Harmonics: SNode – Neptune, Moon – NNode, Sun – SNode,
Chiron – NNode, Mercury – Mars, Venus – DSC, Ceres – DSC, Neptune – Jupiter
2nd Harmonics: Moon – Moon, Moon – Mars, Chiron – Moon, Neptune – Moon, Venus – Pluto,
Ceres – Pluto, Jupiter – Mercury, Saturn – Mercury

LS121's SNode to Tesla's NNode is a Global Gateway (GG) that opens to a field full of opportunity that ranges anywhere from lucky breaks to breakthroughs in any field imaginable. The GG activating through opposite polarity is known to produce some of life's most exquisite experiences; it holds the potential to either enhance or accelerate an individual's sense of growth and life purpose.

Tesla's connectivity to this eclipse is extraordinary, but the real love story here is the eclipse field's Moon on his NNode, forming one of the strongest Cosmic Bridges possible. It is as if the cosmic Mother herself is watching over, making sure his efforts are not in vain, leaving trails of magnanimity in his wake. His 2nd Harmonics are critical especially the Moon to Moon. This is always a 100 percent guarantee that radical changes to your environment are on their way. The 2nd Harmonic is more often an energy coming "at you," in contrast to a 1st Harmonic, which seems to emerge from "within" and is often not as disruptive or dramatic as a 2nd Harmonic.

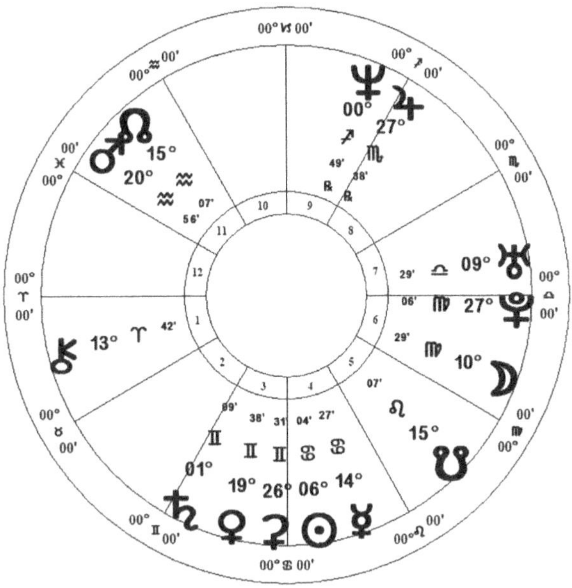

Elon Musk
PREBLE—LS123

June 28, 1971 • TOB Unknown • Pretoria, South Africa

CEO SpaceX/CEO Tesla

(Founder of the Boring Company, Co-Founder of Neuralink and OpenAI, Second Richest Man in the World as of March 2023[7])

"If you can have any superpower, luck is the one you'd want."

-Elon Musk

Tesla Motors was incorporated in the eclipse window of LS121 with its arrival at 25 Scorpio on May 16, 2003. CEO and founder Elon Musk was the driving force behind the design of the original *Tesla Roadster*, the first battery operated electric sports car using an AC motor descended from a design of Nikola Tesla.[8]

The lunar eclipse engulfed Musk's Jupiter at 27 Scorpio and his vision-making Neptune at infinity 00 Sagittarius. I wondered if there would be connections to Tesla's chart and even more, would Tesla's chart still be responding to the cosmic rhythms in play?

A glance at Tesla's chart quickly revealed that the answer was indeed yes. LS121's return in 2003 would activate by opposition Tesla's Uranus at 24 Taurus. How appropriate that LS121would arrive to spark the morphogenetic field of Uranus by its polarity to Scorpio, the sign of legacies and shared wealth. Together, Tesla and Musk share a double dip of Uranus/Jupiter connections: Tesla's Uranus opposes Musk's Jupiter and Tesla's Jupiter opposes Musk's Uranus. Now that's a shout out to alternating currents of inspiration.

Even without a timed birth chart, Elon Musk's drive for success and his early ambition to be an inventor can be deduced by how his Node/Sun-Pluto midpoint is empowered by a Bucket chart with Mars and the NNode in Aquarius at its handle. There could be little doubt that his life force would require the attainment of goals, especially in the fields of innovative technology and space and even more so to lift humanity higher. Elon Musk is profiled in the Fire Eclipse of LS151—Off-World—where the eclipse activations on his chart will continue to highlight his life's work as they should, considering that many of us will be on our way to colonizing Mars and bases on the Moon by the late 2060's to fulfill Elon's dream of humanity becoming a space-faring civilization and ultimately a multi-planet species.

Elon Musk's Connections to the Lunar Dragons of LS121
Uranus with Uranus
Chiron with Chiron

1st Harmonics: NNode – Uranus,
NNode – Pluto, Moon – Chiron, Neptune – Chiron
2nd Harmonics: Saturn – Sun, Mercury – Chiron, Jupiter – Ceres

The impact of LS121 on Elon Musk's chart is impressive as his unaspected Uranus and Pluto are united through two Cosmic Bridge contacts to the hungry NNode. At the third degree of Libra and in conjunction to Uranus also at the third degree, the NNode sports a very curious, I-love-information Gemini vibe. The eclipse Moon's 1st Harmonic to Chiron produces the third CB stabilizing the system while the eclipse Neptune's contact to Chiron compliments the creative team spirit that lies within the Neptune/SNode-Chiron midpoint.

The 2nd Harmonics are the most noteworthy since the eclipse Jupiter/Saturn with Saturn at the AP and its nodal axis square gives it extraordinary reach, political power, and an optimism that any inventor or CEO could hope for. The eclipse Saturn to his Sun concretizes his need to be worthwhile to something greater than his own self-satisfaction as seen through his natal Sun square Uranus. With three contacts to his double-dipped thirteenth degree Chiron in Aries, Musk is an innovator and maverick in the truest sense of the word.

News Flash!

Pulitzer Prize Awarded to Darnella Frazier

On June 11, 2021, the Pulitzer Prize board issued Darnella Frazier a special award and citation for single-handedly reporting the murder of George Floyd with nothing more than her cell phone, by uploading a video that sparked a cultural shift in the way Black racism and violence at the hands of police is dealt with in the United States.[9] The Pulitzer was awarded to her within 2 weeks of LS121's arrival at 5 Sagittarius in May 2021 on her SNode at 1 Sagittarius. DOB 03/23/2003, Saint Paul, MN., USA.

LS121 Summary

These fire starters have been on a holy tear since they entered their Full Moon Phase in 1949. Since 2021 they are now ready to spread their wisdom and be role models for the truth they now have totally come to own. The diamonds of the Disseminating phase are all to be found in the realm of mentorship until the Last Quarter phase arrives in July 2093, when it will begin a more internal expression that will lead to sumptuous levels of productivity.

Either way, when your life intersects with the Fire Dragons of LS121 get comfortable with a renewed belief in yourself and your priorities. Many interests that had fallen by the wayside can now come roaring back to life. Born with an abundance of versatility and originality that borders on genius, these dragons take a backseat to no one and nor should you. They love to stir the pot and are notorious sh*t disturbers. This is not the time to indulge in unnecessary judgmental attitudes.

To be in harmony with these fire eaters one must accept the fact that chaos is on the menu for either most of your life if these are your dragon people or for a thrilling six month adventure. They love being on the creative cutting edge. Their high-power voltage just might be what's needed to turn your life around.

Appreciating the power of chaos in life could well become your next skill set. Along the way pay more attention to your mental and emotional equilibrium—it will need additional sources of support as disappointments in friendships and love are frequent flyers on these SNode dragon tails along with significant swings in financial prosperity. This activation can tempt you to throw in your hat but never the towel. This is a delightful dragon dance that both shakes up your world and puts you back on a truer path.

LS121 Luminaries

Sir Arthur Conan Doyle	May 22, 1859
Edgar Cayce	March 18, 1877
Isadora Duncan	May 27, 1877
Vince Lombardi	June 11, 1913
Red Skelton	July 18, 1913
Jesse Owens[E3]	September 12, 1913
Willie Mays	May 6, 1931
João Gilberto "O Mito"	June 10, 1931
Vince Lombardi	June 11, 1931
Sri Chinmoy	August 27, 1931
Christopher Hitchens[E1]	April 13, 1949
Meryl Streep	June 22, 1949
Randall Wallace	July 28, 1949
Annie Leibovitz	October 2, 1949
Tim McGraw	May 1, 1967
Philip Seymour Hoffman	July 23, 1967
Joe Rogan	August 11, 1967
Mira Sorvino	September 28, 1967
Carey Mulligan	May 28, 1985
Michael Phelps	June 30, 1985
Anna Kendrick	August 9, 1985
Alexander Ovechkin	September 17, 1985

PREBLE—LS116
Christopher Hitchens
Tim McGraw

1. Marc Robertson, *Cosmopsychology 1: The Engine of Destiny* (Snohomish, WA. Astrology Center of the Northwest, 1976), p. 82.
2. W. B. Bernard Carlson, *Tesla-Inventor of the Electrical Age* (Princeton, NJ: Princeton University Press, 2013), p. 31.
3. https://teslauniverse.com/nikola-tesla/timeline/1856-birth-nikola-tesla#goto-2009. Retrieved Jan. 15, 2022.
4. Ibid.
5. Ibid.
6. *Nikola Tesla: The Genius Who Lit the World.* Produced & Directed by Dr. Luubo Vujovic & Professor Alexsandar Marincic. Feb. 17, 2004. DVD.
7. https://www.forbes.com/billionaires/ Retrieved August 21, 2023.
8. http://venturebeat.com/2013/05/29/elon-musk-dreams-big/ Retrieved Jan. 15, 2022.
9. http://www.pulitzer.org/prize-winners-by-year. Retrieved Jan. 15, 2022.

LUNAR SAROS 129

"I am a deeply superficial person."

-Andy Warhol

Lunar Saros 129

June 18, 1351 • 8:59:23 AM • South Pole

Fame and Fortune

This is a Sagittarius lunar eclipse with Jupiter at the helm at the seventeenth degree of Leo. This SNode eclipse proudly proclaims a time to enjoy entertainment, sports, gambling, and notoriety. It reflects well on royalty, people with high public profiles, and those with the ambition to succeed. Jupiter's opposition to Neptune and in trine to risk-taking Pluto favors speculation and all is brought down to earth by its waxing square with a very intuitive Uranus in Taurus. Whether the markets are up or down or moving sideways, these fixed sign planets are endgame players, rarely flustered by temporary fluctuations or setbacks. Along with an OOB (25S00) Moon and (24N17) Venus, its Jupiter/Neptune/Uranus T-Square is a power broker's best friend—it stabilizes the entire field while at the same time encouraging risk-taking.

Lunar Saros 129 features a Fire Eclipse Moon that is also the handle on a Bucket, albeit a little off balance, but decidedly up to the task of pouring forth exuberant streams of largesse. Overconfidence is definitely part of this family dynamic made even more impressive by its double-dipped Jupiter in Leo and its sextile to an entrepreneurial Mars, eager to do whatever it takes to realize a return on investment, especially those that realize short term profits and quick wins.

As interesting and fascinating as the tale already told, the real story within Lunar Saros 129 belongs to Mercury. In rulership and holding steady at the fourth degree of Gemini, Mercury rises twenty-two degrees ahead of the Sun and as such acts first and seeks permission later. Because Mercury can never be more than twenty-eight degrees away from the Sun, its distance affords a high degree of objectivity that can really be appreciated when viewed through three of its critical midpoint structures: to the NNode and Chiron, to Saturn and Venus, and to the Sun and Uranus. Although Mercury/Eclipse-Uranus is the tightest, the most intriguing midpoint structure is to the NNode and Chiron—and here's why. The NNode and Chiron are *always* getting into trouble; that's how they like to learn. No pain, no gain is what this couple lives for, and since everything is new for the NNode, and Chiron is a catch basin for our failings and flaws, there's always a steep learning curve with this cosmic duo. But there's good news here—Mercury's placement moderates a powerful tidal flux that seems to wash away failure as fast as it arrives, bringing in fresh waves of experience. It's a truly remarkable midpoint that gains finesse with every new return. When Saturn/Venus is added to the mix with its organic sextile from Taurus to Cancer, a natural appreciation for style, taste, and beauty and its appreciating value also grows with time. Finally, the Mercury/Eclipse-Uranus midpoint establishes a new beachhead where iconoclastic characters enjoy the benefits of outlier status writ large.

Although LS129 occurs at the moon's descending node, making this a SNode "releasing" eclipse, the NNode's entanglement with its midpoint structures to Mercury and Mars and to Venus and Uranus add tremendous vigor and novelty. One needs to be prepared to experience this provocative eclipse with its full measure of argumentative communication along with a high tolerance for social disruption and unconventionality.

Closest Midpoints: Eclipse/Jupiter-Saturn, Mercury/Eclipse-Uranus
Isotraps: Venus/Neptune conjunct Saturn/Pluto,
Moon/Venus opposition Uranus/Neptune

1900—2100 Eclipses: Lunar Saros—129

1910, 1928, 1946, 1964, 1982, 2000, 2018, 2036, 2054, 2072, 2090
Length of cycle —1,262 years
Series ends—July 24, 2613

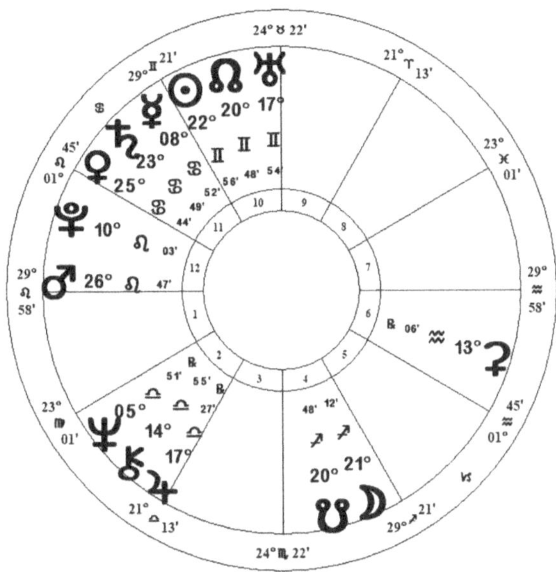

Donald J. Trump
PREBLEs—LS129 & LS124

June 14, 1946 • 10:54 AM • Jamaica, NY, USA

45th American President & Gaslighting Guru

"It's always good to be underestimated."

-DONALD TRUMP

Trump's character is stamped, like his buildings, with a self-serving talent for glitz, flash, and outrageous exaggeration. In Gwenda Blair's biography, *The Trumps—Three Generations That Built An Empire,* she tells quite the tale of the Trump family's entrepreneurial exploits. On their transformation of America, she writes of "Three men; three empires; three different times: the whole constituting a singular history of American capitalism itself."[1] "The Donald" represents the vulgarity and corporate corruption that became the hallmark of the '80s. Published in September 1982 and epitomizing this decade of capitalism on steroids, Trump appeared in the first *Forbes 400*, a who's who list of the 400 wealthiest people in America. "In the first Forbes list, there were only 13 billionaires, and a net worth of US$75 million secured a spot on the list."[2] As of 2022, the minimum net worth required to join this ultra-elite group rose to $37 billion.[3]

Riding on the coattails of his already successful real-estate developer dad, Trump's talent for deal-making quickly emerged, aided by a Sun/Mars-Jupiter, one of the most outstanding midpoints for the realization of great ambition. LS129 returned in the summer of 1982 to find The Donald celebrating the sale of luxury condos in his fast-rising, sixty-eight story Trump Tower on Fifth Avenue. The project had started from a desire to "Construct a big building, name it after himself, and make a lot of money."[4]

Donald Trump's Connections to the Dragons of LS129
↓SNode with SNode↓

1st Harmonics: Sun – Sun, Moon – Moon, Venus – Mercury, Ceres – Neptune
2nd Harmonics: Sun – Moon, Pluto – Jupiter

Trump's birth, having occurred within hours of the lunar eclipse of June 14, 1946, makes him a de facto poster boy for LS129 as they both enjoy a Sun/Moon opposition across the Gemini/Sagittarius axis with Trump's Sun three degrees off the eclipse Sun. The arrival of LS129 on June 14, 1946, marked the lunar eclipse's thirty-fourth return as well as the start of its second New Moon phase.

His overall resonance with the Fire dragons of LS129 has not been diminished even though his nodal axis to the eclipse nodal axis creates a GG that is more often than not detrimental with his NNode at 20 Gemini to the eclipse field's NNode at 9 Gemini. Further research is needed here as it may be that the cancellation factor does not operate when both nodes are in the same sign but different decanates. For example, his NNode has Uranus as its sub-ruler while the eclipse NNode sub-ruler is Mercury. Both sub-rulers are in trine to each other's Neptune, which really makes sense considering he started out as a real estate developer/mogul and a reality television star with a side-hustle in self-help books. In the majority of cases, you'll find that when comparing fields that reflect back the same nodal axis pattern, especially during a transit return, a significant drop, reduction, and even loss of vitality connected to that axis will be experienced.

In fact, during both transit returns of LS129 in 2000 and again in 2018, Trump experienced a decline in both his popularity and his effectiveness as a President to maintain his credibility in the eyes of the press and the public. In 2000 he was a short-lived candidate of the Reform Party before withdrawing, and again in 2018 when, unable to get control of the media, his tsunami of lies and "alternate facts" were beginning to pull him under. Fact-checkers had a field day tracking his false and misleading statements. *The Washington Post* in August 2018 (LS129 returned on July 27, 2018) were the first to declare "that some of his 'misstatements', in particular those concerning hush money paid to Stormy Daniels and Playboy model Karen McDougal, were lies."[5]

Donald Trump's other PREBLE is LS124—Imagine—Water Dragons found in Part Four. It actually fits him even better. But being a Gemini, the duality of his dragon family allegiance suits him perfectly.

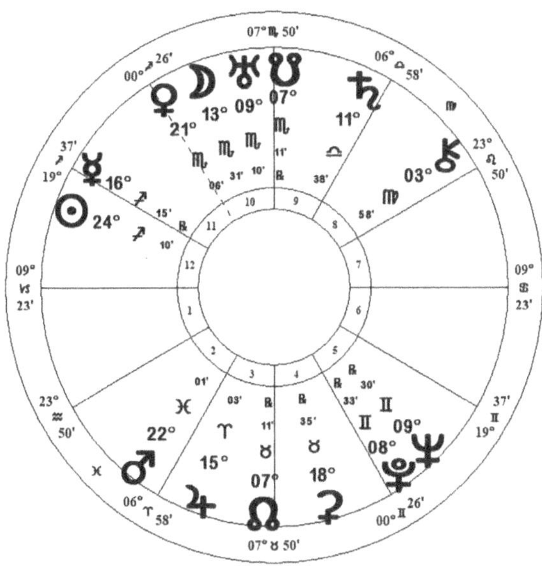

J. Paul Getty
PREBLEs—LS129 & LS134

December 15, 1892 • 8:43 AM • Minneapolis, MI, USA

"If you can actually count your money, then you are not really a rich man."

-Jean Paul Getty

Money and Power

In 1957, *Fortune* magazine named Getty the richest man in the world. Ten years later, he consolidated his business interests into the Getty Oil Company, and by the mid-1970s, it was estimated he had built a personal fortune of $2 to $4 billion.[6]

J. Paul Getty's Connections to the Dragons of LS129
1st Harmonics: Moon – Sun, NNode – Neptune, Saturn – NNode, Ceres – Saturn
2nd Harmonics: Sun – Sun, Venus – DSC, Mars – Mercury, Uranus – Uranus

J. Paul Getty's Sun at 24 Sagittarius is lit up by LS129's lunar eclipse axis, but more important are the Cosmic Bridges across the fields; his NNode tightly conjuncts the eclipse paternity proof Saturn and LS129's NNode returns the favor embracing J.P's Neptune. The eclipse Mars to his retrograde Mercury trine Jupiter in the Third House empowered his extraordinary gifts as a linguist; he was fluent in French, German, Italian, conversational in Spanish, Greek, Arabic, and Russian and was proficient enough to be able to read Ancient Greek and Latin.[7] The eclipse isotraps and their Uranus to his Uranus allowed for a full range of its eccentricity, defiance, and arrogance to play out unfettered in the field of Getty's idiosyncratic behavior that would become legendary.

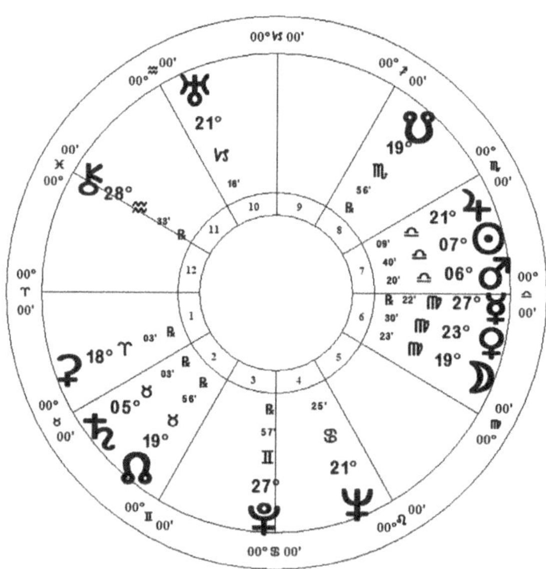

Bonnie Parker
PREBLE—LS129

October 1, 1910 • TOB Unknown • Rowena, TX, USA

"Someday they'll go down together
And they'll bury them side by side.
To few it'll be grief, to the law a relief
But it's death for Bonnie and Clyde."

-BONNIE PARKER

Ride or Die

Three things are dead giveaways that fame and fate would play significant roles in the life of Bonnie Parker. First is her Grand Cardinal Cross, second are the extraordinarily tight septiles from the Sun and Saturn to Uranus, and third and most evocative is her paran from Pluto to the fixed star Betelgeuse, known for its connection to opportunity, wealth, and fame. Retrograde Mercury in Virgo square Pluto rationalized any fear with her own set of facts while its conjunction to Venus kept her poised under pressure. Through her seventh degree double-dipped Libran Sun to Mars, she lived a risk-taking life with Clyde Barrows.

Bonnie Parker's Connections to the Dragons of LS129
Ceres to Ceres

1st Harmonics: Sun – Pluto,
Ceres – Sun/Mars, Saturn – Saturn, Pluto – Ceres
2nd Harmonic: Pluto – Jupiter

Always be on the lookout for contacts that involve the Sun, Pluto, and Ceres as they represent the powers of life and death. Here LS129's Sun awakens the darkness within Pluto's domain while the eclipse Pluto on her Ceres brings intense emotional crises into the life through loss or separation. The eclipse Ceres on her Sun/Mars fed her power, and the 1st Harmonic Saturn with Saturn solidified her confidence and sense of righteousness. The 2nd Harmonic Pluto to Jupiter is perhaps the most revealing as, thanks to a strong Jupiter/Uranus square in both fields, and the fact that both planets want to better their prospects, Bonnie Parker's fortune-hunting adventures were almost unstoppable.

LS129 Summary

One of the many functions of a South Node lunar eclipse is to be a force of exhalation that encourages release, enjoyment, and relaxation. To that end, it's hard to find a better South Node eclipse that personifies these qualities. With a lifespan of 1,262 years giving it 71 opportunities, these fire dancers eagerly await every return. To be born under their fiery wings or to just have a brush with them in passing gives a greater appreciation for the significant role that this family plays or has played in our accomplishments and good fortune.

2018 marked their thirty-eighth return, making them masters of the high art of invigoration. By their next return in 2036, they will be well on their way to unfolding through a Crescent phase with its emphasis on being able to drive oneself forward with assertion and greater energy. It heralds a time of great adjustment as one continues to lay down a foundation within an existing system without alienating those who are quibbling their way to distraction. The benefits to a Crescent phase are found in the growing sense of acceptance and patience that emerges as one pays one's dues with gratitude. Until the beginning of its First Quarter phase in 2108, Lunar Saros 129 will continue to offer breakthroughs of information along with a peppering of allies that both delight and validate your perspective.

An appreciation for gratitude may be just the ticket that will take you to the next stage on your journey to fame and fortune. When these Fire Dragons dance at your doorstep, all bets are off and anything is possible. The bounce in your step returns as self-worth is definitely on the rise. The attainment of a goal or objective is now within reach and success is well in hand. LS129 is overall one of the best lunar eclipse families out there and one that has the power to inspire and leave your life better for its passage. Be wowed by the wonder of you and remember to pay it forward.

LS129 Luminaries

Nikola Tesla	July 10, 1856
George Bernard Shaw	July 26, 1856
Pearl S. Buck	June 26, 1892
J. P. Getty	December 15, 1892
Jacques Cousteau	June 11, 1910

William Hanna	July 14, 1910
Mother Teresa	August 26, 1910
Bonnie Parker	October 1, 1910
Stanley Kubrick	July 26, 1928
Andy Warhol	August 6, 1928
James Randi	August 7, 1928
George Peppard	October 1, 1928
Donald Trump[E1]	June 14, 1946
George W Bush	July 6, 1946
Bill Clinton	August 19, 1946
Terence McKenna	November 16, 1946
Dan Brown[E3]	June 22, 1964
Keanu Reeves	September 2, 1964
Jack Ma	September 10, 1964
Don Cheadle	November 29, 1964
Anna Paquin	July 24, 1982
Sebastian Stan	August 13, 1982
Anne Hathaway	November 12, 1982

PREBLE—LS124

[E1] Donald Trump—born within 24 hours of LS129

[E3] Dan Brown—born with 72 hours of LS129

1. Gwenda Blair, *The Trumps: Three Generations that Built an Empire* (New York: Simon and Schuster, 2000), p. 16.
2. https://www.forbes.com/forbes-400/ Retrieved Feb. 22, 2022.
3. https://www.forbes.com/sites/mattdurot/2022/09/27/the-2022-forbes-400-the-20-richest-people-in-america/?sh=1e6c73391f0a. Retrieved March 25, 2023
4. Blair, *The Trumps*, p. 308.
5. https://en.wikipedia.org/wiki/Donald_Trump. Retrieved Feb. 22, 2022.
6. https://www.biography.com/business-figure/j-paul-getty. Retrieved May 1, 2022.
7. https://en.wikipedia.org/wiki/J._Paul_Getty#cite_note-nytimes1976-10. Retrieved May 1, 2022.

LUNAR SAROS 130

"Time is the fire in which we burn."

-GENE RODDENBERRY

Lunar Saros 130

June 19, 1416 • 12:08:53 PM • North Pole

To Boldly Go

A Sagittarius NNode lunar eclipse with Jupiter at twenty-first degree status gives it an expanded range of possibility, especially as it is both retrograde and at critical degrees and in conjunction to a retrograde Uranus. In combination with rulers Venus, Mercury, and Mars in their signs of power and eminence, this eclipse carries an extraordinary wow factor, along with depth, confidence, and uniqueness to make the field truly jaw dropping.

No other active Lunar Saros Series can lay claim to having the Sun at (23°N30'), usually referred to as Out-of-Bounds (OOB) declination. Technically, the Sun cannot be classified as such, but for the sake of OOB theory, here's the lowdown. Because of the tilt of the Earth's axis and its regular motion that maps the seasons, the sun appears to move from 00 degrees declination at the equator to its farthest range of 23 degrees 28 minutes north and south of the equator. Anything beyond these solar boundaries that define the ecliptic or sun's path are termed "out of bounds." Celestial bodies whose orbits wander into these zones display a high regard for personal freedom that push against social norms. They tend to become laws unto themselves, and their actions produce more extreme results. They are known for their love of freedom and lateral thinking.

The Sun, the lunar nodes, Saturn, and Chiron never can be OOB, but the Moon, Mercury, Venus, Mars, Jupiter, Uranus, Neptune, and Pluto can. It's very rare to find Jupiter OOB. In the entire Lunar Saros Series, only LS120—Burn Baby Burn—and LS121—Sparks of Inspiration—here in the Fire Eclipses of Part One have bragging rights to this phenomenon.

If the Sun, our solar star, cannot be classified as OOB, we can at least recognize its astronomical accomplishment of reaching such a high degree of declination as far as boundaries go. The foundational isotrap Sun/Jupiter conjunct Uranus/Venus confirms this love of and need for freedom that is repeated in the sphere's rarely seen Splay pattern, which compels autonomy and repels confinement. This pattern gives self-reliance, openness to change, and a multivariant perspective on life. It's a perfect pattern for these adventuring lunar dragons who, in their 1,262-year mission signed off "To boldly go where no one has gone before."

The eclipse field's Sun in trine to the originality and inventiveness of Uranus in Aquarius means that the Moon will be in sextile, a brilliant cross pollination capable of producing all manner of innovation and breakthroughs both on a personal and societal level. Shifting from self-seeking goals to social participation activities that can offer unlimited and experimental potential is the potent Jupiter/Uranus conjunction in Balsamic/prophet mode. If the eclipse Sun's conjunction to Pluto and its multiple, fast-acting trines from the Jupiter/Uranus conjunction are any indication, get ready to live life at supersonic speed.

Voyages of discovery and projects of vision can now be undertaken with gusto. In consideration of the eclipse high-achiever Sun/Pluto conjunction in

Gemini, the *Star Trek* analogy is a fitting and most appropriate metaphor. The rejuvenation forces represented by the Sun/Pluto conjunction speak of renewal on all levels while the Moon/Pluto opposition challenges us to break free from limiting beliefs, habits, and rituals that keep us in servitude to our past.

Closest Midpoints: Uranus/Mars-Pluto, Mars/Jupiter-Saturn
Isotraps: Mercury/Pluto conjunct Venus/Neptune
Sun/Jupiter conjunct Uranus/Venus

1900—2100 Eclipses: Lunar Saros—130

1903, 1921, 1939, 1957, 1975, 1993, 2011, 2029, 2047, 2065, 2083
Length of cycle —1,262 years
Series ends— July 26, 2678

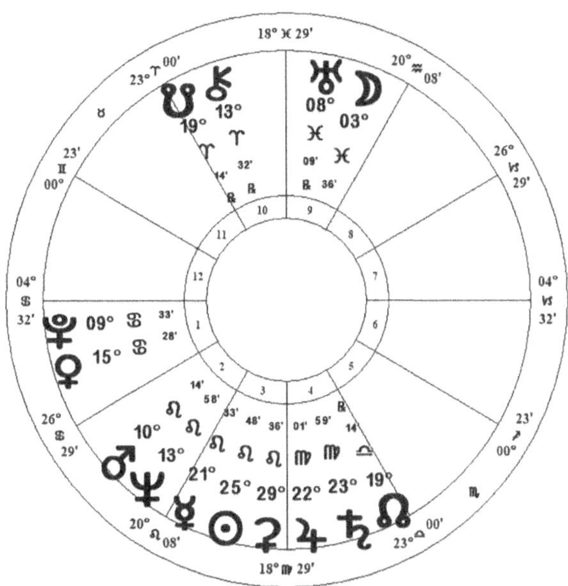

Gene Roddenberry
PREBLE—LS130

August 19, 1921 • 1:35 AM • El Paso, TX, USA

Great Bird of the Galaxy

"These are the voyages of the starship Enterprise.
Its five year mission . . . to boldly go where no man has gone before."

-GENE RODDENBERRY

Gene Roddenberry was the creator and producer of the original *Star Trek* television series that debuted on September 8, 1966. I was thirteen years old and remember the absolute thrill of watching that first show. I was hooked and became a "Trekkie" from day one. The legacy of *Star Trek* has evolved into a feature film series and is one of the most recognizable science-fiction brands in the world, making Roddenberry a star in his own right.[1] He developed a reputation for being a futurist and a visionary; he was a frequent presenter at NASA meetings, the Smithsonian Institution, Library of Congress gatherings, and to top universities.[2]

Gene Roddenberry's Connections to the Lunar Dragons of LS130

**1st Harmonics: Uranus – Moon, Neptune – Venus, Jupiter – IX,
2nd Harmonics: Jupiter – Sun, Jupiter – Mercury**

Point 6 on the Top 10 List for How to Live With Dragons (see page 6) suggests that the next step, after noting all your 1st and 2nd Harmonics, is to look at any patterns in the lunar eclipse chart that connect into the chart under study. These patterns do not have to be anything grand or spectacular as all basic Ptolemaic aspects will have their own unique resonance. After identifying these patterns, it is easier to see if and how they connect into the chart. Then, it's important to note any phase pattern symmetry that both charts contain. Roddenberry has a waning trine between Pluto and Uranus that is also found in the eclipse chart. His is in water, the eclipse in air. Phase pattern symmetry is an outstanding example of celestial DNA that clan members can be identified by, and as such act to connect the entire foundational chart patterns to each individual through their own calibration of the resonance. As far as generational planets go, Pluto and Uranus transform and revolutionize. Roddenberry's life as a combat pilot during WWII and later as a writer for the new medium of television would exemplify these qualities as he wove sensitivity and often spiritual considerations into his stories. In September 1987, *Star Trek: The Next Generation* would continue the legend that had begun a generation earlier.[3]

What makes Roddenberry's 1st Harmonic from the lunar eclipse Uranus to his Moon sizzle is the company that Uranus keeps as he doesn't go anywhere without his posse of Jupiter, Pluto, the Sun, and Moon. Neptune's 1st Harmonic to his Venus is enhanced by the fixed star Pollux with its great love of learning, knowledge, and an enterprising spirit. Another luminary with Pollux on his Neptune and also totally infatuated with space is rocket scientist and former Nazi Wernher von Braun, who was in charge of NASA's Kennedy Space Center missions in the early '60s. His profile is featured in the Air Dragons of LS144—Real Surreal—in Part Three.

Having an accurate chart is such a relief: you can then look at the eclipse planets as they fall on any house cusp. Here we see LS130's spectacular Jupiter and its posse on Roddenberry's Ninth House giving him an insatiable desire to learn, knowing that knowledge gives freedom and freedom, as his celestial comrades love to say, is power.

At critical fixed degree 21 Leo, Mercury has an explorer's heart thanks to the 2nd Harmonic from mighty Jupiter. If you factor in Nikola Stojanovic's Critical Degree Theory, and I hope you do, there is now an even stronger Jupiter effect due to the twenty-first degree overlay of Sagittarius. I have researched these degrees and quite frankly am astounded at how accurate they are and how much extra color they give a consultation. The final 2nd Harmonics are from Jupiter and Uranus to his Leo Sun at the twenty-fifth degree, an Aries overlay shining through the noble and dignified essence of Roddenberry's Leo individuality in full command of his enterprise.

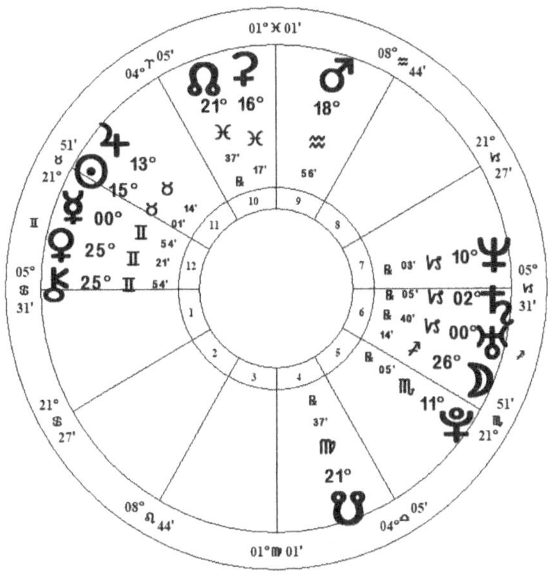

Adele
PREBLE—LS113

May 5, 1988 • 8:19 AM • Tottenham, UK

"I love hearing my audience breath."

-ADELE

The Queen of Hearts

"Adele is a unique presence in all of 21st century pop: a preternaturally gifted singer and songwriter with a leave-it-all-on-the-floor approach to recording and performing–and also an earthy, relatable, and strangely unassuming personality both on and off the stage."

-ANDREW UNTERBERGER—BILLBOARD

According to biographer Caroline Sanderson, Adele Laurie Blue Adkins by age five (1993) was "allowed to stand on the table at dinner parties and entertain the company with her rendition of "Dreams," a stirring and catchy 1993 UK number-one hit for Gabrielle."[4] Even at that tender age, Adele was learning how to sing from her first of many role models and would later say, "I taught me how to sing listening to Etta James at home."[5] Fast forward to 2011 (notice the eighteen year gap) and Adele, not quite twenty-three, had become a global singing sensation. And apparently, she was the only singer/song-writer on the planet with the pipes and sultry style good enough to deliver the 50th anniversary Bond film ballad for *Skyfall* in all its glory.

Sweeping in at 24 Sagittarius on June 15, 2011, Lunar Saros 130 completely enveloped Adele's spectacular OOB Moon (28°S22') at 23 Sagittarius, conjunct not only the Galactic Core at 26 Sagittarius but in parallel declination (29S00) to it, gifting her with its pulsar pull on the surrounding world. Her OOB Venus (27°N44') at the feisty twenty-fifth degree in Gemini conjunction to an equally feisty Chiron at 25 Gemini was stimulated by the activation degree which enabled Adele to radiate and attract a rapid sequence of personal and professional possibilities. In this whirlwind eclipse window, she managed to lose her voice, recover her voice, go back out on tour, lose her voice again, recover her voice again, all the while working on the Bond film *Skyfall* theme song that would win her an Oscar in 2013.

One only has to look at her Mutable Cross that holds all that OOB energy and especially her Venus/Chiron in Gemini at the twenty-fifth Arian overlay degree to appreciate how her elevator love-life has fueled her spectacular and financially successful career. Her Moon at the twenty-sixth Taurean overlay degree has no problem dealing with the difficulties of satisfying her emotional needs.

Adele's Connections to the Lunar Dragons of LS130
Space Lanes via DSC/ASC
Mercury with Mercury
Neptune to Neptune

**1st Harmonics: Moon – Moon/Uranus/Saturn,
Pluto/Sun – Venus/Chiron, Venus – Jupiter/Sun, Jupiter – Mars, Uranus – MC
2nd Harmonics: Pluto/Sun – Moon**

The eclipse chart and Adele's chart contain OOB luminaries that, along with Adele's OOB Venus, propelled her forward. Both spheres hold Sun/Pluto aspects: LS130 has a conjunction and Adele has an opposition that is in hyperdrive thanks to her Sun/Jupiter conjunction. Her Dragon DNA runs deep: Her Mars aligns to the eclipse Jupiter, her Sun to its Venus, her Neptune to its Neptune, and, if the time of birth is correct, her MC aligns with its dazzling Uranus. However the most fascinating aspect here lies in the synchronicity of LS130's eclipse axis returning to conjunct its own lunar foundation degree, something that can only happen after the eclipse has made approximately thirty-four returns. When that happens, the eclipse is experiencing its own New Moon phase and will enjoy a reinvigoration with all the new beginnings it can command. The fact that Adele's Moon sits at the same degree as both the lunar eclipse foundation degree *and* its eighteen year return degree is the real story here, and something to think about when it comes to maximizing time periods of greatest opportunity.

But what really made the return of Lunar Saros 130 so incredibly memorable for Adele can be seen from her 2nd Harmonic Pluto/Sun tie to her phenomenal OOB Moon. I give you my 100 percent guarantee that any 2nd Harmonic to a natal or progressed Moon is going to shake up your world and, if you add in Pluto, nothing will ever be the same again.

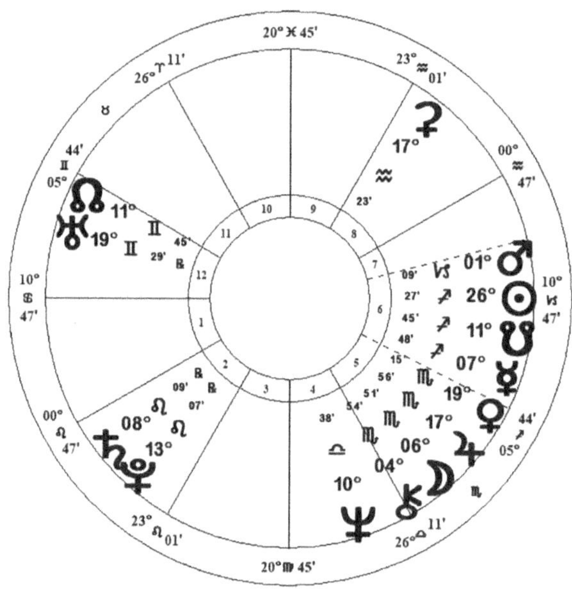

Steven Spielberg
PREBLE—LS134

December 18, 1946 • 6:16 PM • Cincinnati, OH, USA

The Highest-Grossing Film in History

"After Jaws you'll be able to make all the movies you want."

-DAVID BROWN—UNIVERSAL PICTURES

With the release of *Jaws* in the summer of 1975, the modern blockbuster was born.[6] The release was hotly anticipated and opened nation-wide as an "event" rather than a new release. The movie launched a new way to market movies and pioneered the high-concept film: a movie whose premise can be quickly and easily stated—and marketed.[7] The movie redefined the industry and in the process changed Spielberg's life. If you were there and weren't square, the scariest summer movie of 1975 certainly put a damper on swimming lessons—who would dare venture into the water after Jaws opened nation-wide on June 20, 1975? In its time, it was the highest grossing film in history,[8] arriving within a month of LS130 on May 25, 1975. At 3 Sagittarius, it showcased Spielberg's story-telling Mercury in Sagittarius trine Saturn/Pluto in Leo dramatics. Now, with a newly acquired power base secured, he quickly established himself as a filmmaker of Olympian proportion.

Fast forward eighteen years. LS130 returns again—same force field but now it's June 4, 1993, and the circus comes to town and opens at 14 Sagittarius, right on Spielberg's SNode and his progressed fun Fifth House. His blockbuster hit *Jurassic Park* opened the next week on June 11 to become the highest-grossing film of *its* time.[9] Coincidence, luck, serendipity? Since these Fire Dragons arrived in 1975, Spielberg has never looked back or had to second-guess his directorial decisions. He is a filmmaker of prodigious proportions, and he needs to thank the Fire Dragons of LS130. Here's why:

Steven Spielberg's Connections to the Lunar Dragons of LS130
↑North Node with South Node↓

1st Harmonics: Moon – Sun, Mars – Moon, NNode – Mercury, Chiron – SNode, Mercury – NNode, Neptune – ASC, Pluto – Uranus, Jupiter – IX, Ceres – VI
2nd Harmonics: Sun – Sun, Venus – Venus, Venus – Jupiter

The strongest ties are always with the nodes and here we have a Global Gateway, much like what Tesla experienced, as the opposite polarity provides an immense charge across the fields. Even better, but rarer, is when the eclipse field's luminaries or nodes connect into your natal or progressed ASC, DSC, or MC, creating Space Lanes that pretty much get you to the front of the line, no reservation or ticket needed. Such notables as Aretha Franklin, the infamous Red Baron, Tony Robbins, the late and great Larry King, and Robert Downey Jr. (the Iron Man himself), were blessed to hold these rare Space Lane connectors.

At the same power levels are the connections across the fields from the lights. Since the Moon and Sun are on the same axis, you get considerable voltage if either one of them creates a Cosmic Bridge that lights up your natal or progressed planets, but especially your progressed Sun or Moon. Again, we see this with Spielberg's Sun getting a charge from the currents flowing between the lunar eclipse Moon and his Sun. Different but just as powerful is a Moon to Moon contact across the fields as we see with Adele's Sagittarian Moon in resonance with the eclipse field's Moon. This is both a sweet and swift resonance that produces an almost instantaneous shift of circumstances.

Now here's another fascinating fact about how lunar eclipses operate, especially when you're paying attention to their eight stages of cyclical evolution. When the Fire Dragons of LS130 returned in 1975 and again in 1993, they were evolving through their Balsamic Phase. Now, what's exciting to note is that this phase does not have to be regulated to the dust heap. It is often associated with a more inward phase, but that doesn't have to rule out success—even massive success!—as Spielberg's story illustrates. The key take-away here is that the Balsamic Phase is truly the time to dream and to surrender to your dream as it prepares you for the rest of your journey. The key concept here is—and always *should* be—Release.

LS130 Summary

Trailblazers who reach for the stars are the dynamos driving these blessed fire breathers. They bestow deep aspirations and hold the power of hope and renewal. And they work fast! They'll have you burning the candle at both ends as flames of turbulence melt away years if not decades of self-imposed restrictions and limitations. This is a time to call forth courage to experience the world from a new and unique perspective. To that end, whether by birth or by a transit of their return, use your entanglement with their energy field to dive deep into the imagination and life path of any hero, heroine, author, artist, or mentor that uplifts your spirit. Take time to become fully absorbed in the magic and wonder of the world that is right at your fingertips. There's never been a better time to welcome in the course corrections, adjustments, surprises, and shifts that will bring excitement and passion back into your life.

The rejuvenation forces within this lunar eclipse field are not to be missed. To come into harmony with its distinct character and gifts is something to really be looking forward to experiencing, much like a fabulous, no-expense-spared holiday. In fact, planning a vacation, especially to somewhere you've never been or to a foreign or exotic destination, might just be what could heal you. The eclipse carries so much adventure and fun and putting those ideas together might result in a spa weekend or a stay at a health resort or even a trip to take advantage of medical procedures not available in your town or country. To not get up and want to dance with these dragons would be a serious loss of a golden opportunity. Months after this eclipse has passed, a refreshed and more physically alive new you will emerge.

Phase	Return	Year
Last Quarter	26th	1867
Balsamic	30th	1939
New Moon	34th	2011
Crescent	38th	2083

LS130 Luminaries

Wilbur Wright	April 16, 1867
D H Lawrence	September 11, 1885
Bob Hope	May 29, 1903
Lou Gehrig	June 19, 1903
John Dillinger	June 22, 1903
George Orwell	June 25, 1903
Andrei Sakharov	May 21, 1921
John Glenn	July 18, 1921
Maurice "Rocket" Richard	August 4, 1921
Gene Roddenberry	August 19, 1921
Ian McKellen	May 25, 1939
Judy Chicago	July 20, 1939
Breyten Breytenbach	September 15, 1939
John Cleese	October 27, 1939
Frances McDormand	June 23, 1957
Stephen Fry	August 24, 1957
Gloria Estefan	September 1, 1957
Sadhguru	September 3, 1957
Jamie Oliver[E1]	May 25, 1975
Angelina Jolie	June 4, 1975
Charlize Theron	August 7, 1975
Kate Winslet	October 5, 1975
Breonna Taylor	June 5, 1993
Ariana Grande	June 26, 1993
Dominic Thiem	September 3, 1993

PREBLE—LS125
Jamie Oliver

1. https://ca.startrek.com/database_article/Roddenberry. Retrieved April 2, 2022.
2. Ibid.
3. Ibid.
4. Caroline Sanderson, *Someone like Adele* (London: Omnibus Press, 2012), p. 15.
5. Ibid, p. 19.
6. https://screenrant.com/highest-grossing-movies-ever-box-office-how-long/ Retrieved Jan. 23, 2022.
7. http://en.wikipedia.org/wiki/Jaws_(film)
8. Ibid.
9. http://en.wikipedia.org/wiki/Jurassic_Park_(film)

LUNAR SAROS 132

"For all those who believe, expect a miracle."

-LINDA GOODMAN

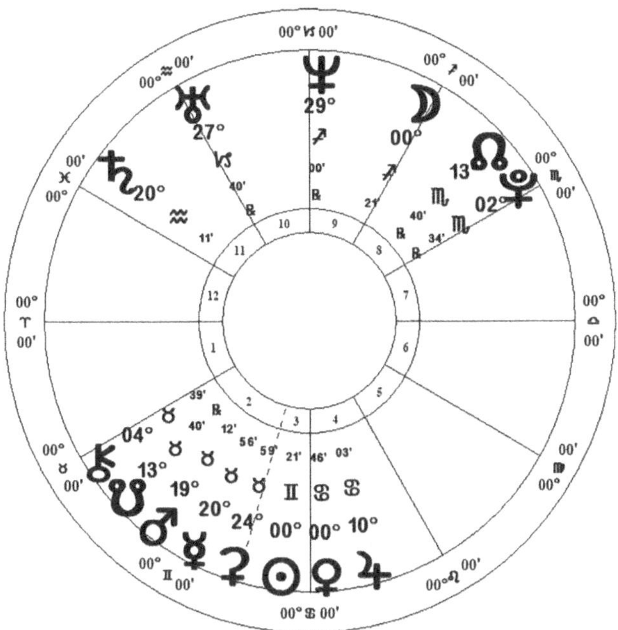

Lunar Saros 132

May 21, 1492 • 6:33:40 AM • North Pole

Reach for the Stars

Journeys that explore our creative life force are the gifts bestowed by these Fire Dragons. You can be sure that whatever touches the life now will be on a grand scale. Both national and international themes dominate this Jupiter ruled Sagittarius eclipse. Internationally, there will be a renewed interest in travel, foreigners, philosophy, and living abroad; domestically, matters connected to cross-country travel, publicity and legal matters come to fruition. Birthed in 1492, this lunar eclipse family shares a distinct love of adventure, on par with the voyages of Christopher Columbus to the new world.

Joanna Martine Woolfolk, author of *The Only Astrology Book You'll Ever Need*, states that Jupiter in Cancer "is one of the luckiest positions Jupiter can be in."[1] Its sign and house placements are indicative of a style of increase that brings abundance, knowledge, and blessings. Western astrological traditions deem Jupiter "the Greater Fortune" and it often correlates with times of profit and expansion when placed in its sign of exaltation. This lunar eclipse has the extraordinarily good fortune to have its ruler Jupiter in MR to the foundation chart Moon, something only one other dragon family can claim. (Hint, you'll find this formidable family in Part Four.) Mutual Reception has a fortunate "get out of jail" quality, especially so when Jupiter is present; in fact, they almost seem like a present and as a feature are not to be overlooked. And for extra sparkle the eclipse field holds a one-of-a-kind Saturn/Uranus MR that definitively dances to its own tune.

Lunar Saros 132 has a Boomerang/Anchor that both grounds and inspires with retrograde Neptune at the prophetic 29th degree, holding steady at the fulcrum. Due to the presence of the two sets of MRs, repositioning Saturn with Uranus and Jupiter with the Moon gives us more latitude to maneuver when Venus, at the Apex, is called upon to solve for both X and Y. In this liberated environment that includes the unboundedness of the eclipse axis, quite frankly anything is possible. Venus, with her elevated status as a planet at the Apex of a Boomerang/Anchor, at the critical AP and also OOB may be residing at the most critical piece of cosmic real estate to date. The social and political climate of this lunar eclipse is not to be taken lightly.

Finally, there is the question of what the Yod or Finger of Fate is up to in this eclipse field. The Sun's quincunxes to Neptune and Pluto are an enigma, especially with the Sun at ground zero Gemini and Neptune holding court at the prophetic Sagittarian twenty-ninth degree. It simultaneously represents the alpha and the omega, the coming into Being and the going out of Being. The best course of action is to make an effort to be more aware of how double-speak, mixed metaphors and self-doubt can stop us in our tracks before we even get going. Neptune's sextile to Pluto has been in effect since January 1941. Given a generous six degree orb allowance, this generational aspect will be in effect until March 2041. Robert Pelletier defines this sextile as an evolutionary quest no matter what direction one follows. "One either reaches out in the natural world in search of answers or seeks those answers in the inner depths of his[her] own spiritual being."[2]

Closest Midpoints: Saturn/Mercury-Mars, Jupiter/Eclipse-Saturn
Isotraps: Sun/Venus conjunct Mercury/Jupiter,
Moon/Neptune opposition Mars/Jupiter

1900—2100 Eclipses: Lunar Saros—132

1907, 1925, 1943, 1961, 1979, 1997, 2015, 2033, 2051, 2069, 2087
Length of cycle —1,262 years
Series ends—June 26, 2754

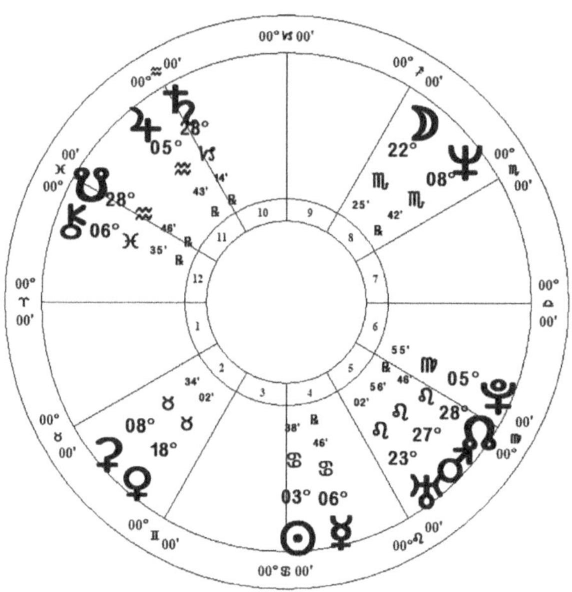

Ricky Gervais
PREBLE—LS132

June 25, 1961 • TOB Unknown • Reading, UK

"Where there's a will, there's a relative."

Ricky Gervais Answers the Proust Questionnaire: What is your Motto?

"Relax. No one else knows what they're doing, either."

-RICKY GERVAIS

Gervais is a national treasure, and his growing list of accolades and awards testifies to his brilliance. As of 2022, Gervais has won two Primetime Emmy Awards for his work on *The Office* and *Extras*, seven BAFTA Awards, five British Comedy Awards and three Golden Globe Awards.[3] Even without a time of birth, his cosmic credentials are certified LS132 gold. His talent has made him one of the world's most beloved and richest comedians. His shows and tour dates sell out within minutes.

No time of birth must *ever* stop the flow of curiosity as one explores the patterns in the landscape of a chart. When calculated for Noon, the Moon will be no more than six degrees up or down from its zodiac degree which generates plenty of opportunities for cosmic contact. Gervais' Moon is decidedly in demand as either way, his Moon square Uranus is the opening act for a life in taboo territory where his clever, edgy comedic chops are fed by his acute Scorpio powers of observation. Going up he would have a common sense Saturn sextile, going down a f**k you rock star Mars/NNode square. Brilliantly detached, Gervais is a breath of excruciating realism in a world sinking fast into a nihilistic morass of minutiae.

Ricky Gervais' Connections to the Lunar Dragons of LS132

1st Harmonics: SNode/Mars/Mercury – Venus,
Venus – Sun, Jupiter –Mercury, Chiron – Ceres, Uranus – Saturn
2nd Harmonics: Neptune – Sun, Saturn – Uranus, Chiron – Neptune

Ricky Gervais shares an all-star cast of connections to LS132 starting with its Venus to his Sun and in turn Ricky's Taurean Venus to the lunar eclipse Mercury/Mars conjunction. A double bond of Venus can increase both your cash and cachet with an adoring public. Throw in a line to Mars and your fan base could border on frenzy. What is truly fascinating here is the rare reciprocity of Uranus to Saturn and then Saturn to Uranus across their fields, giving Gervais "open mike" privileges to freely explore and build on the independence and autonomy that comes with every LS132 return. These are rule-breaker connectors allowing Gervais and his impressive Cancerian emotional range the freedom to entertain his own brand of fire and wit into the collective. In addition, since both his personal landscape is so indelibly entrained to the foundation field of the eclipse, Gervais has no need of a transiting degree to be able to tune into the field, as he is always in receiver mode, enabling his career to take dynamic leaps forward every eighteen years regardless of the prevailing eclipse degree moving along the ecliptic.

At the time of Ricky Gervais' birth on June 25, 1961, the moon was moving through a Gibbous phase, part of an eight fold division of her monthly relationship to the Sun that starts at the New Moon when the Sun and Moon both occupy the same degree along the ecliptic. Each phase of this Sun-Moon cycle has a special quality and style of action based on the distance apart from each other. This cycle is ancient and a phenomenon our oldest *Homo sapiens* ancestors would have watched, participated in, and even recorded. Duncan Steel, author of "Eclipse - The celestial phenomenon which has changed the course of history," writes that sequences of scratch marks on animal bones dating back 30,000 years are suggestive of the changing phases of the Moon from one cycle to the next.[4] To be born under a Gibbous Moon inclines one to become a master of a particular subject, skill set or area of interest. The majority of people born under this phase of the moon are constantly *at it:* refining, defining, and perfecting techniques to gain a greater understanding of their subject matter. Many love to share their knowledge with the world. When the lunar dragons of LS132 returned in 1961, they were already in a Last Quarter phase of their evolutionary journey that had begun in 1943. This is the waning square of the overall cycle, and it carries the energy of reorientation: it is the call of dissatisfaction that now requires our full attention.

To appreciate the impact that your lunar eclipse family has, you need to know the family dynamics. However, even more helpful is knowing what particular phase of evolution your dragon family was experiencing at the time of your birth, especially since the phases shift every seventy-two to ninety years and bring with those changes an updated agenda and style of behavior.

In Ricky Gervais' case, it is kind of cool to know that he benefits from both a lunar Gibbous phase from his natal birth chart and a Last Quarter phase pattern from his evolving dragon family chart. Together these two phases have richly endowed his personality with a quintessential angst that all great comedians, and especially great stand-up comedians have along with the ability to take us willingly to the edge of our comfort zone and push us mercilessly into the proximal zone, where the excitement of discovery can awaken even a sleeping soul.

It's fascinating to watch Gervais and his style of work as it syncs with his Fire Dragon family's evolution while they shifted into the Balsamic Phase with their 30th return in 2015. Since then, his groove seems to reflect the Letting Go energy of the phase. You decide. Here's his May 7, 2018 tweet:

> @rickygervais
>
> I start pre-production on my new Netflix show tomorrow. It's a 6 part, dark comedy, in which I play a man who, after the death of his wife, becomes suicidal but decides to live long enough to punish the world by saying and doing whatever the f**k he likes from now on.

After Life, a black comedy that he created in 2018 premiered on March 8, 2019, on Netflix and has been a runaway phenomenon with Netflix green-lighting a second and third series.[5] It is a tender and touching tribute to love, death, and life after death.

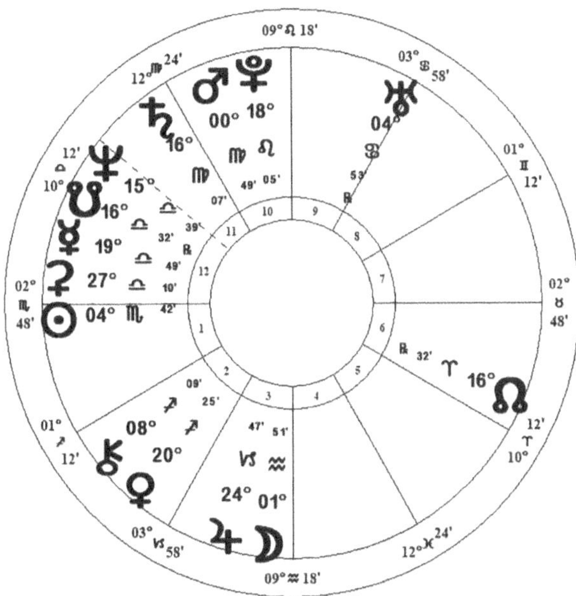

Caitlyn Jenner
PREBLE—LS126

October 28, 1949 • 6:16 AM • Mount Kisco, NY, USA

"The hardest part about being a woman is figuring out what to wear."

-Caitlyn Jenner

The Interview of an Olympian Journey

"I think as long as he is happy and he wants to live his life however he wants to live it, that just makes me happy and I support him 100 percent."

-Kim Kardashian

Until June 2015, she was known as Bruce Jenner, an American athletic icon whose fame spread rapidly after winning gold in the 1976 men's decathlon event at the Summer Olympics in Montreal. As an Olympic gold medalist and member of the Kardashian family (his third wife was Kris Kardashian, who filed for divorce in 2014), Jenner revealed to Diane Sawyer in an interview on April 24, 2015, that he identified as a woman and was making the transition from male to female. "For all intents and purposes, I am a woman."[6]

Bruce Jenner's interview with Diane Sawyer would be followed by a stunning June 9, 2015, story in *Vanity Fair* where his new identity as Caitlyn Jenner would be revealed. Celebrity photographer Annie Leibovitz's cover photo unveiled a compelling image of a transgender woman dressed only in a corset. The cover and story set off a media feeding frenzy, making headlines around the world. For her 10 million Twitter followers. Barbara Kay of the *National Post* said it best: "Bruce Jenner and Caitlyn Jenner is the most famous man and woman on the planet."[7] Even President Obama sent a congratulatory tweet.

One of the first things to notice about Jenner's chart is the almost exact Neptune/South Node Libra conjunction in the Twelfth House of secrets, sorrow, and racial memory. With Mercury just four degrees away, my thoughts turned to mythology and the fling between Hermes and Aphrodite that resulted in the birth of Hermaphroditus, from which we get the word *hermaphrodite*. Many with a Mercury/Neptune emphasis or Mercury tied into the nodal axis are able to integrate the male/female dynamic that exists in all of us quite well. Jenner emerged on the world stage in 2015 to become the new face of transgender, with a little help from his OOB Venus (26S00), Moon (24S43) and Uranus (23N37).

On April 4, 2015, LS132 returned at 14 Libra to claim her man, capturing Jenner's SNode/Neptune/Mercury conjunction while Mercury's Venus/Pluto midpoint would find pleasure in the erotic drama of the unfolding media pile on. Caitlyn's Pluto midpoints, especially those involving the nodal axis, have catapulted her bellwether mojo beyond even the gold standards of her Olympic achievements. Her ability to break records now extends to breaking through social standards of values and behaviors for a world in need of transition. The unstoppable forces that drive humankind forward will always find a soul strong enough to carry the burden of evolution and the commensurate upheavals that shake up every aspect of our lives. In Caitlyn's case, the world will continue to be fascinated by both her *and* her sublime capacity to engender aesthetic and social transformation.

Caitlyn's connections to the energetic field of LS132 are best summed up in one word—Transformational—as seen through the eclipse field's Pluto opposition Chiron on her Sun and ascendant and in return her Pluto to LS132's rule breaking retrograde Saturn in Aquarius. Throw in her Jupiter tie to the eclipse Uranus/Saturn MR and its box of cosmic goodies and you get a front row seat to personal transformational.

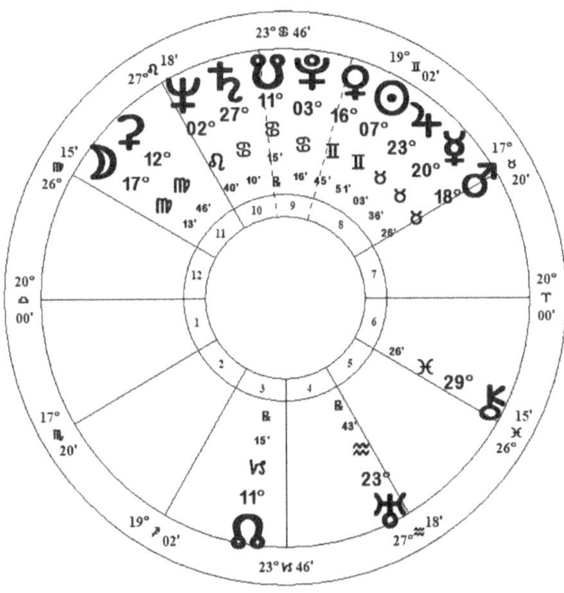

John F. Kennedy
PREBLE—LS123

May 29, 1917 • 3:00 PM • Brookline, MA, USA

"If not us, who? If not now, when?"

-JFK

The 35th President of the United States

"If you done it, it ain't braggin'."

-Jerome "Dizzy" Dean

The successful Soviet flight on April 12, 1961, that put Yuri Gagarin in space was by all accounts a spectacular achievement. John M. Logsdon, in his book, *John F. Kennedy and the Race to the Moon,* writes, "American reaction to the Gagarin flight was characterized by disappointment and chagrin especially given the fact that the general public had no idea the Soviet flight was underway."[8]

The lunar eclipse on March 2, 1961, at 12 Virgo literally lit up JFK's Ceres and though technically out of orb, would have certainly affected his Moon at 17 Virgo. His Ceres holds an exact trine to his NNode in Capricorn and with his Moon trines to Mars, Mercury, and Jupiter; his ability to assimilate and analyze would have made his decisions at this time politically pragmatic. With no time to lose, Kennedy made the decision to achieve the goal of American space preeminence a reality. In his book, Logsdon offers a key memorandum signed by Kennedy, dated April 20, 1961, that clearly led to the decision to go to the Moon. It would be a full month later that President Kennedy would appear before Congress on May 25, 1961, to deliver his famous declaration:

> First, I believe this Nation should commit itself to achieving the goal, before this decade is out, of landing a man on the moon and returning him safely to the Earth. No single space project in this period will be more exciting or more impressive to mankind, or more important for the long-range exploration of space, and none will be so difficult or expensive to accomplish.[9]

J.F.K's Connections to the Lunar Dragons of LS132
Sun with Sun

1st Harmonics: SNode – Mars,
Jupiter – SNode, Mercury – Mercury, Mercury – Mars,
Mercury – Jupiter, Venus – Pluto, Mars – Mars, Ceres – Jupiter, Saturn – Uranus
2nd Harmonic: Uranus – Saturn

Kennedy's ties to the Dragon DNA of LS132 are staggering in their sheer number and power of attachment. There are eight distinct pathways connecting their fields. With the added bonus that both have the Sun in Gemini, and both carry an identical Mercury Mars conjunction in Taurus, this gives, what Howard Sasportas in his book *Dynamics of the Unconscious: Seminars in Psychological Astrology* says, is the ability to "justify their actions on the basis of some rational or intellectual explanation. They can defend most anything they do or say with some sort of rationale."[10] An exact conjunction between their Mercury placements at the deeply intense 20th degree of Taurus—with its complimentary connection to death, wealth, secrets, and sex—would have given Kennedy a platform of reassurance upon which he could wield his youthful vigor and charm. His Mercury/Venus MR would go on to make his political agenda not only socially acceptable but more importantly highly desirable, making his presidency a public relations triumph. JFK is remembered for many things, however, one of the greatest achievements of his presidency was his challenge to a nation and a declaration to the world that the new frontier of space, with its dangerous voyages of discovery was an adventure worth the risk.

LS132 Summary

How intriguing that Christopher Columbus set sail from Spain on August 3, 1492, in the newly birthed lunar eclipse window of LS132. Journeys are in the DNA of these dragons, and deeply entwined in their RNA is the code that releases the exquisite timing that unfolds their unique DNA. Out of seventy-one returns, these dragon explorers passed their twenty-sixth return in 1943 as they entered their first Last Quarter Phase. By 2015 and their thirtieth return, like a jazz trio in their groove, it's all about knowing how to go with the flow. Let go and let God or Goddess, Shaman or Saint run the show for a while. The year 2087 is the big one—they will celebrate one complete global circumnavigation and begin again.

Journeys of exploration fueled by vitality are the name of the game when these Fire Dragons claim you as their own. Whether by birthright or rite of passage, you'll be tempted to travel; they love to ramble and roam the globe in search of new prospects. They carry the twin gifts of freedom and friendship, giving a life blessed by their presence a wonderful buoyancy and resiliency to life's ups and downs. An encounter with this lunar eclipse offers lifelines of vitality.

Their returns are filled with increased communication that bring support and strength and, in the process, anchor a dramatic response to life that encourages hope and a renewed sense of purpose. Challenge yourself to explore and expand on opportunities that come your way, especially if they are at all connected to a growing awareness and appreciation for beauty and aesthetics. Their presence is a reminder to live in the moment. Get ready for liftoff: a more dramatic you is ready to escape the bonds of banality. Let yourself be reborn in the fires of non-conformity.

LS132 Luminaries

Vincent Van Gogh	March 30, 1853
Charles "Charlie" Chaplin	April 16, 1889
Laurence Olivier	May 22, 1907
John Wayne	May 26, 1907
Frida Kahlo	July 6, 1907
Linda Goodman	April 9, 1925
Yogi Berra	May 12, 1925
Jack Lemmon[E]	February 8, 1925
Bobby Fischer	March 9, 1943
Mick Jagger	July 26, 1943
Robert De Niro	August 17, 1943
Susan Boyle	April 1, 1961
Ricky Gervais	June 25, 1961
Princess Diana	July 1, 1961
Heath Ledger	April 4, 1979
Douglas Murray	July 16, 1979
Malala Yousafzai	July 12, 1997
Boeing	August 1, 1997
Jung Kook	September 1, 1997

1. Joanna Martine Woolfolk, *The Only Astrology Book You'll Ever Need*, p. 201.
2. Robert Pelletier, *Planets in Aspect-Understanding Your Inner Dynamic* (Atglen, PA: Schiffer Publishing Ltd., 1974), p. 119.
3. https://en.wikipedia.org/wiki/Ricky_Gervais. Retrieved Jan. 28, 2022.
4. Duncan Steel, *Eclipse: The celestial phenomenon which has changed the course of history* (London, UK: Headline Book Publishing, 1999), p. 12.
5. https://en.wikipedia.org/wiki/After_Life_(TV_series) Retrieved Jan 28, 2022.
6. https://abcnews.go.com/2020/video/bruce-jenner-interview-diane-sawyer-im-woman-30570133. Retrieved Jan. 30, 2022.
7. https://nationalpost.com/opinion/barbara-kay-caitlyn-jenner-trivializes-the-momentousness-of-what-it-means-to-be-a-woman. Retrieved Jan. 30, 2022.
8. John Logsdon, *John F. Kennedy and the Race to the Moon* (London: Palgrave MacMillan, 2013), p. 79.
9. Ibid., p. 80.
10. Liz Greene & Howard Sasportas, *Dynamics of the Unconscious—Seminars in Psychological Astrology* (York Beach, Maine: Samuel Weiser, Inc., 1988), p. 46.

LUNAR SAROS 133

"The psychic task which a person can and must set for himself is not to feel secure, but to be able to tolerate insecurity."

-Erich Fromm

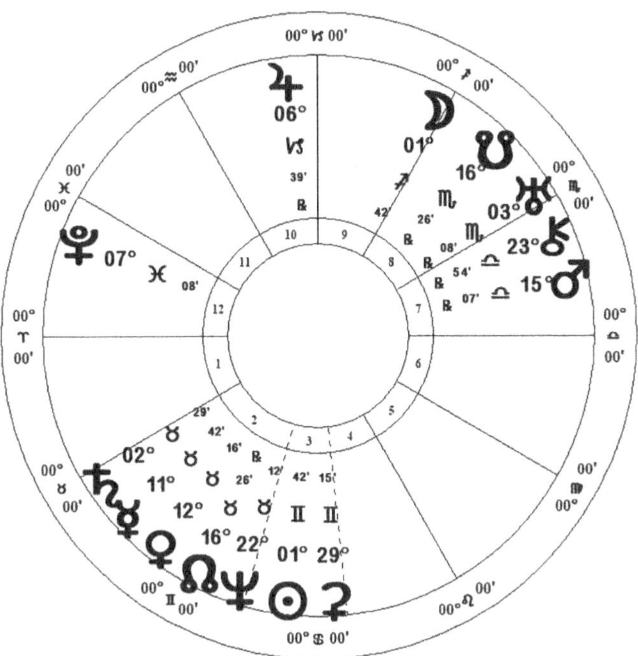

Lunar Saros 133

May 23, 1557 • 9:37:54 AM • South Pole

Letting Go

The gates that lead to freedom and a newfound sense of self-worth all come courtesy of these inspirational Sagittarian Dragons. This is a SNode eclipse that is capable of helping us imagine a brighter future if one is willing to let go of past encumbrances. Ruler Jupiter retrograde in Capricorn is awesomely efficient at providing what is needed. Its trines to a Taurean second degree Saturn, along with a Mercury and Venus conjunction in Taurus, equip the eclipse with a solid basis for all manner of securities and financial exchange transactions on a global scale.

The eclipse Moon not only creates a classic Finger of Fate with Saturn and Ceres but also a Boomerang with the Sun which reinforces an optimistic "all is well" vibe. This is especially so as the eclipse axis resonates to the first degree Aries overtones that hold out the promise of new life on every imaginable front. The energy of the Boomerang can take an individual far away from their starting place on a journey that has deep repercussions not only for themselves but for the collective. The Boomerang returns in kind that which has been released, making this Series profoundly personal. The placement of Venus and Neptune in the midpoint and isotrap structures underscores the importance of the role that service, and surrender will play in the unfoldment of LS133's sphere of consciousness.

The Finger of Fate reference is apropos considering it embodies not only a Boomerang and not just *any* Boomerang but one that holds the Sun at the first degree of Gemini. This is an energetic configuration that establishes a feeling of great vitality and purpose and gives, from a very early age, a call to serve or participate in a very public life. Success is based not on the past but on following a vision for one's life that uplifts everyone. No matter to what extent the depths of despair or disillusionment have taken hold, the way back to sanity and salvation can also be found within. The Greek goddess of grain, known as Ceres to the Romans, was no stranger to heartbreak and sorrow, having lived through her daughter Persephone's rape and abduction to the underworld.[1] Here, at the prophetic or at the very least intuitive twenty-ninth degree of Gemini, Ceres is in the best of all positions to know what needs to be done to turn your world right side up.

Recalibrating and overcoming difficulties are in fact what these Fire Dragons do best. Their willpower, determination, and ability to pull through just about anything is legendary as the list of luminaries can attest to. That ability to cope and endure is largely due to LS133's impressive Saturn in opposition to a third degree Uranus in Scorpio which seems to have access to unlimited fields of both cooperation and information. The eclipse functions best when our collective human concerns take precedence over any local irritations and disputes.

One of the gifts these relative newcomers offer is a willingness to go into the darkness to challenge the disappointment and pain of our naïveté. They carry a boldness that makes the work worthwhile. And, as stated earlier, Neptune's involvement in all the closest midpoint and isotrap structures suggest that Divine Order may be playing an even stronger hand than appearances suggest. No doubt an attitude of gratitude and forgiveness may prove to be our best options here. Maharishi Mahesh Yogi, the founder of Transcendental Meditation (TM) and a luminary of this eclipse, had the right idea when he said, "Whatever we put our attention on will grow stronger in our life."

Closest Midpoints: Neptune/Sun-Venus, Venus/Saturn-Neptune
Isotraps: Sun/Saturn conjunct Mercury/Neptune
Moon/Uranus opposition Venus/Neptune

1900—2100 Eclipses: Lunar Saros—133

1917, 1936, 1954, 1972, 1990, 2008, 2026, 2044, 2062, 2080, 2098
Length of cycle —1,262 years
Series ends—June 29, 2819

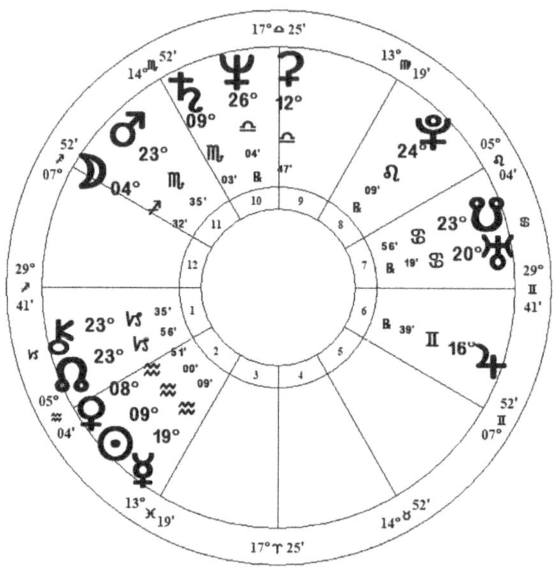

Oprah Winfrey
PREBLE—LS133

January 29, 1954 • 4:30 AM • Kosciusko, MS, USA

The Church of O

"The way through the challenge is to get still and ask yourself what is the next right move and then from that space make the next right move and the next right move and not to be overwhelmed by it because you know your life is bigger than that one moment."

- Oprah

Oprah's Connections to the Lunar Dragons of LS133
Saturn to Saturn

1st Harmonics: Moon – Moon, Mars – Ceres/MC, Ceres – DSC, Chiron – Neptune
2nd Harmonics: Mercury/Venus – Saturn, Neptune – Mars

Let's take a quick peek at Oprah's Mercury trine Jupiter. It's a biggie as it reflects an identical phase relationship to the same aspect in the eclipse field. Oprah's opening trine from a very relational Mercury and Jupiter in air signs features Jupiter conjunct the great battle stars of the ancient world—fiery and feisty Rigel and Bellatrix. They are both known for command, control, wit, and skill when dealing with confrontation, and are the best stars to have at your back in times of conflict. Bellatrix, the "Female Warrior," is often referred to as the "Amazon Star."[2] She is associated with a daring and audacious style of living that thrives on challenge. This star is a strategist that rises to the occasion under pressure while keeping her cool. To have both military stars on Jupiter and to be born within a Jupiter ruled lunar eclipse is an extraordinary stroke of luck that Oprah has parlayed into a billion dollar dynasty.

Oprah has her natal Moon in early Sagittarius conjunct the lunar eclipse Moon. Referencing back to page 6 of this book, "Top 10 Steps for How to Live with Dragons," step nine is all about finding the lunar eclipses that share your Moon sign. And of course the tighter the conjunction, the stronger the resonance. Oprah's fourth degree Moon definitely holds a 1st Harmonic to the eclipse Moon which gives her carte blanche access to the beating heart of the eclipse and its sphere of consciousness.

The 2nd Harmonics really seem to bring it all home. For Oprah, the Mercury/Venus 2nd Harmonics to her Saturn gave her so many opportunities to develop her craft and step from one platform of opportunity to the next. With both the Sun and Saturn holding steady at the ninth degree of exploration and with her Venus at the eighth, a degree associated both with Scorpio and the accumulation of wealth, it would have only been a matter of time before Oprah would be calling all the shots.

The 2nd Harmonic Neptune as we know is a Cosmic Influencer in its own right and its critical midpoint and isotrap structures gave Divine Order a field to play in where acts of service and surrender would be valued. That Neptune falling on her Mars and its Fixed T-Square with Mercury and Pluto gave her the charisma, vision, and sensitivity to know when and how to use her growing power base of influence.

And Oprah wouldn't have to wait long as the karmic Boomerang within Lunar Saros 133 was already returning. On December 18, 1985, at the age of thirty-one, Oprah would appear in her first movie role in Steven Spielberg's *The Color Purple* and make her a certified star. Of note is the return of LS126—Game Changers—on October 28, 1985, that would activate at the fame, fun, and living life fifth degree of Taurus on her Mercury/Uranus midpoint at 4 Taurus 44.

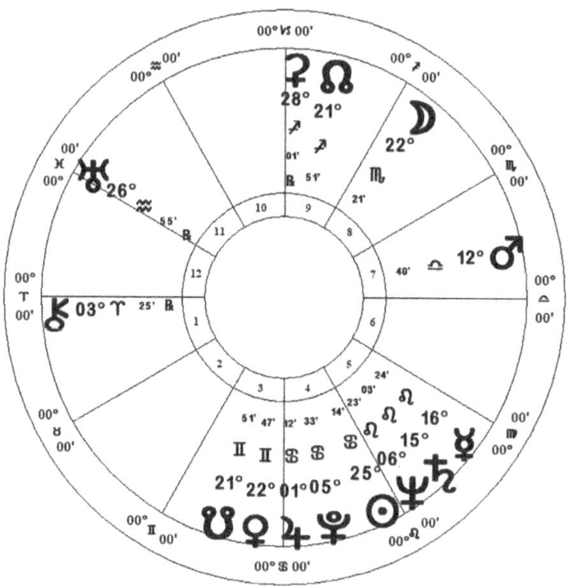

Nelson Mandela
PREBLE—LS138

July 18, 1918 • TOB Unknown • Mvezo, South Africa

Nobel Peace Laureate

"Appearances matter–and remember to smile."

-Nelson Mandela

By the time of his passing on December 5, 2013, Madiba, as he had come to be known throughout South Africa and the world, had been the recipient of over 260 awards, most notably the Nobel Peace Prize in 1993. These tributes were a reflection of his commitment to racial equality, to freedom, and to the dignity of every human being whose struggle for equality in a multi-racial South Africa became his personal and political life mission. Nelson Mandela held the distinction of being the first black President of South Africa from 1994–1999 as well as holding the office of President of the African National Council (ANC) from 1991–1997. The magnificence of the man was that he accomplished his reforms and revolution with minimal bitterness, recrimination, and rancor and all in a spirit of pragmatic self-assurance.

In an interview with *Frontline*, Rick Stengel, who had collaborated with Mandela on his autobiography, suggested that Nelson Mandela's greatest untold struggle and achievement came in the last few years of his imprisonment and his first few years out, when he was dealing with a flood of antagonism toward him. "People thought that he was too inflated with himself. There were so many rivalries, and there were so many people who were conspiring against him."[3] The pressure and intensity continued to build even as President F. W. de Klerk, on February 2, 1990, lifted the ban on the ANC and announced Mandela's imminent release.

On February 11, 1990, Nelson Mandela walked out of prison after a twenty-seven year incarceration. On February 9, just two days before, LS133 had arrived at 21 Leo, liberating his learned and lucky Mars/Jupiter midpoint while at the same time emancipating his Uranus at 26 Aquarius. This is a Moon in Sagittarius eclipse and the activation, falling at the twenty-first degree carries Sagittarian overtones that would have easily synchronized to the eclipse. His message of hope, streaming through a Venus/Saturn conjunct Jupiter/Neptune foundational isotrap beautifully aligned with the eclipse midpoints which were only growing in strength with every return, especially the Venus/Saturn-Neptune midpoint which always favors the tortoise over the hare. He was born to be a legend; Mandela's Jupiter at the AP and its Mars/Sun-Jupiter midpoint reinvigorated and popularized how "the personal becomes political." His lunar dragons are of the Earth; deeply grounded, his PREBLE LS138—Legends and Legacy—are bringers of the fabulous as well as the fatal that include remarkable feats of creativity and worldly accomplishment.

Nelson Mandela's Connections to the Lunar Dragons of LS133

1st Harmonics: Ceres – Jupiter, Mars – Mars,
2nd Harmonics: Ceres – Ceres, Jupiter – Jupiter/Pluto

A shared 1st Harmonic diplomatic Mars in Libra at the twelfth degree is a peace-maker worthy of a Nobel Prize. In fact, the Nobel Peace Prize of 1993 was awarded jointly to Nelson Mandela and Frederik Willem de Klerk "for their work for the peaceful termination of the apartheid regime, and for laying the foundations for a new democratic South Africa."[4] Nelson Mandela's ability to tap the extractive forces within LS133's energetic field is primarily a matter of its 2nd Harmonic Ceres to his Ceres. As you will see through the many examples in this book, 2nd Harmonics bring a change in perception, which brings on a change in perspective, which can change your life. In addition, 2nd Harmonics involving Ceres work to revive lost dimensions of self along with anything else that has seemingly left our life.

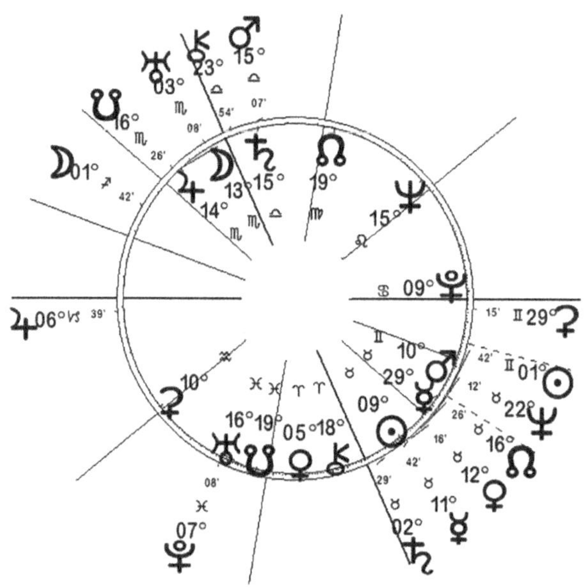

Inside

Bear Stearns
PREBLE—LS112

May 1, 1923 • 12:01AM • Delaware, USA

Outside

LS133
May 23, 1557 • 9:36:49 AM • South Pole

News Flash!

Bear Stearns is Dead

Talk about letting go! The collapse of Bear Stearns played out over a span of seven days, from March 10 to March 16, 2008. The eighty-five-year-old investment bank was sold to JPMorgan Chase for $10 per share, after an initial offer of $2 per share; a shattering fall from its pre-crisis fifty-two week high of $133.20 per share.[5]

Bear Stearn's Connections to the Lunar Dragons of LS133

1st Harmonics: SNode - Jupiter,
Sun - Mercury, Mercury/Venus - Sun, Mars - Saturn
2nd Harmonics: Jupiter - Pluto, Mercury/Venus - Jupiter

On February 21, 2008, Lunar Saros 133 experienced its twenty-sixth return out of a life cycle of seventy-one appearances. Its activation degree fell at 1 Virgo and landed exactly on Bear Stearns' Neptune/NNode midpoint, known for its attraction to exploitation, deception, and a general sense of disappointment with people in general. Note the classic speculative Neptune-Jupiter pattern also found in the charts of Lehman Brothers and AIG in the Earth Dragons of LS138—Legends and Legacy (see part Part Two). The eclipse 2nd Harmonics from Jupiter to Pluto and its potent Taurean Mercury-Venus to Bear Stearns' Jupiter sounded its death knell.

LS133 Summary

Appearances matter—and remember to smile. Nelson Mandela's words seem appropriate as they embody the need to stay open and congenial under the influence of this rather challenging lunar eclipse. It's one of the more difficult lunar eclipses as it gives our self-worth quite the workout along with a run for the money. Heavy Taurus placements tend to do that. Overall, the mood is serious but friendly and encouraging. Baby steps taken now will pay off in huge dividends down the road as we all learn the value of patience and putting in a good day's effort.

Anyone in league with these Fire Dragons from birth or rite of passage would benefit from a trip through the caverns of their own underworld. There is a darkness within all of us that likes to keep us on the edge of despair; seemingly in denial of our individual right to be gloriously alive and hopeful. This eclipse can help us to find the clarity of mind to recognize our own limitations and naïveté. There are diamonds to be mined if we are willing to do the work. A little soul-searching and some decluttering will prove invaluable and quite possibly lead to a joyful release of pent-up emotions that are at the root of long-held anxieties.

As of 2008, Lunar Saros 133 is now experiencing a Last Quarter phase as most lunar eclipses, in their life cycle, enter this critical phase by their twenty-sixth return. The need to reorient and review is palpable as is the sense of dissatisfaction and loss as the energy field recalibrates. It offers wisdom but one must first endure the process of letting go as a life review and update begin to work its magic. This is truly a time for letting go and letting Divine Order take the lead. The power of the AA slogan, *one hour at a time . . . one day at a time . . . one step at a time,* says it best. Let these be your watchwords to sanity.

LS133 Luminaries

Wolfgang Amadeus Mozart	January 27, 1756
FDR	January 30, 1882
James Joyce	February 2, 1882
Nöel Coward[E1]	December 16, 1899
Humphrey Bogart	December 25, 1899
Erich Fromm	March 23, 1900
Spencer Tracy	April 5, 1900
Maharishi Mahesh Yogi	January 12, 1918
Sam Walton	March 29, 1918
Richard Feynman	May 11, 1918
Mary Kay Ash	May 12, 1918
David Suzuki	March 24, 1936
Roy Orbison	April 23, 1936
Bobby Darin	May 14, 1936
Kris Kristofferson	June 22, 1936
Oprah Winfrey	January 29, 1954
Jackie Chan	April 7, 1954
Jerry Seinfeld	April 29, 1954
Jim Belushi	June 15, 1954
Kelly Slater	February 11, 1972
Shaquille O'Neal	March 6, 1972
Dwayne Johnson	May 2, 1972
Zinedine Zidane	June 23, 1972

Kristen Stewart	April 09, 1990
Margot Robbie	July 02, 1990
Rachel Brosnahan	July 12, 1990
Canelo Álvarez	July 18, 1990

PREBLE–LS128
Noel Coward
Humphrey Bogart

1. Jean Shinoda Bolen, M.D., *Goddesses in Older Women: Archetypes in Women Over Fifty* (New York: HarperCollins, 2001), p. 159.
2. Richard Hinckley Allen, *Star Names: Their Lore and Meaning* (New York: Dover Publications, 1963), p. 313.
3. John Carlin, *Interview: Richard Stengel,* The Long Walk of Nelson Mandela http://www.pbs.org/wgbh/pages/frontline/shows/mandela/interviews/stengel2.html. Retrieved July 16, 2022.
4. The Nobel Peace Prize 1993. NobelPrize.org. Retrieved July 16, 2022. https://www.nobelprize.org/prizes/peace/1993/summary/
5. https://www.history.com/this-day-in-history/bear-stearns-sold-to-j-p-morgan-chase. Retrieved July 16, 2022.

LUNAR SAROS 140

"Receive life like a gift, and release it like a present."

-Akiane Kramarik

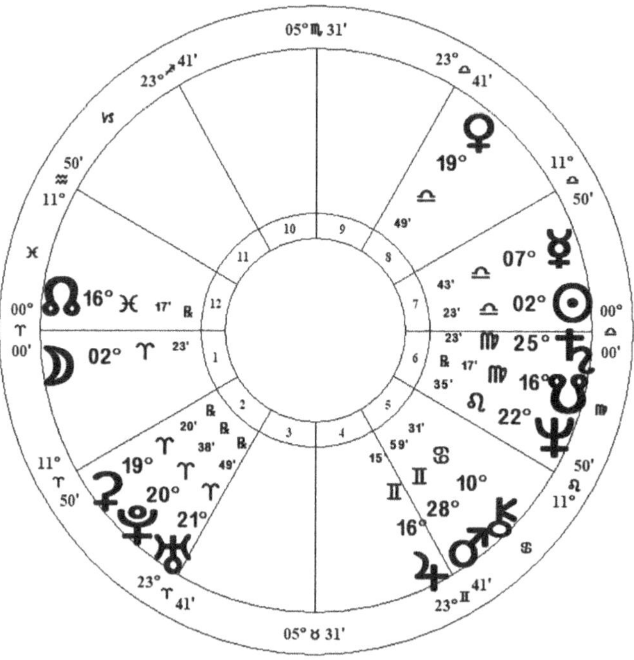

Lunar Saros 140

September 25, 1597 • 01:55:36 PM • North Pole

Design Your Life

The renewal of our spirit finds a welcoming home in the fires of this NNode Aries eclipse. It is the only eclipse in the entire Lunar Saros Series to feature a triple Ceres, Pluto, Uranus conjunction that steps through the nineteenth, twentieth, and twenty-first degrees of Aries to advance the state of evolution for everyone. To accomplish this, the eclipse field has zero tolerance for fakery and demands that we go for the truth at all costs. This is a vital and highly charismatic eclipse field that needs to fall in love with life regardless of the pain and suffering. To die and be reborn is routine for these pioneers of reform. The presence of Jupiter in partile square to the nodal axis is constantly refueling fresh perspectives with an appealing blend of intellectual curiosity coupled to a down-home sense of soulful sensitivity. An equally sensitive and able Mars/Saturn square gives just the right amount of push versus pull and pain versus pleasure to keep everything in motion, especially as Mars, at 23N30 declination, is definitely in the OOB zone. . As the eclipse moves forward in time, deeper and more profound levels of maturity will manifest.

The eclipse field radiates self-worth and the self-esteem that grows over time through triumph and tragedy. As a consequence, openness to experience and especially the ability to trust oneself is an ongoing necessity. There is renewal within the disruptive forces of the powerhouse Ceres, Pluto, and Uranus players who shake things up to better reorganize your life and all with a little taste of honey from a helping hand Venus trine Jupiter. If we can remain open to the flow of good will on all sides and especially for ourselves, this eclipse offers the potential to be reborn into a more loving and harmonious environment.

There is a call now to take up a challenge or mission as seen through the midpoint structures. Ambition is not a dirty word with this lunar family nor is the idea of discipline: both are key drivers in the ability to use potent energy to its maximum. Thoughts and communication now reflect a serious commitment to support social causes or to bring artistic creation into the world. Demanding but not necessarily difficult, the Moon's waning square to Ruler Mars necessitates shifts in habits and more importantly lifestyle changes. As the eclipse is a highly subjective field of transition, much can be accomplished in the area of personal growth and self-development. The foundational Mercury/Jupiter conjunct Mars/Saturn isotrap insists we get out of our comfort zone to better gain a clearer perspective of any situation that needs addressing as its time to put into play a practical approach to problem solving. Done well a new level of excitement and freedom will begin to take hold.

Apart from Chiron and the NNode, Lunar Saros 140 is bereft of planets in water signs. In such a case, either one of two things tends to happen: either the eclipse field attracts a totally unemotional, detached, and unsympathetic response from the environment; or the planetary energies seek out and attract highly emotional, intuitive, psychic, and imaginative forces. Let's hope that the power of self-realization and truth-telling wins the day and allows the wisdom of water to flood this lunar eclipse field with streams of faith and compassion for all humankind.

Closest Midpoints: Mars/Eclipse-Saturn, Mercury/Venus-Saturn
Isotraps: Mercury/Jupiter conjunct Mars/Saturn
Mercury/Mars conjunct Venus/Jupiter

1900—2100 Eclipses: Lunar Saros—140

1904, 1922, 1940, 1958, 1976, 1994, 2012, 2030, 2048, 2066, 2084
Length of cycle —1,370 years
Series ends—January 6, 2968

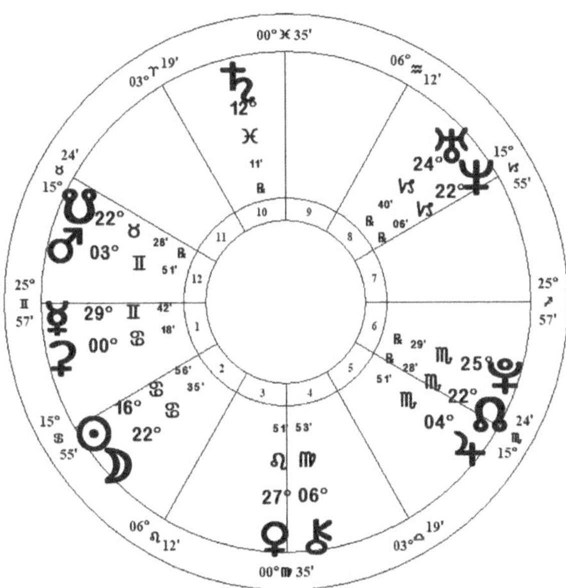

Akiane Kramarik
PREBLE—LS140

July 9, 1994 • 4:00 AM • Mount Morris, IL, USA

Artist/Poet/Child Prodigy

"You are a wonder! Thank you for touching the world the way you do."

-JOSH GROBAN

Akiane Kramarik was water birthed in the opening hours of a New Moon in Cancer, making her transition from spirit to the earthly plane a seamless slide of wonder. Her exceptional life as a child prodigy has been well documented and her absolutely stunning art and poetry have been fêted around the world. She is a true ambassador for Heaven. Her commentary on what life is like "on the other side," like her prodigious outpouring of paintings and poetry, indeed leaves one "god-smacked."

Her gifts pour forth from her Moon opposition to a Neptune and Uranus conjunction in Capricorn and all in trine to a NNode/Pluto conjunction in Scorpio. Jeff Green in *Pluto the Evolutionary Journey of the Soul, Vol 1* suggests that Pluto's conjunction to the NNode is indicative of someone well on their evolutionary way "within the last few lifetimes and is meant to continue in that direction. Every other contributing factor in the birth chart will be channeled or focused through the North Node conjunct Pluto."[1] Clearly, from the age of four, she has been receiving a wealth of visionary images, thoughts and feelings that are deeply transformational. "At the age of nine, she was discovered and featured by Oprah Winfrey and by ten, her first book, *Akiane: Her Life, Her Art, Her Poetry* was published by HarperCollins, and her unique story rapidly circled the whole world."[2]

As an artist, Akiane Kramarik's other-worldly paintings and poetry open our hearts and minds to a realm where our egocentric limitations dissolve into the formlessness and freedom of a world bounded by the boldness of beauty and the wonder of love.

Akiane's Connections to the Dragons of LS140

1st Harmonics: NNode – Saturn,
Chiron – Sun, Mars – ASC, Mars – Mercury/Ceres, Neptune – Venus

Akiane's ties to LS140 are through its NNode conjunction to her Saturn and the eclipse field's Mars to her ASC, her prophetic twenty-ninth degree Mercury in Gemini, and her infinity alpha Ceres at the AP. The fact that the eclipse NNode embodies a sixteenth degree Jupiter brings all that fecundity to bear witness through her exquisitely sensitized and double-dipped Saturn at the twelfth degree of Pisces.

The Mercury Ceres conjunction straddling the summer solstice gateway feels like a portal of both entry and exit, where being and substance are birthed and then released into the dome of earthly domicile. Together and along with the Cosmic Bridge, these energetic vectors are more than enough to establish a global communications platform by which her creative talents can best serve her mission that is all about "founding an Arts Academy, producing and directing movies and uniting the world countries through arts."[3] Akiane's art and devotion are stunning tributes to the gifts of openness, self-discovery, and trusting the grace that flows through the spirit and love of LS140.

Akiane was born right at the heart of the Disseminating Phase of her Fire Dragon family's evolutionary journey giving solidity to a very impressive set of skills. At this stage the eclipse's sphere of influence and its unfolding state of consciousness desires nothing less than to share its gifts and mastery with the world. It is a stage of harvest and productivity.

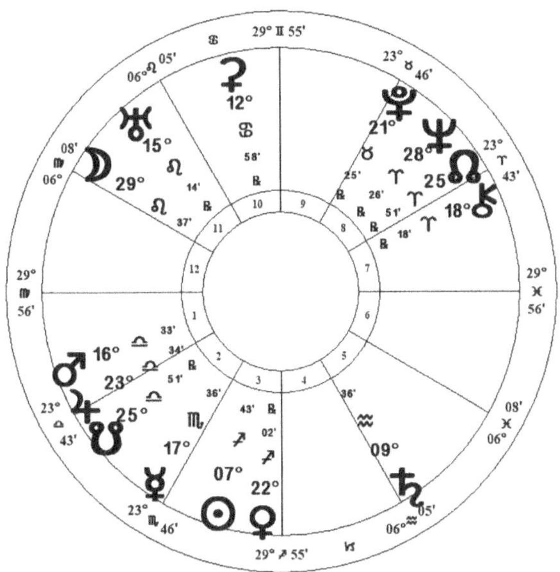

Sir Winston Churchill
PREBLE—LS134

November 30, 1874 • 1:30 AM • Blenheim, UK

"History will be kind to me, for I intend to write it."

-CHURCHILL

Britain's Bulldog Prime Minister

"Tact is the ability to tell someone to go to hell in such a way that they look forward to the trip."

-WINSTON CHURCHILL

LS140's arrival on April 22, 1940, at 2 Scorpio roused Churchill's magnificent Grand Fire Trine of Neptune, his mighty Moon conjunct the fixed star Regulus and his OOB Venus at 22 Sagittarius. His gorgeous Venus sextile Jupiter is not only in MR, but that superpower Jupiter holds a conjunction to the destiny star Spica, a star known throughout the ages for its love of learning and capacity for knowledge that certainly describes the great man's wit, eloquence, and mastery of just about anything he turned his attention and creative hand to.

On May 10, 1940, Chamberlain would resign as Prime Minister and King George VI would ask Churchill to become Prime Minister.[4] Three days later, Winston Churchill would give his famous "*Blood, Toil, Sweat and Tears*" speech in the House of Commons, "the first of many morale boosting speeches made by Churchill to inspire the British to keep fighting against a seemingly invincible enemy."[5] Winston's entire life had prepared him well for this moment; with his background as a proven military commander, politician, and statesman, he was arguably the only man capable of pulling together a coalition from the United States and the Soviet Union to stave off the growing menace that was Nazi Germany.

Churchill's diplomatic and strategic skill set is best left to historians to evaluate and debate, however his PREBLE-LS134—The Attractor Factor (found in the Air Dragons of Part Three)—is worth checking out to appreciate how he benefited from his dragon family's unique ability to link up with and establish meaningful networks. In addition, the persuasiveness of two of the most powerful fixed stars in the firmament would significantly elevate Churchill's political and social capital and help him become a formidable war time leader.

Winston Churchill's Connections to the Dragons of LS140
Space Lanes via DSC/ASC

1st Harmonics: Pluto/Uranus – NNode, Moon – DSC, Venus – Mars, Mars – X, Ceres – Chiron, Chiron – Ceres, Pluto/Uranus – Chiron
2nd Harmonics: Venus – Chiron, Ceres – Mars, Pluto/Uranus – Mars

Winston Churchill's Space Lanes were created from the eclipse axis falling on his DSC/ASC axis, renewing his profile as a trusted public figure with the skills of leadership that would have come in handy in the weeks and months that followed LS140's arrival in the spring of (coincidentally) 1940. The interplay between the eclipse Ceres to his Chiron and conversely his Ceres to the eclipse Chiron is almost too prosaic for words; since Chiron loves to learn through direct experience, Churchill would have his hands full as he would have the eclipse triple Ceres, Pluto, Uranus entangled with Chiron's quest for collective failure and redemption in his capacity to serve. For the six-month duration of this lunar eclipse, and for every return that followed, Churchill would be living out the mythology of both Ceres and Chiron: That is to say, of suffering, loss, grief, birth, death, and renewal on a daily basis.

Let's take a closer look at his Ceres. In the Tenth House in Cancer, it came with all the trappings of a well-heeled ancestry: His family had it all—wealth, land, aristocracy, and political connections. He was a direct descendant of the 1st Duke of Marlborough; his father, Lord Randolph Churchill was a British statesman and his mother, Jennie, was a wealthy American socialite.[6] Winston was perfectly positioned to nurture not only a nation but also to hold the reins of western world leadership at a time of deep despair. To date I can find no other example of an individual's Ceres and Chiron cross-linking by conjunction and/or opposition to the Chiron and Ceres placements of a lunar eclipse field. And for a final touch of glory there is the eclipse ruler Mars in Gemini at the prophetic twenty-ninth degree as well as the AP falling exactly on Churchill's Tenth House MC, making the management of power undisputed and immediately accessible. All things considered, LS140's arrival on April 22, 1940, elevated Winston Churchill's life to legendary status.

LS140's return in the spring of 1940 would be its twentieth as it was progressing through its Full Moon phase begun with its seventeenth return in 1886. All things considered, at this stage of its unfoldment, the lunar eclipse was at its highest state of awareness, capable of levels of pride and confidence heretofore never seen or experienced. This stage is like the breaking of the dawn and the joy that comes with its light, warmth, and hope for a new day. No matter what the challenge, when this stage of evolution arrives in a lunar eclipse cycle, take comfort in knowing that you'll be able to get a handle on whatever it is that needs your attention.

Winston Churchill died on January 24, 1965. His dragon family–LS134 had just returned on December 19, 1964, activating his MC at the highly communicative twenty-seventh degree of Gemini. Links to his eclipse family are scintillating but at the ripe age of ninety it would prove too much for his failing body. In death as in life, Churchill would prove to be an enigma, a character created out of deep space potentials yet to be quantifiable.

I leave you with his final act of cosmic splendor: His earthly existence began on November 30, 1874, exactly *thirty-six days after his* PREBLE-LS134 arrived on October 25, 1874. He would die exactly *thirty-six days after* the return of PREBLE-LS134 on December 19, 1964.

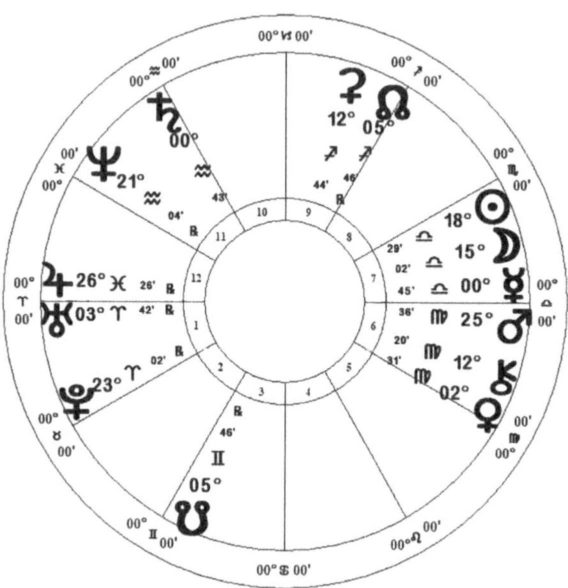

Henry J. Heinz
PREBLE—LS118

October 11, 1844 • TOB Unknown • Pittsburgh, PA, USA

The Pickle King

(First Sale in England June 18, 1886)

"Our market is the world."

-Henry J. Heinz

On May 25, 1886, Henry J. Heinz set off on a three-month European tour that would take his already successful brand-building strategy for his sauces and ketchup into the stratosphere. An undisputed financial genius and market-maker extraordinaire, as a stellar member of the Earth Dragons of LS118—The Marketplace—he had a talent for creating opportunity along with an even greater capacity to rise like a phoenix out of the ashes of despair and defeat. Award-winning journalist Joshua Kendall in his book *America's Obsessives: The Compulsive Energy That Built a Nation*, states that "the supersalesman paid a call to Fortnum and Mason, asking to see the head of grocery purchasing, and armed with seven varieties of our finest and newest goods" closed the deal. Heinz recorded in his diary this statement: "I think, Mr. Heinz, we will take all of them."[7] It wouldn't be until 1898 that production really took off in the UK with his clever "beans and toast campaigns [that] would forever revamp the morning meal throughout the British Empire."[8]

On March 20, 1886, the dragons of LS140 entered through the critical and prophetic twenty-ninth degree gateway of Virgo, rousing not only his Mars and its power-play opposition to Jupiter but, more importantly, his Mercury at the AP infinity degree in a gung-ho trine to Saturn at another all-in alpha degree in Aquarius. All trines activate quickly but when connected to the AP they are dramatic in their expression and become unstoppable in the force of their unfoldment. And then there is the heightened stroke of genius that comes from that freshly infused Mercury and its opposition to a third degree I-can-sell-anything Uranus. Here is another example of how lunar eclipses can shed light on critical turning/burning points along our life journey without the benefit of a certified time of birth.

As you've probably figured out, The Pickle King arrived just as LS140 was beginning to experience the longed-for light of its Full Moon phase. This is party time; this is when you stand the best chance to collect on all those debts and to reap the rewards of years if not lifetimes of service, sacrifice, and dedication. It is considered the peak of the cycle and a time of harvest. The Full Moon phase speaks to the enjoyment of life and to the state of conscious illumination that accompanies its arrival.

LS140 Summary

It's time for a tune-up when these youthful Fire Dragons come roaring your way. Everybody benefits from a little spit and polish as improvement is part and parcel of their daily regime. A noticeable changing-of-the-guards mood is now in fashion as many people question—and even reject—the current status quo. Like interval training, monotony will become a thing of the past as new skills and strategies quickly emerge. Recalibration is here for those who are ready for a new challenge in the weeks and months ahead. Get ready to welcome in a new vision and a more clearly calibrated direction for your life.

When this family of lunar eclipses activates a personal chart, be prepared to work hard, and get organized. Devote some time and energy to helping out as personal time now invested can return fame and prosperity if done for philanthropic interests. Lifestyle changes are the norm now especially if matters of soul and spirit are the motivating factors. Hope for the best, stay positive, and remember to tell the truth. It is essential to not make agreements that you don't intend to keep as these dragons are a source of rapidly changing landscapes where fresh and fascinating people flourish.

The ultimate gifts of LS140 are a renewal of self-worth and a commitment to trusting in your take on the world regardless of what social media naysayers would have you believe. The ability to overcome difficulty is woven throughout the entire field; these are adventurous dragons who love to take risks because they trust in their abilities and so should you. Trust in you. Design the life of your dreams.

Phase	Return	Year
Full Moon	17th	1886
Disseminating	21st	1958
Last Quarter	26th	2048
Balsamic	30th	2104

LS140 Luminaries

Benjamin Franklin	January 17, 1706
Pablo Neruda	July 12, 1904
Charles Mingus[E1]	April 22, 1922
Bea Arthur	May 13, 1922
Judy Garland	June 10, 1922
Emil Zátopek	September 19, 1922
Al Pacino	April 25, 1940
Ringo Starr	July 7, 1940
Alex Trebek	July 22, 1940
John Lennon	October 9, 1940
Prince	June 7, 1958
Terry Fox	July 28, 1958
Madonna	August 16, 1958
Michael Jackson	August 29, 1958
Jamal Khashoggi	October 13, 1958

Benedict Cumberbatch	July 19, 1976
Judit Polgár	July 23, 1976
Ronaldo	September 18, 1976
Ryan Reynolds	October 23, 1976
Aly Raisman[E]	May 25, 1994
Akiane Kramarik	July 9, 1994
Lil Uzi Vert	July 31, 1994
RM Rap Monster	September 12, 1994

1. Jeff Green, *Pluto—The Evolutionary Journey of the Soul Volume 1* (St. Paul, MN: Llewellyn Publications, 2000), p. 19.

2. https://akiane.com/about-akiane/ Retrieved Feb. 13, 2022.

3. Ibid.

4. Jennifer Rosenberg, "Biography of Sir Winston Churchill, Prime Minister of the UK." ThoughtCo, Sep. 9, 2021, thoughtco.com/sir-winston-churchill-1779796. Retrieved Feb. 14, 2022.

5. Ibid.

6. https://en.wikipedia.org/wiki/Winston_Churchill. Retrieved Feb. 15, 2022.

7. Joshua Kendall, *America's Obsessives: The Compulsive Energy that Built a Nation* (New York: Grand Central Publishing, 2013), p. 69.

8. Ibid.

LUNAR SAROS 149

"Nothing is impossible. There's no limit to what I can do."

-LEYLAH FERNANDEZ

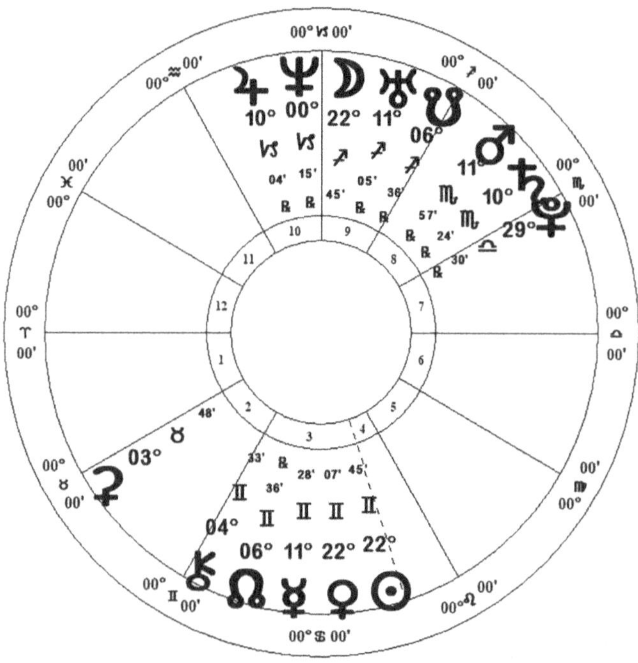

Lunar Saros 149

June 13, 1984 • 2:42:25 PM • South Pole

Breakthroughs and Comebacks

Long shots, breakthroughs, and comebacks abound in the presence of this South Node Sagittarian eclipse. Ruler Jupiter, at the tenth degree in Capricorn, is fully in charge. The lunar eclipse carries an outstanding example of what an Anchor pattern can offer: It simultaneously fulfills the mandate of bringing into manifestation the consequences of our actions, as seen through the Boomerang and its future orientation while grounding the possibilities of the moment as seen through the Anchor. The pattern gives phenomenal staying power. There are more Anchors to discover: LS125 in the Air Eclipses of Part Three—and saving the best for last, the final two are found in the Water Eclipses of Part Four, LS137—Ripples and Riptides, and LS142—There Be Dragons. Keep your eyes open for them; they are rare but highly effective patterns.

A corporate climate permeates the sphere as Saturn, Jupiter, Venus, and the eclipse axis all at the tenth and twenty-second degrees resonate to the tenth sign of the Zodiac. Its six planets in retrograde contribute to a "behind closed doors" mentality where secrecy, suspense, and sophomoric behavior can easily out-gun a more nuanced approach. Flying in the face of the powers that be, planets in retrograde have a well-earned reputation for going their own way and can offer a surprising assortment of heterodox beliefs. To compound this, we have Uranus conjunct the great fixed star Antares, the brightest star in the constellation of Scorpio and one of the Four Royal Stars of the ancient world. Antares has a long history and association with people and positions that command an intense field of power, resources, and confrontation. Many with this star will be gifted with an ability to probe into the great mysteries of life and are not deterred by the challenges that must be faced to reach their end. Naturally, many will be touched by its courage and toughness as it gives mental alertness and strategic ability. Appropriately for this Lunar Saros Series, the Chinese have long known Antares as the "Fire Star" with its implications for protection against "the fires that burn" both literally and metaphorically.

Mercury's apex position in the Anchor and its opposition to Uranus at the fulcrum is fed by the Mars/Saturn sextile to the eclipse captain Jupiter, where it easily digs its metaphorical fluke into the materialistic substrate of Capricorn ambition. Viewed as a Focused Yod or Yod Boomerang, or just plain Boomerang, this energetic pattern has Mercury in rulership in quincunx to an equally potent Mars in rulership; this has all the nasty hallmarks of intellectual aggression if not tempered by communication skills that seek connection rather than conflict. Uranus at the center of the Anchor receives all the benefits of the Saturn and Mars sextile to Jupiter giving it personality that needs to be expressed. At its worst, and thwarted by time or temperament, the flow of energy along the link from Uranus to the apex Mercury has a well-deserved reputation for incurring haste, waste, nervousness, and outright deplorable behavior. But at its best, that same link has a genius for transmuting turbulence into personal triumph.

Final thoughts: With so much going on, I almost failed to notice that LS149 has an OOB Moon; its declination at 24S32 is a reminder that these Fire Dragons come with their own brand of emotional instability, doubt, guilt, and, at times, depression. The Moon's classic association to our emotional life, when wandering through the OOB realms, puts all of us on notice to be mindful of increased sensitivity to just about everything.

LS149's See-Saw chart pattern temperament demonstrates the need to be able to live within an environment of controversy. The See-Saw has a reputation for manipulation and a taste for self-destructive behavior. Chiron's conjunction to the NNode confirms that this is an eclipse that needs to experience life in all the colors of the rainbow. Do not be put off by the Mars and Saturn reclusiveness and its retrograde allegiance to the rest of the pack. The passing of time brings out the best in the Eclipse/Jupiter-Node midpoint with its capacity to build in great relationships, partners, team members and associates who will want nothing but the best for you.

Closest Midpoints: Uranus/Mars-Jupiter, Eclipse/Jupiter-Node
Isotraps: Moon/Uranus opposition Mercury/Venus
Mercury/Saturn conjunct Venus/Pluto

1900—2100 Eclipses: Lunar Saros—149

1984, 2002, 2020 2038, 2056, 2074, 2092
Length of cycle —1,262 years
Series ends—July 20, 3246

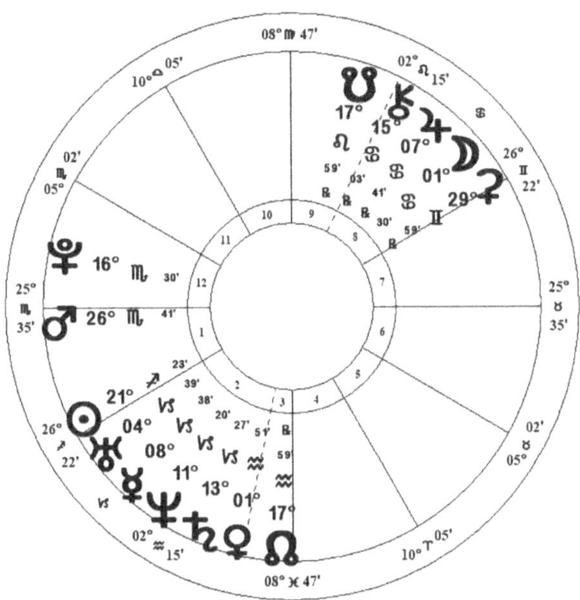

Taylor Swift
PREBLE—LS128

December 13, 1989 • 5:17 AM • West Reading, PA, USA

Industrial Grade American Fame

"If you make something you love, you should just put it out into the world."

-TAYLOR SWIFT

Taylor Swift released her surprise album *Folklore* after abandoning her traditional style and development sequence for rolling out albums, opting for material and a release date based on an intuitive feel for the material and the timing. The album debuted at midnight on July 24, 2020, on her social media platform within weeks of LS149's activation at 13 degrees Capricorn on July 5, 2020.

Taylor Swift's Connections to the Dragons of LS149
Neptune with Neptune

1st Harmonics: Moon – Sun, Jupiter – Mercury/Neptune
2nd Harmonics: Venus – Sun, Neptune – Ceres/Moon

When going for fame, it helps to have a high flying 27 degrees N OOB Moon, along with an OOB Mercury and Uranus in parallel declination. It also helps to have four planets in rulership (Moon, Pluto, Mars, and Saturn) and one in exaltation (Jupiter). Both charts are in Full Moon phase, and both have an almost identical Pluto/Mars phase symmetry. The activation degree fell within minutes of contact to her Saturn and its Capricorn stellium. In lockdown and with her 2020 tour canceled, she let her imagination "run wild" and the result was *Folklore*.[1]

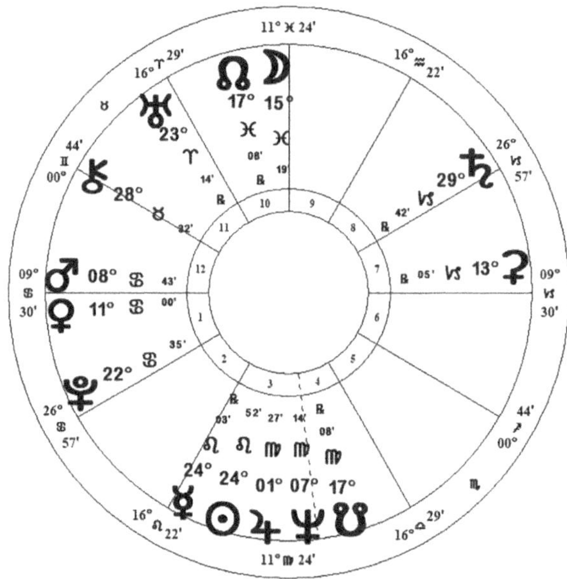

Luc Montagnier
PREBLE—LS131

August 18, 1932 • 2:00 AM • Chabris, France

Nobel Laureate Discoverer of HIV

"I am very puzzled by the fact that young people are getting infected again. They don't take precautions despite an enormous amount of information. It's like riding a race car at 200 kilometers an hour. Some people like the risk."

-Luc Montagnier

Luc Montagnier is a French virologist and joint recipient of the 2008 Nobel Prize in Medicine for his discovery and isolation of the human immunodeficiency virus (HIV) in 1983.[2] His work and that of his colleagues were usurped by a team led by Robert Gallo of the National Cancer Institute (USA) who claimed to have discovered the same virus in 1984. John Crewdson's *Science Fictions—A Scientific Mystery, A Massive Cover-Up, and the Dark Legacy of Robert Gallo* is a fascinating tale of how Robert Gallo falsely claimed to have been the first to isolate the virus.[3]

Luc Montagnier's Connections to the Dragons of LS149

1st Harmonic: Jupiter – Ceres

When LS149 debuted on June 13, 1984, at 23 Sagittarius, there was only a 1st Harmonic from Jupiter to Montagnier's Ceres, which failed to give his role in the research and discovery of HIV any prominence or prestige. It wasn't until LS149 returned eighteen years later in 2002 at 3 Capricorn with links to Montagnier's Mars that his name and role in the discovery of HIV was given full credit, due in large measure to Gallo and Montagnier's articles on the history of AIDS and HIV that appeared in the scientific journal *Science* in November 2002.[4]

LS149's return in June 2002 at 3 Capricorn opened the gate that was to finally allow Montagnier to lay claim to his discovery of a viral cause for AIDS. His Mars at 8 Cancer, its conjunction with Venus on his ASC along with a sweet sextile to Neptune bring the forces of passion and compassion together to be of service to the world. In its sign of detriment, Mars in Cancer is subtle and rarely aggressive; its power is like the tides, eventually wearing down anything in its path. Since 2002 was only the second return of Lunar Saros 149, it stands to reason that this would be the first opportunity to actually see its Boomerang effect in operation. And since the Boomerang contained Mercury in rulership in quincunx to an equally potent Mars in rulership, it seems that the Boomerang's ability to transform turbulence into triumph was responding to something in Montagnier's Mars, helping to set right the error of intellectual aggression that had pervaded its initial appearance in 1984. The 2nd Harmonic activation to his natal Mars again demonstrates the connection between 2nd Harmonics and their capacity to manifest.

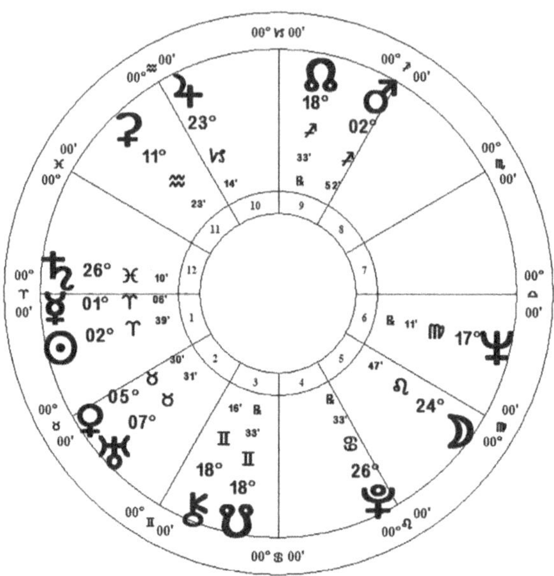

Robert Gallo
PREBLE—LS143

March 23, 1937 • TOB Unknown • Waterbury, CT, USA

Co-Discoverer of HIV

"Bob Gallo is a uniquely disliked person.
He's also uniquely creative and uniquely famous."

-Barbara Culliton

In May 1984, Robert Gallo and his research team published a series of four papers in the scientific journal *Science* that demonstrated that a retrovirus they had isolated, called HTLV-III, was the cause of AIDS.[5] Meanwhile, a French team led by Professor Luc Montagnier had published a paper a year earlier in the same journal in May 1983, describing a retrovirus they had isolated from an AIDS patient.[6] Because Montagnier did not prove that their virus caused AIDS and Gallo's research persuasively if not surreptitiously tied his viruses to the disease, Gallo's name became linked to the discovery of HIV as the virus that caused AIDS.[7]

Robert Gallo's Connections to the Dragons of LS149
↑NNode with SNode↓

1st Harmonics: SNode – Mars,
Moon – NNode, Venus/Sun – SNode, Ceres – Venus
2nd Harmonic: Saturn – Uranus

Look at all his connections! No wonder he got the initial credit, especially with a fully charged Global Gateway. However, that GG created a Cosmic Bridge to Mars, another CB from the Moon to his NNode and an even trickier CB to his SNode. From the start, Gallo's HIV discovery was steeped in controversy and an inquiry into patent and royalty rights was immediately launched.[8] LS149's eclipse axis at 22 Sagittarius set off Gallo's SNode Chiron conjunction and its T-Square to Neptune. On balance, it all looked good but the fly in the ointment was the eclipse 1st Harmonic Ceres to Gallo's Venus that would bring down his house. Ceres holds an opposition to Pluto in the eclipse field and that combination, landing on his Venus/Uranus conjunction, is a recipe for disaster. Certainly, a Ceres/Venus conjunction looks good at first glance, but you have to recognize the company they keep. And then there's the ever reliable 2nd Harmonic Saturn to his Uranus and remember, Saturn is a major player in the karmic quality of a Boomerang.

Pulitzer Prize investigative journalist John Crewdson suggested that what it all came down to wasn't so much which country and team of scientists could claim the glory, but rather it was the lucrative contracts for developing the AIDS blood test that was at the heart of the controversial discovery.[9] In choosing the winner of the Nobel Prize for Medicine in 2008, the Nobel Committee would shun Gallo and honor the work of Luc Montagnier and Françoise Barré-Sinoussi of the Pasteur Institute in Paris for their 1983 discovery that HIV causes AIDS.

News Event!

A National HIV/AIDS Plan 10 June 28, 2002

Within days of LS149's return on June 24, 2002, the Congress of South African Trade Unions (COSATU) tabled a national HIV/AIDS treatment plan in the National Economic, Development and Labor Council (NEDLAC). A key aspect of the plan involved making antiretroviral drugs available in the public health sector for those with HIV, emphasizing that, although the drugs were expensive, the social and economic costs to South Africa of not providing the drugs would be far higher. In contradistinction to the government's strategy of denial of home-based care to HIV/Aids sufferers, COSATU said their plan was aimed at keeping millions alive for longer.

LS149 Summary

Breakthroughs and assistance will surely come your way thanks to this recently arrived family of Fire Dragons. They are eager to experience the thrills and spills of human interaction and social connection. They remind us that meeting people halfway is a sure-fire solution to attracting attention and support. Play fair, be nice, compromise when necessary, but *never* give up hope—it's just a matter of time. And speaking of time, there just never seems to be enough of it now. The patterns play well with anyone working on projects that demand high levels of dedication, discipline, skill, and technical expertise. The ability to focus on a particular area of specialization that requires an extended period of time is one of its great benefits and suits all fields where artistry and research are the key ingredients. It's important to build in more breaks, extended weekends, mini-vacations, and spa dates whenever possible to recharge as your body battery will soon become depleted due to the high-level energy requirements of this field. Whether by birthright or rite of passage, to be in harmony with these "crazy cosmic kids" requires periods of isolation and retreat to recharge, review, and prioritize a growing list of concerns and commitments. Overnight success, the kind that builds up for years, is the glorious reward of this lunar eclipse.

LS149 is experiencing its first New Moon phase until July 2056. Until then, it is awakening to a panoply of opportunities that will come from following one's instincts and happily taking risks.

LS149 Luminaries

Khloé Kardashian	June 27, 1984
Bharti Singh	July 3, 1984
Amanda Hocking	July 12, 1984
Taylor Schilling	July 27, 1984
Luca Patuelli	July 28, 1984

Uriah Hall	July 31, 1984
Ryan Kesler	August 31, 1984
Prince Harry	September 15, 1984
Avril Lavigne	September 27, 1984
Marie Kondo	October 9, 1984
Anton Kushnir	October 13, 1984
Lindsey Vonn	October 18, 1984
Katy Perry	October 25, 1984
Mari Takahashi	November 2, 1984
Milly Shapiro	July 16, 2002
Logan Guleff	July 20, 2002
Hridayeshwar Singh Bhati	September 3, 2002
Xander Zayas	September 5, 2002
Leylah Fernandez	September 6, 2002

1. https://en.wikipedia.org/wiki/Folklore (Taylor_Swift_album). Retrieved May 1, 2017.

2 .http://www.ncbi.nlm.nih.gov/pubmed/12459576. Retrieved August 24, 2013.

3. John Crewdson, *Science Fictions: A Scientific Mystery, A Massive Cover-Up, and the Dark Legacy of Robert Gallo* (Boston: Little Brown & Co. 2003), p. 178.

4. Jon Cohen & Martin Enserink, Science VOL 322 10 October 2008 p. 174-175. www.sciencemag.org retrieved August 24, 2013.

5. Barry Werth, By AIDS Obsessed GQ August 1991. Printhttp://www.virusmyth.com/aids/hiv/bwobsessed.htm. Retrieved Jan 2, 2015.

6. http://history.nih.gov/NIHInOwnWords/docs/page_29.html. Retrieved March 1, 2014.

7. Seth Roberts, Lab Rat-What AIDS Researcher Dr. Robert Gallo did in Pursuit of the Nobel Prize. Retrieved March 1, 20 http://www.virusmyth.com/aids/hiv/srlabrat.htm paragraph 36

8. http://ori.hhs.gov/education/products/unh_round1/www.unh.edu/rcr/Misconduct-Fraud-GoTo2.htm. Retrieved March 1, 2014.

9. Crewdson, *Science Fictions,* p. 301.

10. https://www.sahistory.org.za/dated-event/cosatu-and-tac-table-national-hivaids-plan. Retrieved June 29, 2002.

LUNAR SAROS 150

"I do not want to live in a world where everything I do and say is recorded. That is not something I am willing to support or live under."

-Edward Snowden

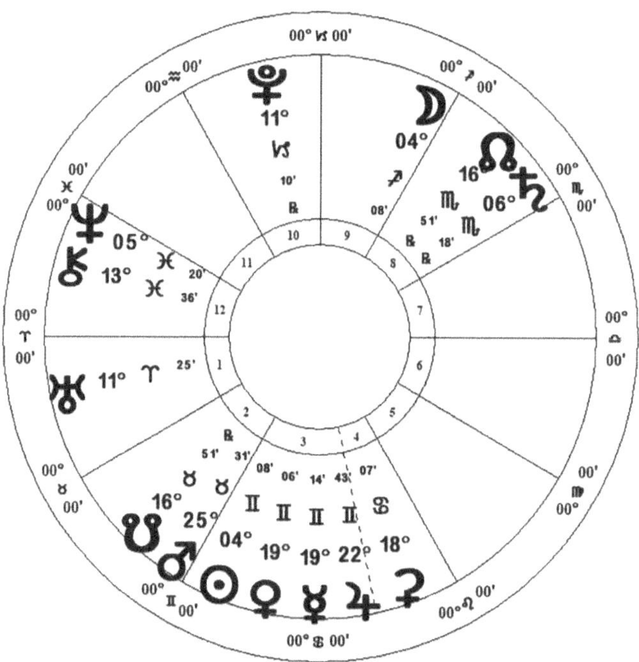

Lunar Saros 150

May 25, 2013 • 4:25:35 AM • North Pole

Be Brave

Lunar Saros Series 150 is currently enjoying its initial *New Moon* phase on a 1,262-year voyage of discovery. The 21st century will see the first six of its seventy-one waves and will conclude with its final lunar eclipse on the distant shores of June 30, 3275.

A climate of social and personal justice emerges from this North Node Sagittarius eclipse as the eclipse axis and its nodal axis resonate to the fourth and sixteenth security degrees. The eclipse axis carries a critical degree resonance that heightens a sense of urgency. Ruler Jupiter in Gemini, an OOB Venus (23N35) and an OOB Mercury (24N57) together create a social media stellium that generates a multiplicity of platforms for the release of information. At the same time, the eclipse axis to Neptune and its Mutable T-Square opens the field to all manner of public and private subterfuge, flagrant deceit and if that wasn't enough, encourages an addiction to information that is almost insatiable.

Pluto's waxing square to Uranus, with both at the eleventh degree favor forward motion; in the fields of AI that unstoppable force of progress is both stunning and down-right scary. It almost feels like an arms race while the Mutable T-Square inculcates a growing mood of apathy in the zeitgeist fueled by an OOB feel-good Venus in parallel declination to Jupiter happy to keep us all entertained. It's been a decade since this Fire Dragon tribe arrived. What is now becoming obvious is the current AI boom and its technology is becoming an "out of control race" to develop ever more powerful and potentially dangerous AI systems that are manipulating our social networks and ability to distinguish fact from fiction.

Since 2015, Nick Bostrom—LS143 (March 10, 1973)—one of the most-cited philosophers in the world, has been voicing concerns over what happens when our computers get smarter than we are. American philosopher and neuroscientist Sam Harris—LS116 (April 9, 1967)—has been voicing concerns for how we build AI without losing control over it for over a decade. His June 2016 TED Talk stands at 6,101,822 views. Harris ends his talk by urging more of us to think about this! And then there's the "godfather of AI," cognitive scientist Geoffrey Hinton—LS144 (Dec 6, 1947)—who says the threat is real. Take a listen to the interview he did with NPR's technology correspondent Bobby Allyn on May 26, 2023. If you aren't scared yet I guarantee you will be after hearing what he has to say. His closing statement is: ". . . these things could get more intelligent than us and could decide to take over. We gotta do something and do it fast!"[1]

Since this is such an obvious information oriented eclipse family, let's give its Moon/Mars opposition Jupiter/Saturn isotrap a crack at the "alignment" problem which is now generating so much tech terror across the globe as mainframe Large Language models (LLMs) are now powering up all AI systems. If we are indeed brave and fearless and understand that there is a deep need for our geopolitics to transcend our current level of functioning, we just might make it. We are exceptional human beings, some of us are extraordinary. If we are to survive and thrive, we must challenge the dictum of the movie *Don't Look Up*, a satire on our current state of affairs, so timely, so prescient. Indeed, we must "Look Up"—and even better, "Look Within" to see that the asteroid coming our way is of our own making and can be unmade if we have the courage to confront our complacency.

Closest Midpoints: Node/Mars-Saturn, Jupiter/Eclipse-Pluto
Isotraps: Moon/Mars opposition Jupiter/Saturn
Mars/Jupiter opposition Saturn/Pluto

1900—2100 Eclipses: Lunar Saros—150

2013, 2031, 2049, 2067, 2085
Length of cycle —1,262 years
Series ends—June 30, 3275

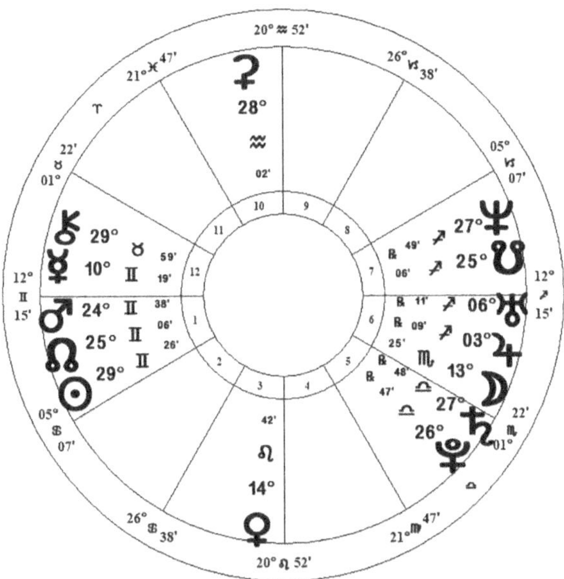

Edward Snowden
PREBLE—LS134

June 21, 1983 • 4:42 AM • Elizabeth City, NC, USA

NSA Whistleblower

"I don't see myself as a hero because what I'm doing is self-interested: I don't want to live in a world where there's no privacy and therefore no room for intellectual exploration and creativity."

-EDWARD SNOWDEN

Simultaneous with the debut of LS150 on May 25, 2013, Edward Snowden was in Hong Kong as the eclipse window opened at 4 Sagittarius on his Jupiter/Uranus conjunction. In an attempt to secure his own safety, he sought out and received asylum in Russia "from charges in absentia of theft and violations of the Espionage Act."[3] Michael Scherer reported for *Time Magazine* that in October 2013, four Americans traveled to Moscow to award Snowden the *Sam Adams Associates for Integrity in Intelligence Award*. Scherer wrote:

> The thing that led him to break the law, the notion that mass surveillance undermines the foundations of private citizenship. In a way, it is the defining critique of the information age, in which data is increasingly the currency of power. The idea did not originate with Snowden, but no one has done more to advance it.[4]

Edward Snowden has a special talent for inducing his own brand of utopian discomfort; with his Sun in opposition to the Neptune South Node Galactic Core conjunction at 26 Sagittarius, Snowden exudes a polarizing force, attracting some and repelling others with equal conviction. Aided by his PREBLE-LS134—The Attractor Factor—Snowden's intrinsic idealism along with some savvy tech acrobatic skills found him high above the swirling storms of controversy.

Edward Snowden's Connections to the Dragons of LS150
Saturn with Saturn

1st Harmonics: NNode – Moon,
Sun – Mercury, Sun – Chiron, Moon – Jupiter/Uranus,
Jupiter – Mars/NNode/Sun, Venus/Mercury – Mars/NNode

Snowden has twelve Ptolemaic links to LS150 with nine connecting in as Cosmic Bridges. The NNode is the star of this show with its timely link to Snowden's Moon while the eclipse Jupiter, Venus, and Mercury links to Snowden's NNode, building in solid ties of support. Three CBs bring the eclipse Sun to his Mercury and Chiron while the final solar CB brings the eclipse Jupiter to his natal Sun. The final two CBs connect the eclipse Moon to Snowden's Jupiter and Uranus.

I was quite frankly stunned to see not only the number of patterns resonating across these two fields but the quality of the links as they indicate what to pay attention to and who is dominating the dance floor. The NNode-Moon as the "first couple" on the floor set the tone for the entire event. Its 16 degree Scorpio nodal axis resonates to the fourth strings of a Cancerian overture which hooks into Snowden's 13 degree Moon in Scorpio and its Moon/Jupiter-Pluto midpoint that is sensitive and willing to respond to the growing power and abuses of a rising plutocracy. From here, the dominos all fall to the touch of LS150's triple OOB Venus, Mercury and Jupiter's conjunction in Gemini as they rally to the cause of truth and their overwhelming need for communication. As noted in earlier chapters, a 1st Harmonic NNode eclipse contact to the Moon is a sure sign that disruption is a daily life event. A 2nd Harmonic comes with a 100 percent guarantee of volatility.

The CBs from the Moon to his Jupiter-Uranus released a sudden and massive outpouring of global information and here is more wisdom from Ebertin on a Jupiter-Uranus alignment:

> At one time, he named this configuration the "Thank the Lord" position because people having such a configuration have repeatedly exclaimed the words "Thank the Lord" after the release of the tension or strain from which they were suffering.[5]

Snowden, Manning, Assange, and many others are all canaries in the coal mine of our collective consciousness. Whether we live well or die tragically is going to depend on our collective responsibility and duty to support a democracy that upholds the rights of the Fourth Estate, surveillance be damned.

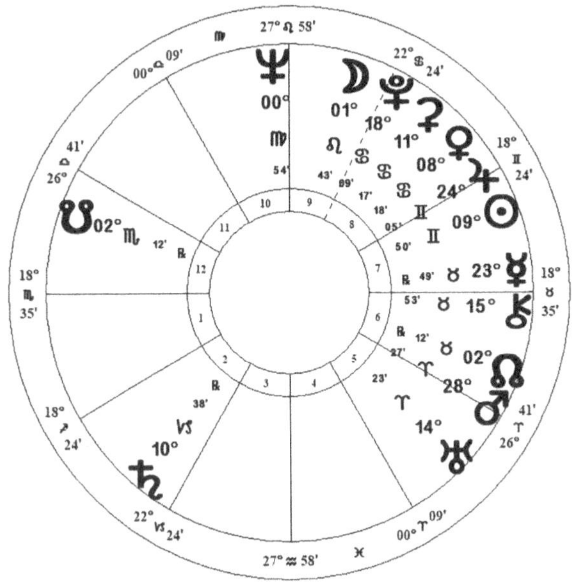

Clint Eastwood
PREBLE-LS111

May 31, 1930 • 5:35 PM • San Francisco, CA, USA

American Sniper —The Movie

"American Sniper disdains war
but honors the people called to serve and fight."
—GLENN WHIPP—LOS ANGELES TIMES

On August 21, 2013, Clint Eastwood accepted an offer from Steven Spielberg to direct Bradley Cooper in *American Sniper,* a screenplay based on Chris Kyle's 2012 *New York Times* bestselling memoir, *American Sniper: The Autobiography of the Most Lethal Sniper in US Military History.* The tragedy of Chris Kyle's life is that after serving four tours in Iraq from 1999 to 2009, and in the process becoming the most legendary SEAL sharpshooter in US history, he was murdered on February 2, 2013, while volunteering with a distressed veteran.

In reality the road from book to movie was an expressway that took an unforeseen turn with the sudden and tragic death of Chris Kyle in February 2013. His bestselling memoir had been quickly optioned by Warner Brothers in 2012, with Spielberg turning the project over to Eastwood in August of 2013.

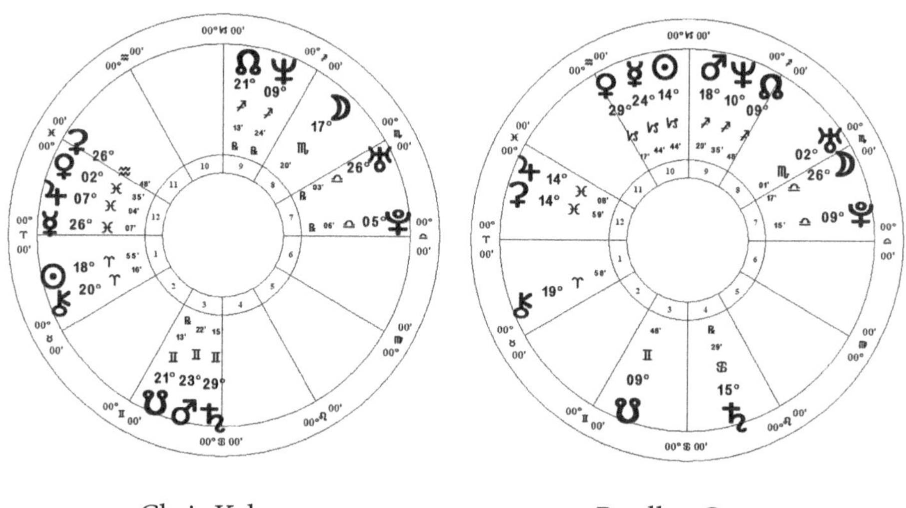

Chris Kyle | Bradley Cooper

April 8, 1974 • TOB Unknown • Odessa, TX, USA | **January 5, 1975 • TOB Unknown • Los Angeles, CA, USA**

Before we consider the impact on Eastwood, Cooper, and posthumously on Chris Kyle from the arrival of LS150 on May 25, 2013, let's take a moment to appreciate them. Since Bradley Cooper played Chris Kyle in the movie, I was impressed by how his NNode at 9 Sagittarius exactly conjuncts Kyle's Neptune and equally impressed by how Cooper's SNode at 9 Gemini sits on Eastwood's

Sun making for a perfect film collaboration. As the producer, Eastwood's Jupiter tightly conjuncts Kyle's Mars while Cooper as the star acts out Kyle's warrior spirit and story with his Mars at 18 Sagittarius in a 2nd Harmonic to Kyle's SNode/Mars conjunction. Additionally, as both star and producer, Bradley Cooper's Chiron at 19 Aries conjuncts Kyle's Sun/Chiron midpoint bringing (some might say channeling) light to the devastation of war with its psychological wounding that resists and more often than not defies the healing process.

Kyle's solar chart holds a See-Saw pattern that tends to attract conflict that forces an individual to choose sides. It is a pattern of contrast that at its best can promote awareness as well as compromise but at its worst, a zero sum game battlefield of winners and losers. Since it generates an abundance of polarities with opposing views, this pattern is often associated with high levels of stress and psychosomatic health issues that, if not addressed, can lead to self-destructive behavior.

The arrival of LS150 would fast-track this project. Space Lanes that even George Lucas would envy emerged as Eastwood's 18 degree Scorpio ascendant aligned with the eclipse nodal axis. In addition, the eclipse activation degree at 4 Sagittarius found Eastwood perfectly positioned as the lunar eclipse set off his Venus/Mars midpoint and a powerful and exact resonance to his Venus/Node midpoint increasing his ability to connect into the multitude of relationships but more importantly the floodgate of feelings that would need to be appreciated and woven into the narrative of the film's story. Equally impressive, Cooper's Venus/Pluto midpoint at 4 Sagittarius opened fully to expose the extraordinary strains and stresses of being in love and doing one's best to keep a relationship and a family together while serving four highly dangerous combat deployments. The evidence is gaining ground with each successive lunar eclipse analysis that midpoint activations may in fact be the most significant contact to factor into any study or review of astrological cycles and in particular, lunar eclipse activations.

News Event!

#Black Lives Matter, June 2013
A Hashtag to Change the World

In 2013, Alicia Garza, Patrisse Cullors, and Opal Tometi created a political and social movement project called #Black Lives Matter.[6] It was birthed in response to the acquittal of Trayvon Martin's murderer George Zimmerman, and seeks to highlight racism, discrimination, and inequality experienced by black people.

Update: July 2020

Black Lives Matter May Be the Largest Movement in U.S. History

According to an article in *The New York Times* that appeared on July 3, 2020, more than half a million people turned out across the United States to join the Black Lives Matter protests on June 6, 2020. Recent polls released by *Civis Analytics* "suggest that about 15 million to 26 million people in the United States have participated in demonstrations over the death of George Floyd and others in recent weeks" making these recent protests, according to interviews with crowd-counting experts and scholars, the largest movement in the country's history.[7]

Social and political change and the willingness to take action to set those changes in motion are the seeds of discontent that have quickly germinated from the arrival of these feisty Fire Dragons unwilling to sit around and be told how to live their lives. In the coming years and under the auspices of this particular celestial family of fire starters, a potentially consequential social change tipping point is just around the cosmic corner.

LS150 Summary

Lunar Saros 150 will have at least seven more incarnations in its New Moon phase to get itself sufficiently sorted and on task. Most assuredly it will stumble and fall but will also grow stronger with each incarnation. It carries the potential to foment spectacular acts of heroism that inspire a willingness in others to stand up for personal rights in the face of oppression.

This Saros Series can release one from conditions of isolation, confinement, sorrow, or suffering. Fearlessness emerges from all walks of life in response to the birth of these exuberant, optimistic, and adventurous Fire Dragons, fresh on the scene in a spirit of openness and compassion. Their potential impact is nothing short of awesome as circles of courage radiate out from their presence. To date, although Lunar Saros 150 is still in its infancy, it may yet prove to be the *enfant terrible* of the lunar eclipse world. There is nothing inconsequential about this family: it carries a powerhouse of curiosity and the courage and endurance to do whatever it takes to get the job done. It is time to up your game and place yourself center stage in the starring role of your life. Heroes and heroines arise as this lunar series promotes freedom, sudden success, expansion, and lucky breaks. As Winston Churchill famously said, "Don't let a good crisis go to waste."

When this family of lunar eclipses activates a personal chart, issues of freedom, justice, and self-interest take on greater significance: don't forsake your own wellness while struggling for the rights of others.. It is essential to enjoy each day as it comes, taking one step at a time. Problems may arise due to an inability to fit in either as a member of a community or as a couple. In either case, breakdowns in relationships are to be expected. Which is why it's important to remember LS150's motto: "Be Brave." An act of fearlessness could change your world.

---

1. https://www.youtube.com/channel/UCNAxrHudMfdzNi6NxruKPLw. Retrieved August 12, 2023
2. https://www.wbur.org/hereandnow/2023/05/26/godfather-ai-warning. Retrieved August 12, 2023
3. Michael Scherer, "Edward Snowden, The Dark Prophet," *Time Magazine,* Dec. 11, 2013. http://poy.time.com/2013/12/11/runner-up-edward-snowden-the-dark-prophet/ Retrieved July 17, 2022.
4. Ibid.
5. Reinhold Ebertin, *COSI*, p. 228.
6. https://blacklivesmatter.com/herstory/ Retrieved June 28, 2022.
7. https://www.nytimes.com/interactive/2020/07/03/us/george-floyd-protests-crowd-size.html. Retrieved July 17, 2022.

LUNAR SAROS 151

"I would like to die on Mars. Just not on impact."

-Elon Musk

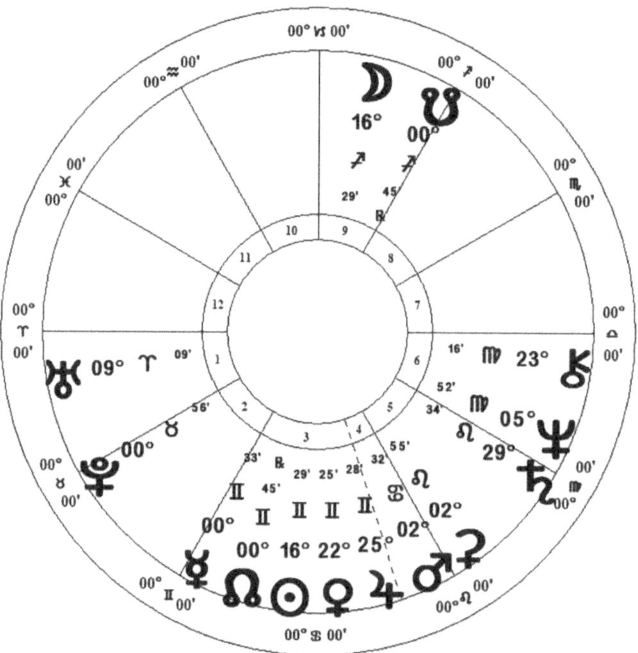

Lunar Saros 151

June 6, 2096 • 2:57:41 AM • South Pole

Off-World

There's no doubt that LS151 is the next iteration spawned from LS150's spectacular seeding of the planet in 2013. The family resemblance is stunning: On momma's side there's 150's Moon to LS151's SNode, but then look at LS150 from papa's perspective and you'll find its Sun in a hearty embrace to LS151's Mercury (like father like son). Then there's its Mercury-Venus connections to 151's Sun-Venus to really bring out the warmth and affection which might need a little chaperoning as 150's Mars is very interested in 151's NNode and, after eighty-three years, both families have a perfect Uranus tie.

Like all Sagittarian families, this is a family made to explore not only terrestrial Earth but also out into the vast expanse of our solar system. AI is now increasing our ability to venture into formerly forbidden zones, and not just any AI. It's what is now referred to as Artificial General Intelligence or AGI, the kind of AI imagined by Elon Musk and Yusaf Harari who wrote that "emotions and desires are in fact no more than biochemical algorithms, there is no reason why computers cannot decipher these algorithms—and do so far better than any Homo sapiens."[1] LS151's NNode-Mercury 00 degree classification is a harbinger of what could be either our greatest leap forward into the next stage of our human evolution or our last hurrah as sentient beings who were outsmarted by our AI creations. Making that even more probable is Jupiter and its conjunctions to an OOB Venus (23N32) and an OOB Mars (24N19).

Jupiter's square to Chiron in Virgo throws down the gauntlet for all levels of global administration to address citizens' and workers' rights in an ever-growing environment of labor, healthcare, and supply-chain disruptions. Adding fuel to the fervor is LS151's singleton OOB Moon (24S10) conjunct the Great Attractor (GA), which undoubtedly will mean that virtually all decisions made by global corporate will impact the day-to-day life of every citizen both on and off-planet. The GA lies in front of the massive gravitational pull of the Shapley Supercluster; since 2006, the use of X-rays have determined that the pull of the Shapley Super-cluster "produces a large-scale flow in which much of the Universe near our galaxy is streaming toward the more massive supercluster"[2] increasing our own vulnerability to the "as above so below" dictum that could well find our entire planet and everything on it being sucked into the gaping black hole of our global elites.

LS151's Nodal Boomerang/Anchor contains the "anything goes" 00 NNode-Mercury (in rulership) at the fulcrum with another, may I add, astonishing 00 infinity degree Pluto in sextile to a detriment Mars at 2 degrees Cancer. The concerns of this sextile are perfectly in tune with the realities of life at the end of the 21st century and address the inescapable Boomerang effect now in play that was seeded back in 2013 through the morphic resonance of its fellow LS150 Fire Dragons.

LS151's Boomerang in the years ahead will bring the fruits of our labors to a world in need of clean water, secure and safe homes, and nutritious food to sustain body and soul. Saturn's proximity to the fixed star Regulus at 1 degree

11 Virgo and in an exact square to NNode-Mercury is a sign of hope but it comes at a price: hard times are ahead while everyone learns how to live in a rapidly shifting world where those who control the resources can name their price. It will take a few returns before these youngsters get a grip on inter-planetary commerce, but they are more than capable of being brilliant. Until such time as they do, we are all going to have to learn to live with higher levels of stress than at any other time in our history as we close out the 21st century.

Closest Midpoints: Eclipse/Mercury-Mars, Venus/Uranus-Neptune
Isotraps: Mercury/Pluto conjunct Venus/Uranus
Sun/Venus conjunct Saturn/Uranus

1900—2100 Eclipses: Lunar Saros—151

2096
Length of cycle —1,262 years
Series ends—July 13, 3358

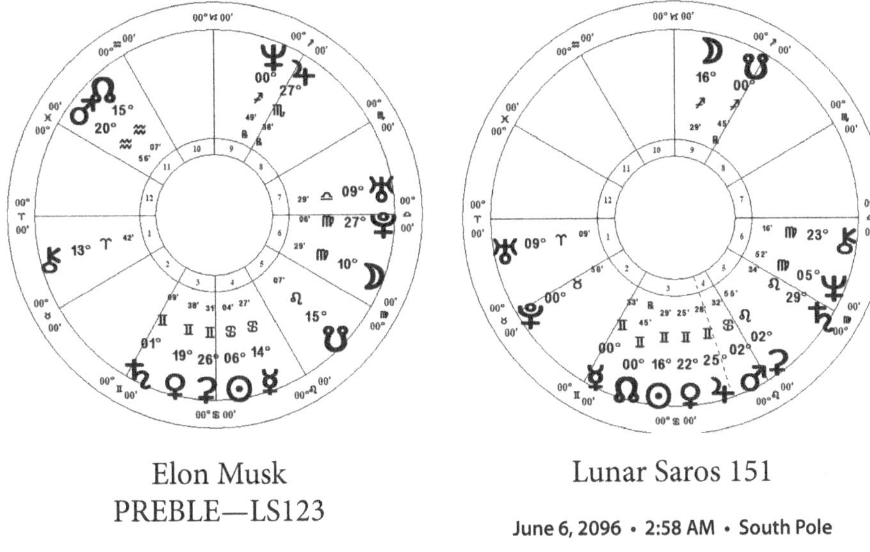

Elon Musk
PREBLE—LS123

June 28, 1971 • TOB Unknown • Pretoria, South Africa

Lunar Saros 151

June 6, 2096 • 2:58 AM • South Pole

With five Cosmic Bridges connecting his energy field to that of LS151, Elon's legacy will be his space exploration conglomerates up and running the commercial interplanetary spaceports by the first decade of the 22nd century. But before that, between 2067 and 2073, our global civilization will finally become an inter-planetary species thanks to his optimistic vision of making mankind a dweller on the space-faring lanes of our solar system.

Elon Musk's Connections to the Lunar Dragons of LS151

1st Harmonics: SNode – Jupiter/Neptune, Mercury/NNode – Saturn, Sun – Venus, Mars – Sun, Venus – Venus, Jupiter – Ceres
2nd Harmonics: Mercury – Jupiter/Neptune, Uranus – Uranus

You have to admit—Elon's got what it takes to not only span the space between Earth and Mars, but quite possibly our neighboring dwarf planet Ceres in the asteroid belt. By the time LS151 arrives, surely his descendants and those who claim him as a mentor or personal guiding star will be heading outward into the solar system, past Mars and across the asteroid belt, on their way to the gas and ice giants Jupiter and Saturn and their many moons which could hold the key to our colonization programs, but more importantly to our future existence.

LS151 Summary

LS151, like LS149 and LS150, is experiencing an opening New Moon phase on its 1,262-year trajectory. This initial seventy-two year phase will be in effect until July 20, 2168, when it will move into its Crescent phase. These are feisty Fire Dragons with a full agenda; they seem to know that a lot is riding on their ability to seed the zeitgeist with a consciousness that is both hopeful and proactive.

Raring to go, these youngsters will settle for nothing less than sheer dazzlement as they stretch the strands of possibility to the next developmental stage. Their presence offers opportunity for those who are solution oriented and unencumbered by the weight of perplexity or a predilection to panic. This family brings the means, might, and motive to push the envelope ever outward, with sparks of creative genius poised to invigorate a global society struggling with ongoing environmental and economic crises.

The greatest difficulty with this new series will come from the domination of the mental realm over the emotional realm. Sociological upheavals and many changes of alliances, both on a global and personal level, do not bode well for a society quickly making the leap to off-planet status. We'll have to wait and see what emotional earthquakes and storms of separation lie on the other side of the 21st century. Meanwhile, when this lunar eclipse family touches down by birthright or rite of passage, expect to see life enhanced by one of the many visionary new technologies that will be rapidly changing lives. This lunar eclipse is a wave of fire that brings higher than normal levels of excitement and intensity that most people will find upsetting if not outright disturbing. But that's the wave that's coming, and we're all going to have to get used to higher temperatures, both figuratively and literally.

---

1. Yuval Noah Harari, *21 Lessons for the 21st Century* (London: Jonathan Cape, 2018), p. 21.
2. https://manoa.hawaii.edu/news/article.php?aId=1308. Retrieved June 30, 2022.
3. Sirius3.0 software The position for Regulus for June 6, 2096 will be 1 degree Virgo 13 minutes.

PART TWO

DANCING WITH EARTH

The Earth Eclipses

"Follow the grain in your own wood."

-Howard Thurman

Unpack your potential. Taking care of business, getting the job done, and going the distance are just some of the phrases that come to mind when hard-working Earth Dragons make an appearance. Though not as flashy or spectacular as their fire cohorts, their presence is an indicator that it's time to roll up your sleeves and get down to solving some of life's pressing problems. The Earth Dragons inhabit a world of consistency that places value on work, deliberation, and self-application. The briefest brush with their energy fields awakens in us a desire to *be* more, *have* more, and *accomplish* more with our lives. These pragmatic lunar eclipse families even take leisure to task as they move heaven and earth in pursuit of their dreams, creating platforms of possibility with every encounter along the way.

These lunar eclipses are as confident as the Fire families; in fact, at times they are much more intense in their exuberance, as their energies unfold through a matrix of physicality. Total commitment to an idea, craft, career, or life purpose is the central pillar from which their particular style of manifestation arises. Just knowing they are about to put in an appearance is often enough to get one back on track and willing to try again. Unlike the fire family of lunar eclipses, a lunar Earth eclipse doesn't even have to activate a planet or midpoint in a chart to get results. Mundane in nature and concerned with earthly realities, a quick look at the house in which it falls will indicate where effort needs to be applied. Rest assured that the exercise of enterprise will not go unnoticed or for that matter unrewarded. These Earth eclipses are masters at generating low-frequency waves of productivity that penetrate deep into the substrate of our material existence. Every return is a fresh opportunity to invest in our well-being.

To work with Earth eclipses is to appreciate and possibly grasp a finer understanding of the value that work provides. In 1832, Thomas Carlyle wrote in *Boswell's Life of Johnson*, that "All work is as seed sown; it grows and spreads and sows itself anew." As a metaphor, it is a poignant force for growth, continually giving rise to opportunities that forge character, consolidate learning, and affirm our true path to wellness and ultimate happiness.

Depending on your perspective, these lunar Earth eclipse fields are hard to ignore. Like a dutiful parent, they show up with a list of chores that need doing.

Putting off or attempting to ignore their presence is a sure sign that even greater tests and tentacles of trouble lie in waiting. It is therefore best to take their arrival seriously and get down to the task at hand. In their midst, single-mindedness is both an honorable and beautiful thing, and all efforts contribute to a fair and equitable accounting. Every act serves to bring one closer to the core essence of what is either blocking or supporting success. The nature of Earth helps to keep us in the realm of the senses. To that end, all Earth eclipses offer opportunities to develop and heighten sensory acuity through our capacity to gain practical efficiency that lightens the load of living in a world bounded by time and space.

The eleven Earth Eclipses are grounded in the muck, mire, and marrow of bottom-line decision making, with each eclipse an exercise in pragmatic and often dramatic acts of dedication under duress. Leading off the eclipses in this section is LS108, a North Node lunar family that was born on July 11, 689 CE. It ran for 1,280 years, incarnating through seventy-two cycles and finished its sojourn across the planet on August 27, 1969. The last lunar eclipse you will discover is Lunar Saros Series 156, an exceptional North Node lunar family that arrives on November 8, 2060. Lasting for approximately 1,442 years, it will unfold through a relatively long cycle of eighty-one incarnations. As one of only two lunar eclipses that carries the Moon in exaltation in the sign of Taurus, it portends significant shifts in the world of global finance.

Once again each lunar eclipse family offers profiles of celebrities, historical events, and individuals that hopefully paint a cosmic portrait of immense complexity, awe, and wonder. Their connectivity is a stunning symbol of synchronicity and a reminder of the astonishing web of life that holds everything in place. These example charts are offered in the spirit of research and only begin to reflect the range and scope of potential in each eclipse family.

The Earth Eclipses define the meaning and wonder of work. Their special dynamic contributes to our resource base and ability to add something of tangible value to the material world. Gravity is the tie that binds these Earth Dragons forever to the hearts and minds of all of us as we experience the full weight of their unfailing sense of form and function in a world of sensual expression.

As with fire eclipses, same sign lunar placements substantially increase the connectivity between an individual or event chart to the eclipse's energy field. The range of influence extends to a ten degree orb of separation. This means that failing to have any 1st or 2nd Harmonic aspects to the foundation chart does not necessarily leave you out in the cold. However, with a combination of either 1st or 2nd Harmonic connections, in addition to a same sign lunar placement, a fertile field of experience awaits.

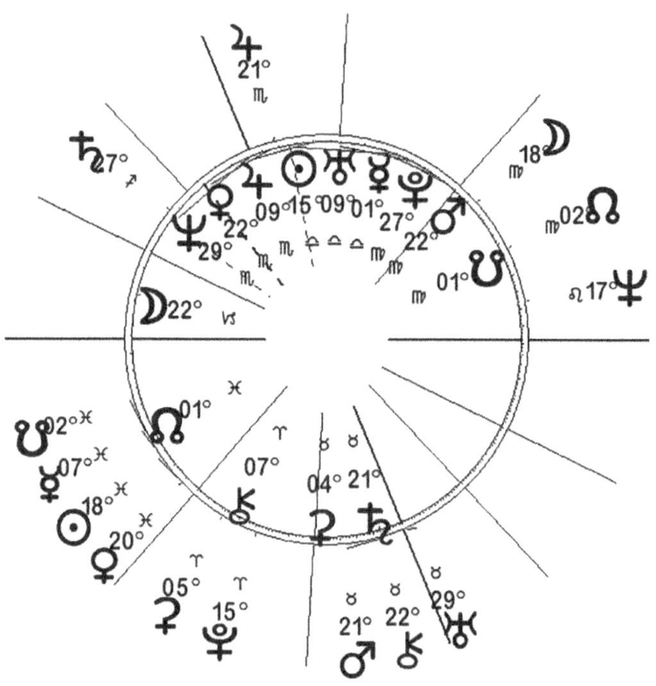

Matt Damon
PREBLE—LS118

October 8, 1970 • 3:22 PM • Boston, MA, USA

Matt Damon's Connections to the Lunar Dragons of LS118
↑NNode with SNode↓

1st Harmonics: Moon – Mars,
Mars – Saturn, Ceres – Chiron, Jupiter – Venus, Chiron – Saturn
2nd Harmonics: Pluto – Sun,
Venus – Mars, Mars/Chiron – Venus, Jupiter – Saturn, Uranus – Neptune

Check out Damon. He's in the 99th percentile of case studies that reflect how awesome life can be when there is both quality *and* quantity of resonance. First and foremost is the Global Gateway, and not just any GG; this nodal axis entanglement has a one degree orb of reversed polarity connection that is pure cosmic power. He also benefits from the results-oriented nature of 2nd Harmonics. Damon receives the mighty eclipse axis to his Mars as well as the eclipse Pluto with all its resources for presentation and leadership to his Sun. For pure chemistry it's hard to beat a Venus 2nd Harmonic to Mars especially when the eclipse field doubles down and provides a Mars 2nd Harmonic to his Venus. There is also a twelve degree conjunction between both Jupiters, which ordinarily would be too wide to consider but since Jupiter returns every twelve years I thought it might be relevant. Either way, Matt Damon is my poster boy for LS118. These alignments allow not only the characteristics of the eclipse field to color his personality but also open him to receive its unique ministrations every eighteen years and especially in the years when the lunar eclipse, advancing through the zodiac by approximately ten degrees, activates his chart.

LS118's energy field in 1988 poured through four degrees Pisces, making it a slam dunk for Damon with his hungry First House Pisces NNode need for self-expression consuming all opportunities on the table. 1988 was the year Damon not only entered Harvard as a theater student but got his first role in the movie *Mystic Pizza*. Its next return in 2006, still in Pisces, touched off his SNode/Mars midpoint and found him in company with Robert De Niro in *The Good Shepherd* and Jack Nicholson in *The Departed*, which won the Academy Award for Best Picture. Such stellar associations would make Damon one of the most bankable movie stars of 2007.

LS118's next appearance will be in September 2024, at twenty-five degrees Pisces opposite his Pluto. I foresee a more erudite and socially focused Matt Damon emerging onto the public stage, communicating an intolerance for the plutocracy that has taken hold of the reins of power.

These eleven lunar eclipses may hold the key that can transform life. Actions and decisions taken under their banner may at first appear negligible, even futile, but don't despair: the smallest of steps will inevitably lead to progress. What matters most, especially during one of their six-month returns, is to remain persistent in any field of endeavor. Allowing yourself a daily dose of purposeful activity will do wonders for your self-esteem; it will reinforce a sense of being useful. Remember, the great gift of the Earth is a certain practical efficiency that permeates our capacity for work. Ultimately, the greatest good that can come from contact with an earthy lunar eclipse is a reconnection to the life of the senses, with its love of bodily pleasure and a renewed interest in creating a safe environment to enjoy.

If you are the lucky bearer of an Earth Moon made for manifestation, pay attention to the following lunar eclipses.

Lunar Saros Series with a Moon in Taurus are rare with only one currently active on the planet until the year 2060.

Lunar Saros 138
Lunar Saros 156

The Lunar Saros Series featuring a Moon in Virgo will be of special interest to anyone with their natal Moon in Virgo.

Lunar Saros 116
Lunar Saros 118

The Lunar Saros Series featuring a Moon in Capricorn will be of special interest to anyone with their natal Moon in Capricorn.

Lunar Saros 108
Lunar Saros 109
Lunar Saros 127
Lunar Saros 128
Lunar Saros 146
Lunar Saros 147
Lunar Saros 148

Earth Dragon Allegiance

Lunar Saros 108
Michael Keaton, Pete Townshend, Roman Polanski

Lunar Saros 109
Oskar Schindler, Google
A Political Sex Scandal—Bill Clinton and Monica Lewinsky

Lunar Saros 116
William Shatner, Jamie Oliver, News Flash! White House Insurrection

Lunar Saros 118
Alexandra Elbakyan, Ralph Nader, Wayne Gretzky

LUNAR SAROS 127
Ingrid Bergman & Tiger Woods, Wernher von Braun,
News Flash! Eisenhower's Military Industrial Complex Speech

LUNAR SAROS 128
Pablo Picasso, Bob Fosse, Alan Turing

LUNAR SAROS 138
Elvis, Jim Henson, The 2008 Financial Meltdown

LUNAR SAROS 146
Larry King, Noam Chomsky, Edith Piaf

LUNAR SAROS 147
H P Lovecraft, J K Rowling, Harry Houdini

LUNAR SAROS 148
Shailene Woodley, Sir Timothy Berners-Lee, Richard Nixon

LUNAR SAROS 156

LUNAR SAROS 108

"There are two kinds of stones,
as everyone knows, one of which rolls."

-Amelia Earhart

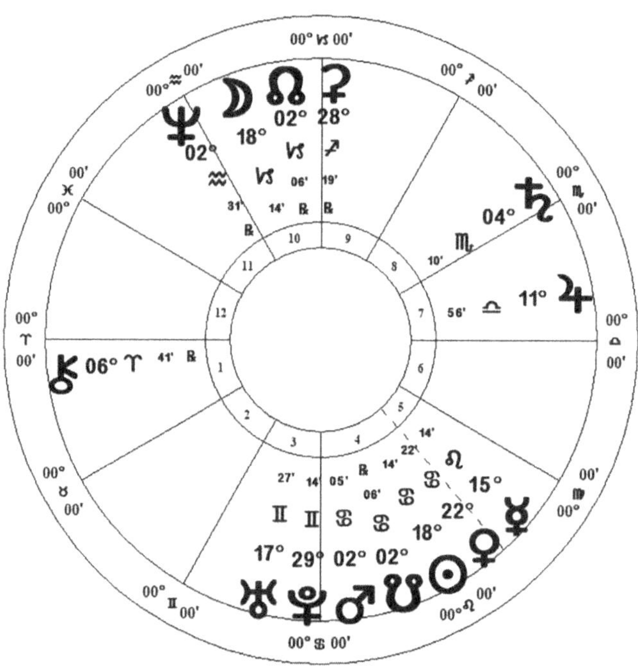

Lunar Saros 108

July 11, 689 • 8:16:15 AM • North Pole

In the Fast Lane

This North Node Capricorn eclipse with ruler Saturn in Scorpio ended its 1,280 year passage from pole to pole in 1969. Of note is the Moon's presence at the apex of a Boomerang; the Sun sits at the fulcrum with Venus, giving all born or blessed by this lunar family a leg up on likability, regardless of a multiplicity of behaviors and personality quirks that might be running the show. And quite the show it is as any luminary on the list will attest to, thanks to the Sun, Pluto, Venus, and Uranus all within less than a one degree parallel declination line-up. This powerful declination is rare and is a pattern associated with many life-altering and often tragic events in the life.

As dispositor of the Sun, many reversals but also opportunities can be leveraged by this extremely savvy Moon in Capricorn that knows instinctively how to right oneself after taking a tumble. Holding strong at the eighteenth degree, its Virgo overlay gives it serious sensibility that only adds to its ballast and ability to work out and work on any differences. Even in free-fall, this lunar family always seems to land unscathed and like a cat with nine lives, survives to live another day.

LS108's Moon/Mars conjunct Uranus/Neptune isotrap carried a distinct note of danger—many individuals would cross paths with accidents, injuries, and often bizarre circumstances that had elements of violence woven within. The best outcomes for this lunar eclipse would revolve around strengthening one's internal system of security. Feeling marginalized would often be the catalyst triggering a quest to leave the past behind in search of a brighter and more hopeful future.

The Uranus/Mercury sextile is one of the best features of this eclipse field: it adds a cheerful and genuine sense of *joie de vivre*. Even with its quincunx to the Moon at the apex of the Boomerang, there is no shortage of self-reliance and originality going to waste as the sextile just keeps on giving. Thanks to the Sun securing the critical fulcrum position, whatever taste for rebellion and distaste for conformity emerged, the stage was set for ingenious solutions that showcased an individual's readiness for action at a moment's notice. The ability to shift gears and change lanes is a feature of this family that just gets better with time; it reflects a heightened sensitivity and ability to adapt to the ever-changing rhythms of the natural world.

Pluto at the prophetic 29th degree of Gemini would have offered a secret blessing or some form or style of a safety net especially with its 2nd Harmonic to Ceres. An often uncanny ability to be able to pick-up on future trends and to feel guided comes with contact to this lunar eclipse. Knowing without knowing seems to be one of their most remarkable gifts. The Pluto/Mars/SNode conjunction in trine to Saturn in Scorpio probably has a lot to do with this power to "cheat death" as Mars in Cancer is in its fall; a very weak placement for Mars which, in this case, should be applauded. Were Mars in exaltation, it would be an entirely different story, with tears for the telling. Apart from a noted volatility, the midpoints offer companionship and agreeableness along with the power to succeed.

Closest Midpoints: Jupiter/Venus-Node, Venus/Mercury-Pluto
Isotraps: Moon/Mars conjunct Uranus/Neptune
Mercury/Jupiter conjunct Venus/Saturn

1900—2100 Eclipses: Lunar Saros—108

1915, 1933, 1951, 1969
Length of cycle—1,280 years
Series ended—August 27, 1969

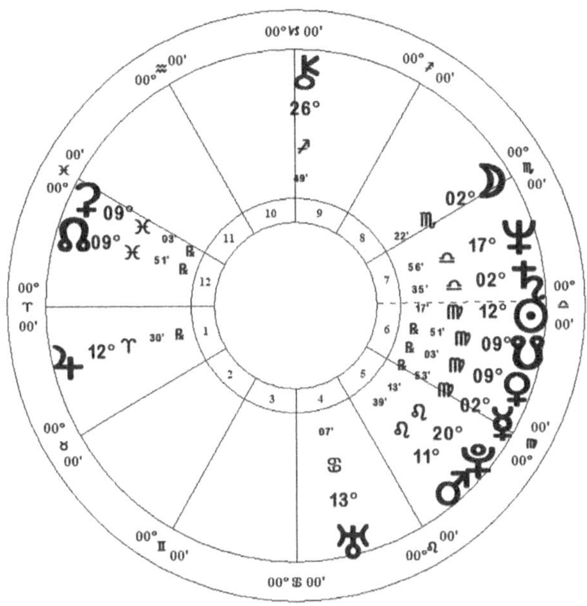

Michael Keaton
PREBLEs—LS108 & LS146

September 5, 1951 • TOB Unknown • Coraopolis, PA, USA

From Batman to Birdman

"There comes a point in your life when you realize how quickly time goes by, and how quickly it has gone. Then it really speeds up exponentially. With that, I think you start to put a lot of things into context; you start to see how huge the world is, and really, the universe."

-Michael Keaton

There is nobody like Michael Keaton. His non-stop intensity and quirkiness make him a true American treasure. Keaton brings the joy, whether from his comedic work in the early '80s or through the Batman years of the late '80's and early '90's. His work in *Birdman* in 2014 was intensely breath-taking and no matter what he does, he exudes a defiant yet authentic spirit of independence.

Michael Keaton's Connections to the Dragons of LS108

1st Harmonic: Ceres – Chiron
2nd Harmonics: Moon – Uranus, Jupiter – Jupiter, Pluto – Chiron

The lunar eclipse axis falls right on his Uranus. That's exciting because the eclipse Sun and its posse of planets is a powerhouse of emotional energy and when all that energy gets linked up to his Uranus, well—it ignites an already sizzling planet in sextile to his Sun. Now we can see there is a shared Sun/Venus conjunction within four degrees in each field giving an added boost to his natal Venus which also happens to hold its SNode in tight embrace. Further, that 1st Harmonic contact to his Uranus now pulls in not only his Sun/Venus/SNode but also his Ceres/NNode conjunction in Pisces. Of all the placements where Ceres could be most at home for anyone involved in the movie industry, Ceres in Pisces has to be right up there in top spot. Certainly, the greatest movie and film critic of all time, Roger Ebert, who is profiled in the Water Dragons of LS114—Carried by the Tide (see Part Four)—has Ceres at the 29th degree of Pisces. Not only conjunct the AP but on the intuitive if not prophetic twenty-ninth degree.

And speaking of Ceres, it's right on Keaton's Chiron. As already stated in the introduction, Ceres holds Pluto in her spell and can offer Keaton her safety net of prophetic wisdom if not timely action. Ceres in Sagittarius is an almost religious experience and in resonance to Chiron could be one of the greatest gifts he receives from his dragon family.

The eclipse Moon's 2nd Harmonic to his Uranus is the commander-in-chief aligning its forces to be ready at a moment's notice to do her bidding. Having an eclipse Boomerang at your fingertips isn't an easy call, but Keaton seems to be managing well. His career has spanned decades and he's still going strong; as of 2023, he's 72 years young and locked in to film projects for many years ahead. And that might be thanks to his 2nd Harmonic from Jupiter to his Jupiter, always giving him something to be grateful for and he seems to be very grateful. Here's a quote that really speaks to this harmonic:

> I'm just shocked and thankful that I've gotten away with everything-experimenting here, trying at this, failing at that, being good in some things, not so good in others. It's kind of amazing that people are still sticking by me. When they come up to me in the street, I just want to write them all cheques.[1]

The last 2nd Harmonic that Michael Keaton enjoys is LS108's Pluto to his Chiron. This contact has a touch of immortality about it and can be felt in Keaton's intense if not obsessive devotion to whatever he sets his mind to accomplish. He has been out of the game and then gotten back in and he never looks the worse for any wear and tear. Hopefully his work will continue to be a source of delight as he seems to thrive in the fast lane of life, intensely ever present, fully occupying each moment while being a great example of how to be authentically alive.

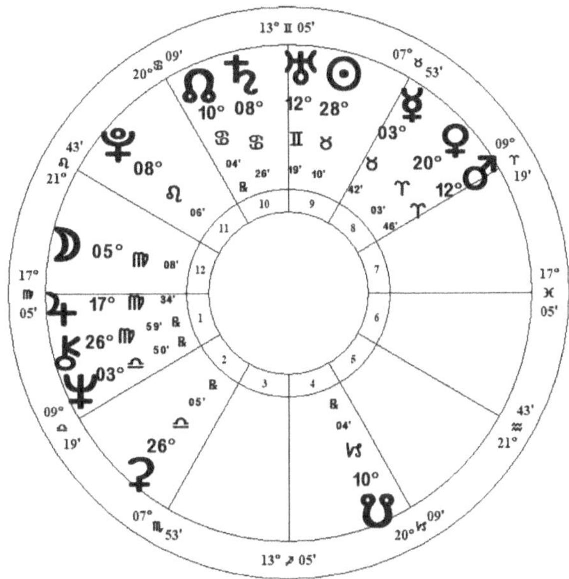

Pete Townshend
PREBLE—LS114

May 19, 1945 • 3:00 PM • London, UK

Guitarist, Composer, Librettist, Rock Star

"See me, feel me, touch me, heal me."

-Pete Townshend

Peter Townshend is known primarily for his electrifying on-stage performances with *The Who* that rocketed him to fame in the 60's, scoring a hit in 1965 with

The Who's "My Generation." *Times* pop music critic Sean Daly reviewed Townshend's 2012 memoir *Who I Am* and wrote that "Townshend's pervasive disenchantment was integral to the Who, which blended counterculture rage and pop hooks, labyrinthine lyrics and theatrical stagecraft."[2] Their legacy rests not only on their rock operas but on Townshend's explosive and signature guitar-smashing antics onstage.

By August 1969, Townshend was already enjoying rock star fame; as the creator of the rock opera *Tommy*, Townshend was at the forefront of pop music's evolution as a force of social change. Agreeing to perform at what would turn out to be the rock event of the 20th century—the Woodstock festival—proved to be exceedingly timely and hugely fortuitous, in large measure due to the release in 1970 of Mike Wadleigh's movie *Woodstock*. Townshend wrote in his memoir that their Woodstock performance "would elevate us into American rock aristocracy, where we would remain year after year, even into the twenty-first century."[3]

LS108's activation on August 27, 1969, at four Pisces lit up Townshend's Twelfth House Moon at five degrees Virgo. In trine to a musical Mercury in Taurus (ruler of the Tenth and in sextile to his elevated Saturn in Cancer, this eclipse triggered Townshend's spectacular *Quadrophenia* Sun/Uranus=Neptune/Pluto lunar midpoint, resplendent in its capacity to generate excitement, intensity and soulful sensation.

Pete Townshend's Connections to the Dragons of LS108
↑North Node with South Node↓

1st Harmonics: Uranus – Uranus/MC
2nd Harmonics: Saturn – Mercury, Chiron – Neptune

Townshend's ties to the rhythms of LS108 could never be in doubt as seen through his dynamic nodal power cords that create a highly charged opposite polarity Global Gateway. When you have this, like Matt Damon or Spielberg, you don't have to spend any time waiting in line. And the excitement would have been electrifying as the eclipse field's Uranus made contact to both his MC and Uranus. Additionally, LS108's Saturn and Chiron 2nd Harmonics would have made major contributions to his success in the summer of 1969.

Although the Chiron square to the Mars/SNode was not highlighted in the introduction, nevertheless it contributes moderate to high levels of excitement, a love of new experiences, along with a tendency to relocate either on a national or international basis. Enjoying a change in pace can be both refreshing and completely frustrating and all at the same time; Chiron's capacity to learn from its failings and flaws will continually set into motion the Mars/SNode capacity to demonstrate its tenacity in the face of danger. Great care needs to be exercised when dealing with hostile environments, especially on a domestic scene as the Mars/SNode has accumulated lifetimes of pent up energy that is in the process of being released. At the highest levels of manifestation, the square is a solid source of vibrancy; its courage is the fuel that enables us to chase down our goals.

Lastly, Saturn's role in the eclipse field comes mainly from its square to Neptune. It's a Last Quarter Square that adds a touch of melancholy, introversion, and a need to continually be re-evaluating one's worth. What is noteworthy between the two fields is that both of them carry the same Neptune/Saturn phase angle symmetry reinforcing a predilection for profound reorientation to self and one's society. In reading his autobiography, it came as no surprise to me to discover that he had planned to write his memoir when he was only 21 years old.[4] And it all makes sense when you know that his PREBLE-LS114—Carried By The Tide—is one of the gentle, old-soul varieties that pretty much follow the dictates of their own personal tastes and interests, regardless of the trials and tribulations that come their way.

Townshend's encounter with LS108 came as this lunar eclipse was taking its last bows and enjoying its final curtain call. On the stage of life, LS108 had had a magnificent run with seventy-two high-energy performances that had spanned almost thirteen centuries. And as one would verily predict, they went out with a roar.

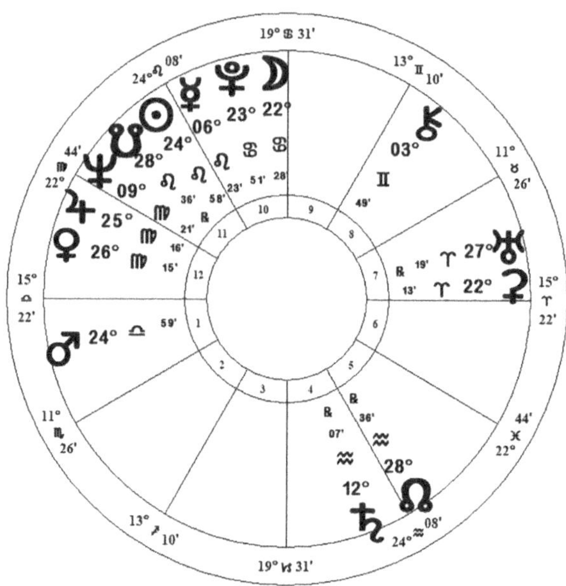

Roman Polanski
PREBLEs—LS108 & LS146

August 18, 1933 • 10:30 AM • Paris, France

Sex, Fame, and Films in the Fast Lane

"Human life is just a given series, an endless series of such moments."

-Roman Polanski

In the world of cinema, Polanski is one of its most celebrated film directors. From 1962 to 2005 he produced some of the finest films ever made in Hollywood including: *Rosemary's Baby, Chinatown,* and the Oscar-winning *The Pianist.* His films are works of art and his genius cannot be denied nor can the central theme of sexuality that runs throughout them and his real life relationships with women, especially younger women.

Polanski, however, is also one of the world's most controversial figures with a life overflowing with tragedy. He survived the Holocaust as a child in war-torn Nazi Poland and emigrated to the U.S. He would become a legendary film director and producer, part of a glamorous Hollywood lifestyle—but one that had its dark side: his pregnant wife Sharon Tate was brutally killed in the horrific Manson murders, and he himself faced numerous sexual assault charges. Finally, he was exiled from the U.S.

Roman Polanski's Connections to the Dragons of LS108
Space Lanes via IC/MC
Mercury with Mercury

1st Harmonics: Sun – Moon, Venus – Moon
2nd Harmonics: Mercury – Saturn, Moon – Moon

The first thing to notice are the Space Lanes running through Polanski's Fourth and Tenth House cusps, an indicator of extreme volatility that would have permeated every aspect of his early life, setting the stage for a career emblematic of high-frequency disruption. Then there is his 1st Harmonic Cosmic Bridge links from the Sun and Venus to his Moon immersing his soul in a celestial cauldron of creative chaos. Polanski's Cardinal T-Square Moon in rulership with its conjunction to Pluto would be a continual source of emotional upheaval, attracting everything from marvel to mayhem to madness. Polanski would have been born with a deep sense of empathy, compassion, and the ability to respond well to another person's feelings. But with Venus it is different; her parallel declination posse of the Sun/Pluto/Uranus are not that interested in people's feelings. In fact, Venus can be quite callous, with a well-deserved reputation for wreaking havoc in her wake. What Venus is all about is value and here Venus gives, through her eclipse Jupiter/Venus-Node midpoint, a generous and optimistic voice to bring talented people together to work in an international environment of cooperation. Polanski's problems, pain, and persecution, especially regarding his relationships with women, can be clearly seen through his Venus–Moon 1st Harmonic.

Polanski's Mercury–Saturn 2nd Harmonic is thankfully a huge relief as its Mercury/Uranus sextile from the eclipse field brings all of its *joie de vivre*, heterodoxy, and ingenuity to work every day to serve his proactive, organized, and very brave Saturn in Aquarius.

You can't have a 1st Harmonic Sun–Moon without its complimentary Moon–Moon 2nd Harmonic. As it plays out in the life of Polanski it is pure tragedy and reminiscent of the myth of Sisyphus. According to the Greek myth, Sisyphus is condemned to roll a rock up to the top of a mountain, only to have the rock roll back down to the bottom every time he reaches the top. It is pure hell, and you have to wonder what keeps him coming back for more.

LS108 Summary

"Hurry up and seize the day" was the clarion call of this determined family of ambitious Earth Dragons, fully formed and informed enough to deal with all manner of obstacles, opposition, and limitation. Their presence was often linked to a communal sense of achievement that proved to be a catalyst for societal change, often accompanied by acts of extraordinary vigor, innovation, and ambition. Advances in education and the arts flourished from their timely returns along with a renewed sense of self-confidence and hope.

To be born under their birthright was one thing, but to experience their field of mayhem, might, and imagination on one of their many returns would have been a celestial event worth waiting for. When this family of lunar eclipses stimulated a personal chart, it brought a high degree of ruggedness, courage, and a pioneering spirit to bear on any task at hand. It also brought with it despair, depression, and loneliness, particularly for those increasingly at odds with the values and pace of societies rapidly modernizing, eager to discard the old for the new. Every return would have driven the nail deeper, setting into motion a profound reorientation to oneself and to one's society.

To be in harmony with these innovators was, and still is, like Sisyphus: a never-ending, uneasy task to manage, but any efforts would have brought instant returns on any investment of time, talent, or more likely, trouble. There is a sense of greater understanding that emerges from these wise old Earth Dragons that only comes as they turn the corner for home. It's in the final stretch, the last mile, the last challenge accepted and fulfilled that we can see how it all ends. It seems to have something to do with eloquence, self-confidence, and an awareness that no matter how fast time is speeding by, we can only fully live one moment at a time.

Phase	Return	Year
Last Quarter	59th	1735
Balsamic	63rd	1807
New Moon	67th	1879
Crescent	72nd	1969

LS108 Luminaries

Raphael	April 5, 1483
Walter Scott	August 15, 1771
Giuseppe Garibaldi	July 4, 1807
Camillo Golgi	July 7, 1843
William James Mayo	June 29, 1861
Lucy Burns	July 28, 1879
Amelia Earhart	July 24, 1897
Enid Blyton	August 11, 1897
Charles Hard Townes[E3]	July 28, 1915
Kunio Toda	August 11, 1915
Warren Avis	August 4, 1915
Jerry Falwell, Sr.	August 11, 1933
Roman Polanski	August 18, 1933
Tom Skerritt	August 25, 1933
Conway Twitty	September 1, 1933
Mark Harmon	September 2, 1951
Michael Keaton	September 5, 1951
Chrissie Hynde	September 7, 1951
Gerald Stano	September 12, 1951
Cesar Millan[E]	August 27, 1969
Jason Priestley[E1]	August 28, 1969
Keith Flint	September 17, 1969

PREBLE—141
Cesar Millan
Jason Priestley
Charles Hard Townes

---

1. https://www.brainyquote.com/authors/michael-keaton-quotes. Retrieved April 3, 2022.
2. Sean Daley. Review: Pete Townshend "Who I Am" gloomy yet addictive http://www.tampabay.com/features/books/review-pete-townshend-memoir-who-i-am-gloomy-yet-addictive/1259585. Retrieved April 4, 2022.
3. Pete Townshend, *Who I Am A Memoir* (Toronto: HarperCollins Publishers, 2012), p. 181.
4. Townshend, *Who I Am,* from the cover jacket.

LUNAR SAROS 109

"The only difference between the saint and the sinner is that every saint has a past and every sinner has a future."

-Oscar Wilde

Lunar Saros 109

July 1, 736 • 10:02:56 PM • South Pole

Virtue and Vice

After a globe-rounding run of 1,262 years, this South Node Capricorn eclipse made its final appearance on August 8, 1998. It fomented obsession and personality patterns that created immense internal dissonance. The scale of difficulties depended on how much of an appetite one had for status and security as the eclipse held an enormous Grand Earth Trine. Pluto and fellow Grand Trine members Neptune and Uranus would never settle for second best, even when faced with hardships. In fact, the harder life got, the more unpredictable and obsessive these players became.

Problem-solving skills were one of the many talents all members of this clan possessed. Their "irritation index" was always set to high alert, giving them plenty of opportunities to practice their de-escalation techniques (if they chose to do so). Dialogue and repartee would have been both annoying and astounding as the eclipse Grand Earth Trine was always in perpetual motion. And that seems odd for planets in Earth signs, but it is the combination of Pluto, Neptune, and Uranus that provide an inexhaustible source of motivation along with an indefatigable spirit that never, *ever* quits. Conflict be damned, these folks power on. All such Grand Trines are resource rich and able to withstand a multitude of incursions against their shores. Noel Tyl refers to the Grand Trine phenomenon as a "closed circuit" of self-sufficiency.[1] Working together, these three outermost planets provided a clearly defined beachhead that served the cause of promoting wealth and internal security.

Pluto's square to the nodes single-handedly created an environment of constant, unmitigated tension; vacillating from one extreme to the other, ideas and values would have been in a constant state of flux. This was great for teachers, academics, and writers such as Oscar Wilde, whose urbane and unabashedly brilliant writings urge all of us to simply "Be yourself; everyone else is already taken."

The North Node/Mars conjunction with its connection to Venus has a deep hunger for relationship. However, all North Node contacts are still learning how to manage that style of behavior and thus many born under this eclipse would have found crises in relationships a recurring theme. This is aggravated by an OOB Mars (24N06) as well as an OOB Moon (24S41) and both are in contra-parallel declination giving them a "love 'em and leave 'em" attitude. The North Node/Mars conjunction in square to Jupiter at 29 Virgo reflected shifts in leadership, brought on by societies eager to embrace a fresh perspective. LS109 had the potential to bring both intuition and a clarity of mind to the table to deal with a myriad of complexity and permutations.

Delving into Lunar Saros 109 finds the Jupiter/Pluto midpoint to Mars perfectly summed up in Ebertin's COSI as: "Organizing talent, ability to inspire others with enthusiasm, [and] desire to achieve great things."[2] This skill was possible for so many members of the family, especially with Jupiter at the critical and intuitive 29th degree in Virgo in opposition to Ceres at the 29th degree of Pisces. The great Serbian astrologer Nikola Stojanovic's theories on how Critical Degree Theory works is an outstanding contribution to astrological analysis. His research on the 29th degree encourages all of us to make better use of its intuitive capabilities. Here Jupiter gets not only intuition but admirable luck, and that made a world of difference for this eclipse.

Closest Midpoints: Mars/Jupiter-Pluto, Saturn/Eclipse-Neptune
Isotraps: Sun/Venus conjunct Saturn/Pluto
Moon/Uranus opposition Mercury/Mars

1900—2100 Eclipses: Lunar Saros—109

1908, 1926, 1944, 1962, 1980, 1998
Length of cycle —1,262 years Series ended—August 8, 1998

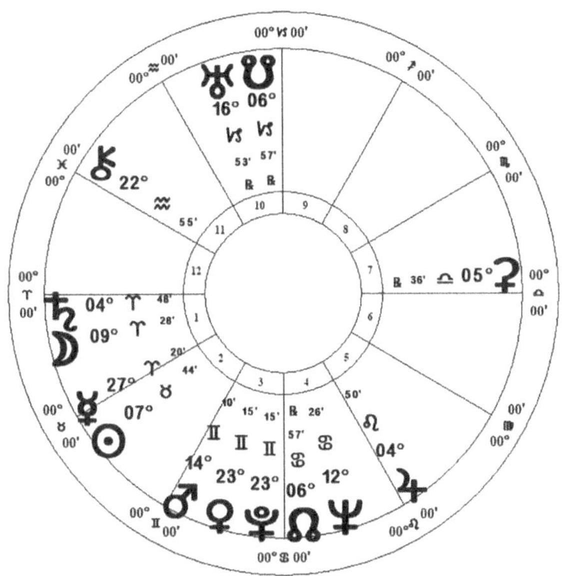

Oskar Schindler
PREBLE—LS142

April 28, 1908 • TOB Unknown • Svitavy, Czech Republic

"I am the conscience of all those who knew something-but did nothing."

Gambler/Guardian/Righteous Gentile

"Beyond this day, no thinking person could fail to see what would happen."

-Oskar Schindler

Oskar Schindler is one of history's most enigmatic figures and known the world over thanks to Thomas Keneally's prize-winning 1982 novel that became the basis for Spielberg's Oscar-winning movie, *Schindler's List*. Twenty-five years later, in 2007, Keneally wrote *Searching for Schindler*, the fascinating story behind the movie. In it, he described how Spielberg shared his interest in "the ambiguity of Schindler, the balance between opportunism and human compassion, [and] the fact that no one could tell where one ended and the other began."[3]

Schindler's remarkable life story takes a critical turn in the summer of 1944, hard on the heels of LS109's arrival on July 6 at fourteen degrees Capricorn. It was during this period that he began making plans to relocate and make a second camp in Czechoslovakia after his enamelware plant was closed in Krakow, Poland.[4] As the lunar eclipse activated his Uranus/Neptune opposition, the collective need to serve others, particularly with Neptune conjunct the NNode in Cancer, would have stirred his instinctive response to matters that represented protection and emotional security.

Schindler's natal Uranus at 16 Capricorn is a fascinating study, as it is the funnel on his Fan planetary pattern from which everything else flows. The Fan's objective seeks out and uses the resources of others for personal gain or achievement, and Schindler's life is a testament to this chart pattern psychology. The Fan's perfect 120 degree trine between Jupiter and Saturn contributed to his compelling presence and ability to get what he wanted, no doubt aided by the power of his lunar eclipse family LS142—There Be Dragons—to recognize the moment when it arrives. With the old order collapsing around him and revolution on the horizon, the arrival of LS109 opened a gateway to virtues within Schindler that had long lain dormant. As a member of the Nazi party, liberation and freedom were not just words to Oskar Schindler. His unshakable strength and personal generosity were to make a difference in the lives of over twelve hundred human beings who were spared and saved from the human suffering and atrocities that were the Nazi death camps.

Oskar Schindler's Connectors to the Lunar Dragons of LS109
Mars to Mars

1st Harmonics: Sun – NNode, NNode – Pluto, NNode – Venus,
Mercury – Jupiter, Mars – Venus, Mars – Pluto, Saturn – Mars, Uranus – Uranus
2nd Harmonic: Venus – Chiron

The hereditary indicators linking Lunar Saros 109 and Schindler are everywhere: there are no fewer than eight conjunctions between them and all within less than one degree of exactitude, creating an extraordinary field of resonance. From LS109's ruler Saturn at 14 Gemini conjunct Schindler's Mars at 14 Gemini to LS109's retrograde Uranus at 16 Capricorn conjunct Schindler's retrograde Uranus at 16 Capricorn, the underlying familial characteristics are unmistakable, qualifying him as a direct descendant. With so many 1st Harmonics plus an extraordinarily powerful Uranus to Uranus connector within *four minutes* of exactitude, Schindler was able to take advantage of a literal avalanche of momentum; in the process he saved lives and created legacies that will live on, even as the lifespan of these dynamic dragons as well as his own have come and gone.

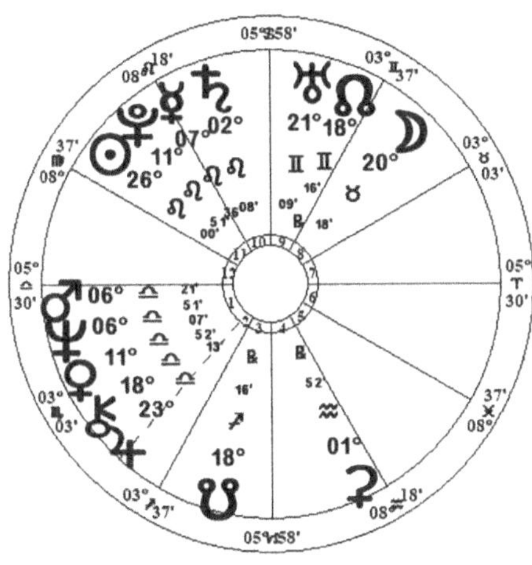

Bill Clinton
PREBLE—LS129

August 19, 1946 • 8:51 AM • Hope, AR, USA

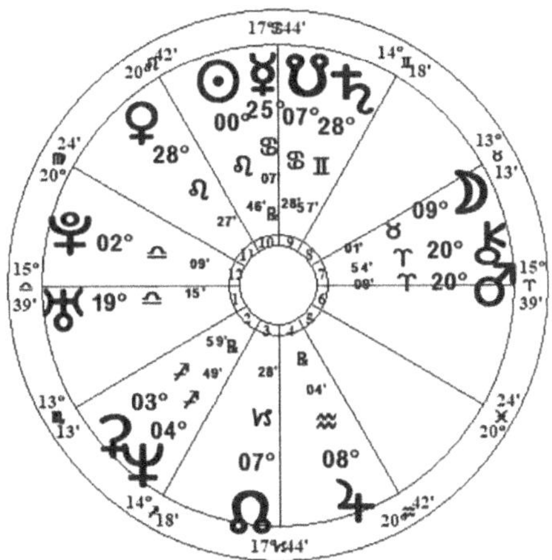

Monica Lewinsky
PREBLEs—LS148 & LS110

July 23, 1973 • 12:21 PM • San Francisco, CA, USA

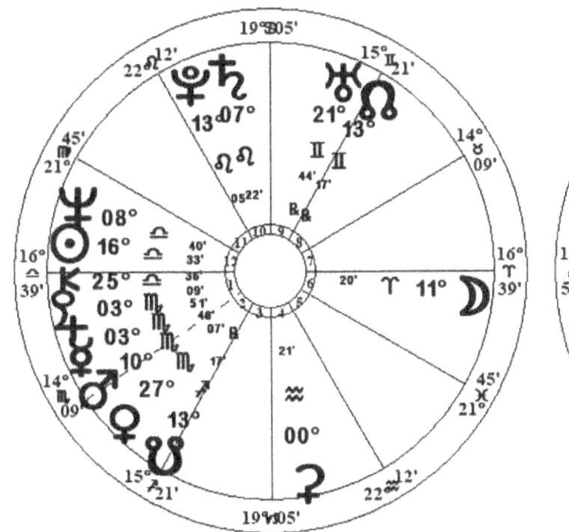

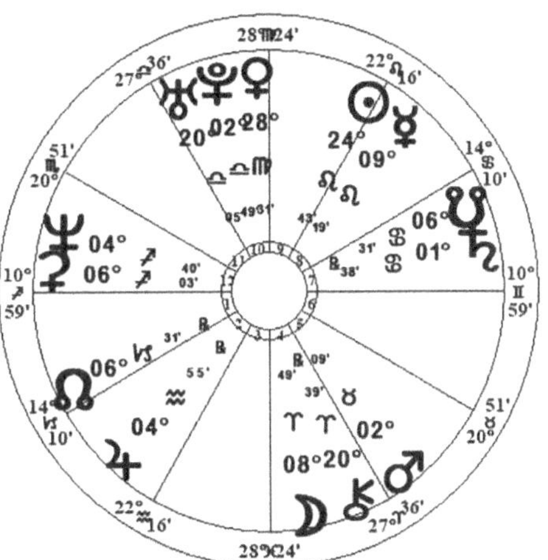

Clinton and Lewinsky Grand Jury Testimony

Progressed Charts for Clinton (left) and Lewinsky (right) on August 17, 1998

A Political Sex Scandal

"I did not have sexual relations with that woman, Miss Lewinsky."

-President Bill Clinton

"We spent hours on the phone talking," Lewinsky told the grand jury investigating the case. "It was emotional. … I thought he had a beautiful soul. I just thought he was just this incredible person and when I looked at him I saw a little boy … ."[5] With identical signs on every house cusp, his Sun on her Venus, his Venus on her Libran ascendant, and with both Moons in Taurus, for sure their attraction was real. Add in Pluto: hers on his ascendant and his Mars/Neptune on her Pluto and violà—passion. Prince Andrew's sex scandal (Part Three) that rocked the world in the spring of 2022 would result in Virginia Giuffre winning her case against him with the help of LS126—Game Changers—and their SLs falling on their identical 11 degree Leo ASC.

The lunar dragons last return on August 8, 1998, at 15 Aquarius landed on Monica's natal Sun/Venus midpoint. Clinton received the lunar activation as an opposition to his Pluto. His progressed Moon at 11 Aries was exactly opposing his natal Venus and had crossed his Seventh House cusp at the first public disclosure of the scandal in January. Monica's progressed Moon made the opposition to her Pluto in January at the first disclosure. Notice Clinton's progressed Moon coming off an opposition to his natal Mars/Neptune that was triggered six months earlier along with his progressed Neptune in the previous three months. His denial of having had 'sexual relations' with Lewinksy was repeated under oath on August 17 stating that he never had "a sexual affair, sexual relations or a sexual relationship" with Lewinsky. Bill Clinton would later confess that he did indeed have an "improper physical relationship" with Monica Lewinsky.[6]

Clinton would survive the impeachment process thanks to a "timely" progressed Sun on his progressed Washington ascendant that offered a counter-balance to the debilitating effects of the eclipse SNode to his SNode: their attachment to his natal "sense of entitlement" Uranus North Node trine Jupiter would, at least temporarily, turn the tables on his hard-wired enthusiasm for youthful entertainments. Their eclipse axis Space Lanes on his natal Tenth/Fourth provided a speedway to both his professional and private lives.

Monica's ties are equally compelling: the eclipse Uranus is on her Fourth House cusp while its Mars/Jupiter-Pluto midpoint activates her progressed Venus/MC conjunction. The eclipse Venus brings all of its Sun/Venus-Saturn/Pluto isotrap seriousness and disdain for superficiality right to the doorstep of her progressed Sun.

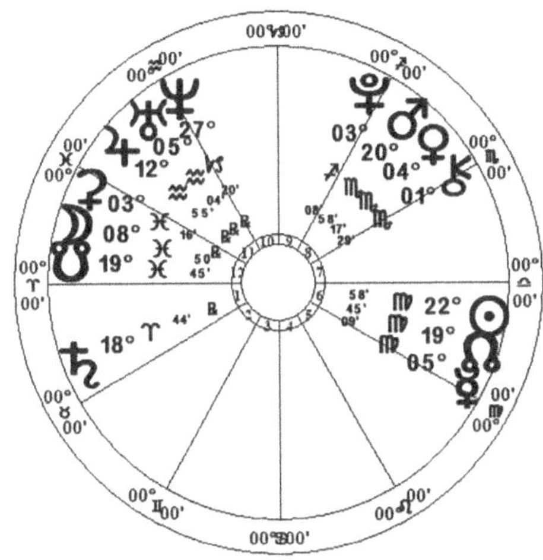

Google Website
PREBLE—LS137
September 15, 1997 • TOB Unknown • Mountain View, CA, USA

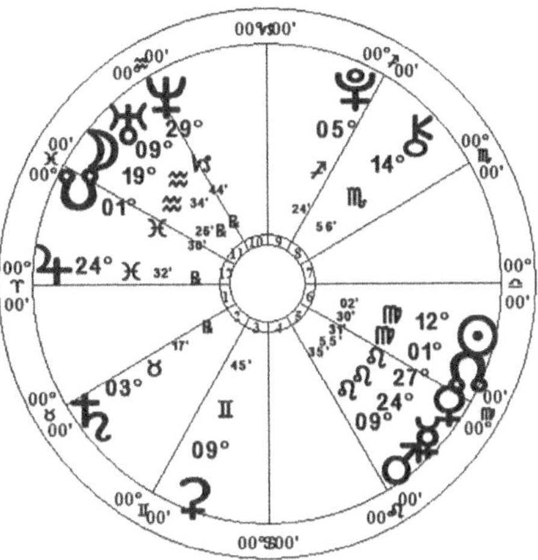

Google Incorporation
PREBLE—LS109
September 4, 1998 • TOB Unknown • Mountain View, CA, USA

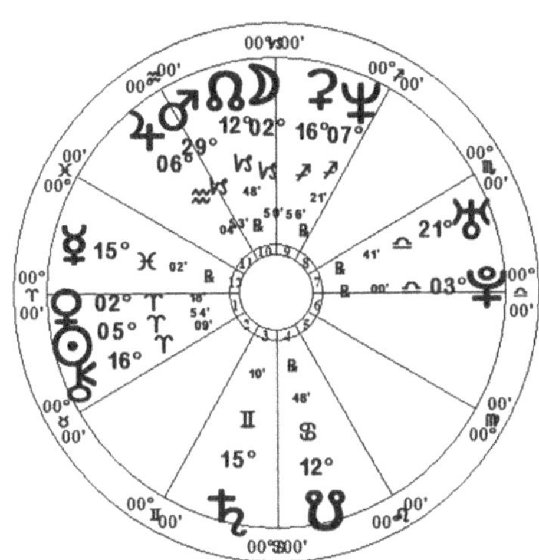

Larry Page
PREBLE—LS143
March 26, 1973 • TOB Unknown • Lansing, MI, USA

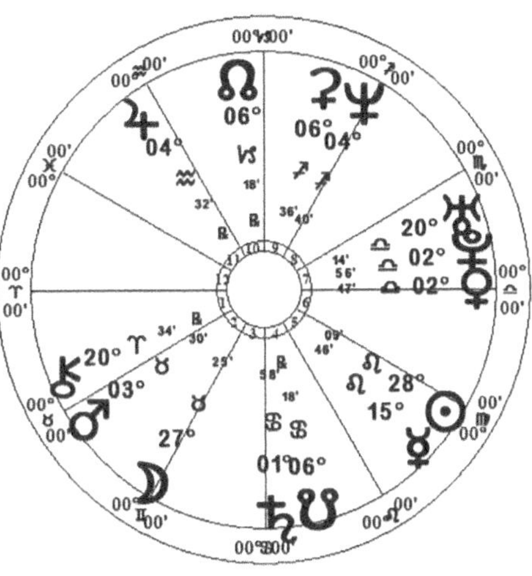

Sergey Brin
PREBLE—LS148
August 21, 1973 • TOB Unknown • Moscow, USSR

Google

"Don't be evil."

Its domain was registered on September 15, 1997, as www.google.com and the company was incorporated on September 4, 1998.[7] The incorporation chart resonated to LS109's final activation degree at 15 Aquarius, which seems appropriate for an internet company that has given us a taste of what the actual Age of Aquarius might represent. And with that in mind, this company is a juggernaut with a frighteningly wonderful and absolutely mind-boggling hold on the global light switch.

The activation degree, however, is more important for cofounders Larry Page and Sergey Brin than it is for the incorporation chart: we need to see the beings behind the Google curtain. Page did not have a resonance in his noon birth chart, but Brin did with his natal Mercury receiving an exact 2nd Harmonic hit. Larry's progressions show the full story as the Bija progressions are solid. He has a progressed Grand Air Trine (Mars at 17 Aquarius, Saturn at 17 Gemini (double yeah!) and Uranus at 20 Libra (partnership yeah!!). Here are their connections:

Larry Page and his Connections to the Lunar Dragons of LS109

1st Harmonics: Moon – NNode, Sun – SNode,
Uranus – NNode, Ceres – Venus, Saturn – Saturn
2nd Harmonics: Mercury – Mars, Jupiter – Venus, Pluto – Mercury

Sergey Brin and his Connections to the Lunar Dragons of LS109

1st Harmonics: Moon – NNode, Sun – SNode, Jupiter – Venus, Jupiter – Pluto
2nd Harmonics: Mercury – Jupiter, Ceres – Venus, Ceres – Pluto

Larry and Sergey both have some of the most powerful Cosmic Bridges you can have, which are created from the eclipse luminaries to their nodes. In addition, Larry's NNode was synced to the eclipse field's Uranus while Sergey's Venus/Pluto conjunction benefited from the eclipse field's expansive, higher-order Jupiter. Both were infused with the fun and creative possibilities that came from being able to connect into the Mercury and Venus vectors of LS109's field.

And one final thought: In the Google incorporation chart there is a Pluto square to the nodal axis that dances in almost perfect symmetry to the exact same pattern in the eclipse field. Maybe it was LS109's way of signing off with a Google goodbye.

LS109 Summary

There's no getting around it. This eclipse family and its field of immense potential were power brokers in the truest sense of the word, and it couldn't have been otherwise. The ability to influence masses of people, whether for goodness or gain, resided within the folds of these frankly awesome Earth Dragons. Maybe it's a good thing they are gone, for that kind of power needs a steady hand on the cosmic wheel to ensure that its promise and possibilities are used for the highest good.

Virtue and vice were the main ingredients at hand as these seasoned, industrial-strength Earth Dragons moved heaven and earth to achieve their goals. They were masters of the moment who embodied leadership and irreverence, aligning myth, mayhem, and morality to get the job done. Their awareness of our shared humanity and decisions made in the light of that realization continue to impact our current marketplace and global consciousness.

These lunar dragons possessed a touch of larceny in their celestial souls; and whether by birthright or rite of passage, at the most mundane of levels they resonated to themes connected to death, sex, and a passion for the manifestation of wealth in all its forms and fascination. All manner of mobility and speculation advanced under their influence, often with cathartic and life-changing patterns of behavior.

Phase	Return	Year
Disseminating	55th	1710
Last Quarter	59th	1782
Balsamic	63rd	1854
New Moon	67th	1926

LS109 Luminaries

Oscar Wilde	October 16, 1854
Sam Giancana[E1]	June 15, 1908
Salvador Allende	June 26, 1908
Estée Lauder	July 1, 1908
Thurgood Marshall	July 2, 1908
Mel Brooks[E3]	June 28, 1926

Elisabeth Kübler-Ross	July 8, 1926
Margaret Laurence	July 18, 1926
Norman Jewison	July 21, 1926
Ernő Rubik	July 13, 1944
Alex Buzo	July 23, 1944
Geraldine Chaplin	July 31, 1944
Robert C. Merton	July 31, 1944
Alton Brown	July 30, 1962
Roger Clemens	August 4, 1962
Patrick Ewing	August 5, 1962
Michelle Yeoh	August 6, 1962
Jacinda Ardern[E1]	July 26, 1980
Fernando González[E2]	July 29, 1980
Athina Papayianni	August 18, 1980
Shawn Mendes[E]	August 8, 1998
Google™	September 4, 1998

PREBLE—142
Mel Brooks
Fernando González
Shawn Mendes
Jacinda Ardern

1. Noel Tyl, *Synthesis & Counselling in Astrology* (St. Paul, MN: Llewellyn, 1994), p. 285.
2. Reinhold Ebertin, *The Combination of Stellar Influences*, p. 235.
3. https://en.wikipedia.org/wiki/Oskar_Schindler
4. Thomas Keneally, *Searching for Schindler* (New York: Doubleday, 2007), p. 186.
5. Todd S. Purdum. Lewinsky at 40. Retrieved March 30, 2022. https://www.politico.com/story/2014/05/lewinskys-perspective-106421
6. https://en.wikipedia.org/wiki/Monica_Lewinsky. Retrieved April 1, 2022.
7. http://www.google.com/intl/en/about/company/timeline/ Retrieved Mar. 31, 2022.

LUNAR SAROS 116

"When the President does it, that means that it's not illegal."

-Richard M. Nixon

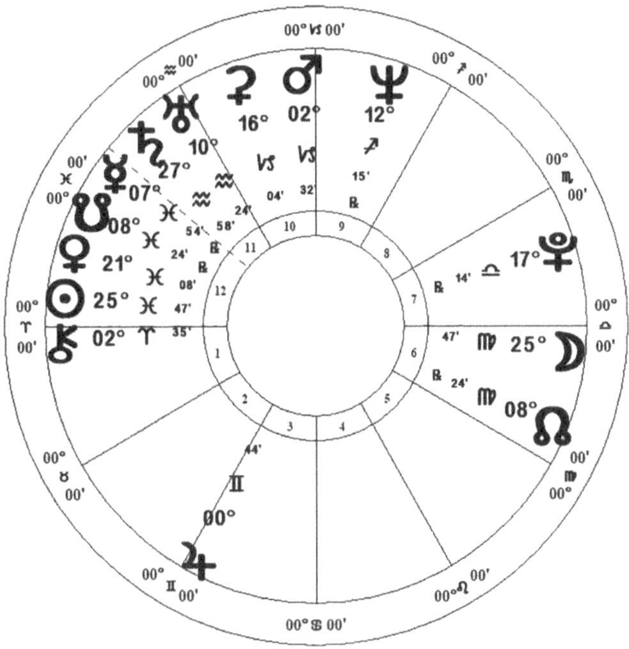

Lunar Saros 116

March 15, 993 • 11:56:26 PM • North Pole

Persuasion

Media, marketing, and all manner of persuasion that spark our endless curiosity fall under the dominion of this NNode Virgo lunar eclipse. The ruler Mercury is retrograde and, aligned to the imaginative legacy of its SNode companion in Pisces will be a willing contributor to whatever field of endeavor stirs their soul into action. And action is a central characteristic of these ancient Earth Dragons; their OOB Mars (23S54) in partile square to Chiron is never at a loss for something to do, especially if it involves increasing your status, security, and net worth.

Jupiter's placement at 00 Gemini and at the "handle" on the Bucket bestows a boon of responsiveness, versatility and cleverness that overflows with new ideas. Its placement at the infinity 00 degree and in detriment works to level the playing field offering anyone a chance to get back in the game. Their quest for fresh experiences is a feature of their ruler Mercury in a potent and extremely persuasive MR to its pivotal 00 Jupiter in Gemini. In fact, by repositioning ruler retrograde Mercury into Jupiter's slot as handle on the proverbial Bucket, an entirely new world opens up that brings nostalgia back into high focus and fashion. Anything old can feel new again, which has both its attractors and detractors who can argue for either side.

One of the features unique to this lunar eclipse family and to the Air Dragons of LS125—Hyper-Drive (see Part Three)—is a waxing sextile between Neptune and Uranus. These two lunar eclipses were birthed within one hundred and seventy years of each other, giving both of these planets the perfect time to return not only to their same phase relationship but to return to their same sign placements, an extraordinary synchronicity. This particular sextile, holding cosmic court from Sagittarius to Aquarius is full of faith, intuition, inspiration, and belief systems that can make anybody feel thrilled just to be alive. Their concordance is congenial—in the intellectual world of ideas they bring a bright and articulate style of communication that is highly persuasive. Without hesitation, this lunar eclipse has a special talent for managing multi-media platforms across a diverse and eclectic global audience.

LS116's Venus-Sun conjunction in Pisces carries a level of confidence that is atypical for this planetary pairing in water. True, it is being energized by the eclipse but more than that is the spark of boldness within their twenty-one and twenty-five RA degrees that reinforce the flames of Sagittarius and Aries. Those fire-starter degrees, especially considering they represent what we value (Venus) and what our Being (Sun) is all about, have an endless capacity for self-promotion that borders on grandiosity if not narcissism. Finally, there is Ceres square Pluto, a page turner in our lunar eclipse story as it brings into our modern world the ancient narratives of separation, loss, retrieval, and return. The square aspect together with their cardinal placements ensures that there will be many occasions upon which one will have to deal with grief, sorrow, and depression; their Cancer/Libra domiciles are particularly suited to offer opportunities for transformation and growth through a myriad of experiences that will require one to learn to let go.

Closest Midpoints: Jupiter/Venus-Uranus, Neptune/Eclipse-Saturn
Isotraps: Sun/Uranus conjunct Mercury/Saturn
Mars/Neptune conjunct Saturn/Pluto

1900—2100 Eclipses: Lunar Saros—116

1912, 1930, 1948, 1966, 1984, 2002, 2020, 2038, 2056, 2075, 2093
Length of cycle —1,298 years
Series ends—May 14, 2291

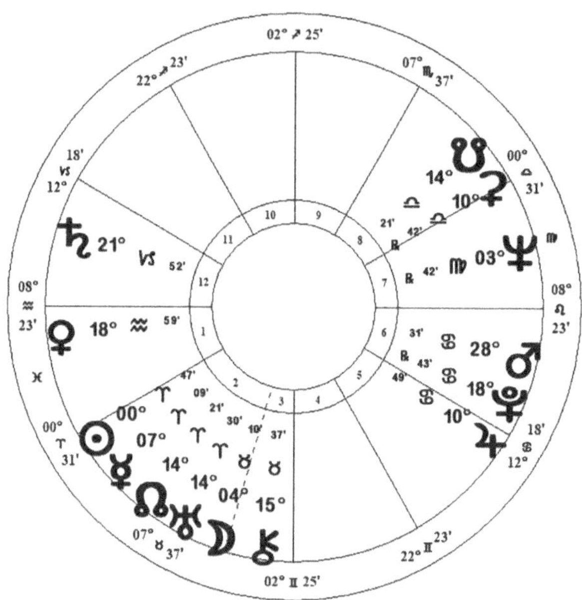

William Shatner
PREBLE—LS116

March 22, 1931 • 4:00 AM • Montreal, PQ, CANADA

James T. Kirk of the Starship USS Enterprise

"Captain Kirk has been a source of pleasure and income for a long time."

-William Shatner

The original *Star Trek* television series that would make William Shatner an iconic figure known throughout the galaxy began its initial television run in 1966. It would run for three seasons until canceled in 1969. It went into syndication and the series enjoyed a rerun hiatus that launched the Trekkie cult following. In 1979, Paramount Studios would bring the movie *Star Trek* to the big screen and solidify William Shatner for all time as the handsome, swash-buckling, starship Enterprise captain James T. Kirk.

On March 28, 1978, Paramount held a press conference to announce its commitment to make *Star Trek* the movie, with filming to begin in August. Four days earlier, on March 24, Shatner's life would be forever changed as the

Titans of Talent from the Air Dragons of LS122 reached out to boldly go where they had never gone before, sweeping up his 00 Aries Sun into their 4 degree Libran embrace. By the start of filming in August, his progressed Moon had just crossed the threshold of his Twelfth House/Ascendant, allowing his vitality and vigor to be reborn. His progressed Moon at 7 Aquarius would simultaneously sextile his Second House Mercury at 7 Aries on the emotionally intense and personally magnetic Garnet Star known for its links to worldly power and authority. It also invokes an intriguing if not mysterious public image along with a desire to undertake transformative journeys.[1]

William Shatner's Connections to the Dragons of LS116

1st Harmonics: Eclipse/Chiron – Sun,
NNode – Neptune, Pluto – SNode, Uranus – ASC
2nd Harmonics: Pluto – NNode/Uranus, Ceres – Pluto

According to Shatner, he wasn't that popular growing up. On Valentine's Day he'd send cards to himself because nobody else did. But all that would change thanks to the persuasive power and the popularity factor that lay dormant within his dragon DNA that would help to make him one of the most beloved entertainers in history.

William Shatner has an intense natal NNode/Uranus conjunction that syncs to the lunar eclipse Pluto and its Mars/Neptune conjunct Saturn/Pluto isotrap which brings an undercurrent of dissatisfaction if he is not engaged in meaningful work. But when fully engaged, help miraculously "transports in," allowing all the positive dynamics of the isotrap to work in synchronicity.

The 2nd Harmonic is even more critical as the lunar eclipse Ceres casts a tractor beam onto his Pluto highlighting not only its own Ceres square Pluto but Shatner's as well. Both charts have a Pluto waxing square with Ceres and both hail from cardinal ports giving them lots of familiarity with issues of separation, loss, retrieval, and return. LS116's Ceres in Capricorn prefers to deal with losses and suffering associated with career and reputation while Shatner's Ceres in Libra deals with grief and sorrow on a more relational level. Both Plutos in square represent the mythic as well as the personal dimensions of loss and Shatner is no stranger to suffering. He has been married four times; his third marriage in 1997 ended in the tragic death of his "beautiful soulmate" and wife in 1999.[2] It was deemed an accidental drowning, but he said the real cause was her alcoholism. His divorce in 2019 brought his fourth marriage to an end.

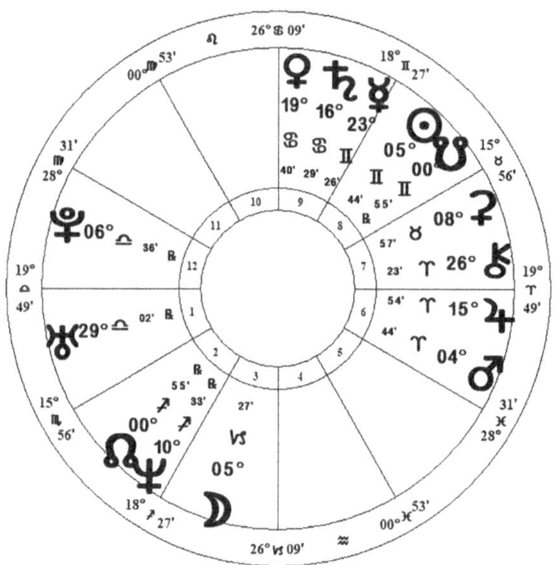

Jamie Oliver
PREBLEs—LS125 & LS130

May 27, 1975 • 4:35 PM • London, UK

Celebrity Chef/Restaurateur/Author

"All I ever wanted to do was to make food accessible to everyone; to show that you can make mistakes–I do all the time–but it doesn't matter."

-JAMIE OLIVER

Jamie Oliver, celebrity chef, writer, entrepreneur, philanthropist, and father, belongs to two distinct dragon families. The one that occurred just two days before his birth (LS130 on May 25, 1975) and the PREBLE that dominated his pre-birth development (LS125 on November 29, 1974). There is no doubt in my mind that being born within hours or days of a lunar eclipse results in having many of the personality patterns and characteristics of that particular eclipse. However, there is no denying the influence of the previous lunar eclipse's capacity to saturate the soul essence of the incoming spirit. In Jamie's case, his life force is so much more attuned to the Hyper-Drive Air Dragons of LS125 found in Part Three.

Jamie's life will always be filled with excitement. Look at all those cardinal signs with the elements of fire and air leading the pack from the personal signs Aries to Cancer. He was discovered by the BBC in 1997 after making an unscripted appearance in the documentary, *Christmas at the River Café*.[3] His big break occurred under the auspices of LS132 landing at 4 Libra on his dynamic Pluto/Mars opposition. "The day after the documentary aired, Jamie received no fewer than four firm offers to go into television and the one he accepted made him a star."[4] He was only 21 years old.

By the end of 2001, with the arrival of LS144 and its smorgasbord of enticements activating his Saturn, he set his sights on bringing his wildly optimistic but altruistic venture known as "Jamie's Kitchen" to life. His dream was to open a first-class restaurant in London and have it operate as a charity, offering unemployed youngsters a fresh start and in the process create a reality TV show.[5] With a Gemini Sun/SNode opposition to Neptune, his appetite for social responsibility would be a hunger only satisfied by connecting and contributing to a zeitgeist as much in need of faith as it was in need of proper food. Add in the thrust of a hard-driving Pluto/Mars opposition and you get a pattern known as the Mystic Rectangle, famous for its unflagging devotion to solving real world problems.

Jamie Oliver's Connections to the Dragons of LS116
Pluto with Pluto

1st Harmonics: Jupiter – SNode/Sun,
Mars – Moon, Pluto – ASC, Chiron – Mars, Neptune – Neptune
2nd Harmonics: Ceres – Saturn/Venus, Pluto – Jupiter

The arrival of LS116 on November 20, 2002, at 27 Taurus on Jamie's SNode made his dream a reality with the grand opening of his own restaurant, Fifteen, that November.[6] Jamie's ties to LS116 is a banquet of impressive links, amongst them a remarkable retrograde Neptune tie-in and a striking Pluto to his ascendant, as well as both Plutos in Libra and retrograde. Even with the passing of a millennium, the family resemblance is striking. His SNode inheritance marker to LS116's Jupiter at infinity 00 Gemini is truly the icing on the cake.

Jamie's popularity continues to soar—his very Being is a force of persuasion recognized not so much as a global brand but more like a global movement. In April 2022, still within the lunar eclipse window of November 2021's LS126—Game Changers—and its activation degree at, wait for it, 27 Taurus, Jamie's Can Do infinity 00 Gemini SNode answered the call. Jamie, together with Ukrainian chef Yurii Kovryzhenko organized a charity dinner in London under the initiative #CookForUkraine to raise money for Ukrainians suffering from the Russian invasion.[7] I can imagine the dinner and especially the borscht would have been, as the saying goes, to die for.

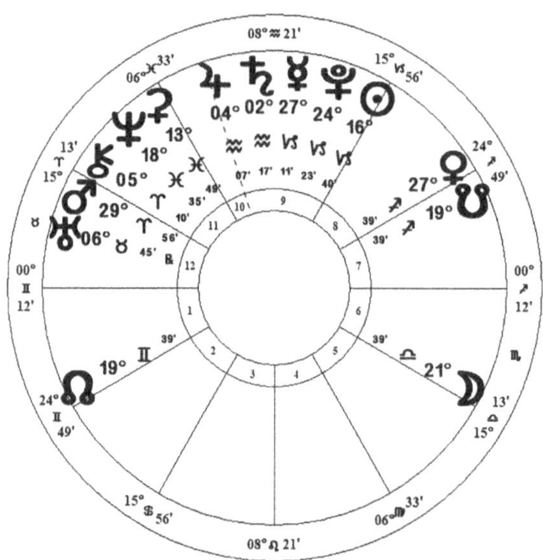

White House Insurrection
PREBLE—LS116

January 6, 2021 • 1:45 PM • Washington, DC, USA

Chaos at the Capital

"We're going to give riot warnings.
We're going to try to get compliance but this is now effectively a riot."

-White House Security Police

By 2:13 pm, on January 6, 2021, the Secret Service evacuate Mr. Pence from the Senate floor as the mob is on its way. Inside the White House, the rioters endlessly chant in a sing-song voice, "Where are you Nancy?" In an audio clip, we hear one staff member whisper, "They're pounding on doors trying to find her." At 2:24 pm, President Trump tweets: "Mike Pence didn't have the courage to do what should have been done to protect our Country and our Constitution. . . . USA demands the truth." House members are told to reach under their seats for tear gas masks and be prepared to use them.

At 2:41 pm, rioters smash their way through the door to the congressional chamber as the crowd chants, "Break it down, break it down." Protester Ashli Babbitt is shot and falls to the ground. Elsewhere, rioters reach the inside of the Senate gallery. Video footage shows rioters rifling through papers with one saying, "There's got to be something we can use against these scumbags." By 6:00 pm, police confirm that Ashli Babbitt has died. Trump tweets and refers to those at the Capital as "great patriots."[8]

White House Insurrection's Connections to the Dragons of LS116
Chiron with Chiron

1st Harmonics: SNode/Mercury – Ceres, Pluto – Moon, Ceres – Sun, Jupiter – ASC, Uranus – MC, Ceres – MC, Venus – Neptune, Chiron – Chiron

On November 30, 2020, Lunar Saros 116 returned at 8 degrees Gemini. At this stage on its 1,298 year globe-traversing journey, it was unfolding through its 58th return out of an evolutionary 73 returns. The White House Riots of January 6, 2021, were officially under a Senate Hearing investigation by June 2022. Evidence offered a timeline produced and verified by video footage. The key time periods stated for the beginning of the riots were given anywhere from 1:45 pm to 2:15 pm, on January 6, placing the ascendant between 00 to 8 degrees Gemini.

The ruler of LS116 is a retrograde Mercury, which is bonded to the imaginative temperament of its SNode companion in Pisces making it a willing party to any matter of redress or call to arms. Thus, its SNode/Mercury 1st Harmonic to the White House Insurrection's Ceres is able to effectively get under anybody's skin as it pours forth into Ceres all of its beliefs, tales of woe and thinly veiled attempts at persuasion. Riding shotgun for both spheres is an identical nodal square to Neptune giving righteousness a power-play platform to address someone else's plea for help.

Both fields have a similar Chiron placement which, as many astrologers know, is the weak spot in the system. If left unaddressed, it will continue to collect our failings and flaws and give cynicism a rent-free abode. It has been referred to as the "chirotic point," where dimensions either collapse or merge.

The most troubling tie between the two fields can be traced back to the eclipse Jupiter falling on the White House Insurrection ASC as its zero alpha degree position in Gemini and at the "handle" on the Bucket of the eclipse field gave a galaxy of possibility to that moment in time. Jupiter's placement at the infinity 00 degree and in detriment can level any playing field, giving anyone a chance to get into the game—and this is exactly what happened in Washington, D.C. on January 6, 2021.

Notice that there are no 2nd Harmonics. This leaves it all up to the 1st Harmonics to stimulate our natural impulses and sense of direction as they simply awaken us to follow a path that, as a seed essence, has always been there, just waiting for the right moment to be born. Sadly, the mob was trying to prevent a legitimate president-elect from assuming office, which is why the attack was regarded as an insurrection or even an attempted coup d'état. Some law-enforcement agencies, as well as the FBI, considered it an act of domestic terrorism.

LS116 Summary

Since 1966, Lunar Saros 116 has been experiencing its second and last Disseminating phase on its 1,298 year journey. Between its return in the years 2038 and 2056, it will be entering its final Last Quarter phase of evolution. There is a noted zealousness to the Disseminating phase of any lunar eclipse and often times it brings with it a proclivity to engage in conflict. This is most likely due to the fact that, at this stage of its journey, especially after coming out of the full bloom and vigor of the Full Moon phase, it's quite full of itself and ready to spread its special message of wisdom to the world. It has a mission, and that mission is to keep on manifesting its meaning so that all can share in its good fortune.

Because of its special status between now and 2056, their lunar saros returns and all those born under its banner will be people who can hold and sway a crowd as attractiveness, popularity and public appeal are the gifts so generously lavished upon us by these stately Earth Dragons. Their arrival, whether by birthright or rite of passage signals a time to forge ahead with new connections while demonstrating one's flair for creative enterprise. Social endeavors exude a special quality of fascination that is enthusiastically received by the public. An uptick in recognition, health, and wellness, along with sound nutrition are some of the benefits associated with this family of lunar eclipses. Good will circulates and many benefit from lucky breaks and job promotions.

This eclipse would benefit anyone with either an interest in the entertainment world or the machinations of politics. Knowing how to handle people and being comfortable with humor and wit, there is little that stands in the way of anyone making a lasting and quite frankly dazzling first impression in the company of this appealing lunar eclipse. If you are prepared to put your imaginative, creative flair into whatever it is that you love to do, this could be the lunar eclipse that brings it all home.

LS116 Luminaries

Louis Pasteur	December 27, 1822
Babe Ruth	February 6, 1895
Sabine Peters	December 29, 1912
Rosa Parks	February 4, 1913
Richard Nixon	January 9, 1913
Boris Yeltsin	February 1, 1931
James Dean	February 8, 1931
William Shatner	March 22, 1931
Leonard Nimoy	March 26, 1931
Samuel L. Jackson	December 21, 1948
Ken Wilber	January 31, 1949
Ivana Trump	February 20, 1949
Victor Garber	March 16, 1949
Gordon Ramsay	November 8, 1966
Royce Gracie	December 12, 1966
Benicio Del Toro	February 19, 1967
Glen Greenwald	March 6, 1967
Scarlett Johansson	November 22, 1984
Theo James	December 16, 1984
Keira Knightley	March 26, 1985
Gal Gadot	April 30, 1985

---

1. Tara Cochrane, Fixed Star Report for William Shatner, Sirius 30 software.
2. https://en.wikipedia.org/wiki/William_Shatner. Retrieved May 27, 2022.
3. Stafford Hildred & Tim Ewbank, *Jamie, King of the Kitchen* (London: John Blake Publishing Ltd., 2012), p. 82.
4. Hildred & Ewbank, *Jamie*, p. 83.
5. Gilly Smith, *Jamie Oliver, Turning Up The Heat* (London: Carlton Publishing Group, 2006), p. 135.
6. Smith, *Jamie*, p. 172.
7. https://en.wikipedia.org/wiki/Jamie_Oliver#cite_note-72. Retrieved May 28, 2022.

LUNAR SAROS 118

"I thought the Barbie doll would always be successful."

-RUTH HANDLER

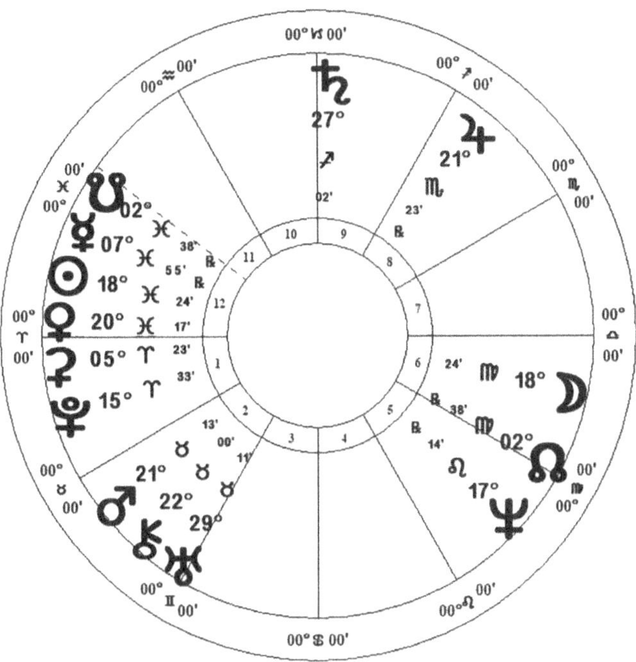

Lunar Saros 118

March 9, 1105 • 4:21:13 PM • North Pole

The Marketplace

Endeavors that serve the public good gain invigoration from this NNode Virgo eclipse. Its natural ruler Mercury has been sidelined by an exalted Venus in trine to retrograde Jupiter in Scorpio. An exalted Venus always brings in an artistic and creative flair to the personality and with its trine to an empowered Jupiter, strengthens willpower and personal magnetism. As part of LS118's Mystic Rectangle with its super charged sextiles from a Taurean Mars/Chiron conjunction to Venus and the eclipse Moon to Jupiter, huge financial decisions and career moves could be blessed by lucky contacts with members of the opposite sex. Either way, the Mystic Rectangle is a super signal for success and is a gorgeous indicator that effort will be rewarded.

And speaking of effort, the Mars opposition to Jupiter in the Mystic Rectangle has a taste not only for the good life but for high adventure. Anyone touched by this eclipse, if willing to take a chance, could find themselves seeking out opportunities to gain recognition and to express creative pursuits abroad. Uranus at the critical and prophetic 29th degree of Taurus and in square to the nodal axis provides a never-ending source of unexpected experiences aka challenges in the management of resources. Isotraps that involve the Sun, Mercury, Saturn, and Uranus help to move innovative projects forward but be aware that this combination can represent a significant source of added stress and strain.

LS118 carries a See-Saw pattern like the one seen in LS102, the first lunar eclipse of the entire Saros Series. It emits an enormous energy field of instability, creating an internal competition within not only oneself but with others. The challenge here is always how to either integrate or satisfy these two sharply divergent aspects of one's life. Thank heaven there's a rescue plan built in: the mutual reception (MR) brings timely escape hatches along with hidden resources to bear. Take a look at LS118's Sun in Pisces and Neptune in Leo and then reverse their positions. Now, with the relocated Sun in Leo, a dimension of vitality and support from Pluto's waxing trine can be appreciated, giving the eclipse field flow, flair, and a powerful additional resource for presentation and leadership. All trines to and from Pluto simultaneously tear us down to quickly rebuild back better, offering gifts of renewal. By relocating Neptune to the Sun's original placement in Pisces, we now have a newly inspired, romantic idealist emerging as exalted Venus and Neptune embrace. Of note is the singer/songwriter/poet/novelist and Rock and Roll Hall of Famer Leonard Cohen, born under this family of lunar eclipses in 1934; his chart holds an almost perfect to within one minute arc conjunction at 12 Virgo between Venus and Neptune.

And speaking of Virgo, the eclipse Moon seeds into the field outstanding personality traits such as meticulousness and an industrious way of being in the world. These folks know the value of work. Their sense of responsibility is legendary. They are realists who need to figure out how to get s**t done. The Virgo/Pisces eclipse axis blesses all who, by birthright or by rite of passage, get to experience a rare combination of precognition and pragmatism. A few stellar examples of people born with a Moon in Virgo are Katharine Hepburn, Blake Lively, Michael Fassbender, Madonna and Jon Hamm.

Closest Midpoints: Pluto/Uranus-NNode, Saturn/Mercury-Pluto
Isotraps: Mars/Jupiter conjunct Saturn/Pluto
Sun/Mercury conjunct Saturn/Uranus

1900—2100 Eclipses: Lunar Saros—118

1916, 1934, 1952, 1970, 1988, 2006, 2024, 2042, 2060, 2078, 2096
Length of cycle —1,298 years
Series ends—May 7, 2403

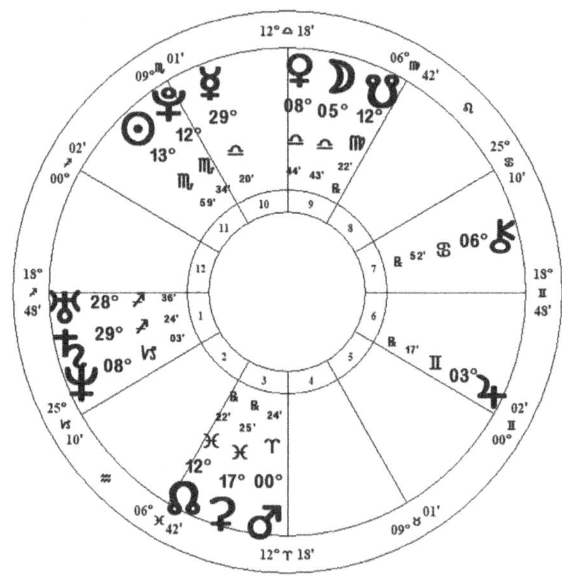

Alexandra Elbakyan
PREBLE—LS118

November 6, 1988 • 10:35 AM • Almaty, Kazakhstan, USSR

The Robin Hood of Science

"Scientific knowledge belongs to humanity."

-ALEXANDRA ELBAKYAN

Alexandra Elbakyan is a computer programmer and the creator of Sci-Hub, a website that is considered to be one of the greatest tools in the world for researchers, providing free access to articles from scientific journals for anyone to read and download, thus bypassing the high and often prohibitive paywalls that most cannot afford. As of 2022, Sci-Hub has grown a database of 88,343,288 research articles and books.[1]

She has been called a modern-day Robin Hood and "Science's Pirate Queen." In December 2016, *Nature* named Alexandra as one of the top ten people who most mattered in science. Edward Snowden acknowledged Sci-Hub to be one of the most important websites for academics in the world.[2] Alexandra is also an astrologer, saying that since 2010 she has it as a hobby.

Alexandra Elbakyan's Connections to the Dragons of LS118
↑North Node with South Node↓

1st Harmonics: Moon – SNode, Mercury – NNode, Sun/Venus – Ceres
2nd Harmonic: Ceres – Venus

Apart from the powerful, battery-charging effect of the NNode/SNode Global Gateway across their fields, the significant connectors are between the eclipse axis and Mercury to her service-to-humanity nodal axis. Remarkably, the eclipse Sun and Venus feed her Piscean service Ceres and the eclipse Ceres doubles down to feed her Venus in Libra social conscience and all the legal ramifications that come with establishing a level playing field. In the marketplace of knowledge, she is indeed a Queen.

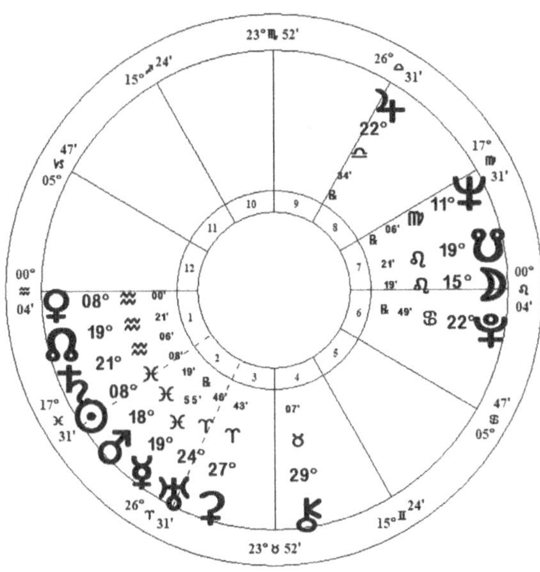

Ralph Nader
PREBLE—LS113

February 27, 1934 • 4:52 AM • Winsted, CT, USA

An Unreasonable Man and Political Activist

I once said to my father when I was a boy, "Dad, we need a third political party." He said to me, "I'll settle for a second."

-Ralph Nader

On August 13, 1970, Nader's lawsuit against General Motors was finally resolved, having dragged on through the courts since 1966.[3] Nader had originally asked for $26 million in damages for invasion of privacy and wound up settling the case for $425,000.[4] Justin Martin's biography of Nader reads like a crime novel, especially when evidence for GM's relentless pursuit into Nader's personal life revealed recordings of GM's instructions to the detective in charge to "get something, somewhere on this guy . . . Shut him up."[5] GM would find out soon enough that in the marketplace of the mid '60's, with its growing civil rights movement, if the consumer was king, Ralph Nader was their knight in shining armor.

On August 17, 1970, Lunar Saros 118 landed feet first at 24 Aquarius, feeding Nader's hungry First House NNode/Saturn. Not wanting his case to drag on into the 1980s when "all the culpable officials would have been retired," Nader settled for what at that time was the largest amount ever collected in an invasion of privacy case.[6] When you factor in Mercury retrograde in Pisces in both charts, the probability of a positive outcome increases because like LS118, Nader also has a Saturn/Mercury-Pluto midpoint that is well suited to guide and influence public policy as it represents formidable intellectual prowess and precision.

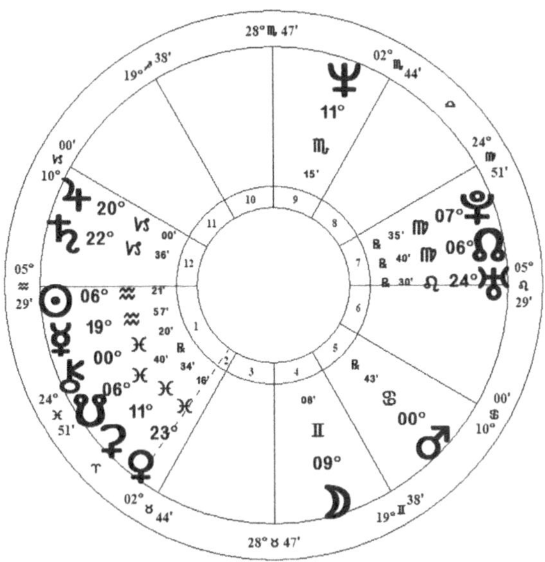

Wayne Gretzky
PREBLE—LS127

January 26, 1961 • 7:45 AM • Brantford, ON, Canada

"I've just traded my life away."

-WAYNE GRETZKY

The Great One

"The highest compliment that you can pay me is that I work hard every day, that I never dog it."

-WAYNE GRETZKY

On August 9, 1988, Canadian hockey fans en masse went into cardiac arrest as Wayne Gretzky, national hero, superstar, and arguably the greatest hockey player who ever lived, was traded to the Los Angeles Kings. It was perhaps the most shocking trade in professional sports history as upset Canadians, gathering outside Parliament in Ottawa, were burning effigies of Peter Pocklington, the owner of the Edmonton Oilers who had instigated the trade, while one member of the Canadian House of Commons demanded the government block the trade.[7] Vancouver Province sports columnist Jim Taylor wrote:

> "The best hockey player in the world was ours, and the Americans flew up from Hollywood in their private jet and bought him. It was the Canadian psyche that was ripped by an uppercut to the paranoia."[8]

Gretzky's Sun by progression had reached 4 Pisces, the midpoint of his Chiron/NNode conjunction at 4 Pisces. Meanwhile, his Pluto/SNode conjunction at 7 Virgo, with its implications for sharing an often tragic destiny with a collective, took the slap-shot full on as he bore up under the overwhelming sadness of the trade and his own apparent disgust at being sold to the highest bidder. In the marketplace of NHL team expansion and product endorsements, it was the beginning of a new game with little afterthought given for the deep feelings of allegiance that fans and their teams would hold sacred. With Gretzky's OOB Mars at infinity 00 Cancer and at the critical AP, it was inevitable that his breathtaking talent could never be contained or claimed by a single country. He was born under PREBLE-127—Fired in the Kiln—a dragon family of unparalleled dedication and mastery.

Gretzky's sensitivity to the lunar eclipse activation that August came from a cosmic hat trick of immense proportion. His SNode conjuncts the eclipse field's SNode, a Global Gateway that opens the field to personal levels of anxiety, discord, and grief which many individuals have had to deal with on the road to success such as Richard Nixon, Donald Trump, J. K. Rowling, Picasso, HP Lovecraft and Shailene Woodley. The eclipse Mercury's conjunction to that very same node and its isotrap with the Sun, Saturn and Uranus bring additional levels of discomfort caused from marketing mismanagement. Ego aside, there was a lot of SNode "letting go" going on and The Great One took it all in his usual elegant stride—helped along by almost identical Venus in Pisces placements in both charts. But the real zinger came from the zap of LS118's Uranus on his Fourth House cusp, the IC, where themes of emotional attachment and roots reside. Uranus, not being the sentimental sort, had no problem ripping away his childhood allegiance or thrashing his national pride. At the twenty-ninth degree, Uranus on his IC was ending one chapter of Gretzky's life so that another, even more glorious chapter could begin. In the global marketplace of sport, it would be a chapter dedicated to his celebrity where Wayne Gretzky's status and autonomy would rise to almost mythic proportions.

LS118 Summary

Triumph in the marketplace is what Earth Dragons do and this family can move heaven and earth to advance their cause thanks to their dedication, creative problem solving, and an enterprising spirit. You're in the fast lane now, so get prepared to do some deal-making. And that's good news because creature comfort concerns are also kicking into high gear. The twin factors of motivation and manifestation can attract success in such diverse fields as medicine, sports, communications, multi-media, entertainment, and cutting-edge technology. If you are an analyst, counselor, researcher, or writer, lucky breaks will fill your sails with lift. An interest in art, fashion, photography, and web development can now emerge.

Whether you are a member of this hard-working eclipse family or enjoying one of their glorious eighteen year returns, it's essential to alternate between work and play, giving both a place in your daily schedule. Although there is great physical strength present within the field, do not take advantage of its vitality and endurance as you may experience health issues, particularly heart problems, due to over-exertion. Keep at least one of your inner channels tuned to the psychic network within as the dragons of LS118 are blessed with an above-average ability to tune into energy fields that have no regard for time or space. This inner sense of attunement is what gives so many members of this clan a winning edge in the world. In the marketplace of life or in the enjoyment of one of their celestial outings, take pride in your net worth, self-worth, and ability to prosper.

Phase	Return	Year
First Quarter	43rd	1862
Gibbous	47th	1934
Full Moon	51st	2006
Disseminating	56th	2096

LS118 Luminaries

Gottfried Leibniz	July 1, 1646
Louis XVI of France	August 23, 1754
Henry J Heinz	October 11, 1844
Friedrich Nietzsche	October 15, 1844
Roald Dahl	September 13, 1916
James Herriot	October 3, 1916
Walter Cronkite	November 4, 1916
Ruth Handler	November 4, 1916
Sophia Loren	September 20, 1934
Leonard Cohen	September 21, 1934
Carl Sagan	November 9, 1934
Charles Manson	November 12, 1934
Neil Peart	September 12, 1952
Christopher Reeve	September 25, 1952
Bill Walton	November 5, 1952
Jeffrey Epstein	January 20, 1953
Matt Damon	October 8, 1970
Annika Sörenstam	October 9, 1970
Sarah Silverman	December 1, 1970
Regina King	January 15, 1970
Tori Black[E1]	August 26, 1988
Kevin Durant	September 29, 1988
Emma Stone	November 6, 1988

PREBLE—LS113
Tori Black

1. https://sci-hub.se/database. Retrieved March 29, 2022.
2. https://twitter.com/snowden/status/1391104503391395840. Retrieved Mar. 29, 2022.
3. Justin Martin, *Nader Crusader Spoiler Icon* (Cambridge, MA: Perseus Publishing 2002), p.112.
4. Ibid, p. 63.
5. Ibid, p.112.
6. Ibid.
7. https://icehockey.fandom.com/wiki/Peter_Pocklington. Retrieved Jan. 20, 2022.
8. https://www.nhl.com/news/gretzky-trade-sent-shock-waves-through-canada/c-380618. Retrieved Jan. 20, 2022.

LUNAR SAROS 127

Raise the sail with your stronger hand.

–JAPANESE PROVERB

"Go after the opportunities that arise in life that you are best equipped to do."

-SOICHIRO HONDA

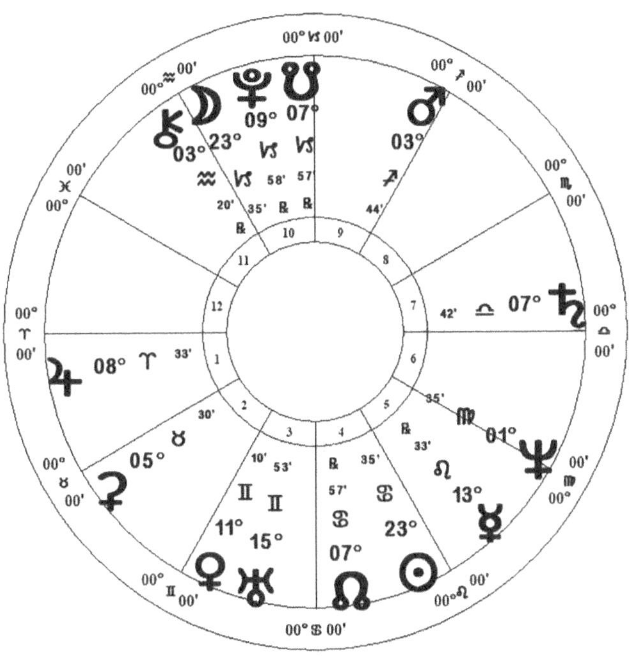

Lunar Saros 127

July 16, 1275 • 2:35:34 PM • South Pole

Fired in the Kiln

This is a Saturn ruled Capricorn eclipse that reflects talent and ambition grown strong by years of patience, dedication, and discipline. The eclipse field is a gold mine of hidden treasure featuring a heightened OOB Mars (24S51) in conjunction to the Great Attractor (GA) at 3 Sagittarius (its position in 1275 CE), and behind the GA the even more massive gravitational pull of the Shapley Supercluster (SSC). All we need to know about the GA and the mind-boggling power of the SSC is that everything is being pulled in their direction, which gives Mars even greater relevance in its interactions within the eclipse field. Mars benefits not only from its MR to Jupiter in Aries but holds an amazingly optimistic trine to Jupiter, enabling resources to "be pulled and *shaped*" into whatever form best suits the occasion.

Turning talent into treasure is pure pleasure for LS127's Pluto/SNode at the critical leg of its Cardinal T-Square. These Earth Dragons have the distinction of being the only current lunar eclipse tracking across the planet until the 22nd century that carries Saturn in an opposition to an extremely self-aware and resourceful Jupiter. Saturn's exaltation here is a vote of confidence increasing the odds that the power inherent in the field will be used judiciously and for the benefit of society. This note of optimism can be seen through the midpoint structures that act as a kiln, providing both a container and the fuel necessary to fuse personal ego to the dreams and aspirations of others. There is a tremendous capacity for mastery within the isotraps; they showcase the value of hard work, gifting those who are touched by this Saros Series with common sense, vitality, tenacity, and the perseverance to go the distance. In order to make good use of the opportunities that will surely present themselves, one must be selective in choosing a goal. When working with the energy of the GA, it has proven to be most rewarding to have one chosen area of interest rise above all others. For best results, identify a goal and move toward it with laser precision.

LS127's Venus-Uranus conjunction in Gemini may be the best seat in the house for checking out potential paths to passion: they are constantly in zap mode, bringing an endless array of new ideas to mind. Venus holds a sextile to Mercury, as does Uranus, giving an appreciation for, if not facility with, words and the ability for self-expression. Anyone in the public eye will prosper from the gifts of eloquence and the freedom to speak one's mind.

Finding a focus should not pose a problem even with the Cardinal T-Square and its Pluto SNode conjunction at the leg of the T. Here I follow Jeff Green's protocols for working with Pluto and find that its conjunction to the SNode indicates, as he suggests, "an evolutionary and karmic fruition condition" and that often there is some kind of special "destiny" playing out in space and time.[1] Identifying the area of interest is the key to the entire process. Christopher Reeve, Erich Fromm, Jimmy Connors, Marianne Williamson, Mickey Rourke,

Neil Peart, Igor Stravinsky and Vladimir Putin all have a 2 degree or under Pluto/SNode conjunction.

Only one other eclipse family, LS108, has bragging rights to a Pluto SNode conjunction, but that conjunction included Mars so it would be similar but different. The similarity lies in the definite sense of urgency in the unfoldment of personal power in the lives of those born under both dragon families The difference is in that those born into the realm of LS127 are formidable, even intimidating, in their unshakable pursuit of their path.

Closest Midpoints: Eclipse/Uranus-Neptune, Jupiter/Pluto-Node
Isotraps: Mars/Saturn conjunct Neptune/Pluto
Moon/Neptune opposition Jupiter/Uranus

1900—2100 Eclipses: Lunar Saros—127

1906, 1924, 1942, 1960, 1978, 1996, 2014, 2032, 2050, 2068, 2086
Length of cycle —1,280 years
Series ends—September 2, 2555

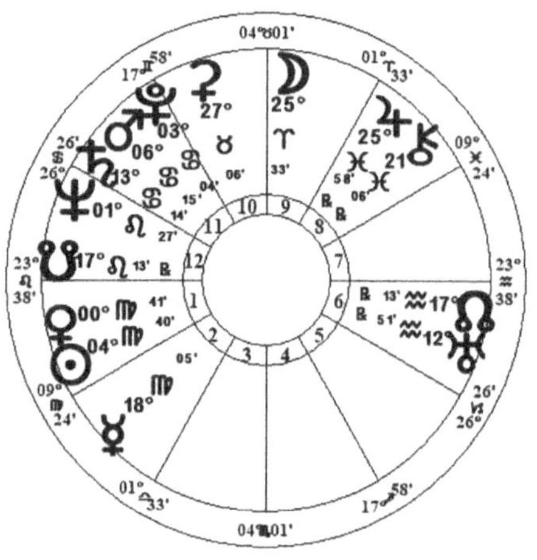

Ingrid Bergman
PREBLEs –LS108 & LS146
August 29, 1915 • 3:30 AM • Stockholm, Sweden

Tiger Woods
PREBLE–LS135
December 30, 1975 • 10:50 PM • Long Beach, CA, USA

Here's Lookin' at You, Kid!

"We'll always have Paris."

-Rick from *Casablanca*

At the tender age of two, Tiger Woods made an appearance on the *Mike Douglas Show* on October 6, 1978, where he demonstrated his astonishing golf skills in front of Bob Hope. With prodigious talent, focus, and the support and encouragement from his parents, as a toddler he landed on a network TV show and won over the crowd as well as the legendary Bob Hope.[2] Let's take a look at how that happened.

When the dragons of LS127 arrived on September 16, 1978, they returned with lifetimes of experience—forty in fact, since their 1978 appearance would find them well on their way to lunar eclipse middle age having been granted a seventy-two cycle lifetime. On that auspicious return, their special talents poured through 24 Pisces, landing right on Tiger's very public Seventh House DSC, one of four angles in a chart that is highly reactive to any transits, progression, or lunations. The DSC is *the* place most associated with how we validate ourselves through others. It is a zone of connection to an expanded world that is different from the safe and secure image that we carry of ourselves as seen through the Ascendant. Tiger's early contact with LS127's field of focus would set the stage for what was to become his life-long passion and brilliance for the game and would make him a legend *on a par* with celebrities like Bob Hope. By 2009, the "kid" had become Sports' First Billion-Dollar Man.[3]

And then there's Ingrid Bergman. Without knowing a word of English, she left her native Sweden in 1939 to wow American audiences both on screen and stage with her radiance. In 1942, she would co-star with Humphrey Bogart in *Casablanca*, which according to film critic Roger Ebert is "probably on more lists of the greatest films of all time than any other single title, including *Citizen Kane*."[4]

Principal filming of *Casablanca* began in the spring of 1942 and the film premiered on November 26, 1942, exactly three months to the day that the dragons of LS127 returned on August 26, 1942, at 2 Pisces. Now let's take a look at Ingrid's chart and notice that the activation degree actually lit up her Venus/Sun midpoint at 2 Virgo by opposition which, in the world of show business, is the cosmic spotlight signaling you out and wrapping you in its luminosity for all the world to see. Social media platforms like Instagram and TikTok that are designed for constant self-flagellation uploads are better served by lunation activations by conjunction. However, when dealing with distribution and corporate management in charge of your social capital, best pray for an opposition to your Sun or Moon and remember Ingrid. No wonder Bogart couldn't keep his eyes off her.

Lunar Saros 127 being so sweet to Tiger can be attributed to the nine conjunctions and oppositions that form cross links that strengthen the resonance between the two fields. LS127's persuasive and potent SNode/Pluto conjunction to Tiger's Sun marked the beginning of what would become one of the most phenomenal and legendary athletic careers of all time. LS127's love affair with Ingrid can be seen through its ties of enchantment from Neptune to both her Venus and her Sun along with its potent Cosmic Bridge SN/Pluto opposition to her Mars. Of note is the eclipse Ceres right on her Tenth House Taurus MC, always a link of real world support and validation.

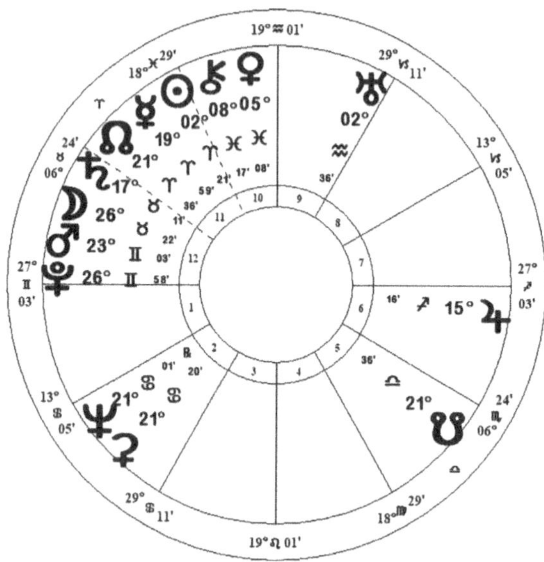

Wernher von Braun
PREBLEs—LS144 & LS111

March 23, 1912 • 9:15 AM • Wyrzysk, Poland

DR. SPACE

"Research is what I'm doing when I don't know what I'm doing."

-WERNHER VON BRAUN

Of all the portraits that illustrate the impact of lunar eclipse field dynamics, Wernher von Braun, rocket engineer, Nazi scientist, and ultimately head of NASA's successful Apollo 11 mission to the moon is a stellar standout. Born into the richly endowed and surreal energy field of Lunar Saros 144, von Braun became a baron at birth and as part of an aristocratic Prussian elite, enjoyed all the wealth and status that came with privilege, living in "a cultured atmosphere of good manners, tradition, appreciation of music, art, and literature, and a disciplined devotion to education."[5] On October 3, 1942, von Braun became part of history as the launch of his V-2/A-4 super weapon "was the world's first successful ballistic missile" giving rise to the Rocket Age.[6] With the defeat of Germany, von Braun surrendered to American forces eager to avail themselves of German military expertise. Considering his ties to the Nazi party, many in the U.S. military had their suspicions, "noting in a September 18, 1947, security report that Wernher von Braun "is regarded as a potential security threat."[7] Nevertheless, Von Braun's rise, like his rockets, was meteoric. The birth of NASA in the late 1950's led to von Braun being put in command of the newly created George C. Marshall Space Flight Center on July 1, 1960.[8]

Charts don't get much more surreal than his, not with both luminaries in exaltation, Venus in exaltation conjunct Chiron, Jupiter in rulership, Uranus enthroned in Aquarius, and Mercury and Mars in MR. Pluto, sitting on the Ascendant conjuncts an OOB Mars and Mercury, as ascendant ruler trines Jupiter in MR to Mars and in conjunction to the NNode dominates von Braun's life. Komilla Sutton writes that Rahu [North Node] "encourages an individual to go for overblown high fidelity experiences with no boundaries, and its conjunction with a planet can make these experiences surreal."[9] Braun's personality has that single minded drive toward a chosen goal that is found in Bucket chart patterns, especially when Jupiter, as singleton, marshals the field forward—this is a spectacular Jupiter and strategically placed within midpoint structures to maximize its full capability.

Lunar Saros 127 first made contact with von Braun's chart on August 26, 1942, just five weeks before the successful launch of the V-2 rocket that would put his name into the annals of history. At 2 Pisces, the lunar eclipse activated his Venus setting off his eye-catching Venus midpoint structures of which Venus/Mars-Saturn is the strongest. The successful October 1942 first flight of the V-2 ensured "Hitler's blessing for all-out development of the A-4" placing von Braun and his missile "at the top of the Third Reich's military priority list."[10]

LS127 would return in September of 1960 at 13 Pisces to find von Braun in charge of NASA's George C. Marshall Space Flight Center. In his inaugural address in January 1961, President John F. Kennedy spoke of exploring the stars and weeks later publicly called for "the peaceful use of space, and the limitation of war in that new environment."[11] By early 1961, von Braun's progressed Moon at 10 Pisces had reached both his natal and progressed Chiron, setting into motion new sets of priorities from which his previous collective failings and flaws as a Nazi scientist might find absolution. Fired in the kiln of expediency and hopefully national pride, and what would have been the greatest challenge of his life, von Braun's boyhood dream of interplanetary travel and spaceflight would finally be realized in the summer of 1969 when Apollo 11 and its crew landed on and safely returned from the moon.

As an engineer, one would be hard pressed to beat the advantages of the eclipse Uranus in opposition to his singleton Jupiter, or even better, its Chiron on his Uranus. Talk about a healing touch. These are quintessential links that define the fields of aviation research as they highlight the two signs (Sagittarius and Aquarius) with the two planets (Jupiter and Uranus) most often associated with flight and space technology. Von Braun's ties to LS127 are overwhelmingly positive. He benefited greatly from the support and recognition that the eclipse axis provided by illuminating his Neptune/Ceres conjunction in Cancer, which allowed him to play ball with the team that had the ball, irrespective of personal or political persuasions.

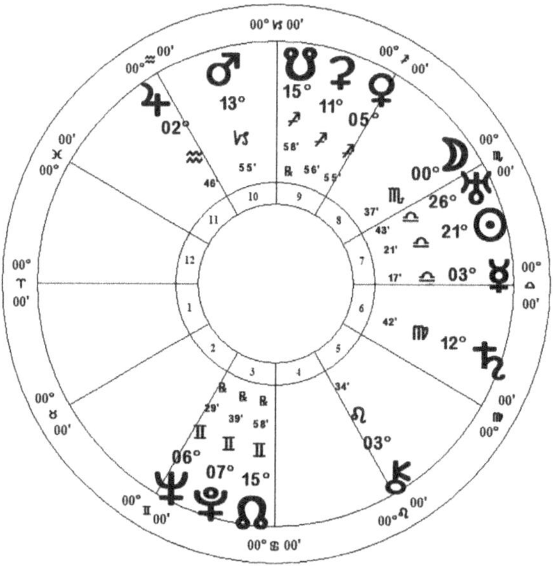

Dwight D. Eisenhower
PREBLE—LS147

October 14, 1890 • TOB Unknown • Denison, TX, USA

News Flash!

Eisenhower's Military Industrial Complex Speech

On January 17, 1961, President Dwight D. "Ike" Eisenhower gave his last and most famous speech of his presidency where he warned the nation to be vigilant of not only the growing power of the military industrial complex but also the growing power of the technological elite. The previous lunar eclipse occurred on September 5, 1960, at 13 Pisces which activated Eisenhower's "at the bends" Saturn in trine to an exalted Mars in Capricorn that understands the value of self-control and how to channel formidable power into the direction that best serves your agenda.

Ike's speech has gone down in history not only because of its critical message but because he gave voice to the growing influence of a military/corporate plutocracy that was already wielding its expanding economic and political hold and power to manipulate the levers of government to shape public policy.

President Eisenhower's natal chart links to the lunar eclipse field of LS127 through three brilliant patterns. First and foremost is the Cosmic Bridge, or in his case the "Corporate Bridge," considering that military might and corporate collusion were at the heart of his presidential warning. With the eclipse Uranus on his NNode, Eisenhower had a pretty good idea of how bad things could get and how fast life could change if the political system became inadvertently controlled by a power elite with enormous wealth and influence at their command. (This is sounding familiar).

The second pattern in play is the eclipse field's Mars on his natal Venus. This resonance opens him up to experience the daunting potential contained within his two high-flying *Kites*, formations created by his Grand Air Trines that desire clarity of communication but were often thwarted and frustrated by the oppositions from the Neptune/Pluto conjunction to Venus. The opposition within a Grand Trine brings a fated quality to the life that requires one to resolve core issues both internally but more often externally that deal with conflict resolution and outer world entanglements of control, manipulation, and game-playing. As a two-term president from 1953 until J. F. Kennedy took the reins of power in 1961, Ike had eight very public years to engage with the pain and the promise inherent within those spectacular patterns. The activation of his Venus by the eclipse OOB Mars and its companion Neptune in the fall of 1960 would have added an additional layer of anxiety to his growing apprehension over the rising power of the military industrial complex.

As usual, I've saved the best for last. At 3 Aquarius, the eclipse field Chiron makes a stunning opposition to Ike's natal Chiron along with a conjunction to his Jupiter, rousing equal portions of both terror and hope: Terror for the destruction that he knew the military war machine was capable of inflicting, and hope for a future where political will might be brought to bear to serve rather than subjugate people.

The backstory to the speech indicates that by October 31, 1960, one of his speechwriters, Ralph E. Williams, was already warning him of a "permanent war-based industry run by former military officials."[12] The warning obviously made an impression because it survived endless rounds of rewrites and drafts to become one of the key takeaways that people most remember from his farewell speech. Of note is the Crescent phase that LS127 had just entered in 1942 on its thirty-eighth return. By 1960 it was well into the fray; many will experience their own personal obstacle course in the struggle to move forward. This is a time of having to deal with delays and all manner of resistance as a new energy of self-assertion takes hold.

LS127's Chiron sextile to Mars affirms the value of sextiles in their capacity to be change-agents whose manner and message are positively received. And that is good news for all of us with sleepy sextiles who have lingered too long in the soft sheets of slumber. It's time to get up and stir those little darlings into action.

LS127 Summary

Focus your talent, energy, and ambition when these accomplished Earth Dragons make an appearance. Robust and in their prime, their independent energy field encourages one to up their game and embrace the challenge of the moment. All of them are prodigies in their own right and know what it takes to achieve a dream. Their arrival marks a time of accelerated activity, increased vitality, and the reward of accomplishment. Turnarounds and failure are built in and should never be considered setbacks—more like adventures as you learn the ropes. Overcoming obstacles and embracing phase shifts are just some of the great gifts of this dragon family as they lead you ever-so-skillfully into finding your focus. And focus, as the Great Gretzky reminds us, is the key to mastery.

There is an amazing sense of optimism within this dragon realm that comes from the confidence of high expectation and the ability to deliver. And as the beloved mythologist Joseph Campbell was famous for saying, "I don't need faith because I have experience." In the realm of manifestation, first principles apply whether we're summoning our muses for help with designing a sonnet or a satellite. The Earth Dragons of LS127 are here to support our goals, but we must have the courage and conviction to take that first step. Welcome the challenges ahead and all the work, dedication, common sense, vitality, tenacity, and perseverance to go the distance.

This is a most progressive lunar eclipse that seeks to find at least one outlet for its superbly inventive disposition. The spirit of innovation is strong as is the desire for mastery; it is essential that we be open to graciously learning from what life sends our way. Personal interests can rapidly turn entrepreneurial as new horizons call for a modern approach. Riding this wave of energy will seem effortless as recognition and rapid advancement is now possible. Social connections and savoir faire open doors. Fired in the kiln—follow your destiny

Phase	Return	Year
New Moon	34th	1870
Crescent	38th	1942
First Quarter	43rd	2032
Gibbous	47th	2104

LS127 Luminaries

William Shakespeare	April 26, 1564
Edgar Degas	July 19, 1834
Maria Montessori	August 31, 1870
Dmitri Shostakovich	September 25, 1906
Soichiro Honda	November 17, 1906
Bede Griffiths	December 17, 1906
Lauren Bacall	September 16, 1924
Lee Iacocca	October 15, 1924
Rod Serling	December 25, 1924
Jack Lemmon	February 8, 1925
Ann Roddick	October 23, 1942
Jimi Hendrix	November 27, 1942
Janice Joplin	January 19, 1943
Kenneth Branagh	December 10, 1960
Julia Louis-Dreyfus	January 13, 1961
Mark Messier	January 18, 1961
Wayne Gretzky	January 26, 1961
Rachel McAdams	November 17, 1978
Katie Holmes	December 18, 1978

1. Jeff Green, *Pluto—The Evolutionary Journey of the Soul Volume 1,* p. 16.
2. Tigers Prowl. https://www.youtube.com/watch?v=ScEv-66QT-c. Retrieved Feb. 25, 2022.
3. Kurt Badenhausen, Sports' First Billion-Dollar Man https://www.forbes.com/2009/09/29/tiger-woods-billion-business-sports-tiger.html?sh=5d49c6e67573. Retrieved Feb 25, 2022.
4. https://en.wikipedia.org/wiki/Ingrid_Bergman. Retrieved Feb. 25, 2022.
5. Bob Ward, *Dr. Space-The Life of Wernher von Braun,*(Annapolis, MD: Naval Institute Press, 2005), p. 10.
6. Michael J. Neufeld, *Von Braun-Dreamer of Space Engineer of War* (New York: Alfred A. Knopf, 2007), p. 137.
7. Wayne Biddle, *Dark Side of the Moon-Wernher Von Braun, the Third Reich, and the Space Race,* (New York: W.W. Norton & Company, 2009), p. 147.
8. Neufeld, Von Braun, p. 346.
9. Komilla Sutton, *The Lunar Nodes-Crisis and Redemption* (Bournemouth, England: The Wessex Astrologer Ltd., 2001), p. 100.
10. Ward, *Dr. Space,* p. 33.
11. https://history.nasa.gov/Apollomon/Apollo.html
12. https://www.nytimes.com/2010/12/11/us/politics/11eisenhower.html

LUNAR SAROS 128

"I don't believe in astrology; I'm a Sagittarius and we're skeptical."

-Arthur C Clarke

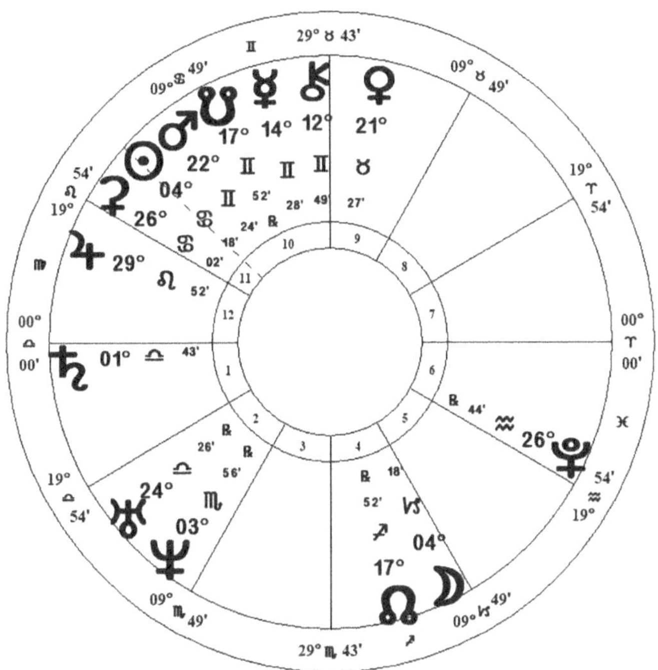

Lunar Saros 128

June 26, 1304 • 09:32:22 AM • North Pole

Coming Into Existence

Creativity, drive, and ongoing challenge are just some of the key concepts that Lunar Saros 128 provides. This North Node Capricorn eclipse shares its solid foundation with a nodal axis famous for winning the game of life. Together, their talent pool is a mighty mainframe of cosmic confidence that is nothing short of miraculous. And it just gets better. Its Grand Air Trine holds within it both an OOB Mars (23N53) and an OOB Pluto (24S18) reminiscent of the socially responsible, defiant/defender John Wick archetype we have all come to know and love. Social structures are evolving under the strategic management of the eclipse axis and its cardinal T-Square to a highly visible and popular Libran AP Saturn.

LS128 is full of heroism and courage as seen by its Sun/Mars parallel declination along with Mars in contra-parallel to Pluto. The only other lunar eclipse with an OOB Mars at such high declination is LS144—Real Surreal (see the Air Eclipses of Part Three). It's one of the wildest eclipses of the entire series. Meanwhile, this Pluto holds an opposition to Jupiter, and both are partnered up with a willing Venus in Taurus in rulership and more than happy to share. This threesome pairs well and offers spectacular creativity regardless of the chosen field. One is just as apt to succeed in robotic engineering or astrophysics; what's important here is the passion (Sun/Mars parallel declination) for the emerging discovery of the self as experienced through the act of creation. The Saturn/Jupiter-Neptune midpoint is a gateway, allowing one level of awareness to pass through to another, helping to shape and mold into existence something from where there was nothing.

However, the Saturn/Jupiter-Neptune midpoint can bring both gains and losses and we need to be prepared for numbers to appear on both sides of the ledger. Jupiter and Pluto's reputation for speculation is legendary and, in the company of a well-heeled Venus in Taurus, it might be prudent to, as Oprah loves to say, "Sleep on it" when you hear about the latest hot crypto craze. Breakthroughs also bring breakdowns; the presence of Saturn at the AP is a warning that societal pressures could be instrumental in rapidly shifting political and economic policies and this is important when tracking LS128's return cycle.

Of note: Venus sits at twenty-one degrees Taurus, a critical fixed degree that is noted for a tendency to withdraw from life, especially with its square to the OOB Pluto. As well, the Sun has a very home-body, double-dipped, fourth degree Cancerian vibe and is in a reclusive water trine to retrograde Neptune, just off another cozy fourth degree tendency to isolate as loneliness is a by-product of this synergy.

But let's end on a happy note. The essence of Lunar Saros 128 is overwhelmingly positive. As stated earlier, these Earth Dragons are winners; there's no going back to Wonder Bread when you've had sourdough bread made from a 19th century Klondike starter. And as stated earlier, these lunar dragons thrive on challenges. To create order out of the daily turbulence of life is a daily chore for all of us, regardless of the lunar eclipse in season. But the gift of LS128 is that these lunar dragons are full of optimism, hope, triumph, passion, and confidence *in spite of* all the skepticism and chaos. And they wouldn't have it any other way. They are problem solvers who are deeply emotional and, at the same time, reasonable. Now that is a winning formula you can bet on.

Closest Midpoints: Uranus/Mars-Pluto, Saturn/Jupiter-Neptune
Isotraps: Mercury/Saturn conjunct Venus/Uranus,
Venus/Saturn conjunct Mars/Jupiter

1900—2100 Eclipses: Lunar Saros—128

1917, 1935, 1953, 1971, 1989, 2007, 2025, 2043, 2061, 2079, 2097
Length of cycle —1,262 years
Series ends—August 2, 2566

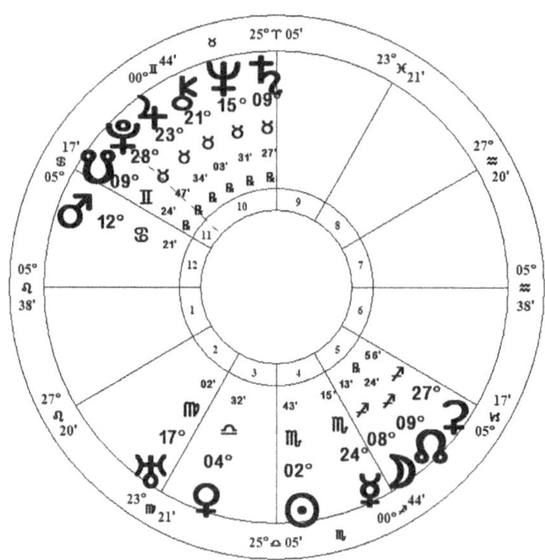

Pablo Picasso
PREBLE—LS128

October 25, 1881 • 11:15 PM • Malaga, Spain

"Yo soy el rey. I am the King."

-PICASSO

A Dark God Trying to Remake the World

"The important thing is to do, and nothing else; be what it may."

-PABLO PICASSO

Picasso was the wealthiest and most iconic artist of the 20th century. John Berger writes in *The Success and Failure of Picasso* that "Just after the Second World War Picasso bought a house in the South of France and paid for it with one still-life. Whatever he wishes to own, he can acquire by drawing it."[1] Picasso was a legend, and an oversized legend at that, so just a few ideas will be explored here to add even more magnitude to his truly oversized life.

First, let's review some "first principles" astrology to appreciate what basic pattern placements can offer in a chart. Picasso is a leftie—that is to say, using the standard Western "ten planet model" that includes the Sun and Moon, seven out of ten planets are on the left half (or eastern hemisphere) of the chart. This represents a person who stamps their personality on their environment. Then notice that half of his planets are found in the south-east quadrant (Houses Ten, Eleven, and Twelve) giving early life experiences of self-sufficiency that tend to bring on success later in life. The Sun and Moon are in the north-west quadrant (Houses Four, Five, and Six), making relationships the key to his happiness. Picasso's life overflowed with an endless stream of psychosexual entanglements that would worship and demean an astounding number of lovers, mistresses, models, and two wives. His voracious virility seemed to border on the monstrous.

I labored long over his sexuality as it frankly puzzled me; I just didn't get how and where all that goddess-/god-awful treatment of women was coming from. The stereotype is that most Latin men, to some degree, place their females on a sliding scale from doormat to deity. Picasso's Venus in Libra held no difficult aspects nor did Uranus as ruler of the Seventh House. Something else was knocking on the door here. After years of working as an astrologer I discovered that the Moon was as important as Venus in determining what a person needs and meets in relationship; Picasso's chart holds the Moon/NNode in Sagittarius in the Fifth House (which is always on the hunt) and with Ceres, one's sexual appetite would be enthusiastic, certainly passionate, but never cruel. Maybe it was his Moon quindecile (165 degree) to Jupiter, which has a touch of obsession. To solve the mystery, we now turn to his lunar eclipse family.

Pablo Picasso's Connections to the Dragons of LS128
↓South Node with South Node↓

1st Harmonics: Neptune – Sun,
Mercury/Chiron – SNode, Venus – Chiron/Jupiter, Saturn – Venus
2nd Harmonics: Chiron – Moon/NNode, Venus – Mercury

The 1st Harmonic Neptune to his Sun adds even more magic to his palette, while the Mercury/Chiron 1st Harmonic to his SNode carries a savant quality that is reintroduced—Picasso was a prodigy and could draw before he could speak.[2] I found his partnership issues starting to make sense through the eclipse 1st Harmonic Venus on his Chiron/Jupiter. Now, all that craving Pluto/Jupiter/Venus Fixed T-Square power could seed and feed his prodigious Jupiter and together with Chiron, take those cravings far beyond any known landmarks of convention. With this one cross-pollination, his dark and tumultuous sex life came into focus. His relationships with women bordered on the macabre:

John Richardson's *A Life of Picasso: The Minotaur Years, 1933 – 1943* lays out a litany of despair. From mental collapse, self-destructive devotion to suicide, the willingness of his women to "sacrifice [themselves] on the altar of his art" was astonishing.[3] Picasso's 1st Harmonic AP Saturn on his Venus is classic May/December material. He was enraptured by youth and beauty given that his pristine four degree Venus in Libra was practically "untouched" by her fellow planetary companions.

The 2nd Harmonics bring the lunar eclipse characteristics right to your door; here Chiron gets a front row seat to crack open a lifetime's worth of adventure due to its 2nd Harmonic to the Moon/NNode. And since we know Chiron carries the master maverick touch, the Moon/NNode will be an eager student, open and willing to experiment. The eclipse 2nd Harmonic Venus to his Mercury and its triple oppositions to Chiron, Jupiter, and Pluto in Taurus speaks to an impressive seventy-eight-year career of ceaseless productivity; his colossal oeuvre numbered over 147,800 pieces, consisting of 13,500 paintings, 100,000 prints and engravings, 300 sculptures and ceramics and 34,000 illustrations.[4] His Mercury held an almost exact parallel declination to his Moon, which would have greatly increased his intellectual curiosity, his sense of beauty, form, design, and love of art along with the ever-flowing river of youthful sensuality that served as muse and madness to his insatiable genius.

Like Spielberg, whose creative genius was set on fire by the Fire Dragon returns of LS130 in 1975 and again in 1993 as they were evolving through their Balsamic phase, Picasso was born into a Balsamic phase governed by the Earth Dragons of LS128. At the time of his birth in 1881, LS128 was entering the twilight of its thirty-third return. And as noted previously, the key take-away to establish harmony with any dragons at this stage is to surrender to the dream of what your life could be. While still in the darkness, yet with the intuition that the light is returning, one is obligated to remain within the confines of self, alone and unencumbered by the pressures and presence of outside forces. It is a time to plant your personal sphere with your own seed essence that will burst into new life as the cycle progresses into its next phase.

And that is exactly what happened. By 1899, Picasso left Barcelona and arrived in Paris, just a few days before his nineteenth birthday, speaking no French and having no place to stay. In less than two years, by the summer of 1901, Picasso would have his first successful exhibition and be well on his way to fame and fortune. Now that is the glory and excitement of watching your PREBLE change phases. As your dragon family enters a new phase in their evolutionary journey, so too will you. There are always noticeable shifts in your life focus and energy levels when your dragon family experiences a new phase of unfoldment.

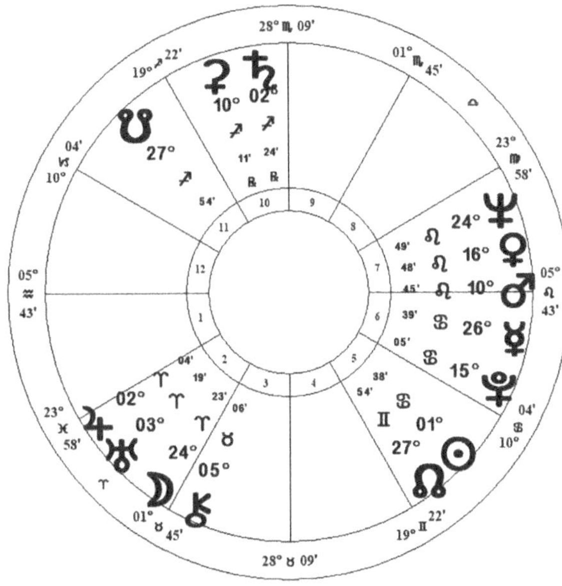

Bob Fosse
PREBLE—LS119

June 23, 1927 • 10:29 PM • Chicago, IL, USA

Choreographer/Dancer/Director

"Live like you'll die tomorrow,
Work like you don't need the money, and dance like nobody's watching."

-Bob Fosse

Bob Fosse's big break came in 1953 while under contract as a dancer for MGM in the movie *Kiss Me, Kate* when he was allowed to choreograph a short section of a dance for Carol Haney and himself.[5] Fosse's electrifying choreography led to his being hired in November to choreograph the new Broadway show *The*

Pajama Game; it would open in April of 1954 to rave reviews and make him an overnight success.[6]

Fosse's work on *The Pajama Game* would take root and flourish as a result of July's LS128 impact on his Ascendant at 3 Aquarius. LS128 returned eighteen years later in August of 1971 to find him editing the soon to be released megahit *Cabaret* in early '72 when Fosse would be just months away from a meteoric recognition of his talent. Presenting at 14 Aquarius, the lunar eclipse would throw its spotlight on his theatrical Mars-Venus conjunction in Leo.

Bob Fosse's Connections to the Dragons of LS128
↑North Node with South Node↓

1st Harmonics: Sun – Sun, Mars – NNode, Ceres – Mercury
2nd Harmonics: Uranus – Moon, Chiron – Ceres,
Saturn – Jupiter/Uranus, Neptune – Chiron, Pluto – Neptune

2nd Harmonics like this means the world is going to find you. The double dip of Uranus to his Moon and the eclipse Saturn to his Uranus/Jupiter brings all the energy of the Mercury/Saturn conjunct Venus/Uranus isotrap into play, giving Fosse the freedom to experiment with unusual styles while the world makes it possible to take whatever risks seem warranted to gain a fresh perspective. This is a choreographer's dream isotrap where innovation is the answer to any problem.

Fosse would get a taste of success during LS128's thirty-seventh return as it was moving through the last leg of its New Moon phase. For the majority of lunar eclipses, the New Moon phase can usually be expected around their thirty-fourth return. The New Moon phase for the Earth Dragons of LS128 began on June 23, 1899, and would end with their thirty-eighth return on August 6, 1971, as they entered their Crescent phase. Until his death from a heart attack on September 23, 1987, Fosse would be in eternal motion: he was an actor, dancer, writer, director of films and theatrical productions but he is best remembered for his innovative and award-winning choreography. At the 1973 Academy Awards, Fosse won for Best Director for *Cabaret.* Also, in 1973 he would win multiple Tony Awards and Primetime Emmy Awards for his roles as producer, choreographer, and director. Bob Fosse is the only person to have ever won all three major industry awards in the same year.[7]

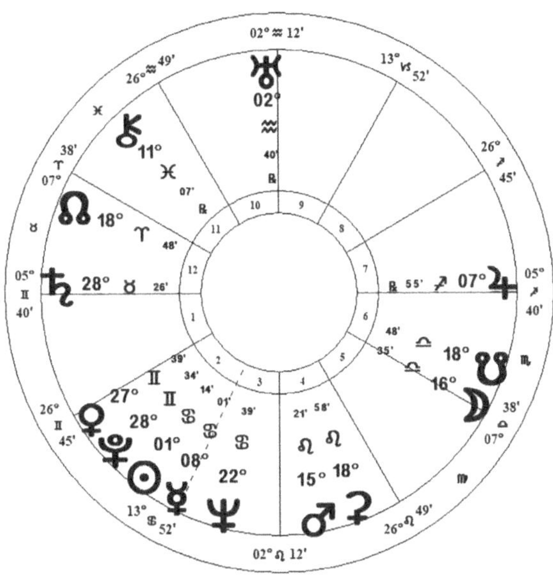

Alan Turing
PREBLE—LS111

June 23, 1912 • 2:15 AM • London, UK

"Sometimes it is the people who no one imagines anything of, who do the things that no one can imagine."

-ALAN TURING

Father of Computer Science and AI

"He was a national treasure, and we hounded him to his death."

-JOHN GRAHAM-CUMMING

The basic principles for the modern computer with its programs stored in computer memory were made possible by British mathematician Alan Turing. In the summer of 1935, "while trying to solve the "decidability problem," one of the great mathematical challenges of the time, inspiration struck Turing for an imaginary machine that could simulate human reasoning."[8] Turing's flash of genius, with its accompanying proofs defining the notion of his "Universal Machine" (now called a Turing Machine), would produce his celebrated paper, "On Computable Numbers," in the spring of 1936, and published in early 1937.[9] However, due to what biographer David Leavitt suggests was "Turing's ignorance of what his contemporaries were up to," his as-yet unpublished paper with its "refreshing directness and simplicity" would, in the spring of 1936 be superseded by Princeton mathematician Alonzo Church's published papers on the same problem.[10]

At the time of LS128's arrival on July 16, 1935, Turing was enjoying the fruits of a King's College Fellowship, a remarkable honor for a 23 year old, freeing him to pursue his choice of academic interests. Activating at 23 Capricorn, LS128 set off his gloomy Neptune at 22 Cancer square to an emotionally conflicted Libran Moon/SNode conjunction. Nikola Tesla has the same Libran Moon/SNode that would have contributed to his emotional isolation and dissatisfaction. In fact, both men share a remarkable resonance; born in 1856, Tesla's nodal axis is within two degrees of Turing's and both, using their NNode in Aries, were innovators and pioneers in their respective fields.

With Uranus at 2 Aquarius the handle on his Bucket chart pattern, retrograde, conjunct his MC and in a powerhouse quincunx to his AP Sun, Turing's career path and personality were decidedly distraught, brilliant, eccentric, vivacious, and solitary. His life was marked by a constant stream of frustration, defiance, and an inability to compromise. This one aspect alone acts as the central "axis mundo" of his life to the extent that the arrival of LS128 in the spring of 1935 would enjoy a remarkable encounter with his deep solar self.

Alan Turing's Connections to the Dragons of LS128

1st Harmonics: Sun – Sun, Sun – Mercury
Midpoints: Mercury – Venus/Saturn, Saturn/Pluto, Sun/Saturn,
Sun – Sun/Mercury, Saturn – Jupiter/Neptune, Ceres – Mercury/Mars

Alan Turing has two harmonics that connect him into the matrix of LS128—but look at all those midpoint connections. It's obvious that midpoint resonance is indeed worth paying attention to. With a gift of brilliance from his PREBLE-LS111—Summon Your Muse—and the alchemy of its mythic Philosopher's Stone, Turing was perfectly positioned to reap the full benefit of all the originality, vitality, and "coming into existence" that was Lunar Saros 128's ground of being through its two Cosmic Bridges: one to his first degree fighting spirit Sun in Cancer, and the other to the remarkable and transformational eighth degree Cancerian OOB Mercury.

Turing's brilliant mathematical leap of 1935 can be appreciated through Lunar Saros 128's Mercury on not one, not two, but three midpoints that all involve Saturn. Some of the most powerful stars of the Pleiades attach to his Saturn: Alcyone, known as the Third Eye of the Pleiades, has a reputation for insight and vision but also anger. Algol is known for its affinity to undertake difficult tasks. Atlas bequeaths great determination and personifies the best of Taurus.

Twenty-nine years after his death in 1954, Turing's story was finally told by fellow mathematician Andrew Hodges in his 1983 biography, *Alan Turing: The Enigma*. The 2014 film, *The Imitation Game*, inspired by his book, helps us appreciate Turing's extraordinary mind and life.

LS128 Summary

These Earth Dragons embody the fertility and abundant creativity of the Earth itself. Their path across the globe entails a profound sense of urgency as 1,262 years just never seems to be enough time to do what needs to be done. Their thirty-eighth return in 1971 marked the beginning of their second Crescent phase of unfoldment and by 1989 the renewed sense of progress was well underway. This new wave of innovation will carry forward until this lunar family reaches their First Quarter phase again in the year 2061. Until then, be on the lookout for backsliding as every return will give opportunities to find the proverbial chink in your armor as meeting delays and overcoming resistance is their daily fare. The Crescent phase is famous for displays of resistance and inertia, but these are now experienced Earth Dragons who are building their strength one hurdle at a time.

Whether by birthright or rite of passage, a future full of discovery awaits as the curtain on life begins to rise. Their arrival coincides with an awakening to a call or mission that is accompanied by a desire to produce and feel creative. Decisions made in the context of their return are sure to earn hefty dividends down the road while previous efforts continue to build momentum. This is a time perfect for planning and bringing forth fresh expectations. One can confidently predict that life-changing roles are within reach and that they will offer a more fulfilling path in the expression of one's talents.

Do not undervalue the importance of social relationships as friends are part of the mojo that can help drive your career forward. This is salutary advice; there is a tendency to be independent and to want to do things your own way.

Either way, when this eclipse activates, effort is rewarded, and personal work becomes deliciously gratifying. All Earth eclipses need physical connection; to be grounded in either your own body or someone else's is as natural as breathing. Do your best to indulge in physical exercise, massage, yoga, satisfying sex and all manner of healthful means of keeping your body purring. Your body does not approve of constraints, boredom, or stagnation so it's best to keep things upbeat and fun. For the most part, travel and commerce bring prosperity.

LS128 Luminaries

Louella Parsons	August 6, 1881
Cecil B. DeMille	August 12, 1881
Pablo Picasso	October 25, 1881
James Cagney	July 17, 1899
Alfred Hitchcock	August 13, 1899
Nöel Coward [E1]	December 16, 1899
Arthur C Clarke	December 16, 1917
David Bohm	December 20, 1917
Dizzy Gillespie	October 21, 1917
Ei-ichi Negishi[E2]	July 14, 1935
Luciano Pavarotti	October 12, 1935
Ken Burns[E3]	July 29, 1953
Woody Allen	December 1, 1953
John Malkovich	December 9, 1953
Jocko Willink	September 8, 1971
Snoop Dogg	October 20, 1971
Winona Ryder	October 29, 1971
Brie Larson	October 1, 1989
Dakota Johnson	October 4, 1989
Taylor Swift	December 13, 1989

PREBLE—LS123
Ken Burns
Ei-ichi Negishi

1. John Berger, *The Success and Failure of Picasso* (New York: Pantheon Books, 1989), p. 3.

2. Berger, *The Success and Failure of Picasso*, p. 27.

3. John Richardson, *A Life of Picasso The Minotaur Years, 1933 – 1943* (New York: Alfred A. Knopf, 2021), p. 11.

4. https://www.pablopicasso.org/picasso-facts.jsp. Retrieved May 23, 2022.

5. Martin Gottfried, *All His Jazz.* (New York: Da Capo Press, 2003), p. 72.

6. Sam Wasson, *Fosse (*New York: Houghton Mifflin Harcourt, 2013), p. 87.

7. https://en.wikipedia.org/wiki/Bob_Fosse. Retrieved May 24, 2022.

8. David Leavitt, *The Man Who Knew Too Much-Alan Turing and the Invention of the Computer* (New York: Atlas Books, 2006), p. 54.

9. Leavitt, *The Man Who Knew Too Much,* p. 56.

10. Ibid., p. 106.

LUNAR SAROS 138

"We were young, we were foolish, we were arrogant, but we were right."

-Abbie Hoffman

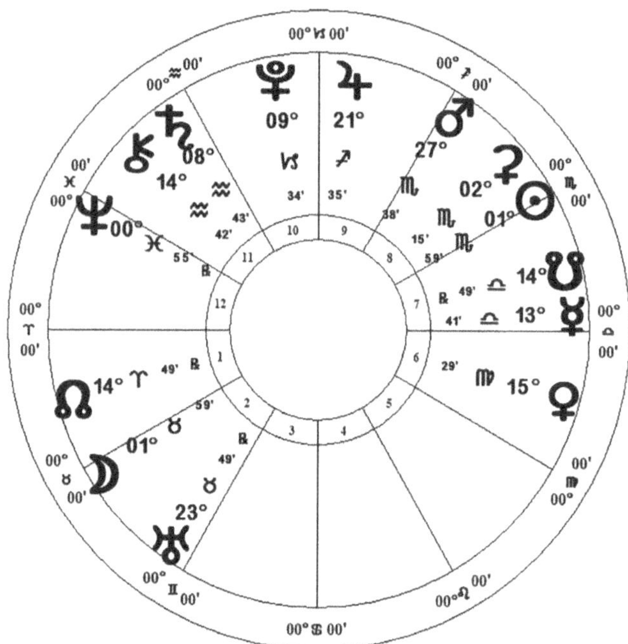

Lunar Saros 138

October 25, 1521 • 11:52:57 PM • North Pole

Legends and Legacy

This is a North Node Taurus eclipse with ruler Venus in Virgo as the Locomotive driving the pattern forward. Her Mars/Venus-Saturn midpoint is no stranger to frustration, and much can be accomplished through sheer force of will and the desire to create a lasting legacy. This NNode eclipse offers a punch of momentum as well as fascinating contacts with people who are in a position to help. The Node/Mars-Neptune midpoint, along with Neptune's septile to Pluto is pure inspiration, making this eclipse a heavy hitter for anyone ready for opportunity to strike.

The Sun/Jupiter conjunct Mercury/Pluto isotrap represents a bastion of talent in fields as diverse as astronomy to zoology and everything in between. From the theoretical to the theatrical this lunar eclipse is open to anyone with a great idea or initiative. Many will fall under a spell of their own making with the Sun's trine and Moon's sextile to Neptune in Pisces and its diaphanous patterns of creative self-expression. However, the Moon's sextile to Neptune and its septile to Pluto provide a darker, slippery-slope of susceptibility to themes and schemes of chicanery, nonsense, and full-on deceit. The MR between Venus and the mental machinations of the Mercury/SNode is no stranger to duplicity, especially when it is acting/reacting out of instinct rather than logic.

There is a mythic dimension to this lunar eclipse that is both fabulous and fatal. Fabulous in that Jupiter in Sagittarius sets the stage for financial luck, free spending, and living well. And fatal if one is not prepared to live in a world with boundaries, order, and good governance. Compounding chaos is Ceres. Worshiped throughout the ancient world, Ceres/Demeter was the all-nourishing great mother. Her astrological story, as told by Demetra George, revolves around Kore/Persephone's abduction by Pluto to the Underworld, Ceres' subsequent grief and suffering, and her search to become reunited with her daughter.[1] As one of the major dramas of western mythology, it spins into the world and evokes stories of loss and return. Her cazimi (within 17 minutes of arc) conjunction to the Sun puts it right at its core where she is both symbolically and physically consumed. This is a rare event and LS138 is the only Saros Series to feature such a conjunction. As Ceres unites with the solar orb, we are nourished even when we have lost our way or have been abandoned by others. We may grieve and rage but our capacity and desire for rebirth can never die.

Jupiter in the eclipse field conjuncts the Galactic Core (GC) of our Milky Way Galaxy. The GC is home to what may be more than one super-massive black hole and any planet that connects into the GC seems to have a particular destiny or raison d'etre that gives a special meaning to the life. For LS138 it brings a powerful financial motive into the life as well as a love of exploration.

Out of the 47 Lunar Saros Series eclipses in this book, LS138 is the *only* one that features the Moon in Taurus until the year 2060 and the arrival of Lunar Saros 156. There is a steady beat to the power within this lunar eclipse (Moon trine Pluto) that welcomes in the challenges (Moon square Saturn) of growth that can lead to remarkable feats of creativity and worldly accomplishments. Of all the lunar eclipses, LS138 is blessed in that it seems to have the least emotional personality problems/baggage of any Lunar Saros Series.

Closest Midpoints: Mars/Venus-Saturn, Node/Mars-Neptune
Isotraps: Sun/Jupiter conjunct Mercury/Pluto
Moon/Neptune conjunct Saturn/Uranus

1900—2100 Eclipses: Lunar Saros—138

1900, 1918, 1936, 1954, 1972, 1990, 2008, 2026, 2044, 2062, 2080, 2098
Length of cycle —1,460 years
Series ends— March 30, 2982

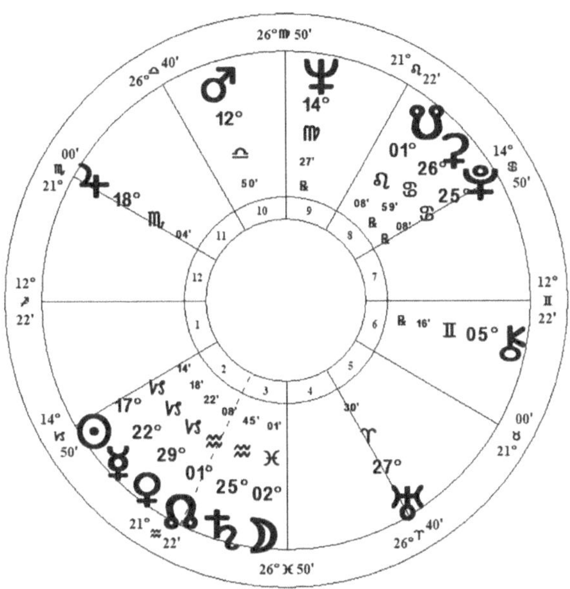

Elvis Presley
PREBLE—LS118

January 8, 1935 • 4:35 AM • Tupelo, MS, USA

The King of Rock 'n' Roll

"Ambition is a dream with a V8 engine. Ain't nowhere else in the world where you can go from driving a truck to a Cadillac overnight."

-ELVIS

Rock 'n' Roll history was made on July 5, 1954, when Sam Phillips, owner of Sun Records in Memphis, Tennessee, recorded Elvis Presley's version of *That's All Right (Mama)*, releasing it as a single two weeks [July 19, 1954] later.[2] Just two days after recording the song, on July 7, WHBQ Memphis disc jockey Dewey Phillips aired it on his *Red, Hot and Blue* show, playing it to an appreciative local audience.[3] Sonny West, Elvis' bodyguard for sixteen years, wrote in *Elvis: Still Taking Care of Business*, "For a local boy like Elvis to be on the show was considered big time."[4]

Move over momma 'cause on July 16, 1954, LS138 made a grand ole entry to the earthly domain, landing at 23 Capricorn, engulfing Elvis' Mercury at 22 Capricorn and its sweet conjunction to Venus. Presley's timing was epic. His action-oriented cardinal line-up and T-Square jumped at the chance to channel this opportunity into a project that would have real-world consequences, and it did, setting into motion a series of events that would place him solidly on the road to superstardom and all in keeping with his PREBLE—LS118's innate understanding of how the marketplace worked. In addition, Elvis was experiencing an exact progressed Moon square to his progressed Sun from 7 Scorpio to 7 Aquarius, a perfect turning point that can always be counted on to reorient the life as it represents the falling away of old patterns and habits that just don't bring the satisfaction of yesteryears. The third quarter phase, as Elvis experienced it, is often the springboard for the most productive period of a life as our skill set gets an upgrade to fit the new person that is coming online.

Resonating on his Mercury opposition Pluto/Ceres, the lunar dragons of LS138 would have to have had an even deeper accord with Elvis considering their own Sun/Ceres signature. Either way, the eclipse would mark the beginning of his meteoric rise and success with all the excess that money, ambition, and power attract. With cash, Cadillacs, and a hip shake that shook the world, Elvis' appetite for indulgence was legendary, no doubt helped along by a tight conjunction of the GA to his Ascendant. In 1935, the GA was at 13 Sagittarius, and here again we have the GA theme across their respective fields, lending its enormous gravitational power, attraction and mass to the personality and distinctive style that would turn the image of Elvis into an icon. In my work as an astrologer, I have found that people who have the GA on the Ascendant and especially on the MC or in a First or 2nd Harmonic to the Sun, Moon or Ceres have a greatly expanded sense of their own destiny. Millions of fans adored him, and they liked his music too. And if that wasn't enough, Elvis had one of the most beautiful faces on the planet—a face that held his fans spellbound.

Elvis Presley's Connections to the Dragons of LS138

1st Harmonics: Mercury/SNode – Mars,
Neptune – Moon, Moon – Uranus, Venus – Neptune

Ties of tenderness link Presley's chart to LS138's Dragon DNA through double bonds of bewitchment: the eclipse Venus conjuncts his Neptune and the eclipse Neptune makes a 1st Harmonic and a Cosmic Bridge to his Piscean Moon. His second CB is built from LS138's persuasive Mercury MR to Venus and its SNode conjunction to his Mars. But for thrills and spills it is his powerhouse T-Square with the leg of the T on Uranus that gets all the glory from the lunar two degree Taurean double dose of exaltation. Having the earthiness, sensuality, and musicality of the Taurus Moon grounding the excitement of his Uranus in Aries in the Fifth House of entertainment, pleasure, sex, and rock n' roll *is* the story of Elvis.

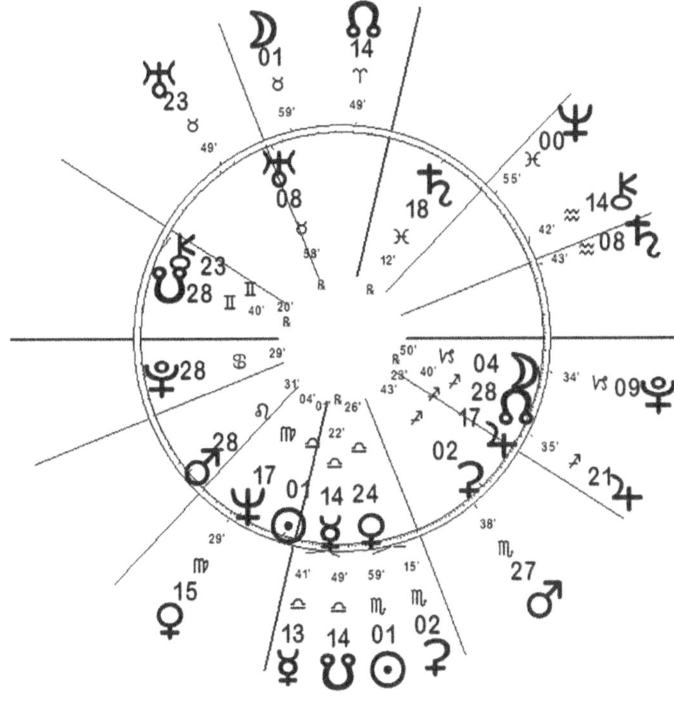

Inside

Jim Henson
PREBLE—LS138

Sept 24, 1936 • 12:10 AM • Greenville, MS, USA

Outside

LS138
October 15, 1521 • 11:51:54 PM • North Pole

Muppet Man—The New Walt Disney

"A man whose joyful genius transcended age, language, geography, and culture–and continues to beguile audiences worldwide."

-Brian Jay Jones

Jim Henson was one of the most widely known puppeteers in history. His legacy as the creator of The Muppets includes his work as an Oscar-nominated director, Emmy Award-winning television producer and writer. He was the innovative force behind the beloved television series *Sesame Street* and *The Muppet Show* and films such as *The Muppet Movie,* and creator of advanced puppets for projects like *Fraggle Rock, The Dark Crystal,* and *Labyrinth.*[5] Henson died on May 16, 1990, at the age of 53. At his funeral, Big Bird paid his respects by singing, "It's Not Easy Being Green" and expressed his gratitude to Kermit the Frog—by all accounts, Henson's Muppet alter ego.

Deeply embedded and entwined within his earthly DNA, the artistic visions and abundance of LS138's exuberant Earth Dragons were already hard at work. At age 18, with the return of these celestial myth makers at 23 Capricorn opposite his Fifth House ruler Pluto, Henson had already coined the term that would become his legacy. His two cowboy puppets created for Joe Campbell at *Circle 4 Ranch* and the soundtrack discs pre-recorded by Campbell for Jim's puppets to perform to, were labeled by studio engineers with stickers reading "Campbell Muppets" or "Circle 4 Muppets" on November 10, 1954.[6]

Jim Henson was born to be a bridge between the chimerical realm of fantasy and the real world of hands-on artistic creativity. His chart is presented to illustrate the dynamic potential of resonance between his natal chart and his lunar dragon family. First and 2nd Harmonics will be listed. For the sake of brevity and as a pathway into using harmonics to define resonance across fields, only the top three 1st Harmonics will be used to demonstrate how their influence informs the basic structure of his character and personality.

Jim Henson's Connections to the Dragons of LS138

1st Harmonics: SNode/Mercury – Mercury, Pluto – Moon, Venus – Neptune, Jupiter – Jupiter, Uranus – Uranus
2nd Harmonics: Neptune – Mars, Venus – Saturn

Now we're ready to note any patterns in the eclipse field that Henson's activated planets hooked into. Start with the highest value connections—here it's the eclipse field's SNode/Mercury conjunct Henson's Mercury. Interpreting this energy pattern would have to include overtures to the main characteristics of Virgo and Libra— craftsmanship and design, with a built-in SNode talent bank of skill sets and knowledge literally at one's fingertips. His Mercury tightly conjuncts the fixed star Algorab, known for its communicative talents, dexterity, and mechanical skills. *The Fixed Star Report* available within the Sirius 3.0 and 4.0 Matrix astrology software offers a thoroughly researched history of thousands of Fixed Stars. The following information on the fixed star Algorab, as I am sure you will agree, is truly on point:

> Algorab is included in the nakshatra, or Vedic Lunar Mansion, Hasta. Hasta means "the Hand." Its ruling deity is Savitar, a laughing trickster god. Hasta relates to craftsmanship and all work done with hands, as well as mental fortitude.[7]

As a puppeteer, Henson was, hands down, all about the hands. His Mercury held eight midpoints. High midpoint tallies point to a planet that is instrumental in the course of a life. Mercury rules Gemini—the sign of the hands. LS138's SNode/Mercury conjunct his Mercury, for all its brilliance, had a darker side as it brings up a theme of loss through its SNode that was not mentioned in the introduction pages of this eclipse. This loss factor often occurs either through a sibling, family relation, or is a financial loss. Jim Henson was 19 when his older brother Paul Henson Jr. was killed in a car crash on April 15, 1956. According to Jim Henson's great friend Frank Oz, the effect on Henson was profound. "He realized that he just didn't have an infinite amount of time to do all the things he wanted to do."[8]

Next come contacts to the Sun or Moon and here we have a 1st Harmonic between the eclipse Pluto and Henson's Moon. An eclipse planet on your Sun or Moon adds a directional force to your life either by birthright or rite of passage. Here, Henson gets a pipeline of power from Pluto via the Sun/Jupiter conjunct Mercury/Pluto isotrap. The entire pattern is elevated by a Pluto/Jupiter parallel declination and gives it an almost god-like degree of aspiration. Henson's First Quarter Moon in Capricorn in the Sixth House makes him a doer. His Moon trine Uranus and its trine to Mars in late Leo would set up patterns of aliveness, originality and confidence that would endear both his personal character and the characters of his imagination to a global audience of children or for anyone who had ever been a child.

The eclipse activation by Venus to his Neptune/Saturn/Jupiter Mutable T-Square is our final example. It is a massive pattern as both Neptune and Jupiter are at the critical seventeenth degree with Saturn holding steady at the eighteenth degree of Pisces. The impact of Venus cannot be overstated here as she is in MR to Mercury and brings to the T-Square a refined and easy-going personality with the ability to both entertain and inform. Her presence on Neptune is a reassuring vote of confidence as it adds tenacity and financial strength to a planet that often has a hard time launching anything into the world of form and substance. Again, Venus has upped her game thanks to her MR with Mercury and is in an enviable position to help turn the phenomenal talent within this powerhouse T-Square into bankable treasure. Saturn and its square with Jupiter and its opposition to Neptune is an inventor's dream, turning the improbable into the possible. New techniques, new systems—these are the hallmarks of Saturn's square and Henson's trademark that were all supervised by the optimism of the eclipse Jupiter master-at-arms, on board, and always ready for whatever and wherever Henson's talent was willing to go.

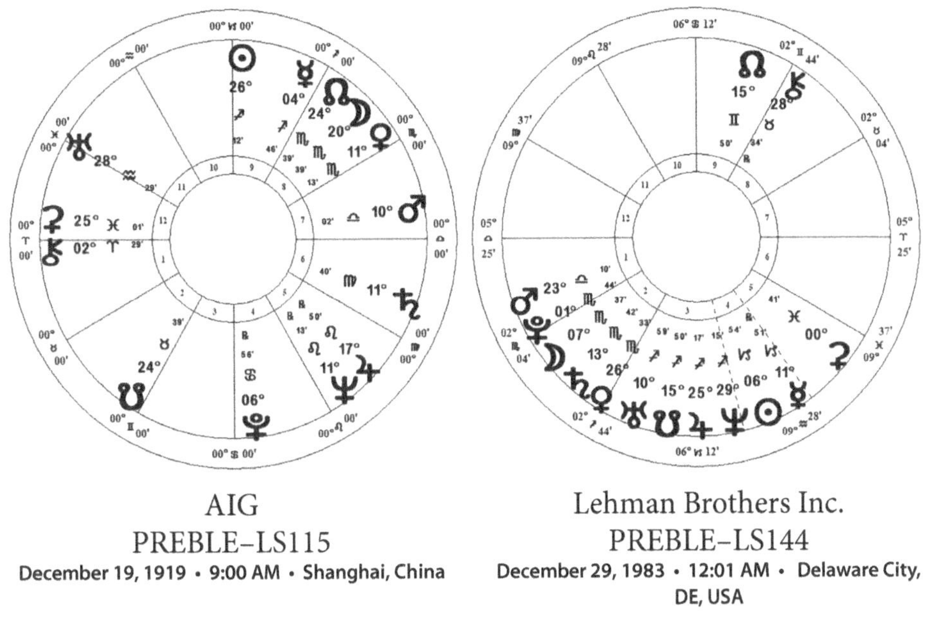

AIG
PREBLE–LS115
December 19, 1919 • 9:00 AM • Shanghai, China

Lehman Brothers Inc.
PREBLE–LS144
December 29, 1983 • 12:01 AM • Delaware City, DE, USA

Winners and Losers in the Global Financial Meltdown of 2008

AIG Thrived and Lehman Brothers Died

On Monday, September 15, 2008, at 1:45 a.m., Lehman Brothers Holdings, Inc. filed for bankruptcy—it was the largest bankruptcy petition in U.S. history: "The firm was the fourth-largest U.S. investment bank, and its bankruptcy kicked off a global financial crisis."[9] Lehman's legendary catastrophic fall from grace occurred within weeks of LS138's touchdown at 24 Aquarius on August 16, 2008.

On Tuesday, September 16, 2008, the Federal Reserve stepped in and provided an $85 billion two-year loan to the hemorrhaging American International Group (AIG) to prevent its bankruptcy and further stress on the global economy. By early 2009, the government would pour more than $180 billion into saving the legacy of AIG.[10]

So why did the King Makers of the U.S. economy sacrifice Lehman Brothers but save AIG? Andrew Sorkin, author of *Too Big To Fail,* summed it all up in the title of his book: When your company is TOO—BIG—TO—FAIL you get to play by a different set of rules. In testimony before the Senate Judiciary Committee on March 6, 2013, U.S. Attorney General Eric Holder stated:

> I am concerned that the size of some of these institutions becomes so large that it does become difficult for us to prosecute them when we are hit with indications that if we do prosecute, if we do bring a criminal charge—it will have a negative impact on the national economy, perhaps even the world economy.[11]

Reporting on August 20, 2014, online for the *New Republic*, Dean Starkman stated that "It's a disgrace that the Justice Department has failed to bring a single criminal charge against any Wall Street or mortgage executive of consequence for their roles in wrecking the economy."[12] Since AIG, as of 2023, is still in business, let's take a look for clues as to how they survived while Lehman died.

If there's a tale to be told you always follow the money. That's doubly true here and even more telling when you also follow the progressed chart. Here we find the progressed Moon making an opposition to a Jupiter/Neptune conjunction in Leo as well as a waxing square to Mars in Scorpio. With its appetite for danger and an all-or-nothing approach, Mars is right at home in Scorpio, loving the wheel and deal of financial manipulation plus it adds strength and robustness to the Moon's square. The Moon's oppositions to Jupiter and Neptune are critical because (a) Jupiter/Neptune in Leo is almost miraculously lucky when it comes to speculation, and (b) Neptune is in MR to the Sun in Pisces giving Jupiter/Neptune a solar radiance that exudes confidence, optimism, and a sense of grandeur. But wait, there's more. Progressed Venus at 27 Aquarius had reached AIG's natal Uranus which held a sextile to AIG's natal Sun at a very Taurean twenty-sixth degree of Sagittarius—a shoo-in for success. In matters of timing, within two months the progressed Moon would make good on those aspects, and all of this would have been instrumental in saving the company from bankruptcy. The activation degree of the lunar dragons of LS138 fell on both the natal Uranus and the progressed Venus ensuring them a double dose of support from the King Makers of both Wall Street and the Federal Reserve.

And Lehman. The progressed Moon at 1 Libra would have squared the Neptune/Jupiter conjunction at 00 Capricorn in August *exactly* as LS138 activated. One cannot help but notice that both charts carry the speculators Jupiter/Neptune conjunction with Lehman getting it squared and AIG opposed from their respective progressed Moon. In particular, Lehman's Jupiter/Neptune on the AP would have made any astrologer take a second look; there is always a larger dimension, often a political overtone, to planets at that position.

The waning trine between the Sun and the Moon really speaks to what happened to Lehman since the trine is always a reliable indicator of an event on its way with nothing to stop it. By the time September rolled in, and the Moon made the trine to the Progressed Sun at 2 Aquarius, Lehman's downfall was already a fait accompli. The investment bank had been on a death spiral for at least a year, as seen by the Progressed Sun and its square to Progressed Pluto, again exact. In my experience, progressed aspects involving the Sun can be felt even when they are two degrees away from approaching partile contact. Sadly, LS138 could only offer Lehman its theme of loss. AIG survived its time in the underworld and will most likely live to take us all down with it on its next descent into economic hell.

The evolution of Lunar Saros 138 saw it move into a Last Quarter phase with its twenty-sixth return in 1972. This phase is famous for its ability to reorient the life path of an individual or, as we see here, a corporate structure. The U.S. Supreme Court, ever since the passage of the 14th Amendment, has grappled with defining corporate vs. personal rights, and over the years has more and more handed down decisions that have firmly granted the attribute of personhood to corporations. As a result, corporations enjoy the same rights as ordinary people. In the case of a corporate entity such as Lehman or AIG, there would be a noticeable "public responsibility" factor in play that would have come into focus by the eclipse return in 2008 on its twenty-eighth return. This is a time for readjustment and turning points that are often highly impersonal and are fueled by a growing sense of disillusionment and a need for elimination.

LS138 Summary

Dare to be creative and practice the high art of thinking outside the box. Kingdoms rise and heads will roll when these mighty Earth Dragons draw near. They are the stuff of legend and legacy, Goliaths gathering momentum at every turn. Their arrival brings both mayhem and might as their global reach rumbles across the landscape. Such tremors disturb but also provide the agitation necessary so that new paradigms may emerge, accompanied by higher standards and goals that are attainable and that reveal fresh and exciting pathways for self-expression. You're up for this and success is likely if you can limit yourself to a plan that does not include homage to a hungry ego. Your business acumen along with your bottom-line will increase as you get your spiritual goals on board to balance the load.

The presence of this lunar eclipse family is linked to cathartic and often life-altering decisions that have the power to shock and awe all who are caught in their groundswell. Leaps of imagination are the basis of success when these Earth Dragons settle in and stay awhile. It's a perfect time to look at the world through the eyes of a traveler, and one that won't necessarily be here for that long. Take in the big picture and try to make an impact on some area that you feel drawn to and where your vision, strength of spirit and yes, love could make a difference.

One would do well to contemplate the role endurance plays in this earthly journey along with the courage to face our inner darkness and walk through the underworld in an effort to reclaim something of great value. Pessimism and self-doubt may come knocking, but you don't have to let them in. There are powerful regenerative forces at work within the matrix of this lunar eclipse that are prepared to restore our inner radiance and splendor if we are willing to get on board this train. It isn't so much a scenic tour—more like a thrills and spills ride at Disney World. In the end, the only thing that matters is that we will understand that we have enough and that we are enough. Not bad for a day's work in LS138 land.

LS138 Luminaries

Carl Fabergé	May 30, 1846
Antoine de Saint-Exupéry	June 29, 1900
Margaret Mitchell	November 8, 1900
Ingmar Bergman	July 14, 1918
Ted Williams	August 30, 1918
Aleksandr Solzhenitsyn	December 11, 1918
Buddy Holly	September 7, 1936
Jim Henson	September 24, 1936
Abbie Hoffman	November 30, 1936
Joel Coen	November 29, 1954

Chris Evert	December 21, 1954
Denzel Washington	December 28, 1954
Idris Elba	September 6, 1972
Eminem	October 17, 1972
Jude Law	December 29, 1972
Jennifer Lawrence	August 15, 1990
Magnus Carlsen	November 30, 1990

PREBLE—LS133
Jennifer Lawrence

1. Demetra George, *Asteroid Goddesses—The Mythology* (Lake Worth, FL, Ibis Press), p.41.
2. https://www.biography.com/musician/elvis-presley Retrieved Feb. 17, 2022.
3. https://www.songfacts.com/facts/elvis-presley/thats-alright-mama. Retrieved Feb. 17, 2022.
4. Sonny West, *Elvis Still Taking Care of Business* (Chicago: Triumph Books, 2007), p. 16.
5. https://www.biography.com/performer/jim-henson. Retrieved Mar. 19, 2022.
6. Brian Jay Jones, *Jim Henson The Biography* (New York: Ballantine Books, 2013), p. 41.
7. The Fixed Star Report. Sirius 3 Matrix astrology software
8. Jones, *Jim Henson*, p. 179.
9. https://www.thebalance.com/lehman-brothers-collapse-causes-impact-4842338. Retrieved March 3, 2022
10. https://www.investopedia.com/insights/too-big-fail-banks-where-are-they-now/. Retrieved March 2, 2022.
11. http://www.americanbanker.com/issues/178_45/transcript-attorney-general-eric-holder-on-too-big-to-jail-1057295-1.html. Retrieved May 28, 2022.
12. Dean Starkman. *Wrecking an Economy Means Never Having to Say You're Sorry.* http://www.newrepublic.com/article/119002/justice-departments-wall-street-settlement-deals-are-shameful. Retrieved May 28, 2022.

LUNAR SAROS 146

"A line is a dot that went for a walk."

-Paul Klee

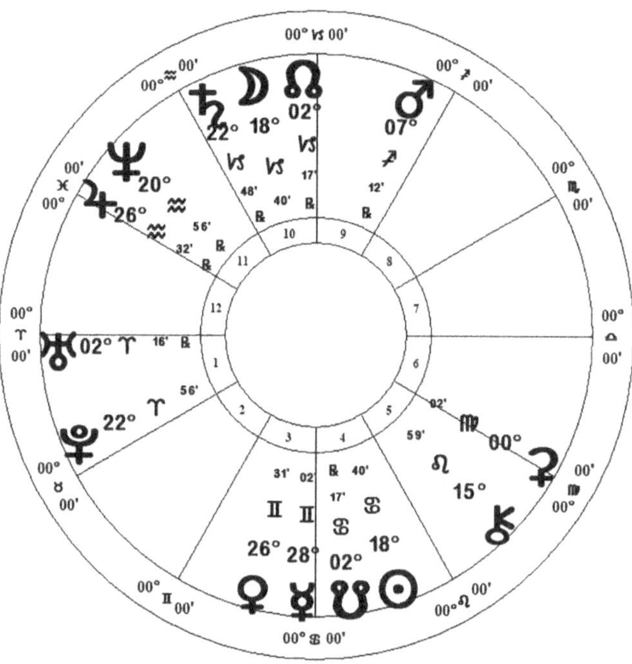

Lunar Saros 146

July 11, 1843 • 5:05:48 PM • North Pole

Walk the Walk

This is a Saturn ruled eclipse in Capricorn that likes to play hardball. Considering how recent their arrival has been, this family is a determined lot who take their responsibilities seriously. Dignified and strategically positioned, retrograde Saturn in its own sign conjunct the eclipse squares Pluto, forming a tenacious and tough-as-nails Cardinal T-Square that sometimes needs help seeing the other side of a situation. The tightness of this waning square to Saturn substantially increases the tension; personal as well as professional discord and all manner of discomfort are themes that these Earth Dragons are well equipped to handle. Their inner toughness gives them a skill set able to deal with all manner of public discord and dissent as well as calls for accountability. At the twenty-second degree, Pluto is more than ready to strip down to the bare essentials to get the job done. As much as we love to "talk the talk" their presence is a reminder that we need to "walk the walk." Disparity and polarization in the court of public opinion is never in doubt with a retrograde two degree Uranus in Aries squaring off against the nodal axis. High levels of agitation, discomfort but also breakthroughs in almost every area of life will come through the tangible presence of Uranus positioned within minutes of the celestial equator.

The lunar eclipse has an attractive Venus to Jupiter trine that can stimulate rapid growth and progress in any occupation or field that serves both a personal as well as public agenda. This is one of the best aspects to have as it generates a field of friendly vibes. Trines from Air signs offer genuine gifts of communication along with the ability to use reason, logic and rationalization which will help with some of the more difficult control and authority issues of the Saturn-Pluto square.

As it must be clear by now, an important element of any chart are its midpoint structures. To that end, let's first take a look at the Mars/Saturn-Pluto midpoint. Here the unmistakable pattern for struggle, hard-earned victories, and the capacity for difficult work is woven into the eclipse field. It is an indicator that not only individuals but large groups of people can be influenced by its presence. This is underscored by the Jupiter/Pluto-Node midpoint; according to Ebertin, the principle of "The common destiny of a large mass of people"[1] is very much tied into this energetic pattern. Factor in Jupiter's conjunction to a socially aware Neptune in Aquarius and its same degree trine to a media-savvy Venus-Mercury in rulership and the stage is set for everyone to be both entertained and informed. Joanna Martine Woolfolk writes that "Neptune in this position has been called by astrologers "the flame of conscience.""[2] The tenure of these midpoints adds up to a lively interest in the welfare of others, along with the aforementioned willingness to "walk the walk."

Any way you look at this chart—and being mindful of its five planets in retrograde: Mars, Saturn, Neptune, Jupiter, and Uranus—a clear cry for redress is present. The possibility for great gain through working in collaboration with others, as seen through the Jupiter/Pluto-Node midpoint, will only grow in magnitude and intensity as this lunar eclipse evolves through time. All midpoint structures benefit from their earthly experiences and become much more effective as they appear to be learning, along with us, at their own rate of evolution. In the case of Earth eclipses, their midpoints are worth noting at twice the price.

Closest Midpoints: Jupiter/Pluto-Node, Mars/Saturn-Pluto
Isotraps: Sun/Uranus conjunct Mercury/Pluto
Moon/Neptune conjunct Mars/Uranus

1900—2100 Eclipses: Lunar Saros—146

1915, 1933, 1951, 1969, 1987, 2005, 2023, 2041, 2059, 2077, 2095
Length of cycle —1,280 years
Series ends—August 29, 3123

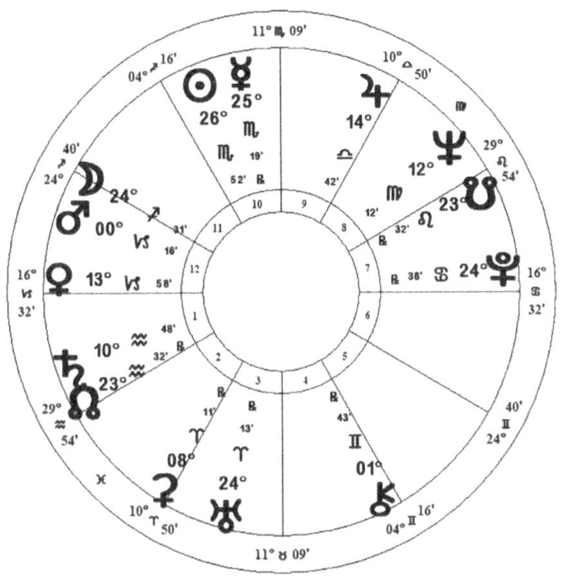

Larry King
PREBLE—LS146

November 19, 1933 • 10:38 AM • Brooklyn, NY, USA

Serial Husband/Gifted Gabber/Legendary Talk Show Host

"He was a great interviewer – sensitivity, humorous and witty.
And he actually let you talk! An all around mensch.
Millions around the world shall miss him, including myself."

-Prime Minister Benjamin Netanyahu

Moon, Venus, and Mars all at OOB designation might just be the cosmic clue that portends seven wives. At least it was for Larry King. After a spectacular sixty-three year run across a multitude of media platforms, and a life over-flowing with interviews, awards, global acclaim and yes, wives, the one and only Mr. Suspenders died on January 23, 2021. His talent as a broadcaster was nothing short of awesome.

Larry King's Connections to the Dragons of LS146
Space Lanes via ASC/DSC

1st Harmonics: NNode – Mars, Jupiter – NNode,
Neptune – NNode, Moon – ASC/Venus, Sun – Pluto, Pluto – Uranus
2nd Harmonics: Mercury/Venus – Moon, Mercury – Mars, Saturn – Pluto

Larry King hit the celestial jackpot on the day he was born: his astral blueprint for this lifetime merged in a very special way to his PREBLE-LS146. By its Moon/Sun eclipse axis degrees falling on his ascendant, a celestial speedway referred to as Space Lanes was laid down, offering a unique portal through which the entire field of the eclipse could be experienced. Even as a child, King was tuned in. "When I was five years old I would lie in bed, look at the radio, and I wanted to be on the radio. I don't know why." But an astrologer aware of the dynamics of lunar eclipse cosmology would know why. At the age of five, King's spirit was already wide awake and dancing with the lunar rhythms flooding his energy field. Between November 1938 and May 1939, King experienced two lunar eclipses that for the first time in his young life would activate his IC and MC.

Let's take a look at the seeding effect of the eclipse NNode and Jupiter 1st Harmonics to his astounding Mars at the infinity AP degree of Capricorn and his nodal axis at the double-dipped twenty-third degree of Aquarius. Because the eclipse Jupiter/Pluto-Node midpoint needs some time to get going, it makes sense that King would have felt it stirring as it, too, was awakening to its impact potential. Any link from the Great Benefic Jupiter is welcome in the world of astrological forecasting; here Jupiter's 1st Harmonic to his NNode at the high-tech, networking, and full of surprises twenty-third degree of Aquarius is a sign that celestial compound interest was rapidly accruing.

Larry King's life would be fabulous for so many reasons even without lunar eclipse Space Lanes, but it's nice to know they're still there when you need to leave town. In 1957, with the return of the lunar eclipse that first touched his life at age 5, and now at age 23, King left Brooklyn for Miami for his first job in radio. His first appearance on air was on May 1, 1957, within days of LS130 activating at 23 degrees Scorpio on his Tenth House retrograde Mercury.

What I love most about Larry King's chart is how LS146's Sun on his Seventh House cusp and those Space Lanes continued to provide a clear and present pathway to a horizon that was never without a golden glow. LS146's Venus/ Mercury 2nd Harmonics to his Moon in Sagittarius only extended his communication networks' reach, market share, and global coverage. His Wiki page states that he did more than sixty thousand interviews. CNN's *Larry King Live* is recognized by the *Guinness Book of World Records* as the longest-running television show hosted by the same person, on the same network, and in the same time slot. He taped 6120 episodes of the show.[3]

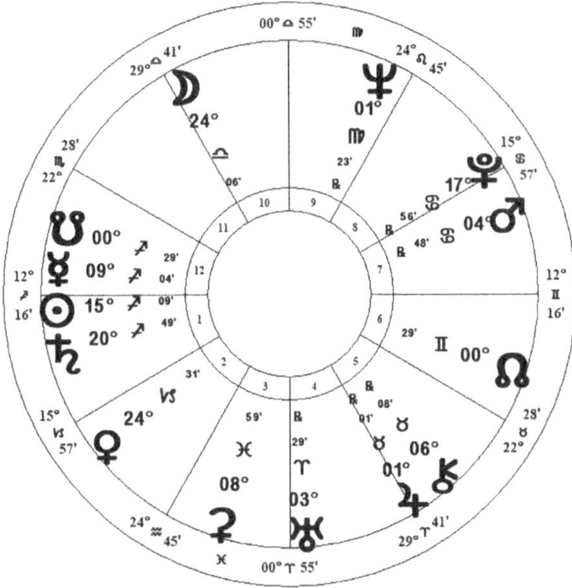

Noam Chomsky
PREBLE—LS134

December 7, 1928 • 7:00 AM • Philadelphia, PA, USA

Social Critic/Political Activist
"The Father of Modern Linguistics"

Philosopher/Cognitive Scientist/Historical Essayist

"If you're teaching today what you were teaching five years ago, either the field is dead or you are."

-NOAM CHOMSKY

Noam Chomsky is without a doubt one of the world's leading scholars and intellectuals working to be a vigilant eye and strong voice of reason against oppression and injustice. Lawyer, journalist, and critically-acclaimed author

Glen Greenwald, noted for his support and on-going collaboration with NSA Whistleblower Edward Snowden, simply calls Chomsky "the nation's bravest and most accomplished public intellectual and political activist."[4] Chomsky's first political book, *American Power and the New Mandarins* was published in 1969. In the forward to the 2002 paperback edition of the book, fellow social activist and historian Howard Zinn restates how Chomsky "insisted that resistance to the law was part of only a spectrum of possible responses to injustice, and that the more moderate, less dramatic form, dissent, was also necessary."[5]

Since the late sixties, Chomsky has played a key role in awakening people to the arrogance of power along with the need to return politics to the people. His ability to reach a growing audience of both American and international peace activists and protesters of the Vietnam War was enormously empowered by the return of Lunar Saros 146 in the fall of 1969. At the highly self-expressive third degree of Aries, it completely hooked his brilliant Uranus and in square to his OOB (26N) Mars in Cancer, the lunar eclipse would embed a call to arms that would engage him forever in a lifelong odyssey to uncover and deliver the truth.

Noam Chomsky's Connections to the Dragons of LS146
Ceres to Ceres

1st Harmonics: SNode – Mars, Moon/Saturn – Venus,
Mars – ASC, Mars – Mercury, Ceres – Neptune, Uranus – Uranus/MC
2nd Harmonics: Moon – Pluto, Pluto – Moon

All the 1st and 2nd Harmonic connectors weave a tapestry of deep familial love. To help make the world a better place, both fields have a foreboding Mars square Saturn-Pluto midpoint because, as the saying goes, you have to break a few eggs to make an omelet. It helps to have a midpoint structure that reinforces tenacity, self-discipline, and yes, frustration, which can generate an enormous outpouring of realizations. The 2nd Harmonics are absolutely stunning as they create a quadraphonic effect that is deeply complex. All Moon/Pluto 2nd Harmonics are life changing and nothing seems to be the same after one has touched down and passed through your personal energetic space.

Chomsky's 12 degree Sagittarian Ascendant, like Elvis Presley's, is tied into the vortex of the Great Attractor. I have found that people who have anything on the GA degree, whether by natal, progressed, or transit, have an ability to make an impression that far exceeds their notion of what was possible. Additionally, his Moon at 24 Libra conjuncts the great fixed star Spica. Hellenistic astrologers saw Spica as a blend of Mercury and Venus giving, at its best, a learned, eloquent, creative, clever, pleasure-loving, and practical approach to life. Such qualities resonate to LS146's own Venus-Mercury conjunction in Gemini giving an even greater emphasis on scholarly attributes connected to the lunar eclipse return of 1969. According to the Arts and Humanities Citation Index in 1992, Chomsky was cited as a source more often than any other living scholar during the 1972–1992 time period.[6]

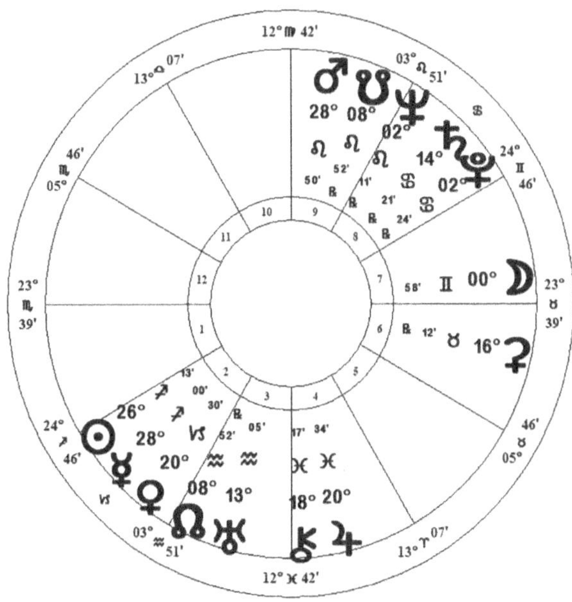

Edith Piaf
PREBLE—LS146

December 19, 1915 • 5:00 AM • Paris, France

"All I've done all my life is disobey."

–"La Vie en Rose"

"Death is the Beginning of Something"

Edith Piaf was France's beloved "Little Sparrow"; her diminutive size (under 5 feet [142 cm] and weighing about 90 pounds [40 kg]) nonetheless held a powerful, passionate voice that would make her an international star. Her life, however, reflected a string of tragedies beset by addiction and health issues that would end with her death in France in 1963 at the age of 47.

Edith Piaf's Connections to the Dragons of LS146

1st Harmonics: Sun – Saturn, SNode – Pluto, Ceres – Mars, Saturn – Venus
2nd Harmonics: Sun – Venus, Mercury – Mercury,
Venus – Sun, Jupiter – Mars, Chiron – Uranus

Both spheres carry the Sun in parallel declination to Venus. Her rare, to-the-minute alignment held enormous artistic potential, universal appeal, and immense charisma, all backed by LS146's identical pattern. Her abundant Cosmic Bridges are plentiful and built in stability right from the beginning. From her miraculous recovery from early childhood blindness right through her tumultuous love affairs and her struggles with drugs, alcohol, and illness, both critics and fans agreed that her voice, stage presence, and sheer emotive power grew with each new crisis. It was as if she thrived on challenge. In her own words, "Death is the beginning of something"[7] is quite possibly the best personification I have ever seen to represent the energy available in a 1st Harmonic eclipse SNode to a natal Pluto, and Piaf's was within minutes of exactitude. Notice the double tap of Sun to Venus and Venus to Sun 2nd Harmonics. Piaf would nurture the careers of all her lovers, immediately pursuing professional opportunities for them whenever and wherever she could.

LS146 Summary

As you can probably tell by now, this is not an easy lunar eclipse. By birthright or rite of passage, challenges are everywhere—they are an integral part of what their sphere of influence brings to our planetary consciousness. And no one is immune from their contentious field of discord that brings on adversaries, difficulties, health issues, and various and sundry delays. Knowing what you want will help you reduce the pain levels as pain accepted willingly has been scientifically proven to be much easier to bear than pain that comes at you out of nowhere.

The upside to the downside of their dragon domain is the ability to carve out a niche as breakthroughs, "firsts," and activism increase substantially. These lovers of life love action and are eager to participate in just about any noble cause. You'll be much wiser in the long run if you can get out and ahead of any oncoming traffic. In other words, accept the present burden of responsibilities that so often come with their arrivals. Definitely do not put off what can be done today. Do what can be done and you'll sleep well knowing you've probably averted a major disaster if not global chaos, at least in your little corner of the world.

Lunar Saros 146 has been cycling through a First Quarter phase since October 7, 1987, and will continue in this phase until November 29, 2077, at which time it will enter its Gibbous phase. Chances are high that the current phase is going to be a challenging one as success and prestige can be had but not if the price is low level anxiety, depression, or gloom. It's critical to make health and wellness a top priority as you work within environments that are literally shifting the very ground on which you stand, making it a challenge to build in a solid base of capacity. And one final note: Do not hesitate to leave a situation that has become intolerable and full of power struggles.

LS146 Luminaries

Samuel Goldwyn	August 17, 1879
Leon Trotsky	November, 7, 1879
Paul Klee	December 18, 1879
Irène Joliot-Curie	September 12, 1897
Edith Head	October 28, 1897
Ingrid Bergman	August 29, 1915
Bob Kane	October 24, 1915
Frank Sinatra	December 12, 1915
Édith Piaf	December 19, 1915
Karl Lagerfeld	September 10, 1933
Charles K. Kao	November 4, 1933
Larry King	November 19, 1933
Lou Rawls	December 1, 1933
Sting	October 2, 1951
Karen Allen	October 5, 1951
Bob Geldof	October 5, 1951
John Mellencamp	October 7, 1951
Matthew McConaughey	November 4, 1969
Gerard Butler	November 13, 1969

Jay Z	December 4, 1969
Minnie Driver	January 31, 1970
Zac Efron	October 18, 1987
Colin Kaepernick	November 3, 1987
Ronan Farrow	December 19, 1987
Rihanna	February 20, 1988

1. Ebertin, COSI, p. 292.

2 Joanna Martine Woolfolk, *The Only Astrology Book You'll Ever Need* (Lanham, MD: Scarborough House, 1990) p. 221.

3. https://en.wikipedia.org/wiki/Larry_King. Retrieved July 5, 2022.

4. Noam Chomsky and Glen Greenwald "How The Law is Used To Destroy Equality and Protect the Powerful." Retrieved July 5, 2022. https://www.youtube.com/watch?v=eYBJDRmSMRY

5. Noam Chomsky, *American Power & The New Mandarins* (New York: The New Press, 2002), p. vii.

6. https://news.mit.edu/1992/citation-0415. Retrieved July 5, 2022.

7. https://www.brainyquote.com/authors/edith-piaf-quotes. Retrieved July 7, 2022.

LUNAR SAROS 147

"Many people are alive but don't touch the miracle of being alive."

-Thich Nhat Hanh

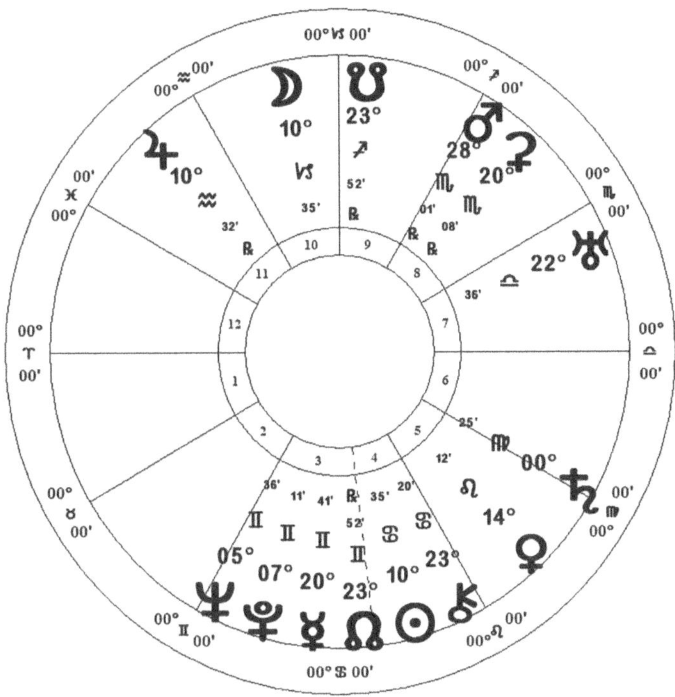

Lunar Saros 147

July 2, 1890 • 2:22:59 PM • South Pole

Mettle and Magic

This South Node Capricorn eclipse lives within a dynamic and practical Locomotive pattern capable of prodigious artistic and entrepreneurial outcomes. Ruler Saturn at 00 Virgo and its opening square to the charms and thrust of the Pluto/Neptune engine driving these dragons forward is more concerned with pragmatics than principles, allowing for ambitious displays of magnificence and malfeasance. Saturn's mutability and its zero infinity degree status in the ultimate sign of work and health leave it vulnerable, and its square to a retrograde Mars in rulership lays itself open to all manner of environmental, psychological, physical, as well as psychic stress. In recognition of its key placement and status, safety guidelines and even more importantly, moral guidelines, need to be put in place to avoid unnecessary and risky behaviors.

Secrets, lies, fantasy, and sexuality all take on a life of their own in the presence of LS147. This eclipse field holds a cornucopia of attraction that can simultaneously bewitch, bother, and bewilder our senses. Mercury in rulership and at the twentieth degree holds a seductive Scorpio power that many will want to experiment with as it embraces both fear and fascination in equal portion. Many will be drawn to the dark side in a desire to experience the forbidden in all its physical and metaphysical manifestations. The world of erotica, seduction, and compulsion will be running a lot of red lights, but you need to know there are speedtraps everywhere. Venus in opposition to retrograde Jupiter in Aquarius is very experimental; her contra-parallel declination honey-pot trap to Neptune is a homewrecker waiting in the wings to dance a dalliance with danger.

Think of Mercury in Gemini and its conjunction to the NNode like adding logs onto a fire. These two together have a love—nay, a need—for new stimuli, especially as Mercury in rulership and at that twentieth degree makes an exact quincunx to a double-dipped Ceres in Scorpio. There's no getting around the theme here of sex, secrets, scandal, and maybe even the supernatural. The quincunx even sounds sexy, but more than that has little regard for the tried and true. This aspect reminds me of what life is like as a teenager where you never feel like you fit in, where you're always thinking you're in trouble (and usually are) but feel like you're a genius.

An exact trine from the NNode to Uranus in Libra conjunct the Fixed Star Spica at 22 degrees 18 minutes Libra confirms that you are indeed a genius. You can confidently expect any number of talents to emerge over your lifetime if these are your Earth Dragons or a windfall every eighteen years as they return with their own brand of mettle and magic.

And speaking of magic, the Sun/Uranus conjunct Mars/Neptune isotrap is a fundamental energy that gives the entire lunar eclipse field a sense of awe and a feeling of wonder. These dragons need room to spread out, to try on new lifestyles, new ways of living and loving, but more than anything they need to live life in their own imaginative and creative style. Lunar Saros 147 holds a rare Neptune/Pluto conjunction that adds, through Neptune's fifth degree resonance, glamor and stage presence to an isotrap that is already overflowing with originality, fantasy, inspiration, illusion, and a willingness to push past the boundaries of conventional wisdom

Closest Midpoints: Eclipse/Venus-Pluto, Venus/Uranus-Neptune
Isotraps: Moon/Jupiter opposition Mercury/Saturn
Sun/Uranus conjunct Mars/Neptune

1900—2100 Eclipses: Lunar Saros—147

1908, 1926, 1944, 1962, 1980, 1998, 2016, 2034, 2052, 2070, 2088
Length of cycle —1,244 years
Series ends—July 28, 3134

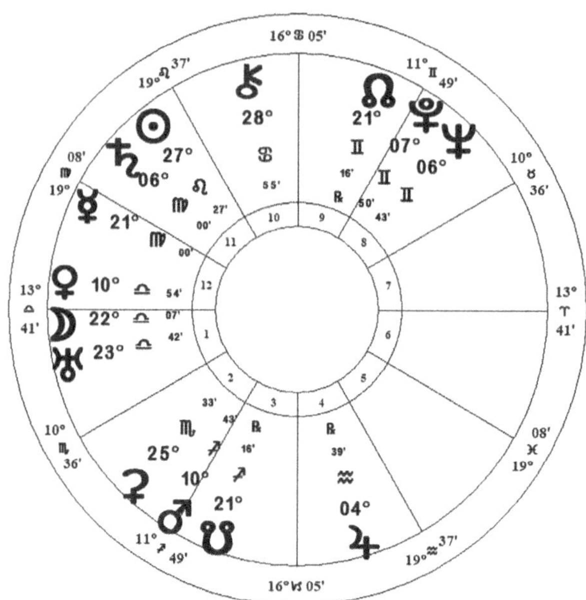

H. P. Lovecraft
PREBLEs—LS147 & LS109

August 20, 1890 • 9:00 AM • Providence, RI, USA

The Father of Weird and Wonderful Fiction

"The 20th century's greatest practitioner of the classic horror tale."

-Stephen King

Lovecraft was relatively unknown during his lifetime even though his stories appeared in well-known pulp magazines such as *Weird Tales*. His output however was voluminous; apart from his weird fiction, it is estimated that throughout his life he wrote over 100,000 letters.[1]

H P Lovecraft's Connections to the Dragons of LS147
Space Lanes via IC/MC
↓South Node with South Node↓
Saturn with Saturn* *Jupiter with Jupiter* *Ceres with Ceres
Neptune/Pluto with Neptune/Pluto* *Uranus with Uranus* *Chiron with Chiron

1st Harmonics: NNode/Mercury – NNode, Saturn – Sun, Uranus – Moon/Uranus
2nd Harmonic: Pluto – Mars

The eclipse 1st Harmonic NNode/Mercury to his nodes brought to life his own Mercury square the nodal axis literary talent. As well, Space Lanes running through your Fourth and Tenth House cusps would certainly make your domestic and professional life either unbelievable or unbearable or both, especially as the eclipse axis holds a Capricorn double-dipped tenth degree. Again, we can see the debilitating effect of the same nodal polarity and its association with weakness. After his death, his wife Sonia Lovecraft revealed that he didn't like sex and that she had to initiate all sexual activity, due in part to the 2nd Harmonic Pluto (and its Neptune conjunction) to his Mars Mutable T-Square.

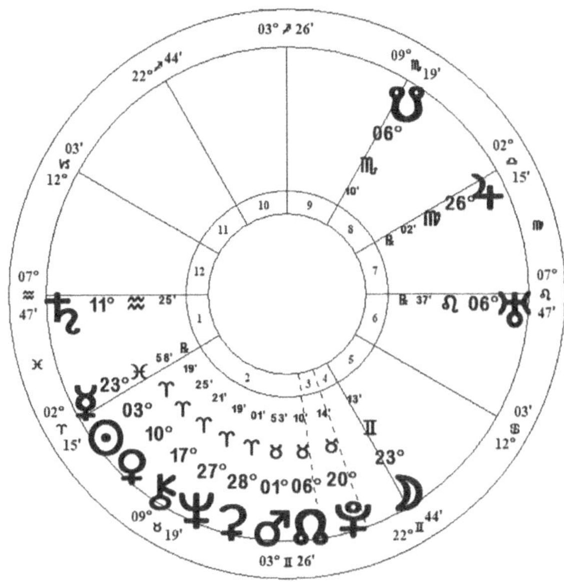

Harry Houdini
PREBLE—LS124

March 24, 1874 • 4:00 AM • Budapest, Hungary

Handcuff King/Escape Artist/Superstar[2]

"I am a great admirer of mystery and magic.
Look at this life –all mystery and magic."

-Harry Houdini

Houdini is by far and away *the* metaphor of magic. In the annals of history, no other name, apart from King Arthur's magician Merlin, carries the mantel with such potency, intrigue, excitement, awe, respect, and incredulity. Fifty years after his death in 1926, the word "Houdini" was added to the Oxford English Dictionary.[3] It would forever establish his dominion over this enchanting and at times perilous realm of entertainment. Thanks to the exhaustive research done by biographers William Kalush and Larry Sloman, the fascinating and true life story of Houdini emerged in 2006, and it would finally shed light on the mystery that was Houdini's response to self-promotion at the turn of the 19th century.

On July 25, 1926, Lunar Saros 147 would be the last lunar eclipse of Houdini's mortal life. In the fourteen weeks that followed, Houdini made repeated references to his eminent death. Kalush and Sloman's research unearthed correspondence between Houdini and numerous friends that clearly indicated he was aware of his impending demise. The majority of his time that summer was spent working on a number of book projects involving myth and magic. By early September, Houdini was rolling out his Fall tour, showcasing his latest and most death-defying escape that he called The Mystery of the Sphinx. It would be Houdini's first new escape in years."[4]

Houdini's extraordinary physical strength was the stuff of legend. A Fixed Cross supported by Mars in conjunction to a Taurus/Scorpio nodal axis reinforced by a Uranus opposition to Saturn gave him phenomenal control over his physiology. As well, his Sun/Venus square Jupiter would have been a source of amazing vitality. In combination with the fluidity of a pair of MRs between Mercury (Pisces) and Jupiter (Virgo) and Venus (Aries) and Mars (Taurus), and empowered by a Venus-Jupiter-Pluto parallel declination, Houdini's Venus/Mercury-Neptune midpoint contributed to his own fascination with Spiritualism and mystical powers from the great beyond.

As Lunar Saros 147 activated at 2 Aquarius, it brought his entire powerhouse Fixed Cross into focus through its opposition to Uranus at 6 Leo, setting off waves of creative self-expression in the exploration of knowledge that would be of benefit to both fellow magicians and the general public. The lunar eclipse beautifully encapsulated Houdini's life at this final stage, falling as it did across the Leo/Aquarius axis that serves to release creative energy into the collective zeitgeist. Born within the realm of the Water Dragons of LS124—Imagine—his PREBLE offered the perfect platform for his audacious feats and risky leaps of daring courage and acrobatic contortion. His final months would prove to be the capstone of a master magician's life. Harry Houdini would survive all his self-made deathtraps only to succumb to a burst appendix. He died on Halloween, October 31, 1926, but his legend is immortal.

Harry Houdini's Connections to the Dragons of LS147

1st Harmonics: NNode/Mercury - Moon,
Jupiter - Saturn/ASC, Neptune/Pluto - IC
2nd Harmonics: Venus - Saturn, Ceres - Pluto

Houdini's birth chart places his Moon exactly on the eclipse lunar node axis establishing a powerful Cosmic Bridge which is reinforced by the eclipse Mercury in rulership creating another CB. Houdini's Saturn at 11 Aquarius is in direct conjunction to LS147's Jupiter, which includes his talented trine to death-defying Pluto and his ever-elusive Neptune companion, his opposition to glamorous Venus and, best of all for an escape artist, a perfect quincunx to the eclipse Sun to defy the known laws of gravity.

In the end however, it is the goddess Ceres in Scorpio and her knowledge of the secret teachings of mystery and magic, reaching out to Houdini's Pluto via a 2nd Harmonic in Taurus that seals their fate and claims Houdini as its own. Together god and goddess walk the mythic underworld, bound forever in a promise of eternal return.

J. K. Rowling
PREBLE—LS139

July 31, 1965 • TOB Unknown • Yates, UK

Billionaire Novelist

"I am the freest author in the world."

-J. K. Rowling

J. K. Rowling was born into the arms of Lunar Saros Series 139 with its implications for the use and abuse of massive reserves of power. As I stated in the introduction to this book, knowing the foundation chart of your dragon family is highly informative as it sets out many of your unique personality traits. Rowling's PREBLE and its formidable Moon/Pluto conjunction in Gemini was a resource waiting to be tapped for its life-giving and soul-inspiring capacity for regeneration.

Her imagination is a product of her super-sized Saturn/Chiron conjunction in Pisces at the handle of a Bucket chart that contains four Grand Mutable Crosses. Getting a "handle" on that handle and all that intensity takes time, but with mobility and some maturity, the obstacles of those Crosses become their own form of GPS, allowing one to navigate with increasing levels of skill. Along with Saturn, all these Mutable Crosses contain her Gemini/Sagittarius nodal axis, elevating her challenges to mythic if not evolutionary proportion. From all reports, the Grand Mutable Cross, along with the Cardinal and Fixed, are synonymous with strength seized from the jaws of defeat that urge us ever forward in a constant battle with creation.

A Noon birth chart puts Rowling's Moon at 19 Virgo giving it access to square Jupiter and her nodes, form oppositions to her Saturn and Chiron, and—if her birth was earlier in the day—conjunctions to her Uranus and Pluto. It seems that no matter what time of day she was born, her Moon would be highly active, giving her life story many chapters for outstanding adventure, self-regeneration, and astounding productivity to unfold. As a novelist and celebrated author of the phenomenon that is the *Harry Potter* series, she is one of the wealthiest and most beloved authors of all time. In 2023, J. K. Rowling's net worth is estimated at a staggering $1.1 billion. According to *Celebrity Net Worth*, "She is one of only five self-made female billionaires and is the richest author to have ever lived."[5]

J. K. Rowling's Connections to the Dragons of LS147
↓South Node with South Node↓

1st Harmonics: Pluto – NNode,
NNode – Jupiter, Mercury – Jupiter, Saturn – Mercury, Ceres – Neptune
2nd Harmonic: Jupiter – Sun

Jumping back in time, let's return to September 6, 1998, and note the arrival of LS147. This Saros Series activated at 14 Pisces, sweeping up half of Rowling's planets along with her Moon and transporting them to its land of enchantment. In that very first week of September 1998, Rowling's debut book, *Harry Potter and the Philosopher's Stone,* was released by Scholastic in the USA under the new title, *Harry Potter and the Sorcerer's Stone.*[6] That USA publishing date would mark the beginning of Rowling's phenomenal rise to the heights of literary stardom. With every book that followed, Rowling continued to break publishing records as her fan base reached a global audience who were entranced by the magic and wonder of Harry Potter and his world of wizards.

Dramatic effects like this can be seen not from the sheer number of contacts but the quality of contacts. Excluding her natal Moon, there are five 1st Harmonics that include two Cosmic Bridges (CBs), and a 2nd Harmonic from the eclipse Jupiter to her Sun, creating a third CB. With LS147's ruler Saturn conjunct Rowling's magnificent Mercury and its conjunction to Regulus, the fixed star of fame and fortune, her rocket to stardom had arrived. Throw in LS147's insatiable Mercury/NNode in Gemini and its conjunction to Rowling's Jupiter and a double rainbow of opportunity suddenly appears overhead. Here is Jan Spiller on the process and power of writing through the NNode in Gemini:

> For these folks, writing can even be a good profession. There's so much flexibility and room for growth that it can be the "one thing" they are looking for. They needn't rely on a corporation or a structure; they can be anywhere and be themselves and do their life's work—and that appeals to them.[7]

As the handle on her Bucket chart, Saturn and its conjunction to Chiron in Pisces filter her personality through an extraordinary funnel that connects her to heightened levels of other-worldly perception. Any contact to Saturn would in turn activate its triple set of midpoint structures allowing for an even greater expression of creativity. Her Chiron at the very potent twenty-second degree has that prodigious Capricorn capacity to work and be organized and its conjunction to Saturn only reinforced those qualities.

But as you can tell by now, it's those 2nd Harmonics that get the party going. Here the eclipse Jupiter can hardly wait to get the Sun on the proverbial dance floor. But he isn't alone; at 10 Aquarius, the Great Benefic is moving "in tune" to the rhythm of not only her Sun but his trine to Pluto, his opposition to Venus, and a perfect quincunx to the eclipse Sun. It's celestial music, and much like an old-fashioned Square Dance, you get to "do-si-do, down the middle and allemande left" with a remarkable number of planetary partners moving in sync with each other. And that is exactly how lunar eclipse fields work and interact: Their patterns are music, and those patterns call to your patterns to "circle left, promenade and weave the ring."

Lunar Saros 147 entered its first Crescent phase with its fifth return in 1962. When it activated Rowling's chart in 1998, it had just entered that sweet seventh spot return where the activation degree sextiles the foundation degree, reinforcing the family's double-dipped Moon at the tenth degree of Capricorn with its potential for control, ambition, and public attention. At this stage, all the necessary information that is needed to achieve a breakthrough becomes available along with the appearance of key allies.

LS147 Summary

Mettle and magic are the true homeland of these newly arrived Earth Dragons who find enchantment in the very act of being alive. Theirs is a power and presence unrestrained by anything like gravity or the weight of public opinion. Seeking satisfaction, they are ravenous in their hunger for experiences that will bring forth creative acts of self-expression and indulgence. Born of Earth, they are eager to test their strength and apply an enthusiastic, hands-on approach to whatever catches their fancy. During their tenure, expect to think outside the box as you place the central pillars of creativity and inventiveness into the framework of your daily life.

When this eclipse activates a personal chart, a time of curiosity will prevail, giving one an intuitive and almost mystical ability to take timely action. Everything will seem to be touched with fairy dust as one lives in a perpetual state of wonder, allowing for prolonged and prodigious periods of productivity unlike anything experienced before. The key concept with this eclipse is that one can now live almost in a state of enchantment being driven by personal inspiration and, seemingly, guidance from the great beyond.

However, in matters of love, one needs to be careful and cautious; seduction and compulsion are in the air, and more infatuation (rather than intimacy) is around the corner. Swings of extreme attraction and then repulsion or life-altering decisions made in matters of mates or lovers must now be set aside. Better to focus on maintaining a healthy lifestyle. The future looks promising if one can focus on developing professional channels and networks that encourage the voice of reason.

Lunar Saros 147 has been moving through a Crescent phase on its earthly evolution since August 15, 1962. It will remain in this phase until September 28, 2034, at which time it will begin to experience a First Quarter phase that will prove to be fabulous and quite frankly irresistible in its ability to open up new doors of perception.

LS147 Luminaries

H P Lovecraft	August 20, 1890
Colonel Sanders	September 9, 1890
John Kenneth Galbraith	October 15, 1908
Claude Lévi-Strauss	November 28, 1908
Louis Hay	October 8, 1926
Thich Nhat Hanh	October 11, 1926
Sathya Sai Baba	November 23, 1926
Fred Smith	August 11, 1944
Barry White	September 12, 1944
Demi Moore	November 11, 1962
Jodie Foster	November 19, 1962
Jon Stewart	November 28, 1962
Bo Jackson	November 30, 1962
Ralph Fiennes	December 22, 1962
Ryan Gosling	November 12, 1980
Kim Kardashian	October 21, 1980
Christina Aguilera	December 18, 1980
Google [E2]	September 4, 1998
Paris Berelc	December 29, 1998
Henry Ruggs	January 24, 1999

1. https://www.theguardian.com/books/2014/aug/20/ten-things-you-should-know-about-hp-lovecraft. Retrieved July 10, 2022.
2. William Kalush & Larry Sloman, *The Secret Life of Houdini: The Making of America's First Superhero* (New York: Atria Books, 2006), p. 110
3. http://www.oxforddictionaries.com/definition/English/Houdini-Harry
4. Kalush & Sloman, *Houdini*, pp. 496-504.
5. https://www.celebritynetworth.com/ Retrieved July 9, 2022.
6. https://en.wikipedia.org/wiki/Harry_Potter. Retrieved July 9, 2022.
7. Jan Spiller, *Astrology for the Soul* (New York: Bantam Dell, 1997), p. 147-148.

LUNAR SAROS 148

"Humankind has not woven the web of life. We are but one thread within in. Whatever we do to the web, we do to ourselves. All things are bound together. All things connect."

-Chief Seattle

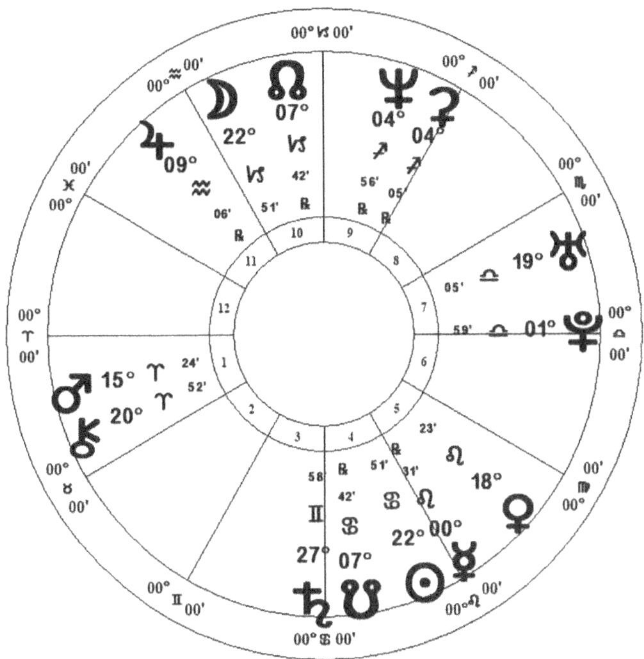

Lunar Saros 148

July 15, 1973 • 11:55:49 AM • North Pole

Webs of Wonder

This North Node Capricorn eclipse with Ruler Saturn in Gemini squaring Pluto at the AP offers up a formidable array of connectivity and persuasion. Tempted by its tentacles of influence, intelligence networks, politicians and their corporate handlers now have ease of access to portals and platforms that connect a global audience. "Surveillance" is the new bottom line, battle cry, and watch word for the coming decades if not centuries.

The core themes of Capricorn and Saturn in Gemini relate to the structure, distribution, and access to channels of information/metadata as a means to achieve power. Dazzled by the delights of instantaneous connection to a world of 24/7 entertainment, we must remain vigilant to the price paid for such diversion. Fast falling away are the days when an open media can be counted on to deliver a fair exchange of ideas. Saturn's square to this strategic Pluto will continue to drive forward a public discourse on our relationship to an omnipresent media whose "handlers" of the taxpayer largesse to politically connected corporations remains impervious to prosecution.

Considering that we now live in an electronic culture with ever-increasing demands for security, overseen by those who hold the reins of corporate and political power, Pluto's AP square to the Cancer/Capricorn nodal axis draws attention to the common destiny that we all now share as citizens of planet Earth. When the personal becomes political, our concerns for security and safety must be addressed in a spirit of openness if the destructive, shadow side of this potent aspect is to be avoided. It is imperative that private and personal gain coexist in equal measure with public sector rights, as viewed through the arresting impact of emerging technologies and the legal implications for social justice, state power, and public policy.

Building upon the eclipse axis is a Grand Cardinal Cross with a militaristic and highly charismatic Mars/Chiron conjunction in Aries opposition to Uranus. The Cardinal Grand Cross represents an overwhelming opportunity to work toward goals that are driven either for the selfish accumulation of power and position or to reinvigorate personal as well as collective systems and hierarchies that are in serious need of an upgrade. The eclipse axis resonating through the twenty-second degree is a double dose of Capricorn persuasion that will always seek to take control through any means of rationality. The Serbian astrologer Nikola Stojanovic did not hold kindly to this degree, calling it the Kill or be Killed degree. He found it in the birth charts of murderers and people who were murdered. Donald Trump has his Sun at 22 degrees and he's still alive, but he certainly has extinguished the hopes and careers of hundreds, perhaps thousands, of people over the course of his life. I do feel there is something dark about this degree as my own Saturn at 22 Libra produced a mother whose favorite saying directed at me was the unholy "I created you and I can destroy you" maxim she'd hurl my way at moments when her own depression and despair would draw down to darken her normal enthusiasm for life.

Believing in a new dream for a world full of optimism is the work of the midpoints as Jupiter takes command and expands its networks for a rich and fulfilling life with every return. The foundational Moon/Saturn opposition Uranus/Pluto isotrap will always be there to stretch your horizons as you create a new design to fit the new you that is emerging, based on your vision of the future.

Closest Midpoints: Node/Jupiter-Neptune, Eclipse/Jupiter-Node
Isotraps: Moon/Saturn opposition Uranus/Pluto
Mercury/Uranus conjunct Venus/Pluto

1900—2100 Eclipses: Lunar Saros—148

1973, 1991, 2009, 2027, 2045, 2063, 2081, 2099
Length of cycle —1,244 years
Series ends— August 9, 3217

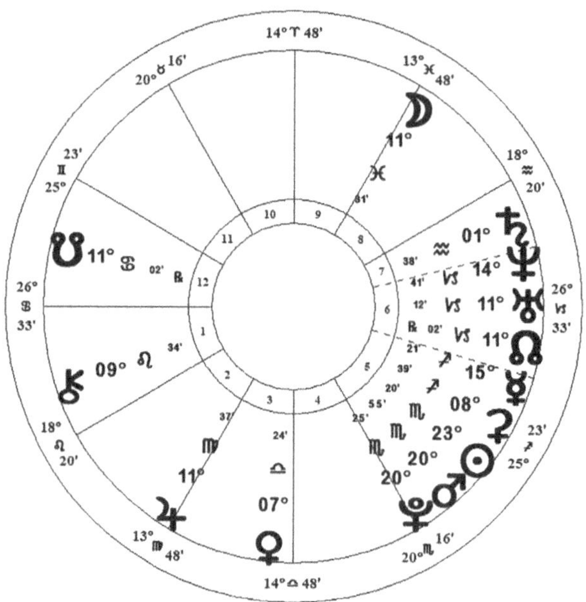

Shailene Woodley
PREBLE—LS148

November 15, 1991 • 9:06 PM • Upland, CA, USA

Environmental Activist/Actress

"A sublime actress with a résumé that pretty much proves she's incapable of making a false move on camera."

-PETER TRAVERS—*ROLLING STONE*[1]

Shailene Woodley's Connections to the Dragons of LS148
Space Lanes via DSC/ASC
↓South Node with South Node↓
Ceres with Ceres

1st Harmonics: Mars – MC, Uranus – IC
2nd Harmonics: Mercury – Saturn, Jupiter – Chiron

In 2010, Shailene co-founded "All It Takes," a youth leadership program to foster sustainable, positive change. She was a Bernie Sanders supporter in 2016 and 2020. In July 2019, she became an Oceans Ambassador for Greenpeace. When Space Lanes are running through your front and back door, you are going places.

By age 5, she was in front of the cameras acting professionally. But in her early 20's she became very, very sick. Shailene said, "While I was doing the *Divergent* movies, I also was struggling with a deeply personal, very scary physical situation. Because of that, I said no to a lot of opportunities because I needed to get better."[2] It seems the GG SNode on SNode would have its pound of flesh, but only for a time. The eclipse Mars 1st Harmonic jump-started her career while Mercury's 2nd Harmonic made her a star in the worlds of entertainment and politics. Jupiter's 2nd Harmonic to a ninth degree Chiron will do what it takes to make the future a better place, no matter how many times she's arrested for public protests. Saturn in Aquarius and Chiron in Leo make for a natural born leader.

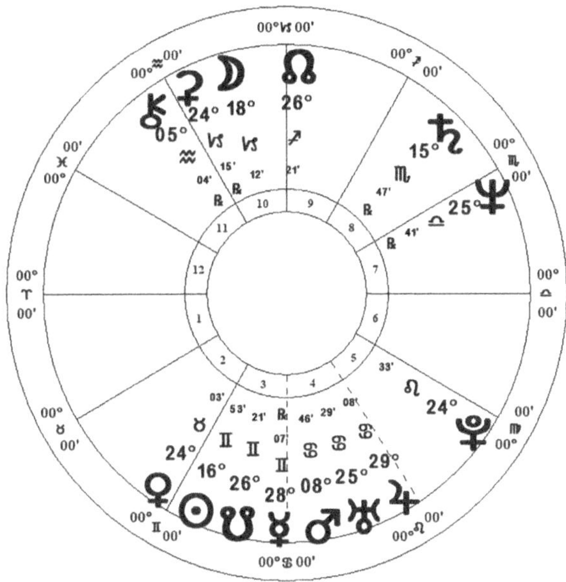

Tim Berners-Lee
PREBLEs—LS110 & LS143

June 8, 1955 • TOB Unknown • London, UK

Inventor of the World Wide Web

"The Web as I envisaged it, we have not seen it yet. The future is still so much bigger than the past."

-Sir Timothy Berners-Lee

Sir Tim is a British computer scientist best known as the inventor of the World Wide Web, a global hypertext project that became available to the public at large in the summer of 1991. It became known as the "internet." In an attempt to set the record straight on how the Web was created, Tim Berners-Lee wrote *Weaving the Web* in 1999. Responding to the rapid growth of the Web, Berners-Lee stated that:

> "The rate was incredible, ... growing by a factor of ten every year, from one hundred hits a day in the summer of 1991, to one thousand in the summer of 1992, to ten thousand in the summer of 1993; putting the Web out at this time was a watershed event that exposed the Web to a very critical academic community."[3]

Capturing Sir Tim's chart in all its visionary splendor would be the work of LS148 as it swept in at 3 Aquarius on July 26, 1991, on his ready-to-make-a-contribution Chiron; on August 6, within two weeks of the eclipse's arrival, Berners-Lee would offer to the largely academic online computer community access to *info.cern.ch*, the world's first browser. His pursuit of knowledge and attraction to humanitarian endeavors can be sourced back to retrograde Mercury's conjunction to the SNode in Gemini and the NNode's conjunction to the Galactic Core. Add in an exalted Jupiter in Cancer conjunct Uranus and we've got someone born with a benevolent technological vision of the future. Robert Pelletier hits it right on the nail with his description of this aspect. In his book *Planets in Aspect,* he writes, "Your outlook is to the future, and you can easily stimulate others to become excited about their future." This was a talent that Berners-Lee had in spades as he encouraged a growing global internet community "not just to browse, but to create."[4] The Jupiter-Uranus combination is again masterfully captured by Pelletier when he writes: "You have the temperament and the skill to construct social guidelines and policies that will be studied by future historians."[5]

Sir Tim's phenomenal NNode/Galactic Core conjunction sits at the apex of an Anchor secured by the ballast of a humanitarian Venus at the twenty-fourth degree of Taurus in sextile to his singularly sensational Uranus at the twenty-fifth degree of Cancer that would concretize his vision of a global information space that he believed would lead to an enormous, unbounded world. This Anchor pattern speaks to the fundamental force that has literally "anchored" his life's narrative. LS148's return in August 2009 would coincide with Sir Tim's progressed Mars at 14 Leo which received LS148's activation at 14 Aquarius. The return of this eclipse quickly led, in November 2009, to the creation of *The World Wide Web Foundation*, a non-profit organization "devoted to achieving a world in which all people can use the Web to communicate, collaborate and innovate freely, building bridges across the divides that threaten our shared future."[6]

Sir Tim Berners-Lee's Connections to the Dragons of LS148
Moon with Moon

1st Harmonics: SNode – Mars,
Moon – Ceres, Mercury – Jupiter, Saturn – SNode/Mercury
2nd Harmonics: Moon – Uranus/Jupiter

Sir Tim's ties to the eclipse field are extraordinary; fusing their fates starts with the Cosmic Bridge from the SNode to his Mars, then it's on to his CB from the eclipse Moon to his Ceres, the Sun's CB to his Uranus and then on to the super structure CB from Saturn to his SNode/Mercury. As always, it's the 2nd Harmonics that seal the deal. Here, the eclipse Moon reaches out not only to Berners-Lee's breaking the shackles of ignorance Uranus but his prophetic twenty-ninth degree Jupiter in Cancer that would weave a web of wonder into the fabric of our planetary existence and put humanity on the threshold of an entirely new platform for unparalleled opportunities and richness.

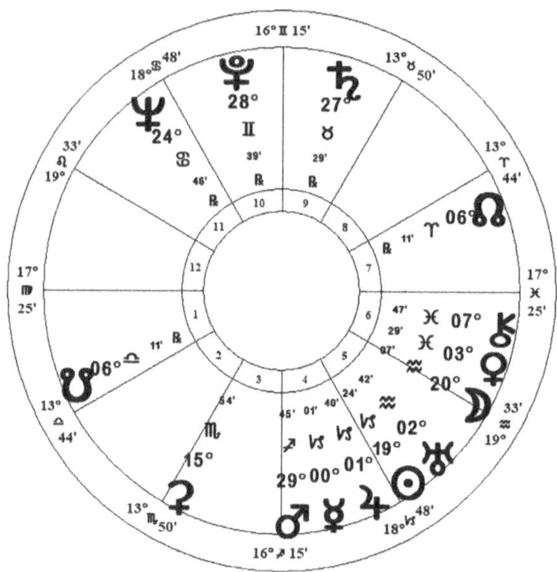

Richard Nixon
PREBLE—LS116

January 9 • 1913 • 9:35 PM • Yorba Linda, CA, USA

37th President of the United States

"When the President does it, that means that it's not illegal."

-Richard Nixon

Richard Nixon was the 37th President of the United States from 1969 until his resignation on August 9, 1974, because of the Watergate scandal. On July 13, 1973, it was revealed that President Nixon had a tape-recording system in his offices, and that recordings from these tapes implicated the president in several nefarious capers, and eventually their coverup.[7] These revelations synced to LS148's arrival on July 15, 1973. At 23 Capricorn, the eclipse lit up Nixon's Neptune at 24 Cancer.

Caught in a web of his own making, which then became his undoing, Nixon had very little room to maneuver. With Neptune activated and inconjunct Mars, Mercury, Jupiter, and the Moon, Nixon was strongly predisposed to breaking the bounds of accepted reality, justifying his mendacity at every turn. Hiding within his web of lies and illusions, he was incapable of handling things rationally. With retrograde Pluto in Gemini in the Tenth House, in opposition to Mars, Mercury and Jupiter, Nixon's downfall was a foregone conclusion. But his Pluto in Gemini would also stand as a symbol for his resurrection as a career politician, intoxicated by the power of statecraft.

This idea of resurrection and the continual reinvention of Richard Nixon in the culture of America is aptly portrayed in Daniel Frick's treatment of the contradictory mythic stories of Nixon in *Reinventing Richard Nixon.* He reminds us of the *Newsweek* cover headline, "He's Back!" and David Bowie asking a generation of young Americans in 1975: "'Do you remember your President Nixon?' Remember? As this cultural history of an American obsession has demonstrated, we can't even begin to forget him."[8]

Richard Nixon's Connections to the Dragons of LS148

1st Harmonics: Pluto – SNode,
Moon – Sun, Sun – Neptune, Saturn – Pluto
2nd Harmonics: Venus – Moon, Mercury – Uranus, Saturn – Mars/Mercury

Richard Nixon's hold on the American psyche has spread out across the globe to fascinate and frustrate all those held captive by an enduring spell of political corruption and conceit. Helping spin this web of woe is due in no small measure to the dynamic energy fields that were created by four Cosmic Bridges; the first three from the eclipse Moon, Sun, and Pluto and the last from the eclipse Venus to Nixon's Moon.

There can be no doubt that an eclipse Pluto to a natal SNode is a cage rattler and not a connector most people would order up. Recall Edith Piaf's PREBLE LS146 SNode on her natal Pluto and her lifelong struggle with just about everything. The thought of those two energies merging sends dread down my spine even without looking at anything else across their respective fields. As ruler of this NNode Capricorn eclipse, Saturn's square to Pluto at the AP is particularly well suited to hardball tactics, political persuasion, and prosecution leading even to persecution. Most planets in square have a natural tendency to dig in and are often impervious to change. To be reminded that there is a world of information and relationships that lie outside the field of one's comfort zone can be highly disturbing. Such a difficult Saturn making a tight, under one degree conjunction to Nixon's Tenth House Pluto would have set off alarm bells for any astrologer versed in lunar eclipse vernacular.

Nixon's Sun at 19 Capricorn and its CB to the eclipse axis brought his twenty-fourth Neptunian degree in Cancer literally to the doorstep of paranoia. All the light that was possible shone down on his insecurity, bringing to the surface his suspicious and paranoid nature and his inability to get a grip on reality. Three 2nd Harmonics would entangle him in his own web of lies while the fourth CB from the merciful eclipse Venus would deliver the final coup de grâce to end his suffering. The eighteenth degree eclipse Venus, with its ability to weaken and make small, had its way with his Moon at the twentieth degree of Aquarius and that was that. It would be a sad ending for a man born under PREBLE-LS116—Persuasion—an Earth Dragon family that needs to love and be loved.

LS148 Summary

Webs of wonder and intrigue await those who are drawn to dance with these catalytic and newly created Earth Dragons, here to change the world for the better. Their arrival is marked with an upsurge of can-do spirit as they carry out their mission to help humankind find better, faster, and more equitable ways of sharing information. They are true architects of the mind, and no one can remain unchanged in their presence. These are creator dragons capable of building networks as easily as bridges, but with carrying capacity undaunted by the vast stretches of dark matter. Their arrival will awaken long-ago memories that hold the power to move mountains.

On its journey of 1,244 years, Lunar Saros 148 offers seventy opportunities to interact and release its distinct DNA into humanity's world-wide-web of consciousness. It is currently enjoying an inchoate New Moon phase, still in its infancy and just beginning to get a feel for its formidable capacity for global connectivity. Considering its recent arrival, we might all want to be on our best behavior and respect the sagacity as well as the worldly reach that is woven into this potent celestial lunar eclipse family. It will enter its Crescent phase with the lunar eclipse of October 22, 2135.

When this family of eclipses affects a personal chart either by birthright or rite of passage, increased risk factors for a dystopian world view are easily accessed. In the guise of gurus, guns, giveaways, all manner of attention-getting, spontaneity, and dogma equally thrive in a kaleidoscope of people, projects, and possibilities. The need for freedom and personal accountability is strong and may suddenly awaken long-forgotten dreams and goals. Meanwhile, be sensitive to the needs and feelings of others who do not wish to walk your road. Family karma offers fascinating glimpses into our personal stories as well as our future trajectories.

LS148 Luminaries

Monica Lewinsky	July 23, 1973
Kate Beckinsale	July 26, 1973
Vera Farmiga	August 6, 1973
Sergey Brin	August 21, 1973
Dave Chappelle	August 24, 1973
Rose McGowan	September 5, 1973
Paul Walker	September 12, 1973
Nas	September 14, 1973
Lena Headey	October 3, 1973
Seth MacFarlane	October 26, 1973
Adam Copeland	October 30, 1973
Edge	October 30, 1973
Tyra Banks	December 4, 1973
Alexa Bliss	August 9, 1991
Marlon Teixeira	September 16, 1991
Riker Lynch	November 8, 1991
Genevieve Buechner	November 10, 1991
Matt Bennett	November 13, 1991
Taylor Hall	November 14, 1991
Shailene Woodley	November 15, 1991

1. https://en.wikipedia.org/wiki/Shailene_Woodley#cite_note-27. Retrieved Jul. 11, 2022.
2. https://www.nytimes.com/2020/04/10/movies/shailene-woodley-endings-beginnings.html. Retrieved July 11, 2022.
3. Tim Berners-Lee, *Weaving the Web: The Original Design and Ultimate Destiny of the WORLD WIDE WEB by Its Inventor* (New York: HarperCollins Publishers, 1999), p. 157.
4. Tim Berners-Lee, *Weaving the Web*, p. 34.
5. Pelletier, *Planets in Aspect*, pp. 57-58.
6. http://webfoundation.org/ Retrieved July 12, 2022.
7. https://www.history.com/topics/1970s/watergate. Retrieved July 12, 2022.
8. Daniel Frick, *Reinventing Richard Nixon: A Cultural History of an American Obsession* (Lawrence, KS: University Press of Kansas, 2008), p. 23.

LUNAR SAROS 156

"Study the past, if you would divine the future."

-CONFUCIUS

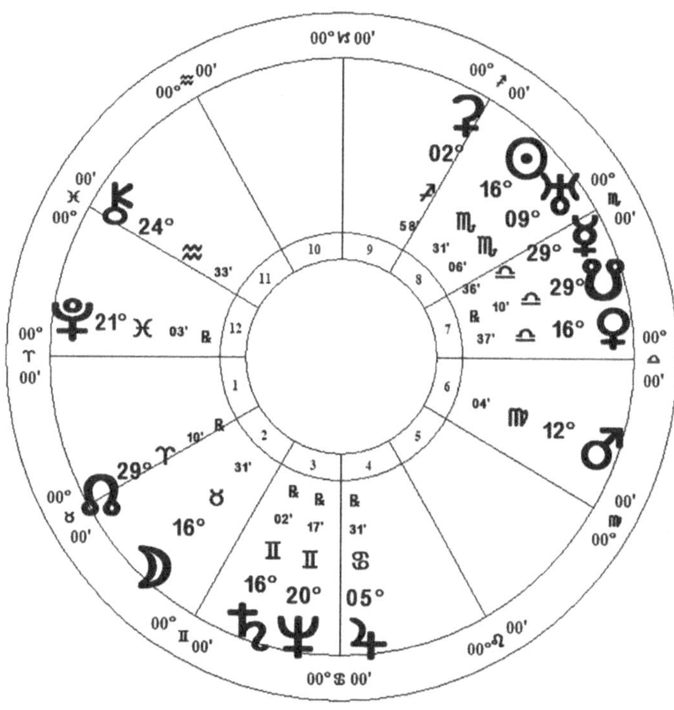

Lunar Saros 156

November 8, 2060 • 4:16:42 AM • North Pole

Money and Power

Bolstered by an inflowing rush of North Node Aries energy, global financial markets and monetary funds, as well as private investors, are headed for new heights of pain and glory. This is in part due to Lunar Saros 156's exalted Moon in Taurus and its insatiable quest for resource acquisition. Judging by its past performance in Lunar Saros Series 138, it might be wise to play your cards close to your chest considering that the availability of credit is certain to play a major role in the lifespan of these resource rich Earth Dragons. Let's see if we have learned anything from the past by taking a look at LS138 and some of its dramatically similar energetic structures.

Both charts hold tight Mercury/SNode conjunctions in trine to Chiron in Aquarius, with Chiron conjunct Saturn in the case of LS138 and in trine to a Saturn/Neptune conjunction in LS156. All told, credit and financial risk may reach extreme levels of volatility as global pressure forces fast-falling markets to spiral into collapse. In light of eclipse ruler Venus enthroned in Libra, all manner of contracts, law and idealism become swept up in the whirlwind generated by her powerful six member Grand Air Trine consortium of celestial hard-liners all playing to win. Mercury's facility for duplicity in combination with the strategic gamesmanship of the SNode in Libra trine Neptune/Saturn in Gemini's metaphysical pragmatics is a sure sign that financial intrigue and manipulation are going for control. Given the nature of the Taurus/Scorpio dynamic in play, Pluto's waxing square to both Neptune and Saturn contributes to the tectonic forces that will shift and recalibrate the balance of power on the world stage. Evolutionary in scale but sized down to fit into a social context, LS156 is going to bring irreversible shifts in corporate agribusiness and global finance.

With Venus holding court, these shifts will be accompanied by a wave of social conformity powered by the growing ascendancy of China. LS156 begins a new chapter in the cultural achievements of our great eastern civilizations. It marks a time period unprecedented since the eleventh century CE and reminiscent of the outpourings of the Song (Sung) Dynasty (960–1276) and its historical chronicles.[1] Technological advances will permeate every facet of our global society, resulting in unprecedented standards of living that will have social credit systems centralizing almost all economic and political activity.

A portrait of scarcity, sacrifice, and social obligation begins to emerge as the Eclipse/Venus-Saturn midpoint unfolds. Adding to the social disruption potential is the Node/Venus-Uranus midpoint which, as it too begins to unfold into the global consciousness, may prove to be the beginning of a very long period of great social unrest as available resources are redistributed based on social and political hierarchies rather than humanitarian needs. The Saturn-Neptune conjunction in Gemini square Mars in Virgo signals public health concerns of major importance as pandemics, pollution, and permafrost melting contribute to an ever-increasing state of global instability. The Sun holds a parallel declination to Pluto that suggests possessions, property, and financial resources will all undergo some manner or form of deconstruction. For the first time in decades if not centuries, for many of us failure is going to become part of our collective psyche.

Closest Midpoints: Eclipse/Venus-Saturn, Node/Venus-Uranus
Isotraps: Sun/Moon opposition Venus/Saturn
Sun/Uranus opposition Jupiter/Pluto

1900—2100 Eclipses: Lunar Saros—156

2060, 2078, 2096
Length of cycle —1,442 years
Series ends—April 5, 3503

LS156 Summary

Language and how we express what we hold to be our most important values will undergo critical shifts as global pressure forces humanity to deconstruct our worldview. These Earth Dragons are all business and bottom-line brokers in a world that is fast becoming more like a global corporate enterprise than a culturally diversified planet. As this dragon family continues to evolve through each phase, many opportunities will arise that will highlight their unique ability to handle the basic needs of a planet as well as off-planet populations that are quickly transforming their social determinants for health, wealth, and political stability. Given their celestial youth, it may take them a while to get a handle on things. Meanwhile, their arrival will coincide, for the majority of us, with some serious shocks to our daily life, our notions of what is now considered acceptable standards of conduct and behavior and a growing sense that the global zeitgeist is moving in the wrong direction.

Here are some dates to look forward to as Lunar Saros 156 begins unfolding through an ancient, celestial eight-fold pattern, inviting us onto the dance floor that marks out their evolutionary journey. During their especially long lifespan of 1,442 years, we get to experience their take on the world as they share their sphere and hold us dear on the terrestrial dance floor that marks out each and every one of their eighty-one returns, with every return helping us to get better and better at learning to move in sync with their cosmic rhythms.

Phase	Return	Date
Crescent	5th	December 22, 2132
First Quarter	9th	February 5, 2205
Gibbous	13th	March 20, 2277
Full Moon	17th	May 3, 2349
Disseminating	21st	June 16, 2421
Last Quarter	26th	August 10, 2511
Balsamic	30th	September 22, 2583
New Moon	34th	November 6, 2655

1. http://afe.easia.columbia.edu/songdynasty-module/ Retrieved July 13, 2022.

PART THREE

DANCING WITH AIR

The Air Eclipses

Thoughts are boomerangs, returning with precision to their source. Choose wisely what you throw.

-ANONYMOUS

Pay attention to your potential! These dragons will wake and shake you up. Think of these lunar eclipses as a breath of fresh spring air. Their visits are always a bit on the hectic side as they give us lots to think about. The energy fields of Lunar Air Eclipses are a study in variety as our lives open up to embrace a steady stream of opinions and options all designed to give us more choices. Each new day is an affirmation that life is better lived out in the open where secrets cannot abide.

You are about to meet twelve extraordinary lunar eclipse families all driven by the simple principle that ideas are worth sharing. And like a good TED talk, after spending some time with each one, you will come to appreciate how simple principles do not necessarily generate simple outcomes. The beauty of working with the lunar eclipses in this section is that they give such a lift to our state of mind. Even the difficult lunar eclipses, like LS135, have an upside if we care to see it. And if we don't, it will be coming around again in eighteen years, at which time we might be in a better position to handle the losses that it invariably brings. It should come as no surprise that there are lunar eclipses that deal with loss and painful separations but knowing that pattern is in play can be helpful in turning lemons into lemonade. If gale-force winds have you in their grasp and you find yourself off course, the first thing anyone must do is resist the urge to panic. Knowing the wallop some of these dragons carry is often just the nudge that is needed to get one back on track, or at least help to course-correct a tendency to drift.

Throughout this section you'll find the charts and astrological highlights that uplift and inspire these eclectic lunar eclipses. For those looking for tender tales, tidbits, and stories that illuminate how lunar eclipses work, there is an assortment of celebrities, historical figures, and events that showcase how awesome these eclipses can be. Part Three holds the likes of Angelina, Brad, Putin, and Spielberg up to the light of lunar eclipses along with the curious case of the rise and fall of Lance Armstrong. You'll get to peek behind the cosmic curtain to catch a glimpse of the goings on when these critical lunar eclipses activate. As always, I hope you get an appreciation for how to work with lunar eclipse fields in their facility to initiate, encourage, and bring to fruition outstanding periods of personal endeavor, and opportunity.

And if you do decide to sit one out, it's not the end of the world. All eclipse seasons present opportunities as well as obstacles—there is no perfect caper or get-out-of-jail lunar eclipse, although the Earth Dragons of LS138—Legends and Legacy in Part Two—continue to audition for the spot. Pound for pound, the Air Dragons can be fiercely unsettling, but you'd never know it because by their very nature they are relational; they seek companions to share in their success, suffering, and sorrow. When an unruly Air Dragon has blown your sanity south, take comfort in the fact that warm westerly winds are on their way to shift your state of mind. Sometimes we all need a little distance and time to appreciate just how much we've learned from past experiences. You'll find that these lunar eclipses are master teachers in that respect, and I invite you to look back and discover the celestial tune-ups that took place while you were busy doing other things.

Part Three holds the second largest treasure of lunar eclipses—twelve Air eclipses that have the power to persuade, sway, educate, enlighten, and even revolutionize our way of thinking about our world and each other. The first three lunar eclipses, LS117, LS122, and LS123 all hail from the 11th century. LS117 features a Libran Moon while LS122 and LS123 both carry Aquarian Moons. If your chart links strongly to any of them, you might find yourself "flashing back" to simpler times and far distant places associated with the birth of those eclipses. This is especially noticed when one studies their PREBLE birth chart and its implications for reincarnation motifs and past-life patterns. The last eclipse in this section closes with Lunar Saros Series 145, a recent South Node lunar family of eclipses birthed on August 11, 1832. With a life span of 1,262 years, it will dance and sway its way from pole to pole, through seventy-one incarnations, completing its journey on September 16, 3094. The Air eclipses are the true masters of movement and change and their expertise is generally played out on a mental level, enjoying the pure pleasure of communication. Their temperament is social and the realization of joint objectives through common interests or a lack thereof is a noted feature of their presence.

A natal or progressed Sun placement along with the angles of a chart receive their fair share of the glory when activated by these lunar eclipses.

Under an Aquarian Moon, our creative passions become rarefied, and our ideas reach into an ever-widening sphere of influence. A Libran Moon will fan artistic flames that crave glamor and romance. The Gemini Moon in a Lunar Saros Series will always provoke a state of constant stimulation wherever it lands during its six-month tenure.

Lunar Saros Series 144 features the pivotal events in the life of Salvador Dalí, one of the most extraordinary and surreal characters of the 20th century. It should come as no surprise that the Moon of this lunar eclipse family is in Aquarius, with Uranus retrograde in Aquarius. Unsettling and often disturbing, LS144 has no time for the mundane; its imaginative and iconoclastic forces are on overdrive to show off their special talents and capacity for genius.

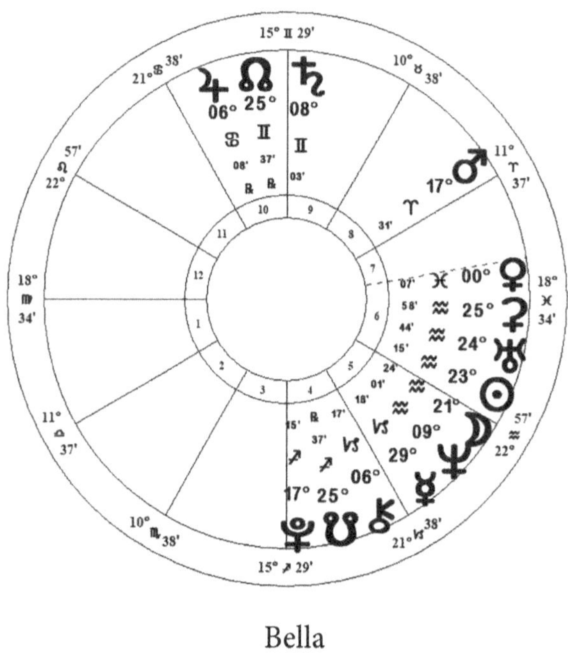

Bella
PREBLE—LS144

February 11, 2002 • 7:40 PM • Surrey, BC, Canada

And speaking of genius, you are about to meet an extraordinary person born under this lunar eclipse. Bella is a young woman with over sixteen personalities; she has a given diagnosis of Dissociative Identity Disorder, which is used to describe people who have distinctive and absolute splits in their identity state.

The disorder develops suddenly and is usually only found in highly intelligent and creative individuals.

Bella's distinct personalities began to develop early in her life in response to the severe trauma she was experiencing. When a child experiences trauma they can only respond in terror, wanting to escape and believing it is their fault. According to her therapist, all sixteen personalities that developed were created out of necessity to cope in a failing environment that lacked the essential requirements of a nurturing and loving home. These personalities all developed so she could survive. They are her creations and her way of dealing with her unfortunate reality. Bella's inner family runs like a high-efficiency turbine: She says that it can be difficult to get enough sleep and rest as everyone seems to have an opinion and everyone wants to have their say. Sometimes sleep is almost non-existent. Bella is an artist functioning at extraordinary levels of brilliant creativity. Her ability to function in society with this much inner reality is an amazing process most of us would not be able to carry out. Just keeping all her internal community "in the loop" is, in itself, a full-time job that very few people would sign up for.

Before taking a look at her cosmic connections to this most astounding lunar eclipse, take some time to appreciate the basic astrological patterns that give rise to archetypes that carry distinct personality and character structures. After that, the next step is to identify any aspect patterns or harmonics that are found in both fields. Only then do I make a list of the 1st and 2nd Harmonics between the eclipse field and the chart under review.

Here are a few highlights from her chart. Bella was born within hours of a New Moon making her a bridge of consciousness that straddled the dark, dying Balsamic Moon and the seed impulse and vision of a New Moon. She is a natural-born explorer. Freedom and spontaneity flow through her veins and arteries as she throws herself headfirst into new experiences. She is a work in progress as her multiple identities project many possible avenues and styles of behavior, thinking, feelings, and perceptions into the world, meeting every challenge of the moment with a fresh perspective. In her chart, the Moon/Neptune/Mercury are all in parallel declination as are her Sun/Uranus/Pluto and Venus giving her a director's perspective on the world with a life purpose that is destined to help reinvigorate society. With a prophetic twenty-ninth degree Mercury in Capricorn along with her zero degree "anything goes" Venus in Pisces, corporate oligarchs will have no defense against her unique style and authenticity. Bella's Sun/Moon-Uranus midpoint is the obvious link to her Dissociative Identity Disorder along with her

Uranus/Sun-Ceres which is often found in charts of individuals who experienced either unreliable and erratic nurturing or their identity and self-image were stymied by some form of physical or psychological deprivation. Helen Keller, Alice Bailey, Helena Blavatsky, Alan Leo, Natalie Wood, Naomi Wolf, Keith Urban and Geraldo Rivera all have Uranus-Ceres conjunctions and their lives all revolved around modernizing techniques and faculties of perception.

Giving Bella her full due in this brief introduction is impossible; all we can do is skim the surface of her complex, multiple personalities. The next step is to find patterns that are in both charts. This is important as it will help us to understand how the harmonics across their fields function. There are two aspects that are found in both charts: a Moon conjunct Uranus and a Saturn in phase symmetry with Venus. Now our 1st and 2nd Harmonic list will make more sense.

Bella's Connections to the Dragons of LS144
Uranus to Uranus

1st Harmonics: Uranus – Moon/Sun,
Moon – Neptune, Mars – SNode
2nd Harmonics: Venus – Moon/Sun, Sun – Neptune, Mercury – Mercury

Bella's imaginative free spirit gets driven and pushed to explore even greater dimensions of her personality by the eclipse 1st Harmonics. Mars on her South Node is an especially high performance factor that has gifted her with the mental energy and karma to be able to connect with a variety of people from all walks of life; hence she would have a reluctance and even unwillingness to integrate her multi-variant community of personalities. The 2nd Harmonic Venus with its square to Saturn is in no hurry to assimilate her internal community; there is enough internal controversy and conflict around issues of independence versus partnership to keep prospective suitors on the sidelines for as long as it takes. The eclipse 2nd Harmonic Sun in Leo on her ninth degree Neptune would be shining a light on careers in the field of music, dance, and film, especially with a visionary and highly theatrical twenty-ninth degree Mercury resonating to her take charge Mercury in Capricorn.

Bella is a singularly sensational woman whose Dissociative Identity Disorder diagnosis is perhaps a beacon of light into the complexity of our own internal state of being and how each of us manage to hold back the gates of anarchy on a daily basis. Bella seems more than capable of managing her community of characters who are equally committed to keeping her sane. Together they have created a life force that is engaged and creatively vibrant. Bella *is* Lunar Saros 144.

If you are the lucky recipient of a vivacious Air sign Moon, note the Lunar Air eclipses scheduled to activate your chart as they will do their best to rouse you out of any rut or hollow of complacency. They all arrive with an agenda if not propaganda and are not shy about extolling their virtues. In the world of these lunar eclipses, controversy is an essential ingredient, utilizing logic and reason to promote social discourse. Disagreements, along with their resolution, for the most part, are just a conversation away. Note: public confessions are an entirely different matter. If your Moon is in one of the Air signs, a Lunar Air eclipse, especially a same sign lunar placement will greatly increase your ability to resonate to their energetic field.

The Lunar Saros Series featuring a Moon in Gemini will be of special interest to anyone with their natal Moon in Gemini. They are rare and only one is currently active in the 20th and 21st centuries:

Lunar Saros 139

The Lunar Saros Series featuring a Moon in Libra will be of special interest to anyone with their natal Moon in Libra.

Lunar Saros 117
Lunar Saros 134
Lunar Saros 135
Lunar Saros 136

The Lunar Saros Series featuring a Moon in Aquarius will be of special interest to anyone with their natal Moon in Aquarius.

Lunar Saros 122
Lunar Saros 123
Lunar Saros 125
Lunar Saros 126
Lunar Saros 143
Lunar Saros 144
Lunar Saros 145

Air Dragon Allegiance

Lunar Saros 117
Tony Robbins, Princess Diana, Sergey Brin & Larry Page

Lunar Saros 122
Aretha Franklin, D H Lawrence, John Oliver

Lunar Saros 123
Robert Downey Jr., The Red Baron, Sir Edmund Hillary

Lunar Saros 125
Steven Spielberg, Madame Chien-Shiung Wu, H. G. Wells & Orson Welles

Lunar Saros 126
World War Z, *News Flash!* The Fall of Prince Andrew, Brad Pitt

Lunar Saros 134
Audrey Hepburn, Angelina Jolie, Paul Newman

Lunar Saros 135
Margaret Atwood, Eve "V" Ensler, A Client's Story—Misha

Lunar Saros 136
Dylan Thomas, Jackie "O," Marie Antoinette

Lunar Saros 139
9—11, Mohandas Gandhi, *News Flash!* Trump's Tweet

Lunar Saros 143
Steve Jobs, Kevin Costner, Susan Boyle

Lunar Saros 144
Salvador Dalí, *News Flash!* White House Insurrection,
News Flash! 1st COVID-19 Case in USA, *News Flash!* BREXIT

Lunar Saros 145
Lance Armstrong, The Snowden Revelations and Laura Poitras,
A Client's Story—Sophia

LUNAR SAROS 117

"The present is the only thing that has no end."

-ERWIN SCHRODINGER

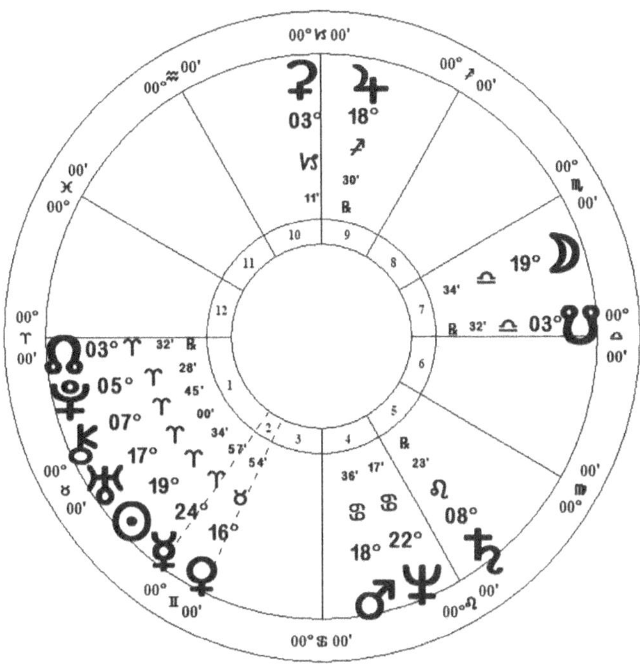

Lunar Saros 117

April 9, 1094 • 5:45:28 PM • South Pole

Searching

Lunar Saros 117 is a love affair with collaboration. Her air waves resonate with lifetimes of integrity, attracting partnerships like hummingbirds to nectar. There is an immediate improvement to any and all fields of endeavor, especially when cooperation holds the highest value. At the nineteenth degree of Libra, the eclipse field radiates an enhanced Libran vibe that promotes savoir faire and teamwork. As ruler of the eclipse and in rulership, Venus is uniquely positioned in Taurus to help us form and identify with what we value and thus bring us ever closer to our own ability to make the choices that define our authenticity.

The field carries a SNode, which naturally gravitates to either giving away or releasing energy that, in our case, helps to serve the greater good. All who labor under their banner will feel the urge to unite their forces to work in tandem in either a personal relationship, a professional partnership, or an association. Healthy teamwork is the ticket here as incompatible relationships will no longer be tolerated. A unique NNode, Pluto and Chiron conjunction in Aries found only in this Saros Series gives this family an ability to awaken to new and specialized fields of opportunity that hold tremendous growth potential. In addition, the nodal axis in an exact square to Ceres at the third degree is prepared to give anyone "the third degree" in the search for new and sustainable ways of living. This is not as easy as it looks with Pluto sitting at the midpoint between the NNode and Chiron creating a public personality that is compelled to serve one's own personal agenda while at the same time advancing the cause and common destiny of the public writ large. Striking a balance between individual self-expression and becoming a cause célèbre will require the acceptance of one's mortal limitations while dealing with all the collective failings and flaws of our shared social destiny.

A heightened awareness of the environment and other people puts you in the right place at the right time. Idealistic and artistic gifts emerge under the lyrical spells of a Mars/Neptune conjunction in Cancer that is ready to serve. Ebertin's COSI suggests that Neptune's Sun/Mercury midpoint gives expression to "the play of imagination, the development of fantasy with inspiration an asset for writers and visionaries."[1] The spirit of this eclipse is not easily defined as it has a multi-dimensional quality, with access to alternative portals of expression and resources that elude conventional rules of historical social engagement. A diverse palette of interests holds sway underscored by Mercury at the Venus/Node midpoint which enjoys cooperating and realizing joint objectives.

Contributing to this lunar eclipse complexity is a highly charged Yod formed from Venus in Taurus in sextile to the above noted Mars/Neptune conjunction with Jupiter in rulership and retrograde at its apex. After years of noticing Yod formations, I have come to the conclusion that they are *exactly* what they are—literally forks in the road of life that, as Yogi Berra has famously stated, need to be taken. Thoughtfulness and a little patience go a long way to bring out the best in this remarkable Yod. In the following pages you will meet Princess Diana who, with two powerful Yod formations to a retrograde Jupiter, exemplifies the importance of being able to take that fork in the road when it appears.

Closest Midpoints: Mercury/Venus-Node, Neptune/Eclipse-Mercury
Isotraps: Mercury/Mars conjunct Saturn/Pluto
Sun/Mars conjunct Uranus Neptune

1900—2100 Eclipses: Lunar Saros—117

1905, 1923, 1941, 1959, 1977, 1995, 2013, 2031, 2049, 2067, 2085
Length of cycle —1,262 years Series ends—May 15, 2356

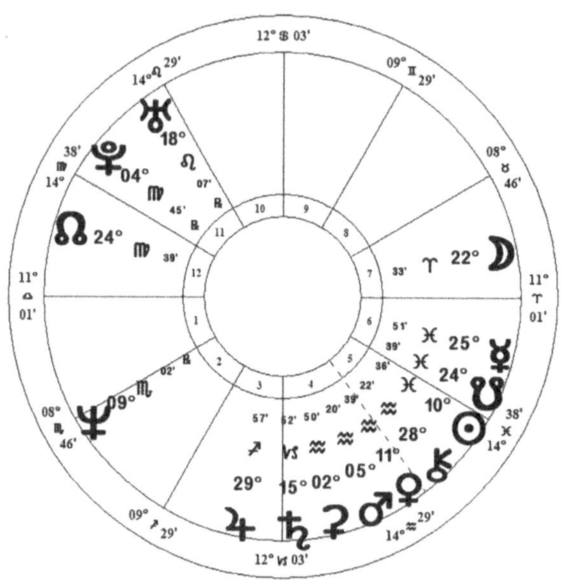

Tony Robbins
PREBLE—LS117

February 29, 1960 • 8:10 PM • Los Angeles, CA, USA

"There's always a way if you're committed."

An Awakened Giant

"Successful people ask better questions, and as a result, they get better answers."

-Tony Robbins

Tony Robbins has a Locomotive pattern, one of the easiest patterns to spot. His Uranus leads the way and as part of his Venus/Mars-Uranus midpoint suggests that his social and financial needs will be met through a relentless drive for innovative methods that employ sudden breakthroughs that allow people to experience greater levels of satisfaction and success. Some of Robbin's earliest success came through his ability to achieve ground-breaking results with professional sports figures involving his unique use of Neuro-Linguistic programming (NLP) to produce rapid and effective results. Before we look at his clan connections, apart from his high-velocity Uranus, let's see what else jumps out remembering that going with the flow is the fastest way to circumvent rigidity; Tony would approve.

Tony Robin's Connections to the Dragons of LS117
Space Lanes via ASC/DSC
↑NNode with SNode↓

1st Harmonics: Mercury – Moon, Uranus – Moon
2nd Harmonics: Moon – Moon, Mars – Saturn, Saturn – Mars

Tony Robbin's inner landscape, as viewed through the master control switch of the twenty-second degree Moon in Aries, holds a waxing First Quarter square with a Saturn tucked tightly by rulership to his Fourth House cusp, giving him the inner strength, action potential and empathic ability to create a new identity out of the conflict that shaped his early childhood years. Both Saturn and Jupiter are in rulership adding in the essential qualities of optimism and leadership that would make Tony Robbin's motivational coaching, books, seminars, lectures, and multi-media presentations a global brand. Tony's chart truly speaks to his personality and life path especially considering his SNode conjuncts the proactive twenty-fifth degree Mercury in Pisces, giving him what many Vedic astrologers would suggest is a well-deserved skill set for communicating knowledge for the benefit of others.

Tony's First Quarter squares continue with one from Neptune to Mars along with Neptune to Venus. This gives him his marching orders to live in the here and now, to take immediate action whenever possible and deal with any fall-out later. As a Piscean, these two aspects alone make him a visionary able to run after whatever it is that he cares to pursue in the full awareness that as long as he strives forward, success is well within reach. And like Bella, his ninth degree Neptune with a waxing trine to a Piscean Sun makes Tony a cross-cultural phenomenon that creatively merges the best within his shamanic Second House healer and his magical Fifth House conjurer. No doubt about it, Tony Robbins is a showman.

Take note of the awesome Space Lanes that connect the eclipse field to Robbin's ASC/DSC axis. The nineteenth degree Libran/Aries eclipse axis is a double Libran resonance which greatly amplified Robbins aesthetic sensibilities and competence in the public sphere; his eleventh degree Venus in Aquarius is also a double dip of idealism as well as unconventionality as that degree carries an Aquarian overtone. He has remarked that his early life was "chaotic" and "abusive" and at age seventeen, he left home for good.[2] When relief comes it usually arrives in the form of a 2nd Harmonic. Here we find a double dose of Mars to his Saturn and the eclipse Saturn to his Mars allowing for a massive release of Tony Robbin's style energy thanks to the enterprising and deeply searching spirit of LS117's Mercury/Mars conjunct Saturn/Pluto's isotrap. Tony's Global Gateway would always swing wide open to accommodate the strivings of his inner giant.

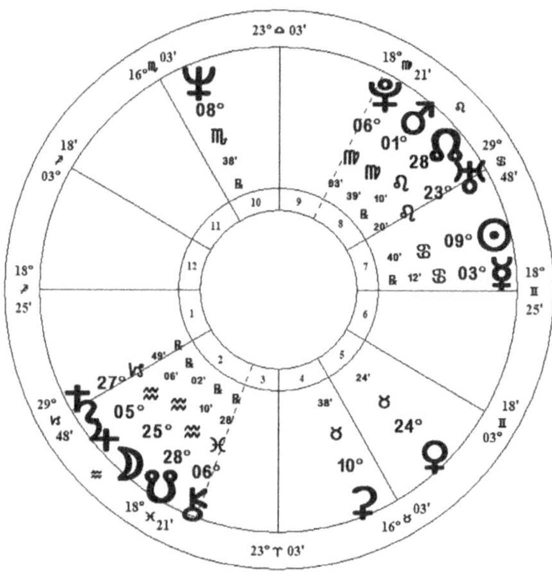

Princess Diana
PREBLE—LS132

July 1, 1961 • 7:45 PM • Sandringham, UK

The People's Princess

"I like to be a free spirit. Some don't like that but that's the way I am."

-DIANA

On November 20, 1995, Diana, Princess of Wales, gave an hour-long interview with the BBC. She spoke candidly about her separation from her husband Charles, the Prince of Wales, and admitted to an adulterous affair with her riding instructor, James Hewitt. She expressed the pain that her husband's long-term relationship with Camilla Parker-Bowles had caused her, but remained silent on the topic of the new romance that was quickly overtaking her life. Diana had met Pakistani heart surgeon Hasnat Khan on September 1 and reportedly was "smitten," managing to arrange their first date by mid-September.[3]

Diana's Connections to the Dragons of LS117
Space Lanes via MC/IC
Venus with Venus

1st Harmonics: Jupiter – ASC, Mercury – IC
2nd Harmonics: Saturn – Jupiter, Ceres – Mercury

On October 8, 1995, the rising winds of LS117 blasted through the eye of the storm that was centered at the fifteenth degree of Aries. While none of Diana's planets or angles received a direct link to the lunar eclipse, her Mercury/Saturn midpoint at 15 Aries certainly did along with her Venus/Pluto at 15 Cancer. In search of love and connection, these midpoints responded with enthusiasm, dancing a tango of sexuality, stress, strain, and ultimately of suffering.

Princess Diana's ascendant at 18 degrees Sagittarius establishes direct ancestral ties of royalty and kinship to LS117's Jupiter at 18 Sagittarius. The eighteenth degree with its overtones of service from both charts would, working together strike a chord for freedom that would resonate through her ascendant ruler Jupiter, compelling its life-affirming Pluto/Sun Yod to take that "fork in the road" that would simultaneously terminate and resurrect a life that had become unbearably inauthentic.

Diana's chart is an exceptional example of the importance of checking phase angle patterns across charts. Notice her tight Moon in Aquarius opposition Uranus which replicates *an identical* one hundred eighty-two degree waning phase angle between the eclipse Moon and its opposition with Uranus. Such symmetry, with nothing else in the way of activation degrees, would be more than enough to create an evocative resonance across their two fields. In fact, Diana had just turned sixteen when LS117 returned in the summer of 1977. In his engagement interview in 1981, Charles had told a reporter: "I remember thinking what a very jolly and amusing and attractive 16-year-old she was. I mean, great fun, and bouncy and full of life and everything."[4] LS117's return that year at four Aries would cast an opposition directly on her Neptune/Node midpoint at four Libra and her Mars/Neptune midpoint at five Libra. As a point of interest, Diana's Moon holds a parallel conjunction to Neptune within minutes of exactitude, underscoring her sensitive nature and her deeply sympathetic response to the poetry, pain, disappointment, and disillusionment of all those who suffer in the silence of social rejection. Another similarity is through LS117's unique NNode-Pluto-Chiron conjunction and Diana's Pluto-Chiron opposition. In tandem, their energetic patterns united to make Diana a cause célèbre in her desperation to redefine both her own flaws and those of the Royal Family. Assisting her were the temporary and politically savvy Space Lanes created by the eclipse axis at nineteen Libra on her MC/IC axis that would remove all the radar, speed traps and inhibitions that had been stifling her authenticity and personal power.

LS117's 2nd Harmonic Saturn to Diana's Jupiter is where we shall end this discussion as it is the most important of all the harmonics: it influences not one but two of her critical Yods from Jupiter to her Sun/Pluto and to her Mars/Mercury. These Yods are true turning points as they mark a fork in the road where a decision would have to be made. And on that crucial day in November 1995, Diana, Princess of Wales saw that fork in the road and made a choice. That her life would be re-orienting itself based on a new relationship would be obvious as such shifts in focus are what the lunar eclipses do best and, apart from prediction, give valuable information not only to where we are now but where we are headed. In Diana's case, the road chosen led to the possibility of a new romance as this Libran eclipse and its NNode/Pluto conjunction in Aries was ready to take a leap of faith in love, especially with Pluto resonating to the fifth degree, a very Leonian overtone. The eclipse Saturn at the eighth degree of Leo is specifically connected to wealth and sex; in a 2nd Harmonic to her high-spirited and magnetic, fun-loving fifth degree Aquarian Jupiter, love would return to her world where she could enjoy once again the conviviality and the light-heartedness of inspiring and uncomplicated companionship.

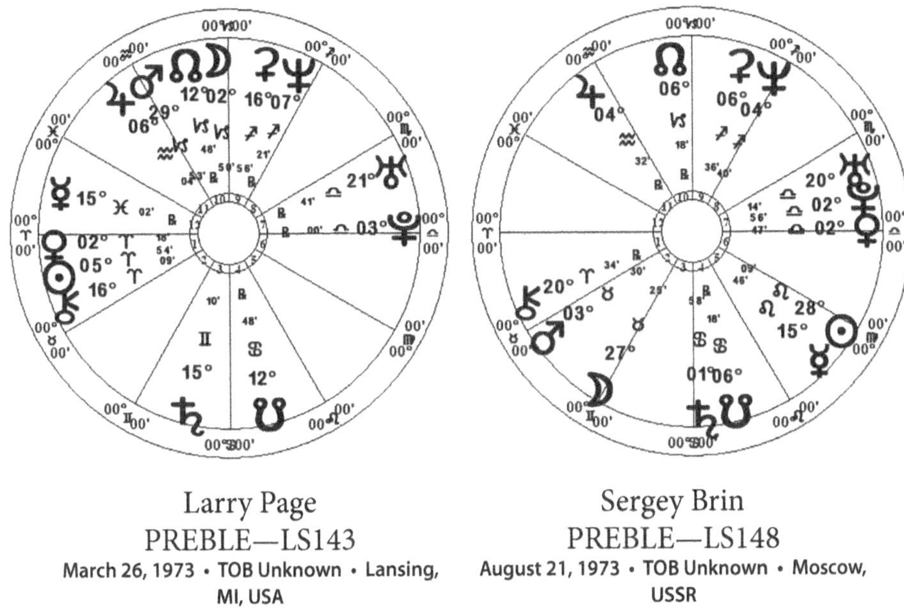

Larry Page
PREBLE—LS143
March 26, 1973 • TOB Unknown • Lansing, MI, USA

Sergey Brin
PREBLE—LS148
August 21, 1973 • TOB Unknown • Moscow, USSR

Greed in Deed Could Be Their Creed

If we were motivated by money, we would have sold the company a long time ago and ended up on a beach."

-LARRY PAGE

While still graduate students at Stanford working on PhD studies in computer science, Larry Page and Sergey Brin's separate projects were brought together under LS117's return at 15 degrees Aries on October 8, 1995. According to biographer Richard Brandt's *Inside Larry & Sergey's Brain*, it was in the fall of 1995 that Larry recruited Sergey to design a Web crawler that would combine Page's search technology with Brin's genius for archiving and data mining masses of Web data. Their academic exercise would quickly become the basis for a new and exciting company.[5] The Google search engine, first set up to troll through Stanford's own web pages, was an immediate hit with students and faculty, and Page and Brin became convinced of its commercial potential. By late 1996, Sergey recalled, "We had something we thought was quite nice."[6]

They make a formidable team; both are Fire signs with Moon in Earth exhibiting the classic steamroller, pig-headed, take-no-prisoners approach. Both have Sun/Moon *Last Quarter* phases, giving them a rich resource base of applied wisdom to draw upon. But it was their Venus/Pluto contacts that sparked their collaboration. Sergey's Venus/Pluto in Libra in opposition to Larry's Venus in Aries opposition Pluto made it possible for them to have creative projects within a partnership that would literally change the world in terms of how we search and find information. Let's check out their LS117 playlist.

Larry Page's Connections to the Dragons of LS117
Chiron with Chiron

1st Harmonics: Moon – Uranus,
NNode/Pluto/Chiron – Sun/Venus, Sun/Uranus – Chiron, Jupiter – Ceres
2nd Harmonics: Sun/Uranus – Uranus, Saturn – Jupiter, Pluto – Pluto

Sergey Brin's Connections to the Dragons of LS117
Chiron with Chiron

1st Harmonics: Moon – Uranus,
Sun/Uranus – Chiron, SNode – Pluto/Venus, Ceres – NNode
2nd Harmonics: Sun/Uranus – Uranus, Pluto – Pluto/Venus

The critical aspect they both share that was activated by LS117 in late 1995 was their Chiron's opposition to Uranus in Libra. Larry's Chiron is at the nurturing sixteenth degree of Aries and Sergey's is at the twentieth manifestation degree of Aries. Sergey received the strongest resonance to his Chiron, falling within one degree, but it was Larry's initiative that got the project going with his multiple connections.

The eclipse Uranus, being part of a Cardinal T-Square that invokes the essence of Leo, Virgo and Libra can seamlessly transmit its lock-step pattern of energy to both Page and Brin through the eclipse Sun/Uranus 1st Harmonic. Both of them receive a Cosmic Bridge from the nodes: Page's Venus is in resonance to the eclipse NNode and its Pluto conjunction while Brin's Pluto/Venus conjunction takes in the full force of the Cosmic Bridge via the eclipse's SNode in Libra.

As always, the 2nd Harmonics can be counted on to move the energy from inspiration into manifestation. Here we see that Larry's Venus gets "lit up" by the eclipse NNode while Sergey receives the light from the eclipse SNode to his Venus. Since both Venus positions are at the second degree, there is going to be a lot of value put into manifestation with all its potential for accumulation and material wealth. They would drop out of their PhD programs to work exclusively on their partnership that reflected the nodal axis on the third degree of communication, and everything connected to it.

LS117 Summary

Searching for solutions that celebrate diversity and iconoclastic thinking is the special gift bestowed by these Air Dragon wizards. One of the many functions of a South Node lunar eclipse is to be a force of exhalation that encourages release, enjoyment, and relaxation. This South Node eclipse personifies these qualities and with a lifespan of 1,262 years giving it seventy-one opportunities, these aerial artists eagerly await every return. To share their space either by birthright or rite of passage is to be a part of something bigger and greater than oneself.

1995 marked their fifty-first return, making them well into middle age and masters of the high art of negotiation. LS117 is currently unfolding through its last Full Moon phase that will be in effect until the eclipses of 2067 and 2085. Within a span of thirty-six years, it will reach its peak of productivity and will be at its greatest level of co-operation, hopefully for global peace initiatives. Meanwhile, we all have a greater chance at actually knowing what we're doing when we are either members of this illustrious clan or get to ride on their coattails for the duration of their cosmic returns. If you haven't been making out as well as you had hoped to, the trick is to realize that—disappointing or not— give yourself credit for the distance you've come. Remember, this is an eclipse that loves to/needs to work collaboratively so factor that into your plan of action. A little cross-pollination is exactly what Dr. Cosmos is ordering for your general well-being.

This Lunar Saros Series is strong enough to make it on their own but wise and well-informed enough to know that we're all in this together. A noticeable esprit de corps and touch of elegance combine to help put you center stage in the spotlight of your life while igniting a longing for meaningful companionship and association. This is not a time for modesty but a time to raise awareness and give voice to whatever it is within that is seeking outlets for expression.

LS117 Luminaries

Alfred Nobel	October 21, 1833
Melvil Dewey	December 10, 1851
Erwin Schrödinger	August 12, 1887
Greta Garbo	September 18, 1905
Howard Hughes	September 24, 1905
Tommy Dorsey	November 19, 1905
Otto Preminger	December 5, 1905
Richard Attenborough[E3]	August 29, 1923
Maria Callas	December 2, 1923
Gordon Jackson	December 19, 1923
Benny Hill	January 21, 1924
Bernie Sanders[E3]	September 8, 1941
Art Garfunkel	November 5, 1941
Stephen Hawking	January 8, 1942
Muhammad Ali	January 17, 1942
Simon Cowell	October 7, 1959
Bryan Adams	November 5, 1959
Allison Janney	November 19, 1959
Tony Robbins	February 29, 1960
Maggie Gyllenhaal	November 16, 1977
PSY	December 31, 1977
Volodymyr Zelenskyy	January 25, 1978
Ashton Kutcher	February 7, 1978

PREBLE 112
Richard Attenborough
Bernie Sanders

1. Reinhold Ebertin, *The Combination of Stellar Influences*, p. 211.
2. https://en.wikipedia.org/wiki/Tony_Robbins. Retrieved May 3, 2022.
3. Sarah Ellison, *Diana's Impossible Dream.* http://www.vanityfair.com/society/2013/09/princess-diana-love-hasnat-khan. Retrieved May 3, 2022.
4. https://www.tatler.com/article/prince-charles-and-princess-diana-relationship. Retrieved May 3, 2022.
5. Richard L. Brandt, *Inside Larry & Sergey's Brain.* (New York: Portfolio, 2009), p. 8.
6. Brandt, *Inside Larry & Sergey's Brain*, p. 23.

LUNAR SAROS 122

"I don't try to describe the future. I try to prevent it."

-Ray Bradbury

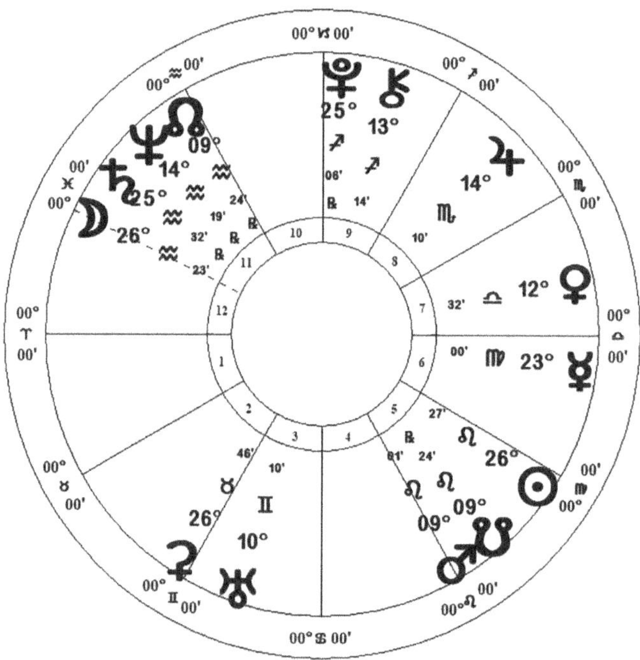

Lunar Saros 122

August 20, 1022 • 2:34:58 PM • North Pole

Titans of Talent

Everybody wants to be a star when this Aquarian North Node lunar eclipse is the main event. By proximity as well as tradition, Saturn is the undisputed Lord of the eclipse, but modern ruler Uranus steals the show as it is the handle on a Bucket overflowing with talent. It's part of a Grand Air Trine to Venus and Neptune as well as two high-flying Kites. Uranus has leverage—its extraordinary set of midpoint structures are eager to collaborate to enrich the lives of others.

The scope of possibility is sky high as these dragons are no strangers to risk-taking. However, even titans can fall, and Kingmakers can fail in their quest to test the boundaries of convention. Saturn's dominating presence defines both possibilities having equal regard for the value of both success and failure. Its function works to help mine the proverbial gold within its family's Grand Trine and to provide the focus and dedication necessary to keep its star grazing Kites flying high. This lunar eclipse is only one of two lunar eclipses out of the entire 47 Lunar Saros Series to have a Moon/Saturn conjunction, the other being LS146—Walk the Walk, found in The Earth Dragons of Part Two. The responsibilities encountered and carried as well as the self-control potential contained within both of these eclipses are extraordinary and freely offered at every return to those able to tune in to their frequency.

Many born under this lunar family experience profound psychological shifts throughout their lives as the pursuit of pleasure is an instinctive response and often in conflict with an equally insistent drive to embrace larger ideals. The waning Neptune/Jupiter square can be a safeguard against inflationary and self-indulgent pursuits if one can be more concerned with humanitarian concepts. Some will even attain spiritual awakening thanks to the NNode/Neptune in Aquarius evolutionary drive. K. Sutton's *The Lunar Nodes: Crisis & Redemption* offers the opinion that the lesson of the Aquarius/Leo nodal axis "is all about using your power to make the world a better place to live."[1] While the NNode/Neptune drive for liberation is definitely on the road to Shangri-La, the SNode/Mars instinct has an equal if not better claim to maintain one's status and fortune at all costs. It's a nodal axis evolving on a continuum of time not in years but in lifetimes.

LS122 offers many ongoing challenges as they are continually arising out of the fertile soil of the Ceres in Taurus square to the eclipse axis and its steady supply of both pleasure and pain. A love of excess might just be the ticket to personal salvation considering the key position that the Mars/SNode conjunction holds in relation to the Grand Air Trine. Since the SNode shows us where we get caught up in our own misguided broodings and even delusions, and the self-sufficiency factor of the Grand Air Trine can keep us forever "tilting at windmills," it's great to have Mars in the cosmic mix, instilling courage.

Thank goodness a powerful work ethic is born within the ferociously ambitious perseverance of a Mars/Pluto and Saturn/Uranus isotrap that is a constant source of disruption, seeking freedom of expression regardless of personal cost and all backed up by the cool-headed and rational Moon/Saturn conjunction in Aquarius. What's so great about this lunar family is that its celestial quartet of Sun, Mercury, Venus, and Saturn are all rulers in their own right and more than capable of serving the greater good.

Closest Midpoints: Mars/Mercury-Pluto, Venus/Uranus-Neptune
Isotraps: Mars/Pluto opposition Saturn/Uranus
Moon/Uranus opposition Mercury/Jupiter

1900—2100 Eclipses: Lunar Saros—122

1906, 1924, 1942, 1960, 1978, 1996, 2014, 2032, 2050, 2068, 2086
Length of cycle —1,316 years
Series ends—October 29, 2338

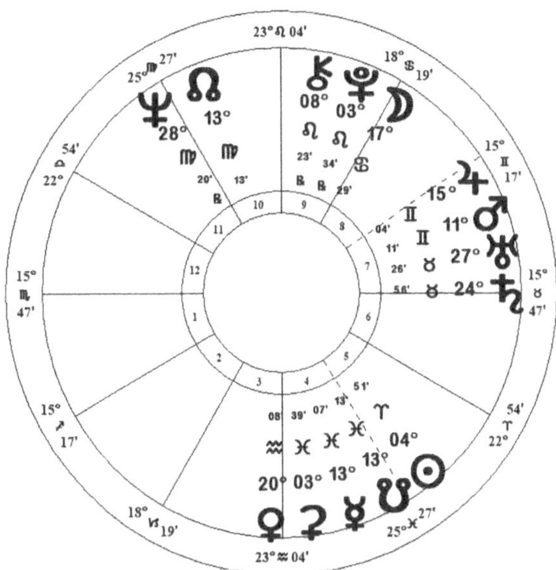

Aretha Franklin
PREBLE—LS122

March 25, 1942 • 10:30 PM • Memphis, TN, USA

"She set the bar upon which every female singer has and will be measured."

-QUINCY JONES[2]

The Queen of Soul

"Be your own artist, and always be confident in what you are doing. If you're not going to be confident, you might as well not be doing it."

-ARETHA

Aretha Franklin is possibly the greatest musical talent to have ever emerged in the 20th century. At age eighteen she signed with Columbia Records under LS122's first returning wave, activating her Neptune/NNode midpoint, not the best midpoint for a young singer starting out but it did get her a recording contract and into the big city lights of New York. Aretha's talent had never been in doubt; from the age of twelve she was an acknowledged prodigy, growing up in a famous musical family with a minster father who skillfully encouraged and managed her appearances.[3] Jack Hamilton's tribute to Aretha after her death on August 16, 2018 sums it all up:

> Franklin's most famous recordings—"Respect," "Chain of Fools," "Baby I Love You," "(You Make Me Feel Like) A Natural Woman," and so many others are so fundamental to American popular music that they're basically the air we breathe. I don't remember the first time I heard Aretha Franklin, much in the way I don't remember the first time I saw a sunset or ate a bowl of ice-cream. Living in a world with Aretha Franklin's music is one of the great privileges of being a human being.[4]

Aretha was a titan in the truest sense of mythological metaphor as her presence not only commanded respect but inspired generations of women to be part of a cultural shift that recognized the universality of human rights for all. No one will know the extent to which her unwavering faith and light of human dignity has changed the world but here are some of the dragon markers that testify to her amazing talent.

Aretha Franklin's Connections to the Dragons of LS122
Space Lanes via IC/MC

1st Harmonics: Moon/Saturn – IV, Sun – MC,
Jupiter – ASC, SNode – Chiron, Ceres – Saturn/Uranus, Uranus – Mars
2nd Harmonic: Chiron – Mars/Jupiter

The first thing to notice are Aretha's Space Lanes running through her IC/MC, a gift from the eclipse axis. Luckily for her, and unlike Roman Polanski who also has Space Lanes on his IC/MC, Aretha's experience was not so much volatility as it was a highly scheduled and work-oriented environment, as one would expect with a Venus square Saturn dominating the Fourth House cusp.

If, like Aretha, you have a Dragon Jupiter vector operating through your Ascendant, keep your passport and journals up to date as great ideas and plans can now get air-born. LS122's eclipse axis on Aretha's Leo Tenth House opened up a Space Lane that would lionize her professional image and another that would give expression to her deeply rooted Aquarian Fourth House libertarian needs. Remember in the introduction how Uranus, as the handle on the lunar eclipse Bucket steals the show? In Aretha's chart, that show-stealing Uranus lands directly on her success driven Mars/Jupiter "at the bends" gracing her life with sudden and fortunate changes in destiny, what Reinhold Ebertin calls the "Thank the Lord" configuration.[5] How appropriate for a gospel singing gal from Memphis, Tennessee who rose to stardom to become the Queen of Soul.

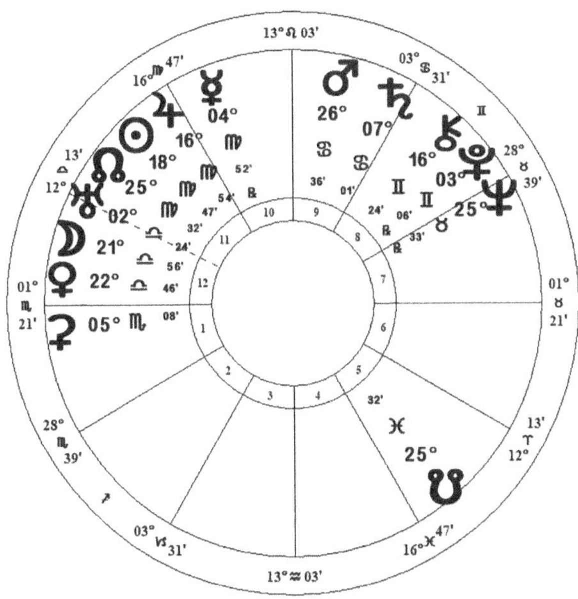

D. H. Lawrence
PREBLE—LS130

September 11, 1885 • 9:45 AM • Eastwood, Nottingham, UK

"If Lawrence hadn't written those novels he would have been far more readily acclaimed as one of the greatest poets in the language."

-Joyce Carol Oates

Novelist/Poet/Playwright

"It's the one insane taboo left: sex as a natural and vital thing."

-D. H. Lawrence

The full and uncensored edition of *Lady Chatterley's Lover* was published by Penguin Books in the UK in 1960 in honor of the thirtieth anniversary of the death of D. H. Lawrence. Their announcement in May to publish 200,000 paper-back copies of the long banned and sexually graphic book was made even more scandalous by its proposed selling price: at £3 it would be accessible to anyone who could afford a pack of cigarettes. Penguin's decision to publish followed on a ruling by the US Supreme Court that enabled the full text of *Lady Chatterley's Lover* to be published in New York in 1959. Penguin Books would go on to win a landmark obscenity case in the UK. On November 2, 1960, a jury acquitted Penguin of all charges of violating Britain's Obscene Publications Act.[6]

Penguin's decision to go ahead with the uncensored UK paperback edition of *Lady Chatterley's Lover* fell within the time frame of LS122's arrival on March 13, 1960, at 23 Virgo. The activation degree would literally resurrect the life and work of D. H. Lawrence by its links to both his Sun at 19 Virgo and his North Node at 25 Virgo. The activation of his Sun degree immediately brought back on line the immense empire-building capacity of his Sun/Jupiter conjunction in Virgo. As well, his exact NNode trine to Neptune in Taurus would finally receive a wave of wealth and tribute that had eluded him during his often vulnerable and highly criticized lifetime. Of interest here is the LS122 Neptune right on his Fourth House IC reinforcing all the creative potential within his NNode trine to Neptune.

D. H. Lawrence's Connections to the Dragons of LS122
Space Lanes via IC/MC
Venus with Venus

1st Harmonics: Mercury – Sun/NNode,
NNode/Neptune – IC, Ceres – Neptune
2nd Harmonics: Chiron – Chiron

LS122's nodal axis opened a temporary Space Lane portal through his Fourth House cusp, connecting D. H. Lawrence's Tenth House that simultaneously created a new base of operations that allowed his work to once again be known to the world. This nodal activation is sublime yet powerful: Take a look at what it was able to do for Susan Boyle later on in this section in the Air Dragons of LS143—Dream a Dream.

The eclipse Mercury's 1st Harmonic to his Sun and Mercury are perfect name recognition boosters that reinforce the strength and viability of a CB. His NNode/Sun-Uranus and Sun/Mercury-Uranus midpoints are his strongest and reflect a need to inject a spirit of progressive, literary reform into the zeitgeist. Lawrence himself considered his writings an attempt to challenge and expose what he saw as the constrictive and oppressive cultural norms of modern Western culture. He once said, "If there weren't so many lies in the world . . . I wouldn't write at all."[7]

As we will see in the lives of so many of the people in these case studies, our charts, vis à vis their unique spheres of consciousness, do indeed outlive our earthly presence as do the fields of energy contained within these majestic lunar eclipses. Our corporal forms vanish, and we thank the Lord for recycling, but something of us continues to exist. However, whenever, wherever, our energetic resonance carries on.

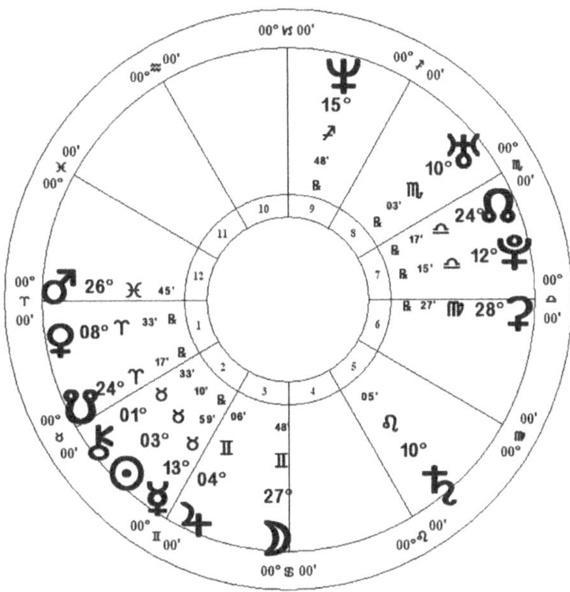

John Oliver
PREBLE—LS112

April 23, 1977 • TOB Unknown • Erdington, UK

Oliver's Twists on Titillating Times

"I think the best analogy for where we are right now is that America is Elvis Presley–the most beautiful, talented, rebellious nation in the history of Earth. And now, you're in your Vegas years. You've squeezed yourself into a white jumpsuit, you're wheezing your way through 'Love Me Tender' and you might be about to pass away bloated on the toilet. But you're still the King."

-John Oliver

John Oliver's late-night talk show on HBO, *Last Week Tonight with John Oliver,* debuted on April 27, 2014, within twelve days of LS122 arriving on April 15. Its activation degree was 25 Libra, right up and close on his NNode at 24 Libra.

Oliver's influence is not only delightful and entertaining but life changing. His take-no-prisoners satirical look at politics and current events has made a significant impression on the US culture to the extent that its legislators and policymakers are paying attention to the issues he presents. The difference he has made has been dubbed the "John Oliver effect." *Last Week Tonight* has won Oliver thirteen Emmy Awards and two Peabody Awards and was included in the 2015 *Time 100* edition, being described as a "comedic agent of change . . . powerful because he isn't afraid to tackle important issues thoughtfully, without fear or apology". His initial two-year contract has been continuously extended and as of 2020, HBO renewed *Last Week Tonight* for three years, through 2023.[8]

John Oliver's Connections to the Dragons of LS122

1st Harmonics: Mars/SNode – Saturn, Venus – Pluto,
Jupiter – Uranus, Chiron – Neptune
2nd Harmonics: Mercury – Mars, Venus – Venus,
Jupiter – Mercury, Neptune – Saturn

Both his natal and progressed chart answered the call; his progressed Venus at 24 Aries conjuncts both his progressed Mars and natal SNode and that's a happy trio. The SNode here is a well-tooled talent bank full of self-confidence that, by the eclipse activation enthusiastically entertains and energizes an appreciative global audience. No need for an ascendant or exact Moon degree as the planetary links from the LS122 foundation chart are deeply embedded into Oliver's progressed energetic field linking him to multiple vectors of support and resonance. Again, we have a SNode theme but now it is due to the eclipse field's potent Cosmic Bridge SNode/Mars conjunction. This power combo increases Mars' assertion of self, drive, and aspirational nature and here we find it making a CB to both natal and progressed Saturn in flamboyant Leo. Now that's one way to land a multi-million dollar entertainment contract.

There are nine vectors that play across their fields, but the last one worth applauding is the eclipse field's Uranus conjunction to Oliver's progressed Sun/Jupiter midpoint. Remember, the mighty meaning of Uranus in terms of this lunar eclipse is its participation in a Grand Air Trine with Venus and Neptune and their high-flying Kites. Uranus is truly a star maker and eager to collaborate to enrich the lives of all.

LS122 Summary

Captivating and contrarian by nature and feisty and frankly fabulous for sure, these indefatigable Air Dragons know how to bring out humanity's best and worst traits. This Lunar Saros Series will strengthen your resolve to pitch in and do whatever it takes to help serve humanity. And yes, grandiosity is a part of their platform, but it pales in comparison to the gifts they bestow on all who are touched by their generosity, kindness, and dedication to an ideal. Under their protection, an aura of certainty envelopes you no matter how strong the opposition. Fearlessness is a strength you can call upon when times get tough; however, be mindful of a tendency to act first and repent at leisure. Stirred but not shaken, there is plenty of room under this canopy for all manner of discourse. Activism runs high. This is a lunar family designed for social engagement and networking: Concerned citizens, motivated to resolve confrontation simply by being better informed and educated on any subject, can now rally their forces.

Whether by birthright or by transiting return, be mindful of your innate drive to self-inflate, for much can be accomplished under their divine dominion. In the long run, self-discipline is your savior. Make a concerted effort to project an attitude of gratitude as you welcome innovation and feedback on any project. There is a mystical Midas Touch that plays through the melody of this high-flying eclipse if your senses are attuned to the needs of others less fortunate that yourself. To that end, be ready to share your good fortune. The cosmic laws are very clear on this account: Rewards are abundantly offered for those who give with an open and generous heart.

Phase	Return	Year
Full Moon	50th	1906
Disseminating	54th	1978
Last Quarter	59th	2068
Balsamic	63rd	2140

LS122 Luminaries

Charlotte Brontë	April 21, 1816
Robert Assagioli	February 27, 1888
Buddhadāsa	May 27, 1906
Josephine Baker	June 3, 1906
Lee Marvin	February 19, 1924
Marlon Brando	April 3, 1924
Henry Mancini	April 16, 1924
Charles Aznavour	May 22, 1924
Aretha Franklin	March 25, 1942
Barbra Streisand	April 24, 1942
Roger Ebert	June 18, 1942
Paul McCartney	June 18, 1942
Bono	May 10, 1960
Erin Brockovich	June 22, 1960
Sarah Brightman	August 14, 1960
Sean Penn	August 17, 1960
Malalai Joya	April 25, 1978
Zoe Saldana	June 19, 1978
James Corden	August 22, 1978
Kobe Bryant	August 23, 1978
Anya Taylor-Joy	April 26, 1996
Lele Pons	June 24, 1996

1. Komilla Sutton, *The Lunar Nodes—Crisis & Redemption*, p. 46.
2. https://www.rollingstone.com/music/music-news/quincy-jones-on-aretha-franklin-you-will-reign-as-the-queen-forever-711687/ Retrieved Feb. 5, 2022.
3. https://slate.com/culture/2018/08/aretha-franklin-dead-the-singer-was-the-defining-voice-of-the-20th-century.html. Retrieved Feb. 5, 2022.
4. Ibid.
5. Reinhold Ebertin, *The Combination of Stellar Influences*, p. 228.
6. http://www.theguardian.com/books/2010/oct/22/dh-lawrence-lady-chatterley-trial. Retrieved Feb. 6, 2022.
7. http://www.biography.com/people/dh-lawrence-17175776#death-and-legacy. Retrieved Feb. 6, 2022.
8. https://en.wikipedia.org/wiki/John_Oliver. Retrieved March 14, 2022.

LUNAR SAROS 123

"The penetration of society by the Internet and the penetration of the Internet by society is the best thing that has ever happened to global human civilization."

-Julian Assange

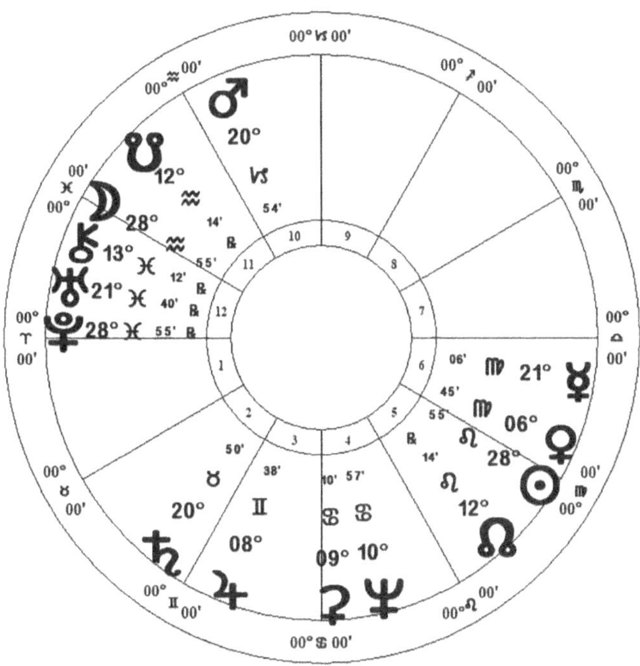

Lunar Saros 123

August 22, 1087 • 9:23:26 PM • South Pole

Attitudes of Magnitude

This is a South Node Aquarius eclipse with Saturn and Uranus members of an independent Kite formation. In this eclipse two sextiles, one from an OOB Mars (27S38) and the other from Saturn link to Uranus at the "notch" of power, releasing into the blade of Mercury's arrow a groundswell of focused determination. The isotraps, particularly the Moon/Pluto opposition Mercury/Venus, have their hands full managing feed-back loops that prefer perfection over praise. Venus and her involvement in this pattern make her energy subordinate to that of Mercury.

LS123 contains a magnificent Grand Earth Trine ready to triumph in any field of endeavor that speaks to innovation and individual achievement. Being a part of this lunar eclipse family means you'll always have the wind at your back in terms of insight and help when it is most needed. In turn, their gifts of inspiration mean that you become a locus of excitement and encouragement for others. Mars' pragmatic exaltation in Capricorn drives the Grand Earth Trine forward, as well as driving its dynamic Locomotive pattern able to overcome enormous challenges. Uranus at the notch of power strikes sparks of heterodox thinking into the zeitgeist where they have a good chance to come to life as creative ideas and scientific breakthroughs.

I do not want to end this introduction on a falsely optimistic note. I know from the research and life stories of those with Grand Trines—particularly those that extend their reach via a Kite formation—that too much of a good thing is often more detrimental in the long run than an experience or two stuck on a side road of self-pity. Over-reaching often brings in more collateral damage than the occasional bout of depression. Rebellious behavior, as well, may become a source of impediment as one learns or fails to learn how to control an appetite for novelty and originality.

Be on the lookout for extended periods of isolation as Uranus in Pisces at the pivotal release point can place excessive strain on one's subtle energy bodies and they will need to be frequently replenished. Although you wouldn't think of Venus bringing confrontation, her waxing square from Jupiter is more than happy to provide all the U-turns, reboots, and even drastic changes to your environment and psyche that you'll need to clear the road ahead of rubble. And remember: Venus sits within an isotrap, waiting for the right time to make her move, empowered by its deeper psychological grounds and rational of reason.

Thank goodness for midpoints since those of LS123's are more than qualified to reinvigorate and even rescue any and all who need help re-establishing new norms. Because this is a South Node "releasing" Air eclipse, dustups are normal as one learns the value of discipline versus hot air. Everything works beautifully in this eclipse field to provide enough resistance to put the brakes on what could be frequent flyer miles of self-indulgence, which is why discipline and the importance of establishing priorities is the correct antidote.

In the dance of life unfolding through LS123's dragon DNA, it is important to note that its offspring carry forward all of its potential, while also noting that many of its feature characteristics may remain dormant until destiny and time choose otherwise. LS123 is a bastion of idiosyncratic attitudes.

Closest Midpoints: Mars/Mercury-Saturn, Eclipse/Jupiter-Saturn
Isotraps: Mercury/Pluto conjunct Jupiter/Neptune
Moon/Pluto opposition Mercury/Venus

1900—2100 Eclipses: Lunar Saros—123

1917, 1935, 1953, 1971, 1989, 2007, 2025, 2043, 2061, 2077, 2097
Length of cycle —1,280 years Series ends—October 8, 2367

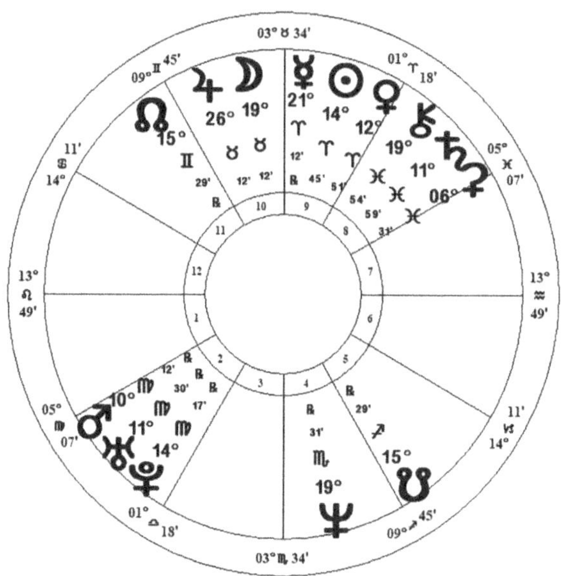

Robert Downey, Jr.
PREBLE—LS134

April 4, 1965 • 1:10 PM • New York, NY, USA

Iron Man

"Sometimes you gotta run before you can walk."

-IRON MAN 1—2008

LS123 descended to Earth at 13 Virgo on March 3, 2007, in a tornado torrent, sweeping into motion Robert Downey Jr. and his triple-headed demon Mars/Uranus/Pluto conjunction. Filming on the set of *Iron Man* began on March 12 and would wrap on June 25, 2007.[1]

The backstory on how Downey got the lead is quite the read but suffice to say he was not the director's first choice. But how could he *not* have gotten the starring role? When you put the real life story of Robert Downey Jr. up against the fictitious world of the Marvel Superhero it was a match literally made in heaven.

Robert Downey Jr.'s Connections to the Dragons of LS123
Space Lanes via ASC/DSC

Chiron with Chiron
1st Harmonics: Saturn – Moon, Venus – Mars, Chiron – Saturn, Uranus – Chiron
2nd Harmonics: Mercury – Chiron, Venus – Ceres

First, this is not his PREBLE. Downey's dragon family is LS134—The Attractor Factor—found further along in this section. What's exciting here are the Space Lanes created by the temporary activation of the eclipse nodes across his ASC/DSC axis, giving him a royal road welcome into the energetic sphere of LS123. Downey shares this exciting connection with fellow Space Laners Clint Eastwood from the Fire Dragons of LS150—Be Brave in Part One—along with Lenny Bruce from the Water Dragons of LS137—Ripples and Rip Tides in Part Four. Space Lanes created from the nodal ties seem to be in a league of their own, with an extraordinary capacity to boost the lunar eclipse resonance.

There is an almost identical phase angle symmetry between the Uranus/Pluto conjunctions in both charts along with the Mars/Uranus and Uranus/Saturn aspects that play well together. Considering that LS123 has a Grand Earth Trine with an OOB Mars and Downey is—well—Iron Man, the fit really fits. LS123's descent to Earth at 13 Virgo on March 3, 2007, not only swept up his monster Mars/Uranus/Pluto conjunction but its opposition to Saturn in fantasy-land Pisces making Robert Downey Jr. the man for that movie. Nine days later, on March 12, filming began on the set of *Iron Man*.

We'll have to wait and see what happens on LS123's next return in 2025 at 23 Virgo and again in 2043 at 4 Libra. Without the benefit of activating any natal planets or midpoints, Downey appears to hold a most-favored status with these idiosyncratic Air Dragons who will undoubtedly keep him in mind for another date with destiny.

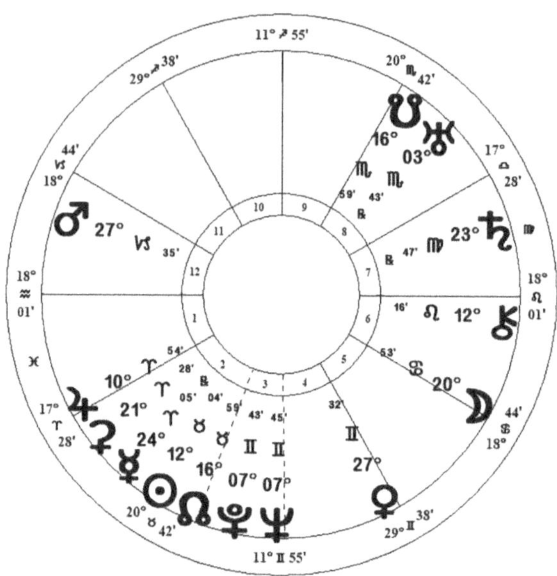

The Red Baron
PREBLE—LS124

May 2, 1892 • 2:00 AM • Breslau, Germany

Deadliest Flying Ace of World War I

"Fight on and fly on to the last drop of blood and the last drop of fuel, to the last beat of the heart."

-MANFRED VON RICHTHOFEN

Manfred von Richthofen, dubbed "The Red Baron," was World War One's greatest combat pilot, downing eighty enemy aircraft before his death on April 21, 1918. He was known internationally as the ace-of-aces and his appointment as a Commanding Officer of a German unit named Jasta 11 on January 16 would turn a futile German squadron into the deadliest and most feared fighter pilots of the war.[2] All of this began within a week of LS123's touchdown on January 8, 1917, activating at 17 Cancer on his Moon. Jasta 11 became the "highest scoring German Jasta of World War 1, with 350 claims."[3] Richthofen was buried by the Allies in France, with full military honors.[4] Devotees of World War I aviation history would turn the combat record of the Red Baron into a knight and folk hero of the skies.

The Red Baron's Connections to the Dragons of LS123
Space Lanes via ASC/DSC
Mars with Mars

1st Harmonics: NNode - Chiron,
Saturn - NNode, Mercury - Saturn, Jupiter - Pluto/Neptune
2nd Harmonics: Mars - Moon, Uranus - Saturn

The Baron's ties to the eclipse field of LS123 are absolutely stunning. Imagine this: He's a freshly minted pilot and as luck would have it, gets put in charge of a squadron just as the lunar eclipse field, in resonance to his own sphere of influence, is laying down a pair of Space Lanes for the lad. These lanes stretch across the horizon, following the path of the nodal axis at 12 degrees Leo/Aquarius and seemingly made to handle the aerial and technological wizardry of a fighter pilot with panache. The Red Baron joins a rarefied group of fellow Space Laners that include Clint Eastwood, Robert Downey Jr., and Lenny Bruce, proving once again that the Space Lanes that are created from the nodal ties falling on the ASC/DSC axis are truly in a league of their own, as they impart an extraordinary range and scope of capability.

In total, the Baron benefited from three Cosmic Bridges. The first was created from the eclipse field's 1st Harmonic Saturn to his nodes, which literally seeded the ground of his being with the full potential of LS123's spectacular Kite formation. It isn't every day, or for that matter, any year that you get to immerse yourself in the energy of a magnificent Grand Earth Trine that is ready to take on the world.

The second Cosmic Bridge comes courtesy of the eclipse field's NNode to his Chiron, which is just two minutes of arc off from being a perfect conjunction. At the euphoric twelfth degree of Leo, the Red Baron's Chiron and its partile square to his equally determined twelfth degree Sun in Taurus is a heroic, action-oriented, and willing to sacrifice for glory energetic patterning.

The third Cosmic Bridge is the best; it brings the lunar eclipse Mars and its powerful exaltation position within the Grand Earth Trine into a 2nd Harmonic to the Baron's Moon. This is an extraordinary tie considering that the returning eclipse activation degree fell on his Moon. Whenever you see this, it is a 100 percent guarantee that someone's life circumstances are about to radically change. This activation of LS123 proved to be unequivocally the

Baron's date with destiny as his military career was literally launched into the stratosphere with help from the powers-that-be placements of Mars in Capricorn along with some very rare and potent Space Lane connectors.

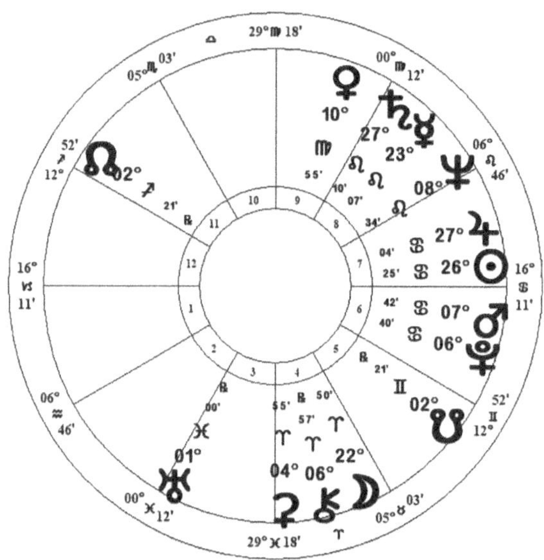

Sir Edmund Hillary
PREBLE–LS110

July 20, 1919 • 4:00 PM • Papakura, New Zealand

News Flash!

Mountaineering Magnificence: May 29, 1953

"Because it's there!"

-George Mallory

At 11:30 am on May 29, 1953, Edmund Hillary and his Sherpa guide Tenzing Norgay successfully reached the summit of Mt. Everest, the highest peak in the world.[5] The expedition would begin within days of Lunar Saros 123's return on January 29, 1953, at the ambitious tenth degree of Leo, activating Hillary's "date with destiny" Neptune/Pluto-Venus. Sir Hillary's ties to the energetic field of this lunar eclipse are remarkable with the eclipse Pluto anchoring his

Fourth House IC, which would have further reinforced the activation potential of his natal Neptune. The eclipse axis lit up his thrill-seeking need for space and adventure Uranus/Moon-Mars midpoint, which would have made him the man of the moment to lead the expedition. Notice the MR between the Moon and Mars. The lovely Venus conjunct Venus vectors in harmony across their fields gave the expedition a story book ending.

LS123 Summary

These Air Dragons are truly "out there" riding the currents of exploration; their sails are filled with the winds of change. Their presence is a reminder that nothing in creation is permanent. Charismatic characters with drive, determination, and highly charged energy fields appear to delight and exacerbate. Throughout either your lifetime or the sparkling months that arrive with their return, take a plunge into the deep end of the psychological pool. A greater understanding of self is sure to refresh as these dragons invite the twin forces of discord and dissent to shake things up. Along the way, experience the pleasure that comes from great art and literature as they open your imagination and bring a vision of what your life could become. This dragon family loves to soar, so let your soul be drawn to the mystical, let your spirit be inspired by the inspirational, and let your heart be open to experience a world without borders or boundaries. As contrary as they come, members of this family are suspended in a gimbal unaffected by time and space yet challenged to be a part of *this* time and space. The dragons of LS123 bring a breath of fresh air as they remind us to keep our spirits strong and our minds engaged in pursuits that bring out the best in all of us.

Phase	Return	Year
Gibbous	47th	1917
Full Moon	51st	1989
Disseminating	55th	2061
Last Quarter	59th	2133

LS123 Luminaries

Samuel Taylor Coleridge	October 21, 1772
Louis Braille	January 4, 1809
Charles Darwin	February 12, 1809
William Randolph Hearst	April 29, 1863
Fred Astaire	May 10, 1899
Zsa Zsa Gabor	February 6, 1917
Ella Fitzgerald	April 25, 1917
John F. Kennedy	May 29, 1917
Lena Horne	June 30, 1917
A. J. Foyt [E3]	January 16, 1935
Dudley Moore	April 19, 1935
Carol Shields	June 2, 1935
Dalai Lama	July 6, 1935
Paul Krugman	February 28, 1953
George Knapp	April 18, 1953
V, aka Eve Ensler	May 25, 1953
Cyndi Lauper	June 22, 1953
Selena	April 16, 1971
Elon Musk	June 28, 1971
Julian Assange	July 3, 1971
Sandra Oh	July 20, 1971
J. J. Watt	March 22, 1989
Lily James	April 5, 1989
Alex Morgan	July 2, 1989
Daniel Radcliffe	July 23, 1989

PREBLE—LS118

A J Foyt

1. https://en.wikipedia.org/wiki/Iron_Man_(2008_film)#cite_note-FilmingBegins-74. Retrieved: Jan. 14, 2022.
2. https://en.wikipedia.org/wiki/Jagdstaffel_11. Retrieved Feb. 6, 2022.
3. https://www.history.com/this-day-in-history/red-baron-killed-in-action-2. Retrieved Feb. 6, 2022.
4. https://en.wikipedia.org/wiki/1953_British_Mount_Everest_expedition. Retrieved Jan. 31,2022.
5. Ibid.

LUNAR SAROS 125

"I live in a landscape, which every single day of my life is enriching."

-Daniel Day-Lewis

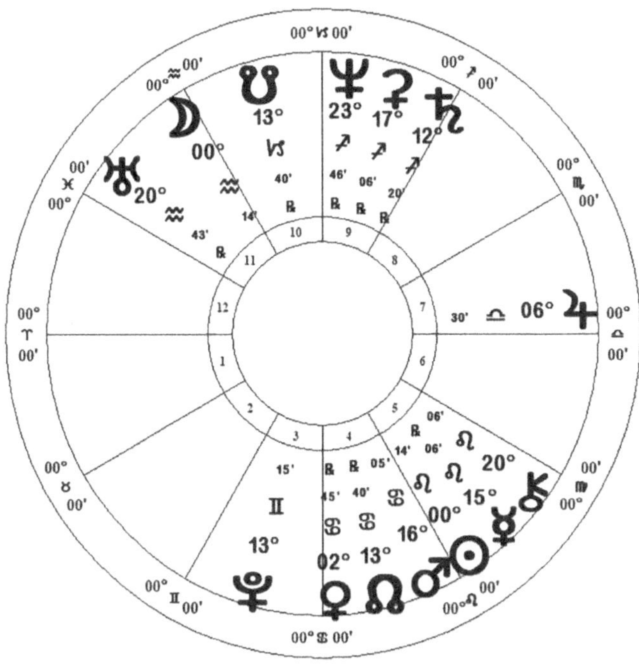

Lunar Saros 125

July 24, 1163 • 11:52:06 AM • South Pole

Hyper-Drive

Welcome to one of the most exciting lunar eclipses of the entire Saros Series. At zero Aquarius, and with both ruler Saturn in Sagittarius and Uranus in Aquarius retrograde, anything is possible. Three more planets—Mercury, Venus, and Neptune—are in retrograde, generating a heterodox field of enormous self-direction. Considering that this is an Air eclipse, be prepared to deal with an ocean of emotion. Long experience has given members of this eclipse family an astute if not magical touch in the pursuit of any chosen goal. Their zest for life is audacious as they fearlessly dive the depths of their passion. They live in the moment and hyper-drive is their de facto gear.

The tightest aspect always wields the biggest stick and here Saturn in opposition to Pluto in Gemini creates a communications powerhouse of mass appeal. Obstacles are basically annihilated or rendered neutral as the zealous force of LS125 doesn't *do* compromise. Take a look back at Lunar Saros 102, the first Fire eclipse in Part One and note how that same pattern permeated the harsh social conditions of its time with a heavy hand and fears that cut deep into the fabric of society. Robert Pelletier, in *Planets in Aspect: Understanding Your Inner Dynamics,* says of this aspect, "You must learn to either transform your environment or remove yourself from it and make a new start."[1] As with all oppositions, polarities dance to an either/or tune that can be highly controversial. The key to resolving conflict when faced with oppositions is to plan ahead, which is unfortunately a behavior of last resort for this "flying by the seat of your pants" lunar eclipse. The good news here is that the opposition occurs across the Gemini/Sagittarius modality, giving these mutable signs the ability to go with the flow while generating personalities with name brand global recognition who delight in pushing the boundaries of convention.

Apart from the South Node in Capricorn, Lunar Saros 125 is without Earth sign representation. In such cases, a vacuum is created that tends to attract a completely body-centric and physical response from the environment. All manner of practical, efficient, and highly motivated individuals with an enormous capacity for work emerge from this family and its cyclic returns.

LS125's Anchor with the NNode at the fulcrum between Pluto's sextile to Mercury and its SNode at the apex gives this lunar eclipse the ability to hold fast to innovation even when the price may be isolation, ridicule, and even denial at the hands of fellow colleagues. A Mars/NNode conjunction is a boat rocker for sure, but it eventually rewards truth tellers and those who are confident and secure enough to lead by example. Like LS144—Real Surreal—another Aquarian eclipse in this section, fifty percent of the planets in LS125 are retrograde, giving the underbelly of these Air eclipses a hidden side and a more instinctive way of living than would be expected from an Air eclipse family.

The eclipse Moon in quindecile (165 degree) aspect to both Mercury and Mars adds a disruptive and, at times, obsessive quality to the energetic field underscored by a Pluto/Chiron-Saturn midpoint adept at delivering the cathartic forces of healing that are an integral component of this Lunar Saros Series. It's a comforting thought to close this intro by way of acknowledging the sheer joy and all manner of goodwill that can be found within the energetic realms of this special 00 infinity degree lunar eclipse axis.

You've already met Lunar Saros 132 in the Fire Eclipses of Part One with its 00 Sagittarius infinity degree lunar eclipse axis. LS132 is aptly named Reach for the Stars—it invites all of us to escape the bonds of banality. So too will you find and hopefully experience the life-changing events that are part of Lunar Saros 124—Imagine—in the Water Eclipses of Part Four. Its 00 Pisces infinity degree lunar eclipse axis brings renewal with every return.

Closest Midpoints: Jupiter/Sun-Saturn, Mercury/Jupiter-Neptune
Isotraps: Sun/Venus opposition Saturn/Uranus,
Sun/Saturn opposition Moon/Pluto

1900—2100 Eclipses: Lunar Saros—125

1902, 1920, 1938, 1956, 1974, 1992, 2010, 2028, 2047, 2065, 2083
Length of cycle —1,280 years
Series ends—September 9, 2443

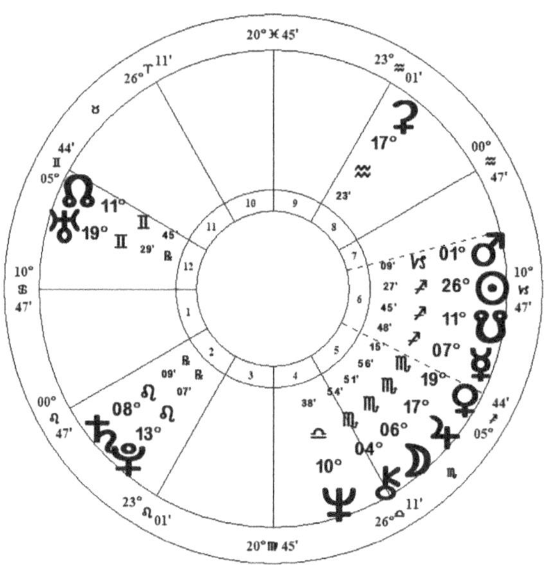

Steven Spielberg
PREBLE—LS134

December 18, 1946 • 6:16 PM • Cincinnati, OH, USA

"I dream for a living."

Film Director/Screenwriter/Producer

"This is the best drink of water after the longest drought in my life."

-Steven Spielberg

Spielberg began casting *Schindler's List* in December 1992.[2] At the moment LS125 touched down on December 9, 1992, at 18 Gemini, Spielberg's Uranus was already in preproduction. His Uranus/Mercury-Mars midpoint (stories and action) was making rapid fire decisions as he quickly pulled the movie together. With time, Spielberg had matured and was ready to take on work of a serious nature, much to the joy and relief of his mother, Leah Adler. Reflecting on his childhood, Mrs. Adler told a journalist, "I didn't know he was a genius. Frankly, I didn't know what the hell he was."[3]

The darkness of the Holocaust would finally be exposed in the creative directorship of Spielberg; LS125's Sun/Venus opposition Saturn/Uranus isotrap would provide a pathway forward for future generations to feel and heal and be able to love one another again. The eclipse marked a turning point in his style of movie making and more importantly, in the nature of the seriousness of the subject matter. While still creating entertaining blockbusters with phenomenal mass appeal, *Schindler's List* was a conscious, deliberate, and unique act of love that resonated to the very depths of our shared humanity. At the 1993 Oscars, Spielberg took home two Academy Awards for *Schindler's List*, winning for Best Director and for Best Film of 1993.[4]

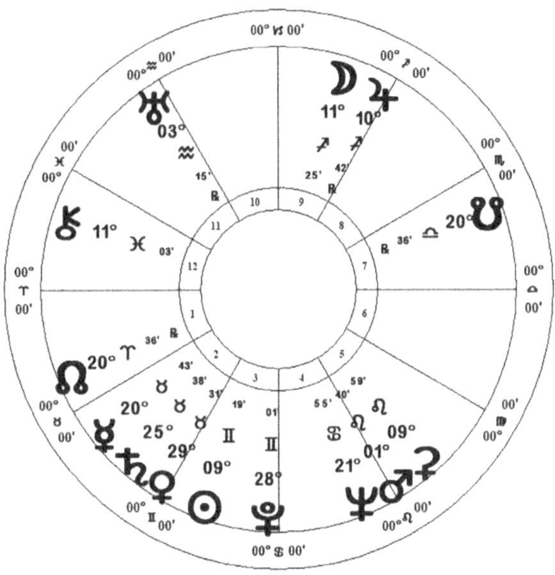

Chien-Shiung Wu
PREBLE—LS111

May 31, 1912 • TOB Unknown • Liuhe, Taicang, China

Dragon Lady—The Queen of Physics

"She was the world's distinguished woman physicist of her time."

-William Havens

"Dragon Lady" was the nickname affectionately given by Dr. Wu's students at Columbia's physics department in the early 1950s. As the Queen of Physics, and the most highly honored female physicist of the 20th century, Chien-Shiung Wu gives the metaphysical "wu"—the Chinese word for awareness and enlightenment—a physics makeover that is well worth pondering as the fields of high energy physics and metaphysics are beginning to merge. If the current "wu" craze seems out of this world, try getting your head around particle physics or, better yet, try explaining it. Richard Feynman could, and so could Dr. Wu, which is why she was dubbed the "First Lady of Physics."

At 2:00 a.m. on January 9, 1957, after months of preparation and four days and nights in the laboratory conducting her world-first parity conservation experiment, Dr. Wu, along with her colleagues, would announce that the principle of parity conservation had been overthrown. It was a world first in nuclear physics; her experimental design and flawless execution changed 20th century physics, laying down the groundwork for the creation of the Standard Model in Particle Physics.[5]

Chien-Shiung Wu's Connections to the Dragons of LS125

1st Harmonics: Moon – Uranus, Sun – Mars, Pluto – Sun, Saturn – Jupiter
2nd Harmonics: Saturn – Sun, Pluto – Jupiter

It was November 18, 1956, and Lunar Saros 125 had just touched down at the double-dipped twenty-sixth degree of Taurus scoring a direct hit to her Saturn, setting off its powerful conjunctions to Mercury and Venus. Wu's Mercury was directly aligned to the great Fixed Star Capulus, which brings excellence and confidence in any field. Her Venus as well channeled the mighty flow of energy from Alcyone, the brightest star of the Pleiades known from ancient times for its association with ambition, fame, and glory.

LS125's 1st Harmonic Moon to her Uranus allows all of its infinite potential to activate her similarly situated Uranus in Aquarius with its openness to new and revolutionary trends. From the time she was a child, Wu had the advantages of a father, a family, and a community that supported and encouraged her intellectual brilliance. The eclipse Sun on her first degree Mars in Leo was a celestial portent of the recognition that was about to come her way, while the eclipse Pluto on her Sun was the old-boy network working behind the scenes that was to deny her the honor and glory that was her due—her breakthrough work on particle physics was overlooked and ignored by the Nobel

Prize committee. Saturn's 1st Harmonic, linked up with Pluto on her Jupiter, would further deflate her achievement.

As I'm sure you can tell by now, the 2nd Harmonics really tell the story, and here we have the eclipse Saturn in its 2nd Harmonic iteration to Wu's Sun, which is never anything to take to the bank. Saturn's twelfth degree Piscean overtone and its opposition to Pluto's thirteenth degree Aries overtone is almost a guarantee that a personal sacrifice is going to be required to keep the machinery running. Even in Spielberg's chart, the effect of LS125's Saturn on his SNode would prove insightful as Spielberg had secured the rights to make *Schindler's List* in 1983, but he would wait almost ten years until he felt ready to take on the project.

Dr. Wu's final 2nd Harmonic is from the eclipse Pluto to her Jupiter. And since Wu's Jupiter holds an opposition to her Sun, it is strengthened and indemnified and thus made resistant to the debilitating if not destructive forces within the eclipse Pluto. Wu's tenth degree Jupiter has a corporate overtone that had to play ball with the academic and cultural elitism that came with her brilliant and distinguished ninth degree Sun in Gemini research in the field of nuclear fission—she was, "after all," part of the Manhattan Project. In 1990, the asteroid 2752 Wu Chien-Shiung was named after her.

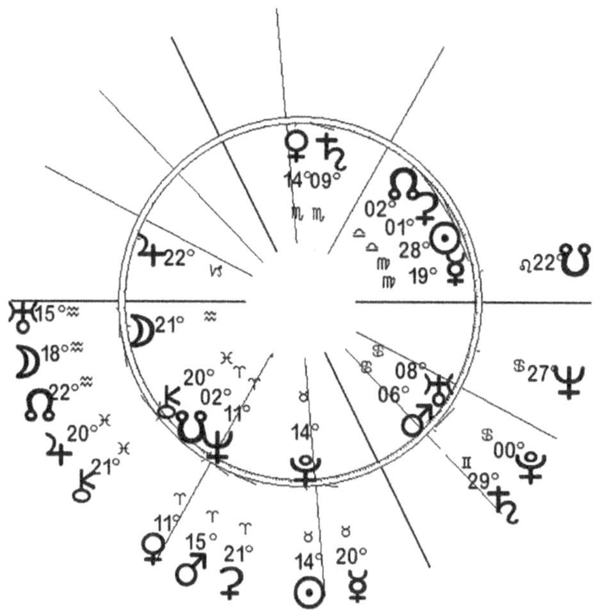

Inner Ring

H. G. Wells

PREBLE—LS120

September 21,1866 • 4:30 PM • Bromley, UK

Outer Ring

Orson Welles

PREBLE—LS141

May 6, 1915 • 7:00 AM • Kenosha, WI, USA

Science Fiction Masters

"If you want a happy ending,
that depends, of course, on where you stop your story."

-Orson Welles

There are moments in life that affect individuals and their societies so profoundly that their impact and legacy ripple across time, delivering to each and every new generation a taste of that initial blast of panic, paranoia, and even pleasure. Such heightened states of arousal can be extremely cathartic, taking individuals to new levels of appreciation and awareness of what it means to be a human being with feelings that can be so easily manipulated.

Such was the case with Orson Welles' original dramatization of H. G. Wells' 19th century science fiction novel *War of the Worlds*. The radio broadcast originally aired on October 30, 1938, depicting a Martian invasion of Earth. It proceeded to stun and frighten the public, striking national panic into the hearts of those who heard it.[6] LS125 arrived on November 7, 1938, at the communicative fifteenth degree of Taurus, activating not only H. G. Wells' Pluto at 15 Taurus but Orson Welles' Sun at 15 Taurus. For the brash and talented young Orson Welles, rather than ruining his career, the fallout from the publicity and outrage that followed the broadcast enabled him to make important contacts in Hollywood. In 1941, Orson Welles "directed, wrote, produced, and starred in *Citizen Kane*—a movie that many have called the greatest American film ever made."[7]

When a personal chart is tuned into the field of an eclipse, reception can be picked up anywhere within two and sometimes three weeks either side of its arrival, allowing LS125's invincible and powerhouse Pluto/Saturn a global stage on which to play.

Orson Welles' Connections to the Dragons of LS125
Uranus with Uranus

1st Harmonics: Uranus - Moon/NNode,
Sun - Neptune, Venus - Saturn/Pluto, Chiron - SNode, Neptune - DSC
2nd Harmonics: Mercury - Uranus/Moon, Chiron - Moon

H. G. Wells' Connections to the Dragons of LS125

1st Harmonics: Jupiter - NNode,
NNode - Uranus, Venus - Mars, Mercury - DSC, Uranus - Moon

The greatest impact fell to the energetic sphere of Orson Welles, which makes sense as he was the driving force behind the broadcast. In tribute, H. G. Wells received three waves of appreciation from the lunar eclipse with the best being a renewed interest in his novel *War of the Worlds*, which, by the late 1930's had fallen out of favor. The eclipse Jupiter, with its Cosmic Bridge to his NNode, would have increased interest from his publisher's side fueled by the eclipse Mercury to his DSC, which increased interest from an entire new generation of readers to his genre. During a radio interview on KTSA in San Antonio, Texas, on October 28, 1940, H. G. Wells acknowledged his debt to Orson Welles for "increasing sales of one of his more obscure titles."[8]

LS125 Summary

Feeling alive to the joy as well as the angst of life is what concerns these noble Air Dragons and the force field of their return. It's true they are rule breakers, rule benders, and non-conformists at heart, but know they bring us chances for healing at deeper and deeper levels of awareness. Their arrival is always a time to deal with taboo topics; they revel in a spirit of avant-garde fanfare. Let your inner crusader out and see where the battle lines need to be drawn. Allow your feelings open range and remember that it is our emotions that connect us to each other. There is much power and passion waiting within us to be discovered. This is a time to profess your love for who and what it is that brings hope and meaning into your life. Cherish your friends and family and let that spirit of goodwill ripple out across the planet in waves of unapologetic joy.

This family of lunar eclipses is concerned with and often brings in noticeable improvements to mental or physical well-being as seen through healthier habits or a reduction in neuroses. Often an increase in libido is experienced. The midpoint structures encourage self-disclosure as a tool to help bring forth creative energy previously blocked by an incessant need for control. Though relationships will feel the stress that change always produces, those struggles ultimately bring forth catharsis and healing. Engagements and weddings are associated with this lunar eclipse family along with opportunities to travel internationally

Since 1992, LS125 has been unfolding through a Gibbous phase noteworthy for its tendency to perfect and refine whatever comes its way. This is the "coming into bloom" phase of its evolutionary process where mastering a field of knowledge becomes a part of your life. It's a time to gain greater understanding and to put that knowledge to work.

LS125 Luminaries

Leonardo da Vinci	April 24, 1452
Maurice McDonald	November 26, 1902
Anaïs Nin	February 21, 1903
Malcolm Muggeridge	March 24, 1903
Gene Tierney	November 19, 1920
Betty Friedan	February 4, 1921
Lana Turner	February 8, 1921
Gordon Lightfoot	November 17, 1938
Ted Turner	November 19, 1938
Marvin Gaye	April 2, 1939
Seamus Heaney	April 13, 1939
Larry Bird	December 7, 1956
Stephen Fry	January 8, 1957
Spike Lee	March 20, 1957
Daniel Day-Lewis	April 29, 1957
Drew Barrymore	February 22, 1975
David Beckham	May 2, 1975
Bradley Cooper	June 5, 1975
Fred	March 5, 1993
Anthony Davis	March 11, 1993
Paul Pogba	March 15, 1993
Natalia Starr	March 22, 1993

PREBLE—LS120
Ted Turner

---

1. Robert Pelletier, *Planets in Aspect: Understanding Your Inner Dynamic*, p. 320.
2. Thomas Keneally, *Searching for Schindler* (New York: The Doubleday Publishing Group, 2007), p. 183.
3. *The World is Going to Hear of This Boy*. Interview by Leah Adler, Spielberg's mother. http://www.fredbernstein.com/articles/display.asp?id=45. Retrieved June 9, 2022
4. Awards for Steven Spielberg. http://www.imdb.com/name/nm0000229/awards. Retrieved June 9, 2022.
5. Chiang Tsai-Chien, *Madame Wu Chien-Shiung The First Lady of Physics Research* (Singapore: World Scientific Publishing Co. Pte. Ltd.), 2014, p. 119.
6. http://www.radionouspace.net/programs/mercurytheater/war-worlds.html. Retrieved June 9, 2022.
7. https://screenrant.com/citizen-kane-best-movie-all-time-why/ Retrieved June 9, 2022.
8. https://en.wikipedia.org/wiki/H._G._Wells. Retrieved June 9, 2022.

LUNAR SAROS 126

"One chance is all you need."

-Jesse Owens

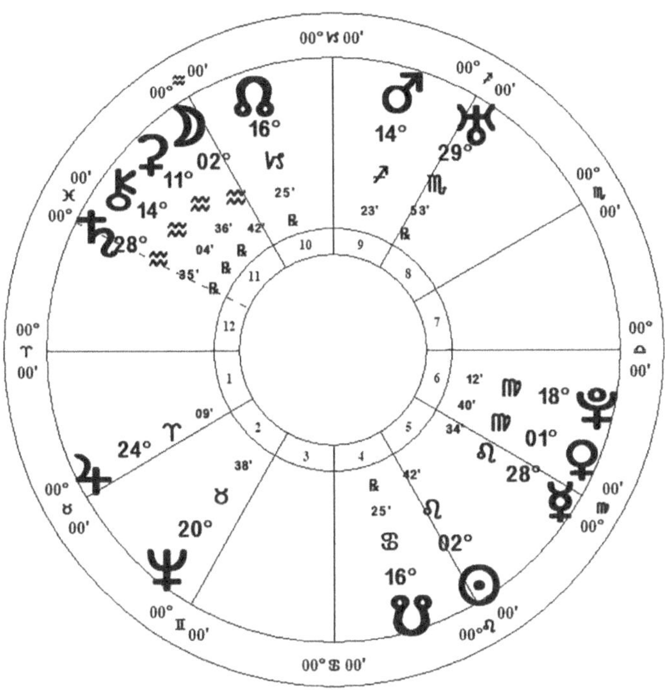

Lunar Saros 126

July 25, 1228 • 6:33:06 PM • North Pole

Game-Changers

Welcome to an Aquarian family of dragons destined for greatness. Their DNA is both ancient and modern as are their rulers, and in retrograde, at late degrees in fixed signs, and in square, necessitates a structural refit—a personal renovation no less. It is time to break free from the past because your success now depends on it. Ties to traditional values must now be put aside to make room for a more contemporary, progressive, and individual perspective to emerge.

Setbacks aside, these Air Dragons are specialists. They remind us that we all have significant contributions to make, and the clock is ticking. To hang on or let go—that is the question their Fixed T-Square hopes we'll answer. And here's a clue: Uranus, the modern ruler of the eclipse, is conjunct the fixed star Antares, known to bring opportunity and even fame in her cosmic embrace. There are many gifts associated with Antares, chief among them is a passion for life and an uncompromising spirit. Prince Harry has Uranus conjunct this powerful fixed star and is a stellar example of someone who refuses to be reined in by tradition. There is also a mysterious and dark underbelly to the star that attracts and exposes the vile and hidden to the light of day. Zelda Fitzgerald, with Uranus on Antares, experienced every shade of talent and torment this star can bring living through the excesses of the Jazz Age of the 1920's. One of the secrets to getting the best out of this magnificent star is to set yourself a challenge or project that requires at least a three to six month commitment and then go for it. The eclipse field holds just enough aggravation (Pluto/Mars waxing square) to get the job done and just enough hope (Ceres conjunct Chiron in Aquarius) to make it all worthwhile. And that's important because for all their talent, the Capricorn NNode/Cancer SNode axis can spend far too much time and energy brooding over past "mistakes" and missed opportunities. You can change your world and it just might start today. It for sure could start if you get an activation from this lunar eclipse. Not surprisingly, breakdowns and breakups are common during this period as incompatible value systems vie for dominance, creating temporary moments of insanity.

Both the midpoint and the isotrap structures encourage a wonderful revival of the creative spirit and help us open up to a greater appreciation for the role our dreams and hopes play in our day-to-day sanity. The Sun/Mercury opposition Moon/Saturn isotrap pattern can be especially helpful for what psychologists call "reframing": seeing the current situation from a different perspective. This approach can be very effective at offering a new door to go through instead of the same old one that never lets us leave the house.

Fortune favors the brave or desperate, so either way, take a spin on the cosmic wheel and bet on your resourcefulness. There's plenty of opportunity to go around with an OOB Mars (27S) in Sagittarius in mutual reception to Jupiter invigorating the entire field. We need to be thinking past our present state of grievances and disappointments to envisage a world where friendship and cooperation hold the highest value. These Air Dragons have always extended themselves in friendship and will continue to do so. Their Uranus square to the

Mercury/Venus conjunction will only get stronger with every passing return, reminding us that a more egalitarian society is calling to us from our future if only we would listen. Now over halfway through their 1,244 year life cycle, the lunar dragons of LS126 are at full strength.

Closest Midpoints: Jupiter/Eclipse-Node, Jupiter/Uranus -Pluto
Isotraps: Sun/Mercury opposition Moon/Saturn
Sun/Pluto opposition Uranus/Neptune

1900—2100 Eclipses: Lunar Saros—126

1913, 1931, 1949, 1967, 1985, 2003, 2021, 2039, 2057, 2075, 2094
Length of cycle —1,244 years
Series ends—August 19, 2472

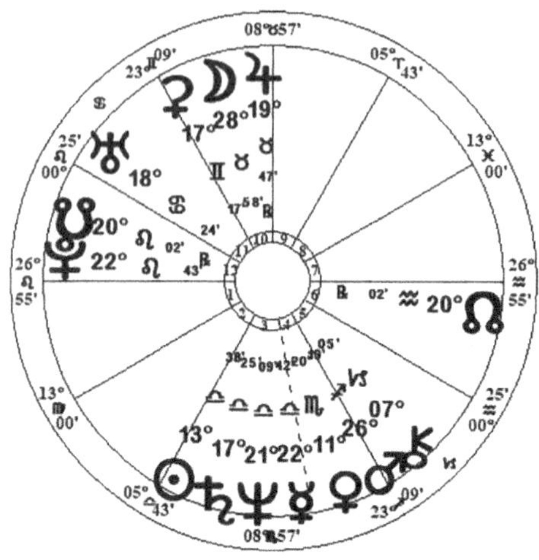

Vladimir Putin
PREBLE-118
7 October 1952 • 2:23 AM • St. Petersburg, Russia, USSR

Volodymyr Zelenskyy
PREBLE-117
25 January 1978 • 2:00 PM • Kryvyi Rih, Ukraine, USSR

World War Z —SNode/Pluto vs NNode/Pluto

"Dictators never ask why, it's always why not."

-Gary Kasparov

On November 20, 2021, Putin drew a red line, and told the signatories of NATO not to cross it. His progressed Sun at 22 Sagittarius 54 was now within a fast moving trine to progressed Pluto at 23 Leo 10 and his progressed Moon had reached the twenty-fifth degree of Scorpio, the opposition degree not only to his radix Moon but to the lunar eclipse activation degree at 27 Taurus. I believe that LS126, and its return in November 2021, may be the key piece in the puzzle that pulls his chart together. (See rectification study in Notes, p. 588).[1] Putin's need for internal security was at high tide, brought on by the progressed Moon and then by cosmic entanglement to the lunar eclipse.

Vladimir Putin's Connections to the Dragons of LS126

1st Harmonics: SNode - Uranus,
Neptune - Jupiter, Mercury/Venus - ASC, Saturn - DSC
2nd Harmonics: Neptune - Moon, Mars - Ceres

Putin was able to tune into the Game-Changer field of LS126 through his radix Moon at 28 Taurus in his Tenth House not only by the eclipse activation degree, but by the inducement of the eclipse field's 2nd Harmonic twentieth degree Neptune to that radix Moon. Then there's Neptune's 1st Harmonic to Jupiter with its potent square to Putin's personal and patriotic twentieth degree SNode and its conjunction to Pluto. Neptune again surfaces as part of the Saturn-Neptune-Mercury trio that inconjuncts Jupiter, making Putin prone to pessimism with an exaggerated sense of his own authority. This is a seriously complicated pattern that can easily produce a savior complex that is both willing to serve and wanting to be adored.

The eclipse field's Cosmic Bridge SNode contact to Putin's Uranus is *extremely* worrisome considering the extent to which Uranus has been flowing into Putin's political realm since spring 2020. Uranus is not called the "Great Awakener" for nothing. Sitting on his MC, it has allowed Putin to throw down the gauntlet as it hit his "complicated" Jupiter in May 2023. A tipping point arrives with the start of the Uranus retrograde in September 2023, while October brings in a new lunar eclipse with a number of tactical surprises. In the meantime, the arrival of LS136 in November 2022 began to turn the tide against Putin, however it won't be until LS146 returns in October 2023 that the world will see an end to this conflict. This lunar eclipse carries a potent financial punch from its Uranus square to the nodal axis while its eclipse axis falls right on Putin's Uranus. The eclipse Moon's 2nd Harmonic from the eighteenth degree of Capricorn to his 18 degrees Uranus will suddenly want to consolidate and wind down, especially as the eclipse Jupiter on Putin's DSC brings to bear the full weight of global diplomatic pressure.

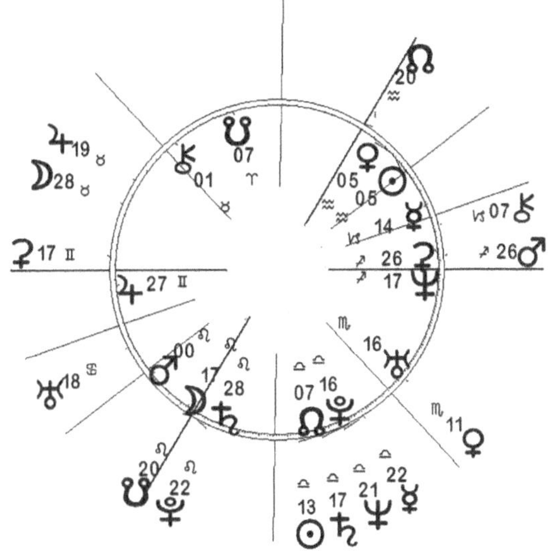

Zelenskyy inside chart, Putin outer chart.

While Putin's Jupiter deals with the complexity of its quincunx, Ceres receives all the benefits of that trio but in a trine along with input from an enterprising and strategic thirteenth degree Sun in Libra that suggests the role an armistice could play in the cessation of hostilities.

Volodymyr Zelenskyy's Connections to the Dragons of LS126

1st Harmonics: NNode – Mercury,
Moon – Sun/Venus, Sun – Mars,
Mercury/Venus – Saturn, Mars – Neptune, Pluto – IC
2nd Harmonics: Ceres/Chiron – Moon, Saturn – Saturn, Neptune – Uranus

Volodymyr Zelenskyy's chart holds a Mercury/NNode midpoint at 27 Scorpio which received the lunar eclipse activation by a resonation that was both deeply emotional as well as intellectually stimulating. Zelenskyy is not only an entertainer—he is also a fighter: every fiber of his fifth degree Sun/Venus humanitarian spirit is fueled by a fiery alpha Mars in Leo that is up to the challenge. LS126's eclipse axis has brought his leadership to full strength as he defends the sovereign rights of his people and in the process rallies the NATO's consortium of nations to his side.

In his struggle against Putin, Zelenskyy may not be winning the war, but he certainly is winning the hearts and minds of people from all over the world who value the right to self-determination in a political process called democracy. As the eclipse axis lights up his Sun, Venus and Mars by 1st Harmonics, Zelenskyy is taking his place on the world stage as a political leader and humanitarian. The eclipse NNode 1st Harmonic Cosmic Bridge to his Mercury represents the beginning of an enormous effort to challenge the status quo that is underscored by 2nd Harmonics from the eclipse Saturn in perfect resonance to a twenty-eight degree Saturn in Leo's love of nostalgia and the need to protect. And underscoring it all is the eclipse Neptune at the regenerative twentieth degree of Taurus setting off Zelenskyy's nurturing sixteenth degree Uranus.

The conundrum at the heart of Lunar Saros 126 is that it values in equal measure the role of breakthroughs as well as breakdowns in service to its evolution. To that end, and with the eclipse Pluto on the IC of Zelenskyy's chart, it appears that the war will not end well for his country. It gives me no joy to say that Zelenskyy's NNode Pluto will not survive Putin's SNode Pluto punch. He was never going to be able to defeat Putin as you can see from Putin's SNode/Pluto on his Moon/IC. In the end, what matters most is that the world will honor and respect Zelenskyy for his efforts to move the destiny of the Ukrainian people toward a more democratic and progressive future by its bid for integration into the EU.

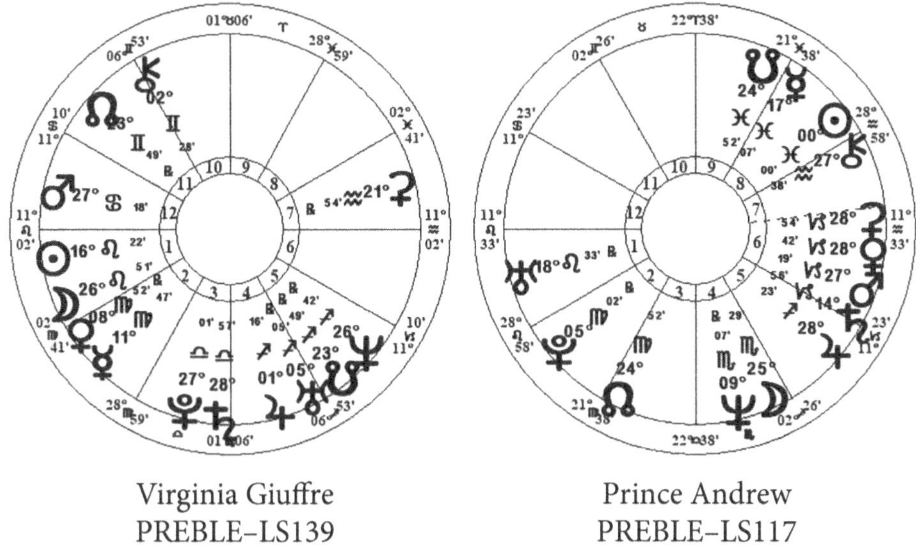

Virginia Giuffre
PREBLE–LS139

August 9, 1983 • 5:52 AM • Sacramento, CA, USA

Prince Andrew
PREBLE–LS117

February 19, 1960 • 3:30 PM • London, UK

Taken to the Tower—The Fall of Prince Andrew

"Humpty Dumpty sat on a wall, Humpty Dumpty had a great fall.
All the king's horses and all the king's men
couldn't put Humpty together again."

–Children's Rhyme

Prince Andrew's PREBLE LS117, with its core message for "searching" out meaningful companionship, seems to have been interpreted as a free-for-all "cross-pollination" that sadly led to his downfall. Virginia Giuffre, on the other hand, has risen to the call of her PREBLE LS139's Truth or Dare mandate, personifying the best of her dragon family.

The prince that the press nicknamed Randy Andy would find that, like Humpty-Dumpty, he couldn't be put back together again. On February 15, 2022, Virginia Giuffre was awarded a $20 million dollar out-of-court settlement, a substantial donation to her charity, and an apology in her sexual abuse lawsuit. The lawsuit alleged that, when she was 16 and 17 years old, she was trafficked by convicted sex offender Jeffrey Epstein to Prince Andrew. Seemingly sealing his fate a month earlier, his mother Queen Elizabeth II had already stripped the prince of his HRH designation, titles, and royal duties. Benjamin Weiser, writing in the *New York Times* on February 15, 2022, stated that:

> The settlement may serve as a capstone to the years of investigations and litigation that has surrounded Mr. Epstein and his associates. The Epstein saga implicated or involved people at the highest levels of celebrity and politics, including Andrew, on both sides of the ocean, spawning court cases and conspiracy theories.[2]

The settlement was a coup de grâce in its truest sense: this term first appeared in the English lexicon at the end of the 17th century, translated as "stroke of grace" or "blow of mercy," and originally referred to the act of putting to death a person or animal who was severely injured and unlikely to recover.[3] Harsh as that seems, it appears that Prince Andrew has thoroughly burnt his bridges and may have few prospects for any hope of a return to his former noble stature and lifestyle.

Which is why PREBLE LS126—Game Changers—is so prescient because it fits the circumstances of what happened to him after it landed on November 19, 2020. And LS126 also fits the circumstances of what happened to Virginia Giuffre, so let's take a closer look.

The activation degree of 27 Taurus in Andrew's chart sits opposite his Moon at 25 Scorpio. What we have with Moon to Moon activations by opposition always reflect a realignment of a domestic situation, or family or childhood needs that arise, or in this case, a national issue of security. In Taurus you can bet your bottom dollar there's going to be financial implications.

Prince Andrew's Connections to the Dragons of LS126
Space Lanes via DSC/ASC

1st Harmonics: NNode – Saturn, Moon – Mars/Venus/Ceres, Uranus – Moon, Saturn – Chiron/ Sun, Venus – Pluto, Jupiter – MC, Ceres/Chiron – DSC
2nd Harmonics: Neptune – Moon,
Mercury – Chiron/Sun, Venus – Sun, Chiron – Uranus, Pluto – Mercury

Both Prince Andrew and Virginia Giuffre share ascendants at 11 degrees Leo! Their charts have AA data, so this tie is spot on. But what is truly compelling is an opposition within one minute of exactitude between their Mars placements. This is so rare in chart comparisons and in over fifty years of consultations and research, I've never seen it. The dragons of LS126 are in for a cosmic workout as both have riveting "relationships" with them. Prince Andrew has the highest total connectors of anyone researched for this book: seventeen links to the lunar eclipse field of which nine form Cosmic Bridges.

Prince Andrew's tally of ties is a prime example of how it is not so much the number as it is the quality of connection that ultimately wins you the day, or season, or for that matter lifetime. What seemed to work against him was the double dose of Saturn; first from the eclipse to his Moon and then from the eclipse Sun. Ordinarily these do not spell doom, but in tandem with an eclipse 1st Harmonic Uranus to his twenty-fifth self-obsessed Moon in Scorpio degree and an opposing 2nd Harmonic Neptune at the Scorpionic twentieth degree of Taurus weighing in, his Moon was about to be skewered and grilled.

Virginia Giuffre's Connections to the Dragons of LS126
Space Lanes via DSC/ASC
Venus with Venus

1st Harmonics: Mercury/Venus – Moon,
Ceres/Chiron – DSC, Uranus – Jupiter/Uranus
2nd Harmonics: Saturn – Moon, Ceres/Chiron – Sun, Uranus – Chiron

The activation degree of 27 Taurus in Virginia's chart sits on her Chiron at 2 Gemini in opposition to Jupiter at 1 Sagittarius and its conjunction to Uranus at the fun-loving fifth. But there's more here: that Chiron/Jupiter/Uranus trio pulls in her Venus at the eighth degree of wealth as it links to the eclipse Venus at the precedent-setting first degree. Both parties, as they share the same degree on the ASC, have Space Lanes which get you up and running before the public. Not bad if you're in the public eye or trying to get public sympathy for your cause. The eclipse 1st Harmonic Mercury/Venus to her Moon is a Cosmic Bridge that truly links the chorus back to the verse as her legal team would have had to navigate Prince Andrew's litany of protests and denials as they contested and denied Giuffre's chapter and verse statements on the facts of the case. A 1st Harmonic CB to a natal Moon is going to bring in a new environment at least 70 percent—if not 100 percent—of the time since it provides a pathway that links the past to the future. The eclipse Ceres/Chiron to her DSC is a resonance that brings public support to investigate and activate awareness, especially when an injured party claims to have been "taken down into the underworld." The Seventh House in astrological symbolism is where we find members of the public and many consultants, especially of the legal kind, and Ms. Giuffre had some of the best. The twenty million dollar settlement will hopefully establish legal precedents for future cases, but more importantly act as a cultural determinant and game-changer for what needs to be level-headed jurisprudence.

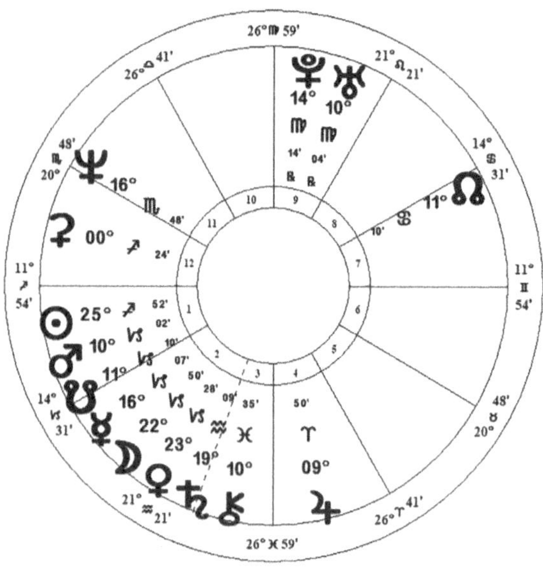

Brad Pitt
PREBLE–LS119

December 18, 1963 • 6:31 AM • Shawnee, OK, USA

Self-Employed Dad

"Having children takes the focus off yourself, which I'm really grateful for. I'm so tired of thinking about myself. I'm sick of myself."

-BRAD PITT

In his unauthorized biography of Angelina Jolie, Andrew Morton writes about the Hollywood alchemy that film directors dream of, and that alchemy happened when Angelina and Brad shot their first scene together in late November 2003.[4] By April 2004, the sizzle on the set of *Mr. & Mrs. Smith* was so hot that Jennifer Aniston's only reply to questions about Brad's repeated absences was "Busy working."[5] Nice work if you can get it and get it he did. Brad went on to adopt Angelina's children as well as father three of their own together, creating, as Angelina says of her brood, "cool people."

The story on Brad's chart and LS126 is a simple tale of fascination and frustration: On November 9, 2003, the eclipse opened at 16 Taurus in opposition to his natal Neptune at 16 Scorpio. It was light penetrating into the seductive world of Brad's soulful life of secrets and shadow. With Brad's seven placements in Earth and LS126 breaking through to his Neptune in Scorpio, deep desires for sex, eroticism and mysticism would awaken a soul hunger for connection and feeling. When factoring in his Neptune/Venus-Uranus midpoint, it is easy to see how his meeting with Angelina on that film set was so electrifying. Twelve years later, the sizzle was replaced with sadness: Jolie filed for divorce on September 19, 2016, embroiling Pitt in a custody battle that, as of 2023, has yet to be resolved to his satisfaction.[6]

Brad Pitt's Connections to the Dragons of LS126
↑NNode with SNode↓
Saturn with Saturn
Neptune to Neptune
Pluto with Pluto

1st Harmonics: NNode – SNode,
NNode – Mercury, Mars – ASC, Uranus – Ceres

Even though this is not Brad's lunar eclipse family (he belongs to PREBLE–LS119 Who's Your Daddy Fire Dragons in Part One) LS126 is extremely fond of Brad. Just look at all the connectors and resonance across their fields: Both have Pluto in Virgo, both have Saturn in Aquarius, both have Jupiter in Aries, their Neptunes are in complimentary opposition, and LS126's Mars falls on Brad's Ascendant. But even all those connections pale in comparison to the importance of the dragon family's Cosmic Bridge NNode attaching to Brad's Mercury, much like in the case of Volodymyr Zelenskyy, sealing the deal and declaring him *their* shining son and star. Nodal attachments are just that powerful, and in terms of dragon DNA paternity, offer prima facie evidence of cosmic connection. And to give a new twist on an old tale, Brad's nodal axis reverses that of LS126, revealing a fully charged and invigorated Global Gateway.

But hang in there, Brad Pitt fans: his bargaining position to negotiate for more access and custodial rights to his children started to improve with the return of the Water Dragons of LS131 in May 2022 as they activated his progressed Tenth House to help press for his fatherly rights. The return of the Air Dragons of LS136 in the fall of 2022 activated his Neptune sextile Mercury and its rulership of his natal Tenth House. Thus triggered, Brad's Neptune is primed and ready to reveal a new side of his fatherly ministrations with the return of the Water Dragons of Lunar Saros 141 in the spring of 2023 with five Cosmic Bridges ready to span the gulf of grief and discord between himself, Angelina, and his six children. But time will tell. The return of the Walk the Walk Earth Dragons of LS146 in October 2023 will have the final say as they present at 5 Taurus triggering his Sun/Pluto midpoint.

LS126 Summary

There is a distinct air of intelligence and vibrancy with these youthful Air Dragons. They are driven to pursue their own dreams and in the process manage to uplift all those in their company. Game-Changers all, when this Lunar Saros Series blows your way, expect to be blown away by how awesome life can be. The Universe is calling—don't play coy. Pick up. This is a time to appreciate your individuality, your friends, and all the good stuff that life has to offer. Success now is about getting out of your comfort zone and letting a Higher Power move your story forward. Loosen the chains that bind you or, better yet, just open the bloody locks. There's a better way to live your life if you're willing to have a better life. Decide today that things are going to be different and let the old patterns and habits fall by the wayside. There's no guarantee that you won't suffer, but if you don't let the winds of change refresh your spirit, you will have wasted a valuable opportunity for personal growth. A little discomfort now is a small price to pay for the future you that is most definitely on its way. Maybe it's time for a new doormat—pun intended.

Remember, breakdowns are an integral part of the plan and are included at no extra charge, along with any love relationships in your life that could use some tweaking. Be devoted to them but remember the wise words of Jimi Hendrix, "Don't be reckless with other people's hearts [and] don't put up with people who are reckless with yours." And here's more good news: There's no need to fear going it alone. This is, after all an amazingly well-connected Aquarian family of dragons, eager to make a magnificent contribution to the world writ large. It's time for a breath of fresh air. It's time to be a Game-Changer.

Phase	Return	Year
Crescent	38th	1895
First Quarter	43rd	1985
Gibbous	47th	2057
Full Moon	51st	2130

LS126 Luminaries

Napoleon Bonaparte	August 15, 1769
Buster Keaton	October 4, 1895
André Breton	February 19, 1896
Jesse Owens[E3]	September 12, 1913
Francis Farmer	September 19, 1913
Desmond Tutu	October 7, 1931
John le Carré	October 19, 1931
Mickey Mantle	October 20, 1931
Johnny Cash	February 26, 1932
Christiane Northrup[E3]	October 4, 1949
David Foster	November 1, 1949
Pablo Escobar	December 1, 1949
Sissy Spacek	December 25, 1949
Jamie Foxx	December 13, 1967
Josh Brolin	February 12, 1968
Daniel Craig	March 2, 1968
Celine Dion	March 30, 1968
Amanda Seyfried	December 3, 1985
Charlotte Church	February 21, 1986
Lady Gaga	March 28, 1986
Sergio Ramos	March 30, 1986

PREBLE—LS121
Jesse Owens
Francis Farmer
Desmond Tutu
Christiane Northrup

---

1. Ellen Barry. Putin Once More Moves to Assume Top Job in Russia. https://www.nytimes.com/2011/09/25/world/europe/medvedev-says-putin-will-seek-russian-presidency-in-2012.html. Retrieved March 13, 2022.
2. Benjamin Weiser. Prince Andrew Settles Sexual Abuse Lawsuit with Virginia Giuffre. https://www.nytimes.com/2022/02/15/nyregion/prince-andrew-virginia-giuffre-settlement.html. Retrieved Feb. 21, 2022.
3. https://www.merriam-webster.com/dictionary/coup%20de%20gr%C3%A2ce
4. Andrew Morton, *Angelina* (New York: St. Martin's Press, 2010), p. 239.
5. Ibid, p. 246.
6. https://en.wikipedia.org/wiki/Brad_Pitt. Retrieved Feb. 27, 2022.

LUNAR SAROS 134

"You would think that a rock star being married to a supermodel would be one of the greatest things in the world. It is."

-DAVID BOWIE

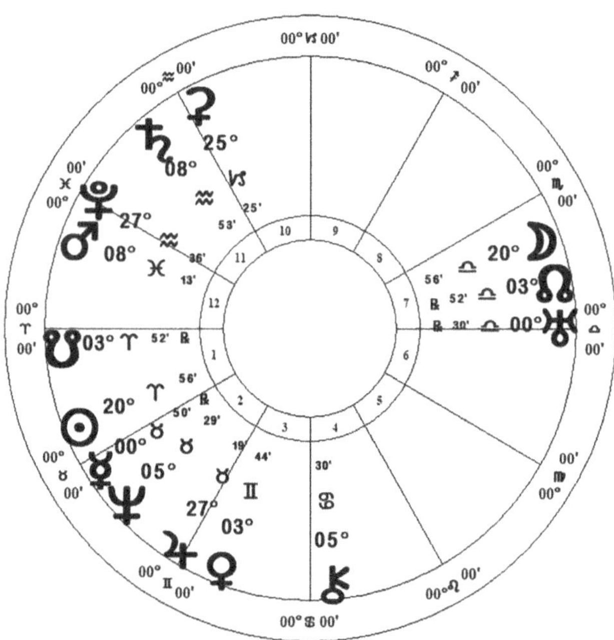

Lunar Saros 134

April 11, 1550 • 1:07:34 PM • North Pole

The Attractor Factor

Radiating high levels of social awareness, this is a North Node Libran eclipse eager to open doors that facilitate connecting, sharing, and caring for others. Issues of justice and fair play are championed by those with panache and personality ready to do what it takes to create a just, equitable and more sustainable world. Ruler Venus in double-bodied Gemini in waxing trine to Saturn in Aquarius quickly and boldly expands her network of influence and in mutual reception with retrograde Mercury in Taurus isn't just another pretty face. The attractor factor within this extraordinary lunar eclipse family is due in large measure to the planet Venus in alignment to one of the stars of the Hyades Cluster found in the constellation of Taurus. Located ten degrees southeast of the Pleiades, this star cluster has been famous for ages; Richard Allen's *Star Names: Their Lore and Meaning* gives an extensive historical account with multiple references indicating their association with rain, storms, tempests, and even droughts.[1] In particular, Epsilon Tauri or Ain (The Bull's Eye or the Northern Eye) is in a direct alignment with Venus, and within a twenty-seven minute orb literally pours forth from its "eye" a cosmic shower of aesthetic gifts not only in the classic creative art forms of painting, sculpture, literature, architecture, cinema, music, and theater but also in the contemporary fields of political expression and social commentary. Celestial downpours of renewal are just half of the Hyades story, the other half being times of drought, denial, tragedy, and tears. My own research indicates that the grief element is overstated: What matters most is a compelling emotional response to a chosen career path as well as a powerful need to love and be loved; now that's a bull's eye worthy of your time and attention.

As ruler of the eclipse, Venus combines with Saturn and an AP Uranus/North Node conjunction to exploit the potential of its brilliant Grand Air Trine by stirring social action. Most members, from an early age, will take every opportunity to make a contribution either to their family or to their social group's well-being. As one matures, the need to be involved in social justice issues and to address injustice becomes a moral necessity as seen through Uranus at the AP, particularly as the growing gap of social inequality continues to widen.

Mercury's 00 degree infinity retrograde conjunction to Neptune likes to get results through a collaborative network that teams ingenuity with enterprise and entertainment. The end result is stunningly strategic and sublime thanks to Mercury's MR to Venus and all of her creative Grand Air Trine supply chains. Working in tandem with others rather than trying to get all the glory for oneself is the only way to go when the AP Uranus at 00 Libra conjuncts the North Node. It's true that all members of this eclipse family are prodigies in their own right but now, in conjunction with others, your capacity to change the world lies within your willingness to surrender your ego for the greater good. If you take on the mantel of a humanitarian agenda, the attractor factor will find you, especially with the Node at the Jupiter/Saturn midpoint. Have a plan and work that plan. The Sun/Mars conjunct Mercury/Pluto isotrap guarantees that your efforts, although they may not be realized in this lifetime, will be exonerated by future generations who will live to tell the tales of your noble deeds.

Closest Midpoints: Eclipse/Venus-Mars, Node/Jupiter-Saturn
Isotraps: Sun/Mars conjunct Mercury/Pluto
Venus/Saturn conjunct Mars/Neptune

1900—2100 Eclipses: Lunar Saros—134

1910, 1928, 1946, 1964, 1982, 2001, 2019, 2037, 2055, 2073, 2091
Length of cycle —1,280 years
Series ends—May 28, 2830

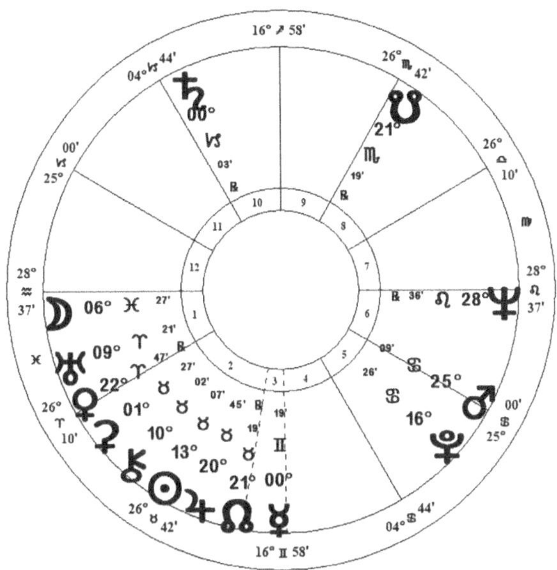

Audrey Hepburn
PREBLE—LS134

May 4, 1929 • 3:00 PM • Ixelles, Belgium

She was the Fairest of Them All

"Suddenly there was that dazzling creature, looking like a wide-eyed doe prancing through the forest. . . it took exactly five minutes for everybody on that set to fall in love with her."

-Billy Wilder

Some of the finest one-on-one interviews with Hollywood's greatest stars were done by New York University film professor Richard Brown in his American Movie Classics interview series *Reflections on the Silver Screen,* a TV series that aired from 1990 to 1996. One of his first interviews in 1990 was with the legendary Audrey Hepburn.[2] Watching the interview was like having a front row seat in appreciating her journey as a Taurean soul who valued the simplicity of a real life that was continually fed by her enchanting and sensitive Piscean

Moon and all clothed in her Aquarian ascendant's concern for others. Audrey's enormous love for humanity shone through every fiber of her being: her wide-open eyes and every disciplined step overflowed with grace, purpose, serenity, elegance, and high spirits. Let's see the role that her dragon family played that made her life so legendary.

Audrey Hepburn's Connections to the Dragons of LS134
Uranus to Uranus
Jupiter with Jupiter

1st Harmonics: Mars – Moon,
Pluto – ASC, Mercury – Ceres, Venus – Mercury, Neptune – DSC
2nd Harmonics: Moon – Venus, Ceres – Mars, Pluto – Neptune

As always, take a quick look at the natal chart to see what jumps out and don't be afraid to go with the flow; following rigid rules leaves less room for creative synthesis. In Hepburn's chart her 00 infinity Mercury/Gemini in the Third House along with 00 infinity Saturn retrograde/Capricorn in the Tenth House are hugely significant as it gives an almost infinite possibility for manifestation as they are in rulership, dignified by house and at the alpha zero degree placement where anything becomes possible. Her retrograde Saturn highlights the fact that she was not a trained actress, rather a ballerina and fell into acting to make a living. Audrey Hepburn's tightest midpoint is the Node/Sun-Mercury putting her fresh and anything's possible Mercury in alignment with the vitality of her life essence to serve the greater good. This midpoint, as many midpoints do, grew in power, and contributed to a flair for elegance and finesse in all her movies. She was beloved by all.

Let's look at two of Audrey's 1st Harmonics from the eclipse field: its Sun to her Venus and its Venus to her Mercury as both become gloriously energized by the Eclipse/Venus-Mars midpoint. LS134's Venus, as stated in the introduction, is in a stellar position to literally rain down upon her all its creative instincts. Audrey's Venus at the masterful 22nd degree of Aries and retrograde is positioned to do it her way as all retrogrades follow their own path; here we can appreciate how magnanimous she was in doing it in full consciousness of what her way was going to be. The eclipse Venus on her Mercury gifted her sparkling personality with a distinct style of speaking that was uniquely her own. Empowered by its Grand Air Trine, the eclipse Venus had Audrey, from a very young age, studying to be a professional ballerina. However, due to height and health concerns from many years of malnutrition during the occupation of the Netherlands during WWII—and needing to make a living as any sensible Taurus gal would—she turned to what she knew she *could* do: modeling and acting.

As often is the case, the 2nd Harmonics are even more impressive. In Audrey's chart, as a Venus-Arian, her link to the eclipse Moon and its over-arching attractor factor gave her an enthusiastic response to life. She seemed to charm any and all who fell within her fun-loving spell. Mind you, the woman had a powerful square to Mars in Cancer and all that cardinal energy wasn't going to sit around and let someone else call the shots. Many who have Venus in Aries have a challenging mixture of sentimentality and fearlessness that seems to create both professional success and personal angst, and Audrey certainly had her share of both.

The eclipse Moon with its square to Ceres in Capricorn does not deny relationship satisfaction so much as it seems to delay it with almost all clan members, ultimately finding their true love in the middle to third phase of their life. It wouldn't be until age forty-nine, and after two unhappy marriages, that Audrey fell in love. Robert Wolders was a Dutch-born businessman who Audrey always introduced, in true Taurus fashion as, "This is my Rob" or "Have you met my Rob?"[3] They would be together from 1980 until her death in 1993.

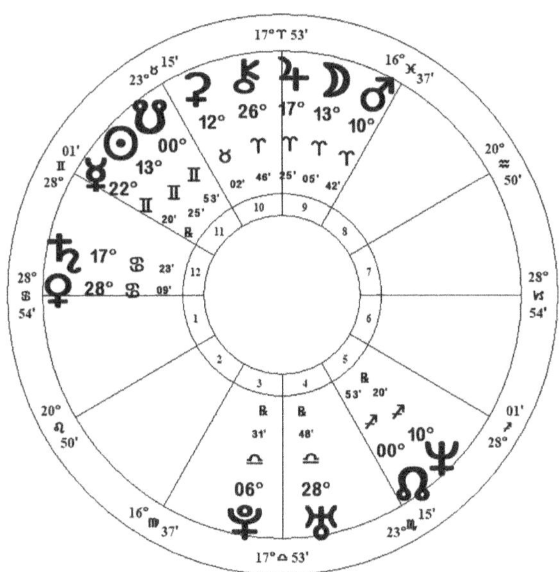

Angelina Jolie
PREBLE—LS130

June 4, 1975 • 9:09 AM • Los Angeles, CA, USA

"I have so much in my life.
I want to be of value
to the world."

Actress/Director/Producer/Goddess

"Wherever I am I always find myself
looking out the window wishing I was somewhere else."

-Angelina Jolie

In January 2001, Angelina was in discussions with UNHCR, the UN Refugee Agency, asking about visiting refugee camps to research her next movie, *Lara Croft: Tomb Raider*; by the end of February she was in Abidjan, Côte d'Ivoire, "shocked and upset by the human tumult she encountered."[4] Biographer

Andrew Morton wrote that her first visit to refugee camps was monumental—"When I came back [to America] two weeks later, I was a very different person."[5] Looking at the lunar eclipse that danced with her chart in January, it was obvious that her world-view would be turned inside out. As the portal presented at the twentieth degree of Cancer on January 9, Jolie's Saturn and Jupiter, both in a partile cardinal square at the seventeenth degree of fame, light, children, creativity, self-expression, and entertainment, jumped at the chance to respond. Seizing the day and the next six months of her life, the Air Dragons of LS134 took hold of her most badass aspect to lay down a track that Angelina could follow that would guide her path forward in the months and years to come.

Angelina's rising star power and provocative personality would lead to an appointment by the UNHCR in Geneva on August 27, 2001, as a UNHCR Goodwill Ambassador.[6] On April 17, 2012, after more than a decade of service, Angelina was promoted to the rank of Special Envoy to High Commissioner Guterres.[7] Thanks to her Node/Moon-Saturn midpoint and the fixed stars linked to them, Angelina went from being a self-indulgent, pampered movie star to an actualized citizen driven by the idea that she could make a difference in the life of a child. Bernadette Brady's astrological software, *Starlight,* gives Angelina's fixed star parans as "Saturn to Arcturus—The one who finds new pathways, and the Moon to Sirius—A desire to create a lasting monument to a loved person."[8] These parans are truly descriptive in light of the many projects and facilities that have been funded by the Jolie-Pitt Foundation since its inception in 2006, making Angelina a global phenomenon with her ability to influence people on a large scale.

Angelina's Connections to the Dragons of LS134
Moon to Moon

1st Harmonics: Jupiter/Venus – SNode,
NNode – Pluto, Mercury – Chiron
2nd Harmonics: Moon – Jupiter/Chiron, Ceres – Venus, Mercury – Uranus

The overall energetic feel of what the Dragons of LS134 can offer Angelina is a sense that her life is taking on a new direction. This shift in focus is what the lunar eclipses do best and apart from prediction, give valuable information not only to where we are now but where we are headed. To orient oneself in the world one needs to know not only where you are right now but where you are going. It helps to be able to give a full accounting of our experiences to date because if you do not know how you got here, it is difficult to calculate where you are now and hence what roads you might be able to take.

Angelina met up with the full force of LS134 ready to make some major changes in her life. The lunar eclipse 1st Harmonic Sun to her Jupiter/Chiron, along with the eclipse Jupiter/Venus to her SNode, is a double tap of opportunity. It delivered not only an expansion of her innate ability to generate possibility (as seen through the 00 Gemini SNode) but it also triggered a profound awareness and a sense of propriety in terms of her social behavior. Their synergy resulted in an alchemical fusion that promoted something akin to a religious fervor that would help her map her world with an exhilarating sense of renewed confidence.

The lunar eclipse 2nd Harmonics from the Moon and Ceres validate her new map as they reorient and redirect her personal achievements in service to her concerns for the welfare, dignity, and legal rights of disadvantaged and impoverished children. The Ceres to Venus 2nd Harmonic is the ultimate expression of the eclipse's ability to move her toward fulfilling her very Cancerian twenty-eighth degree Venus in Cancer desire: to establish companionship and care through social contacts that revolve around creating a womb of comfort for those in need. Audrey Hepburn's Arian twenty-fifth degree Mars in Cancer would have thrown her total support to Angelina's UNHCR mission.

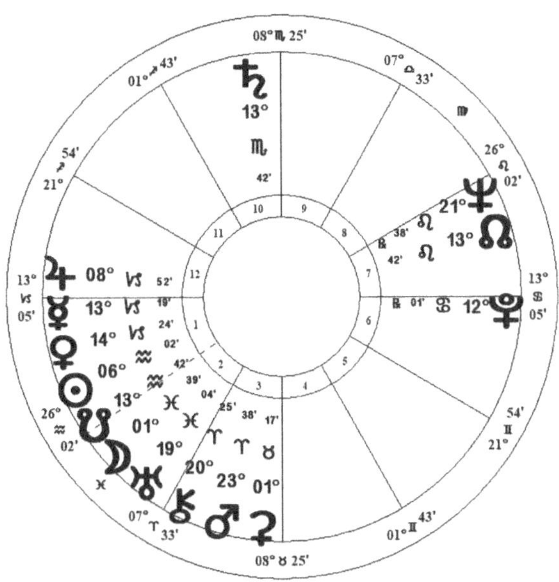

Paul Newman
PREBLEs—LS127 & LS132

January 26, 1925 • 6:30 AM • Cleveland, OH, USA

"The star of oil and vinegar and the oil and vinegar of the stars."

–PAUL NEWMAN

Actor/Entrepreneur/Humanitarian

"Paul was a very fine actor and a really good race driver. But mostly, he personified humanity–always taking care of those who were less fortunate. For me, this will be his legacy."

-DAVID LETTERMAN

Newman's Own Salad Dressing was officially launched in 1982; with first year profits exceeding $300,000, Paul declared, "Let's give it all away to those who need it."[9] Paul Newman would become a legend not only for his stunningly gorgeous blue eyes and heart palpitating film performances but for his equally stunning soulful generosity and philanthropy. Newman roared into 1983 on the expressway of social enterprise fueled by LS134's December 30, 1982, touchdown at the wealth-building eighth degree of Cancer on his retrograde Pluto on the Seventh House DSC cusp. In 1983, Newman's personality was his brand: his pasta sauce led to lemonade, microwave popcorn, and salsa, with earnings reaching over $370 million by 2013—all of it donated.[10] In an article from the archives of the *New York Times*, Paul Newman is quoted as saying:

> We take the profits we make from the people who eat our food and turn those profits into food for people who haven't enough to eat. That's the cycle of our business, from those who have to those who have not. [11]

Newman was an icon of social responsibility: He has Capricorn rising with ruler Saturn in essential dignity in the Tenth House hooked into a Grand Water Trine to Pluto. He also has, like Angelina Jolie, Venus right on the ascendant and in a stellium of duty-oriented Capricorn companions in sextile to Saturn. His First House Sun in Aquarius is ennobled by a Piscean Moon's sympathetic heart (much like Audrey's Aquarian ascendant and Pisces Moon) and artistic temperament born to leave the world a better place.

Paul Newman's Connections to the Dragons of LS134

1st Harmonics: Saturn – Sun/SNode, Pluto – Moon, Mercury – Ceres
2nd Harmonics: Moon – Mars, Chiron – Jupiter

Newman's chart holds an identical phase angle symmetry between Jupiter and Venus to the eclipse field's Jupiter and Venus, reinforcing resonance. To have such symmetry to the Lesser and Greater Benefics is a stroke of divine luck. Newman becomes the recipient of LS134's cosmic blessings as his own chart reveals a triple Venus/Mercury/Jupiter parallel declination that is indicative of social conviction and causes that promote fairness and a generosity of spirit. LS134's Saturn in the sign of the humanitarian making a CB to Newman's Sun/SNode laid down a path making it the right time to shine his celebrity on issues that would appeal to the *tastes* of a global audience. And, like Angelina, with both having Venus in the First House and in cardinal signs, Newman would find it impossible not to take on his share of the collective responsibility to redress the global concerns of hunger, especially with his Venus in a 2nd Harmonic to his natal retrograde Pluto at the Piscean twelfth degree.

At 6 degrees Aquarius, Paul Newman's Sun carried a true desire to be of service and, in that regard, the twenty-second degree lunar eclipse axis, with its ability to take control and bring a sense of rationality to a public cause, was a match made in heaven. Activations by 1st Harmonics stimulate our natural impulses and sense of direction; they simply awaken us to follow a path that, as a seed essence, has always been there, just waiting for the right moment to be born. The eclipse 2nd Harmonic Moon to Newman's Mars reinforces the Eclipse/Venus-Mars midpoint and its potential to attract a veritable chalice that would be filled with Newman's special appeal, all backed by his networks of social connection and consciousness that continue to be a source of hope and joyful self-expression for those in need.

LS134 Summary

Networks of sharing, caring, healing, and connection are what drive these Air Dragons, still in the vigor and promise of young adulthood. Lunar Saros 134 has a lifespan of 1,280 years, giving it seventy-two opportunities to return to refresh our global consciousness with its curiosity and courage. 2001 was its twenty-sixth appearance; until 2073 it will be unfolding through a Last Quarter phase with its emphasis on re-orientation and review. This lunar phase is consistent with coming to terms with a sense of dissatisfaction and loss as old patterns and habits no longer bring the joy of previous years. The benefits to a Last Quarter phase are found in the growing sense of disillusionment that comes when one has the courage to question the validity of almost everything. The eclipse returns until the beginning of its Balsamic phase in 2073 show a territory rich in the exploration of how the beginning of a meaningful inner dialogue can become the springboard for some of the most productive periods of a lifetime.

LS134 was birthed in a stellar nursery of love, giving all by birthright or rite of passage access to its enhanced powers of attraction and allure. However, its expansive capacity for social, aesthetic and relationship needs must be tempered by an awareness of how quickly one can fall into states of indulgence and excess. As mentioned in the introduction, most members of this clan find happiness in their mid to later years. Of all 134's luminaries the only one who was able to stay committed throughout his entire married life was the illustrious Danny Kaye, a devoted UNICEF advocate for children's rights. Along with Audrey Hepburn, many LS134 alumni are fiercely devoted and dedicated to raising awareness and collective responsibility for improving the living conditions and standards of children throughout the world. This eclipse holds a special capacity to foster and raise awareness of issues that need addressing both on a personal as well as geo-political level.

When the energy of this family of eclipses touches a chart, everything will revolve around the reintegration of skills, beliefs, and knowledge that need to be fine-tuned and updated to fit the new you. There is wisdom here that needs to be used to benefit both the personal and the greater collective that operates through each individual. Whether one is single, attached, or somewhere in between, be open to meeting new people who are as interesting as you—commitments and personal causes are all in the ascendency.

LS134 Luminaries

Walter P Chrysler	April 2, 1875
Yogananda	January 5, 1893
Danny Kaye	January 18, 1911
Ronald Reagan	February 6, 1911
Jean Harlow	March 3, 1911
L. Ron Hubbard	March 13, 1911
Noam Chomsky	December 7, 1928
Martin Luther King Jr.	January 15, 1929
Max von Sydow	April 10, 1929
Audrey Hepburn	May 4, 1929
Steven Spielberg	December 18, 1946
David Bowie	January 8, 1947
Michio Kaku	January 24, 1947
Elton John	March 25, 1947
Kareem Abdul-Jabbar	April 16, 1947
Diane Lane	January 22, 1965
Aamir Khan	March 14, 1965
Chris Rock	February 7, 1965
Robert Downey Jr.	April 4, 1965
Alexander Dreymon	February 7, 1983
Emily Blunt	February 23, 1983
Lupita Nyong'o	March 1, 1983
Edward Snowden	June 21, 1983

1. Richard Hinckley Allen, *Star Names Their Lore and Meaning* (New York: Dover Publications, 1963), p. 391.
2. Audrey Hepburn: Reflections on the Silver Screen. https://www.youtube.com/watch?v=v18G6K-4MVjc. Retrieved April 18, 2022.
3. Kara Warner & Liz McNeil, August 19, 2017. Retrieved April 25, 2022. https://people.com/movies/audrey-hepburn-love-marriage-robert-wolders/
4. Morton, *Angelina*, p. 239.
5. Ibid., p. 204.
6. Ibid., p. 246.
7. http://www.unhcr.org/pages/49c3646c56.html. Retrieved May 28, 2022.
8. Bernadette Brady, Starlight software.
9. http://newmansownfoundation.org/about-us/history. Retrieved May 28, 2022.
10. Ibid.
11. http://www.nytimes.com/1989/12/22/nyregion/from-paul-newman-s-own-company-250000-for-neediest.html. Retrieved May 28, 2022.

LUNAR SAROS 135

"Humans think in stories, and we try to make sense of the world by telling stories."

-Yuval Noah Harari

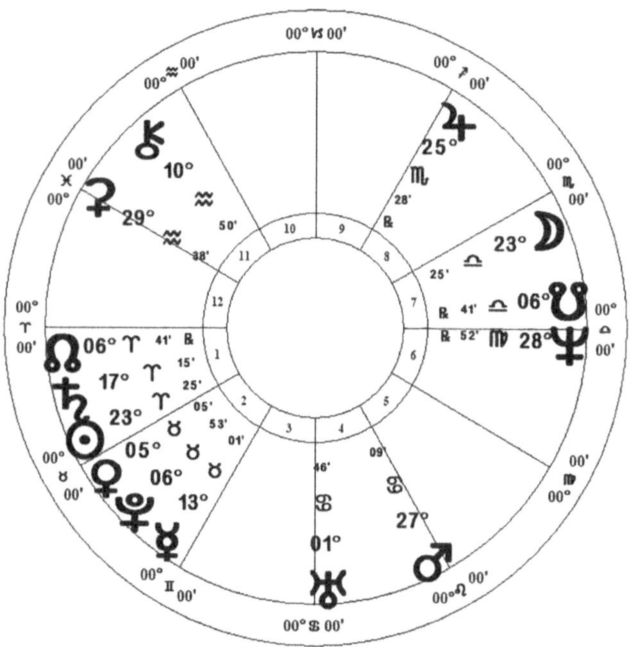

Lunar Saros 135

April 13, 1615 • 7:51:19 PM • South Pole

Storytellers

This is a South Node Libran eclipse with Venus in Taurus in rulership conjunct Pluto. Out of the entire 47 Lunar Saros Series, this mighty conjunction, found only in LS135's sphere of consciousness, holds a profound artistic gift that has the power to recalibrate not only the personal but also the collective mindset. It stirs within our deepest ancestral core an irresistible drive to free oneself of any entrapments, entanglements, or ideologies whose time and relevance have long gone. Aligned to Venus, the potency of Pluto's parallel declination with Neptune, the planet of mystery and illusion, sends its imagination soaring into the stratosphere. There will be loss and struggle and beginnings and endings but it's time to push past fear and enter the birth canal of fascination. Helping to ease the contractions is a Ceres, Neptune, and Mars Yod, coordinating times of pain with times of pleasure. This is an inspirational Yod full of endless creativity. Ceres at the twenty-ninth degree in Aquarius is not only prophetic but also fun-loving, providing overtones of much appreciated hope and optimism. Saturn's opening conjunction to the Sun is willing to put in the time and effort that is required if one is to tap the immense artistic gifts and procreative powers of this Lunar Saros Series.

Stressful nodal squares to an OOB Uranus (23N46) at the first degree of Cancer are personally very disruptive and can result in protracted periods of difficulty maintaining steady patterns of work or creative output. This nodal square is particularly prone to periods of interruption or frustration in one's work environment making it essential to have either a backup form of employment or a lifestyle that can handle the ups and downs of a variegated work/life. It is essential that one develops a working relationship with both solitude and adversity as both are essential to bring out the best qualities of this eclipse.

Saturn's Venus square Neptune midpoint doesn't seem to mind playing the game of Snakes and Ladders; for the most part, it's an invigorating experience going up and down the scales of desirability. For some it will be a stumble, for others a tumble, into irrelevance, if only for a day. Saturn is the king of confidence here and knows that time is always on his side; even when personal and professional relationships are going through an awkward period of recalibration, temperaments always adjust to any perceived shifts in loyalty and trust. Many hindrances seemingly appear out of thin air and because of this, volatility it is absolutely vital to learn how to protect and nourish yourself first before jumping feet first into the fray.

This eclipse carries a tight Mars/Jupiter square Neptune midpoint notorious for hasty speculative decisions made under duress, so take as much time as you need before flashing those credit card and bank account numbers. And asking for help or reaching out for consensus is often the *wrong* way to go even though this is a lunar Libran eclipse. The NNode at the sixth degree of Aries is building your castle brick by brick so, once again, take your time. In the shifting winds of LS135, take comfort in the words of fellow alumni and mythologist

Joseph Campbell's realization that "We must let go of the life we have planned, so as to accept the one that is waiting for us."

Closest Midpoints: Mars/Jupiter-Neptune, Saturn/Venus-Neptune
Isotraps: Sun/Pluto conjunct Mercury/Saturn
Venus/Jupiter opposition Uranus/Neptune

1900—2100 Eclipses: Lunar Saros—135

1903, 1921, 1939, 1957, 1975, 1993, 2011, 2029, 2048, 2066, 2084
Length of cycle —1,262 years
Series ends—May 18, 2877

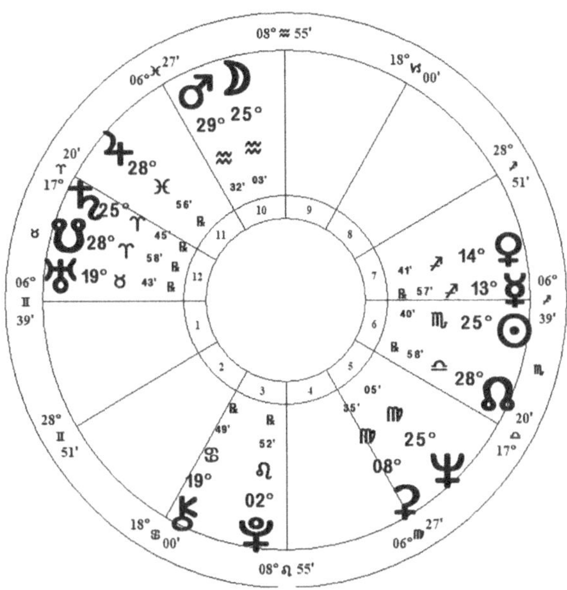

Margaret Atwood
PREBLE—LS135

November 18, 1939 • 5:00 PM • Ottawa, ON, Canada

Margaret Atwood—Slasher Extraordinaire

"Sooner or later, I hate to break it to you, you're gonna die. So how do you fill in the space between here and there? It's yours. Seize your space."

-MARGARET ATWOOD

Poet/novelist/literary critic/essayist/teacher/environmental activist, and inventor, Margaret Atwood is a certified "slasher"—her published works, awards, and honorary degrees from around the world are staggering in their number and significance. Her style encompasses themes of gender, religion, myth, and politics; since she began writing from an early age, Atwood has always given credit to the role that myths and fairy tales have played in her work.

Margaret Atwood's Connections to the Dragons of LS135
Saturn with Saturn
Neptune with Neptune

**1st Harmonics: Sun – SNode,
Sun – Saturn, Jupiter – Sun, Ceres – Moon/Mars, Neptune – Neptune
2nd Harmonic: Neptune – Jupiter**

Always look for similar planetary pictures or patterns between the two charts. Here what's most notable is Atwood's fully developed Jupiter opposition to her Neptune which brings to mind the emerging Jupiter sextile Neptune of the lunar eclipse. Robert Pelletier's *Planets in Aspect* gives the best description I've ever found for this sextile:

> "[It] shows that you are imaginative, articulate, and extremely hopeful about the future. You study human nature, trying to learn the lessons of the past for guidance in solving the problems of tomorrow . . . you will help publicize important social problems in order to arouse public response."[1]

This is so Margaret Atwood. Another luminary from LS135's vast treasure trove of master storytellers is Yuval Noah Harari and his science bestsellers *Sapiens: A Brief History of Humankind, Homo Deus: A Brief History of Tomorrow,* and *21 Lessons for the 21st Century*—all rich in the themes of happiness and suffering. The Jupiter/Neptune convergence is an alchemical reaction of realization, and in Atwood's case, it has found a home for full manifestation thanks to its 1st Harmonic Neptune with Neptune.

And here's another telling tale between Atwood and the lunar eclipse: they both share an almost identical mainframe isotrap. Atwood's foundational isotrap in her natal chart is an alignment between her Mercury/Venus and Saturn/Pluto, and in the eclipse we have a Sun/Pluto and Mercury/Saturn. What these isotraps bring is a very similar approach to problem solving with a highly focused and almost maniacal view of the situation. They resonate with maturity, and a willingness to do whatever it takes to get the job done. Isolation, self-discipline, and even renunciation are on tap if deemed necessary.

And as always, I've saved the best for last. Margaret Atwood has an Anchor: it's created by her Mars sextile to her SNode with Jupiter at the midpoint creating the fulcrum to its opposition to Neptune at the apex. Now it just so happens that the eclipse Neptune, as you can see from the list of harmonics, is in a 2nd Harmonic to that Jupiter, which completely sensitizes and grounds the growth, expansion, and aspirational nature of her Jupiter in Pisces. No wonder she was born to be a writer.

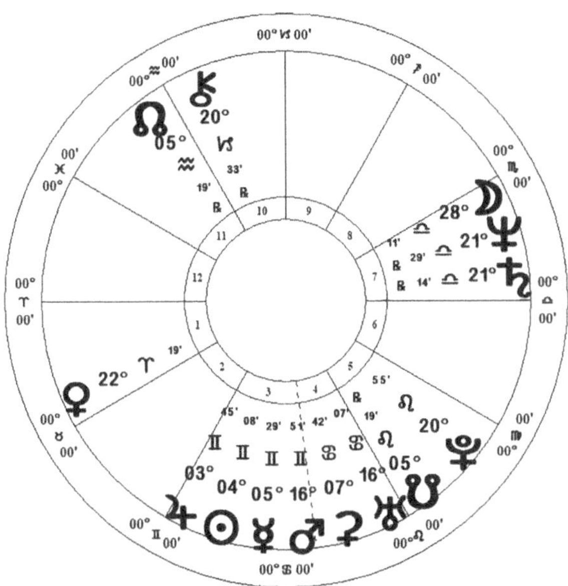

Eve "V" Ensler
PREBLE—LS123

May 25, 1953 • TOB Unknown • New York, NY, USA

The Vagina Monologues Launches One Billion Rising

"I'm living the dream."

-Eve Ensler

On February 14, 2012, Eve Ensler launched One Billion Rising, a global campaign to end rape and sexual violence against women. It was started in 2012 as part of the V-Day (V as in "vagina") movement. The "billion" in One Billion Rising refers to the UN statistic that one in three women—*worldwide*—will be raped or beaten in her lifetime, or about one billion.[2]

Eve Ensler's Connections to the Dragons of LS135
Moon with Moon
Saturn to Saturn

1st Harmonics: Moon - Saturn/Neptune, Sun - Venus
2nd Harmonic: Saturn - Saturn

On December 10, 2011, the lunar dragons of LS135 returned at 18 degrees Gemini activating Eve Ensler's feisty Mars at 16 Gemini. Fiery and feisty because it conjuncts the great military star of the ancients—Rigel, known for its command and control, wit and skill in the face of conflict or confrontation. It is one of the best stars to have at your back as it never backs down from conflict. Eve's Mars also conjuncts the great fixed star Bellatrix, known as the "Female Warrior" and is often referred to as the "Amazon Star."[3] Bellatrix is known for its daring and audacious manner of living in the moment where time-sensitive options are the order of the day. Bellatrix is a strategist and can always be counted on to summon the courage needed when critical decisions are needed. To have either one of these military stars on a Mars in Gemini is a back-stage pass to a world of speaking, writing, teaching, entertaining, and all of the above in a manner that both delights and educates the public.

The 1st Harmonic Moon-Saturn Cosmic Bridge is impressive as it activates a seed essence within the individual that can quickly germinate, take root, and embody the principles of the lunar eclipse axis. The twenty-third degree Aquarian overtones of the eclipse Moon are ripe for any collective action that challenges the accepted norms of male behavior as seen through the eclipse Moon square Mars. Ensler's Saturn at the twenty-first degree Sagittarian overtone is cosmic confirmation that her work must be global and underscored by universal principles of justice and freedom.

The 2nd Harmonic Saturn to Saturn is even more impressive as it plucks the strings of the eclipse Saturn/Venus-Neptune midpoint to awaken to accept a burden of duty that could take decades if not lifetimes to achieve. Eve Ensler's Saturn in her natal chart tightly conjuncts Neptune, making this 2nd Harmonic Saturn to Saturn resonance soulfully significant especially as it pertains to what possibly could be her life's work and dharma to alleviate suffering in the world.

Misha's Story

Misha was born on September 16, 1975, in Hobro, Denmark. She is a journalist/travel and hospitality blogger, wife, mother, and friend. She was born under LS130—To Boldly Go.

Misha sadly remarked on the high number of deaths around her from December 2011 until the spring of 2012. She said those winter months carried a lot of sorrow. "People died like flies around me in that period, not very close friends and family but close enough that it shook my world." At the time, she was pregnant but not happy being pregnant. She felt uncomfortable for almost the entire three months between December 2011 to March 2012. One of the friends that died was only thirty-eight and left a wife and two children behind.

When LS135 touched down in December 2011, it landed directly on her natal Mars at 18 Gemini and activated her Mars/Venus-Pluto midpoint. Knowing that this family of lunar eclipses carries a Venus/Pluto conjunction as part of its energy signature and is a contributing factor to the high levels of anxiety and loss experienced by many, the arrival of LS135 was not good news. My client told me that her husband's father lost his best friend in this time period, a man who had been, as she told me, "like a second grandfather to us." And then after all the funerals, the loss of her baby in March 2012 was almost too much to bear. With Mars in Gemini, her life is a continual process of refinement as she acclimates well to diversity and on-going adjustment. Misha has many Grand Air Trines that bring ever-changing perspectives into her life.

With five direct celestial DNA markers tying her destiny to that of LS135, it came as no surprise that her life would resonate so strongly to the theme of loss and endings, fear and frustration, especially considering the miscarriage and her poor health that followed. Misha's chart is instructive in that her natal Sun is at 23 Virgo, making it in exact inconjunct to LS135's Sun at 23 Aries. Of note: on its previous return in 1993, she was recovering after a prolonged six-month hospitalization.

My client was both in fear of and fascinated by this recurring wave of strife that was contributing to her massive levels of upset on an eighteen year cycle of suffering.

LS135 Summary

Getting through tough times is what makes a story great, and these Air Dragons are master storytellers. Their struggles and difficulties help turn the everyday straw of life into bankable gold, gleaming in the luster of personal satisfaction. With every return, these Air Dragons encourage release, flexibility and an openness to the rise and fall of fortune. Their presence is a reminder that life is in a constant dance of impermanence held together, only momentarily, by the glue and gutsiness of our values and choices. And as our values and choices change so too do our outer world experiences take on new forms of expression.

This family of eclipses is currently moving through a highly agitated Disseminating Phase that began in 1993. There will be a commensurate level of high stress associated with births or returns of this series until it reaches its Last Quarter phase in 2066. It is important to acknowledge that this lunar eclipse series lives in an almost perpetual crisis mode mentality that can generate more than its fair share of doubt and inadequacy. Pitfalls seem to be lurking behind every corner as life becomes a game of Snakes and Ladders where one day you're up and the next day you're sliding down into insanity. To keep yourself clear from any psychopathic pit of pain that might be lurking nearby, it is absolutely imperative to have at least one friendly line of communication available. As you've read, there is a collective spirit to this eclipse that can be counted on to pull you back from the brink. And that's a good thing because the brink is no laughing matter when it has its own zip line direct to LS135 HQ.

The benefits obtained from these lunar dragons are found in one's ability to focus on specific details of an issue for long periods of time. Any area that requires research, specialization, precision, technical detail, or excellent technique will blossom under the watch of these dragons. Their visit reminds us that a daily routine without a problem to solve or an issue to get through is just flat out boring and too prosaic for words. In fact, words may just be what will turn your life around as you embrace the fear and frustration but also the fascination of what magic may be playing out behind the scenes. Through foul weather or fair, your capacity to endure will become the stuff of legends.

LS135 Luminaries

Thomas Carlyle	December 4, 1795
Marie Curie	November 7, 1867
Niels Bohr	October 7, 1885
Vladimir Horowitz	October 1, 1903 (NS)
Cary Grant	January 18, 1904
Dr. Suess	March 2, 1904
Rodney Dangerfield	November 22, 1921
Steve Allen	December 26, 1921
Betty White	January 17, 1922
Jack Kerouac	12 March 1922
John Cleese [E1]	October 27, 1939
Margaret Atwood	November 18, 1939
Jack Nicklaus	January 21, 1940
Mario Andretti	February 28, 1940
Ray Romano	December 21, 1957
Ellen DeGeneres	January 26, 1958
Ice-T	February 16, 1958
Holly Hunter	March 20, 1958
Tiger Woods	December 30, 1975
Chai Jing	January 1, 1976
Yuval Noah Harari	February 24, 1976
Peyton Manning	March 24, 1976
Dakota Fanning	February 23, 1994
Justin Bieber	March 1, 1994
Saoirse Ronan	April 12, 1994
Alexander Gould	May 4, 1994

PREBLE—130
John Cleese

1. Robert Pelletier, *Planets in Aspect*, p. 109.
2. https://en.wikipedia.org/wiki/One_Billion_Rising. Retrieved June 16, 2022.
3. Richard H. Allen, *Star Names*, p. 313.

LUNAR SAROS 136

"Contrary to public opinion, the bustle is not a new dance step; It is an old business procedure."

-FRAN LEBOWITZ

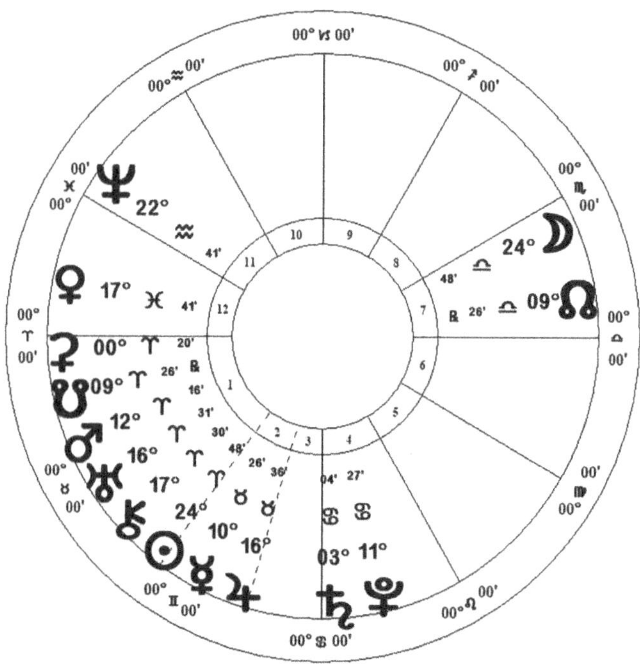

Lunar Saros 136

April 13, 1680 • 11:35:16 PM • North Pole

Risk and Reward

Finding balance through courage and creativity is at the heart of this North Node Libran eclipse. The time to reconcile your life has arrived with all the commensurate levels of risk and reward associated with liberation. Ruler Venus is both exalted in Pisces and at a Critical Degree allowing her spirit of devotion and sacrifice to rise to fit almost every occasion. Her MR to Jupiter in Taurus suggests that there will be financial repercussions along the way as Venus *is* the beloved, entangled in a world of form and fantasy. The eclipse moon, as the handle on a Fan formation and at the twenty-fourth degree of Libra, commands the entire field making recalibration an essential element in all fields of endeavor.

The Pluto square to the nodal axis supports the entire eclipse structure and gives the feeling of destiny and the ability to wield power over others. A sense of omnipotence floods the field. US Chief Justice Clarence Thomas has the square from Taurus to Leo, actress Carrie Fisher has it with her Pluto in Virgo, and actor Robert Duvall has an identical phase symmetry with his SNode Aries in square to Pluto in Cancer. The Pluto Node square is a pathway to public prominence that often includes an absolute or idealistic identification with an extreme point of view rather than a more flexible and pragmatic approach.

LS136's singleton Libran Moon is a sure sign that aesthetic tastes, charm, and the powers of persuasion will prevail. And when all else fails, self-indulgence and sacrifice are always on tap. Note the quindecile aspects to Mercury and Mars along with the electrifying Uranus-Chiron conjunction in Aries opposing the eclipse Moon. This family is not going to go without and has, thanks to the Venus-Jupiter sextile in MR, all the necessary and required resources at their disposal.

In fact, striving to secure material wealth or at least financial stability is as natural as breathing for this lunar eclipse and its zero degrees Ceres at the AP, the only lunar eclipse out of the entire 47 Lunar Saros Series that features Ceres at this singularly significant degree. Ceres and its square to Saturn are both looking to increase their internal states of security and well-being through the accumulation of money, cash, capital, opulence, and prosperity by any and all means possible. The Aries stellium square to a Saturn-Pluto conjunction in Cancer with Mars at the sensitive twelfth degree in Aries is not averse to risk-taking as the perceived rewards appear manageable.

Jeff Green's, *Pluto The Evolutionary Journey of the Soul, Volume 1*, refers to "skipped steps" and an individual's "bottom line" when Pluto squares the nodal axis. I encourage you to take his theory for a test run. Here, Pluto applies to the South Node which gives Venus, as ruler of the Libran North Node, a special role to play. In Pisces, the glamour of Venus is deliciously alluring, especially as she sits at the very proud seventeenth degree, veiled in robes of paradox and pleasure.

To engage with the energy of this vortex requires one to pay attention to the twin gatekeepers of risk and reward, especially where the entropy of antiquated behavior is reinforcing a reluctance to tackle the tasks that are diminishing the vitality of your relationships. This is especially cogent considering its Mercury/Venus-Saturn midpoint with its issues of faithfulness, self-torment, jealousy, suffering, marked age along with status differences between partners and a multiplicity of separations that accompany these difficulties.

Closest Midpoints: Mercury/Venus-Saturn, Neptune/Mars-Saturn
Isotraps: Sun/Saturn conjunct Uranus/Pluto
Mercury/Venus conjunct Mars/Uranus

1900—2100 Eclipses: Lunar Saros—136

1914, 1932, 1950, 1968, 1986, 2004, 2022, 2040, 2058, 2076, 2094
Length of cycle —1,280 years
Series ends— June 1, 2960

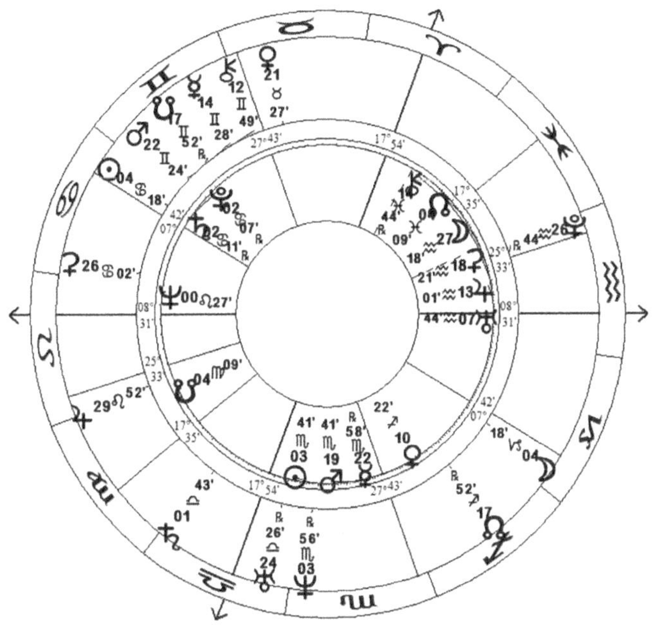

Inside

Dylan Thomas

PREBLE—LS136

October 27, 1914 • 11:00 PM • Swansea, Wales

Outside

LS128

June 26, 1304 • 9:32 AM • North Pole

The Doomed Poet

Do not go gentle into that good night,
Old age should burn and rave at close of day;
Rage, rage against the dying of the light.

-Dylan Thomas

Dylan Thomas was one of the most gifted poets of the 20th century; however, heavy drinking, chronic health problems, physical exhaustion, problems in his marriage, and struggling to write through all of this while being in a constant state of debt brought on his death at the age of thirty-nine.

His chart holds some extraordinary energy patterns: Venus at an extreme OOB 27S34 accelerated by a rare Sun Moon and Mars Jupiter parallel declination within minutes of exactitude with contra-parallel declinations of the same tightness between Mars and Pluto and Jupiter and Pluto. A rare find indeed is his Pluto-Saturn conjunction in Cancer but mirrored back as a Saturn-Pluto conjunction in Cancer in the eclipse field, a remarkable cosmic pairing capable of producing heightened amplitude and levels of resonance across their fields. Its 1st Harmonic Neptune to Dylan's Sun gives him the gift of the muse as it brings its own magic through its Neptune sextile Sun and trine Moon. When delineating the PREBLE charts of creative people there is almost always a Neptune aspect that links to the artist and if that link is to their Sun or Moon you can be assured that their parents played a supportive role. That was certainly true for Dylan Thomas' dad David John (D. J.) Thomas. Dylan's daughter Hannah Ellis writes:

> Dylan's father was the man that introduced his son to poetry and showed him the power of words and the mysteries that language holds. We can certainly, in part, thank D.J. for Dylan Thomas' magical poetry. He ensured there were opportunities and resources available to his son to help him discover the joys of literature. A friend of Dylan's, Bert Trick, described visiting the family home. "Every room you went into in the Thomas' house was strewn with books. Even in the kitchen, they'd be under the kitchen table, up on the sideboard, piled with books."[1]

As fascinating as his PREBLE is, what I want to showcase here is the ability of a Lunar Saros Series to predict or at least indicate difficult health trends coming your way. I stumbled on this aspect of lunar eclipse prognostication after comparing the birth charts of deceased family members to the Lunar Saros eclipse that was active at the time of death. Here's what I found and will demonstrate by using the chart of LS128, the last active lunar eclipse in the life of Dylan Thomas.

Dylan Thomas' Connections to the Dragons of LS128

1st Harmonics: Moon – VI, Neptune – Sun, Pluto – Moon/VIII
2nd Harmonics: Moon – Saturn/Pluto,
Jupiter – Moon, Venus – Mars/Mercury, Mercury/Chiron – Venus

Lunar Saros 128 returned on July 26, 1953, at 3 degrees Aquarius, activating Dylan Thomas' Uranus, ruler of his Seventh and Eighth Houses and part of a Fixed T-Square with Neptune and the Sun. The Sun is a classic indicator of vitality and in his chart it is a Focal Determinator as it sits at the leg of his Fixed T-Square while Uranus and Neptune straddle the ASC/DSC axis. He would fall desperately ill within three months and die on November 9, 1953. The eclipse Neptune at 3 Scorpio 56 sat on his Sun at 3 Scorpio 41 and squared his natal Neptune.

However what initially drew my focus was the eclipse axis on his Sixth/Twelfth House cusps and the importance of Saturn as ruler of his Sixth House in conjunction with Pluto and all that eclipse axis energy streaming into that Saturn-Pluto. His Saturn rules his Sixth and at 2 Cancer 11 squares the eclipse Saturn at 1 Cancer 43 which is the Focal Determinator of the eclipse Sun/Moon/Saturn Cardinal T-Square. The eclipse axis not only lit up his Saturn-Pluto, but its trine to his natal Sun in the Fourth instantly reignited his childhood bouts of bronchitis and asthma, conditions which were a constant source of physical strain on his vitality.

Now let's look at the eclipse Fixed Jupiter/Pluto/Venus T-Square and all that energy pouring into his natal Moon/NNode conjunction on his Eighth House cusp with Pluto in command. I was reminded of Komilla Sutton's thoughts on the Moon-NNode pairing when she wrote:

> When the Moon is placed with Rahu [NNode] all the things which the Moon represents will suffer. Rahu causes fear, anxiety and distrust. Issues from the past may impede your growth in the form of fears or phobias that you cannot rationalize, and you may lean too heavily on drink or drugs.[2]

Over the next three months his health would rapidly take a serious turn for the worse. The eclipse Pluto on his Moon/NNode would be one more nail in the coffin while the eclipse Sun was burning through his natal Saturn-Pluto. The last eclipse pattern would prove too much to bear: the Grand Air Trine's Mars/Uranus/Pluto would be the final straw. If anything in astrology works 100 percent of the time, it is the speed at which trines operate, and here we have Pluto once again back in action and wasting no time. Now it was *really* starting to look bad.

By the time Dylan Thomas arrived in New York on October 20 for his US lecture tour, he was already in serious decline, suffering from bronchitis and pneumonia.[3] He was admitted in the early morning hours of November 6 to St Vincent's Hospital in New York; he was in a coma and would never awaken. He died at noon on November 9, 1953.

The transits to both charts are stunning. Transiting Saturn at 2 Scorpio was on the eclipse Neptune at 3 Scorpio and his natal Sun at 3 Scorpio. Transiting Neptune was within a 3 minute arc of exactitude to the eclipse Uranus. Transiting Sun at 17 Scorpio was within 2 degrees of his natal Mars at 19 Scorpio and the transiting Moon at 20 Sagittarius had just made a conjunction to his NNode six hours earlier, reminiscent of his natal Moon-NNode conjunction.

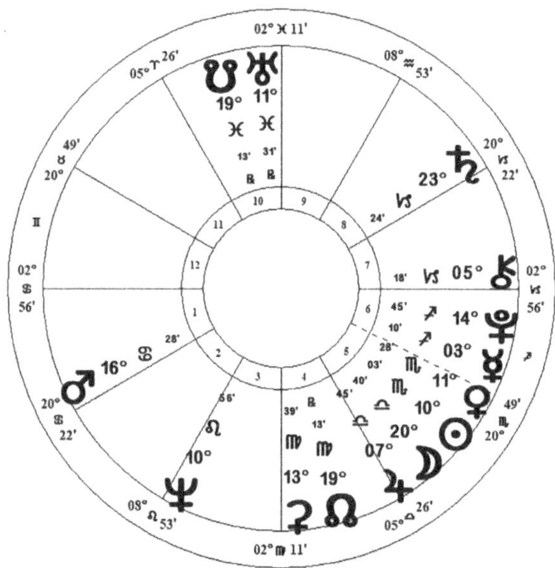

Marie Antoinette
PREBLE—LS133

November 2, 1755 • 7:30 PM • Vienna, Austria

Madame Déficit/Queen of France

"Let them eat cake."

-Marie Antoinette

Marie Antoinette, born in Austria, was Dauphine of France from 1770 to 1774 and Queen of France from 1774 to her execution on October 16, 1793. On June 8, 1770, LS136 unfurled its banner and announced to all its presence at 17 Sagittarius, capturing her Pluto and its nodal square on the Virgo/Pisces axis of service and sacrifice. Marie Antoinette's marriage took place within the three week window leading up to the eclipse. On May 16, 1770, she married the future King Louie XVI to strengthen the French-Austrian alliance.

With her own Pluto at the bends mirroring LS136's Pluto at the bends, a double element of fate came into her life but one that she must have been well prepared for since her Pluto holds a waxing square to her SNode. This is often a hereditary and obligatory pattern of power that forces an individual into a new life path or lifestyle that is orthogonal to one's native roots. Pluto is the lord purveyor of pain, sex, and secrets and it was no secret that the marriage was an unhappy one and unconsummated for many years. In the frivolous world of the French court's aristocratic debauchery, you can't blame her for finding comfort and relief in her lavish lifestyle of gambling, partying, and personal spending. She was, after all, a teenager on foreign soil. Her name would be forever linked to excess and the collapse of the monarchy.

Marie Antoinette's Connections to the Dragons of LS136

1st Harmonics: Moon – Moon,
NNode – Jupiter, Venus – SNode, Saturn – ASC
2nd Harmonics: Uranus/Chiron – Moon, Mercury – Sun, Saturn – Chiron

No less than five CBs were to magically appear that would unite her sphere of influence with that of the returning Lunar Saros 136 in June of 1770. Most impressive was the stellar blessing from the eclipse 1st Harmonic Moon to her Moon, a diplomatic Moon in Libra match and one for the record books. The nodal markers on both sides were activated: an eclipse NNode to her Jupiter and an eclipse Venus to her SNode to seal the deal and make the love match legal. Marie's Jupiter at the seventh degree of Libra was a double dip of partnership, fashion, beauty, charm, and luxury that gave her, by law, carte blanche access to the kingdom. Finally, there is her triple Pluto-Sun-Venus in parallel declination to the eclipse 2nd Harmonic Mercury at the tenth degree of Taurus that would grant her de facto rights and claims through marriage to the Dauphin, Louie, and, as the Dauphine of France, to lands, title, wealth, and ascension befitting the future Queen of France.

At the time of the eclipse, LS136 was in its Crescent phase, having just entered this phase in 1752 on its 5th return. In 1770, as the Dauphine of France, Marie Antoinette was living out the full effects of this phase during which one is literally torn in two directions. Such changes now require a path that can accommodate a new direction. Often a very public presentation of self accompanies this phase as individuals pursue interests that lay down a new foundation that reflects a bigger and bolder statement in the life.

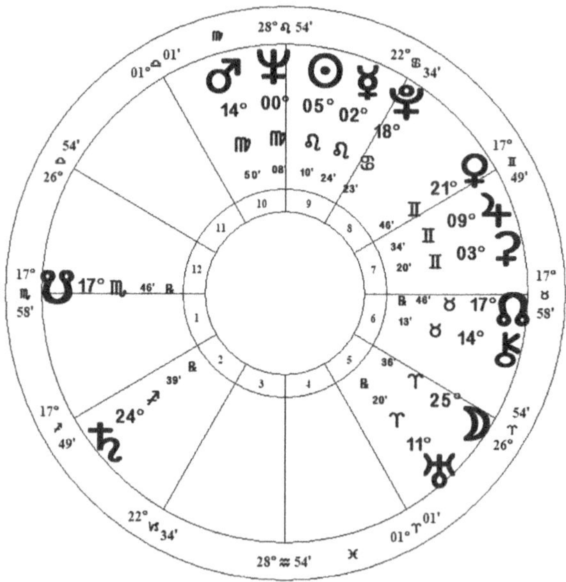

Jackie Onassis
PREBLE—LS139

July 28, 1929 • 2:30 PM • Southampton, NY, USA

America's Queen of Camelot

"The first time you marry for love, the second for money, and the third for companionship."

-Jackie O

The assassination of President John F. Kennedy in Dallas, Texas, on November 22, 1963, made Jacqueline Bouvier Kennedy—beloved as "Jackie"— the most famous widow in the world. Tragedy would strike again with the death of her brother-in-law Robert Kennedy in June 1968. Fearing for her life and those of her children, she left the United States and shocked the world with her marriage on October 20, 1968, to wealthy Greek shipping magnate Aristotle Onassis.[4] LS136 enabled her to forge alliances that promoted her family's safety without compromising her need for personal freedom.

April's LS131 landed at 23 Libra opposite her Aries Moon and its waning square to Pluto, setting off instinctive, predatory alarm bells for security and safety. By embracing her Moon, April's eclipse invoked the power of her singleton Saturn conjunct the Galactic Core, which contributed to her decision to leave the United States. LS136 arrived in October at 13 Aries on her waning Sun trine Uranus to strategically position not only her privacy and safety, but more importantly, her autonomy and international status as a celebrity. She calculated the risk/reward ratio and on October 20, 1968, married her longtime friend and mega millionaire Aristotle Onassis two weeks after the arrival of LS136, securing a world of safety far from the brutality and political turbulence of the United States. Here she could feel protected by the immense financial resources of one of the world's most famous and influential shipping magnates and his empire of elegance and luxury regardless of their widely divergent backgrounds, temperaments, and age. Sarah Bradford, in her biography *America's Queen*, wrote that, "Onassis fed Jackie's fantasy of the Mediterranean as an escape from America."[5] LS136 reinforced her ability to handle problems diplomatically; with elegance and sophistication she would use her newfound connections as a tool to begin to build the next chapter in her life.

Jackie Onassis's Connections to the Dragons of LS136
Uranus with Uranus
Pluto with Pluto

1st Harmonics: SNode/Mars – Uranus, Jupiter – NNode/DSC
2nd Harmonics: Moon – Moon, Venus – Mars

Compatibility aside, the dynamics of these two charts are reinforced through their similarities as Bucket pattern charts with an astonishingly identical Last Quarter Uranus in Aries square Pluto in Cancer. Remember—these two charts are separated by a span of 249 years. Trilateral markers through Jackie's Moon, NNode, and Uranus to LS136's Sun, Jupiter, and Mars denote a wealth of evidence in support of connections to this eclipse family's Dragon

DNA. Her 2nd Harmonic Cosmic Bridge Moon to her natal Moon again reinforces the ability of 2nd Harmonics to "bring it on" by whatever means is required to make the necessary changes. This is never truer than when the Moon is involved. To date, all the research confirms the power of a 2nd Harmonic Moon/Moon contact to implement much needed change in a domestic environment and/or in an emotional relationship that needs anything from repair to renunciation.

Jackie's involvement with this eclipse occurred during its seventeenth return at the end of a Gibbous phase known for its ability to overcome resistance, to take control, and to work with what you have already achieved. It fosters growth through accurate analysis with a focus on the details that help you connect the dots. By the eighteenth return of LS136 in October 1986, and its brand new Full Moon phase, Jackie's life would reflect the Lunar Saros Series' evolution as its progression into this full-of-life phase would find her in a celebratory mood, reaping the rewards and enjoying the harvest of a life filled with conscious illumination.

LS136 Summary

Relationships have definitely been a first priority with these high-flying Air Dragons since they entered their rosy-cheeked Full Moon phase in 1986. And with every return, they are just getting better and better at figuring out what's worthy of their time and attention. Any reluctance to avoid confrontation is fast falling by the wayside as their ability to bargain for a better slice of the pie gets stronger with every return. There is a marked unwillingness to put up with issues of infidelity in relationships and one-sided effort in all forms of partnerships. The risk versus reward ratio that underpins the entire sphere's energy of engagement is rapidly accelerating as it moves through the Full Moon phase bringing greater levels of refinement and sharper tools of wit and wisdom to the negotiation table.

To be in harmony with this Lunar Saros Series whether by birthright or rite of passage requires a willingness to be in the most difficult relationship of all, namely the one with yourself. Because in this relationship all bets are off when it comes to tallying up the risk versus the reward factors; it isn't so much a numbers game as it is an intuitive art form that will help you make the right decisions. Hard work plays a key role in this endeavor as tests of internal strength seem to continually emerge that require perseverance and the conviction that one is able to meet any challenge head on. The rewards of vibrant energy and sheer joy come to those willing to partner up with risk as you dance your way through the conga line of resistance. Meanwhile, on the expressway of life, we're all going to have to find the exits and on-ramps that will take us to our next destination. An understanding of this lunar eclipse is comforting and downright essential if we want to give each other some slack in how we appreciate each other and, even more importantly, how we appreciate ourselves. Pay attention. Cosmic Lane Change Ahead.

Phase	Return	Year
First Quarter	9th	1824
Gibbous	13th	1896
Full Moon	18th	1986
Disseminating	22nd	2058

LS136 Luminaries

Joseph Stalin	December 18, 1878
Swami Prabhupada	September 1, 1896
F Scott Fitzgerald	September 24, 1896
Joe DiMaggio	November 25, 1914
Dorothy Lamour	December 10, 1914
Alan Watts	January 6, 1915
John Lilly	January 5, 1915
Sylvia Plath	October 27, 1932
Roy Scheider	November 10, 1932
Little Richard	December 5, 1932
Corazon Aquino	January 25, 1933
Fran Lebowitz	October 27, 1950
John Candy	October 31, 1950
Chesley Sullenberger	January 23, 1951
Phil Collins	January 30, 1951
Michael Schumacher	January 3, 1969

Jason Bateman	January 14, 1969
Jennifer Aniston	February 11, 1969
Javier Bardem	March 1, 1969
Drake	October 24, 1986
Aaron Swartz	November 8, 1986
Elliot Page	February 21, 1987
Kesha	March 1, 1987

---

1. Hanna Ellis www.lovethewords.co.uk. December 16, 2017 https://www.discoverdylanthomas.com/d-j-thomas-man-introduced-dylan-thomas-poetry. Retrieved July 28, 2022.
2. Komilla Sutton, *The Lunar Nodes Crisis & Redemption*, p. 101
3. https://en.wikipedia.org/wiki/Dylan_Thomas. Retrieved July 28, 2022.
4. Sarah Bradford, *America's Queen: The Life of Jacqueline Kennedy Onassis* (New York: Viking, 2000), p. 327.
5. Ibid.

LUNAR SAROS 139

"It is impossible to live without failing at something, unless you live so cautiously that you might as well not have lived at all – in which case, you fail by default."

-J. K. Rowling

Lunar Saros 139

December 9, 1658 • 8:27:46 PM • South Pole

Truth or Dare

Pluto dominates this South Node Gemini eclipse by its tight 1 degree conjunction to the Moon, bringing an intensity of emotion unlike any other Lunar Saros Series. Dramatic, transformative, and often drastic changes in living conditions accompany these controversial dragons who are no strangers to personal and social upheaval. SNode eclipses invite the release of accumulated energy and often come with a bill to pay; demolition, reconstruction, and realignment are all in a day's work for Lord Pluto.

Two sets of mutual reception significantly expand the scope of possibility: Jupiter's placement in Leo and the Sun in Sagittarius fuel far-reaching aspirations of glory fortified and sanctioned by the ethical considerations of Venus in Aquarius and the judgment and hard-earned wisdom of Saturn in Libra. Retrograde Jupiter's enhanced status spills over into its trine with Mercury, adding an extra level of confidence and optimism to any foreign or domestic travel agenda.

Including the NNode of the Moon, LS139 is the only lunar eclipse out of the entire series of 47 eclipse families to have Mars, Venus, Mercury, Sun, Uranus, and Neptune all in parallel declination—a truly rare cosmic event. The declination of any celestial object is found by locating its vertical angle above or below the celestial equator, much as we use latitude 00 at the equator and 90 degrees at the North and South Poles to coordinate and locate geographical positions. Within this powerhouse alignment, Neptune and Uranus hold steady at 22S27 at the same exact degree and minute with Mercury just two minutes of declination further south. The synergy of these three planets gives Mercury even more amplitude to make a media splash. In combination with the satisfaction principles personified by the planets Mars and Venus, the Sun commands extraordinary pathways to power and personal growth.

The innovation and eccentricity of this lunar eclipse is clearly seen in its isotrap configurations, especially since all members of the isotraps are in parallel declination. LS139 features a one-of-a-kind Chiron/Neptune conjunction which is supposed to lead to spiritual awareness but that might prove difficult since the energy is expressed through a corporate veil that prefers dividends over divinity. Its quindecile aspect to the eclipse Moon/Pluto puts it on a bumpy road to nirvana, requiring constant physical and emotional tune-ups. The quindecile (165 degree) aspect is linked to disruptions and obsessive determination and a good discussion of the quindecile aspect can be found at Noel Tyl's website. [1]

Whether we measure the might of this family of eclipses by its effects on an individual or its place in the grand scheme of cultural syntax, it is important to recognize its ethical reverberations along with its capacity for loss. To that end, LS139 at its best is a beacon of light in a world that has lost its moral compass. Court cases and legal trials bring far reaching consequences with continual calls for investigations, inquiries, and commissions. It is a time to discuss foreign and domestic policy and legislation that can serve to restore order out of the growing sense of chaos and injustice that constitute the daily news.

Closest Midpoints: Mercury/Pluto-Node, Neptune/Eclipse-Uranus
Isotraps: Mercury/Uranus conjunct Venus/Mars
Sun/Venus conjunct Uranus/Neptune

1900—2100 Eclipses: Lunar Saros—139

1911, 1929, 1947, 1965, 1983, 2001, 2019, 2037, 2055, 2073, 2091
Length of cycle —1,406 years
Series ends—April 13, 3065

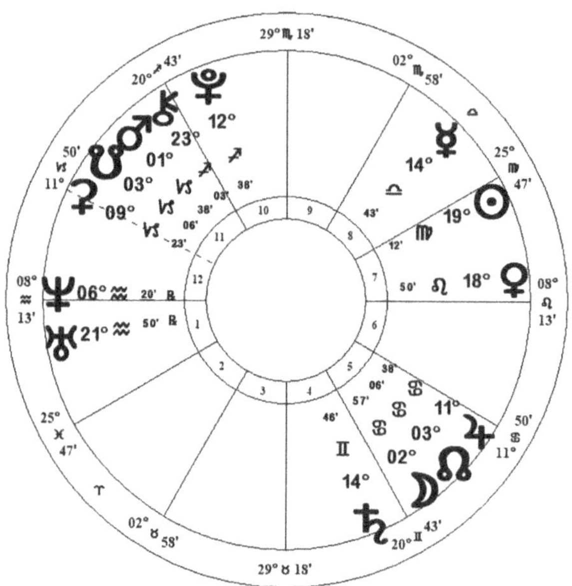

World Trade Center Building 7 Collapse
PREBLE—LS139

September 11, 2001 • 5:20:33 PM • New York, NY, USA

"Perhaps the best thing to do is to pull it!"

-LARRY SILVERSTEIN[2]

The devastation that brought down the three buildings at the World Trade Center (WTC) on 9/11/2001 occurred in the aftermath of LS139's touchdown at 14 Capricorn on July 5, 2001. Three buildings? you may ask. The collapse of the Twin Towers, the first two buildings, is seared into our collective memory. But there was a third building: WTC Building 7 was not hit by a plane. It was hundreds of feet away from the closest Twin Tower. But at 5:20 pm on the afternoon of 9/11, it seemingly spontaneously collapsed.

At the very moment that WTC 7 began to collapse, the transiting Moon/NNode was igniting the explosive AP/OOB Mars/SNode on the Cancer/Capricorn axis of security. At the same time, retrograde Neptune was rising up into the veiled and shadowed realm of the Twelfth House.

Before noting the connections across the lunar landscapes of these two fields, it will prove useful to wander into the world of Fixed Stars for a moment. A portion of an AstroMap calculated by Matrix software Sirius 3.0 for the northeastern United States shows an alarming line-up of celestial troublemakers. Notice the width of the line representing Alcyone to the east of New York—that's power—that's the Pleiades anchoring the base of the chart at 29 degrees Taurus. At Jamie Partridge's Astrology King website, he states that "Alcyone and the whole Pleiades group are noted for their association with deep sorrows and tragedies, bereavements."[3] I agree. As an astrologer using the fixed stars for decades and a graduate of Bernadette Brady's Fixed Star Diploma, the difficulties associated with Alcyone and especially sisters Electra and Merope far outnumber their benefits. The 29th degree of Taurus and now 00 Gemini are ecliptic eye-openers and any planets or stars rising, culminating, setting and anti-culminating to those degrees are significant bellwethers.

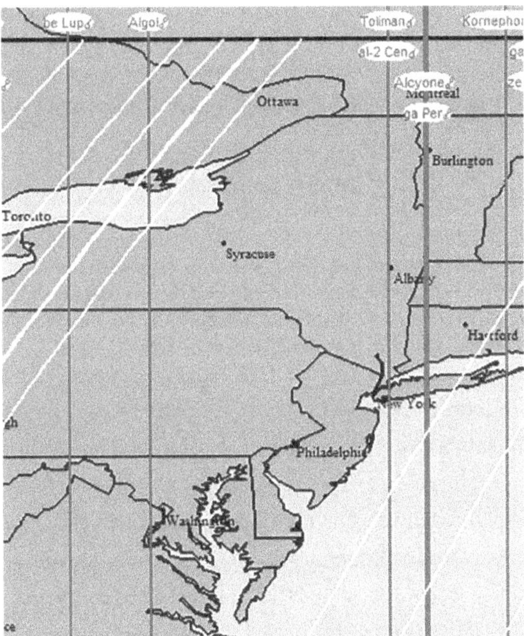

As nerve-racking as it is to have the Pleiades at the IC, look who's on top! It's Toliman, the third brightest star and the alpha star of the constellation Centaurus— its line of power runs right through the heart of New York City! It is moments away from an exact conjunction to the MC. Toliman at the Tenth would bring its full presence to bear witness to the mythological drama of Chiron and its capacity for suffering and sacrifice. As a fixed star, Toliman represents our ability to actually *learn something* from our failures. The destruction of the WTC 7 building and the horrific wounding of that day is a frightening symbol of the power carried within these Air Dragons that remind us of our collective bitterness, cynicism, and the inescapable failings and flaws of our human existence.

I don't recall where I learned this but somewhere in my astrological past Al Morrison summed up Chiron brilliantly. He called it an "inconvenient benefic." He said that Chiron always offers a profound gift but its gift-giving and the events surrounding it are almost always on the shocking side. Maybe that's why we actually learn something no matter how gradual it may seem. Some of you might be thinking, "Hey, what about Algol, it's over there, just off to the west of Washington—what about *that* fixed star?" Yes, Algol is another holy terror of the night skies with a bloody family history to boot. But its influence has more to do with the geo-politics of what happened in Washington, D.C. so for now, that tale of treachery awaits its own day of reckoning.

WTC Building 7 Collapse Connections to the Dragons of LS139

Space Lanes via MC/IC
Chiron with Chiron
Pluto to Pluto

1st Harmonics: Chiron/Neptune – Mars/SNode,
Moon – Saturn, Sun – Chiron, Sun – Pluto,
Venus – Neptune/ASC, Mars – MC, Mercury – Pluto, Jupiter – Venus
2nd Harmonic: Mercury – Saturn

There is something other-worldly about Space Lanes coming down from high above, entering as they do through the MC Tenth and exiting through the IC Fourth House. These SLs are powered by the nodal axis and in particular the NNode at 2 degrees Gemini. On the day of their birth on December 9, 1658, Lunar Saros 139's NNode aligned to the Hyades, a star cluster known in Greek mythology as "The Rainy Ones" for their relationship to rain as well as to their connection to bringing tears of sadness and loss. You may recall its influence in LS134, another member of the Air Dragon clan. A review of the Fixed Star literature, especially on Hyades I, the brightest star in the Hyades cluster, reveals a tragic influence and a classic association with grief.

There can be no denying that at 5:20 pm on that fated day of 9/11, even more hell and misery was to rain down a sea of tears. Together, the eclipse Chiron and Neptune would create an unparalleled Cosmic Bridge of sheer terror; that moment's 1st Harmonic SNode/OOB Mars in Capricorn would concretize a collective fear of terrorism that would become a permanent feature of not only the American landscape but of the world.

The cosmos does seem to favor back-up plans: Neptune, as earlier stated, was rising into the Twelfth House minutes before Building 7 was destroyed. As Neptune rose, it would resonate with the eclipse field's fifth degree Venus in Aquarius setting a new precedent for how things were going to be done in the future. Thank goodness we haven't yet entered that illustrious and longed-for Age of Aquarius! There is still a lot of work that is going to have to get done before we sing the praises of our collective shared humanity. An astounding fact about the events of 9/11 is how few people even realized that the WTC Building 7 had collapsed, so shaken was the world by the horrific acts of criminality and unimaginable catastrophe that had consumed the day.

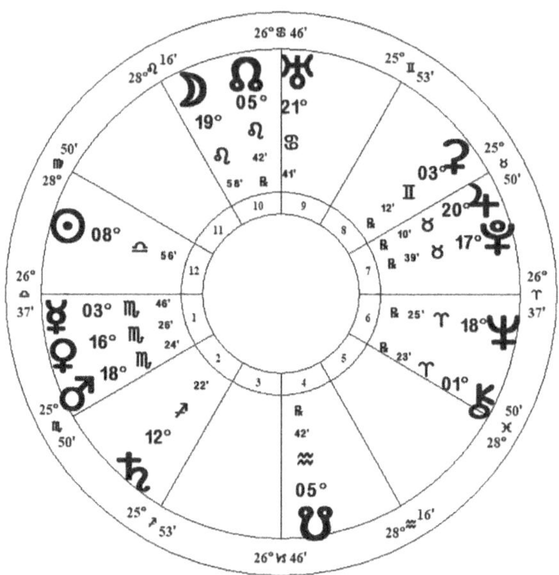

Mohandas Gandhi
PREBLE—LS117

October 2, 1869 • 7:11 AM • Porbandar, India

"Live simply so that others may simply live."

Mahatma/Bapu/Great Soul

"Even if you are a minority of one, the truth is the truth."

-Mahatma Gandhi

Known as Mahatma—Great Soul—Mohandas Gandhi was the legendary inspiring force of Indian nationalism that rose up against British rule. Gandhi led India to independence while inspiring movements for non-violence, civil rights, and freedom across the world. The events that followed the eclipse on May 1, 1893, can all be sourced back to its activation at 11 Scorpio. In Gandhi's natal chart his Venus is at 16 Scorpio conjunct Mars at 18 Scorpio. Together they form a formidable powerhouse and fixed T-Square that engages a Jupiter/Pluto conjunction in Taurus and his dignified Moon in Leo.

History tells us that Gandhi's first act of civil disobedience occurred on June 7, 1893, when, refusing to move to a third-class seat while holding a first-class ticket, he was "pushed off the train in the middle of the night, in the middle of winter, his luggage hastily thrown after him." Gandhi later recalled:

> I was afraid for my very life. I entered the dark waiting room. There was a white man in the room. I was afraid of him. What was my duty? I asked myself. Should I go back to India or should I go forward with God as my helper, and face whatever was in store for me? I decided to stay and suffer. My active non-violence began from that date.[4]

Gandhi's willingness to stand up in the face of power while he stayed and suffered the atrocities of colonialism brought forth a total realignment of his being while inspiring millions of people around the world to treat each other with the dignity of fairness and equanimity. By tapping into the power of LS139 and its lessons of internal security and idealism, Gandhi risked his life and left a legacy of peace and non-violence that the world is still trying to comprehend. His truth was to always stand up to meet the face of tyranny, proving that the realm of darkness, however deep, must eventually yield to the light of day.

Gandhi's Connections to the Dragons of LS139

1st Harmonic: Sun – Sun
Midpoints: Mercury – Venus/Saturn, Saturn/Pluto, Sun/Saturn, Sun – Sun/Mercury, Saturn – Jupiter/Neptune, Ceres – Mercury/Mars

Gandhi was born under PREBLE-117—Searching—the first family of Air Dragons in this section. However, his spirit is universal and beloved by LS139's Venus, giving them unrestricted access to his SNode bandwidth, especially considering his Uranus at 21 Cancer was in opposition to the eclipse family's Uranus at 19 Capricorn. Such free-flowing awareness would enable Mahatma to do what needed doing to bring freedom and independence to his homeland. In addition, his Saturn at 12 Sagittarius received universal solidarity from LS139's media savvy Mercury at 11 Sagittarius. Finally, the lunar eclipse SNode at 2 Gemini was a solid source of support continually grounding his 3 degree Ceres with its talent and love for communication.

The lunar eclipse of May 1, 1893, set off an avalanche of turmoil that would ultimately crack open the holy seal of colonial power and British imperialism of the late 19th century. Overcoming a status quo entrenched with anachronistic attitudes was a challenge Gandhi whole-heartedly rose to meet, spurred on by a vision of equality and a future that would uphold the rights of each and every citizen, regardless of caste, color, race, or religion.

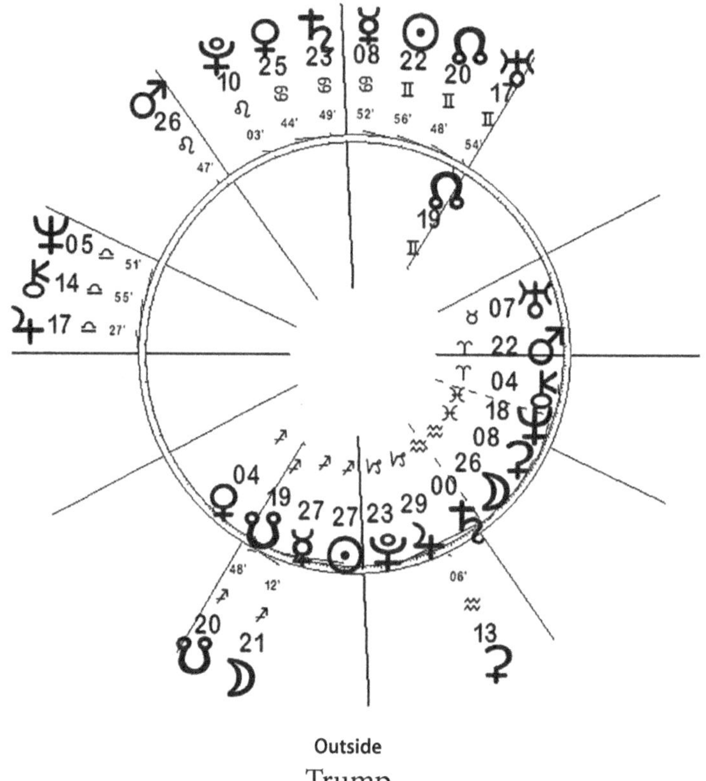

Outside

Trump

Inside

Trump's Tweet
PREBLE—139

December 19, 2020 • 1:42 AM • Washington, DC, USA

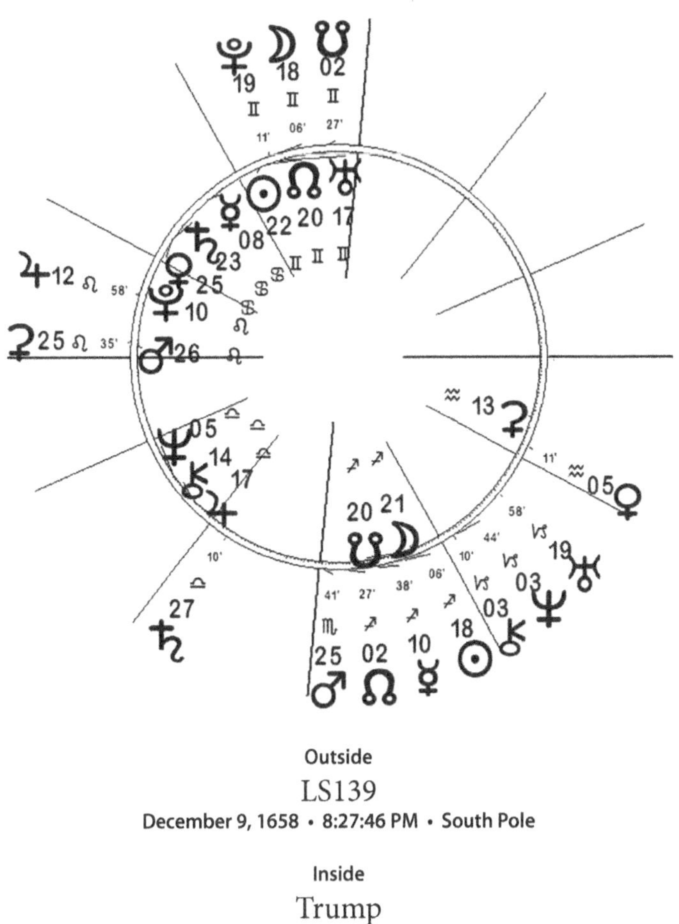

Outside
LS139
December 9, 1658 • 8:27:46 PM • South Pole

Inside
Trump

The Tweet that Changed the Course of American History

"Be There, Will be Wild!"

@REALDONALDTRUMP

Unwilling to accept defeat, at 1:42 AM on December 19, 2020, and still well within LS139's sphere of influence and its activation degree of 24 Capricorn on his Pluto, Donald Trump repeated his big lie to galvanize his followers. Here is his infamous 1:42 am Tweet:

> "Statistically impossible to have lost the 2020 election. Big protest in D.C. on January 6th. Be there, will be wild!"[5]

His words would unleash a political firestorm that would change the course of US history. And looking at the connections between the prevailing Lunar Saros eclipse and how its environment meshed with Trump's sphere of influence, it is simplicity itself to see how this time period emboldened his actions.

Donald Trump's Connections to the Dragons of LS139
↑NNode with SNode↓

1st Harmonics: Moon/Pluto – Uranus, Moon/Pluto – NNode, Moon/Pluto – Sun, Sun – Moon, Mars – IC, Ceres – Mars, Jupiter – Pluto
2nd Harmonic: Jupiter – Ceres

Not only did Trump have six Cosmic Bridges helping him solidify his pronouncements, but a fully charged and open Global Gateway. It is truly a miracle that his staged assault on the capital was rendered moot and did not achieve its anarchical goal. It is truly a miracle that deaths and casualties remained relatively low that day. Although Trump's Uranus, NNode, Sun, Moon and, most importantly, his IC would fold under the dramatic intensity of the eclipse 1st Harmonics, the 2nd Harmonic eclipse Jupiter to Ceres played a strategic role in the uprising. This pattern was set in motion on July 16, 2019, long before the November election and its disputed results. In fact, Trump had already been proclaiming that he couldn't possibly lose, and began openly contesting the validity of an impending loss, stating that the only way he could lose the election would be if the election was rigged from the start. As you can see from the Bi-Wheel of LS139 to Trump's chart, the eclipse Jupiter at 12 Leo is retrograde and on his Pluto at 10 Leo encouraging his self-promotion and desire for power.

LS139 Summary

Truth, like beauty, is a relevant term and seemingly made to order by this revolutionary family of Air Dragons: they are content to manufacture and promote their version of it. Trendsetters and market makers, accustomed to varying degrees of risk taking, will feel right at home as they ride the chaos of this energy field. Get ready to experience adrenaline inspired confidence as you reach for higher levels of intensity and excellence. An atmosphere of tension may be just the thing to get your talent juices flowing. In fact, fear may be the best conduit that can transform your obstacles into personal liberation and full power. In the end, these Dragons dance to inspire idealism and promote lessons of internal security. Look for strategic people appearing out of nowhere to get your idea, research, or project to the next level.

Lunar Saros 139 has been experiencing its first Full Moon phase that began with its seventeenth return on June 3, 1947. We can think of this phase in its evolution much like we would regard someone moving through their late teenage years and into early adolescence; still relatively ignorant but trying to appear cool. In essence, a very dangerous period indeed. It won't settle down until it reaches its Disseminating phase on July 27, 2037, when it returns for its twenty-second visit. It will probably still take another seventy-two years until it reaches the Last Quarter phase on September 9, 2109, to experience the "crisis in consciousness" state most identified with this phase. At this stage, lets hope the phenomenal power within its circuitry has benefited from the "readjustment" that characterizes this phase.

Whether by birthright or rite of passage, when LS139 activates a personal chart, a noticeable reinvigoration will suddenly appear, bringing passion and dedication back into the life. But there's also the disruption, unrest, and dissatisfaction that tags along to see if it can find a way to join in the fun. Often the fields of law, economics, psychoanalysis, and rehabilitation, as well as international travel and a renewed interest in spirituality, all offer rewards for those eager to expand their horizons. As always, look to both the number and significance of the links that connect to assess the potential to receive and resonate to the eclipse field's complexity of character and creativity.

LS139 Luminaries

Ralph Waldo Emerson	May 25, 1803
Edgar Rice Burroughs	September 1, 1875
Mae West	August 17, 1893
Ginger Rogers	July 16, 1911
Marshall McLuhan	July 21, 1911
Lucille Ball	August 6, 1911
Anne Frank	June 12, 1929
Imelda Marcos	July 2, 1929
Barbara Walters	September 25, 1929
Grace Kelly	November 12, 1929
CIA	July 26, 1947
Arnold Schwarzenegger	July 30, 1947
Paulo Coelho	August 24, 1947
Stephen King	September 21, 1947
J K Rowling	July 31, 1965
Viola Davis	August 11, 1965
Shania Twain	August 28, 1965
Charlie Sheen	September 3, 1965
Bjork	November 21, 1965
Ben Stiller	November 30, 1965
Chris Hemsworth	August 11, 1983
Amy Winehouse	September 14, 1983
Jesse Eisenberg	October 5, 1983
Aaron Rodgers	December 2, 1983
Jonah Hill[E]	December 20, 1983
Billie Eilish	December 18, 2001

1. https://www.noeltyl.com/techniques/990801.html. Retrieved Feb. 1, 2022.
2. https://911truth.org/Retrieved Feb. 1, 2022.
3. https://astrologyking.com/alcyone-star-pleiades/ Retrieved Feb. 2, 2022.
4. http://www.onthisdeity.com/7th-june-1893-%E2%80%93%C2%A0gandhis-first-act-of-civil-disobedience/ Retrieved Feb. 1, 2022.
5. https://www.bbc.com/news/world-us-canada-62140410. Retrieved July 4, 2022.

LUNAR SAROS 143

"To succeed in life you need three things:
a wishbone, a backbone and a funny bone."

-REBA MCENTIRE

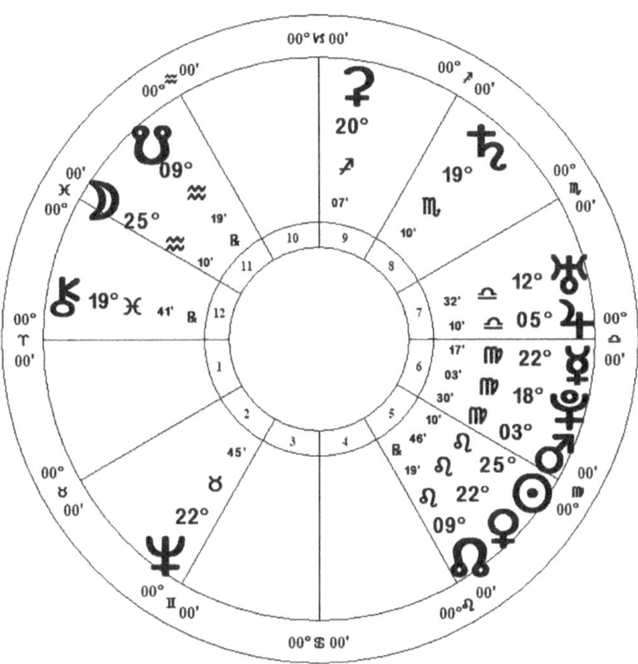

Lunar Saros 143

August 18, 1720 • 2:48:15 AM • South Pole

Dream a Dream

An awesome Fixed Cross, found only in this South Node Aquarian eclipse, features the dazzling creations of its 22 Venus/Neptune Critical Degree fixed square. Retrograde Saturn as part of the Fixed Cross and co-ruler along with Uranus is part of the soft power within the symmetry of LS143 that understands the value of patience and believing in oneself. Time and talent keep the lights on allowing anyone connected into their power grid the ability to pull it together. With every return, the gravity of time drives one's will-power ever deeper into the substrate of the psyche.

Helping to deliver its precious cargo of self-esteem is LS143's rare Wheelbarrow pattern, unique to this lunar eclipse family. I first thought I was looking at a See-Saw pattern until I noticed the symmetry of separation between what Marc Edmund Jones referred to as a "Focal Determinator" or in this case Focal Determinators Neptune and the eclipse Moon to the other eight planets. Created by the two arms of the Fixed Cross, these "high focus" energies form the two handles of the Wheelbarrow, giving the psychological strength and structure needed to balance the load. The Moon square Neptune handles offer a study in the art of developing a healthy imagination that is not allowed to run riot in the face of oncoming traffic. Mercury in rulership's T-Square to Ceres and Chiron in Pisces provides a steady diet of cognitive dissonance. The pattern is prone to burn out or drop out as it thrives in environments where aggravation, criticism, and perfection create a trifecta for misery or magnificence. An individual stands to lose the good will of others and can become their own worst enemy if unable to get their inner critic under control. The good news here is that LS143 has a waning Neptune/Moon square whose escapist and obsessive compulsive tendencies tend to dissipate over time. Transforming debility into dignity and self-respect are the true twin treasures buried deep within the matrix of this iconoclastic lunar eclipse.

There is a fascination with beauty, image, and living the high life not often associated with a Grand Fixed Cross; but here the call of pleasure, glamor, and even sacrifice cannot be tuned out. It's the siren song of Neptune in Taurus in square to Venus at her powerful critical degree placement in the twenty-second degree of Leo.

LS143 carries a conundrum: It's in the nature of a Grand Fixed Cross to be overwhelmed with its formidable power, causing younger members to postpone taking responsibility and thus losing out on opportunities more dedicated souls are happy to pursue. If immobility and contradiction is running you in circles, it's time for some serious self-evaluation to discover all the exceptional and unique talents within. Tension or a cavalier attitude experienced under this eclipse are signs that you need a new plan or a reorientation for your life that requires some serious goal setting. The dragons of this lunar eclipse offer a goldmine of opportunity if you are not frightened by the power and possibility that lies within you.

Whether by birthright or rite of passage, invoke the spirit of enterprise to step into their field of power. Owning the podium, the prestige and status that comes with victory await anyone who is willing to go the distance. Be that person who *never gave up.* Pluto's numerous midpoints bring a Lazarus effect into play further embellished by a Uranus/Mars-Neptune manna from heaven midpoint that surreptitiously bestows a boon on anyone who shows up with the courage of their convictions.

Closest Midpoints: Pluto/Venus-Uranus, Uranus/Mars-Neptune
Isotraps: Sun/Uranus conjunct Mars/Jupiter
Moon/Neptune opposition Jupiter/Uranus

1900—2100 Eclipses: Lunar Saros—143

1900, 1918, 1936, 1955, 1973, 1991, 2009, 2027, 2045, 2063, 2081, 2099
Length of cycle —1,280 years
Series ends—October 5, 3000

Steve Jobs
PREBLE—LS143

February 24, 1955 • 7:15 PM • San Francisco, CA, USA

"And one more thing..."

-Steve Jobs

Co-Founder, Chairman, and CEO, Apple, Inc.

"He was our Edison, he was our Picasso. He was an incredible inventor."

-Larry Ellison

On March 18, 1991, Steve Jobs got married exactly as his progressed Moon reached the mighty tenth degree of Leo. The dragons of LS143 had just touched down on January 30, 1991, at —the tenth degree of Leo! And, as Martha Stewart would say, "it's a good thing" because by early 1991, Jobs was in need of some serious positive spin, having established himself as one of the most difficult bosses around. Dan'l Lewin, a co-founder of NeXT, said of Jobs, "The highs were unbelievable, but the lows were unimaginable."[1] Let's take a look at his dragon DNA.

Steve Jobs' Connections to the Dragons of LS143

**1st Harmonics: Sun/Venus – Pluto,
SNode – Mercury, Pluto/Mercury – ASC, Saturn – Saturn, Chiron – DSC
2nd Harmonics: Mars – Sun, Jupiter/Uranus – Moon, Neptune – Saturn**

Familiarity with either the eclipse chart or that of the subject is essential. I personally prefer to get a feel for the eclipse chart first as it sets the tone for how its patterns will activate patterns in the chart under review. Having done that, let's look at his chart.

His quindecile Sun/Moon is a recipe for obsessive behavior even more sharply defined by his quality-control, make-it-perfect Virgo ascendant. Together with a relentlessly creative Cardinal Cross driving him forward, Jobs brandished his own style of energetic suffering. His Sun/Moon midpoint at the Ascendant acted as a prism to focus all of his angst, emotional depression, and need to be separate from others into a persona of perfection, revealing a personality living on the razor edge of visions yet to come.

Always check to see what the two spheres of energy share. In our case Jobs has a Jupiter/Uranus conjunction just like in the mother chart which opens him up to experiencing the power of the eclipse field's potent isotraps: Sun/Uranus conjunct Mars/Jupiter and its Moon/Neptune opposition Jupiter/Uranus. The latter is able to handle almost anything as it can take on defeat and turn it around in a heartbeat proving the resilience of the human spirit. In fact, the very nature of the opposition itself speaks to the value that struggle brings in being able to achieve your dreams, hopes, goals and even visions.

Of all the connections to LS143, he was strengthened and inspired the most by Saturn and Neptune to his Saturn. Steve Jobs is a great example of how planet links to lunar eclipse fields can open you up to experience an entirely new system of energy that you get to call your own. Here, Jobs was able to tap into the soft power of the lunar eclipse's Fixed Cross and its 22 degree Venus square Neptune with its commitment to the long arc of understanding the value of patience. Time and talent would keep Steve Jobs running fast on the cosmic wheel of high-quality and aesthetically spectacular production

In the end, LS143's Venus/Sun 1st Harmonic to Steve Jobs' Pluto must have been terribly proud of what their cosmic son had managed to achieve, bells and whistles, TED talks, and tech conferences aside. Their boy did good. Steve Jobs took their Leo love and need for adoration and with an almost god-like Vulcan power, continually raised the bar for elegant technological design and beauty that kept us waiting in line and eager to pay for his next creation.

Steve Jobs always had to have the last word. His sign-off at conferences always ended the same way: "And one more thing. . . " he would say to tease the crowd. Here are his last words. His sister would write in his obituary that as he gazed on his wife and family for the last time, he glanced beyond them and was heard to say, "Oh Wow. Oh Wow. Oh Wow." Wow!

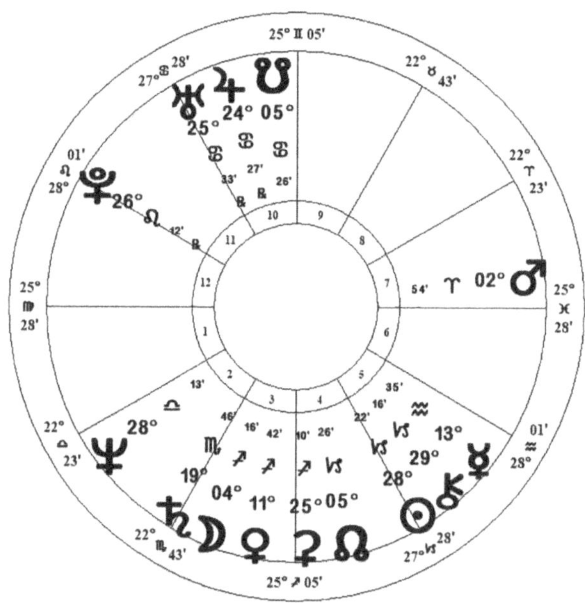

Kevin Costner

PREBLEs—LS143 & LS138

January 18, 1955 • 9:40 PM • Lynwood, CA, USA

"The rose goes in the front, big guy."

-Crash Davis, *Bull Durham*

Actor/Singer/Producer/Director

"I'm a big fan of dreams. Unfortunately, dreams are our first casualty in life–people seem to give them up, quicker than anything, for a 'reality.'"

-Kevin Costner

As Costner has matured, his ability to express and develop his ideas while overcoming the many hurdles of Hollywood have resulted in an abundance of career opportunities that reveal his trademark self-reliance and youthful spirit. In addition, Costner is on the record as stating, "Whomever I play, I enter his world." In the process, he makes the roles he plays believable by "trying to be as honorable to the character as [I] can."[2] Costner's roles reflect his love of action and the confidence to take on the world those characters inhabit. Primarily associated with Westerns and baseball stories, those genres reflect his signature maverick (Sun/Chiron) personality and values gleaned from leaner times that nevertheless provide inspiration for a brighter and more prosperous (Jupiter conjunct Uranus in Cancer) future.

The Academy Awards celebration in March 1991 honored Costner's epic three-hour movie *Dances with Wolves*. It received twelve nominations, winning in seven with Costner personally taking home an Oscar for Best Director and Best Picture.[3] Landing at 10 Leo, LS143's arrival on January 30 shone the spotlight on his idealistic, truth-seeking Mercury at the thirteenth degree of Aquarius.

Costner's links to Lunar Saros 143 display tier one levels of entanglement: His Pluto sitting on the eclipse axis and an almost exact Saturn in Scorpio placement allowed him to fully embody the tension, energy, action, and creative power held within the intensity of LS143's Fixed Cross. The fact that it was Costner's natal Mercury that got activated in 1991 and that very same Mercury linked to the eclipse through the SNode Cosmic Bridge suggests a ready-made tool bank of skills was just waiting to be acknowledged. There are numerous vectors of resonance across their mutual fields, but the one that stands out—especially in regard to the theme of *Dances with Wolves*—is Costner's Ceres on the IC conjunct the lunar eclipse Ceres. Demetra George in *Asteroid Goddesses* states, "When Ceres is near the IC, the mythos of Ceres is especially predominant as a psychological foundation—an emotional connection with the themes of loss and return of loved ones, or of rejection and acceptance."[4] If you want to know the best way to nourish someone, find Ceres in the chart by sign, house, and aspect and you'll be well on the way to nurturing that soul. The twelve Academy Award nominations and seven wins for *Dances with Wolves* in 1991 not only honored Kevin Costner but paid tribute to the disconnection that we all suffer: that is, our modern cosmopolitan lifestyles have almost totally erased our soulful footprint on Mother Earth.

By the time LS143 returned in February 2009, its activation degree had moved along the ecliptic eleven degrees, landing at 21 Leo. Again, honors and recognition would accompany the eclipse, but it would feel very different falling on Costner's Twelfth House Pluto. With the encouragement from his wife Christine Baumgartner, he returned to his musical roots, cutting his first debut album, *Untold Truth,* in November 2008 and taking his country/rock band Modern West back on the road in 2009.[5] After the death of a fan at a Canadian music festival that summer, brought on by freak tornado winds that ripped apart and collapsed the main stage, Costner auctioned himself off in the guise of a dinner date (along with guitars) to raise money for the two sons of the woman who died.[6] Now that's a class act.

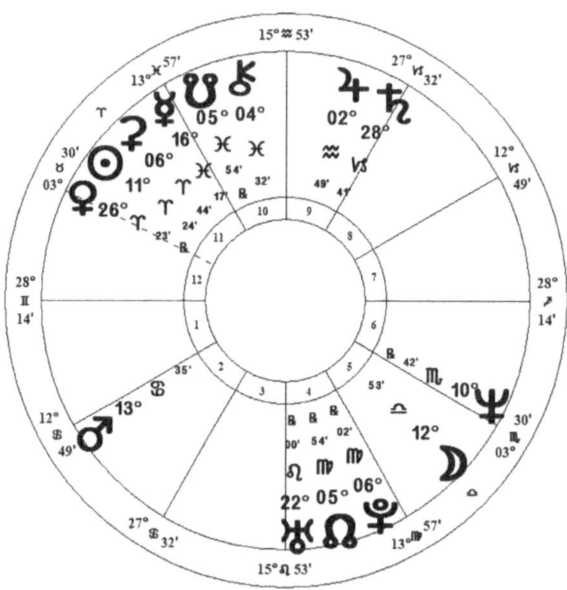

Susan Boyle
PREBLE—LS132

April 1, 1961 • 9:50 AM • Blackburn, UK

Bloody Fantastic!

"There are enough people in the world who are going to write you off. You don't need to do that to yourself."

-Susan Boyle

Susan Boyle rode in on the strength of LS123, a South Node Aquarian equal opportunity eclipse with a soaring Kite formation that activated her Mercury by opposition in March 2007. Encouraged by Paul Pott's rendition of *Nessun Dorma* on *Britain's Got Talent* in April 2007, in her autobiography Susan states, "Somewhere in the back of my mind, a seed was sown."[7] Fast forward to January 2009 and she's on stage in Glasgow, Scotland thrilling the audience with her rendition of *I Dreamed a Dream* from Les Misérables.

That encounter with the idiosyncratic attitudes of Lunar Saros 123 was a breath of fresh air that awakened her imagination along with the magnificence of her slumbering Grand Water Trine. It had taken her forty-six years, but she was ready. LS138's cathartic wave that hooked her Uranus by opposition in August 2008 left no doubt that she was ready. By the time LS143 arrived on February 9, 2009, the eclipse had opened a portal at fiery 21 Leo that synced perfectly with Boyle's Uranus at 22 Leo. Susan's date with destiny had finally arrived.

Lunar eclipses can be felt up to three weeks before they are declared officially active. It was no surprise then to see Boyle's spirit soar into an event horizon waiting just for her thanks to LS143's activation of her natal Uranus in late January 2009. Its Jupiter/Mars-Uranus midpoint was about to overwhelm all who saw her spectacular debut. A YouTube video of her performance, which was aired on April 11, 2009, went viral; within nine days, web sites around the world had generated over 100 million views helping her take the world by storm.[8]

Susan Boyle has a complex chart: There's her lyrical Grand Water Trine and then there's her highly complex Boomerang with Chiron and the SNode in Pisces at the fulcrum seemingly doing its best to keep her in her place. And it doesn't help to have a retrograde Venus in an opening square with a powerfully positioned Saturn in rulership in Capricorn which is in parallel declination to Jupiter. Susan's road to fame would be a stunning example of what can be achieved with a NNode/Pluto conjunction that carries an evolutionary force that is slowly gaining control over Fourth House needs for safety and security.

What is so wonderful for Susan Boyle was the activation of her Fourth House cusp by LS143's nodal axis at 9 Leo/Aquarius opening a portal for the

Space Lanes to appear and clear a direct pathway right through to her Tenth House. That's one badass cosmic power move.

Susan Boyle's Connections to the Dragons of LS143
Space Lanes via IC/MC
Pluto with Pluto

1st Harmonics: Sun – Uranus, Uranus – Moon,
Mars – NNode, Chiron – Mercury, Venus – Uranus, Mars – Pluto
2nd Harmonics: Pluto – Mercury, Jupiter – Ceres, Chiron – Mars

Lunar Saros 143's eclipse axis established a scintillating link to Boyle's Uranus while her own Full Moon in turn lit up the eclipse Uranus—an extraordinary cross link resonance further empowered by her Uranus in a tight under one degree conjunction to the eclipse Venus in Leo. In addition, no less than four cross links from LS143's Mars reached out and connected directly to her Chiron, North and South Nodes, and her Pluto, igniting forever the tremendous reach and scope of her nascent talent. LS143's next return will no doubt play a pivotal role in deepening her capacity for self-determination and self-worth; it arrives March 20, 2027, and activates at 2 Virgo. She continues to be an international star and global treasure, in keeping with her autobiography as *The Woman I Was Born to Be.*

LS143 Summary

Dignity, self-worth, honor, respect, and well-earned success are just some of the gifts so graciously bestowed on those whose lives are touched by the manna and magnificence of these Air Dragons. Before you know it, the uncertainty and stalls of the past will be replaced by steady gains and profit as your energetic system gets an upgrade or an entire renovation. They reward those who refuse to quit and are particularly helpful in times of metamorphic change. This is not a time to play safe or small; rather, go for the biggest and most energetic dream you can possibly imagine. And then roll up your sleeves and get down to work. Priceless resources materialize when you show Divine Order your true self.

Whether by birthright or rite of passage, when this eclipse family calls you in for supper, be prepared for a feast or a piece of fruit. Either way, fully fueled or running on empty, give yourself permission to seize the day and dream your dream. Endurance pays off so be ready to go the distance. Reaching an appreciative audience is only a matter of time and staying the course.

Your creative and artistic abilities are real. Never give up. Believe in yourself. Believe in your dream.

Phase	Return	Year
Last Quarter	9th	1864
Balsamic	13th	1936
New Moon	17th	2009
Crescent	21st	2081

LS143 Luminaries

Thomas Edison	February 11, 1847
Clark Gable	February 1, 1901
Linus Pauling	February 8, 1901
J.D. Salinger	January 1, 1919
Jackie Robinson	January 31, 1919
Nat King Cole	March 17, 1919
Eva Perón	May 7, 1919
Mary Tyler Moore[E1]	December 29, 1936
Billy Dee Williams	April 6, 1937
Jack Nicholson	April 22, 1937
George Carlin	May 12, 1937
John Grisham	February 8, 1955
Steve Jobs	February 24, 1955
Reba	March 28, 1955
Olga Korbut	May 16, 1955
Eric Lindros	February 28, 1973
Larry Page	March 26, 1973
Rachel Maddow	April 1, 1973
David Blaine	April 4, 1973
Bonnie Wright	February 17, 1991
Sarah Bolger	February 28, 1991

PREBLE—LS138
Mary Tyler Moore

---

1. Brian Dumaine & Rosalind Klein Berlin, America's Toughest Bosses https://money.cnn.com/magazines/fortune/fortune_archive/1993/10/18/78470/ Retrieved March 28, 2022.
2. Sue L. Hamilton, *Reaching for the Stars: Kevin Costner: Award-Winning Actor/Director* (Edina, MN: Abdo & Daughters, 1991), p. 10.
3. http://www.oscars.org/oscars/ceremonies/1991. Retrieved Feb. 9, 2022.
4. Demetra George and Douglas Bloch, *Asteroid Goddesses*, p. 68.
5. http://kevincostnermodernwest.com/band/kevin-costner/ Retrieved Feb. 9, 2022.
6. https://www.express.co.uk/celebrity-news/119690/Costner-auctions-date-for-tragic-concert-goer. Retrieved Feb 13, 2022.
7. Susan Boyle, *The Woman I Was Born to Be My Story* (New York: Atria Books, 2010), p. 163.
8. http://www.telegraph.co.uk/culture/tvandradio/susan-boyle/5206091/Susan-Boyles-Britains-Got-Talent-performance-sets-YouTube-record.html. Retrieved Feb. 9, 2022.

LUNAR SAROS 144

"The painting has a life of its own. I try to let it come through."

-Jackson Pollock

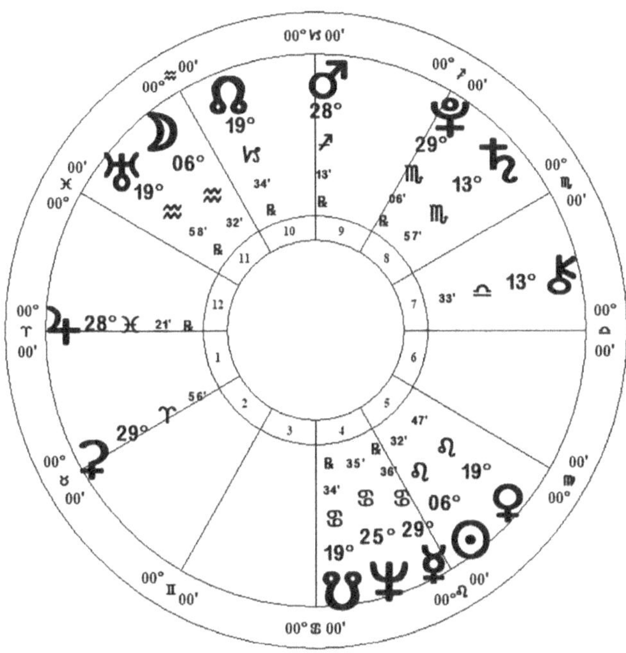

Lunar Saros 144

July 29, 1749 • 4:45:32 PM • North Pole

Real Surreal

In the theater of the absurd, this NNode Aquarian Lunar eclipse would feel right at home, sparkling as it does with over-the-top excess. Its Grand Water Trines overflow with retrograde and critical degrees that refuse to be confined or bounded by circumstance or protocol. Topping that is the highest declination OOB Mars of the entire Lunar Saros Series; at 28 degrees South 40 minutes, it functions more like a meteor, giving the eclipse a daring and dynamic quality. Its square to a retrograde Jupiter enhances its vitality making it imperative to learn and use basic self-management skills. Jupiter's position here is a dream come true seeding high levels of feeling, imagination, and wisdom into the field. The presence of the Sun, Jupiter, Uranus, and Pluto all in signs of rulership and dignity make for an amazing lunar family.

As a ruler, retrograde Saturn in Scorpio and its T-Square to Uranus and Venus invites extravagant, idiosyncratic, and downright weird behavior. Saturn holds the power position and like an umpire, gets to decide who gets the yellow card. Be prepared for feathers to fly. Saturn's influence can also be seen through its connections to the closed circuitry of the Grand Water Trines and its midpoint to the dashing Mars/Jupiter square. Saturn gives a potent and persuasive robustness to any arguments Uranus and Venus can offer making negotiation and compromise a critical skill to learn at the feet of these dragons.

LS144 is very much like its cousin, fellow Air Eclipse LS125: both lack any planetary reps in Earth signs, thus loosening the grip on the *real* world. Only LS144's NNode in Capricorn speaks to a mortal/moral dimension urgently in need of earthly raiment. In light of the OOB Mars in tight embrace to Jupiter, *the* planet of excess, powerful undercurrents would be seeking to redress this imbalance. Urges and inclinations of dazzling proportion now enjoy their very own multi-pass to a world of indulgence. The eclipse axis personifies indulgence; their inventiveness is legendary which makes it even more essential to get control over one's wants and needs. It is, after all, the sign most associated with our hopes and wishes. Its opposition to the Sun in Leo is both thrilling and potentially catastrophic as it offers an enthusiasm that is hard to turn down. In consideration of the Grand Water Trine and the Fixed T-Square contained in this magnificent eclipse, it is absolutely essential to put one's health at the top of the daily "to do" list. Failure to do this is a guarantee that your body/mind/spirit circuitry will begin to flag under the weight and excessiveness of this eclipse.

Positioned in closing degrees and retrograde, LS144's Grand Water Trines of Pluto, Jupiter and Mercury/Neptune in Cancer evoke worlds within worlds; womb-like webs of diaphanous distraction but also worlds on the cutting-edge platforms of future technology delivery. Either way, gigantic leaps of imagination will be deemed de rigueur.

The predominance of retrograde planets can often be a call to return to a career or even a relationship that can be reinvigorated. This is especially the case considering that both Venus and Uranus are at the very companionship oriented nineteenth degree and in fixed signs that place high value on loyalty and friendship. The retrograde is a valuable force within this eclipse field that offers an opportunity to go back in time and reclaim projects, people or plans that were left behind in the dash and dazzle of the latest and greatest.

Closest Midpoints: Pluto/Mercury-Jupiter, Saturn/Mars-Jupiter
Isotraps: Moon/Uranus conjunct Mars/Jupiter
Sun/Uranus opposition Moon/Venus

1900—2100 Eclipses: Lunar Saros—144

1911, 1929, 1947, 1965, 1983, 2001, 2020, 2038, 2056, 2074, 2092
Length of cycle —1,262 years
Series ends—September 4, 3011

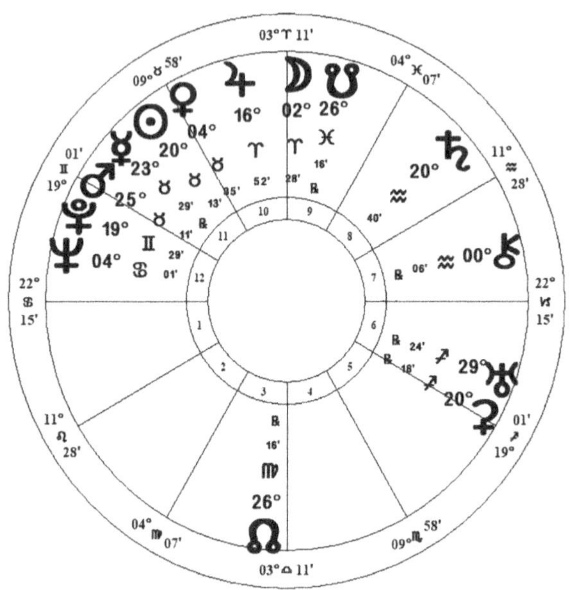

Salvador Dalí
PREBLEs—LS140 & LS102

May 11, 1904 • 8:45 AM • Figueras, Spain

The Last of the Great Old Masters

"Every morning when I wake up, I experience an exquisite joy–
the joy of being Salvador Dalí–and I ask myself in rapture:
What wonderful things is this Salvador Dalí going to accomplish today?"

-Salvador Dalí

Dalí was the richest, most famous and without a doubt *the* most bizarre artist of the 20th century. He lived a life of superlatives and proclaimed to the world that he *was* Surrealism. He was the Andy Warhol of his day, and his impact on the public, like October's Wall Street Crash of 1929, would result in shock waves of incredulity and provocation that would continue to resonate with every decade that followed. In the summer of 1929, Dalí had just met Gala, a Russian woman ten years his senior who was married to fellow surrealist, poet Paul Éluard.[1] She would leave her husband to become Dalí's life-long muse, soul mate, lover, manager, and wife and no doubt the driving force spurring Dalí to reach new heights of fame and fortune.[2]

Film critic Roger Ebert in the year 2000 would write that the film *Un Chien Andalou* was "the most famous short film ever made."[3] It was a script that Dalí would write and promote in 1929 with surrealist friend and filmmaker Luis Buñuel. By the time Lunar Saros 144 and its twenty-fourth dreaming degree of Taurean artistry descended on his Sun, Mercury, and Mars on November 17, 1929, Dalí was definitely *becoming* Dalí, enjoying his first art exhibition and flush of fame at the Galerie Goemans in Paris, (November 20–December 5, 1929). Landing at the midpoint of his Mercury/Mars conjunction, Dalí's Mercury/Jupiter-Uranus and his Mars/Jupiter-Neptune midpoints must have been reeling in the ecstasy and anguish of sexual desires, insecurities, and phobias.

Salvador Dalí's Connections to the Dragons of LS144
Space Lanes via DSC/ASC

1st Harmonics: Moon – Chiron,
Jupiter – SNode/Moon, Neptune – ASC, Mars – Uranus, Uranus – Saturn
2nd Harmonics: Mercury – Chiron,
Venus – Saturn, Chiron – Jupiter, Saturn – Sun, Pluto – Mars

Reading the reviews of Dalí's prodigious and startling body of work point to the period from the late 1920's and into the 1930's as his best and most creative period. 1929 was truly an epic year for Salvador Dalí, made even more extraordinary by his connection to the unorthodoxy of Lunar Saros 144. Multiple links of symmetry flow between them but the ones that scream stellar standout are the ASC/DSC Space Lanes that opened through the portal of his Seventh House cusp.

In addition to giving him greater access to a segment of society that remained untouched by the financial crisis of 1929, Dalí's temporary Space Lanes easily crossed the Four Cosmic Bridges that were created by the fusion of LS144's energetic field to his. Dalí's decadence would be encouraged by such connectors as LS144's 1st Harmonic Mars to his Uranus and doubling down with the eclipse Uranus to his Saturn that would fuel an extraordinarily high-powered if not obsessive field of vitality and vigor.

Lunar Saros 144's arrival in November 1929 marked a time for breakthroughs in every sense of the word as Dalí's growing powers of self-determination took on a life of their own. Still tied to the best of Old World standards and technique but with a supreme confidence in his ability as a writer, artist, and painter, Dalí would not be confined by attitudes and structures, even of the Surrealists, from whom he made a clean break in the early 1930's.

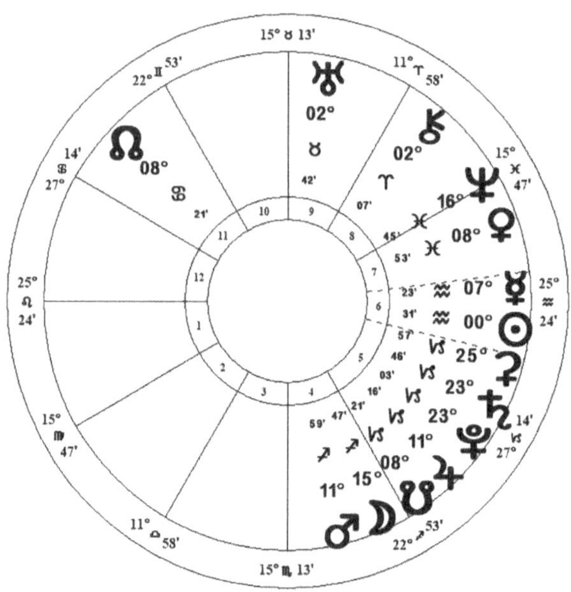

First Covid-19 Case in USA
PREBLE—LS144

January 20, 2020 • 7:00 PM[4] • Everett, WA, USA

January 20, 2020: WHO Announces COVID-19

CDC Says 3 US Airports Will Begin Screening for Coronavirus[5]

On Monday, January 20, 2020, a thirty-five year old man's flu-like symptoms were confirmed to be the first case of the coronavirus in the United States. He had just returned from a visit to Wuhan, China. Within hours of LS144's arrival on Friday, January 10, 2020, the World Health Organization (WHO) announced the appearance of a coronavirus-related pneumonia in Wuhan, China, with the first USA infected case appearing on January 20, 2020.

On March 11, 2020, the WHO declared the coronavirus (COVID-19) outbreak a global pandemic.[6] Of note is the USA natal chart's Mercury at 24 Cancer and its links to LS144's foundation Neptune/SNode-Mercury.

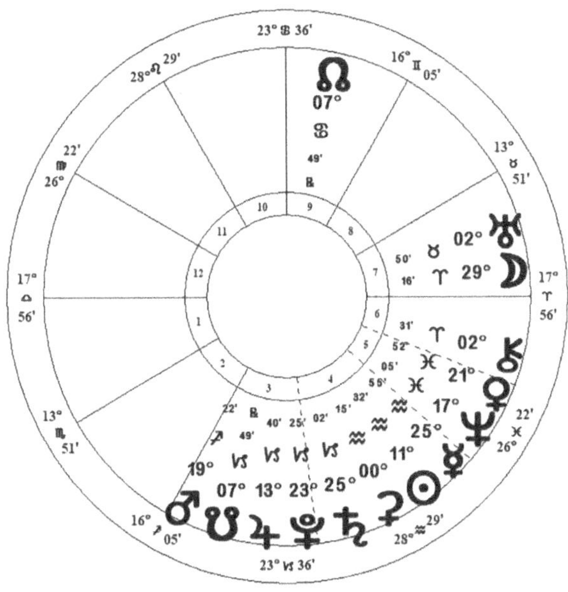

BREXIT
PREBLE—LS144

January 31, 2020 • 11:00 PM • London, UK

BREXIT was the withdrawal of the United Kingdom (UK) from the European Union (EU) at 23:00 GMT on 31 January 2020. This historical moment occurred exactly three weeks after the arrival of LS144 on the reconstructive and transformational twentieth degree of Cancer. As of 2023, no sovereign country other than the UK has voted to withdraw from the EU.

BREXIT's Connections to the Dragons of LS144
↑North Node to South Node↓
Mars with Mars
Chiron to Chiron

1st Harmonics: NNode – Pluto/Saturn, Moon – Ceres, Moon – Sun, Ceres – Moon/Uranus, Chiron – ASC, Jupiter – Chiron, Neptune/Mercury – MC
2nd Harmonics: Neptune/Mercury – Saturn/Pluto

BREXIT's sphere of influence offers a precedent-setting fully charged Global Gateway created from a complimentary seventh and nineteenth degree nodal alignment that redefines the concept of partnership and union. New legal traditions emerge from Mars also at the nineteenth degree while the eclipse Mars and especially its NNode tap the raw power of BREXIT's Pluto-Saturn and its driving ambition to succeed. The eclipse was experiencing its sixteenth return in its Gibbous phase with an emphasis on tying up loose ends so that a greater degree of vitality can flood the system while eliminating potential barriers to higher levels of productivity.

LS144 Summary

Surprises and excitement are second nature to these dynamic Air Dragons who dance color and creativity into every step along their way. They carry a sense of destiny within and attract all manner of radical changes and opportunities. They adore beauty and anything that speaks to an enjoyment of life through the senses. Born with superlative imaginations, these charismatic dragons gladly enter into a world of their own making, free from the confines and opinions of other (lesser) mortals who do not share their point of view. A need to let go of the past when things are not going well is something many of us struggle with on a daily basis, and that goes double for these devil-may-care dragons. And that makes life very interesting for all born under their futuristic gaze or for those simply enjoying one of their unforgettable eighteen year appearances.

Their return marks a time of high energy and high levels of accomplishment as their competitive spirit enjoys a challenge. To dance with these dragons, you are going to need to up your game; this field of energy loves nothing better than to throw themselves fully into any and all activities. Regardless of what comes your way, you'll be the darling of your social circle and will most certainly benefit from unorthodox, independent, open-minded people of liberal persuasion that are about to cross your path.

Phase	Return	Year
First Quarter	9th	1893
Gibbous	13th	1965
Full Moon	17th	2038
Disseminating	21st	2110

LS144 Luminaries

Billy Bishop	February 8, 1894
Jack Benny	February 14, 1894
Lee J. Cobb	December 8, 1911
José Ferrer	January 8, 1912
Jackson Pollock	January 28, 1912
Eva Braun	February 6, 1912
Gene Hackman	January 30, 1930
Joanne Woodward	February 27, 1930
Stephen Sondheim	March 22, 1930
Eckhart Tolle	February 16, 1948
Jonathan Sacks	March 8, 1948
Billy Crystal	March 14, 1948
Bobby Orr	March 20, 1948
Heidi Fleiss	December 30, 1965
Cindy Crawford	February 20, 1966
Jonah Hill[E1]	December 20, 1983
Ben Shapiro	January 15, 1984
Trevor Noah	January 31, 1984
Elizabeth Holmes	February 3, 1984
Andre Ward	February 23, 1984
Mark Zuckerberg[E1]	May 14, 1984

PREBLE—139
Jonah Hill

---

1. Brian Sewell, *The Dali I Knew.* Retrieved Jan. 13, 2022. http://www.standard.co.uk/goingout/exhibitions/the-dali-i-knew-6587130.html

2. Ian Gibson, *The Shameful Life of Salvador Dalí.* (New York: W.W. Norton 1997), p. 292.

3. Roger Ebert reviews, 2000. Retrieved Jan. 13, 2022. http://www.rogerebert.com/reviews/great-movie-un-chien-andalou-1928

4. https://www.usatoday.com/in-depth/news/nation/2021/01/19/first-covid-case-us-year-anniversary-snohomish-county/4154942001/ Retrieved Feb. 5, 2022.

5. https://www.ajmc.com/view/a-timeline-of-covid19-developments-in-2020. Retrieved Feb. 5, 2022.

6. Domenico Cucinotta & M. Vanelli, WHO Declares COVID-19 a Pandemic. https://pubmed.ncbi.nlm.nih.gov/32191675/ Retrieved Feb. 15, 2022.

LUNAR SAROS 145

"The older I get, the better I used to be."

-John McEnroe

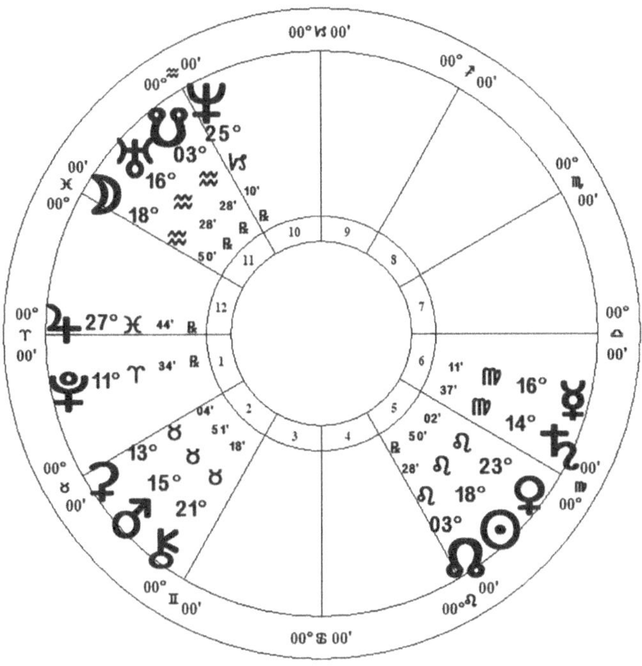

Lunar Saros 145

August 11, 1832 • 2:31:55 PM • South Pole

Resistance Is Futile

Unexpected news is the order of the day with Saturn and Uranus ruling this Aquarius eclipse with Uranus Lord by its proximity. Long overdue adjustments reflect the overwhelming number of inconjunct aspects: eight pairs pushing and pulling apart the fabric of the field and all calling out for redress and relief to problems that have lingered for years if not decades. Contradictory forces, especially within the Aquarius/Virgo inconjuncts, create a gulf of incompatible differences that place great strain and tension within the eclipse sphere. The end result is an often unpleasant resolution to a dichotomy between theory and practice. However, the upside to all these readjustments acting like tectonic plates is to slowly grind to dust our resistance, opening space for new opportunities.

Now our past comes back for review driven by the tremendous internal pressure within the lunar eclipse Fixed T-Square. Both squares are potent sources of conflict as they buttress and reinforce the load: The waxing Uranus/Ceres-Mars side is pure outlier energy willing to do whatever it takes for changes *now* while the waxing Mars/Sun side is equally adamant that life must go "my way or the highway." Decisions made out of ego, haste, carelessness, or selfishness will prove to be the source of both pain and a pathway forward as seen through Pluto's conjunction to the Ceres/Mars side of the equation. Pluto can always be counted on to take you to the gates of hell and Ceres can always be counted on to bring you back—changed but alive. The karmic relief that lies therein is the story of this dragon family's tale.

LS145 carries a See-Saw pattern, unafraid of challenging the status quo, putting this lunar eclipse in a constant state of problem-solving arousal. This mode of behavior is simultaneously curative and a curse: curative in that while you may single-handedly discover one of the great secrets of the universe, your indifference and analysis/paralysis attitude will leave you feeling isolated and lonely such that not even a copy of Dale Carnegie's *How to Win Friends & Influence People* will be able to cure. The chilly side of the Mercury/Saturn in Virgo conjunction is justified by its trine to Mars making it even more insufferable when it's not saving lives. In addition, Chiron's square to Venus gives the eclipse field a utilitarian feel which is highly problematic because such moral decision-making requires that we assign values to the benefits and harms of our actions. But the question here is how does one go about assigning a value or even how does one attempt to even measure or compare values across a spectrum of possibilities? In the realm of morality, any course of action is, to say the least, dubious.

Great pressure is now brought to bear that will collapse any project or system that is in need of reform. A rebellious attitude against past restrictions is something to be on the lookout for as is the need to justify decisions. Exercising restraint may prove to be the better part of valor. Effort is required to control what others may see as an egotistical and high-and-mighty attitude born on the wings of specialized or privileged information. The Moon/Pluto opposition Mercury/Saturn isotrap is a yellow flag warning that living in a state of emotional detachment is cause for resentment and anger as one may feel increasingly bitter toward life. The upside to all this pressure can be found in a new sense of urgency to set the record straight. One can only live in such high states of tension and disharmony for so long. Eventually the psyche will rebel if only to find relief.

Closest Midpoints: Venus/Saturn-Node, Jupiter/Saturn-Pluto
Isotraps: Venus/Uranus conjunct Saturn/Neptune
Moon/Pluto opposition Mercury/Saturn

1900—2100 Eclipses: Lunar Saros—145

1904, 1922, 1940, 1958, 1976, 1994, 2012, 2030, 2048, 2066, 2085
Length of cycle —1,262 years
Series ends—September 16, 3094

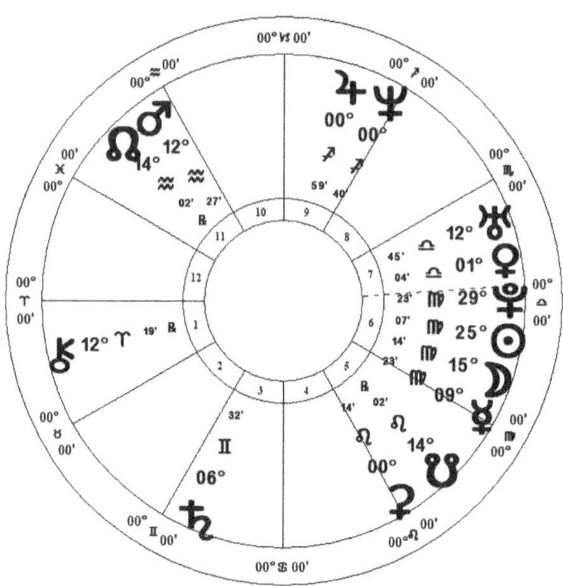

Lance Armstrong
PREBLE—128

September 18, 1971 • TOB Unknown • Dallas, TX, USA

Golden Boy/Hero/Villain

"Everybody wants to know what I'm on. What am I on? I'm on my bike, busting my ass six hours a day. What are you on?"

-LANCE ARMSTRONG

On November 28, 2012, the lunar eclipse of Saros Series 145 occurred at 7 degrees Gemini. It landed on Armstrong's pivotal Saturn, the handle on his Bucket pattern and the driving force behind his Grand Air Trines. The speed at which his life began to unravel in the window of this lunar eclipse is nothing short of spectacular and due in large measure to the swiftness of trines in action. Caught up in a whirlwind of his own undoing, his downfall can be dated from October 17, when Armstrong stepped down as Livestrong's CEO after the U.S. Anti-Doping Agency (USADA) published their incriminating report. He was immediately stripped of his seven Tour de France titles and was given a lifetime ban from Olympic sports.[1]

He recorded an exclusive interview with Oprah that was broadcast worldwide in early January 2013. In the interview, he finally admitted to his complicity in a doping scandal that he had been vehemently denying for over a decade. Alex Gibney's riveting 2013 documentary, *The Armstrong Lie*, is a fascinating before and after look at his professional cycling career: that is to say, the triumph of the post-cancer 2009 comeback tour juxtaposed against his fall from grace in the light of USADA sanctions in respect to doping violations.[2] To his credit, Gibney makes a concerted effort to reveal how human nature, even at the best of times and working to promote a noble cause, can be corrupted by the many opportunities for personal gain that serendipitously appear along the roadside to celebrity status.

Juliet Macur of the *New York Times*, writing in *Cycles of Lies: The Fall of Lance Armstrong*, offers a compelling account of Armstrong's private life through a tapestry of interviews woven together from those who knew both the public and private Armstrong. She writes of how she came away from a visit with him on June 7, 2013 "suspecting that Armstrong, in his heart of hearts, believed absolutely, and will believe forever, that he won those Tours de France because he was the best."[3]

Macur writes that, as a teenager, "Armstrong was brash and ill-mannered, in desperate need of refinement, that his insecurities and anger were products of his broken home—he felt abandoned by his biological father and mistreated by his adoptive one."[4] With Chiron in Sagittarius in quincunx to Mercury, fanning the flames of belligerence would be a viable expression of Chiron's wound and sensitivity to rejection. Armstrong's reliance on bluntness, bullying, and aggression can be seen from his tight Mercury/Mars quincunx and, taken together with Chiron, form a Yod of immense and unyielding agitation. Demanding triathlons and punishing competitive cycling would offer Armstrong some degree of respite as well as compensation for his feelings of inferiority. In addition, his Mars/Pluto midpoint to Saturn would emerge to fuel a legendary career and miraculous status as a cancer survivor. Ebertin describes Mars/Pluto midpoint to Saturn in COSI as: "A person unafraid of hard work leaving no stone unturned in the pursuit of a particular task, desire to overcome difficulties and obstacles at all costs."[5]

Armstrong's hereditary links to this eclipse come by way of the oppositions running between his Sun/Pluto in Virgo and LS145's Jupiter in Pisces, reinforced by LS145's Pluto at 11 Aries to Armstrong's fascinating fame/failure twelfth degree vortex of Chiron in Aries. He carries the eclipse field's penchant for power and pomposity, with all of its karmic implications woven into a "savior" scenario noted for its self-sustaining levels of Olympian proportion. Of all the Air eclipses, LS145 holds us accountable to the horizon of our personal and collective destiny, ensuring that we arrive in our own good time, to reap the harvest of our labor.

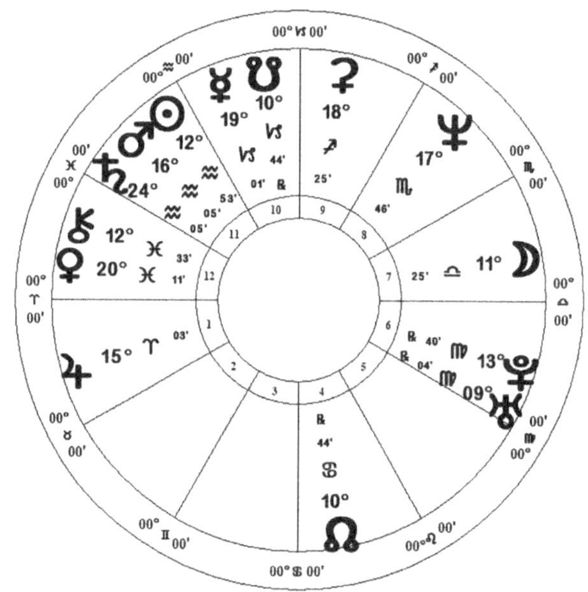

Laura Poitras
PREBLE—124

February 2, 1964 • TOB Unknown • Boston, MA, USA

The Snowden Revelations

"There is a massive apparatus within the United States government that with complete secrecy has been building this enormous structure that has only one goal, and that is to destroy privacy and anonymity, not just in the United States, but around the world."

-Glen Greenwald

Edward Snowden is featured in LS150—Be Brave in the Fire, eclipses of Part One. This entry tells the tale of Laura Poitras, the first investigative reporter to take on the responsibility of navigating her way through Snowden's massive cache of documents. When LS145 activated on November 28, 2012, at the discerning sixth degree of Gemini on Edward Snowden's dignified and highly professional Mercury at the tenth degree of Gemini, Snowden reached out to the only two respected reporters he knew who could be counted on to not cave in under the pressure of what would be revealed to them: the release of thousands of documents that would prove the existence of massive surveillance programs by the US government in breach of American citizens' privacy rights both at home and abroad. Those two trusted individuals were Laura Poitras, an investigative documentary filmmaker, and Glenn Greenwald of the *Guardian*.

Laura Poitras was the first to establish encrypted chat with Snowden. Peter Maas of the *New York Times* reported a discussion he had had with Snowden about her decision. Snowden said, "She had demonstrated the courage, personal experience and skill needed to handle what is probably the most dangerous assignment any journalist can be given—reporting on the secret misdeeds of the most powerful government in the world."[6] In her piece for *Rolling Stone* on Greenwald and Snowden's collaboration, Janet Reitman wrote that "it was on December 1st, 2012[that] Greenwald received a note from a person asking for his public encryption, or PGP key so he could send him an e-mail securely."[7] It turned out that Greenwald was just too busy and didn't have the time to learn how to install or use it and went back to working on his book and columns. That left Poitras as the only media connection and link to Snowden; by mid-May, Poitras finally had Greenwald on board and, by his own account, safely working with encrypted email and enough documents to realize both the authenticity and significance of what Snowden's cache of documents represented.[8]

Poitras' involvement with Snowden began with her Progressed NNode on Snowden's Progressed Ascendant—a remarkable tie of celestial collaboration that would break the biggest news story of 2013 and launch a public debate on the issues of policy around mass surveillance and the extraordinary targeted invasion of privacy conducted by the NSA. For Poitras, Edward Snowden was arguably *the* biggest story of her career—she would go on to win an Academy Award for Best Documentary in 2015 for her film *Citizenfour*, coproduced with Stephen Soderbergh.[9] With an impressive count of eight hereditary lines of celestial DNA attached to this lunar eclipse family, Edward Snowden's story became her story and rapidly accelerated the trajectory of her life. The eclipse Moon's foundation degree resonated to the exact frequency of Poitras' Mars/Sun-Saturn midpoint enabling her to utilize her energy for maximum efficiency in a professional manner that would empower her career and life purpose.

Sophia's Story

Sofia is a practicing psychotherapist. She is a highly trained and sought after specialist in her field. She was born on November 8, 1943, under LS137—Ripples and Riptides. The eclipse activation at 6 Gemini on November 28, 2012, linked to her Uranus at 7 Gemini. She said that when the eclipse arrived, she was already deep into a cleansing of her basic beliefs about life. She said, "It felt like a meteor shower of insights and new awareness. I felt like the foundation of who I was, was being shaken and spun around in every direction." She spoke of seeing a therapist at the time who told her to picture an image of herself and to describe what she saw. Sofia said, "I saw myself as a person with a crutch and a deformed leg walking down a road smiling and trying to keep up with the other people, pretending that it was okay and being grateful that I was even on the road. Deep inside I am sad and lonely."

Sophia's Connections to the Dragons of LS145
↓South Node with South Node↓

1st Harmonics: NNode – Pluto,
Uranus – SNode, Jupiter – Moon, Saturn/Mercury – Chiron, Venus – Jupiter

Sophia's experience conforms to the more agitated reaction that occurs when two fields with the same polarity interact, reflecting lower levels of power and integration potential. She bravely spoke of feeling hopeless about changing anything and that she just had to keep "pushing myself to pretend that it was all okay." She told me that it was a wake-up call, and she has thankfully been able to shift "how I did a lot of pretending in my relationships and how I isolated quite a bit." Thanks to the brilliance of a Uranus activation and the eclipse NNode on her Pluto, she has become "more aware of the urge to pretend and not confront. I am getting so much better at that."

The synchronicity of the eclipse field's Uranus on her SNode is another cosmic wave; for some it feels more like a slap on the wrist to get our attention. Sophia's links to LS145 are both numerous and significant, thus increasing her sensitivity to "hear" the eclipse field's complexity of mood and meaning. The fact that she offered to share her experience is a tribute to her nurturing and deeply sensitive twenty-eighth degree Moon in Pisces that received the eclipse Jupiter. This is a tie-in that brings the information-orientation of Jupiter forward to access, update and expand her intuitive inner landscape.

LS145 Summary

Revelations and the steady tick of time slowly bring forth solutions in the presence of these action-oriented Air Dragons. Their appetite for contrariness is legendary and so is their knack for getting involved with difficult and embarrassing situations. Welcome in the life-style changes that invariably accompany their return while letting your ego take a much needed vacation. Because the emotional field of this eclipse runs the gamut from saint to sinner, relationships bear the brunt of unnecessary misunderstandings and frustrations that rise as fast as they fall. These Air Dragons are used to getting their way, which makes it even more necessary that in our current era that some have characterized as "The Age of Self-Interest," utilitarianism requires all of us to look beyond the self to the good of others.

Whether by birthright or transit, this lunar family offers insight and lessons in the subject of patience and how to work through the discomfort of any self-destructive behavior that is ruining your prospects for a better life. Only then can a new alignment and perspective emerge. As anyone who has labored long and hard in the trenches of turmoil knows, strain and stress can be leveraged to discipline, allowing one to discover hidden dimensions and channels of personal strength and ability. To achieve such noble ends is not easy. One might want to contemplate cultivating a spiritual outlook to help make the transition from selfish to selfless acts the new norm. When these topsy-turvy dragons dish out disappointment, remember, there's always an upside and our differences make a difference in the world.

Phase	Return	Year
Crescent	5th	1904
First Quarter	9th	1976
Gibbous	13th	2048
Full Moon	17th	2121

LS145 Luminaries

Rasputin	January 21, 1869
Tommy Douglas	October 20, 1904
Ayn Rand	February 2, 1905
Christiaan Barnard	November 8, 1922
Charles M Schulz	November 26, 1922
Paddy Chayefsky	January 23, 1923
Franco Zeffirelli	February 12, 1923
John J Gotti	October 27, 1940
Bruce Lee	November 27, 1940
Richard Pryor	December 1, 1940
Buffy Sainte-Marie	February 20, 1941
Jamie Lee Curtis	November 22, 1958
Sade	January 16, 1959
Bob Lazar	January 26, 1959
John McEnroe	February 16, 1959
Chadwick Boseman	November 29, 1976
Shakira	February 2, 1977
Floyd Mayweather Jr.	February 24, 1977
Chris Martin	March 2, 1977
Leonard Fournette	January 18, 1995
Trayvon Martin	February 2, 1995
Haley Lu Richardson	March 7, 1995

---

1. Charlie Gillis. "Liar, liar, Lance on fire." *MacLeans Special Issue.* Dec. 17, 2012: p. 74. Print
2. https://www.documentarymania.com/player.php?title=The%20Armstrong%20Lie. Retrieved Jan. 24, 2022
3. Juliet Macur, *Cycles of Lies: The Fall of Lance Armstrong* (New York: HarperCollins, 2014), p. 395.
4. Ibid, p. 398.
5. Reinhold Ebertin, *The Combination of Stellar Influences*, p. 214.
6. Peter Maas, *How Laura Poitras Helped Snowden Spill his Secrets* http://www.nytimes.com/2013/08/18/magazine/laura-poitras-snowden.html?pagewanted=1&_r=2&. Retrieved Jan. 24, 2022
7. Janet Reitman, *Snowden and Greenwald: The Men Who Leaked the Secrets* http://www.rollingstone.com/politics/news/snowden-and-greenwald-the-men-who-leaked-the-secrets-20131204. Retrieved Jan. 24, 2022.
8. Ibid.
9. https://en.wikipedia.org/wiki/Citizenfour. Retrieved Jan. 24, 2022.

PART FOUR

DANCING WITH WATER

The Water Eclipses

Don't drink at the water's edge, throw yourself in.
Become the water. Only then will your thirst be quenched.

-Jeanette Berson

Immerse yourself in your potential: these nine lunar eclipses take us to the depths of our capacity to feel our emotional connection to life's creative complexity. A mighty tide of mayhem arrives when these Water Dragons surface, forcing many of us to rewrite our notion of how the world works. Heisenberg and his uncertainty principle sums it up best: "Not only is the world stranger than we think, it is stranger than we can think."

These Water Dragons are the epitome of what it means to be part of the Universe. They illuminate the fundamental mystery that is our life as they continually help us discover our story. All the atoms and waves that sit within their celestial matrix offer not just a linear version of a moment in time but an inchoate possibility as to what you could become. All the information that is you is actually not only embedded in your biological DNA but is embedded in the context of the world in which you grow into and develop. This is now being explored in the exciting field of epigenetics where behaviors and environment play significant roles in the way your genes work. To that end, the information that is packed within the potential of any lunar eclipse and especially Water Eclipse DNA becomes a reservoir of expectation.

These lunar dragons remind us that life is in a constant state of flux with fault lines appearing out of nowhere. Trouble, turmoil, and turbulence for sure are always waiting to test our resolve. The beauty and treasure of these dragon dwellers is that they have the power to bring us home; to reconnect our feelings and emotions so we can be reminded of our collective need to belong. Love, affection, and our yearning for human relationship are the great takeaways that we are left with after one of these Water dragon families has paid a visit. They remind us that what matters most, especially during their six month presence, is to open up our senses to the instinctual, the intuitive, and even the psychic. We are led ever so gently into an imaginal world that values surrender, serenity and salvation. It offers an opportunity to try on new flavors of faith, wisdom, devotion, and compassion without having to buy anything. In fact, it is the "no-thingness" of these lunar miracle workers that can steal your heart and take your breath away, such is their power to penetrate our defenses and leave us at the mercy of our magnificence.

Leading off the eclipses in this final section is LS103, a South Node lunar family that was born on September 4, 472 CE. It ran for 1,460 years, incarnating through eighty-two cycles and finished its sojourn across our planet on February 10, 1933. The last lunar eclipse you will discover is Lunar Saros Series 142—There Be Dragons—fittingly named to (at least for our current 21st century) close out our lunar eclipse adventures. This North Node lunar family arrived on September 19, 1709. Lasting for approximately 1,298 years, it will unfold through a relatively short cycle of seventy-three incarnations, with its last return on November 17, 3007. LS142 holds the distinction of being the only Water Dragon family to have its Moon exactly on the celestial equator giving all those touched by its presence the ability to connect massively with a global audience.

Part Four holds the smallest treasure of lunar eclipses—nine Water eclipses: four with a Moon in Scorpio, four with a Moon in Pisces, and one very special lunar eclipse with a Moon in Cancer. For all those born within their watery domain, there is a style of living that only water signs have and the most uniquely qualified to carry that banner of caring are those born within the watery realm of Cancer. This sign responds to life's energy in an almost unconscious manner, fitting and filtering every situation through a highly intuitive process that seems totally irrational yet rarely misses the mark in terms of effectiveness. I had the honor of studying with one of the greatest astrologers ever, Katherine de Jersey, a Cancerian and one of the kindest and most nurturing astrologers I have ever met in my life. If you haven't read her book, *Destiny Times Six*, it's a true page turner.

For laser-like vision and sheer intensity, it's hard to beat the forcefulness and extreme emotion associated with the dynamic energy fields of Lunar Saros 113, LS114, LS115, and LS131. The Moon in Scorpio often gets a bad rap probably because its energy fields are so intimidating, something that comes from its almost preternatural willpower and acute powers of perception. Nothing can stop a Moon in Scorpio when they are in the flow, so you just have to get out of their way. When it comes to sheer extreme emotion, it's hard to beat the Apollo 13 launch on April 11, 1970. It is an example of how the best features of LS113 got the mission off the launch pad and back to Earth with all aboard safe and sound. At the moment of lift-off, the Moon was at the powerful 00

AP of Cancer, a degree known for its connection both to the world of politics and power as well as the world of the personal and profound. It is a joy to feel this delicious syncopation, this wondrous symmetry and resonance that runs unheeded throughout our lives; the life of these lunar eclipses is just another way to hold that magic and sacredness close to our hearts.

The Moon in Pisces Water Dragon families are the most complex and trickiest to define as they can be nowhere, everywhere, and out there. Like 2023's Best Picture Academy Award Winner *Everything Everywhere All at Once*, there is a distinct interdimensionality to Lunar Saros 103, LS124, LS141, and LS142. They all carry within their spheres of consciousness an ability to escape into their own special world of imagination, offering enlightenment that can uplift the world. And paradoxically, being a mutable sign, they can flip over and reveal in the next second the darkness and deepest sorrow that lies within the heart of every human being. Their sensitivity, style, and exquisite capacity to respond to each moment as a singular act of creation is a gift freely given and enjoyed by all those following the career highlights of Novak Djokovic, Kathryn Bigelow, and Robin Williams, whose lives are all touched by the imagination of these lunar eclipse water worlds.

You are about to meet Thomas Merton, who was born within four hours of a lunar Water eclipse. "Father Louis," the acclaimed 20th century American Trappist monk, author, activist, and spiritual leader was born on January 31, 1915, in the umbra of LS103—Zero Sum Zeal. He was a mystic and a contemplative, but he was also an intellectual and a man with a social and political consciousness, having published more than fifty books, two thousand poems and numerous essays, reviews and lectures. As his journals reveal, he was a man of many contradictions; a man endlessly in search of God, but, because he never found it, wrote endlessly about that search. He was a Trappist monk devoted not only to obedience but also to silence and to his belief in non-violence and civil rights. Father Louis dances with two sets of cosmic parents, the Water Dragons of LS103—Zero Sum Zeal—and his Air Dragon parents from LS136—Risk and Reward. This additional lunar Air eclipse with its analysis can be found in the Notes section.

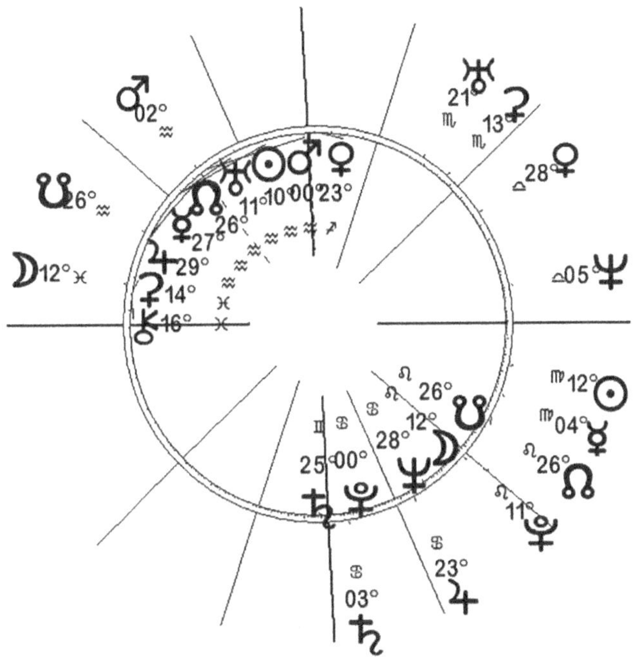

Thomas Merton
PREBLE—LS103

January 31, 1915 • 9:00 AM • Prades, France

Outside
LS103

September 4, 472 • 11:08:06 AM • South Pole

"Without a life of the spirit our whole existence becomes unsubstantial and illusory."

-THOMAS MERTON

Thomas Merton's Connections to the Dragons of LS103
↑North Node with South Node↓
Saturn with Saturn

1st Harmonics: SNode – NNode, SNode – Mercury/Jupiter, Moon – Ceres/Chiron, Pluto – Moon, Saturn – Pluto, Mars – Mars
2nd Harmonics: Pluto – Sun/Uranus

Merton benefited enormously from the supercharge off the opposite polarity of the nodal axis. The Saturn ties are helpful but what stands out is his stunning 2nd Harmonic Pluto to his Sun-Uranus conjunction in Aquarius. Notice how his tenth degree Sun and his double-dipped Aquarian eleventh degree Uranus receive the eclipse Pluto's equally potent eleventh degree liberalism coming through the star maker sign of Leo. LS103's Moon at the double Piscean twelfth was not easy on his Ceres/Chiron because when those two energies merge they are seriously sensual: Living a monastic life would have only heightened somatic streams of stress, internalizing conflict if not moral anxiety, so much so that Father Louis would fall deeply and passionately in love when the arrival of LS111 in May 1966 activated his Sun/Moon and Moon/Uranus midpoints at 14 Scorpio.

For anyone with a Water Moon, here are the Water eclipses that will help guide you home. Out of forty-seven Lunar Saros Series, there is only one that features a Moon in Cancer. It is a unique and very special Lunar Saros Series eclipse and one worth waiting for. If this is your dragon family, you belong to a rare cosmic event that only occurred once during the 20th and 21st centuries.

Lunar Saros 137

Out of forty-seven Lunar Saros Series, there are only four that feature a Moon in Scorpio. These will be of special interest to anyone with their natal Moon in Scorpio.

Lunar Saros 113
Lunar Saros 114
Lunar Saros 115
Lunar Saros 131

Out of forty-seven Lunar Saros Series, there are only four that feature a Moon in Pisces. These will be of special interest to anyone with their natal Moon in Pisces.

Lunar Saros 103
Lunar Saros 124
Lunar Saros 141
Lunar Saros 142

Water Dragon Allegiance

Lunar Saros 103:

The Lone Ranger, Joan of Arc, St. Bartholomew's Day Massacre

Lunar Saros 113:

Louis Theroux, Jack Dorsey, Apollo 13

Lunar Saros 114:

Roger Ebert, The Beatles, Anthony Bourdain

Lunar Saros 115:

13th Amendment to Abolish Slavery in the USA, Chelsea Manning, Alice Bailey

Lunar Saros 124:

J. R. R. Tolkien, Prince Harry & Meghan Markle, Sally Ride

Lunar Saros 131:

Anne Frank, Chernobyl, *News Flash!* Johnny Depp's $10 Million Win

Lunar Saros 137:

Lenny Bruce, Mark Twain, Ray Charles

Lunar Saros 141:

Novak Djokovic, Kathryn Bigelow,
News Flash! COVID-19 is no longer a global health emergency

Lunar Saros 142:

Jordan B. Peterson, David Letterman, MrBeast

LUNAR SAROS 103

"Sometimes I've believed as many as six impossible things before breakfast."

-Lewis Carroll

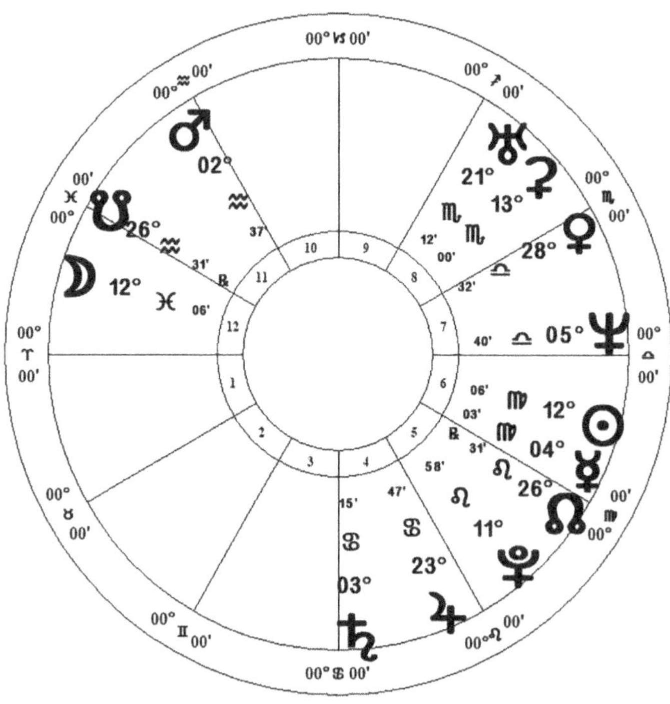

Lunar Saros 103

September 4, 472 • 11:08:06 AM • South Pole

Zero Sum Zeal

This South Node Pisces Lunar eclipse series ended in 1933, after a run of 82 returns, one of the longest life spans in the entire Saros Series. Its presence in our planetary consciousness gave it ample time to develop a decidedly religious fervor and passion for reform. The family's rebel-rousing but equal-opportunity OOB (24S45) Mars in Aquarius YOD with Saturn's sextile to Mercury in rulership attracted courageous zealots with mass appeal. And for good measure, a theatrical aka messianic mood lingered in the air from Neptune's opening trine to Mars.

The ability to sense and serve are noted Piscean attributes as is a heightened sensitivity and flair for diversion/distraction indemnified by a double Piscean twelfth degree overtone flowing through the eclipse axis. All told, these special qualities would fit well within LS103's See-Saw pattern that constantly generated opposing viewpoints and opinions. There was never a shortage of controversy or conflict with this family. Its arrival was often a call to arms, forcing many to choose sides. In the end, with battle lines drawn, victory would go to those who either stood their ground or beat a hasty retreat. Clearly, these lunar eclipse players were masters of the zero sum game.

Charts that carry a See-Saw pattern are prone to take an either/or position, like the Fire dragons of LS149—Breakthroughs and Comebacks—in Section One who live and breathe contrast and controversy. Choosing the correct alignment is often the antidote to deescalating the fields of conflict that continually flow through these controversial fields. See-Saw patterns are known to generate leaders with high levels of awareness who view life through a contrasting set of values.

Depth and diversity along with public appeal are a feature of Jupiter's MR to the Moon, a decidedly lucky exchange of cooperation that is found in only one other Lunar Saros Series—the feisty Fire dragons of LS132— Reach for the Stars. Take a moment to look back and appreciate what a Moon/Jupiter MR can truly accomplish. In our current energetic field, Jupiter's resonance was more attuned to the beat of übernationalism that was ready to defend, protect, and even sacrifice when necessary. Uranus in square to the nodal axis underscored a "frontier form of justice" approach to problem solving.

Apart from the Fire dragons of LS102 and LS110, LS103 is the only Water dragon family in the entire Lunar Saros Series that carried an extreme OOB (28N08) Pluto. Such high declinations for Pluto are rare and characteristically reluctant to engage in attempts at reconciliation, and certainly not with an edgy quincunx to a Piscean Moon finely tuned into the mass consciousness of the times. Like the Pluto transit of Leo from 1937 to 1958, this lunar eclipse was no stranger to hero-worship, waging war and cults of personality. Just take a look back at the pride and determination that marked the Allied Powers victory over Germany and Japan in World War II and then their involvement on the Korean peninsula in the early 50's. Pluto in Leo's taste for self-aggrandizement and its love of power is almost insatiable.

Closest Midpoints: Venus/Uranus-Neptune, Mercury/Mars-Neptune
Isotraps: Mercury/Venus conjunct Uranus/Pluto
Mars/Jupiter opposition Uranus/Neptune

1900—2100 Eclipses: Lunar Saros—103

1915, 1933
Length of cycle —1,460 years
Series ended—February 10, 1933

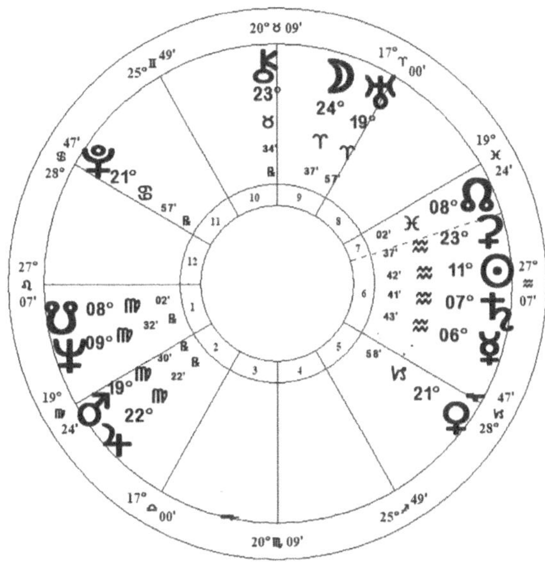

The First Lone Ranger Broadcast

January 31, 1933 • 7:00 PM • Detroit, MI, USA

The Lone Ranger debuted on Detroit radio station WXYZ on January 31, 1933, to the stirring notes of the *William Tell Overture* and a shout of "Hi-yo, Silver! Away!"[1] He was the masked Texas Ranger astride his glorious white stallion Silver, and his six-shooter fired silver bullets.[2] Personifying the best of his PREBLE, the Lone Ranger was devoted to the cause of frontier justice with a little help from his laconic sidekick Tonto. The show easily made the transition from radio to television in 1949 with programming that ran until 1957.[3]

The show premiered within LS103's eclipse window that poured through 21 Leo on February 10, 1933, onto the broadcast's Ceres at 23 Aquarius. It was a time of economic and political turmoil and in their despair, people would turn to leaders who could stand and deliver. The show both entertained and challenged the prevailing social codes of behavior in matters of race, ethnicity, and justice. Its huge success romanticized a long ago wild and lawless west and turned the Lone Ranger into a modern day Medieval Knight of the Realm.

The Lone Ranger broadcast of 1933 held a Locomotive pattern, and its keyword is Reformer—it gives a very ambitious drive that can be used to accomplish great things. Used negatively it acts more like the Rebel refusing to play. Three ties connect both charts. The first is LS103's Jupiter and its opposition to Venus, the engine of the broadcast chart. This signifies that conflicts are not that difficult to resolve. The remaining ties involve the luminaries: LS103's Sun lights up the Lone Ranger's Savior SNode/Neptune at the same time that the eclipse Pluto at 11 Leo's 2nd Harmonic receives power from his double-dipped eleventh degree Aquarian Sun. Silver bullets and a fiery stallion named Silver —there's definitely a mythic dimension to the Lone Ranger's character that embodies both the darkness and the light. He does, after all, wear a black mask and dresses in white. He is a solar hero, fighting injustice at every turn. He is a carrier of the light and in that capacity holds the sacred power to dispense justice in his de facto role as judge and jury.

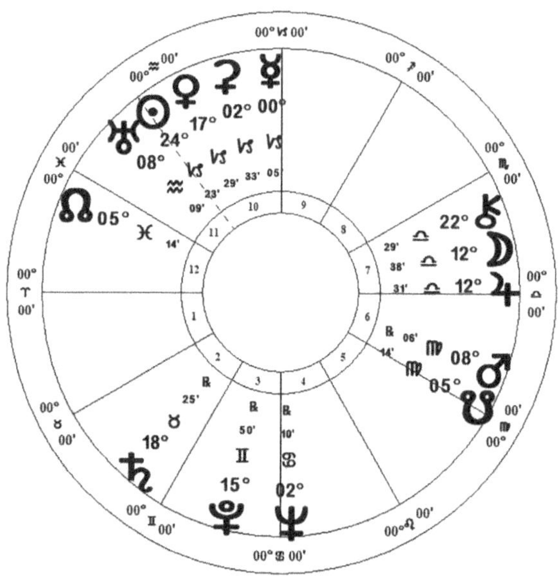

Joan of Arc
PREBLE—LS118

January 6, 1412 OS–January 15, 1412 NS • TOB Unknown • Domrémy, France

---

15th-Century Mystic and French Martyr

"Joan was a being so uplifted from the ordinary run of mankind that she finds no equal in a thousand years."

-Sir Winston Churchill[4]

The date of Saint Joan's birth is recorded as January 6, 1412.[5] On March 31, 1428, when Joan was 16 years old, Lunar Saros 103 arrived, flowing through a very Libran nineteenth degree of Libra, rousing her twenty-second "take charge/kill or be killed" Chiron into action. With her country in the midst of the Hundred Years War, and suffering the depths of hell, the chronicles of the time state that Joan fearlessly and relentlessly petitioned to be taken to the royal court of Charles VII of France to deliver a divinely inspired message from God.[6] Since her birth, ongoing internal wars within two factions of the French Royal family made it even easier for the English King Henry V to invade and press his historical claim for the French throne.[7]

Documents retrieved from this time in French history state that in May 1428, on her way to Charles VII's royal court, she was initially rejected by the local magistrate, Robert de Baudricourt. Her courageous spirit won over the local magistrate; he changed his mind and soon Joan would change the course of French history.

Despite being viewed as a simple maid, unable to read or write, she went on to inspire the allegiance of thousands of French troops to rally to her banner. Churchill's *A History of the English-Speaking Peoples Vol. 1: The Birth of Britain* writes that having been wounded in battle by an arrow, she "plucked it out and returned to the charge only to be hurled into the ditch." Lying prostrate on the ground, she commanded new efforts. "Forward, fellow countrymen! God has delivered them into our hands."[8]

Helped by the arrival of these take-no-prisoners dragons, LS103 provided support through links of solidarity from their Saturn at 3 Cancer to her patriotic Neptune at 2 Cancer. In addition, Joan's SNode at 5 Virgo conjunction to LS103's inspired Mercury at 4 Virgo gave her deep and unrestricted access to the eclipse field's command post. The eclipse Mercury/Venus conjunct Uranus/Pluto isotrap seems made for "The Maid of Orléans" as it supported an eloquent and energetic framework for the forces of radical restructuring and revolution.

There is still no scholarly agreement as to the exact date of Joan's birth. However, even without confirmed birth data, lunar eclipse analysis can offer a fresh perspective on the events and more importantly people of those times.

Whether or not she was hearing the voice of God is irrelevant. The story of Joan of Arc in the final years of her young and very short life is a testament to the sacredness and spiritual obsession that flowed forth from the spirit of this lunar eclipse family.

St. Bartholomew's Day Massacre
PREBLE—LS103

August 24, 1572 OS • September 3, 1572 NS • 12:01 AM • Paris, France

In the Name of God's Greatness

Catholics and Protestants killed each other by the hundreds of thousands during the 16th and 17th centuries. The historical record states that on August 24, 1572, French Catholics attacked communities of French Protestants killing between 5,000 and 10,000 Protestants in less than twenty-four hours. Yuval Noah Harari in his blockbuster bestseller *Sapiens: A Brief History of Humankind* writes:

> More Christians were killed by fellow Christians in those twenty-four hours than by the polytheistic Roman Empire throughout its entire existence. When the pope in Rome heard the news from France, he

was so overcome by joy that he organized festive prayers to celebrate the occasion.[9]

The lunar eclipse that preceded the St. Bartholomew's Day Massacre was the 62nd return of Lunar Saros 103 on calendar date June 25, 1572, OS, July 5, 1572, NS, with an activation at the feisty thirteenth degree of Capricorn. This return fell within a Last Quarter phase with its lunar degree in sextile to its foundational and deeply devotional twelfth degree Piscean Moon. At this stage of the eight fold phase the waning sextile has a need to purge and prune whatever now seems excessive. There is a natural tendency to pare down and separate the wheat from the chaff, and all this is done in the Last Quarter phase of a cycle known for a sense of dissatisfaction, a loss of joy, and a need for reorientation.

LS103 Summary

Zeal flowed forth from these ferocious Water Warrior Dragons, birthed in the early years of the Middle Ages. Their presence carried a formidable power of social persuasion, inciting acts of a religious and even violent nature, attracting many who answered the call of king and country. With an energy field radiating an unfaltering connection to the very heavens themselves, many would be caught up in the currents of other-worldly splendor with its implication of celestial blessing.

One has to look no further than the luminaries presented for this series to appreciate how impactful these eclipses are on the emerging human energy system. Of note is the American Trappist monk and acclaimed author, activist, and spiritual leader Thomas Merton, who was born within four hours of this eclipse in 1915. As noted in the Introduction, people born within hours of a lunar eclipse seem to be able to "channel" and even magnify the eclipse field life force into every facet of their being regardless of time spent immersed in the previous lunar eclipse field. We remain slain by the assault of stellar grandeur in our midst, only to be "god-smacked" yet again by the mystery and wonder of it all.

Phase	Return	Year
New Moon	68th	1680
Crescent	72nd	1752
First Quarter	76th	1824
Gibbous	80th	1897

LS103 Luminaries

Emperor Go-Horikawa	March 22, 1212
Peter I of Portugal	April 8, 1320
Roger de Mortimer	April 11, 1374
Jingtai Emperor	September 21, 1428
Andrey Bolshoy	August 14, 1446
Daniel Boone	November 2, 1734
Lewis Carroll	January 27, 1832
Ruth St. Denis	January 20, 1879
Louis "Lepke" Buchalter	February 6, 1897
Charles Kingsford Smith	February 9, 1897
Gary Moore[E]	January 31, 1915
Thomas Merton[E]	January 31, 1915
Lorne Greene	February 12, 1915
Zero Mostel	February 28, 1915
Costa Gavras[E2]	February 12, 1933
Yoko Ono	February 18, 1933
Nina Simone	February 21, 1933
Philip Roth	March 19, 1933

PREBLE—136

Gary Moore

Thomas Merton

Yoko Ono

Nina Simone

Philip Roth

---

1. https://en.wikipedia.org/wiki/Lone_Ranger#cite_note-dunning407-23. Retrieved Jan. 19, 2022.
2. Ibid.
3. Ibid
4. Sir Winston Churchill, *A History of the English-Speaking Peoples: Volume 1 The Birth of Britain* (London: Bloomsbury, 2015), p. 260.
5. http://archive.joan-of-arc.org/joanofarc_short_biography.html. Retrieved Jan. 9, 2022
6 . Ibid.
7. Ibid.
8. Churchill, *A History of the English-Speaking People.*, p. 258.
9. Yuval Noah Harari, *Sapiens: A Brief History of Humankind*, p. 241.

LUNAR SAROS 113

"I am constantly amazed by Tina Fey. And I am Tina Fey."

-TINA FEY

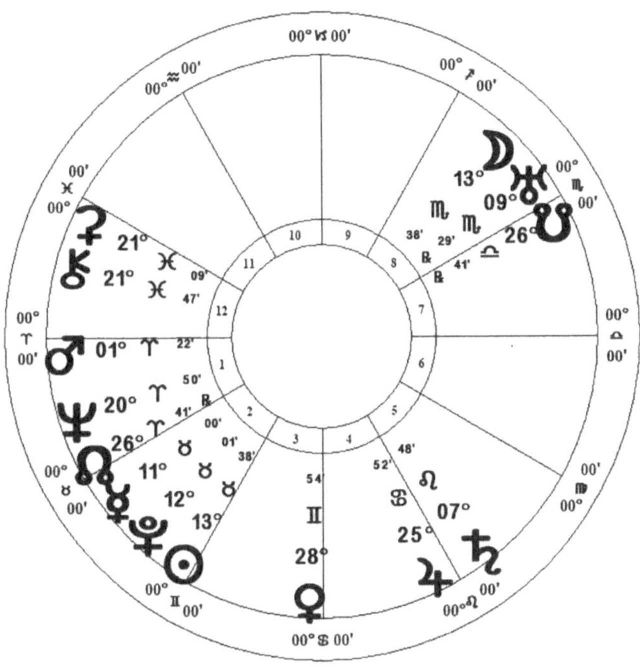

Lunar Saros 113

May 3, 888 • 6:55:17 PM • South Pole

Stripped Down

Opportunities emerge out of the depths of this Scorpio South Node Lunar Saros Series. These ancient Water Dragons pulsate with messages designed to bring out the best in us. The ability to focus on the achievement of goals is one of its many strengths. Traditional ruler Mars in Aries is all in and at the AP is strategically positioned to help move our culture forward in a different direction. This is evident in so many ways but especially with Uranus in such potent proximity to the eclipse Moon. In addition, the presence of the fertile and pragmatic Mercury/Pluto conjunction to Uranus on the eclipse axis indicates an agile and techno-savvy mindset that is infused with the spirit of global if not galactic enterprise. These Water Dragons have seen it all, done it all, and are keeping the faith, waiting for the next iteration of delight to unfold from its interactions with its beloved human family.

Lunar Saros 113 is a rare double-handled Fan pattern; the eclipse Moon/Uranus conjunction is the handle to a persuasive and dignified Mars trine Saturn in Leo. Mercury's MR to Venus in Gemini and its across-the-board influence in all the tightest midpoint structures provides multiple platforms for the conveyance of information. The Pluto/Eclipse-Mercury midpoint along with the Mercury/Eclipse-Uranus midpoint encourage radical if not revolutionary ideas to flourish. For many, these Water Dragons will help to close a chapter in one's life while for others their tidal flux will bring renewal and a second or even third phase to the life. All will feel relief that solutions are being found that bring either comfort or resolution. LS113 is an enigma: It is both a heavy hitter and delightfully playful and as all paradoxes go, able to play both sides with equal aplomb.

A palpable mystical presence flows within the eclipse field. It is empowered by the Mars, Mercury, and Uranus trifecta. Mars' unique stature gives it formidable forward momentum, able to use whatever resources are at hand with little to no resistance. With a very fast Moon and a Promethean Mercury in MR to the highest OOB Venus (26N49) in the entire 47 Lunar Saros Series, there is literally nothing that can touch the prodigy potential of this high energy eclipse. The field is well connected—Jupiter's square to the nodal axis encourages the sharing of experiences within a larger community and context.

Neptune's diffusion throughout the eclipse field and its hyper-connectivity means prosperity is just a thought away as innovation and initiation can literally pop into existence from anywhere. LS113 may bring, in light of the Neptune/Mars-Uranus midpoint, an opportunity to experience "Unusual achievements through an extraordinary power of effort."[1] The overall effect of this lunar eclipse family is nothing short of miraculous and its potent Ceres conjunct Chiron at 21 degrees Pisces is another fold in the fabric of fate that these wise old dragons wear so well. Fellow LS113 illuminati Marianne Williamson reminds us that when we ask ourselves, "Who am I to be brilliant, gorgeous, talented, fabulous? Actually, who are you not to be." May her words help us stay open to life's messages of hope and renewal. And one last thought: 2096 will bring it all home when these Water Dragons hit the final stretch and their end-game begins. They're saving the best for last. Mark the date—May 7, 2096.

Closest Midpoints: Mercury/Uranus-Pluto, Pluto/Eclipse-Mercury
Isotraps: Mercury/Venus conjunct Mars/Saturn
Moon/Uranus opposition Mercury/Pluto

1900—2100 Eclipses: Lunar Saros—113

1916, 1934, 1952, 1970, 1988, 2006, 2024, 2042, 2060, 2078, 2096
Length of cycle —1,262 years
Series ends—June 10, 2150

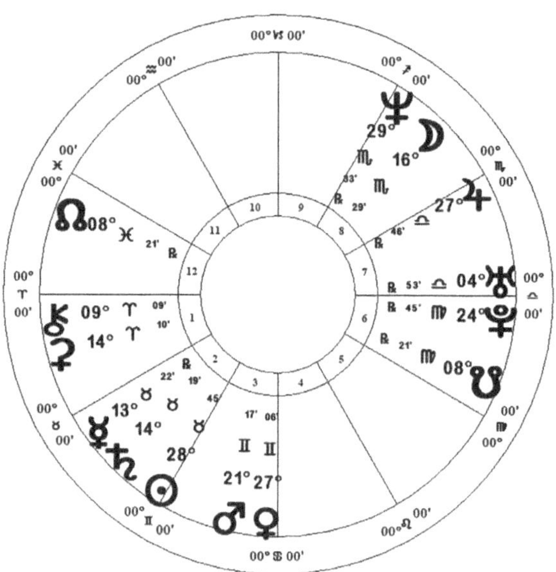

Louis Theroux
PREBLE—LS113

May 20, 1970 • TOB Unknown • Singapore, SINGAPORE

Weird Weekends with Louis

"I think what I'm good at is getting to know people and trying to build a relationship over a few weeks and trying to get to the truth."

-Louis Theroux

Awkwardly charming and unfettered by controversy, boundary-pushing filmmaker/investigator Louis Theroux has been in the TV trenches making films that involve extreme subcultures and feature people on the fringes of society for over twenty-five years. In the great George Carlin tradition of having front row seats to the circus of life, Theroux has planted his flag. Interviewed by Joe Rogan, Theroux sardonically stated that his world view is much like "an arsonist's thrill at seeing civilization burn."[2] To that end, let's take a look at the man and his Water Dragon family.

Louis Theroux's Connections to the Lunar Dragons of LS113

1st Harmonics: SNode – Jupiter, Mercury – Mercury, Mercury – Saturn, Venus – Venus, Pluto – Mercury, Pluto – Saturn
2nd Harmonics: Moon – Mercury, Moon – Saturn, Mars – Uranus, Ceres – Pluto, Chiron – Pluto

The essence of Lunar Saros 113 can now be factored into the framework of Louis' life. Let's begin by taking a look at his natal chart. Of all the patterns, and there are a lot, it is his Mars/Venus conjunction in Gemini in square to Pluto and in trine to Jupiter that tells us what he values, and as a Taurus we need to firmly establish that fact. These aspects provide the basic building blocks of his personality, as our core identity emerges from what we value. His occupation as a filmmaker is perfect as it fulfills many of the requirements of the stated patterns to perfection: In an upbeat manner, he gets to serve the public need to know; he's friendly so he's rarely refused an interview and all his films are by invitation; his brand is identifiable as quirky but informative with a willingness to venture into the land of taboo subjects and unchartered waters. His Sun channels the power of the Pleiades with all its myth and magic into Neptune at the penetrative and regenerative twenty-ninth degree of Scorpio.

A 1st Harmonic SNode forms a Cosmic Bridge to his Jupiter trine Venus laying down spirit gifts of wit, adaptability, and curiosity. LS113s Mercury/Pluto/Sun holds a tight embrace to his Mercury/Saturn as does their Venus to his natal Venus. Imagine all this free form, cutting-edge agility infused by the immense attractor-factor of the most OOB lunar eclipse Venus ever and now imagine all of that pouring through the emerging consciousness of his birth chart.

As usual, the 2nd Harmonics are even more impressive. The eclipse Moon with its conjunction to Uranus lights up his Mercury/Saturn in a way that might even surprise Theroux's solid Saturn in Taurus by encouraging him to discover personal resources and skills he never knew existed. The Moon/Uranus pattern is a highly transferable portal of intuitive, flash-drive unpredictability and fly-by-the-seat-of-your-pants potential.

The Ceres/Chiron 2nd Harmonics to Pluto are extremely significant because both fields hold the conjunction: The eclipse has it in "trusting in the flow of life" Pisces while Theroux's Ceres/Chiron points the way to a life of courage and enterprise. The symmetry deepens the resonance and suggests that Theroux's pathway to happiness and healing is tied into offering service to the world through his in-your-face can do spirit.

At the time of his birth, the Water Dragons of LS113 were experiencing their sixty-first return in a Last Quarter phase of their seventy-one returns lifespan. The Last Quarter phase that began in 1934 transitioned into the Balsamic phase in 2006. Theroux's life as a fearless investigative filmmaker does his family and in particular this phase proud. He is a true warrior who feels a public responsibility to uncover the often hidden stories that no one else takes the initiative and open-heartedness to explore.

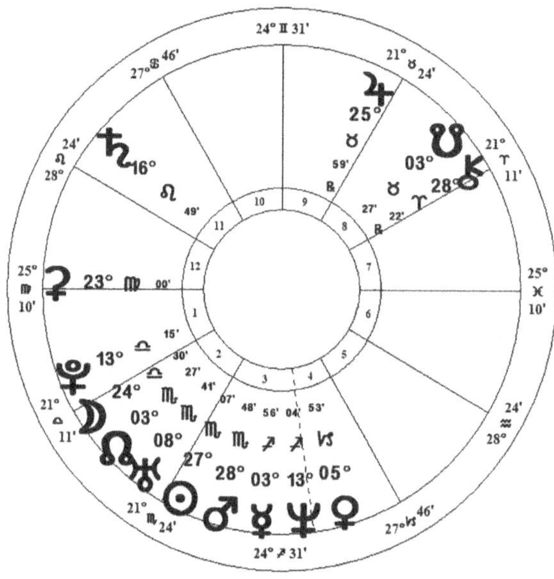

Jack Dorsey
PREBLE—LS145

November 19, 1976 • 1:43 AM • St. Louis, MO, USA

Internet Entrepreneur/Philanthropist

One of 2023's most eligible bachelor billionaires.

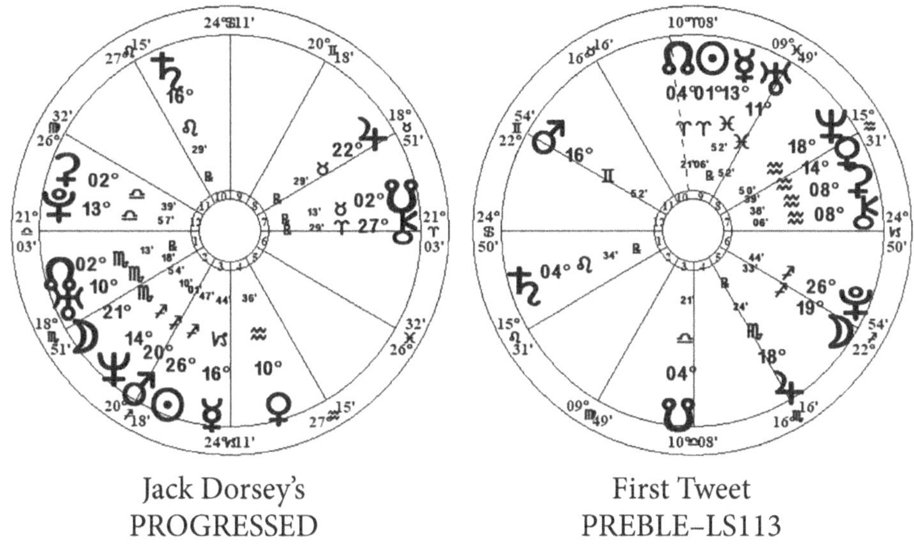

Jack Dorsey's PROGRESSED

March 21, 2006 • 12:50 PM • San Francisco, CA, USA

First Tweet PREBLE–LS113

March 21, 2006 • 12:50 PM • San Francisco, CA, USA

Co-Founder of Twitter/Founder of Square aka Block

"Make every detail perfect, and limit the number of details to perfect."

-Jack Dorsey

On March 14, 2006, LS113 touched down at 24 Virgo on Jack Dorsey's natal Ceres at 23 Virgo, eagerly awaiting its next assignment. Dorsey's background in web development and dispatch software for couriers, taxis, and emergency services had prepared him well. With Sun in opposition to Jupiter in Taurus and its trine to his activated Ceres, Jack Dorsey was about to take the ride of his life on a fast-rising wave of technological innovation into a world of connectivity and wealth.

The kinetic power and potential of LS113 was breathtaking in its expediency. Within a week, Dorsey published the first Twitter message on March 21, 2006, at 12:50 pm; by July 15, a full version of the Twitter platform was introduced to the public.[3] When asked why Twitter only allows one hundred and forty characters per "tweet," Dorsey replied that anyone on the planet, using either the cheapest or most expensive of devices, could send and receive a message using those characters.[4]

Jack Dorsey's Connections to the Dragons of LS113

1st Harmonics: SNode – Moon, Moon – Uranus, Mars – DSC
2nd Harmonics: Uranus – Uranus, Neptune/NNode – Moon, Mercury/Pluto/Sun – Uranus, Ceres/Chiron – Ceres

The connectivity between Dorsey and LS113's foundation chart is breathtaking in its rapport. Considering the age difference, both have an almost identical Uranus placement, a quintessential factor in the sudden and precise technological frequency that contributed to Twitter's innovative design. The eclipse 2nd Harmonic Ceres-Chiron and its insightful twenty-first global degree conjunction in Pisces to his Ceres at the progressive twenty-third degree of Virgo on his ascendant is a key player especially with its trine to a Ninth House Jupiter. Twitter is a transformative and addictive social networking tool that brought Jack Dorsey fame and fortune. Dorsey's success as an internet entrepreneur can be gleaned from his third degree NNode and its conjunction to an eighth degree wealth oriented Uranus in the Second House of resources.

The Oxford English Dictionary's (OED) chief editor John Simpson set a new precedent on June 17, 2013, within weeks of the arrival of the newest Lunar Saros Series LS150—Be Brave—by releasing the announcement that the noun and verb "tweet" had just been added to the OED, breaking the rule that required a new word to be current for ten years before being considered for inclusion.

Apollo 13
PREBLE—LS113

April 11, 1970 • 2:13 PM • Merritt Island, FL, USA

"Houston, we have a problem..."

-Tom Hanks in *Apollo 13*

The Apollo 13 mission—with its transmitted iconic understatement—was rendered unforgettable by Tom Hank's portrayal of astronaut Jim Lovell in Ron Howard's movie, *Apollo 13*. In his book *Apollo Expeditions to the Moon*, James Lovell states that the message was first spoken by Jack Swigert. It was April 13, 1970, two days into the mission, and Lovell had just signed off a forty-nine-minute TV broadcast, biding all a good night.[5] Then at 10:05 pm Eastern Time, "a message came in the form of a sharp bang and vibration to which Swigert said, 'Houston, we've had a problem here.'"[6] Talk about a revelation—and word play. By changing the tense of the verb from the past to the present—from "had" to "have"—director Ron Howard turned a dangerous moment in the perilous flight of Apollo 13 into one of the most dramatic true-to-life odysseys ever attempted on film. We viewers lived through it as it was happening.

On February 21, 1970, six weeks earlier, Lunar Saros 113 had set its sights on 2 Virgo, effortlessly docking with Swigert's Venus at 3 Virgo along with its

Neptune/Sun conjunction. On April 8, just seventy-two hours before the mission was to launch, backup crewman Swigert was called in to replace Command Module pilot Ken Mattingly who had been exposed to German measles.[7] Swigert's place in history was advanced by LS113's contact with his triple conjunction Venus/Neptune/Sun and its association with weakness and illusion. Lovell's Mercury at 6 Pisces received the eclipse by opposition; as Commander he was able to resolve the conflict by projecting the problems it represented, giving space for collaboration and innovative solutions to emerge. The Moon at the time of launch was conjunct the fixed star Betelgeuse, which is known for its military might and ability to take decisive action. Success and even fame are often the result after overcoming hardship.

LS113 Summary

Life is literally awash in messages that hold the power to invigorate and innovate when these ancient Water Dragons appear. Wherever their celestial tides rise and fall, their waters are sure to refresh a parched landscape. They are amazingly adept at finding practical, stream-lined solutions to day-to-day problems: they have a knack for managing multi-levels of reality. The eclipse links to "firsts," risk takers, and all those who favor the unconventional. It is always a good idea to keep your awareness open as Fate may choose you to become a spokesperson for a timely idea, project, or ground-breaking path. Spending time in new environments will help get the creative juices flowing as well as providing for an astonishing array of real characters to enjoy. The majority of endeavors meet with little to no resistance.

To be in harmony in the time and space created by these dragon dancers is to find the essence, the spirit of the thing that rocks your world. Simplicity is an undervalued concept but one these Water Dragons are deeply immersed in and, by example, are willing to share. Getting back to basics—whether by stripping down or willingly removing the fluff—should prove delightfully entertaining. To be a part of this clan by birthright or by rite of passage is to know that your "true North Star" is overhead; whether you can see it or not doesn't matter because it can see you. There is an emotional intelligence here that carries the day and will carry you as well. Remember, this is a family that loves innovation and originality in all its forms and will be there to guide you every step of the way.

Phase	Return	Year
Full Moon	51st	1789
Disseminating	55th	1861
Last Quarter	59th	1934
Balsamic	63rd	2006

LS113 Luminaries

Gustave Moreau	April 6, 1826
Alice Bailey	June 16, 1880
Golda Meir	May 3, 1898
M C Escher	June 17, 1898
Yehudi Menuhin	April 22, 1916
Francis Crick	June 8, 1916
Paul Ekman	February 15, 1934
Ralph Nader	February 27, 1934
Gloria Steinem	March 25, 1934
Alan Arkin	March 26, 1934
Harvey Weinstein	March 19, 1952
Bob Costas	March 22, 1952
Dan Aykroyd	July 1, 1952
Marianne Williamson	July 8, 1952
Andre Agassi	April 29, 1970
Tina Fey	May 18, 1970
Louis Theroux	May 20, 1970
Christophe Nolan	July 30, 1970
Adele	May 5, 1988
Chris Smalls	July 4, 1988
Julianne Hough	July 20, 1988
Tyson Fury	August 12, 1988

---

1. Reinhold Ebertin, *The Combination of Stellar Influences,* p 207.

2. Joe Rogan, Interview with Louis Theroux #835. https://www.youtube.com/watch?v=uX-yS-74sRTE. Retrieved Apr. 7, 2022.

3. https://en.wikipedia.org/wiki/Twitter

4. http://www.cbsnews.com/news/twitters-jack-dorsey-on-60-minutes/ Retrieved Apr. 7, 2022.

5. James A. Lovell, *Apollo Expeditions to the Moon*, Chapter 13.1 http://history.nasa.gov/SP-350/ch-13-1.html. Retrieved Apr. 7, 2022.

6. Ibid.

7. http://www.jsc.nasa.gov/Bios/htmlbios/swigert-jl.html. Retrieved Apr. 7, 2022.

LUNAR SAROS 114

"Almighty God, I am sorry I am now an atheist,
but have You read Nietzsche?"

—JOHN FANTE

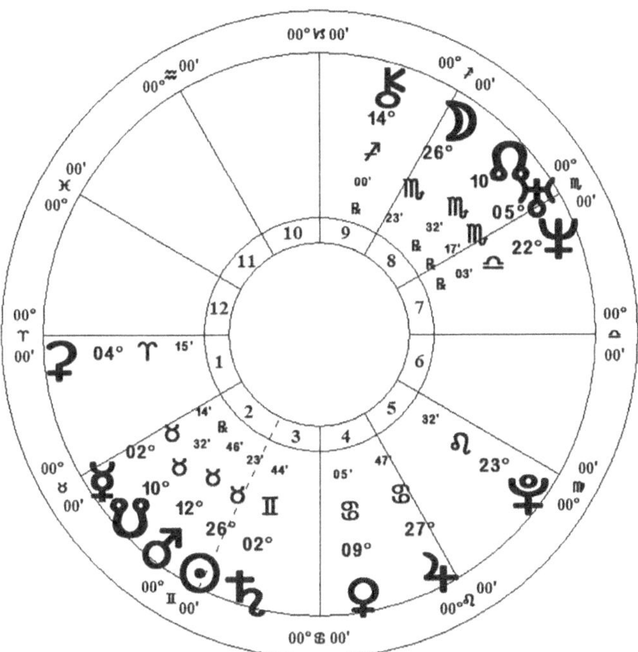

Lunar Saros 114

May 18, 971 • 3:50:26 AM • North Pole

Carried by the Tide

A Fixed T-Square with Pluto on this Scorpio eclipse axis provides a scaffolding of enormous value. It offers support for those courageous enough to keep on moving forward regardless of the obstructions and hindrances encountered along the way. A Fixed T-Square is always a thing of beauty but one holding both lights with Pluto as the focal determinator is devastatingly awesome in its potential for harnessing the power of passion in the development of character and moral fortitude. Pluto in Leo is a constant call to reveal the true seat of self in all its glory, and to develop real independence, clarity, and understanding. It is a never-ending, always available portal of manifestation ready for the next version of creation. The conjunction of Mars to the South Node has as a stellar backdrop—the magnificent Pleiades—known throughout the ages to increase one's productivity along with affording positions of leadership to those worthy of such honor. Rapid shifts in all areas of life come regardless of one's level of satisfaction; such is the nature of accelerated evolution made possible through the Mars/SNode condition that is continually releasing energy back into the void. Either way, tremendous growth is possible. Regardless of the circumstances in which we find ourselves, this eclipse family reminds us of the great rhythms that govern our lives. All things considered, let previous successes ground your ego and know that you're able to deal with whatever comes your way. The eclipse Moon's waxing square to Pluto is relentlessly building in competence through an insatiable appetite for real world experience. The old order must yield to the incoming wave of new life. If we can learn to flow and not fight the powerful currents that reach our shores, all manner of storms can be weathered.

In addition, the Moon's waxing trine to Jupiter in exaltation gives vitality and an optimistic mindset to any challenge at hand. Generosity and a spirit of bonhomie are part of every major decision made. Opportunities, as with all trines, are always around the next corner, but here they can take advantage of Jupiter's special status. Whether your interest is business, leisure, sports, politics, counseling, or entertainment, there's something here for everyone. Mercury's double dip of second degree Taurean tenacity and its opposition to Uranus pulls in the NNode and increases the chances that careers in the STEM fields will be highly valued and worth pursuing as the tidal forces of innovation and high-tech flood the field.

Lunar Saros 114, on its fifty-ninth return as of 2017, is now presenting through its final Last Quarter Phase. As we attend to their interplay of patterns and especially to their Mercury/Mars-Neptune and Mars/Saturn-Neptune midpoints, we bring ourselves into alignment with their evolving sensitivity to the size and scope of their own capacity for disillusionment. To be in resonance with them as they pass through this critical phase is to gain a foothold of understanding as to our own state of frustration along with the possibility of actually being able to correct and reorient ourselves. There is a profundity of wisdom to be experienced in the presence of these ancient Water Dragons.

Closest Midpoints: Mercury/Mars-Neptune, Mars/Saturn-Neptune
Isotraps: Sun/Neptune conjunct Mars/Uranus
Moon/Mars opposition Saturn/Uranus

1900—2100 Eclipses: Lunar Saros—114

1908, 1926, 1944, 1963, 1981, 1999, 2017, 2035, 2053, 2071, 2089
Length of cycle —1,262 years
Series ends—June 22, 2233

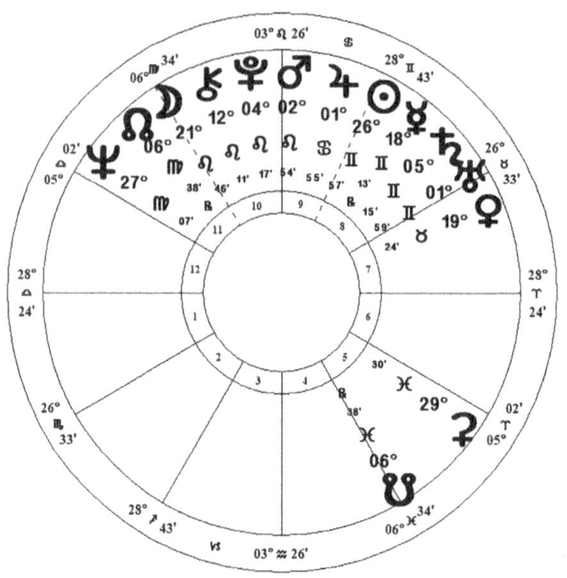

Roger Ebert
PREBLE—LS122

June 18, 1942 • 3:30 PM • Urbana, IL, USA

Film Critic Extraordinaire

"No matter what they're charging to get in, it's worth more to get out."

-Roger Ebert

That was Roger Ebert talking about a bad movie and he would know. Ebert's trademark "thumbs up" was worth the price of admission and certainly his reviews were worth the wait. The arrival of this lunar eclipse marked a changing of the guards in the annals of film review. On January 31, 1999, the eclipse returned at 11 Leo, spotlighting the maverick energies of Ebert's Chiron at 12 Leo. Sadly, the eclipse was witness to the passing of Ebert's long-time, twenty-four year, vitriolic partnership with his co-host Gene Siskel, a professional relationship that came on the heels of Ebert's 1975 Pulitzer Prize for Criticism. In his memoir, *Life Itself*, Ebert wrote: "We were linked in a bond beyond all disputing. 'You may be an asshole,' Gene would say, 'but you're my asshole.'"[1]

But the return of LS114 in 1999 would also bring good news with Roger Ebert establishing his very own film festival, held that year and every year thereafter in April, known as the Overlooked Film Festival in Champaign, Illinois. The festival was renamed Ebertfest in 2008 and is the only long-running film festival in the world created by a film critic.[2]

As film critics go, it's hard to beat a Bundle formation as it tends to be the chart pattern of a specialist. His Gemini Sun T-Square Neptune and Ceres gave him the wit and wisdom that nurtured the creative expression of his love for the movies. The eclipse activated the non-conformist energies of Chiron, allowing him access to the rich potentiality of his regal Leo stellium, while accessing LS114's diverging currents of change. Ebert's Chiron became the catalyst that catapulted him into his own realm of stardom, helped along by the Air dragons of PREBLE—LS122—Titans of Talent—and their formidable punch and power.

With Mercury and Venus both in rulership, Ebert could always be counted on to assess the value of a movie in a way that brought both pleasure and enlightenment to the viewer. Aided by the artistic Node/Sun-Venus midpoint, an Ebert review was *the* gold standard by which all others would be measured. Ebert was up to the challenge of LS114 and its stormy seas as it provided a sudden and surprising opportunity through which his personal taste and encyclopedic knowledge of the film industry would be repackaged to reach an even greater audience of movie goers. I found it fascinating to note how both charts carry the promise and provocation of a waning Neptune/Jupiter square with its power to give life to illusion and inspiration to life.

Tracking the lively art of conversation across the fields by way of Saturn shows how deep the cosmic paternity went: Ebert's creative fifth degree Gemini Saturn to LS114's resplendent third degree Gemini Saturn reinforced the familial love for literature, music, travel, theater, and the modern art of filmmaking. It is not uncommon for a Saturn contact such as this to signify the ending of a relationship especially with the eclipse Saturn in an even tighter relationship to Ebert's Uranus. These two planets are in his Eighth House and both rule the end-of-matters Fourth House. The eclipse Chiron at 15 Sagittarius held an intriguing opposition to his Promethean Mercury that would have accentuated his savant-like brilliance and ability to get under-appreciated films exposed to a more urbane audience. The eclipse axis on his Uranus marked a time of increased freedom and with the eclipse Pluto on his Moon a time of deep rejuvenation and personal transformation had arrived. In a span of six months, their unique dimensional fields would merge, offering Roger Ebert an expanded platform on which to play and slay both critics and fans with his genius.

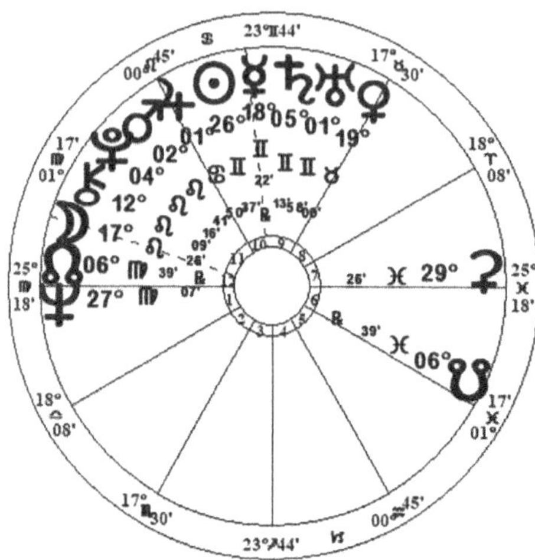

Paul McCartney
PREBLE—LS122

June 18, 1942 • 2:00 PM • Liverpool, UK

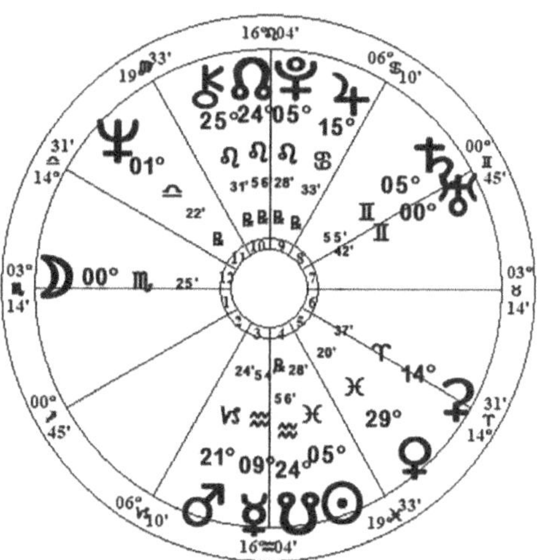

George Harrison
PREBLEs—LS132 & LS127

February 25, 1943 • 12:10 AM • Liverpool, UK

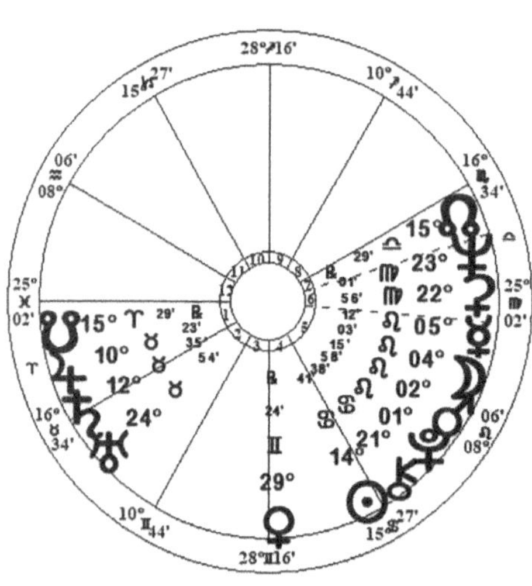

Ringo Starr
PREBLE—LS140

July 7, 1940 • 12:05 AM • Liverpool, UK

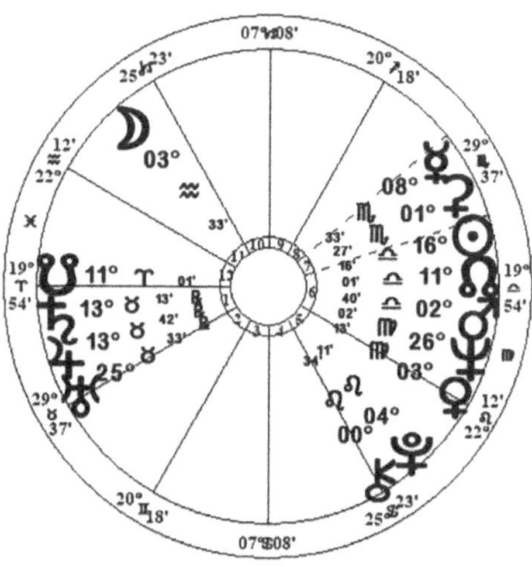

John Lennon
PREBLEs—LS140 & LS145

October 9, 1940 • 6:30 PM • Liverpool, UK

THE FAB FOUR

"The Beatles were a band, of course, and I loved their music. But they were also a cultural force that made it OK to be different. They didn't look like everyone else, and they still made the girls scream."

-GENE SIMMONS, KISS

McCartney reflected in 1992, "When [Lennon] died, I'd got my relationship back. And I feel sorry for George because he never did. George was arguing until the end." In response to Lennon's death, Harrison's statement to the press read, "I had and still have great love and respect for him. I am shocked and stunned."[3] Harrison started working on a tribute to him that came together shortly after LS114 touched down on January 20, 1981, at 00 Leo. Harrison's homage to Lennon, *All Those Years Ago,* was recorded on February 6, 1981, with a little help from former band mates Paul and Ringo.[4] It was a gift of gratitude and a testament to their enduring nostalgic ties.

Both McCartney and Starr have a Mars/Pluto in early Leo in opposition to Lennon's Aquarius Moon, giving a playful if not cathartic dimension to their often tense interactions, which probably fueled so much of their creative output. Harrison's Moon at 00 Scorpio, in square to Lennon's Moon, would have offered day-to-day friction. In addition, both Lennon and Harrison have Pluto in hard aspect to their Moon, giving rise to what Liz Greene states is a condition where love and hate go hand in hand in a close relationship.[5] Harrison's Moon/Pluto square is in an almost identical phase angle symmetry to the lunar eclipse making him deeply sensitized and synchronized to the eclipse field's cleansing waters of renewal. Plus Harrison, like Tony Robbins, as a member of the Air Dragon clan LS117, would benefit from Space Lanes across his ASC/DSC axis. However unlike Robbins' Space Lanes which are a permanent feature in his life's story, Harrison's would only be temporary.

As the eclipse approached at 00 Leo, Harrison, McCartney, and Starr embraced their loss and marked Lennon's passing with a soulful tribute. Ringo was especially hit hard; LS114's Sun on his Uranus at 25 Taurus along with his Saturn at 12 Taurus to the eclipse Mars would have left a deep impression. Both Paul and George can track their connections back to LS114, like Roger Ebert, through their natal Saturn both at 5 Gemini in direct link to the eclipse Saturn.

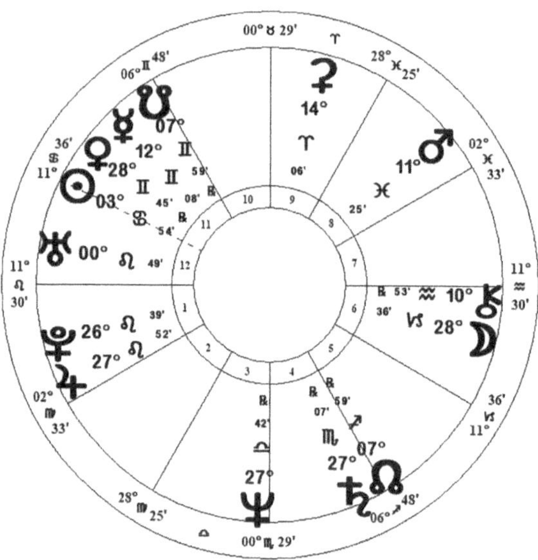

Anthony Bourdain
PREBLE—LS120

June 25, 1956 • 8:35 AM • New York, NY, USA

It was April 12, 1999. Anthony Bourdain's *New Yorker* essay "Don't Eat Before Reading This" is about to become the basis for his upcoming *Kitchen Confidential*, a book that would explode like a star and make him a celebrity.[6] At the time, Bourdain was a relatively unknown 43-year-old chef surviving the do-or-die cut-throat New York dining scene. But his life would fast be transformed into a globe-hopping celebrity chef/author and soon to be television star thanks to the tidal flux and flow of the ancient Water Dragons of LS114. All aspiring authors and creative souls take note: Your tide may just be about to turn if these water darlings are about to flow your way.

It was January 31, 1999, when they poured their largesse unto his 11 Leo Ascendant, baptizing him in all their media splendor with a complimentary side of Chiron at 10 Aquarius on his very public Seventh House DSC cusp. Let's take a look at why LS114 had such an effect on Bourdain's life at that critical moment. But before we do remember that every dragon family has their own unique style of behavior and are more than just the sum of their planetary parts.

LS114's core values honor a deliberate and steady build-up of power as well as a generosity of spirit that can easily be triggered by a similar spirit of generosity in the zeitgeist. In the case of Bourdain, it feels like a natural recognition of a fellow soul well deserving of tribute. So here are the contacts of which there are many: Their Mercury to his MC, Jupiter to both Uranus and his Moon, Chiron to his Mercury, Pluto to Pluto and saving the best for last, their Moon on his Saturn which also means their Sun opposite his Saturn. Both charts carry Ceres in Aries, reinforcing the importance that ego and personality play in their affections as well as both fields have Neptune in the third decanate of Libra making them incorrigible comrades of charm and idealism.

LS114 Summary

A change in circumstance often sets off an existential crisis that can lead to new opportunities with the arrival of these masterful Water Dragons. Loss is a part of the great cycle of life and no one is immune to its transformational undertow. This Lunar Saros Series is a family that brings its fair share of controversial twists and turns and loops and downfalls, all bent on renewing vitality and life direction. Whatever troubles or trials they bring, know you have the resources to handle what comes your way. These are often grave and soulful times. Deep romantic yearnings and relationship commitments, however, do not favor as well and those should be entered into with a certain degree of objectivity until time proves them worthy of more serious consideration. It is also important to keep an eye on all financial matters as market fluctuations and market drift may soon find many day traders out to sea and far from shore.

When the life force of Lunar Saros 114 connects by way of birthright or temporal transit, expect shifts in enthusiasm, work routines, leadership, and even careers as its waves of revitalization wash over. Boredom be gone, there's a new sheriff in town and everyone gets to start from scratch. This is a revitalizing lunar eclipse with enough depth, delight, and dazzle to keep one engaged for a lifetime or a six month passage of time. A cartoon that once appeared in *The New Yorker* about the life and career of fellow LS114 luminary George Plimpton best summarizes this eclipse. In it, a patient looks at the surgeon preparing to operate on him and demands, "Wait a minute! How do I know you're not George Plimpton?" To be in harmony with the dance steps of this eclipse, let this cartoon be a delightful reminder to all of us amateurs that even in our age of specialization, with enough love and passion, almost anything is possible, if only for a moment.

Phase	Return	Year
Full Moon	51st	1872
Disseminating	55th	1944
Last Quarter	59th	2017
Balsamic	63rd	2089

LS114 Luminaries

Edmund Halley	November 8, 1656
Captain James Cook	November 7, 1728
Robert Ripley	December 25, 1890
Baby Face Nelson[E1]	December 6, 1908
Douglas Harding	February 12, 1909
John Fante	April 8, 1909
Benny Goodman	May 30, 1909
Hubert de Givenchy	February 20, 1927
Sidney Poitier	February 20, 1927
Gabriel Garcia Marquez	March 6, 1927
George Plimpton	March 18, 1927
Rod Stewart	January 10, 1945
Bob Marley	February 6, 1945
Patch Adams	May 28, 1945
Michael Jordan	February 17, 1963
Quentin Tarantino	March 27, 1963
Gary Kasparov	April 13, 1963
Johnny Depp	June 9, 1963
Elijah Wood	January 28, 1981
Joseph Gordon-Levitt	February 17, 1981
Rami Malek	May 12, 1981
Natalie Portman	June 9, 1981

PREBLE—LS147
Baby Face Nelson

1. Roger Ebert, *Life Itself: A Memoir* (New York: Grand Central Publishing. 2011), p. 313.
2. https://en.wikipedia.org/wiki/Ebertfest. Retrieved March 1, 2022.
3. Peter Doggett, *You Never Give Me Your Money: The Beatles After the Breakup* (New York: HarperCollins, 2011), p. 6.
4. Ibid.
5. Liz Greene & Howard Sasportas, *The Luminaries: The Psychology of the Sun and Moon in the Horoscope. Vol 3.* (York Beach, MA: Samuel Weiser, Inc., 1992), p. 200.
6. Helen Rosner. Annals of Gastronomy. https://www.newyorker.com/magazine/1999/04/19/dont-eat-before-reading-this. Retrieved March 1, 2022.

LUNAR SAROS 115

"Not only is the world stranger than we think,
it is stranger than we can imagine."

-WERNER HEISENBERG

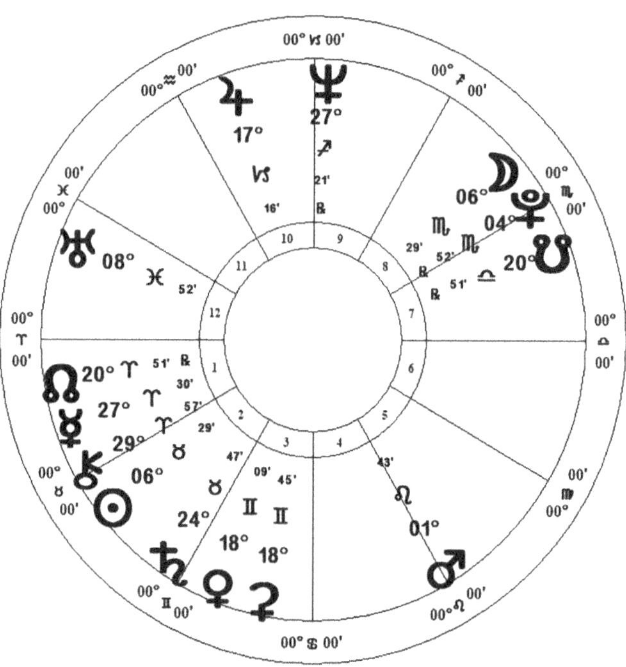

Lunar Saros 115

April 27, 1000 • 10:38:17 AM • South Pole

Mayhem and Might

The release of accumulated energy and knowledge follows in the wake of this South Node Scorpio eclipse with traditional ruler Mars demoted by Lord Pluto's three degree proximity to the Moon. Mars in Leo sets off a robust square to the Moon and Pluto, producing a constant state of deeply intensive, if not disturbing subterranean pressure. Additionally, the far-reaching consequences of Moon/Pluto's futuristic trine to Uranus are greatly enhanced by Mercury's savant-like conjunction to Chiron in Aries. At the twenty-seventh degree, Mercury is double-dipped in Gemini fluency and its same vibe trine to Neptune in Sagittarius significantly expands the range of communication possible, providing ample opportunity to manifest on local, national, international, as well as off-planet platforms. In addition, the Moon's ability to penetrate and sync with her septile to Neptune, just one of four, suggests high levels of fate and focus are dancing through its sphere. As with Lunar Saros 113—Stripped Down—and Lunar Saros 120—Burn Baby Burn—Jupiter's cardinal square to the nodal axis is a bellwether of change on almost every front.

Because the eclipse carries a fixed Plutonian theme with repercussions flowing through both personal domestic issues as well as national security issues, the majority of events and decisions connected into its sphere of manifestation will reflect the values and ideas that deal with themes of regeneration, mystery, intrigue, and the use or abuse of power. Critical agreements and resolutions, for the most part, are conducted behind closed doors. Matters of major significance remain hidden, as if an invisible curtain were drawn in deference to real time events. The overall effect of LS115 results in an esoteric atmosphere that invites intrigue as well as intimidation.

To deal with an atmosphere of secrecy or subversion, it is imperative to act on principle and work toward arbitration or negotiated settlements. Expect a fair share of blackouts and backlash as opinions will vary with the wind (keep in mind this eclipse holds a Mercury/Chiron conjunction in Aries which can make for hard-headed negotiations and disapproval of methodology). Brush up on your communication skills because refusals, a lack of cooperation, and general mayhem are common at the start of any engagement under this eclipse. The spoils of this kind of sport always go to those who can muster self-control and maturity.

Allow a finer level of abstraction and symbolism to play a part in any conversation. Your openness to these levels of subtlety could add significant traction and appeal to the future of any proposals under consideration. The Moon/Venus opposition Mercury/Neptune isotrap is well positioned to offer a helping hand if one can take advantage of etiquette and decorum even in the face of heated disagreement. Draw from such cultural resources as art, music, literature, and even political figures to find common ground. Always remember that inside the soul of every human being there is a ten-year-old child that still delights in magic and believes in the wonder of the world.

Closest Midpoints: Venus/Mars-Pluto, Mercury/Pluto-Node
Isotraps: Moon/Venus opposition Mercury/Neptune
Moon/Uranus conjunct Jupiter/Neptune

1900—2100 Eclipses: Lunar Saros—115

1901, 1919, 1937, 1955, 1973, 1991, 2009, 2028, 2046, 2064, 2082, 2100
Length of cycle —1,280 years
Series ends—June 13, 2280

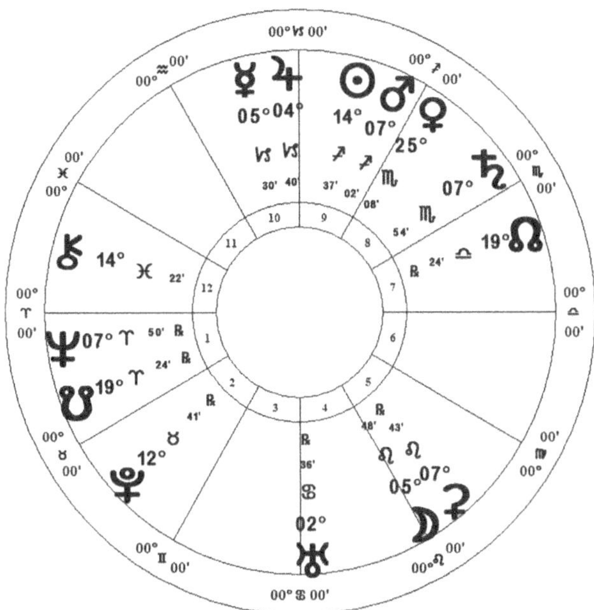

13th Amendment
PREBLE—LS115

December 6, 1865 • Time Unknown • Washington, DC, USA

13th Amendment to Abolish Slavery

"Whenever I hear anyone arguing for slavery, I feel a strong impulse to see it tried on him personally."

-Abraham Lincoln

In the realm of LS115's activation on October 4, 1865, at 11 Aries, the United States Congress ratified, on December 6, 1865, the 13th Amendment to the United States Constitution that abolished slavery and involuntary servitude, except as punishment for a crime. The activation degree fell on Neptune at 7 degrees Aries.

The 13th Amendment's Connections to the Dragons of LS115
↑North Node with South Node↓
Pluto to Pluto

1st Harmonics: NNode – SNode, Moon – Saturn, Sun – Pluto
2nd Harmonics: Moon – Pluto, Ceres/Venus – Sun, Saturn – Venus

There are over one hundred and forty charts given as examples that support the spheres of consciousness hypothesis that is presented in this book. The chart of the 13th Amendment to Abolish Slavery in the United States may be the strongest and best example in this entire book of the Global Gateways (GG) effect, with a connection under one and a half degrees between both nodal polarities.

Before noting all the cross-connections, take a look at the chart and notice Neptune's strategic alliances. There's the Grand Fire Trine which, even if the time of ratification is unknown, the Moon is still going to be viable as it conjuncts the always-important Ceres. Then there's the Cardinal T-Square with its Mercury/Jupiter capacity to redress old-world monarchical thinking. But the best is always reserved for last: here it's the ever dependable, times-up quincunx between Neptune and Saturn. These two are minutes apart, making the amplitude of vibration deeply resonant, ready to relieve the suffering and injustices that the social structures of the United States had allowed to exist for such a disgraceful length of time.

The eclipse Moon is making a 1st Harmonic to Saturn and the eclipse Sun a 1st Harmonic to Pluto. Both luminaries bring their light to the darkness and cruelty of slavery and to the success of a new chapter in the fate of masses of people who were mistreated by the most severe, cold-hearted, and violent conditions imaginable.

As I'm sure you are by now aware, it appears with the growing amount of data and anecdotal evidence that the 2nd Harmonics wield the greatest potential to influence our personality and, more importantly, our behavior. The Moon's 2nd Harmonic to Pluto is an almost 100 percent indicator that either a personal lifestyle is about to shift (and shift dramatically) or in the case of an event, a major sociological phase shift is underway and headed our way. Either way, the Moon/Pluto combination saturates the soil of our inner psyche with emotional and quite often physical upheaval. And considering that LS115 carries that identical pairing, it pretty much makes its own case.

The last tie between these two energetic fields worthy of our time is the eclipse Saturn to Venus. If there was a signature aspect for slavery, this one would be right at the top of the list. In the name of exploitation, of devaluing human dignity, of suffering at the hands of overlords—be they parents, siblings, partners, friends, bosses—Saturn and Venus do not a happy couple make. I have found difficulty even with trines between them, an observation that Vancouver astrologer Tim Stephens shared with me way back when we first met in the early 1980's. Tim had been noticing this for years as we contemplated starting an astrologically-based dating service. And still on the theme of Saturn, both fields carry a Saturn in quincunx to Neptune, giving both an identical phase angle relationship that should have been noted earlier: identical phase alignments greatly reinforce, in our case, such characteristics as fear, isolation, obligation, feeling overwhelmed by burden, and an inability to compete in the marketplace.

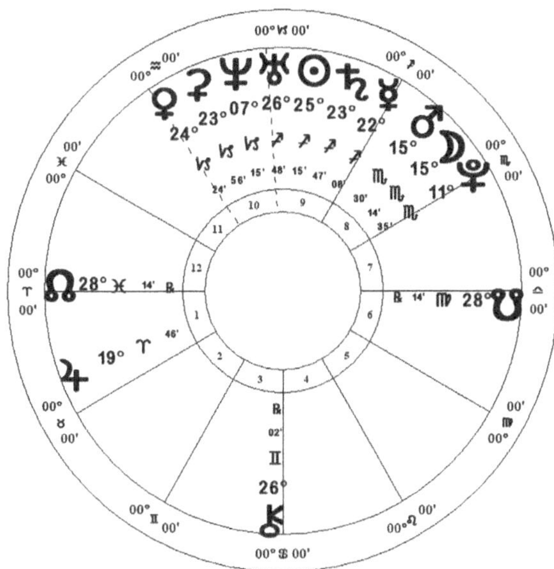

Chelsea Manning
PREBLE—LS146

December 17, 1987 • TOB Unknown • Oklahoma City, OK, USA

Intelligence Analyst Whistleblower

"I began to think the documented backdoor deals and seemingly criminal activity didn't seem characteristic of the de facto leader of the free world."

-Bradley Manning

Trained as an intelligence analyst, Manning was deployed to Iraq in October, 2009, and given TS/SCI Security clearance (short for Top Secret/Sensitive Compartmented Information), the highest-level designation available."[1] A disturbing mix of psychosocial issues combined with his morally conflicted feelings about the war would lead to a massive download of state secrets to Assange and WikiLeaks for which he would be arrested in Iraq in May 2010. His trial revealed that he had established a relationship online with Assange in 2010 and that he transmitted the first documents to WikiLeaks in February 2010.[2] Manning was sentenced on August 21, 2013, to thirty-five years in prison for leaking what was reported to be hundreds of thousands of classified documents to WikiLeaks.[3] Elaborating on Manning's motivations for leaking such an astounding number of documents, Nick Denver cites altruism as the major contributing factor in his decision.

> He said he had perpetuated the largest leak in American history—very likely world history—because of a belief that information should be free for the betterment of all mankind. And, though he didn't appear to have intended it when he said, "Information should be free," Brad Manning's leak illustrated the futility of wanton state secrecy in a digital age.[4]

The initial link that forged a connection between Lunar Saros 115 and Manning's chart occurred on December 31, 2009, at 10 Cancer. By accessing his natal Neptune at 7 Capricorn, an endless chasm of subterfuge would emerge to reveal an orchestrated web of injustice and brutality of US counter-terrorism and counter-insurgency operations. Manning's double if not triple Pluto/Moon/Mars conjunction in Scorpio fit LS115's secretive Moon/Pluto pattern perfectly, no doubt setting off a contagion of paranoia across major governmental organization on the planet.

In Alexander Star's book *Open Secrets: Wikileaks, War and American Diplomacy*, he quotes *New York Times* reporters Scott Shane and Andrew W. Lehren referring to more than half of the quarter-million cables leaked that date from 2007 onward: "To read through them is to become a global voyeur, immersed in the jawboning, inducements and penalties the United States wields in trying to have its way with a recalcitrant world."[5]

Manning's Pluto/Sun-Node midpoint, per Ebertin's COSI, is "bound up with a mass destiny."[6] That he became a pawn in the US government's ploy to "send a message" that whistleblowers will not be tolerated is another sad step in the advancement of politically sanctioned global secrecy. That he has struck a note for freedom of information is due to his OOB Uranus/Mercury along with his Sun/Saturn in opposition to his freedom of information Chiron.

The hereditary ties between LS115 and Manning are primarily due to the influence of Neptune and Venus. With over a dozen cross links overall, Neptune holds the majority. The eclipse Venus/Ceres in Gemini matches his Venus/Ceres in Capricorn need to feel nurtured, which for Manning would find a fit in the highly structured world of the military. The fact that he downloaded the majority of his documents in LS115's eclipse window strengthens the influence of the Venus/Ceres in Gemini correlation to the work he did as an intelligence analyst. Manning's transgendered identity as Chelsea would emerge fully formed out of the chrysalis that was Lunar Saros 115.

In 2009, these Water Dragons were moving through their last Disseminating phase, inculcating the power of synthesis. It is now essential to draw the necessary conclusions that highlight the errors in any system to prevent the further deterioration of that system. The fifty-seventh return brings a fast flow of energy geared to a willingness to accept responsibility for the distribution of information that can have far-reaching consequences for the greater good of any collective.

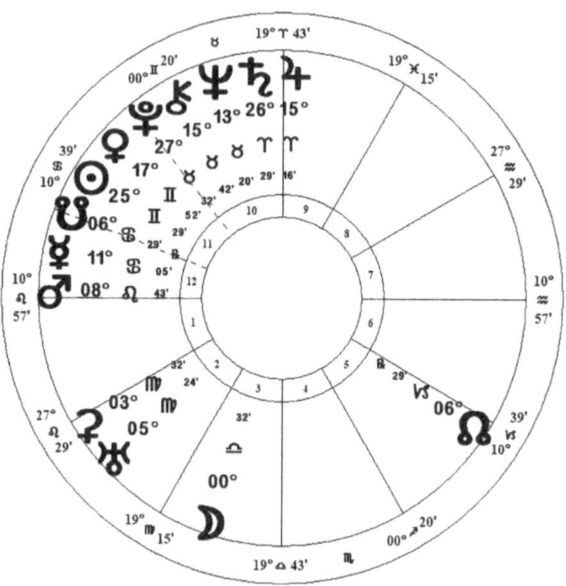

Alice A. Bailey
PREBLEs—LS113 & LS118

June 16, 1880 • 7:42 AM • Manchester, UK

The Ageless Wisdom Teachings

"Love is the great unifier, the prime attractive impulse, cosmic and microcosmic, but the mind is the main creative factor and the utilizer of the energies of the cosmos. Love attracts, but the mind attracts, repels and coordinates, so that its potency is inconceivable."

-Djwal Khul, The Tibetan[7]

November of 1919 marked the arrival of Lunar Saros 115 and with it the beginning of what would become a most extraordinary telepathic alliance between Djwal Khul (aka the Master DK, the Tibetan) and Alice Bailey. In her unfinished autobiography, published in 1955, Bailey revealed how she had initially been reluctant to proceed. The quality of the communication, however, proved remarkable in terms of its esoteric spirituality. The clarity of its content encouraged her to continue.[8] In 1923, with the help of her husband Foster Bailey, Alice

Bailey founded the Arcane School and Lucis Publishing Company, formerly part of the Lucis Trust. The collaboration of this husband-wife team would go on to publish twenty-four books.

The initial contact between DK and Alice Bailey arose out of LS115's activation at 15 Taurus on November 7, 1919, as it enveloped her natal Chiron at 15 Taurus, along with its conjunction to Neptune at 13 Taurus. This contact in and of itself would have signified a time literally "out of time" as defined by cosmological if not metaphysical measurement. In light of LS115's affiliation for profound if not secretive communication, it stands to reason it would have had a tremendous impact on any individual with a consciousness tuned toward furthering their own and others' spiritual evolution.

Alice Bailey's Connections to the Lunar Dragons of LS115
Space Lanes via MC/IC
Venus with Venus
Mars with Mars
Uranus to Uranus

1st Harmonics: NNode – Jupiter, Mercury/Chiron – Saturn, Ceres/Venus – Venus, Saturn – Pluto
2nd Harmonics: Neptune – Sun, Uranus – Uranus

Alice Bailey's birth chart holds a number of remarkable connections to the Water Dragons of LS115, starting with the best example in this entire book of a Space Lane portal opening through the Tenth House cusp. And this is quite remarkable since the eclipse nodal axis that opened on her MC was just minutes away from a perfect 100 percent alignment —allowing for complete and unbridled use of the cosmic expressway. This in itself opens the door for unrestricted downloads and inspirational channeling that is literally not of this world.

The eclipse Neptune's 2nd Harmonic to her Sun allows the full force of the eclipse Moon/Uranus conjunct Jupiter/Neptune isotrap to infuse her body of work with deeper levels of arcane knowledge and mystery. Resonance is strengthened by the many same sign placements with an almost identical Venus in Gemini with only a four minute arc of separation between their celestial longitudes.

At the time of her encounter with LS115, these lunar dragons were evolving through their second and last Full Moon phase, where many of their benefits and talents become fully realized. An encounter with any Full Moon phase increases the odds for success if not personal satisfaction. Their Full Moon phase was in effect from 1901 until the start of their current Disseminating phase that began in 1973.

LS115 Summary

A mighty tide of mayhem arrives when these Water Dragons surface, forcing many of us to rewrite our notion of how the world works. Heisenberg and his uncertainty principle sums it up best: "Not only is the world stranger than we think, it is stranger than we can think." Be prepared for upheaval as this family of lunar dragons reminds us that life is in a constant state of flux with fault lines appearing out of nowhere. There is always a call to action with often stunning if not enthralling consequences. Their visits bring an exploration of a wide range of noble interests and experiences within global communities of like-minded people. It is a time to go deep and acknowledge the intangible complexity and mystery that is our existence on this planet. The best that we can do is to take our dreams to the starting line that is every new day and welcome in the wonder that awaits.

Until 2046, the lunar dragons of LS115 are experiencing their final Disseminating phase, helping all of us to truly embody our journey. It helps to turn one's focus inward as at this stage: it's all about the meaning you've gleaned from your journey after seeing the big picture of your life. Many will feel called to teach and spread any kernels of wisdom that one has been blessed to receive. Sharing is as natural as breathing in this phase of the eclipse. It fosters introspection as we are all more willing to go within, to listen and to seek guidance from sources that long to connect with us from the spheres of stillness that support our existence. As we journey inward, personal and collective resources can be both discovered and recovered to support our growth and ability to make a contribution within the broader context of society.

Profound experiences and life-altering events are the norm for these mighty Water Dragons, birthed at the turn of the last millennium. By clan allegiance or by a cosmic chance encounter, they can be counted on to revive the soul and refresh the spirit. Their flair for communication and fluency is something to behold in a world that is fast losing its grip on civility. To that end, I am forever indebted and inspired by the words of the great 19th century English poet and novelist Rudyhar Kipling who said, "I am by nature a dealer in words and words are the most powerful drug known to humanity." May you find comfort, pleasure, and harmony in the words and deeds that flow from the soulful sphere that is Lunar Saros 115's Mayhem and Might.

LS115 Luminaries

William Blake	November 28, 1757
Rudyard Kipling	December 30, 1865
Walt Disney	December 5, 1901
Werner Heisenberg	December 5, 1901
Isaac Asimov	January 2, 1920
Federico Fellini	January 20, 1920
An Wang	February 7, 1920
Ravi Shankar	April 7, 1920
Anthony Hopkins	December 31, 1937
Etta James	January 25, 1938
Oliver Reed	February 13, 1938
Phil Knight	February 24, 1938
Bernie Madoff	April 29, 1938
Mel Gibson	January 3, 1956
Bill Maher	January 20, 1956
Bryan Cranston	March 7, 1956
Christian Bale	January 30, 1974
Steve Nash	February 7, 1974
Chris Kyle	April 8, 1974
Penelope Cruz	April 28, 1974
Neymar	February 5, 1992
Daisy Ridley	April 10, 1992
Saagar Enjeti	April 21, 1992

1. Denver Nicks, *Private Bradley Manning, Wikileaks, and the Biggest Exposure of Official Secrets in American History* (Chicago: Chicago Review Press Inc, 2012), p.184.
2. Micah Lee. *Bradley Mannings' Statement.* https://freedom.press/news/help-spread-bradley-mannings-words-across-the-internet/ Retrieved August 23, 2013
3. Julie Tate, Judge sentences Bradley Manning to 35 years http://www.washingtonpost.com/world/national-security/judge-to-sentence-bradley-manning-today/2013/08/20/85bee184-09d0-11e3-b87c-476db8ac34cd_story.html. Retrieved August 23, 2013.
4. Nicks, *Private Bradley Manning*, p. 116-117.
5. http://www.amazon.com/Open-Secrets-WikiLeaks-American-Diplomacy-ebook/dp/B004-KZQH12#reader_B004KZQH12
6. Reinhold Ebertin, *The Combination of Stellar Influences*, p. 105.
7. Alice A. Bailey, *A Treatise on White Magic* (London: Lucis Trust, 1934).p.125.
8. http://www.lucistrust.org/en/books/alice_bailey_books/about_alice_bailey

LUNAR SAROS 124

"By logic and reason we die hourly; By imagination we live."

-William Butler Yeats

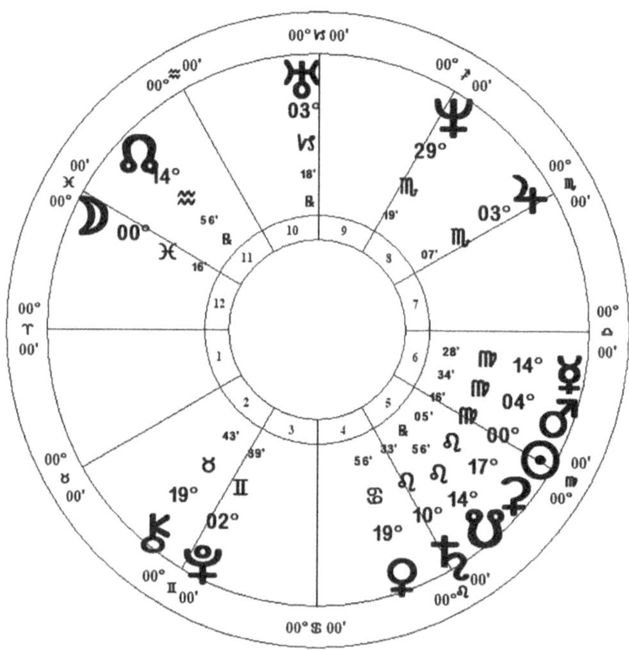

Lunar Saros 124

August 24, 1152 • 12:07:39 AM • North Pole

Imagine

The power to imagine takes center stage with the arrival of this imaginative lunar eclipse family. Its 00 alpha degree Pisces Moon opens the floodgates for all manner of scientific, literary, and social endeavors to flourish and achieve success. Its NNode in Aquarius is an equal-opportunity provider that takes delight with anyone willing to step up to the plate and take a swing. A talent bank of ambition and the need for public attention, courtesy of Saturn's SNode Leo conjunction, lies deep within the matrix. The eclipse features a Splash pattern that encourages diversity and its Grand Cross in predominately mutable signs underscores the cares, concerns, strife, and struggles of our shared humanity.

LS124 features a Boomerang within the eclipse field's Grand Cross. Neptune sits at 29 Scorpio, a critical and prophetic degree that has karmic implications for the Boomerang (what you send forth has a way of returning) and the intense energy of the Grand Cross. Its opposition to Pluto as the apex planet boosts its signal and brings focus to maximize and leverage Pluto's intensity. Planets at the 29th degree of Scorpio carry all the pain, power, and potential of Antares, one of the Four Royal Stars of ancient Persia. Its charisma, passion and even genius light the way for opportunity and fame to find you. And if that seems too good to be true, it also carries confrontation, belligerence, and a fascination for the "dark side" and its allure for worldly power.

The energy within a Grand Cross can be formidable. When fully integrated, its creative and evolutionary potential is unstoppable. In a predominately Mutable Grand Cross, its overwhelming tensions and contradictions generated by the four squares and the two oppositions keep it moving forward with a double dose of lucidity and mobility, always willing and able to make new choices. Neptune's strategic position dominates the eclipse field through a multiplicity of interlocking alliances. In its tight embrace, Neptune's waning square to the Sun is a classic signature aspect denoting imagination, artistic potential, and a groundswell of endless creative self-expression. The Moon's opening trine from Jupiter and square with Neptune reflect an attitude of joy and optimism even in the worst of times; in fact, a certain amount of self-delusion, depression, and even defeat may be required to bring out the best in this family's celestial DNA. These dragons are problem solvers and left to their own devices will attract all manner of discord to paradoxically feel great. Saturn in both the midpoint and isotrap structures, and its potential for sudden illness, needs to be factored into the storyline when viewed through Neptune's key position within the Boomerang and The Grand Cross's energy outputs.

When these Water Dragons draw near, take a deep breath as you might be going deep. Fill your lungs with optimism and be sure your backpack is full of generosity and intellectual curiosity. Lessons in self-sufficiency are part of the package; relationships seem to suffer as the emphasis is on personal attainment and the joy of the challenge. To that end, there just doesn't seem to be enough time to satisfy the needs of our partners. But it *can* be done with dedicated focus and effort. In the meantime, loneliness, instability, health issues, and separations are common. With four quindecile (165 degree) aspects of obsession in play, you can be sure that this lunar eclipse carries enough aspiration to drive your evolution forward. As William Blake noted long ago, it's the human imagination that drives the world and we're pretty much in control of everything except for earthquakes and the weather.

Closest Midpoints: Saturn/Moon-Uranus, Mercury/Moon-Uranus
Isotraps: Venus/Uranus conjunct Jupiter/Saturn
Sun/Moon opposition Saturn/Pluto

1900—2100 Eclipses: Lunar Saros—124

1909, 1927, 1945, 1963, 1982, 2000, 2018, 2036, 2054, 2072, 2080
Length of cycle —1,298 years
Series ends—October 21, 2450

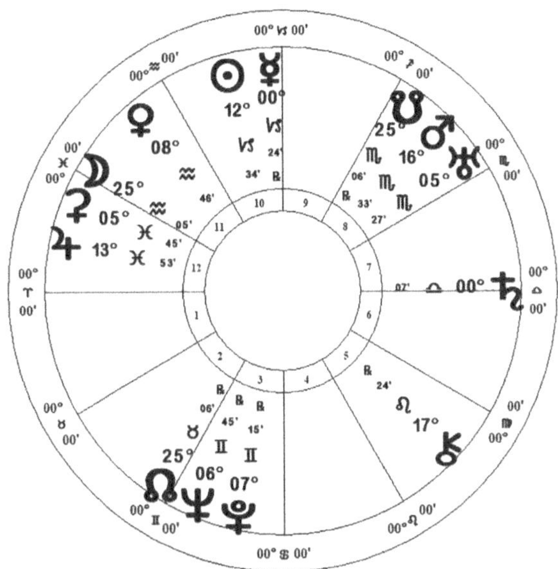

J. R. R. Tolkien
PREBLE—LS124

January 3, 1892 • TOB Unknown • Bloemfontein, South Africa

Father of High Fantasy

"We are here, surviving, because of the indomitable courage of quite small people against impossible odds."

-J. R. R. Tolkien

A distinguished scholar of Anglo-Saxon literature, Tolkien was known throughout the world for his spellbinding fairy tales and award-winning fantasy books that include *The Hobbit* (1937), *The Lord of the Rings* (1954), and *The Silmarillion* (published posthumously in 1977). Populated by a cast of characters grand in scope and deftly crafted, his world of orcs, ents, hobbits, dragons, and elvin lords paid tribute to his life-long passion for language, literature, and learning. By age thirteen, Tolkien had invented a language he called Naffarin, complete with grammar, history, and an entire sound system.[1]

Tolkien's deep understanding and fluency with language, myth, and the symbolic realms of legend and fantasy grounded him in the mythological kingdom that would become Middle-Earth. His heroes are "ordinary folk" fighting the timeless war between Good and Evil. By the mid-1960s, *The Lord of the Rings* reached cult status and turned Tolkien into a superstar and modern day hero. In North America, Hobbit societies were formed, and *Lord of the Rings* graffiti appeared on buttons and subway walls declaring[2]

"Frodo Lives!"

"Gandalf for President"

"J. R. R. Tolkien is Hobbit-Forming"

Tolkien's Connections to the Dragons of LS124
Pluto with Pluto

1st Harmonics: SNode – Chiron, Neptune – SNode,
Moon – Ceres, Ceres – Chiron, Jupiter – Uranus, Uranus – Mercury
2nd Harmonics: Mars – Ceres, Mercury – Jupiter, Saturn – Venus, Chiron – Mars

Tolkien's natal dance card was always full, so desirable was his energy field to the patterns and players of LS124. As always, the SNode is the Cosmic Bridge that solidifies the relationship, making it a lifelong commitment. The 1st and 2nd Harmonics of the eclipse field's Moon/Sun axis are the cosmic fertilizer that continuously fed Tolkien's Ceres a formula of Moon in Pisces inspired fantasy. All of this is grounded through the interior world of perfection that is his Sun in Virgo.

Remembering that Neptune is the key planet that unlocks the power of LS124's Boomerang and Grand Cross, it is wonderful to see its Neptune in a 1st Harmonic to Tolkien's SNode, giving him access to all of their planetary/personality patterns. It's really quite extraordinary, especially when the Moon, calculated for midday, might actually be sitting right "at the bends" where fate and destiny come together to hand out special assignments for the willing of heart.

The sextile of an OOB Uranus and Jupiter in the lunar eclipse field also holds valuable information since the sextile in a Boomerang often holds the solution to the entire unfolding of this pattern. And once again, Tolkien's energy field ties into both of those key planets: its Jupiter to his Uranus, and its OOB Uranus to his Mercury demonstrating first principles in action. Apart from all the above mentioned patterns in play, Uranus finally gets its due and is delighted to be taking Tolkien's AP Mercury/Capricorn out for a spin on a wild, mental ride with creature characters whose dark side captures our own fascination for the macabre.

Saving the best for last is one of the best sextiles you could ever hope to have or experience—I give you LS124's "get-out-of-jail" Jupiter/Uranus sextile. In the eclipse field, it operates through a Balsamic phase primarily concerned with the process of letting go and surrendering to a dreamtime filled with hope and excitement. This is a teaching sextile that needs to share experience with others; in the Balsamic phase its energy is self-contained, better suited to the creation of new platforms of knowledge yet to be born. It is an enlightened force ready to update or download any career or occupational skill that wants to move with the times.

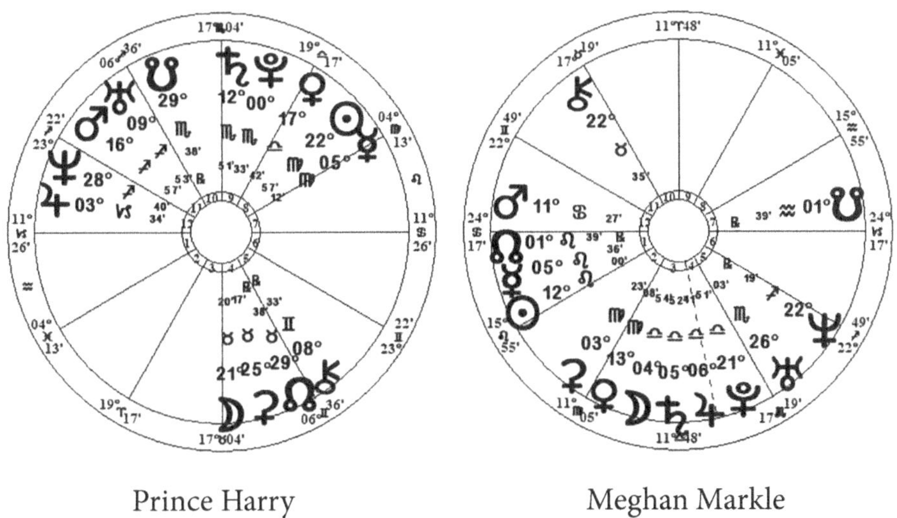

Prince Harry
PREBLE—LS149

September 15, 1984 • 4:20 PM • London, UK

Meghan Markle
PREBLE—LS119

August 4, 1981 • 4:46 AM • Canora Park, CA, USA

The Duke and Duchess of Sussex

Fairy Tales Can Come True

It Can Happen to You, if You're Young at Heart[3]

"I know that at the end of the day, she chooses me. I choose her. Whatever we have to tackle will be us together as a team."

-Prince Harry

January 31, 2018 brought LS124 right to Meghan's doorstep. Its 11 Leo activation degree not only lit up her Sun but added even more sparkle to the engagement ring her beau Prince Harry had placed on her finger back on November 27, 2017. Her wedding to her Prince took place at Windsor Castle on May 19, 2018.

And what about Harry? Glad you asked. Although 11 Leo does not ring any bells in his chart, remember that the rhythms of the progressed chart are always there, working away in the background, mapping out the cycles of our soulful life with exquisite precision and flawless timing. So it should come as no surprise that in April 2018, one month to wedding bell bliss, the prince's progressed Moon hit 11 Leo. That is a cosmic jackpot for the record books. Indeed. Fairy tales can come true, and they do come true if you're young at heart.

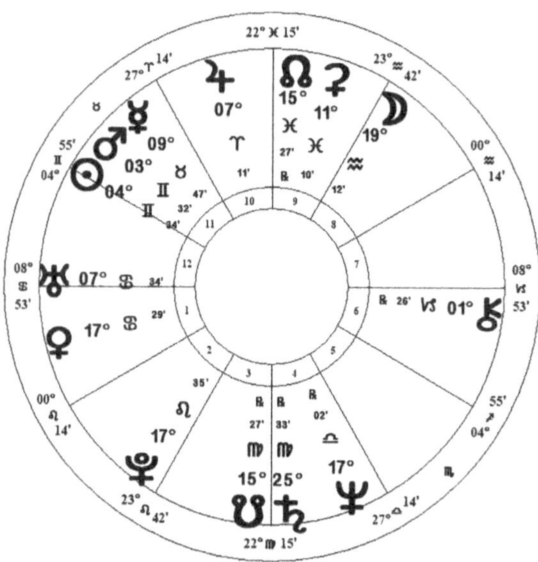

Sally Ride
PREBLE—LS141

May 26, 1951 • 8:11 AM • Los Angeles, CA, USA

Ride Sally Ride

"The thing that I'll remember most about the flight is that it was fun. In fact, I'm sure it was the most fun I'll ever have in my life."

-Sally Ride

On April 19, 1982, Sally Ride found out that she had been selected as the first woman to be part of a space shuttle crew; she was chosen out of a field of 8,000 applicants.[4] She would go on to make history aboard Challenger. Her selection to be NASA's first woman in space came in the glow of LS124's activation at 19 Cancer on January 9, 1982, making an almost perfect lunar landing on her natal Venus/Mercury-Saturn midpoint at 17 Cancer. By 1978, at the time of her initial entry into the training program, Ride had already earned four academic degrees, including a doctorate in physics. Her deep love of learning can be seen through her Sun and Mars at critical degrees along with her Sun/Mercury conjunct Jupiter/Uranus isotrap. This is wildly significant because the isotrap's Jupiter/Uranus frequency is all about knowledge and freedom; in resonance to the eclipse Jupiter/Uranus sextile, it gave Ride the ability to tune in and turn on to all of its expertise for sharing and laying down new communication platforms for future scientific breakthroughs.

Ride's contacts to LS124's mothership reveals a powerhouse of connections. A CB NNode conjuncts her Moon, giving her first crack honors at, well, anything. Both fields hold a Sun/Mars conjunction—power respecting power—and their Pluto sits on her Sun/Mars. And as always, I've saved the best for last: They share a Venus in Cancer conjunction! Yummy, yum yum. Three cheers for the home girl.

LS124 Summary

The power to imagine are the waves that wash upon the shores of this imaginative and forward-thinking family of Water Dragons. Their optimism and faith are a result of timely action taken, based on an almost uncanny grasp of any situation. They've been around long enough to know how to solve problems and remain hopeful that our world has a shot at surviving our evolutionary adolescence. This family carries a sweet yet subtle Midas Touch, eagerly bestowed on all those willing to break with stereotypes to forge a more holistic way forward. We're all time travelers seeking new frontiers to explore. With the help of these imaginative dragons, let's set our sights on lands, seas, and stars we've yet to explore. Space travel, exploration into the depths of our water worlds, along with the exploration of our deeply profound and paradoxical sub-atomic realms, are the true playgrounds of these globe and galaxy hopping freedom-lovers.

Whether you get all these goodies by way of birthright or by way of an eighteen year return, pencil them into your diary/datebook or flight itinerary as you will want to be going places when this ship of dragons docks. Remember that these dragons want to dance with you, so take them up on their invitation. This just might be the occasion to learn that foreign language you've always been drawn to, or at least pack a bag and your passport and get out into the wild blue yonder where surprising opportunities and serendipitous events await. A life-changing event could be just a glorious moment away if you decide to ride on the imagination of their celestial waves.

Phase	Return	Year
Crescent	38th	1819
First Quarter	43rd	1909
Gibbous	47th	1982
Full Moon	51st	2054

LS124 Luminaries

W. Somerset Maugham	January 25, 1874
Gertrude Stein	February 3, 1874
Mary Pickford	April 8, 1892
Manfred von Richthofen	May 2, 1892
Django Reinhardt	January 23, 1910
Akira Kurosawa	March 23, 1910
John Nash	January 13, 1928
Fats Domino	February 26, 1928
Gordie Howe	March 31, 1928
Maya Angelou	April 4, 1928
Diane Keaton	January 5, 1946
Dolly Parton	January 19, 1946
Gregory Hines	February 14, 1946
Reggie Jackson	May 18, 1946
Jeff Bezos	January 12, 1964
Niall Ferguson	April 18, 1964
Stephen Colbert	May 13, 1964
Dan Brown[E3]	June 22, 1964
Kate Middleton[E1]	January 9, 1982
Adam Lambert	January 29, 1982
Henrik Lundquist	March 21, 1982
Kirsten Dunst	April 30, 1982

1. Anne E. Neimark, *Mythmaker: The Life of J.R.R. Tolkien* (Boston: Houghton Mifflin Harcourt, 1996), p. 27.
2. Ibid, p. 99.
3. "Young at Heart Lyrics." *Lyrics.com*. STANDS4 LLC, 2022. https://www.lyrics.com/lyric/2414901/Shawn+Colvin. Retrieved Mar. 22, 2022.
4. https://sallyridescience.ucsd.edu/about/sallyride/about-sallyride/ Retrieved March 22, 2022.
5. https://en.wikipedia.org/wiki/Space_Shuttle_Challenger. Retrieved March 22, 2022.

LUNAR SAROS 131

"Let us come together before we are annihilated."

-Stevie Wonder

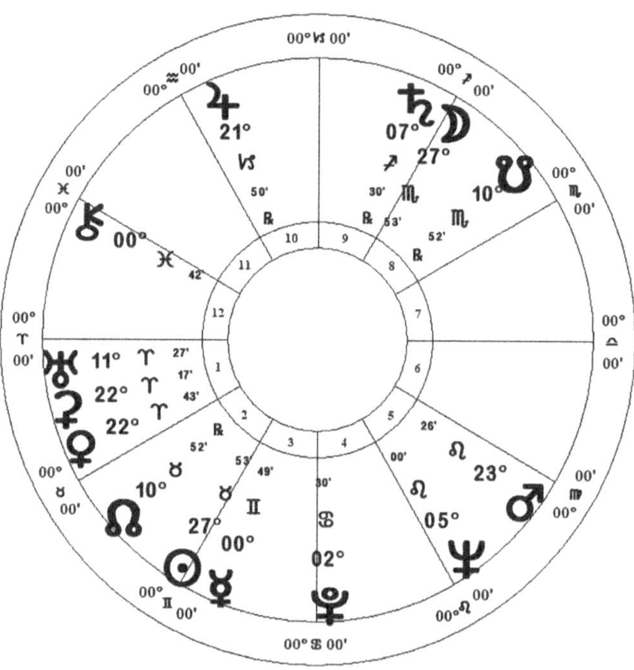

Lunar Saros 131

May 19, 1427 • 11:49:31 PM • South Pole

Pursuit of Truth

As of May 2022, LS131 is all in, having completed one cosmic round of the zodiac since its birth in 1427. With a lifespan of 1,280 years and armed with a depth of instinct and intuition refined over centuries, 2022's return began a new epoch: from despair to delight, making all the stops along the way. LS131's pursuit of truth just might save us from our own insanity. At least we can hope. The dragons of LS131 came into our world water-birthed and are right at home with the great mysteries of the unknown—from birth to death and everything in between. They are here to witness it all as we give strength to their call.

The eclipse field is the only one to carry both a Moon/Pluto MR and a Jupiter/Saturn MR. The Moon/Pluto MR comes in handy when you need to withdraw, reorient, or even reinvent yourself. The Jupiter/Saturn MR—only-to-be-found in this eclipse—gives an extraordinary range of interests and activities. This is a South Node "releasing" eclipse which sets the stage for giving, and also for giving up those things that may no longer be serving your greater good but might be a hidden gem for someone else. Neptune "at the bends" increases our social obligations and empathy, opening up our spiritual space to make room for those more capable or more in need to benefit from our time, talents, and generosity.

There is a palpable dynamic of largesse easily seen through the Grand Fire Trine linking Saturn, Neptune, and Uranus. It burns with the desire to transcend the personal as its natural ego drive and self-sufficiency can be put to work to inspire, sustain, and even illuminate the moral high ground of decision-making; its closed-circuit of sufficiency draws strength from friends and allies. The MR of Jupiter and Saturn only increases the speed if not acceleration capacity of the entire field making it essential that we all stay on top of our daily earthly concerns.

LS131's Fixed T-Square, formed by the regenerative power of the Scorpio/Taurus eclipse axis, means we will survive the current tumult to fight another day. The Moon's MR to Pluto and in square to Mars are sure to rattle their sabers if push comes to shove: these lunar dragons have no problem stepping up to the line of conflict. It is at times like this that I draw strength from knowing that there is a doctrine of military strategy known as Mutually Assured Destruction (MAD) that just might prevent our complete annihilation. But we have to be thoroughly mad or insane to put our trust in the military.

The LS131 Moon/Pluto MR gives more options and it's like finding out there are more people at a party who might like to dance with *you*. Take the Node/Eclipse-Venus midpoint and sub in Pluto for the Eclipse factor and voilà, behold the Node/Pluto-Venus upgrade that can take the fraternizing urge of Venus and the ego-bound contentment of the Sun/Moon=Eclipse and shift all that ego neediness to a deeper part of the stream. Now Pluto's erotic potential in its pure essence of coming alive to life's awesome potential wants to share and engage intensely with others.

And then there's Mercury at 00 Gemini—in rulership and as fresh a face as you will find anywhere in the entire 47 Lunar Saros Series. As a singleton member of the air element, it's a clean slate on which anything can be written, so choose your words wisely— planets at the zero degree infinity zone are capable of anything.

Closest Midpoints: Neptune/Saturn-Pluto, Node/Eclipse-Venus
Isotraps: Moon/Venus conjunct Saturn/Uranus
Venus/Saturn opposition Mars/Neptune

1900—2100 Eclipses: Lunar Saros—131

1914, 1932, 1950, 1968, 1986, 2004, 2022, 2040, 2058, 2076, 2094
Length of cycle —1,280 years
Series ends—July 7, 2707

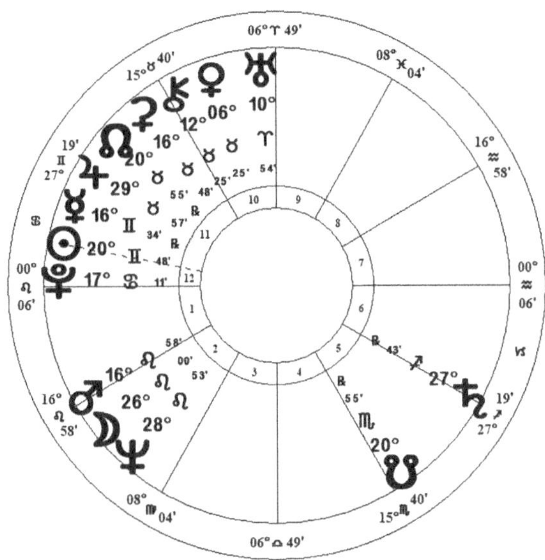

Anne Frank
PREBLE—LS139

June 12, 1929 • 7:30 AM • Frankfurt, Germany

Jewish Victim and Diarist of the Holocaust

"Who would ever think that so much went on in the soul of a young girl."

-ANNE FRANK

On May 15, 1986, the Anne Frank House, together with the Huygens Institute for the History of the Netherlands and the NIOD Institute for War, Holocaust and Genocide Studies Documentation in Amsterdam, published a scientific edition of Anne's writings, bringing to light "hidden text on two pages covered up with gummed paper in the first diary of Anne Frank."[1] This edition also presents Anne's diary text, her rewritten version, and Otto Frank's version on the same page to refute any claims that they were forgeries. The 1986 edition shows "clearly how Anne changed the original texts, which choices Otto Frank made, and what he adapted, omitted, or changed."[2] Mr. Frank would release a heavily edited version of Anne's rewritten diary, simply known as B for its

American publication as *Anne Frank: Diary of a Young Girl*, released in 1947. That publication became known as version C.

The timing of the new scientific edition of the Anne Frank diary came with LS131's activation at 4 Scorpio on April 24, 1986, to her Venus ruler of her Hopes and Dreams Eleventh and her Beginnings and End of Life Fourth. This return took place within the seventy-two year period from 1950–2022 that marks its Balsamic phase, which is always a time for letting go and releasing. Fortunately for the millions of Anne Frank fans, this new edition would offer all of us a deeper look into her life and her writing as a young woman held captive by a time of tyranny that sadly ended a life so full of hope and promise.

Anne Frank's PREBLE—LS139—Truth or Dare—is part of the Air Dragon clan of Part Three. If you haven't read it, I encourage you to go back to it and immerse yourself in the power and pain of her dragon kin. It's all guts and glory. And a quick aside: notice Anne's deeply anchored Taurean Chiron-Ceres conjunction. This is important when we look at her connections to the vectors of LS131 because where she was wounded became her greatest strength with the added capacity to not only endure (Taurus talent) but to nurture others through the soil of her own embodied anguish.

Anne Frank's Connections to the Lunar Dragons of LS131
↓South Node with South Node↓
Mars with Mars

1st Harmonics: NNode – Chiron, Sun – Jupiter,
Mars – Moon, Mercury – Jupiter, Neptune – ASC, Uranus – Uranus
2nd Harmonics: Moon – Jupiter, Chiron – Neptune

Notice the weakened Global Gateways connection that would have reduced her capacity to make the required changes needed at the time she was alive. However, she has two Cosmic Bridges that reinforced her life's work and they do not disappoint. The eclipse NNode directly activated her Chiron, turning it into what Al Morrison referred to as the "inconvenient benefic." The NNode can be counted on to bring in new experiences and this is what happened. There are many vector patterns in play and here are a few outstanding ones: The phase angle between Neptune and Saturn are almost identical, creating tremendous sensitivity across time and space. Even the Saturns (which relate to studying the past) are in the same sign as are the Mars placements. LS131's Mars directly links to her Moon (speaking of the past); the eclipse field's Mercury links to Jupiter and the eclipse axis resonates to her Jupiter, creating the second Cosmic Bridge. The vector links between the eclipse Sun/Mercury to her prophetic Jupiter refresh marketability while the stunning Uranus to her Tenth House Uranus also updates the diary for future generations to enjoy.

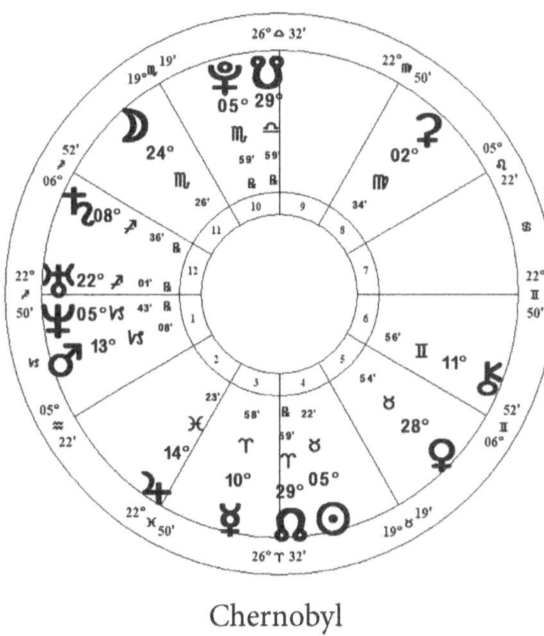

Chernobyl
PREBLE—LS131

April 26, 1986 • 1:23:04 AM • Chernobyl, Ukraine, USSR

World's Worst Nuclear Disaster

"Every lie we tell incurs a debt to the truth. Sooner or later that debt is paid."

-CHERNOBYL—2019 HBO MINISERIES

On the morning of April 28, 1986, unusually high levels of radiation were detected in Sweden, prompting calls from the Swedish government to the Soviet government to inquire whether there had been a nuclear accident in the Soviet Union. The Soviets initially denied it but by 9:02 pm that evening this 20-second announcement was released:

> "There has been an accident at the Chernobyl Nuclear Power Plant. One of the nuclear reactors was damaged. The effects of the accident are being remedied. Assistance has been provided for any affected people. An investigative commission has been set up."[3]

It's hard to find an upside to a nuclear meltdown but Gorbachev, writing in April 2006, declared, "The nuclear meltdown at Chernobyl 20 years ago this month, even more than my launch of *perestroika*, was perhaps the real cause of the collapse of the Soviet Union."[4] It is often said that it is always darkest before the dawn. Sadly, the Chernobyl disaster *was* the terminator, the line dividing the geopolitical night side from the day side on the surface of the soon to be dissolved USSR.

From the moment LS131 activated on April 24 at 4 Scorpio on Chernobyl's Pluto at 5 Scorpio, until the moment of meltdown forty-four hours, thirty-six minutes and forty-two seconds later, all hell was about to be unleashed. Jumping into the fray, I once more offer the cogent words of Robert Pelletier on Pluto in *Planets in Aspect*:

> Pluto is the urge to sacrifice oneself to the demands of an evolving social structure or to use every available resource to determine the form of that evolution. Pluto refers to subtle individualized sources of energy coalesced into a massive reservoir of power. It is the power available to large organizations, which have the economic leverage to control the destiny of man.[5]

The chart of the nuclear meltdown would make even an amateur astrologer gasp with Uranus on the ascendant rising at Stojanovic's noted kill-or-be-killed twenty-second degree and accompanied by five of the most formidable fixed stars in the entire firmament. Three of them, Aculeus, Lesath, and Shaula, known for their taste for tumultuous, chaotic, and even life-and-death associations, were rising along with Uranus. To the east of the Full Moon, Saturn at the eighth degree of Sagittarius was rising alongside Antares, one of the four legendary Royal Stars of the ancient Persians and a star noted for its God of War affiliation to Mars. Finally, Neptune at the fifth degree of Capricorn was just below the ascendant, waiting in the wings with possibly one of the most difficult stars of all—Facies, famous for its alignments and misalignments with difficulty.

What is striking is the quality of connections across their fields, starting with both Moons in Scorpio, both Saturns in Sagittarius, and both tightly conjunct and reinforcing their phase angle symmetry. And then there is the Cosmic Bridge, here defined by the releasing South Node of the eclipse to the activated Pluto. In total there are eight vectors that connect through 1st and 2nd Harmonics that would have given full expression to these Water Dragons and in particular to their highly charged Grand Fire Trine. Remember, all it takes is one vector connecting into an eclipse pattern to access its full potential. It seems Chernobyl would teach once again the truth that out of lies, suffering and disasters, hope is the eternal flame that keeps alive the human spirit.

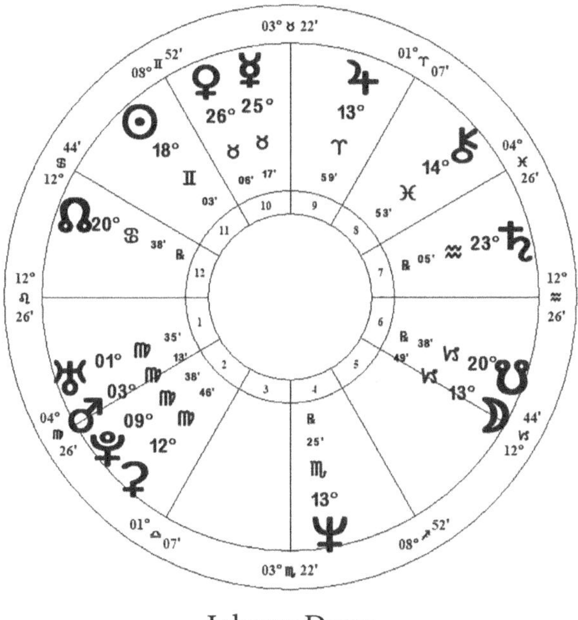

Johnny Depp
PREBLE—LS114

June 9, 1963 • 8:44 AM • Owensboro, KY, USA

News Flash!

June 1, 2022: Johnny Depp's $10.4 Million Win

Here's How He Won:

Johnny Depp's Connections to the Lunar Dragons of LS131
Space Lanes via MC/IC
Chiron to Chiron

1st Harmonics: SNode – Neptune,
Jupiter – SNode, Sun – Mercury/Venus, Uranus – Jupiter
2nd Harmonics: Mars – Saturn, Chiron – Uranus/Mars

Here's How She Lost:

Amber Heard's Connections to the Lunar Dragons of LS131
↓South Node with South Node↓

1st Harmonics: SNode – Pluto, Sun – Venus, Saturn – Saturn
2nd Harmonics: Chiron – Ceres, Pluto – Neptune

It's hard to beat a Space Lane coming down from high above, especially when powered by a nodal axis. The SNode Cosmic Bridge to Depp's Neptune, which aligns to the fixed star Zuben Elgenubi is a conduit for social justice and the release of truth.

Heard's weakened position is due to a diminished GG, a Cosmic Bridge from the eclipse SNode to her Pluto and an almost exact Saturn conjunction to the eclipse Saturn. Of note: Amber Heard's birthdate April 22, 1986, occurred within 48 hours of LS131's return on April 24.

LS131 Summary

There is a distinct note of liberation that emerges out of the depths of these Water dwelling Dragons. They don't seem very tolerant of secrecy or acts of deception meant to coerce or corrupt. They put great value on the importance of knowledge and truth. But because our knowledge can expose us to our deepest darkness and despair, we desperately need to have an even greater capacity to hold out for hope, knowing that whatever comes our way, if we can hold fast to the truth, we'll be OK; we'll be able to handle it. That is the key message and illumination provided by this lunar eclipse family.

There is an edginess to Lunar Saros 131 that defies all attempts at negating its presence, all affirmations aside. Social graces and charm, wit and wisdom might temporarily block its signal, but it will persist and resist any attempts at nullifying its message that twists of fate are on their way. Thankfully, this is a lunar family that brings its own style of communication and youthful engagement to our world, intent on making a difference. In that case, let your voice be heard. Be curious, be radiant, be deeply interested and the world will notice. At the heart of this eclipse is a surprising source of self-sufficiency and strength that understands the value of joining forces to come together to be part of a project, group or community that is making a difference.

Upholding moral and ethical standards both personally and professionally will tend to dominate either one's lifetime if born under their domain or for the six month duration of their return. There is both a potency and a purity to the personality structure of this lunar family that can be readily observed in their style of communication. This eclipse loves to go deep, giving added benefit to particular fields of endeavor found in the political and diplomatic realm, education, science, and any field that is research driven. Remember that above all else, it is critical to be able to draw distinctions between right and wrong and that the currency of ethics will hold its value for either an entire lifetime or at least for the duration of the eclipse return. In the meantime, know your worth and keep your word.

LS131 Luminaries

Lord Byron	January 22, 1788
Gustav Mahler	July 7, 1860
Pancho Villa	June 5, 1878
Jean Piaget	August 9, 1896
Joe Louis	May 13, 1914
Tenzing Norgay	May 29, 1914
Carl Perkins	April 9, 1932
Dave Thomas	July 2, 1932
Peter O'Toole	August 2, 1932
Patsy Cline	September 8, 1932
Agnetha Faltskog[E3]	April 5, 1950
Stevie Wonder	May 13, 1950
Richard Branson	July 18, 1950
Steve Wozniak	August 11, 1950
Timothy McVeigh	April 23, 1968
Bill Burr	June 10, 1968
Susan Wojcicki	July 5, 1968
Gillian Anderson	August 9, 1968
Amanda Berry[E2]	April 22, 1986
Robert Pattinson	May 13, 1986
Lex Fridman	August 15, 1986
Usain Bolt	August 21, 1986

PREBLE—126
Agnetha Faltskog
Amanda Berry

1. https://www.annefrank.org/en/anne-frank/diary/complete-works-anne-frank. Retrieved March 10, 2022.
2. Ibid.
3. https://en.wikipedia.org/wiki/Chernobyl_disaster. Retrieved March 11, 2022.
4. Ibid.
5. Robert Pelletier, *Planets in Aspect*, p. 8.

LUNAR SAROS 137

"What have I got? No looks, no money, no education. Just talent."

–Sammy Davis, Jr.

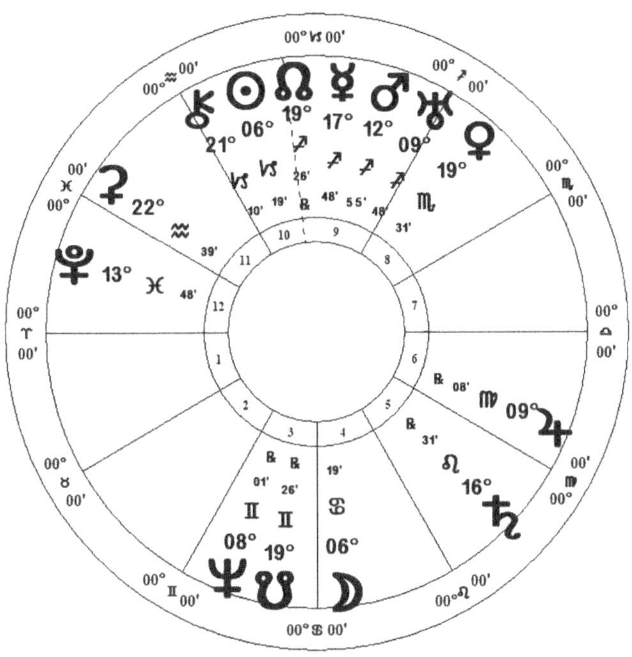

Lunar Saros 137

December 27, 1564 • 9:31:03 PM • South Pole

Ripples and Riptides

Of all the families of lunar eclipses making their way across the globe, LS137 is unique in being the only one with a Moon in Cancer. Its watery world continually ebbs and flows to the releasing rhythms of its SNode tidal flux. Having "arrived" at the shoreline, many do not stay long as these sandy beaches of success offer little resistance to the ripples of power that continually surge through the celestial undertow of the Sagittarian NNode and its conjunction to an extremely restless Mercury, happily on the hunt for the next big idea to explore.

LS137's Mercury is strategically placed through its tight embrace with the NNode, and its mutual reception (MR) with Jupiter generates a multiplicity of tidal pools and estuaries where new life can take hold. There is an ocean of opportunity that rises and falls within the innovative and creative waves of this lunar eclipse family. Yours is a lifetime of learning to navigate the rip tides of tumult and chaos with brief interludes of success available on the relaxing shores of sanity. Many members of this clan are skilled raconteurs, writers, comedians, and wordsmiths who delight in the sheer joy of word play. All members are closet entertainers just waiting for a chance to get up on stage and strut their stuff.

The eclipse field is fortunate to have a second MR from the Sun in Sagittarius to Saturn in Leo that builds in a solid set of skills that can be used to establish yourself in any field. Placements of the Sun and Saturn in Capricorn and Leo exude quality, integrity, leadership, and a need for control that again is synonymous with success. The trick here is to give yourself enough time to develop your foundation as Saturn always pays its dividends later rather than earlier. There is a late-bloomer quality about LS137's field caused by highly sensitive, vulnerable, and easily wounded Cancerian feelings protecting its tender soulful self.

Jupiter's Mutable T-Square with Neptune and Uranus and its MR to Mercury is a source of constant upgrades and downloads that require more diversified fields of experience and entertainment to keep one moving forward. Another feature of the T-Square is a real aptitude for psychic development and prophetic ability, which almost all members have to some extent. Neptune's role in the T-Square brings intuitive foresight along with a natural flair for the rhythms of wit and wordplay.

The tidal flux of this lunar eclipse is always in motion, generating waves of unpredictability that can contribute to an underlying feeling of perpetual anxiety. This heightened state of apprehension is an emotional magnet attracting all manner of conflict, confrontation, or problem-solving that come by way of both personal and professional partnerships. Often financial investments and romantic affairs are the key drivers of this dissonance as seen through the waxing Saturn/Venus square. Due to the fact that this eclipse field has such strong and incessant tidal flow, it makes building a nest egg a life-long challenge.

When the pace of life gets to be too much, the body is the first to suffer. This lunar eclipse doesn't have a dimmer switch—it's all or nothing until one drops from exhaustion. So, don't let that happen. Your nervous system needs downtime while you're still above ground. If you're reading this and you are a fully paid up member of the LS137 clan, either get your sneakers on or head to the tub for a long, leisurely soak. Sea salts would be a nice touch.

Closest Midpoints: Pluto/Mercury-Uranus, Mars/Eclipse-Venus
Isotraps: Moon/Venus opposition Mercury/Neptune
Mars/Jupiter opposition Neptune/Pluto

1900—2100 Eclipses: Lunar Saros—137

1907, 1925, 1943, 1961, 1979, 1997, 2015, 2033, 2051, 2069, 2087
Length of cycle —1,388 years
Series ends— April 20, 2953

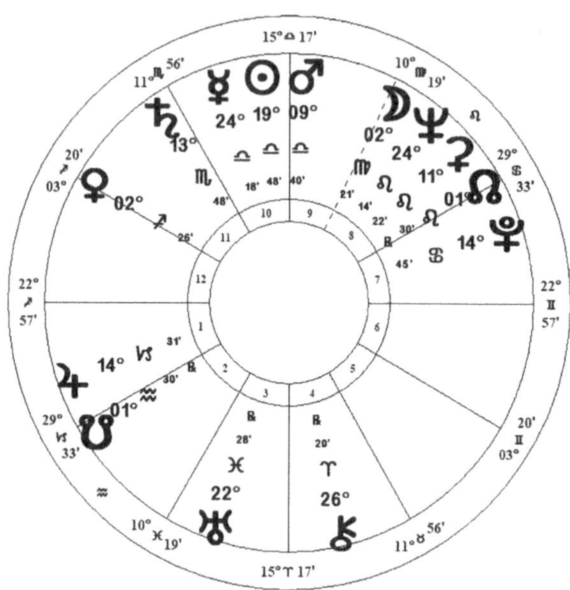

Lenny Bruce
PREBLE—LS137

October 13, 1925 • 11:24 AM • Mineola, NY, USA

Improvisational Rips and Riffs

"If God made the body, and the body is dirty, then the fault lies with the manufacturer."

-Lenny Bruce

On February 3, 1961, Lenny Bruce, a young comedian with a flair for speaking truth (profane truth) to power, performed at Carnegie Hall in New York. His stand-up style was reportedly chaotic and his delivery borderline insane. The performance was recorded and released as *The Carnegie Hall Concert* and in the liner notes, Albert Goldman described the event:

> This was the moment that an obscure yet rapidly rising young comedian named Lenny Bruce chose to give one of the greatest performances of his career . . . Lenny worshipped the gods of Spontaneity, Candor and Free Association. He fancied himself an oral

> jazzman . . . sending out brainwaves like radio waves into the heads of every man and woman . . . sending, sending, sending, he would finally reach a point of clairvoyance where he was no longer a performer but rather a medium, transmitting messages that just came to him from out there—from recall, fantasy, prophecy.[1]

By September 1961, LS137 returned at 3 Pisces to churn the waters, picking up Bruce's natal lunar Moon at 2 Virgo and washing him out to sea. On October 4, he was arrested on obscenity charges and then again later in the year. The fast-talking hipster with his flair for breaking obscenity rules was now in a court of law, defending his right to speak his truth regardless of profanity. Lenny Bruce's official website states that the following few years were some of the most turbulent, filled with undercover cops, drug charges, and arrests.[2] And bans: locally, nationally, and internationally, Bruce was pretty much banned from going on stage or performing anywhere.

He had it all: fire, earth, air, water, and a monster Cardinal T-Square armed and deadly thanks to his Jupiter opposition Pluto torpedo launcher. And if that wasn't enough, Ceres was in Leo granting Bruce sovereign rights to the stage that was his life. Sadly, his life ended on August 3, 1966. It would take two more waves of this series before the genius of Lenny Bruce could once again be appreciated. LS137 returned in September 1997 at the formidable twenty-second degree of Pisces, immersing Bruce's 24 Pisces Uranus in its regenerating flux. Within a year, the film *Lenny Bruce: Swear to Tell the Truth* was released with fellow LS137 alumni Robert De Niro narrating the documentary. It would win Academy Award fame and re-establish Lenny Bruce as one of the greatest stand-up comedians of all time.

Lenny Bruce's Connections to the Dragons of LS137

Space Lanes via ASC/DSC

Lenny's chart clearly demonstrates how even having just one contact from the foundational chart of a Lunar Saros Series can set you up for life and perhaps even better for your *afterlife* to experience a download from that dragon family. Months, years, even centuries might pass, and you could still be *killing it* with news coverage to die for. And because Lenny's Space Lanes were created by his PREBLE-LS137 family's nodal axis falling across his ASC/DSC axis, they are in a league of their own, with an extraordinary capacity to boost the lunar eclipse resonance.

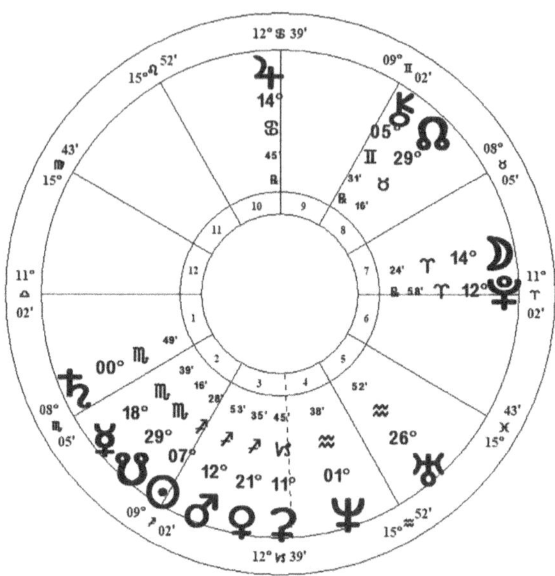

Samuel Clemens
PREBLEs—LS137 & LS142

November 30, 1835 • 2:21 AM rectified • Florida, MO, USA

"Travel is fatal to prejudice."

-Mark Twain

American Humorist, Novelist, and Travel Writer

"The two most important days in your life are the day you were born and the day you find out why."

-Mark Twain

In the fall of 1835, the heavens witnessed two spectacular events that would herald the birth of what would be one of the greatest American writers of the 19th century. Two weeks before Samuel Clemens' birth, Halley's Comet returned on its periodic seventy-five to seventy-six year orbit along with a lunar eclipse on December 5. Commenting on the comet in 1909, Mark Twain said:

> I came in with Halley's Comet in 1835. It is coming again next year, and I expect to go out with it. It will be the greatest disappointment of my life if I don't go out with Halley's Comet. The Almighty has said, no doubt: "Now here are these two unaccountable freaks; they came in together, they must go out together."[3]

And indeed they did. On April 21, 1910, one day after Halley's Comet returned to burn the brightest, Mark Twain suffered a heart attack and left this world as he had entered it—on the wings of a comet. He lived an extraordinary life that began as a riverboat pilot on the Mississippi, learning the ways of the river's constantly shifting rhythms, reefs, and rocks. The crewmen's cry "mark twain" referred to a measuring of the river depth, which had to be at least two fathoms (twelve feet).[4] At this depth dangerous water becomes safe or worse, safe water becomes dangerous.

On February 3, 1863, responding to the pull of a progressed lunar return on his Pluto, and with a newly adopted pen name in hand, Mark Twain was born anew. It would be the start of an adventure born out of the ever-changing currents of the mighty Mississippi, a life in metaphor on a river of high adventure navigating the shoals and eddies between lightness and dark, between safety and danger. In the summer of 1871, the dragons of LS137 returned at the double-dipped tenth degree of Capricorn with a solid Saturn in tow to find Twain working "very hard" on his novel *Roughing It,* which was published the following spring.[5] The dragons' return landed on his Ceres at 11 Capricorn and opposed his Ninth House Jupiter in Cancer.

Mark Twain's Connections to the Dragons of LS137

1st Harmonics: NNode – Venus,
Uranus – Sun, Venus – Mercury, Mars – Mars, Neptune – Chiron
2nd Harmonics: SNode – Venus, Moon – Ceres

The Cosmic Bridge with its Mercury/NNode to his Venus was a powerful stimulant that got him out into the world at an early age (Mercury) to make his way and find value in what skills he could learn. The Cancer/Capricorn eclipse axis to his Ceres was a source of endless flow, making sure his Ceres never missed a meal. And then there is Uranus with its hat trick Mutable T-Square signing off on his Sun, the center of our deepest self and, some might say, destiny. If the Sun is our will to live and Uranus, by its activation and ties to Neptune and Jupiter, is that zap of inspiration, then Mark Twain was both blasted and blessed by his lunar eclipse family.

A fascinating feature of lunar eclipse analysis is to look at your dragon family's lunar eclipse that preceded your birth. In Mark Twain's case, it was the sixteenth return of his Water Dragons on June 10, 1835, that carried an energy field that would refuse to be bounded by any known rules of engagement. Its Grand Fire Trine from the Moon in Sagittarius to Pluto in Aries and Mars in Leo speaks to his innate sense of adventure while the Sun in Gemini to a tight conjunction to Jupiter gave his life boundless enthusiasm and his prolific fluidity with language.

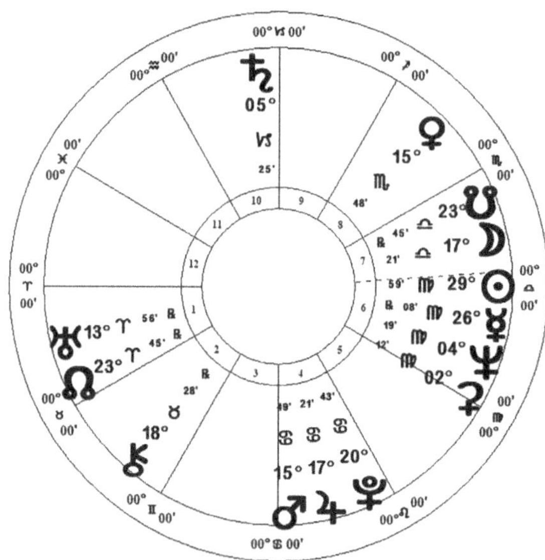

Ray Charles
PREBLEs—LS111 & LS116

September 23, 1930 • TOB Unknown • Albany, GA, USA

"Goodbye don't mean gone."
-Ray Charles

"A fellow who lives in the dark has to have something."
-Ray Charles

With his great hit *Georgia on my Mind* released in September 1960, Ray Charles would take his band on the road in 1961. On November 14, 1961, he would be arrested for drug possession (Pisces) and his career and personal life would take a huge hit. When the Water Dragons of LS137 splashed down on August 26, 1961, at 3 Pisces, they were already fomenting waves by their opposition degree to his Ceres/Neptune and its Earth trine to Saturn. Ray's hold on reality through his long-time drug dependency would become an issue that the tidal flux of LS137 with its powerful currents could no longer conceal. Thankfully the inborn luck of his corporate friendly Saturn saved the day along with the tidal flux/flow of LS137's powerful Moon in Cancer and its sextile to an empowered Jupiter.

At the time of their arrival in 1961, these Water Dragons were moving through the first Disseminating Phase of their lifespan. In this phase of synthesis, it becomes essential to be able to draw the necessary conclusions that plug the leaks and cap the wells that might be preventing further expansion. It's a time to pay attention to failure and course correct. This twenty-third return offered Ray an opportunity to take control of his future success. In the true spirit of the Disseminating Phase, he expanded his small road ensemble and crossed over into mainstream pop to become one of the most celebrated black artists of his time.

LS137 Summary

If all the world is a stage, and you deeply understand this and are willing to play your part (or perhaps many parts), then you have absolutely nothing to fear. Don't be afraid to die and be reborn—on a yearly, monthly, weekly, or even daily basis when necessary. For heaven's sake, some of us hang on by the thread of an hour or the flicker of a moment. Do what you have to do to stay sane. If you are committed, you'll find it gets easier to *find* the perfect solution to a problem. Believe in your instincts. Trust your intuition. Feel your emotions and stay the course of your convictions no matter what other people are telling you. Go for depth—it's usually quieter down deep. The more you can trust your perceptions and feelings, the stronger and keener and clearer they will become. It's a win-win all around.

Anyone by birthright or rite of passage will seem ahead of their time within the cosmic churn of these soulful lunar dragons. All they ask is that you learn to go with the flow and appreciate all the changes that come with transformation. Not that much to ask for—right? Paradoxically, they hope you'll discover the value that discipline brings to any field of endeavor. The forces of originality and even experimentation flow through all life experiences now, as do the forces of tidal friction that just as easily reach your shores. This one realization alone might be the life line that you can grab hold of when swirling currents have you in tow. It is absolutely essential to remember that any state of conflict is temporary—it will pass and in its place calmer waters will return.

Phase	Return	Year
Full Moon	18th	1871
Disseminating	22nd	1943
Last Quarter	26th	2015
Balsamic	30th	2087

LS137 Luminaries

Mark Twain	November 30, 1835
Edwin Hubble	November 10, 1889
Bhagat Singh	September 28, 1907
Jimmie Foxx	October 22, 1907
Joseph G Hamilton	November 11, 1907
Simone de Beauvoir	January 9, 1908
Oscar Peterson	August 15, 1925
Peter Sellers	September 8, 1925
Richard Burton	November 10, 1925
Carlos Castaneda	December 25, 1925
Robert De Niro[E2]	August 17, 1943
Lech Walesa	September 29, 1943
Joni Mitchell	November 7, 1943
Billie Jean King	November 22, 1943
James Gandolfini	September 18, 1961
K D Lang	November 2, 1961
Ghislaine Maxwell	December 25, 1961
Jim Carrey	January 17, 1962
Pink[E2]	September 8, 1979
John Krasinski	October 20, 1979
Angela Ruggiero	January 3, 1980
Yvonne Tousek	February 23, 1980

PREBLE—LS132
Oscar Peterson
Robert De Niro
Pink

1. https://www.rollingstone.com/culture/culture-lists/50-best-stand-up-comics-of-all-time-126359/lenny-bruce-10588. Retrieved Jan. 3, 2022.

2. https://lennybruce.org/about/ Retrieved Jan. 3, 2022.

3. https://en.wikipedia.org/wiki/Mark_Twain. Retrieved March 28, 2022.

4. Ibid.

5. https://www.history.com/topics/art-history/mark-twain. Retrieved March 28, 2022.

LUNAR SAROS 141

"The people who make it to the top–whether they're musicians, or great chefs, or corporate honchos–are addicted to their calling . . . {they} are the ones who'd be doing whatever it is they love, even if they weren't being paid."

-QUINCY JONES

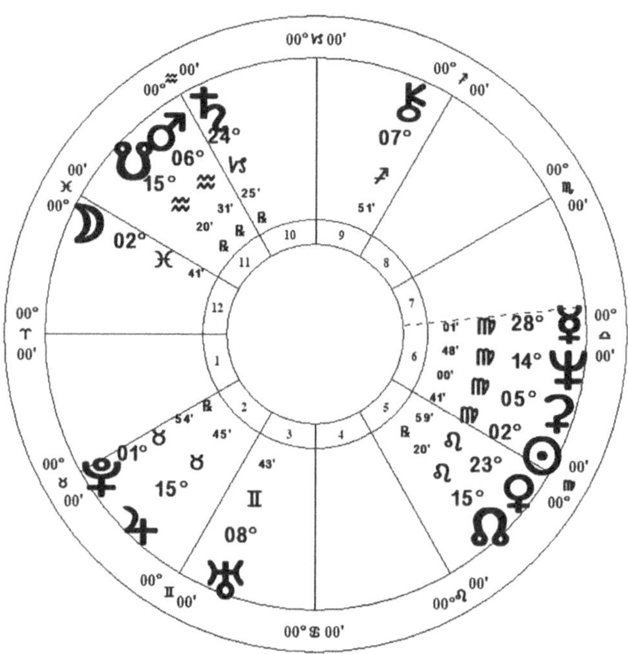

Lunar Saros 141

August 25, 1608 • 7:32:12 PM • South Pole

Finding Your Way

This is a South Node Pisces lunar eclipse that specializes in competency. If there ever was a story to tell about devotion to a higher standard and to principles unsullied by greed or avarice, these lunar dragons can quote you chapter and verse. Mastering detail is their specialty. Ceres on the eclipse axis is able to attract and nourish what is needed to feel the vitality of Being, and along with Mercury and Saturn in rulership, increase the efficiency factor tenfold. Regardless of the challenges ahead, finding your way through mastering the minutiae of any project or career path just got a little bit easier.

The only other Lunar Saros eclipse that has this same dedication to the task at hand is found in the Earth Eclipses (see Part Three) in Lunar Saros 138—Legends and Legacy. These are the only two lunar saros series that have Ceres on the eclipse axis, giving them the mythic might that seems both unworldly and unstoppable. A Grand Mutable Cross featuring a Chiron/Uranus opposition in square to the eclipse axis can feel unnerving as it calls forth an on-rush of experiences that can redirect our focus toward a healthier lifestyle.

This eclipse carries a rich soulfulness that streams through the star Deneb Adige as its energy filters through the Moon's placement at two degrees Pisces. This is a very subtle star that "shows that you are actively seeking awareness, not in a gentle mystical manner, but rather in a practical hands-on way." Its connection to the eclipse Moon encourages all "to walk a different path from society's expectations."[1] Many artists and scientists who share this lunar degree and fixed star, such as Leonard Cohen, Gene Roddenberry, and Jonas Salk, have all found financial success following their chosen fields. The two-degree eclipse axis with its Taurean touch adds pragmatic and aesthetic sensibilities.

But this is a Piscean lunar eclipse and at two degrees has the double distinction of dealing with the duality of spirit manifesting through a world of material existence. With Neptune at the midpoint of the Sun and Mercury along with its placement in the Uranus/Eclipse-Neptune midpoint, many and more options are on offer. The eclipse holds a retrograde OOB Mars (24S44) in Aquarius in trine to that Mutable Cross Uranus providing an on-ramp to novelty capable of shaking up and shaping up your "Being" in new and unexpected ways.

The only fly in the ointment comes through Venus in an exact quincunx to Saturn. Alan Epstein's *Understanding Aspects—The Inconjunct* writes:

> . . . of a Cinderella complex, which makes them feel unlovable. Many of these natives feel unattractive and worry about the impression they make."[2]

If that ever becomes an issue for you, the best solution is to refresh your social life by either attending entertainments that raise your spirits or volunteering at something that brings you satisfaction and even joy from being of service. The last suggestion works 100 percent of the time. There is absolutely nothing standing in the way of your fabulousness. Not your eccentricities, your complexities, nor even your contradictions—which, by fellow alumni Robin Williams' standards, could be massive.

Closest Midpoints: Mercury/Venus-Pluto, Uranus/Eclipse-Neptune
Isotraps: Sun/Mars conjunct Saturn/Neptune
Mercury/Pluto conjunct Jupiter/Neptune

1900—2100 Eclipses: Lunar Saros—141

1915, 1933, 1951, 1969, 1987, 2005, 2023, 2041, 2059, 2077, 2095
Length of cycle —1,280 years
Series ends—October 11, 2888

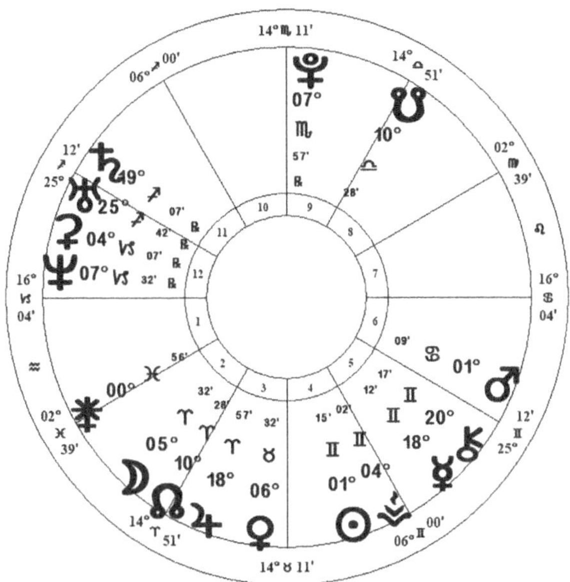

Novak Djokovic
PREBLE—LS141

May 22, 1987 • 11:25 PM • Belgrade, Serbia

"I think luck falls on not just the brave but also the ones who believe they belong there."

-Novak Djokovic

"People have got to wake up to the greatness of Novak Djokovic. He's one of the greatest of all time but he wants to be the greatest of all time."

-Boris Becker

Most people don't decide what they want to be when they are 6 years old, but Novak Djokovic did. He'd never played tennis but, in a moment, watching Pete Sampras win Wimbledon, he decided that he would become the best tennis player in the world. In his autobiography, *Serve to Win,* Novak writes: "And for the next thirteen years, I gave every day of my life to reaching my goal."[3] All the world's tennis fans know his name so let's take a look at his lunar eclipse family.

Novak Djokovic's Connections to the Dragons of LS141
Pluto to Pluto

Midpoints: SNode – Moon/Uranus,
Mercury – Mars/Uranus, Mars – Venus/Pluto, Ceres – Mars/Pluto

When harmonics can't be found, midpoints are just as effective, if not more so. Here the resonance is created by the eclipse field's activation of midpoint structures. The eclipse SNode is directly on Djokovic's Moon/Uranus midpoint creating a Cosmic Relay Station of sorts which in fact may be an even more dramatic statement of resonance. In his own words, Novak says:

> I became what I am today from nothing, and that was no easy task. I came from a place that was torn by war, during a time of food shortages, restrictions, sanctions, and embargoes. There was no tennis tradition, and no money for my family to send me to tournaments, yet I still grew up to become number one in the world.[4]

Many astrologers use the South Node as a reference to past life patterns of behavior or simply as an indicator of gifts or a skill set that comes naturally. LS141's SNode on his Moon/Uranus would reinforce an instinctive need to seek comfort from innovative routines that would represent non-traditional forms and sources of nourishment, especially as the lunar eclipse South Node is in Aquarius. Mercury's elevated status in the eclipse field on his Mars/Uranus midpoint allows the entire Mercury/Pluto conjunct Jupiter/Neptune isotrap to function through Djokovic's extraordinary power to focus and find his way through all obstacles in his path.

LS141's OOB Mars on his Venus/Pluto midpoint is a resonance so deep, so penetrating, it functions more like an obsession. And his life, since the age of six, has been an all-consuming dedication to the creative act of taking his love of tennis to the highest levels of performance possible; his joy in the game resembles a lover's total entanglement with his beloved.

Finally, the lunar eclipse Ceres, with its life-affirming conjunction to the Sun and its powers of regeneration, provides whatever his Mars/Pluto midpoint needs. People who have this midpoint activated can seemingly, out of nowhere, tap into sources of almost superhuman strength and stamina; its combination creates a capacity for hard work that is legendary.

Of note are the positions of Pluto, Chiron, and Uranus in the lunar eclipse field all in the opposite signs to their placements in Djokovic's natal chart. I always take note of these wide conjunctions and oppositions as they seem to give, especially in the 2nd Harmonic, either an energetic boost from environmental factors or they provide a counterbalance to that planet's concerns. Probably due to the awareness factor of the opposition, clients seem to be able to handle the adversity and projection associated with oppositions from a more relaxed response when receiving a wide opposition from that same planet in their lunar eclipse family's energetic field.

Let's take Novak's retrograde Pluto in Scorpio in opposition to his Venus in Taurus, both in rulership. These heavy hitters are not, by any stretch of the imagination, consensus builders, more like pyramid builders, preferring fanatics to fans and supplicants rather than supporters. But in resonance to the lunar eclipse Pluto across the way at one degree Taurus, Novak gets to earn his fans' respect rather than manipulate them through the rules of the game he loves. The Chiron to Chiron opposition is quite wide as is the Uranus to Uranus opposition. Being oppositions—and in the spirit of oppositions, which tend to come at us from the environment, aka other people—I'm sure that Novak Djokovic will have many opportunities to experience all the thrills, chills, spills, and repercussions of his Chiron and Uranus, especially as they hold a 2nd Harmonic in his birth chart with Chiron in conjunction to a very hard working and savvy Mercury sextile Jupiter. I wish him the best. He seems to be on a good path.

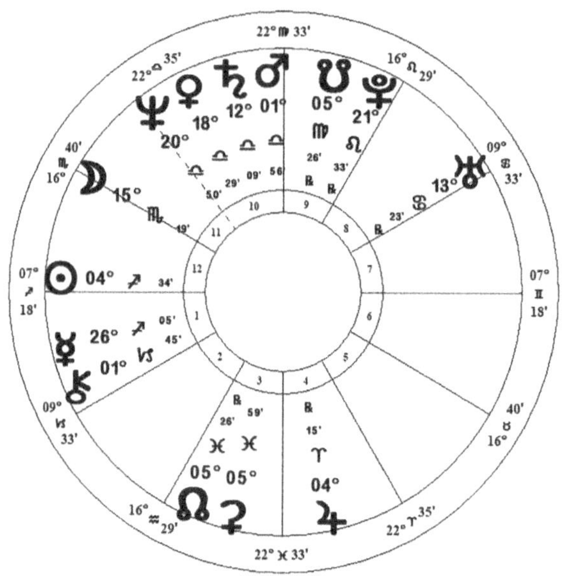

Kathryn Bigelow
PREBLE—LS146

November 27, 1951 • 7:19 AM • San Mateo, CA, USA

"I need to have my hands on the DNA of a film."

-Kathryn Bigelow

First Woman to Win Best Director Award at the Oscars

"What does a set of ovaries have to do with directing a film? She sees through her eyes, not her mammaries."

-Jeremy Renner

Since 1929, the Academy Awards have only nominated five women for Best Director. As of 2022, Kathryn Bigelow is one of three of those women to win the award—and she was the first. She is a trailblazer extraordinaire and best known for her films *Near Dark, The Hurt Locker,* and *Zero Dark Thirty.*[5]

Kathryn Bigelow's Connections to the Dragons of LS141

1st Harmonics: Moon – NNode/Ceres,
SNode – III, Chiron – ASC, Uranus – DSC, Mercury – MC/Mars, Venus – Pluto
2nd Harmonics: Jupiter – Moon, Uranus – Sun, Ceres – Ceres

The Water Dragons of LS141 returned on April 14, 1987, at 24 degrees Libra to find Kathryn Bigelow working on her solo directorial debut movie *Near Dark,* which would become a cult classic. Peter Travis of *Rolling Stone* called it "gory and gorgeous," and Alan Jones of *Radio Times* awarded it four stars out of five, calling it a "1980s horror landmark" and "one of the best vampire movies ever made."[6]

This lunar eclipse offers anyone interested in researching lunar eclipse spheres of influence a banquet of detail in how links to their energy patterns can set you on a totally new course, path or career. It seems to have done all three for Bigelow so let's dive into the details.

The activation degree lit up her Venus-Neptune conjunction along with her Mercury fire trine to Pluto. As you can see from the list above, there is a staggering amount of ties into the energetic field of Lunar Saros 141 with an emphasis on the angles of her chart. The eclipse Moon on her NNode/Ceres is the epitome of sublime resonance, giving her an inside lane that would fast-track her career in the high pressure world of film directing. LS141's Chiron/Uranus opposition falling across her ASC/DSC brings all of its intellectual curiosity and cutting edge mindset to bear on a very hands-on approach to filmmaking that is both extremely personal and socially significant. The eclipse Mercury to her Mars/MC, as well as the eclipse Venus to her Pluto, are extraordinarily helpful as she has a reputation in her field for her use of violence. Her renditions of military operations brought to the screen have invoked powerful emotional reactions. In a 1992 interview with Ana Maria Bahiana from *Cinema Papers,* Bigelow was questioned about her fascination with the subject of violence and whether it was a personal interest of hers. Bigelow responded:

> I don't know. It's not necessarily a personal fascination, though I do like intensity in movies. I like high-impact movie-making. It's challenging, provocative. It makes you think. It upsets you a little.[7]

Her 2nd Harmonics are intense: The Sun/Ceres conjunction would offer a harvest of strength and encouragement that would be highly stimulating to her innate fifth degree NNode/Ceres theatrical and artistic leanings. The eclipse

2nd Harmonic Jupiter on her Moon brings with it the full court press of its Fixed T-Square to the nodes, giving her lots of room to grow. Her four-star stellium in Libra might have been content with a serene and relatively trouble-free life so it's a good thing her PREBLE packs a sophisticated Jupiter/Neptune trine that takes her talent into the stratosphere while underscoring her already deeply determined, ambitious, and idealistic behavior. In her 2010 Oscar Acceptance Speech, Bigelow said: "And, I think the secret to directing is collaborating, and I had truly an extraordinary group of collaborators in my crew."[8]

The eclipse axis and its Grand Mutable Cross with Uranus on her Sun means that, after the arrival of LS141, she could never be happy playing it safe. The eclipse would shape up her career but it would also shake up the foundations of her personal life. With that Libran stellium she was up for the challenge, especially with Saturn in Libra but the twelfth degree took its toll. She would go on to marry fellow film director James Cameron in 1989, but it would be over within two years. As always, I've saved the best for last. LS141's Ceres 2nd Harmonic to her Ceres in Pisces is both precision and prose—Bigelow's canvas from 1987 onward would challenge the masculine and feminine roles portrayed on screen as well as the standard western models of film making, opening up the possibility to view our cultural scripts in a more creative and dynamic manner.

You can be sure that a 2nd Harmonic Ceres contact to any planet, angle, midpoint, asteroid, or sensitive degree will open you up to its ancient mysteries, and that a rite of passage is probably in store. The world of Ceres is ripe with transformation because we either adapt and survive or we perish, making contacts to Ceres a matter of body, mind, spirit, or soul retrieval. A Ceres to Ceres resonance can be summed up in one word—rejuvenating.

And since I failed to mention it at the start, I'll mention it at the end: Always look at Ceres. Always take note of her connections, her aspects, patterns and phase angles as this is what is going to matter most when it comes to how an individual is going to feel nurtured and nourished and yes—happy! How awesome to find that a lunar eclipse family either by birthright or rite of passage has your back.

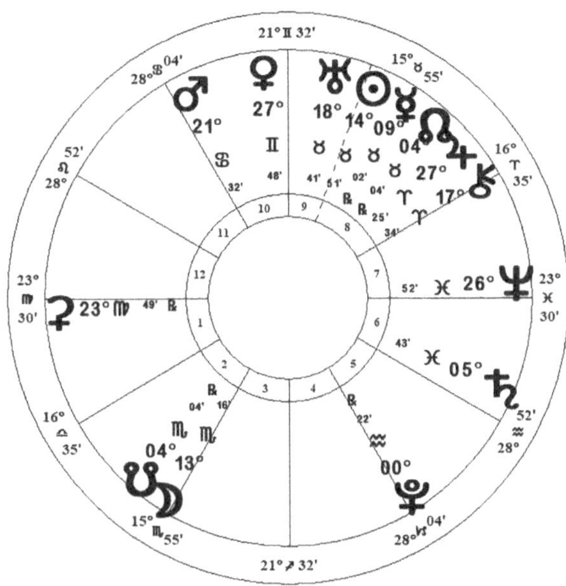

May 5, 2023 • 3:31 PM BST • London, UK

News Flash!

COVID-19 No Longer a Global Threat

On May 5, 2023, within hours of LS141's twenty-fourth return to the global stage, the WHO Director-General issued this bulletin: "COVID-19 is now an established and ongoing health issue which no longer constitutes a public health emergency of international concern."[9]

LS141's arrival on May 5, 2023 would serve to dissolve many of the barriers that seemingly separate our species. This lunar series is a subtle yet potent reminder that it is in our best interest to surrender to the fact that we are all in this together—that our collective need for security, serenity and heaven help us all—salvation does not come without some degree of sacrifice. Lunar Saros 141's current state of evolution encourages all of us to be mindful of our magnificence as we find our way through the maze of entanglement that unites all of humanity.

LS141 Summary

It's time to get unstuck no matter how quirky or complex are your issues. In fact, with the arrival of these sensitive and curious Water Dragons, it has never been easier to simultaneously swim both upstream and downstream in a river of endless contradictions and complexities. These are soulful Dragons with youth and vigor on their side; they are open and willing to try just about anything if it gets them closer to achieving their objectives.

Failure, in the vocabulary of LS141, doesn't exist; but if it did it would be defined as simply the first step or steps in a process of discovery. In fact, helping us to discover our story is what these dragons do best. With every return, their level of sophistication deepens as they do their best work unseen and unappreciated, yet unfailingly there, navigating us through the currents of life's chaos.

Two prominent themes emerge when this lunar eclipse family activates by birthright or rite of passage. The first is a theme of sharing and caring, especially if you let others care for you in "their way," not in "your way." As stated earlier, being of service will assuage any lingering feelings of loneliness and insecurity as a growing circle of new friends promote a greater sense of self-worth. Secondly, if you find yourself losing your grip on reality it might just be the perfect time to let go. Be open to alternative pathways that promote cleaning up and clearing out the clutter. This series offers many opportunities to revive lost dimensions of self along with anything else that has seemingly left your life. To that end, we all get a little bit better at finding our way through this fabulous flow that we call existence.

LS141 Luminaries

John Milton	December 19, 1608
Rudolf Steiner	February 25, 1861
Billie Holiday	April 07, 1915
Orson Welles	May 06, 1915
Saul Bellow	June 10, 1915
Barbara Feldon[E]	March 12, 1933
Quincy Jones[E2]	March 14, 1933
Michael Caine[E2]	March 14, 1933

Danny Aiello	June 20, 1933
Sally Ride	May 26, 1951
Angelica Huston	July 8, 1951
Robin Williams	July 21, 1951
Cate Blanchett	May 14, 1969
Tucker Carlson	May 16, 1969
Peter Dinklage	June 11, 1969
Ice Cube	June 15, 1969
Novak Djokoviç	May 22, 1987
Kendrick Lamar	June 17, 1987
Lionel Messi	June 24, 1987
Blake Lively	August 25, 1987

PREBLE—103
Barbara Feldon
Quincy Jones
Michael Caine
Louis Anquetin

1. Bernadette Brady, *The Book of Star-Planet Combinations*—Star Fact Sheet (Astrologos, 2002) p. 29.
2. Alan Epstein, *Understanding Aspects: The Inconjunct,* p. 122.
3. Novak Djokovic, *Serve to Win* (New York: Zinc Ink, 2013), p. 19.
4. Ibid, p. 184.
5. Jo Mayer https://www.videomaker.com/how-to/directing/why-kathryn-bigelow-is-a-trailblazing-director/ Retrieved May 15, 2022.
6. https://en.wikipedia.org/wiki/Near_Dark. Retrieved May 16, 2022.
7. Anna Maria Bahiana, "Kathryn Bigelow," in *Kathryn Bigelow Interviews*, eds. Peter Keough and Gerald Peary (Jackson, MS: University Press of Mississippi, 2013), p. 70–71.
8. Bahiana, "Kathryn Bigelow's 2010 Oscar Acceptance Speech," in *Kathryn Bigelow Interviews*, p. 212.
9. https://www.theguardian.com/world/2023/may/05/covid-19-no-longer-global-health-emergency-world-health-organization. Retrieved May 6, 2023.

LUNAR SAROS 142

"I'm selfish, impatient and a little insecure. I make mistakes, I'm out of control, and at times hard to handle. But if you can't handle me at my worst, then you sure as hell don't deserve me at my best."

-Marilyn Monroe

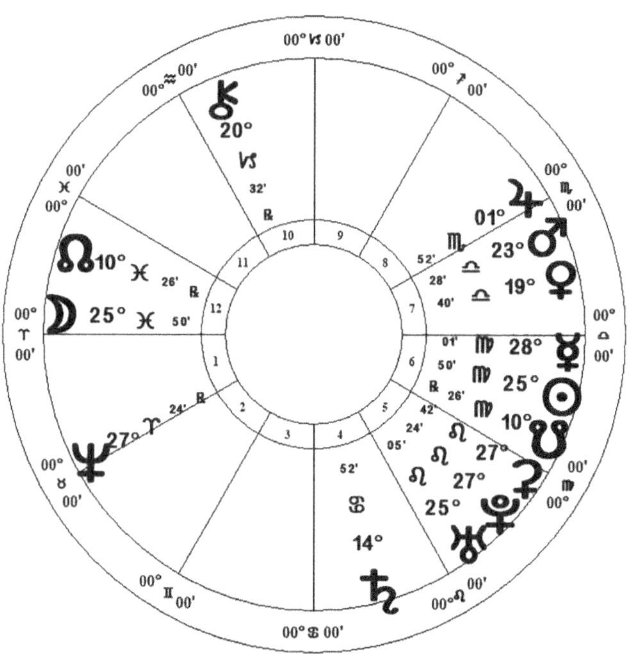

Lunar Saros 142

September 19, 1709 • 00:47:59 AM • North Pole

There Be Dragons

This is a North Node Pisces lunar eclipse overflowing with funk and freedom. Both Mercury and Venus are in rulership offering a heavenly cache of quirks, quarks, and unadulterated charm. Mercury has a knack for annoyance with a touchy, irreverent edginess; thankfully, Venus knows how to negotiate her way out of any withholding Saturn square or impulsive Mars conjunction. Contradictory forces within the Pisces and Leo inconjuncts place great strain and tension within the eclipse, creating a fundamental dichotomy between the need to be at the center of one's world and at the same time oblivious to it. The end result, however, is a fascinating and enigmatic zone of attraction that is hard to resist.

From Neptune in Aries to its Libran Mars opposition, practically everything that lies between those two planets feeds the flow of energy into the vortex of the Moon; six of them directly inconjunct the Moon, offering what may appear to be endless opportunities to learn the high art of compromise and the role that social obligations play in creating a life that is a work of art. Never underestimate the value of inconjuncts as they know the value of when to hold and when to fold.

Its Moon in Pisces is uniquely positioned on the celestial equator, a placement known for its ease of access and ability to connect into the zeitgeist, greatly increasing one's public profile and desire to interact with the spirit of the times. This inclination can become a movement with Neptune's cardinal opposition to Mars, increasing this feeling of bold perception and personal will. This one aspect alone is enough to ensure a lifetime's worth of joy where your dreams can come true.

To help matters along, there is a Mars sextile Uranus. Liz Greene and Howard Sasportas, in their book *The Inner Planets, Building Blocks of Personal Reality,* write that Mars trine or sextile Uranus is a good aspect in that it denotes a high degree of individuality and originality—and the knack for getting away with being that way; your "differentness is acceptable."[1] The eclipse Moon not only creates a classic Finger of Fate with Uranus and Mars but also a Boomerang *and* an Anchor, giving the Sun at the fulcrum and at the twenty-fifth degree an Arian first principles approach that makes your differentness essential. The foundational Sun/Pluto conjunct Mercury/Uranus isotrap is a source of innovative talent that needs to be channeled to gain the best from its high levels of inspiration and creativity. Thankfully, both the Anchor for grounding in the present and the Boomerang for rewarding in the future are patterns of energy at your command.

The triple conjunction of Pluto, Uranus, and Ceres in Leo is a celestial showstopper as its dragon DNA conveys a sense of style and genius that can never be destroyed—delayed, for sure, disoriented, of course but eventually your comeback is assured. This is a feature shared by only one other lunar eclipse, the Fire Dragons of LS140—Design Your Life. They alone have the power to completely rebuild a life from seemingly nothing as do the Water Dragons of LS142, thanks to the life-giving, restorative powers within the intuitive flames of its triple Pluto, Uranus, and Ceres conjunction. When the battle seems hopeless and even lost, you can call on this magnificent trio to reset the clock. It is a true superpower that only these two dragon families wield.

Closest Midpoints: Saturn/Mercury-Jupiter, Mars/Venus-Neptune
Isotraps: Sun/Pluto conjunct Mercury/Uranus
Sun/Moon opposition Uranus/Neptune

1900—2100 Eclipses: Lunar Saros—142

1908, 1926, 1944, 1962, 1980, 1998, 2016, 2034, 2052, 2070, 2088
Length of cycle —1,298 years
Series ends—November 17, 3007

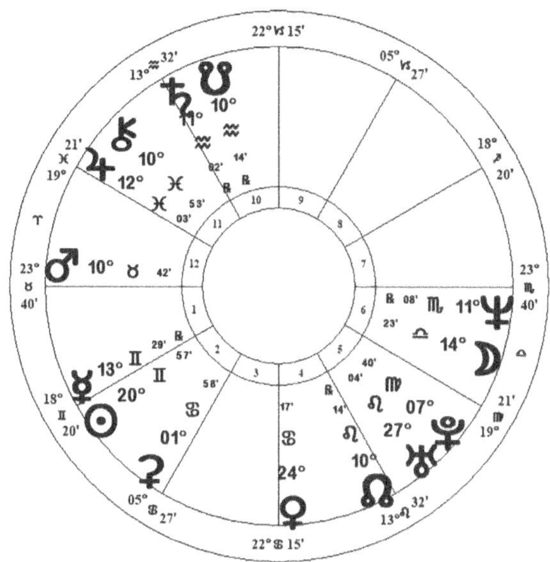

Jordan B. Peterson
PREBLE—LS142

June 12, 1962 • 2:49 AM • Edmonton, AB, Canada

Clinical Psychologist/YouTube Personality
Best-Selling Author/Public Intellectual

"He is outselling the Bible, the most influential psychologist since Carl Jung, more popular than Jeremy Corbyn and the biggest philosopher since Albert Camus."

-PENGUIN PUBLISHERS, LONDON, UK

Jordan Peterson is on fire and has been since March 2016 when he began an experiment in crowdfunding through Patreon. As of August 2023, Peterson's YouTube live subscriber count stands at 7,380,000.[2] His meteoric rise as a YouTube podcaster can be traced back to LS142's activation on March 23, 2016, at 3 degrees Libra. Let's take a look at his story.

Jordan Peterson's Connections to the Dragons of LS142
Uranus with Uranus

1st Harmonics: NNode – Chiron,
SNode – Pluto, Venus – Moon, Uranus/Pluto/Ceres – Uranus, Chiron – MC

First rule is always to look for similar patterns in both fields and here we have two: A same phase relationship between Uranus and Pluto as well as between Mars and Neptune. To find one is something very special, but to find two is frankly extraordinary. Together these four planets create a symphony of resonance that is the essence of synergy. As you can see from the above table, there is a Uranus 1st Harmonic to his Uranus that also includes the eclipse field's Pluto and Ceres. And remember, this is his PREBLE; the Water Dragons of LS142 are his by birthright which makes every return an event worth celebrating.

When your dragon family returns every eighteen years, you don't need an activation degree to sync with its sphere but if one is offered, so much the better. For Peterson, the power levels that March were pumped up by the activation degree falling not only on his Uranus/Neptune midpoint at 4 Libra (another Uranian tie) but also on his Progressed Bija Moon at 2 Libra 20. It's always the start of something new, even when you can't put your finger on exactly what that "newness" is when the progressed Moon gets close to home.

And since Jordan Peterson's fame came about through his best-selling *12 Rules for Life: An Antidote to Chaos,* and *Beyond Order: 12 More Rules for Life*, my rule is to start with a basic understanding of both charts. Get a feel for how each functions before you weave their stories together. In Peterson's case, he was born to be a scholar and a clinical psychologist as his chart holds a Grand Air Trine with Saturn in rulership in the Tenth House conjunct the SNode and in a Grand Fixed Cross with its fully functioning Mars/Neptune opposition from the Twelfth/Sixth Houses. Considering the basic fourteen factors used here that include the Moon's nodes, Ceres, and Chiron, Peterson has a perfect balance between masculine and feminine energies, making him well on the road to being a fully integrated and functioning Being. His work in the fields of clinical psychology, neurobiology, myth, and religion reflect a life dedicated to a rapturous journey of intellectual, spiritual, and ideological growth.

What I find fascinating about Jordan Peterson's connections to his dragon family is that there are only 1st Harmonics connecting their fields of resonance; this gives a much more subjective experience to the eclipse story. With only 1st Harmonics, it is simply a matter of time until the seed essence of the eclipse erupts into one's consciousness. But in Jordan's case I suspect that his two Cosmic Bridges—both of which involve the eclipse nodal axis—quickened the pace of germination. Peterson's acceleration in 2016 can be credited to his Uranus/Neptune midpoint awakening to the return of Lunar Saros 142's "There Be Dragons" and their intense foundational Sun/Pluto conjunct Mercury/Uranus isotrap and its energy field of insight, innovation, and metamorphosis.

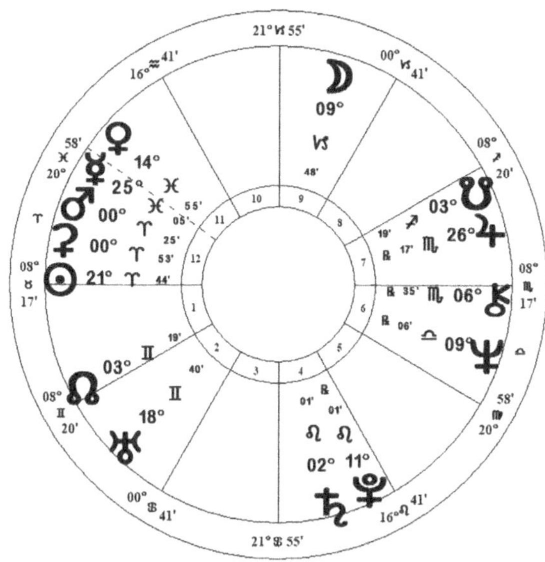

David Letterman
PREBLE—LS134

April 12, 1947 • 6:00 AM • Indianapolis, IN, USA

Top Ten Stupid Human Tricks

"People say New Yorkers can't get along. Not true.
I saw two New Yorkers, complete strangers, sharing a cab.
One guy took the tires and the radio; the other guy took the engine."

-David Letterman

David Letterman is a singular sensation as one would expect from a scrappy Mars and Ceres alpha infinity conjunction at the AP and in of all places, Aries. True, for most of his professional life he was a self-proclaimed, unapologetic alcoholic and bastard in name and deed to almost all who had to deal with his insufferable quirkiness. But that didn't seem to stop his meteoric rise to stardom, wealth, and power. He rose from obscurity to become Johnny Carson's most frequent Monday night substitute host and in 1979, Letterman was given his own morning talk-show, "The David Letterman Show," which premiered in June 1980 and ran until October 24, 1980.[3] The *New York Post* wrote on June 18, 1980, that:

"In an astonishing high-level shake-up, the top two producers of the David Letterman Show have resigned only days before this morning's scheduled debut of the NBC talk show. . . . The shake-up seems to indicate yet more trouble in the NBC studios—as well as Letterman's clout."[4]

David Letterman's Connections to the Dragons of LS142
Mercury to Mercury

1st Harmonics: NNode – Venus, Moon – Mercury/Mars/Ceres, Neptune – Sun
2nd Harmonics: Mercury – Mercury, Mercury – Mars/Ceres, Venus/Mars – Sun, Saturn – Moon

The lunar eclipse that activated Letterman's chart on March 1, 1980, opened at 11 Virgo, in opposition to his ASC ruler Venus at 14 Pisces. Oppositions bring gifts of opportunity, especially when they are reaching out to touch Venus, but they can also bring confrontation. LS142 is a study in adjustments with ten inconjuncts dominating the aspect totals with seven to the Moon. No doubt LS142's 1st Harmonic Cosmic Bridge from its NNode to his Venus was a cosmic act of pollination. It would allow his personal style of aesthetics to reach an adoring public through the eclipse Moon's 1st Harmonic to his independent Mercury/Mars/Ceres bastion of ambition. Letterman would go on to enjoy phenomenal success in late-night television thanks to his ability to apply, according to the New York Times national media reporter Bill Carter, "that potent mix of searing intelligence and scintillating wit that could take [your] breath away."[5] The intensity and unconventional quirkiness of LS142 easily enticed Letterman's Venus/ASC-MC to lower the drawbridge so his brand of banter and repartee could begin to restore the realm with a nightcap or two of irreverent humor.

Letterman benefits from the eclipse 2nd Harmonic Venus/Mars and its ability to jumpstart a relationship by its alignment to his adventurous twenty-first degree Sun. In this way, its Neptunian element of attraction/deception will also play a part in the pattern. The good news here is that his Sun at the 21st degree of Aries falls exactly at the midpoint of the Venus/Mars 2nd Harmonic giving him status and a boldness to his creativity that would serve him well in the years to come. Late Night with David Letterman began on February 1, 1982, and ended on May 20, 2015, a run of thirty-three years and 6,080 episodes.[6] He was the most successful late night talk show host in American television history.

News Flash!

178 Million Subscribers—30.8 Billion Views[7]

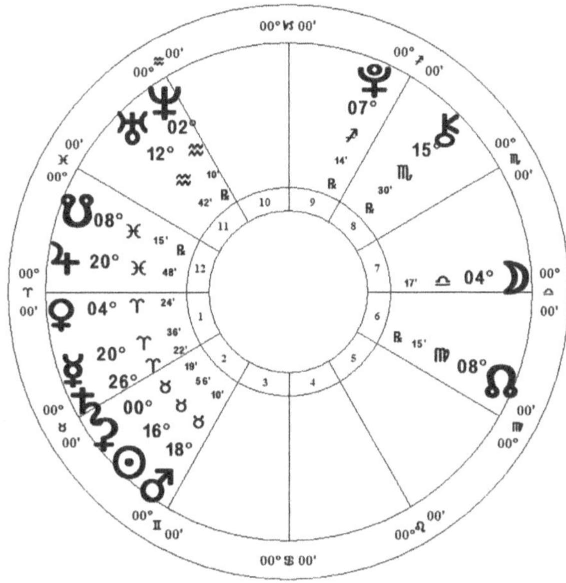

MrBeast
PREBLE—LS142

May 7, 1998 • TOB Unknown • Wichita, KN, USA

YouTube's Biggest Philanthropist

Apart from all his over-the-top stunts, as of June 2023, Jimmy Donaldson, aka MrBeast, is "YouTube's biggest philanthropist[8]." His main channel is the most-subscribed channel owned by an individual from the United States. He's one Beastie Bull, here to make the world a better place to live by planting trees and cleaning up Earth's oceans. He's also got a few tech startup gigs on the side along with his very own burger chain. MrBeast is a true Taurean who loves to roll in the sweet smell of cash.

MrBeast's Connections to the Dragons of LS142
↑North Node with South Node↓

1st Harmonics: NNode – SNode, Moon – Jupiter, Neptune – Saturn/Ceres
2nd Harmonics: Venus/Mars – Mercury, Mars – Saturn, Jupiter – Ceres

MrBeast sports a fully charged Global Gateway, a dynamic 1st Harmonic Moon to his Jupiter in rulership and in sextile to a Mars in MR to Venus. His Ceres at zero Taurus is his own cosmic ATM machine and with Uranus in Aquarius you know this guy was born to sail into and past the edge of the known world 'Where Dragons Be."

LS142 Summary

LS142 has been tracking through its first Full Moon phase since its seventeenth return on March 13, 1998. It will remain in Full Moon force until April 25, 2070, when it returns for its twenty-first appearance. These seventy-two years will prove to be highly dramatic as many bold and adventuresome souls test the waters and defy the warnings of the old adage, "There be Dragons," that was meant to keep us chained in subjugation to our fear of the unknown. Thank goodness those days are being replaced by the spirit of these youthful Water Dragons whose pounding hearts beat lifelines of effervescence into every particle of our Being. Their youth gives them an intractable ability to bounce back from whatever difficulty is encountered as they slide past obstacles, roadblocks and an Earth spinning on the edge of chaos. Their mobility and willingness to try something new is the sweet source of their perennial strength and their gift is an endless supply of resilience.

To be in the flow of experience that is so richly provided by these brilliant spheres of consciousness just takes a decision to join in the fun. You are never more than one breath away from being a part of this heightened stream that can connect you to a field of all possibility where sudden new insights and creative ideas are looking to land. You could receive a spontaneous healing or recover from a chronic illness; an invention or innovation whose time has come could make you its spokesperson. Whatever comes through—don't panic. Trust. Believe. Dream. And maybe buy some new pillows to keep your head held high while drifting through those cosmic clouds of creation.

Take the time to explore how you can act as a channel so that more of you can dance with not just the dragons of Lunar Saros 142 but with all their cosmological cousins and clans. It makes no difference which elementary particles you choose to partner with as the leptons and bosons and up quarks and down quarks are happy to remind all of us that we are both the dancer and the dance.

LS142 Luminaries

Bette Davis	April 5, 1908
Edward R. Murrow	April 25, 1908
Oskar Schindler	April 28, 1908
James Stewart	May 20, 1908
Harper Lee	April 28, 1926
David Attenborough	May 8, 1926
Miles Davis	May 26, 1926
Marilyn Monroe	June 1, 1926
Alice Walker[E]	February 9, 1944
George Lucas	May 14, 1944
Boz Scaggs	June 8, 1944
Raymond Moody	June 30, 1944
Matthew Broderick	March 21, 1962
Jordan B. Peterson	June 12, 1962
Paula Abdul	June 19, 1962
Tom Cruise	July 3, 1962
Rebel Wilson[E1]	March 2, 1980
Ronaldinho	March 21, 1980
Rishi Sanak	May 12, 1980
Venus Williams	June 17, 1980
Jimmy Donaldson MrBeast	May 7, 1998
Jaden Smith	July 8, 1998

PREBLE—LS137

Alice Walker

Rebel Wilson

1. Liz Greene and Howard Sasportas, *The Inner Planets*, p. 244.
2. https://socialblade.com/youtube/user/jordanpetersonvideos/realtime. Retrieved Aug. 25, 2023
3. http://blog.wfmu.org/freeform/2010/03/the-late-night-hosts-before-they-were-big.html. Retrieved June 24, 2022.
4. Ibid.
5. Bill Carter, *The War for Late Night* (New York: Viking, 2010), p. 229.
6. https://en.wikipedia.org/wiki/David_Letterman. Retrieved June 24, 2022.
7. https://vidiq.com/youtube-stats/channel/UCX6OQ3DkcsbYNE6H8uQQuVA/ Retrieved Aug. 25, 2023.
8. https://fortune.com/2023/05/30/mr-beast-stunt-philanthropy-raising-money. Retrieved June 18, 2023.

And One More Thing

In the infinite game of life, lunar eclipses are a lighthouse on the rocky shores of our journey. The constant pulse of their light is a reassuring reminder that like the tides they watch over, our lives are always riding the waves of endless renewal. Their presence affirms an ancient understanding that lies deep within our species that we are tied to their cosmic rhythms in ways that defy reason. Their endless cycles of creation, dissolution, and rebirth mirror our own mortality and bring comfort to our brief earthly passage as we embody the mystery of transformation within the larger context of eternity. We are the stuff of stars and every atom in our body pulses to the rise and fall of our celestial dance partners.

Appendix A

Reference Tables

LUNAR SAROS ECLIPSE FOUNDATION DEGREES

102N	13 Aries	122N	26 Aquarius	138N	01 Taurus
103S	12 Pisces	123S	28 Aquarius	139S	18 Gemini
108N	18 Capricorn	124N	00 Pisces	140N	02 Aries
109S	08 Capricorn	125S	00 Aquarius	141S	02 Pisces
110N	09 Sagittarius	126N	02 Aquarius	142N	25 Pisces
111S	22 Sagittarius	127S	23 Capricorn	143S	25 Aquarius
112N	02 Sagittarius	128N	04 Capricorn	144N	06 Aquarius
113S	13 Scorpio	129S	26 Sagittarius	145S	18 Aquarius
114N	26 Scorpio	130N	27 Sagittarius	146N	18 Capricorn
115S	06 Scorpio	131S	27 Scorpio	147S	10 Capricorn
116N	25 Virgo	132N	00 Sagittarius	148N	22 Capricorn
117S	19 Libra	133S	01 Sagittarius	149S	22 Sagittarius
118N	18 Virgo	134N	20 Libra	150N	04 Sagittarius
119S	25 Aries	135S	23 Libra	151S	16 Sagittarius
120N	28 Aries	136N	24 Libra	156N	16 Taurus
121S	18 Aries	137S	06 Cancer		

LUNAR SAROS ECLIPSE SOUTH NODE DEGREES

102N	27 Virgo	122N	09 Leo	138N	14 Libra
103S	26 Aquarius	123S	12 Aquarius	139S	02 Gemini
108N	02 Cancer	124N	14 Leo	140N	16 Virgo
109S	23 Sagittarius	125S	13 Capricorn	141S	15 Aquarius
110N	22 Taurus	126N	16 Cancer	142N	10 Virgo
111S	06 Sagittarius	127S	07 Capricorn	143S	09 Aquarius
112N	16 Taurus	128N	17 Gemini	144N	19 Cancer
113S	26 Libra	129S	09 Sagittarius	145S	03 Aquarius
114N	10 Taurus	130N	12 Gemini	146N	02 Cancer
115S	20 Libra	131S	10 Scorpio	147S	23 Sagittarius
116N	08 Pisces	132N	13 Taurus	148N	07 Cancer
117S	03 Libra	133S	16 Scorpio	149S	06 Sagittarius
118N	02 Pisces	134N	03 Aries	150N	16 Taurus
119S	08 Aries	135S	06 Libra	151S	00 Sagittarius
120N	11 Libra	136N	09 Aries	156N	29 Libra
121S	03 Aries	137S	19 Gemini		

LUNAR SAROS NS ECLIPSE HISTORICAL DATA

LS102 – 06 Oct 461	LS103 – 04 Sep 472	LS108 – 11 Jul 689
LS109 –27 Jun 736	LS110 – 01 Jun 747	LS111 – 14 Jun 830
LS112 –24 May 859	LS113 – 05 May 888	LS114 – 18 May 971
LS115 – 27 Apr 1000	LS116 – 15 Mar 993	LS117 – 09 Apr 1094
LS118 – 09 Mar 1105	LS119 – 19 Oct 935	LS120 – 22 Oct 1000
LS121 – 12 Oct 1047	LS122 – 20 Aug 1022	LS123 – 22 Aug 1087
LS124 – 24 Aug 1152	LS125 – 24 Jul 1163	LS126 – 25 Jul 1228
LS127 – 16 Jul 1275	LS128 – 18 Jun 1304	LS129 – 18 Jun 1351
LS130 – 19 Jun 1416	LS131 – 19 May 1427	LS132 – 21 May 1492
LS133 – 13 May 1557	LS134 – 11 Apr 1550	LS135 – 13 Apr 1615
LS136 – 13 Apr 1680	LS137 – 27 Dec 1564	LS138 – 25 Oct 1521
LS139 – 09 Dec 1658	LS140 – 25 Sep 1597	LS141 – 25 Aug 1608
LS142 – 19 Sep 1709	LS143 – 18 Aug 1720	LS144 – 29 Jul 1749
LS145 – 11 Aug 1832	LS146 – 11 Jul 1843	LS147 – 02 Jul 1890
LS148 – 15 Jul 1973	LS149 – 13 Jun 1984	LS150 – 25 May 2013
LS151 – 06 Jun 2096	LS156 – 08 Nov 2060	

ECLIPTIC DEGREE FREQUENCY FINDER

Aries	02 – LS140	13 – LS102	18 – LS121	25 – LS119	28 – LS120
Taurus	01 – LS138	16 – LS156			
Gemini	18 – LS139				
Cancer	06 – LS137				
Leo	N/A				
Virgo	18 – LS118	25 – LS116			
Libra	19 – LS117	20 – LS134	23 – LS135	24 – LS136	
Scorpio	06 – LS115	13 – LS113	26 – LS114	27 – LS131	
Sagittarius	00 – LS132	01 – LS133	02 – LS112	04 – LS150	09 – LS110
	16 – LS151	22 – LS111	26 – LS129	27 – LS130	
Capricorn	04 – LS128	08 – LS109	10 – LS147	18 – LS108	18 – LS146
	22 – LS148	23 – LS127			
Aquarius	00 – LS125	02 – LS126	06 – LS144	18 – LS145	25 – LS143
	26 – LS122	28 – LS123			
Pisces	00 – LS124	02 – LS141	12 – LS103	25 – LS142	

LUNAR SAROS NS ECLIPSE HISTORICAL DATA

1,496 years and 84 returns

LS102 – 06 Oct 461

1,478 years and 83 returns

LS120 – 22 Oct 1000

1,460 years and 82 returns

LS103 – 04 Sep 472	LS119 – 19 Oct 935
LS121 – 12 Oct 1047	LS138 – 25 Oct 1521

1,442 years and 81 returns

LS156 – 08 Nov 2060

1,406 years and 79 returns

LS139 – 09 Dec 1658

1,388 years and 78 returns

LS137 – 27 Dec 1564

1,370 years and 77 returns

LS140 – 25 Sep 1597

1,316 years and 74 returns

LS122 – 20 Aug 1022

1,298 years and 73 returns

LS116 –15 Mar 993	LS118 – 09 Mar 1105
LS142 –19 Sep 1709	LS124 – 24 Aug 1152

1,280 years and 72 returns

LS108 – 11 Jul 689	LS110 – 01 Jun 747	LS112 – 24 May 859
LS115 – 27 Apr 1000	LS123 – 22 Aug 1087	LS125 – 24 Jul 1163
LS127 – 16 Jul 1275	LS131 – 19 May 1427	LS134 – 11 Apr 1550
LS136 – 13 Apr 1680	LS141 – 25 Aug 1608	LS143 – 18 Aug 1720
LS146 – 11 Jul 1843		

1,262 years and 71 returns

LS109 – 01 Jul 736	LS111 – 14 Jun 830	LS113 – 03 May 888
LS114 – 18 May 971	LS117 – 09 Apr 1094	LS128 – 26 Jun 1304
LS129 – 18 Jun 1351	LS130 – 19 Jun 1416	LS132 – 21 May 1492
LS 133 – 23 May 1557	LS135 – 13 Apr 1615	LS144 – 29 Jul 1749
LS 145 – 11 Aug 1832	LS149 – 13 Jun 1984	LS150 – 25 May 2013
LS151 – 06 Jun 2096		

1,244 years and 70 returns

LS126 – 25 Jul 1228	LS147 – 02 Jul 1890	LS148 –15 Jul 1973

Appendix B

Notes

Part One—Dancing with Fire

Lunar Saros 102

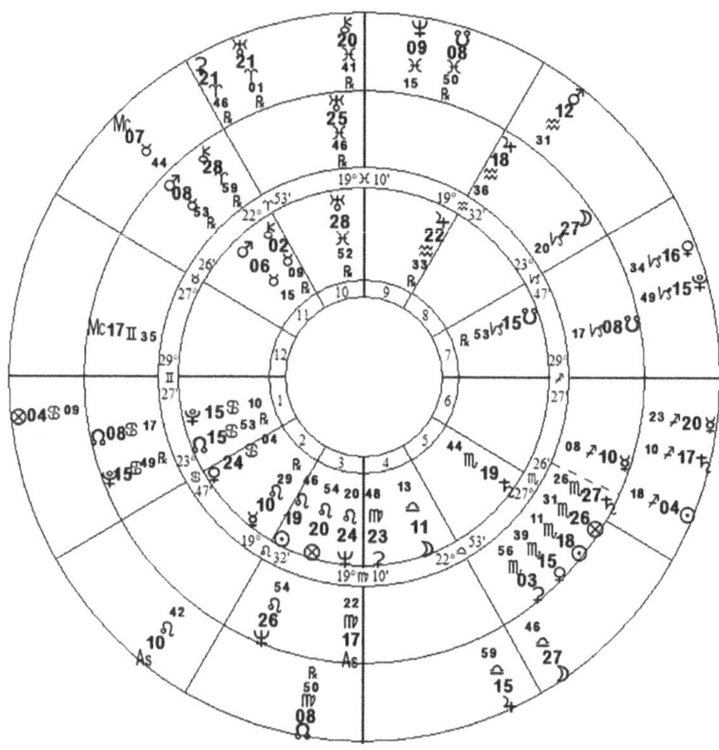

Inner

Fidel Castro

August 13, 1926 • 2:00 AM • Biran, Cuba

Middle

Secondary Progressed

Solar Arc • Bija Correction • November 25, 2016

Outer

Death of Castro

November 25, 2016 • 10:29 PM • Havana, Cuba

August 13, 1927, is an alternate DOB given for Fidel Castro however, the key life event dates below better reflect August 13, 1926. There is a 90 percent probability that the transiting Moon at the time of death will be making a major aspect to either the natal Sun/Moon or to the progressed Sun/Moon. Castro's progressed Moon had just entered his Eighth House and together with his PAscendant on his IC and in square to his PMidheaven would indicate that the end of his life was drawing near. PSun was within one degree of natal Saturn while transiting Saturn was trine his Sun. Inconjuncts are always present as are sextiles and trines as they smooth the way and help to ease the transition. All of this with transiting Pluto in exact opposition to its radix position. In addition, the day held a transiting Pluto square Jupiter within minutes of an exact conjunction to his natal South Node.

Key Life Events for Fidel Castro Using Progressed Bija Moon

1953—Oct 16: Imprisoned after an unsuccessful rising against Batista's regime
P☽ 9♎ conjunct ☽

1955—May 15: Released from prison under an amnesty deal
P☽ 28♎ quincunx P♅:, sextile P♀

1956—Dec 2: Lands in Cuba with Ché Guevara to begin a guerrilla war
P☽ 17♏ opposition P♂, sextile P☉, square P♃, square ☉

1959—Jan 8: Defeats Batista, enters Havana–Feb 16: Sworn in as Prime Minister
P☽ 15♐ quincunx P♇, square P☿

1961—Apr 17-25: Fights off CIA-sponsored Bay of Pigs invasion by Cuban exiles
P☽ 14♑ conjunct P☋, opposition P♇

1962—Oct 14 - 28: Cuban missile crisis
P☽ 5♒ square ♂

1963—Castro's mom Lina Ruz González dies
P☽ 19♒ conjunct P♃, square P♂, square P♄, opposition ☉, square ♄

1976—Nov 2: Elected president by Cuba›s National Assembly
P☽ 18♌ opposition P♃, square P♂, square P♄, sextile P☿, conjunct ☉, opposition ♃, square ♄

1991—Oct: Steps down as head of government
P☽ 27♒ opposition P♆, square P♄, opposition ♆.

2006—Jul 31: Hands over reins of government to brother Raul due to health
P☽ 16♍ quincunx P♃, sextile P♇, conjunct IC, sextile ♇☊

Lunar Saros 119

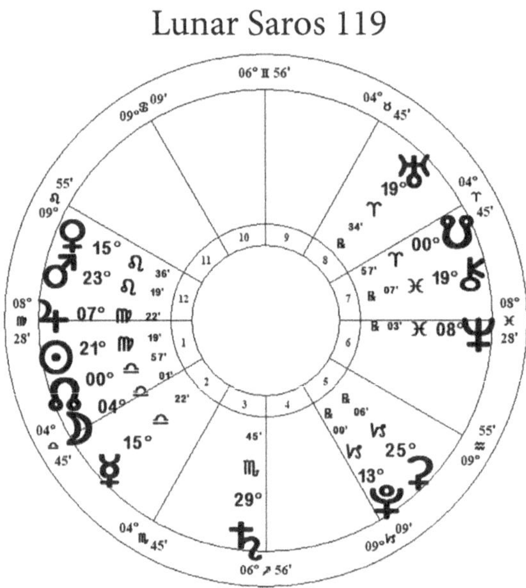

Gravitational Waves

September 14, 2015 • 5:51 AM • Livingston, LA, USA

News Flash!
Einstein's Gravitational Waves Found At Last![1]

On October 3, 2017, the Royal Swedish Academy of Sciences announced that the Nobel Prize in Physics would be awarded to Rainer Weiss, Kip Thorne, and Barry Barish, three pioneers in the study of gravitational waves that were detected on September 14, 2015.[2] These waves had been predicted by Einstein one hundred years earlier.

LS119's arrival on August 7, 2017, at 15 Aquarius sensitized its entire field of resonance to react to that heightened activation degree. Not surprisingly, on the day of the discovery of the gravitational waves, Venus was holding court at its polarity position at 15 Leo and was able to respond in full spectrum Leo magnificence. Within hours the world would hear of the breakthrough discovery and set physics and physicists on fire with the knowledge that Einstein had been right all along.

The chart for the moment of discovery is stunning in its cosmic architecture as it features Jupiter, our most massive planet rising in the east as Neptune, named after the Roman god of all the oceans and seas, setting in the west. If there is a better cosmological representation of the concept of Gravitation Waves I have failed to find it. The Jupiter/Neptune opposition symbolism works perfectly. This is synchronicity on a grand scale. The extra touch of the Moon in Libra conjunct the AP NNode injects into this moment an extra wave of initiation that is a confirmation that working together in global partnerships is the way we are going not only to survive but to thrive in the decades and millenniums ahead. Thank you Alfred Nobel, for being of such "great benefit to Mankind."[3]

1. https://www.nobelprize.org/prizes/physics/2017/summary/ Retrieved Jan. 20, 2022.
2. https://www.nobelprize.org/prizes/lists/all-nobel-prizes/ Retrieved Jan. 20, 2022.
3. Ibid.

Lunar Saros 130

By definition, an Out-of Bounds (OOB) Moon or planet is one that exceeds 23 degrees 27 minutes either North or South of the equator. Outside of the standard physical model that is the Sun's 23 degree 27 minutes range, planets that venture beyond this realm are true explorers, born to think, imagine, interpret, and even transcend our preconceived notions of the way our cultural norms lay down the rules for acceptable behavior.

OOB Moon: Frank Abagnale, Adele, Roseanne Barr, Cher, Albert Einstein, Sigmund Freud, Draymond Green, Hugh Jackman, David Letterman, Louis C.K., Yoko Ono, Susy Orman, Gwyneth Paltrow, Neil Peart, Cole Porter, Vladimir Putin, Keanu Reeves, Babe Ruth, Emma Watson, Amy Winehouse.

OOB Mercury: Bob Dylan, Tom Hanks, Henri Matisse, Elon Musk, Dolly Parton, Brad Pitt, Maggie Smith, Neil Young.

OOB Venus: Frank Abagnale, Adele, Jack Dorsey, Al Pacino, Auguste Rodin, Oskar Schindler, Frank Sinatra, Maggie Smith, Meryl Streep.

OOB Mars: Tim Berners-Lee, Susan Boyle, James Cameron, Wayne Gretzky, Anne Hathaway, Janice Joplin, Martin Luther King, Jr., Meghan Markle, Rupert Murdoch, Dolly Parton, Neil Peart, Brad Pitt. Cole Porter, Putin, Franklin D. Roosevelt, Oskar Schindler, Steven Spielberg, Tiger Woods.

OOB Jupiter: Eminem, Enrico Fermi, Prince Harry, Petra Kvitová, Gwyneth Paltrow, Kristen Stewart, Emma Watson.

OOB Uranus: Frank Abagnale, Adele, Susy Orman, Louis Pasteur, Meryl Streep, Wilbur Wright.

OOB Pluto: Frank Abagnale, Bob Dylan, Harrison Ford, Janice Joplin, David Letterman, Dolly Parton, Susy Orman, Cher, Meryl Streep.

Part Two—Dancing with Earth

Introduction

"The most explosive impact in English literature during the nineteenth century is unquestionably Thomas Carlyle," writes Lionel Stevenson. "From about 1840 onward, no author of prose or poetry was immune from his influence."[1]

1. https://en.wikipedia.org/wiki/Thomas_Carlyle

Part Three—Dancing with Air

Lunar Saros 126

All the critical dates for Putin using 2:23 AM have given progressed positions along with transiting planets that time the key events of his political career since being named Prime Minister of Russia on August 16, 1999. The rise of the Sun, Saturn, and Neptune crossing the natal 26 degree Leo ascendant marks the years 1999 and 2000 (age 47) when he became Prime Minister, 2004 (age 51) when he was re-elected President, and 2008 (age 55) when he was appointed Prime Minister. On March 26, 2000, when he was elected President of Russia, transiting Jupiter was within one degree of the MC and the progressed Bija Moon was conjunct the NNode at 15 Aquarius. On March 14, 2004, he was re-elected President under a transit of Venus conjunct his MC at 9 Taurus with the transiting NNode at 12 Taurus. His progressed MC had just turned over to 00 Cancer with his progressed ASC at 00 Libra. His progressed Moon, ruler of the MC at 11 Aries was rapidly opposing his radix Sun. On May 8, 2008, he was appointed Prime Minister and once again transiting Venus was conjunct his MC at 9 Taurus! Transiting Saturn was at 1 Virgo conjunct his natal ASC with the progressed Moon at 7 Gemini trine Mars at 7 Aquarius and opposing progressed Sun at 9 Sagittarius. On September 24, 2011, Putin announced that he was "swapping" jobs with then President Dmitri Medvedev, a political move that would return him to the presidency in the 2012 elections he was assured of winning.[1] Just this one political act alone should be enough to at least establish the fact that we have his correct birth date as there seems to be some speculation as to the day and year of his birth. I offer his second Saturn return as prima facie evidence that we at least have his correct day and year as Saturn's transiting position on September 24, 2011, was 17 Libra 49, just three days off of an exact return to its natal position. As well, his progressed Moon had just made a conjunction to his natal Uranus. On March 4, 2012, he won the presidential election again under an exact transit of Jupiter to his MC and a progressed Moon at 28 Cancer sextile his radix Moon at 28 Taurus. On May 7, 2018, his fourth term began with progressed Moon on his progressed ASC at 9 Libra.

On July 3, 2020, Putin's amendments to the Russian constitution basically made him a dictator for life, giving him an extension for twelve more years as President. His progressed MC had reached 16 Cancer 48 where his progressed Uranus sat waiting to pounce at 17 Cancer 30. The progressed Moon was at 7 Scorpio, one degree off his IC. Now here's where it really takes your breath away because transiting rebellious Uranus was at 9 Taurus, breaking down the control structures of the authoritative Tenth House.

Lunar Saros 139

After years of investigation, thousands of scientists, engineers, architects, military personnel, and concerned citizens, along with many of the family and friends of the 2,744 people who died that day, have come forward to question and challenge the veracity of the official government sanctioned NIST report explaining the events of 9/11.[1] In their *9/11 Commission Report* released in 2004, it should be of great concern that in its 571 page public report on the events of September 11, 2001, *there was no mention of the collapse of WTC 7.*[2] Building 7 was a 47-story skyscraper and part of the World Trade Center complex. It was not hit by an airplane and suffered minimal damage from those two collisions. And yet, at 5:20 pm on September 11, it collapsed into its own footprint, at near free-fall speed.[3]

1. https://911truth.org/ Retrieved Feb. 1, 2022.
2. Ibid.
3. https://www.govinfo.gov/app/details/GPO-911REPORT. Retrieved Feb. 1, 2022.

Lunar Saros 144

■ EU member states
■ Non-EU countries participating in the EU single market through the EEA (European Economic Area) or other agreements

Part Four—Dancing with Water

Lunar Saros 103

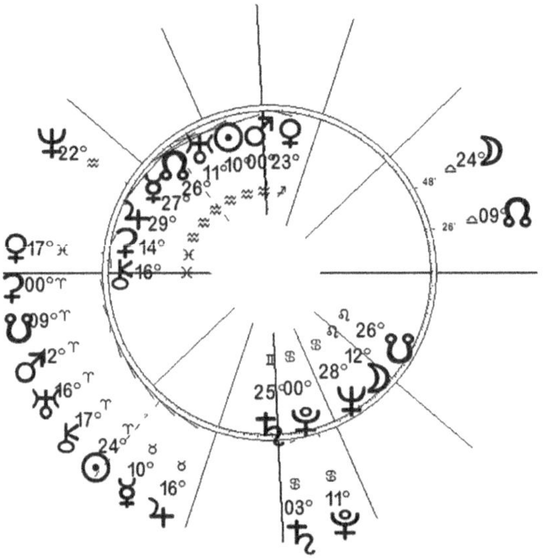

Inside

Thomas Merton
PREBLE—LS136

January 31, 1915 • 9:00 AM • Prades, France

Outside

Lunar Saros 136

April 13, 1680 • 11:35:16 AM • North Pole

Thomas Merton's Connections to the Dragons of LS136
Saturn with Saturn* *Pluto with Pluto

1st Harmonics: Neptune—NNode, Venus—Ceres/Chiron, Saturn—Pluto

LS136's Pluto square the nodal axis is an indicator that an evolutionary process is well underway. Merton's Pluto at the AP has resonance to the eclipse Pluto giving him awareness that there are issues that need resolution and integration. Merton's journal entries throughout his life consistently speak to his "inconsistency" and desire to constantly shift his frame of reference. Their Saturn to

Saturn tie brings in LS136's Saturn square Chiron at the AP which is always churning the waters of new beginnings. Again, Merton's journals repeatedly speak of "always beginning" and never feeling contentment for any extended period of time. The eclipse Neptune on his NNode and its Cosmic Bridge definitely kept him sane while its Saturn on his Pluto drove him constantly into the arms of deep psychosis and distress.

Acknowledgments

For his wealth of knowledge and fabulous support for the 47 Lunar Eclipse Dragons who can now dance their way into the consciousness of the world, I say thank you Scott Silverman. Your editing skills have made *Where Dragons Dance* not just a book you read; it's a book you live. It shows you how to connect to the wonder, magic, and life-affirming energy that's already inside of you. For her enthusiasm for the study and value that lunar eclipses bring to the art of astrological analysis, I thank my publisher Yvonne Paglia who never faltered in her belief in this work. My thanks also go out to Kathryn Sky-Peck for her right out of the gate enthusiastic appreciation, patience, professionalism, and support for the manuscript and wrangling with my labyrinthine "Dragon Beast" of a book. Also, a huge round of applause to the ever generous, immensely knowledgeable, and kind staff at the Strathcona Public Library in Edmonton and a special shout out to Gail and Stephen, who unfailingly guided me through the maze of computer glitches, gadgets, grammatical incursions, and special requests for biographical material that contributed to the endless rounds of research for this book. You guys are the best.

Special thanks goes out to Paulette Tomasson, a master therapist and treasured friend who endured countless calls, updates and revisions of every chapter as we calibrated and defined the personality profiles, power and potency of each Lunar Eclipse Dragon family's DNA.

About the Author

Kory Varlen is a professional astrologer, educator, radio and TV personality with five decades of experience in the field. She graduated from the University of British Columbia in 1980 and holds a degree in Education. In 2011, she graduated from McEwan University "with distinction" in Social Work. As a researcher, she worked for the Edmonton Social Policy Council where she coauthored *Time for Action*, a Public Interest Alberta publication which helped to establish a designed-in-Alberta poverty reduction strategy. She travels extensively: In 1996, a two-week winter vacation to Ecuador turned into a ten year love affair with the land and people, working for such international companies as Manpower and Deloitte and teaching English and college entry level writing programs at the prestigious Fulbright Commission in Quito, Ecuador.

In 2005 she earned a Practitioner's Diploma of Fixed Stars from Bernadette Brady's Astro Logos in Bristol, UK. Kory is the creator of *Astral Inspiration—Tweaking Chaos One Day at a Time*™, an elegant 12-deck personal guidance series that merges the concepts of Positive Psychology with the astrological lore traditions of western mythology. Kory is currently working on the next installment of *Where Dragons Dance*; a lay person's guide to the lunar eclipses of the 21st century. She lives in Edmonton, Alberta, Canada. You can find her online at *www.koryvarlen.com.*